CORPORATE SOCIAL RESPONSIBILITY
The Corporate Governance of the 21st Century

the global voice of
the legal profession

International Bar Association Series

CORPORATE SOCIAL RESPONSIBILITY

The Corporate Governance of the 21st Century

General Editor:

Ramon Mullerat

Authors:

Daniel Brennan

Richard Brophy

James E. Brumm

Emilio J. Cardenas

Hans Corell

Jonathan Goldsmith

Ivor Hopkins

Michael Hopkins

Donald J. Johnston

David Kinley

Paola Konopik

Reinier Lock

John Lowry

Josep M. Lozano

Claes Lundblad

Jonathan Lux

Felix Martin

Annemarie Meisling

Ramon Mullerat

Gerald Milward-Oliver

Felix Ntrakwah

Isaiah Odeleye

Maria Prandi

Jakob Ragnwaldh

James Roselle

Phillip H. Rudolph

Jerome J. Shestack

Marcelle Shoop

Richard Taylor

Rosamund Thomas

Sune Skadegard Thorsen

Mark Walsh

Stephen B. Young

KLUWER LAW
INTERNATIONAL
and
International Bar Association

A C.I.P. catalogue record for this book is available from the Library of Congress.

ISBN 90-411-2324-5

Published by:
Kluwer Law International
P.O. Box 85889
2508 CN The Hague
The Netherlands

Sold and distributed in North, Central and South America by:
Aspen Publishers, Inc.
7201 McKinney Circle
Frederick, MD 21704
USA

Sold and distributed in all other countries by:
Extenza-Turpin Distribution Services
Stratton Business Park
Pegasus Drive
Biggleswade
Bedfordshire SG18 8TQ
United Kingdom

Printed on acid-free paper

Website: www.kluwerlaw.com

Printed in the Netherlands.

INTERNATIONAL BAR ASSOCIATION
the global voice of the legal profession

In its role as a dual membership organisation, comprising 16,000 individual lawyers and over 190 Bar Associations and Law Societies, the International Bar Association (IBA) influences the development of international law reform and helps shape the future of the legal profession. Its Member Organisations cover all continents and include the American Bar Association, the German Federal Bar, the Japan Federation of Bar Associations, the Law Society of Zimbabwe and the Mexican Bar Association.

Grouped into two Divisions – the Legal Practice Division and the Public and Professional Interest Division – the Association covers all practice areas and professional interests. It provides members with access to leading experts and up-to-date information as well as top-level professional development and network-building opportunities through high-quality publications and world-class Conferences. The IBA's Human Rights Institute works across the Association, helping to promote, protect and enforce human rights under a just rule of law, and to preserve the independence of the judiciary and the legal profession worldwide.

The principal aims and objectives of the IBA are:
- To promote an exchange of information between legal associations worldwide
- To support the independence of the judiciary and the right of lawyers to practise their profession without interference
- Support of human rights for lawyers worldwide through its Human Rights Institute

The IBA works towards these objectives through three main areas of activity:
- Services for individual lawyer members through its Divisions, Committees and Constituents
- Support for activities of Bar Associations and in particular, developing bars
- Support of human rights for lawyers worldwide

Further Information

Contact: International Bar Association, 10th floor, 1 Stephen Street, London, W1T 1AT, United Kingdom. Tel: +44 (0)20 7691 6868. Fax: +44 (0)20 7691 6544. E-mail: member@int-bar.org. Website: www.ibanet.org

TABLE OF CONTENTS

Foreword   xiii
Emilio J. Cardenas

About the Editor and Authors   xv

PART I – PRESENTATION

Chapter 1
The Global Responsibility of Business   3
Ramon Mullerat

PART II – GENERAL OVERVIEW

Chapter 2
Business Ethics   31
Rosamund Thomas

Chapter 3
CSR and Corporate Governance   37
Mark Walsh & John Lowry

Chapter 4
The Soul of the Corporation   61
Gerald Milward-Oliver

Chapter 5
Corporate Social Responsibility and
Public Policy   77
Felix Martin

Chapter 6
Corporate Social Responsibility in a Changing Corporate World   97
Jerome J. Shestack

**PART III – THE MAIN OBJECTIVES OF CORPORATE
SOCIAL RESPONSIBILITY**

Chapter 7
The Triple Bottom Line: Building Shareholder Value   113
James Roselle

Chapter 8
Labour Standards and Corporate Social
Responsibility: The Need for a Planetary Bargain   141
Michael Hopkins & Ivor Hopkins

Chapter 9
Corporate Social Responsibility and
the Environment – Our Common Future   159
   Marcelle Shoop

Chapter 10
Corporate Social Responsibility and Human Rights   183
   Josep M. Lozano & Maria Prandi

Chapter 11
Corporate Social Responsibility and
International Human Rights Law   205
   David Kinley

**PART IV – WORLDWIDE INITIATIVES ON CORPORATE
         SOCIAL RESPONSIBILITY**

Chapter 12
The Tripartite Declaration of Principles Concerning
Multinational Enterprises   217
   Phillip H. Rudolph

Chapter 13
The Global Sullivan Principles of Corporate Social
Responsibility   221
   Phillip H. Rudolph

Chapter 14
The Caux Round Table Principles for Business:
Decision-Making Matrix for a More Moral Capitalism   225
   Stephen B. Young

Chapter 15
The Global Compact   235
   Hans Corell

Chapter 16
Promoting Corporate Responsibility:
The OECD Guidelines for Multinational Enterprises   243
   Donald J. Johnston

Chapter 17
The UN Norms on the Responsibilities of
Transnational Corporations and other Business
Enterprises with Regard to Human Rights   251
   Jakob Ragnwaldh & Paola Konopik

Chapter 18
Corporate Social Responsibility and
Corporate Governance: New Ideas and
Practical Applications   263
   Daniel Brennan

PART V – REGIONAL PERSPECTIVES

Chapter 19
The European Initiatives   279
Jonathan Lux, Sune Skadegard Thorsen & Annemarie Meisling

Chapter 20
A European Perspective   299
Sune Skadegard Thorsen & Annemarie Meisling

Chapter 21
The Central Role of Lawyers in Managing, Minimizing,
and Responding to Social Responsibility Risks – A US Perspective   311
Phillip H. Rudolph

Chapter 22
Africa's Unique Challenge: Linking Economic Growth,
Infrastructure Reforms and Corporate Responsibilities   321
Reinier Lock

Chapter 23
The Japanese Perspective   337
James Brumm

Chapter 24
Corporate Social Responsibility and
Human Rights – The Ghana Experience in the
Gold Mining Industry   347
Felix Ntrakwah

PART VI – CODES OF CONDUCT

Chapter 25
The History, Variations, Impact and Future of
Self-Regulation   365
Phillip H. Rudolph

Chapter 26
Some Legal Dimensions of Corporate Codes of Conduct   385
Claes Lundblad

PART VII – LAWYERS AND CORPORATE SOCIAL
RESPONSIBILITY

Chapter 27
Social Responsibility and the Lawyer in the 21st Century   403
Jerome J. Shestack

Chapter 28
Lawyers' Responsibility for Advising on
Corporate Social Responsibility   417
Jonathan Goldsmith

Chapter 29
Corporate Social Responsibility in Lawyers' Firms   433
  Richard Taylor and Richard Brophy

Chapter 30
Corporate Social Responsibility and the In-house Counsel   447
  Isaiah Odeleye

**PART VIII – CRITICISM OF THE CORPORATE
                SOCIAL RESPONSIBILITY MOVEMENT**

Chapter 31
Criticism of the Corporate Social Responsibility Movement   473
  Michael Hopkins

PART IX – CONCLUSIONS

Chapter 32
A Few Concluding Remarks   485
  Ramon Mullerat

PART X – ANNEXES

Annex 1
The ILO Tripartite Declaration of Principles Concerning
Multinational Enterprises and Social Policy   489

Annex 2
The Global Sullivan Principles   497

Annex 3
The Caux Round Table Principles for Business   499

Annex 4
Amnesty International Guidelines for Companies   505

Annex 5
Social Accountability 8000   511

Annex 6
OECD Guidelines for Multinational Enterprises   517

Annex 7
The Global Compact Launched by the United Nations   527

Annex 8
The ICC's Nine Steps to Responsible Business Conduct   529

Annex 9
Global Reporting Initiative Guidelines   533

Annex 10
CCBE Guide for European Lawyers advising on
Corporate Social Responsibility Issues   541

Annex 11
UN Norms on Responsibilities of Transnational
Corporations and other Business Enterprises with
regard to Human Rights 549

Index 555

FOREWORD

This excellent and illuminating book, edited with sweeping vision by Ramon Mullerat, allows the reader, with such wisdom in its pages, to step back from the normal rush of his or her daily business to consider how some leading legal scholars and practitioners think about, and chart on a long-term basis, the issue of corporate social responsibility.

The International Bar Association is very proud to co-publish with Kluwer Law International and to present this book both to its members and to the world's legal community at large.

At a time when global cooperation is growing in many areas, such as commerce, investment, banking, crime prevention, human rights, or the environment, this innovative and stimulating book, full of new perspectives and measured judgements about risks involved, shows that effective governance definitely requires corporations to constantly take into account their different social responsibilities.

It will, I believe, help anyone interested in its subject to shape his or her thinking or perceptions on an issue of great importance, providing a comprehensive and detailed account of how the subject has unfolded, as well as a vital background to its growth and development.

Topics treated include the new worldwide and regional initiatives as well as comments on the impact of 'Codes of Conduct' and some perspectives of particular professional importance, such as the links existing between corporate social responsibility and the environment or human rights.

Written by a diverse cross-section of lawyers for lawyers and anyone else involved or interested in business, this engaging as well as comprehensive and opportune book, enlivened by the authors' personal experiences, debunks well-known myths and fears which often prevent people from seeing the reality it describes. It is also packed with interesting chapters dealing with the particular role of lawyers on the issue, thus making it far more profound than a mere reporting of events and trends.

Ramon Mullerat's star-quality cast has provided a thoughtful and provocative work as well as a multifaceted and up-to-date professional tool for all those interested in keeping pace with today's evolving business climate. This therefore is, and will be, a book to consult.

Emilio J. Cardenas
President of the International Bar Association

ABOUT THE EDITOR AND AUTHORS

Ramon Mullerat (editor)
Ramon Mullerat O.B.E. is a lawyer in Barcelona and Madrid, Spain; Avocat à la Cour de Paris, France. He is an Honorary Member of the Bar of England and Wales and an Honorary Member of the Law Society of England and Wales. Ramon Mullerat is Professor at the Faculty of Law of the Barcelona University and an Adjunct Professor of the John Marshall Law School, Chicago. He is a Former President of the Council of the Bars and Law Societies of the European Union (CCBE) and a Member of the American Law Institute (ALI) alongside being a Member of the American Bar Foundation (ABF). He is a member of the board of the Institute for North American Studies and former Chairman of Commission 2020 of the International Bar Association (IBA), Co-Chairman of the Human Rights Institute (HRI) of the IBA, Member of the Board of the London Court of International Arbitration (LCIA) and Chairman of the Editorial Board of the *European Lawyer*. He is the author of numerous books, articles and publications and he writes and lectures frequently around the world on company/commercial law, arbitration law and legal ethics.

Daniel Brennan
Lord Brennan QC is a former Chairman of the Bar of England and Wales and he was appointed a life peer in the year 2000. He has been a QC since 1985 and he currently sits as a Deputy High Court Judge. He is a member of the Bars of the Republic of Ireland and of Northern Ireland and the London Court of International Arbitration. Lord Brennan is Advisor to United Nations Global Compact and a member of the Global Governing Board of Caux Round Table on CSR. He is on the Panel of Consultants to World Bank for Latin America and South and East Asia, Co-Chair of the IBA Committee on Globalisation of the Legal Profession, Member of the American Law Institute, an Associate member of the American Bar Association and President of the European Circuit of the Bar of England and Wales. In 2001 Lord Brennan was the Leader of the IBA Legal Delegation on Justice Issues in Sri Lanka and he has co-operated with a number of Latin American states on development of judicial independence and training, law reform and the role of lawyers in modern society. In the House of Lords, he is a member of the Select Committee on the European Union which deals with European economic and political issues and also a member of the Sub-Committee on European Law and Institutions.

Richard Brophy
Richard Brophy has been the Community Affairs Co-ordinator at CMS Cameron McKenna since September 2003, overseeing its pro bono, employee volunteering and charitable giving schemes. After completing a degree in English Literature at King's College London in 1997 he worked in business support at a

leading London architectural practice, followed by a similar role at the prestigious Bartlett School of Architecture, University College London. After a period working for Hobsbawm Macaulay Communications – a specialist PR agency advising charities, not-for-profuts, NGOs, media and arts clients – he joined the Education department at the Royal Institute of British Architects. At RIBA, Richard ran a series of charitable trusts, developed their web presence and other information tools, event managed an international student design award and played a key role in projects designed to widen access to the profession. His own volunteering work includes serving as a management committee member at Hackney Community Law Centre advising specifically in PR, media management and other communication issues.

James E. Brumm

Jim Brumm is Executive Vice President and General Counsel of Mitsubishi International Corporation in New York. He is a director of Mitsubishi International Corporation and was a director of Mitsubishi Corporation of Japan from 1995 to 2002. Mr Brumm is also a member of the board of Tembec Inc., a Canadian forest products company, where he serves on the Audit Committee and Chairs the Corporate Governance Committee. Mr Brumm is President of the Mitsubishi International Corporation Foundation and serves on the boards of Forest Trends, the American Bird Conservancy and Sanctuary for Families. He is also on the Corporate Advisory Boards for Earthwatch Institute, Inc., the Global Forest and Trade Network and the New York Botanical Garden. His responsibilities include environmental issues and CSR. He practised with law firms in New York and Tokyo for seven years. He is active in the Association of the Bar of the City of New York where he was Chair of the Committee on International Trade and Chair of the Task Force on International Legal Services. He is currently the Association's representative to the IBA where he served on a Task Force on International Multijurisdictional Commercial Practice. He graduated magna cum laude with a Bachelor's Degree in Political Science from California State University at Fresno in 1965 and graduated from Columbia University School of Law in 1968.

Hans Corell

Hans Corell, presently Ambassador in the Swedish Ministry for Foreign Affairs (MFA), was Under-Secretary-General for Legal Affairs and the Legal Counsel of the United Nations from March 1994–March 2004. Having received his law degree from the University of Uppsala in 1962, he served first as court clerk and later as judge until 1972. That year, he joined the Ministry of Justice, where he was engaged in legislative work on real estate, company law, maritime law, administrative law, and constitutional law. He became Director of the Division for Constitutional Law in 1979 and Head of the Legal Department in 1981. From 1984 until March 1994, he served as Ambassador and Head of the Department for Legal and Consular Affairs in the MFA. He was a member of Sweden's delegation to the United Nations General Assembly 1985–1993 and had several assignments related to the Council of Europe, OECD and the CSCE (now OSCE). Together with two other rapporteurs, he was author of the 1993 CSCE proposal for the establishment of the International Tribunal for the former

Yugoslavia. In 1998, he was the Secretary-General's representative at the Rome Conference on the International Criminal Court. Hans Corell holds an honorary Doctor of Laws degree at the University of Stockholm (1997).

Jonathan Goldsmith

Jonathan Goldsmith is the Secretary General of the Council of Bars and Law Societies of Europe (CCBE), which represents over 700,000 European lawyers through its member bars and law societies. The CCBE deals with a wide range of EU and global issues, such as anti-money-laundering legislation, an EU-wide Code of Conduct, competition matters affecting the legal profession, and GATS. He is an English solicitor. Jonathan Goldsmith began his legal career in the UK Citizens Advice Bureaux as advice worker (1978–1980) and community lawyer (1980–1986). After that, he joined the Law Society of England and Wales, first as Deputy Head, Communications and then, from 1995–2001, as Director, International, promoting the interests of solicitors abroad.

Ivor Hopkins

Ivor Hopkins is Senior Partner with MHC International Ltd, a company that specialises in research and advisory services on Corporate Social Responsibility (CSR). His particular areas of expertise in CSR are SMEs, sport and sustainable tourism. He has a background in sales and marketing, having worked in the sports industry for nearly 20 years – 10 of them in Germany – before joining MHC International Ltd. He designs and run Masterclasses and seminars on CSR issues and has made many presentations on CSR to, amongst others, the Asian Development Bank (Manila), ILO, SEEDA (South East England Development Agency), ESCP-EAP University (Paris), Cumberland Lodge (Windsor) and the Inter American Development Bank (Panama City). He regularly writes articles on CSR issues (including MHCi's Monthly Features) and is currently driving a Sustainable Tourism project for a German tour operator. He is Visiting Research Fellow in CSR to the Middlesex University Business School, London, and holds an MA from Manchester University.

Michael Hopkins

Michael Hopkins is CEO and Chairman of MHC International Ltd. (London and Geneva), a research and service company that specialises in social development issues for the public and private sector alike (see www.mhcinternational. com). Michael is also a part-time Professor at Middlesex University Business School and is co-Founder and Chairman of the International Centre for Business Performance and Corporate Responsibility (see http://mubs.mdx.ac.uk/Research/Research_Centres/icbpcr/index.htm). Michael holds First and Masters degrees in Mathematics and Statistics and a Doctoral Degree in Labour Economics from the University of Geneva, Switzerland. He is currently leading the ILO, Geneva team on corporate social responsibility as follow-up to ILO's World Commission on the Social Dimensions of Globalization.

Donald J. Johnston

Upon taking office as Secretary-General of the OECD in 1996, Mr Johnston moved from a career as a lawyer and politician who spent 10 years in the Canadian Parliament and served as a Cabinet Minister in a number of senior portfolios. In 1988, Mr Johnston ended a decade of political life to become legal counsel to the Canadian law firm, Heenan Blaikie, of which he was a founder in 1972. Mr Johnston was a Member of Parliament from 1978 to 1988. He served in the Cabinet, first as President of the Treasury Board, and then as Minister of State for Economic and Regional Development, Minister of Science and Technology, Minister of Justice and Attorney General of Canada. In 1990 Mr Johnston was elected President of the Liberal Party of Canada. In 1992, he was re-elected and held the post through the election in 1993 that returned the Liberal Party to power. Mr Johnston studied Arts and Law at McGill University, graduating from law in 1958 as the Gold Medallist. He studied at the University of Grenoble on a scholarship. He taught fiscal law at McGill University. He has written many articles on taxation, law and public affairs and is the author of several books including a best-selling political memoir.

David Kinley
David Kinley has been a legal academic and practitioner for 15 years specialising in human rights law. At the time of writing, he is professor of International Law, and founding Director of the Castan Centre for Human Rights Law at Monash University in Melbourne, Australia: www.monash.law.edu.au/castan-centre. In April 2005, however, he fills the position of the inaugural Chair in Human Rights Law at Sydney University. He has taught at a number of universities in Australia and has been a Visiting Fellow at several universities. He was awarded a Senior Fulbright Scholarship in 2003, which he pursued at Washington College of Law, American University, Washington DC during 2004. He has lectured and delivered speeches in a host of countries worldwide and has also worked for many years as a consultant and advisor in international and domestic human rights law. He is author/editor of four books including: *Human Rights in Australian Law* (Federation Press; 1998), in addition to the publication: *Human Rights Explained* at: http://www.hreoc.gov.au/hr_explained/index.html. He is also author of some 50 articles, book chapters, reports and papers published internationally on a range of legal matters, but especially on human rights law.

Paola Konopik
Paola Konopik is an Associate in the Corporate Accountability practice group of Mannheimer Swartling in Stockholm, Sweden. Paola Konopik specializes in CSR and has written and lectured on CSR issues. She is a graduate of Stockholm University. Paola Konopik is a Fulbright scholar and earned her LLM degree from Columbia University in New York.

Reinier Lock
Reinier Lock spent the first 24 years of his life in Southern Africa. In his five years at university in South Africa, followed by a year as a financial journalist in Johannesburg, he witnessed first hand, and fought against, the injustices of apartheid. After his exile from South Africa for anti-apartheid activities, Reinier studied at Oxford (BCL) and the University of California at Berkeley (LLM); and he received a Diploma in Human Rights Law from the University of

Strasbourg. He practised business law in San Francisco, and then served in several legal positions in the US Department of Energy and as Legal Advisor to a Commissioner of the Federal Energy Regulatory Commission. Since returning to private practice in 1990, he has worked primarily in the areas of energy and infrastructure development, project financing, and infrastructure regulation. This work brought him back to South Africa after 28 years in exile; and he has subsequently worked extensively in the SADC region and, more recently, in the ECOWAS region, of Africa. Reinier has been very active since the early 1980s in the American Bar Association and, since the early 1990s, in the International Bar Association (IBA). He has served on the Board of Directors of a state-wide rural cooperative electricity corporation in the US. He has recently spoken at IBA conferences in Lagos and in Calgary on the challenges of CSR in the infrastructure areas. He assumed the Chair of the IBA's Section of Energy, Environment, Natural Resources and Infrastructure Law (SEERIL) at the IBA's Auckland conference in October 2004.

John Lowry
John Lowry teaches Corporate Law and Insurance Law at University College London. He has taught law in the USA and practised in Canada specialising in corporate litigation. He has written widely in domestic and international journals on directors' fiduciary obligations and shareholder remedies and he is co-author of a number of books including *Limitation of Actions* (1988); *Company Law* (2003); *Insurance Law: Doctrines and Principles* (1999) and *Insurance Law: Cases and Material* (2004). He is also a Contributing Editor to *Cole-Browne on Companies* and Company Law section editor for the *Journal of Business Law*. John Lowry has delivered papers at the University of Cologne, the LSE, the Institute of Advanced Legal Studies, the Russian Federation Securities Commission, the University of Hong Kong and All Soul's College Oxford. In 2001 he was a Visiting Fellow at the University of Connecticut.

Josep M. Lozano
Josep M. Lozano was awarded a PhD in Philosophy by the University of Barcelona and a degree in Theology by the Theology Faculty of Catalonia. He also holds a degree in Executive Management from ESADE Business School. He is currently Full Professor at the Department of Social Sciences at ESADE and Director of the Institute for the Individual, Corporations and Society (IPES). His academic and professional activity focuses on the fields of Applied Ethics and Corporate Social Responsibility. Josep Lozano's five major books to date include *Danone en Ultzama* and *Ethics and Organizations* (Kluwer). He is Director of the Observatory on Ethical, Ecological and Social Funds in Spain. He is co-founder of Ética, Economía y Dirección (the Spanish branch of the European Business Ethics Network); member of the international council of Ethical Perspectives. Mr Lozano was the ESADE representative in the consortium of European universities that created the European Academy of Business in Society (EABiS). He was member of the Catalan Government's Commission on Values, and of the Spanish Ministry of Employment and Social Affairs' Commission of Experts on CSR. He was awarded as Runner-up in the Faculty Pioneer Awards by Beyond Grey Pinstripes.

Claes Lundblad

Claes Lundblad is a partner of Mannheimer Swartling, Stockholm, Sweden. He heads the firm's Arbitration and Litigation Practice Group. Claes Lundblad's expertise lies in international arbitration in disputes concerning joint ventures, general contract matters, financing, energy and shipping. Mr Lundblad acts both as an arbitrator and as counsel. He has published various articles on arbitral and procedural issues. Mr Lundblad is the Swedish member of the ICC Court of Arbitration, a member of LCIA, AAA, IBA (Committees D and O) and other professional organizations. Mr Lundblad also practises in the CSR area having written and lectured on CSR-related issues.

Jonathan Lux

Jonathan specialises in maritime, energy, marine insurance, international trade and general commercial litigation and has been involved in many landmark cases. He acts for the major P&I Clubs, their ship-owner or charterer members, oil industry interests, cargo sellers and buyers as well as the major insurers. Jonathan is a leading expert advising bunker suppliers, ship-owners, and charterers. He is a Council Member of the International Bunker Industry Association and former co-ordinator of its working group on dispute resolution. He has been a pioneer in the introduction of ADR (principally mediation) into his fields of practice. He is an accredited mediator (CEDR, the Academy of Experts and ADR Net) and leads the firm's ADR Group. He is also a practising Arbitrator and Fellow of the Chartered Institute of Arbitrators and member of the British Academy of Experts. He is also one of an Arbitrator on the Panel of Arbitrators of the China Maritime Arbitration Commission (CMAC). Jonathan is editor of *Classification Societies* and co-author of *The Law of Tug, Tow and Pilotage, The Law and Practice of Marine Insurance and Average, Bunkers* and *Corporate Social Responsibility*. Jonathan chairs the Advisory Panel on Corporate Social Responsibity of the International Bar Association and is former Chairman of the IBA's Maritime and Transport Law Committee. Jonathan is a member of the Steering Group of the London Shipping Law Centre and is listed in Chambers Global Directory as a leading international shipping lawyer in London. He was instrumental in setting up and then served for two years as senior partner of the Hamburg office of Ince & Co, retuning to London in 2004.

Felix Martín

Felix Martín was born in Málaga, Spain in 1969. After completing his school studies in Spain he read Law at Exeter College, Oxford. He qualified as an English solicitor in 1993. He also holds a MBA from Manchester Business School. He has worked as a lawyer for Slaughter and May, Edge & Ellison, Marriott International, Inc. and most recently as Corporate Counsel for a leading international Food and Drinks manufacturing company. Felix in involved in a number of educational initiatives for young people in London. He is the president of the London Alumni Association of Manchester Business School and has made a number of contributions to specialist magazines on management topics.

Annemarie Meisling

Annemarie Meisling, LLM MA Consultant at Corporate Responsibility Ltd. Specialized in Human Rights Law, European Union Law, Corporate Social

Responsibility and sociology. Annemarie Meisling provides services to business, organizations, governments and development agencies on human rights and CSR. She has previously been employed at Lawhouse.dk, the Danish Ministry of Foreign Affairs and worked as a consultant for the Danish Red Cross. E-mail ameisling@lawhouse.dk

Gerald Milward-Oliver

Gerald Milward-Oliver is CEO of The Anima Organisation, a company formed in 2004 to contribute to the exploration and understanding of issues related to organizational culture. He has spent the past 30 years helping organizations 'find their voice'. He has worked with some of the largest corporations in the world, as well as for multinational and governmental institutions and charitable organizations. Since 1981, he has been principal of GOcomms, a business specializing in a broad range of communications projects. From 1984–1989, he was also a director of one of the UK's leading motivation and incentive companies.

Based in Bradford on Avon, Wiltshire, Gerald Milward-Oliver is a Fellow of the Royal Society of Arts, a director of the international charity Rights and Humanity, Chairman of the Bradford on Avon Development Trust, a member of the Advisory Council for the Wiltshire Music Centre Trust and a Governor of St Laurence School.

Felix Ntrakwah

Mr Felix Ntrakwah is the senior partner of Ntrakwah & Co., a corporate law firm in Accra. He started private practice in 1981 when he resigned from the civil service as an Assistant Registrar General in charge of companies, trademarks and patents. Mr Ntrakwah obtained his LLB degree from the University of Ghana in 1973. He is a member of the Ghana Bar Association and the Chartered Institute of Arbitrators (UK). He is a director of Ghana Commercial Bank Limited and the Chairman of Financial Investment Trust. He is also the Chairman of Mondex Ghana Limited. Mr Ntrakwah is the founder of the Corporate Law Institute of Ghana. Mr Ntrakwah has written on various topics including Corporate Governance in Ghana, Banking Litigation in Ghana, Legal Issues in Privatization in Ghana, and Public concerns about privatization in Ghana. He has given lectures at professional seminars on topics including the following; Observations in the Development of Corporate Law Practice in Ghana, The Legal Practitioner and the Delivery of Justice, the Position of the Board of Directors of a Ghanaian company and Due Diligence in Ghana.

Isaiah Odeleye

Mr Odeleye started his career as a Legal Practitioner with the Lagos State Ministry of Justice. In 1983, he left the Ministry of Justice and went in to private legal practice. In 1984, he joined The Shell Petroleum Development Company of Nigeria Limited as a Legal Assistant. He has been involved in various legal matters relating to oil and gas business and operations. He has served the company in various positions, and currently, he is the Company Secretary of The Shell Petroleum Development Company of Nigeria Limited. Mr Odeleye is a member of the Nigerian Bar Association, the International Bar Association, the Nigerian Gas Association and the Christian Lawyers Fellowship of Nigeria.

He is a member of the National Executive Committee of the Nigerian Bar Association, and a member of the Gas Committee of the IBA's Section on Energy and Natural Resources Law (SERL). Mr Odeleye has presented papers at several Conferences and Seminars including the Conferences of the Nigerian Bar Association, the IBA, SERL etc.

María Prandi

María Prandi is an Assistant Professor and doctoral researcher at IPES (ESADE) where she is conducting research on business and human rights. Fellowshipped by the John Hopkins University, she is currently a PhD Candidate in International Relations at the Autonomous University of Barcelona where she also lecturers on business and human rights. She has authored articles on business, human rights and corporate codes of conduct. Maria Prandi has worked as an external consultant on human rights and participated at the United Nations Commission on Human Rights and Sub-commission on the Promotion and Protection of Human Rights (Geneva) following, among other issues, the agenda on business and human rights.

Jakob Ragnwaldh

Jakob Ragnwaldh is a Senior Associate in the Litigation and Arbitration practice group of Mannheimer Swartling, Stockholm, Sweden. He is also a member of the firm's Corporate Accountability practice group. Mr Ragnwaldh specializes in international commercial arbitration, acting as counsel in arbitrations worldwide. A graduate of Lund University, Mr Ragnwaldh has also earned a law degree from the University of Panthéon-Assas, Paris II, France. Mr Ragnwaldh is a member of the Swedish Bar Association.

James Roselle

James Roselle is associate General Council to Northern Trust Corporation, based in Chicago, Illinois. Prior to joining Northern Trust, he served as in-house counsel to Bank One Corporation and its predecessor banks for over 30 years, most recently holding the position of Senior Vice President and Business General Counsel to the Commercial Bank. Most of his career has been spent on legal matters involving international business and financial regulatory compliance. Mr Roselle established Bank One's Asia Regional Counsel Office in Hong Kong and served on the Board of Governors of the American Chamber of Commerce in Hong Kong. Mr Roselle has been a member of the IBA and is a member of the ABA, where he serves on the Council of the Section of International Law. He also serves on an ABA Task Force on Gatekeeper Regulation and the Legal Profession. He has spoken and written on anti-money laundering, corporate governance, letters of credit and other banking topics. Mr Roselle received a BA from Northwestern University and a J.D. from the University of Virginia School of Law.

Phillip H. Rudolph

Phil Rudolph is a partner in the Washington, D.C. Office of Foley Hoag LLP, where he is active in the firm's International and CSR Practice Groups. Prior to joining Foley Hoag, Phil was a Vice President at McDonald's Corporation, where he served in several capacities, including those of US and International General Counsel, and Head of Vendor Compliance. Phil served on McDonald's Social Responsibility Steering Committee, which provided strategic advice and counsel to senior management, and he assisted in the drafting and publication of McDonald's first Social Responsibility Report in 2002. He has written on CSR issues for legal and other publications, and speaks at conferences around the world on issues of sustainability and corporate responsibility. He has also participated as a member of the faculty of 'Managing Ethics In Organizations,' co-sponsored by the Ethics Officers Association and the Center for Business Ethics at Bentley College. Before he moved to McDonald's, Phil was a partner in the D.C. office of Gibson, Dunn & Crutcher LLP, where he specialized in antitrust litigation and counselling. He graduated magna cum laude with a bachelor's degree in political science from the University of California at Irvine in 1980. In 1983, he received his JD from the University of Chicago Law School.

Jerome J. Shestack

Mr Shestack was President of the American Bar Association (1997–1998). He chairs the Litigation Department of Wolf, Block, Schorr and Solis-Cohen LLP. A renowned trial lawyer, he is regularly cited by the *National Law Journal* as one of America's '100 Most Influential Lawyers'. He Chairs the ABA's Center on Human Rights, is a Counselor to the American Society of International Law and a Commissioner of the International Commission of Jurists. He served as Chairman of the IBA Standing Committee on Human Rights. He was US Ambassador to the United Nations Commission on Human Rights under President Carter. He founded the New York-based 'Human Rights First'. President Clinton appointed him to the Council of the Holocaust Memorial Museum, where he chaired its Committee on Conscience. Mr Shestack graduated from Harvard Law School where he was editor-in-chief of the *Harvard Law School Record*. He has authored more than 200 articles for law journals and editorial pages. He is a member of the Order of the Coif, a Fellow of the American College of Trial Lawyers, the American Academy of Appellate Lawyers and the International Academy of Trial Lawyers.

Marcelle Shoop

Marcelle Shoop is Director of Sustainable Development for RioTinto Subsidiary, Kennecott Utah Copper Corporation, a copper mining, smelting and refining operation near Salt Lake City, Utah, US. In her role she is responsible for leading efforts to integrate sustainable development into Kennecott's business model. This includes managing corporate social and environmental reporting, environmental auditing, and certain environmental legislative and regulatory issues, as well as coordinating the company's climate change policy issues. Ms Shoop also serves as legal counsel for the company primarily concerning Superfund matters, and her past practice has covered waste, water and air matters, closure and compliance programs. In 2003, she received the Attorney of the Year Award from the Energy, Natural Resources and Environmental Law section of the Utah Bar Association. Prior to joining Kennecott, Ms Shoop was in private practice with Holland & Hart in Cheyenne, Wyoming. Prior to entering private practice, she clerked for the Honorable Ewing T. Kerr, United States District Court, District of Wyoming. Ms Shoop received her Juris Doctorate in 1984 from the University of Wyoming College of Law and is admitted to practice in Utah, Wyoming and Colorado.

Richard Taylor

Richard Taylor is counsel to CMS Cameron McKenna having been a partner of the firm since 1974. His practice developed from general corporate work into a specialized anti-trust practice in EU and UK competition law. He has represented clients (including a number of well-known multinationals) on a wide variety of matters including international merger control, antitrust compliance and proceedings before courts, tribunals and competition authorities and he has written extensively on competition law related topics. He was the founder and first chairman of CMS, the transnational legal services organization linking eight law firms and practising in 23 jurisdictions. He has also served as Chairman of the Law Society's European Group, is a member of the IBA and serves on the Competition Commission of the International Chamber of Commerce. Richard has been responsible for a number of his firm's key client relationships and also pro bono activities.

Rosamund Thomas

Dr Rosamund Thomas is Director of Centre for Business and Public Sector Ethics, Cambridge, UK: see www.ethicscentre.org. She is an expert in CSR, Business Ethics, and Business Management. Dr Thomas read these subjects at the University of Birmingham (UK); Harvard University to doctoral and post-doctoral levels (USA); and taught at the London School of Economics and Political Science (1978–83). In 1983 she accepted a Senior Research Fellowship in the Faculty of Law of the University of Cambridge, before becoming Director of the Centre for Business and Public Sector Ethics in 1988. Dr Thomas has given evidence and Conference assignments to distinguished bodies, and is also a well-known author, and editor. Her published books include *The British Philosophy of Administration; Espionage and Secrecy: The Official Secrets Acts 1911–1989 of the United Kingdom*; ed. *Government Ethics*; and ed. *Environmental Ethics*. Dr Thomas has originated five Modules on 'Ethics and Anti-Corruption', published by Centre for Business and Public Sector Ethics, 2004, and is listed in 'Who's Who in the World' 2004 for her contribution to the betterment of contemporary society.

Sune Skadegard Thorsen

Sune Skadegard Thorsen is the owner of the law firm Lawhouse.dk (DK) and Director in Corporate Responsibility Ltd. (UK). He has given lectures and high-level presentations worldwide addressing academia, business, governments and NGOs. He has build an extensive network in the field and advised leaders like Shell, Novozymes, and Novo Nordisk, the latter also as in-house Senior Adviser. His clients also include Governments, Development Agencies, Non and Inter-Governmental Organizations. His work includes a wide range of pro bono work in the field. He is an adviser to the Business Leaders Initiative on Human Rights (www.blihr.org), member of the Board of the Danish Centre for International

Studies and Human Rights (www.dcism.dk), the Board and Council of the Danish Institute for Human Rights (www.humanrights.dk), the Council of the Bars and Law Societies of the European Union – CSR working group (www.ccbe.org), the International Advisory Network of the Business & Human Rights Resource Centre (www.business-humanrights.org) and several other initiatives. He is Chairman of the Danish Section of the International Commission of Jurists (ICJ). He has written and published numerous articles and papers in the field, confer www.lawhouse.dk.

Mark Walsh
Mark Walsh is a Corporate and Securities partner at Sidley Austin Brown & Wood LLP, an international law firm. He spent seven years in the firm's New York office (1986–94) and five years in its Hong Kong office (1994–99), and has been based in London since 1999. He is admitted to practice in New York, English and Hong Kong law, and is a member (non-practising) of the Irish bar. One of Mr. Walsh's areas of specialty is corporate governance. He works regularly with non-US companies that file reports with the SEC concerning the requirements of the Sarbanes Oxley Act, including UK and other European companies subject to competing requirements under the Combined Code or other EU codes. Since the collapse of Enron, Mr. Walsh has published articles on corporate governance in the *International Company and Commercial Law Review*, the *Sweizerische Zeitschrift für Wirtschaftsrecht, The Lawyer, Legal Week, Investor Relations* and *Legal Business' Finance 2002*. He was a principal contributor to LNTV's April 2003 Programme (949), *'Directors' Responsibilities and Liabilities – Sarbanes Oxley, Higgs and Smith'*. Mr. Walsh has law degrees from University of Dublin (Trinity College) and London (Queen Mary College) and has a diploma in international commercial arbitration from the Centre for Commercial Law Studies.

Stephen B. Young
Stephen B. Young has been Global Executive Director of the Caux Round Table since 2000. He was educated at Harvard College, graduating magna cum laude, and at the Harvard Law School, graduating cum laude. Stephen B. Young was an Assistant Dean at the Harvard Law School and Dean and Professor of Law at the Hamline University School of Law. Mr Young has taught jurisprudence, corporate finance and the law of fiduciary relationships. Mr Young has practised law, both transactional and litigation, in New York City and Minnesota. His book, *Moral Capitalism*, was published by Berrett-Koehler of San Francisco in 2003.

PART I
PRESENTATION

Chapter 1

THE GLOBAL RESPONSIBILITY OF BUSINESS

Ramon Mullerat

I am very grateful to Kluwer Law International Publishers and the International Bar Association for having asked me to invite a number of miscellaneous authors coming from different quarters but all of them excelling in their professions and enthusiastic with the idea of putting together their views on Corporate Social Responsibility (CSR) to help the world to be more human.[1]

I read once that a group of six blind men watched an elephant. Someone asked the first blind man: 'What does an elephant look like'? 'Like a pillar', said the one who had been grabbing the elephant by one of its legs; 'like a snake', said the one who had just grabbed the tail; 'like a fan', the one who had touched the ear; 'like a hose' the one who had grabbed the trunk, and so on and so forth. With CSR something similar happens. Each one of us has a different concept or at least prioritizes some of its aspects according to our particular background and views: an economic theory, an ethical aspiration, a legal regulation, a market tool, a management risk instrument and so on and so forth.

As it happens, CSR, as something new, is still a vague, imprecise and even misty concept. Undoubtedly there are already some good definitions. CSR is a concept whereby companies voluntarily decide to respect and protect the interests of a broad range of stakeholders while contributing to a cleaner environment and a better society through an active interaction with all. CSR is the voluntary commitment by businesses to manage their roles in society in a responsible way (International Chamber of Commerce). CSR is the commitment of businesses to contribute to a sustainable development by working with employees, their families, the local communities and society at large to improve their quality of life (World Business Council for Sustainable Development). CSR is the cooperation with government, civil society and businesses, etc. However, as a doctrine still in its infancy, it still has undefined contours. CSR also poses important questions still difficult to resolve.

---

[1] I would also like to thank Alba Botines, Professor Joaquim Forner, Kathy Mathews, Lauda Morales, and Rui Nascimento, whose help has been invaluable in the compilation of this book.

Ramon Mullerat (ed.), Corporate Social Responsibility: The Corporate Governance of the 21st Century, 3–27.
© 2005 *International Bar Association. Printed in the Netherlands.*

Probably the first question consists of deciding whether CSR is part of business ethics, of corporate governance or something different. The reality is that CSR is often confused with the recent efforts to restore 'corporate responsibility' after the traumatic events of Enron and the plethora of scandals that occurred in the US, followed by the suit in the EU, which shook the confidence in the effectiveness of the governance, disclosure systems of corporations and the laws governing the role of executive officers, directors, auditors and lawyers and designed to enhance the public trust in corporate integrity and responsibility. I do not share this view and believe that we must distinguish between corporate governance, which is a binding and enforceable law, and CSR, which is ethical, voluntary, non-enforceable rules. That does not mean that both rules do not have areas in common and do not overlap and intertwine with one another and are not interchangeable. On the one hand, labour infringements, environment sustainability and human rights are the domain of both law and ethics, which they inspire, regulate and influence such human interests. On the other hand ethical rules are often metamorphosed into legal rules (i.e. many irregularities committed by the directives of Enron and other recent scandals were violations of ethical rules; what the Sarbanes–Oxley Act has done is to transform and legally penalize many of such ignored ethical rules). Finally, some CSR instruments, like voluntary codes of conduct, might cease to be self-imposed ethical rules, to be converted into required and binding duties.

Another important issue, and of a higher calibre, is the Hamlet-type and hotly debated proposition, whether CSR should remain a set of voluntary principles of corporate behaviour or should it rather be the object of binding and enforceable legislation. The authors in this book constantly refer to this dilemma with great interest and persuasive arguments. Many consider that CSR should not be legislated and they allege important reasons for this. On the other hand others, especially NGOs, think that many refutable practices cannot be truly eradicated unless imposed by legally enforceable rules. They believe that environmental damaging emissions of CO_2 cannot be stopped unless international agreements were not put in place and that the fraudulent corporate behaviours in the US would continue was it not for the Sarbanes–Oxley Act. I agree with this. But legal rules can never wholly replace ethical principles. We must remember Lucien's story: Jupiter and a countryman were walking together, discussing with familiarity the subject of heaven and earth. The countryman listened with attention and acquiescence while Jupiter strove only to convince him, but happening to have the hint of a doubt, Jupiter turned partially round and threatened him with his thunder. 'Ah ha!', said the countryman, 'Now Jupiter I know that you are wrong; you are always wrong when you appeal to your thunder!'. I do not believe in a manichean solution, and think that both voluntary and mandatory rules are necessary and may co-exist to regulate specific matters depending on the different areas or objectives.

A subordinate issue to the previous one is to determine whether the violation of voluntary self-imposed standards of conduct (i.e. codes of conduct) should engender legal liability for the violator or, in other words, can the violator be legally sued for damages? Can a corporation who has signed and publicized, internally and externally, that it complies with high labour, environmental or human rights standards, just break one of them with impunity, or is that conduct legally punishable?

Everybody recognizes that CSR is also good for business. How to combine CSR principles and ethical doctrine with the evident CSR effects of marketing and window-dressing. In more simple words, ethics or marketing? Do corporations subscribe to CSR programs by conviction, or do they do it to entice employees, or to encourage consumers to buy their products or even to avoid the boycott of their products? In morals, two sorts of repentance for the sins are distinguished: the contrition and the attrition. The first one is the sincere remorse for wrongdoing, the sinner is sorry to have sinned because sin is an offence against the good God. In the attrition, the repentance is motivated by fear of punishment rather than by love of God, the sinner is sorry because he fears the pains in hell. The first is much better. But eventually what is important is that the sinner does not sin any more irrespective of the motive. The important thing for corporations is to engage in some of the many CSR activities. So much the better if it is by conviction, but it is also desirable if they do that for other less laudable reasons.

Undoubtedly CSR is already inspiring the corporate governance and management at the dawn of the 21st century. However, the CSR movement is still full of imprecision which needs definition and determination on its notion, shape and effects as it prospers throughout the world. It is precisely these issues that are explicitly discussed in this book.

Most of the contributors have been trained in law and that is why many of their remarks are conceived from a legal perspective and addressed to jurists. That does not mean that the book's contents will not be interesting and helpful for businessmen, politicians, journalists and many others interested in business law and ethics. On the contrary the book contains meaningful and inspiring insights for all those who are preoccupied with the role and duties of business in the modern world.

Chapter 2 'Business Ethics', has been written by Rosamund Thomas, who is Director of the Centre for Business and Public Sector Ethics, Cambridge, UK. Rosamund Thomas introduces us to the world of ethics (the 'obedience to the unenforceable' as the Institute of Global Ethics has defined it). The author asks herself whether 'business ethics' concerns just morality or does it extend to wider social and environmental responsibility and corporate governance. She reminds us that there are several types of values, including economic values (such as 'equity'), political values (like 'democracy'), social values (such as 'equal opportunity') and moral values. She distinguishes between 'business ethics', which is concerned particularly with moral values, and CSR, which focuses more on the social, environmental and sustainability issues than on 'morality', although both movements have converged to an extent, with ever increasing responsibilities being added to both, such as anti-corruption practices, and even the liability of directors for 'corporate manslaughter'. Dr Thomas considers that corporate governance is part of 'business ethics' even though it is phrased in factual terms related to the roles and responsibilities of the board of directors. Most countries have seen the damage, which can be caused to their business and government institutions by the breakdown of moral values, particularly 'trust' and 'integrity', but also 'truthfulness', 'openness' and others. This chapter skilfully explores business ethics in depth. Rosamund Thomas affirms that inspiration through leadership, example, and establishing a culture of morality, based on good practices – and training – are more likely to charge the moral motor of the corporation than coercion or quantitative tools.

In Chapter 3, Mark Walsh and John Lowry address 'CSR and Corporate Governance'. Mark Walsh is a corporate and securities partner at Sidley Austin Brown and Wood law firm and specializes in CSR and John Lowry is a professor of Corporate Law and Insurance Law at University College, London. Walsh and Lowry assert that while the term corporate governance is of recent origin, laws with corporate governance objectives have existed for well over a century. With the passage of the Sarbanes–Oxley Act in 2002, the US regime is primarily statute and rule based, whereas in the EU there is still much greater reliance on voluntary or semi-voluntary codes of conduct ('soft law'). The authors recognize that CSR principles aim to make today's large public companies responsible members of the community. To ensure that, in addition to complying with the minimum requirements of the law, the companies conduct their activities in an environmentally sensitive manner, they pay their taxes in full and on time, they respect their employees and pay and treat them fairly wherever they may be based, they source their raw materials from companies that also follow sound labour and environmental practices and they otherwise act ethically in their dealings with the outside world, whereas corporate governance is more concerned with the enhancement of shareholder value and the protection of shareholders interests. Walsh and Lowry make a brilliant summary of corporate governance in the US, the UK and the EU, separately analyzing corporate governance and directors, management, shareholders and third parties. They conclude that corporate governance matters have been focussed on the protection of shareholders interests but the themes – strict checks and balances on senior management, greater involvement in the supervision of management by directors, avoidance of conflict of interest and imposed disclosure to investors – must inevitably further the interests of those seeking to promote wider CSR objectives and that there is a need for further harmonization of global corporate governance and requirements.

Gerald Milward-Oliver, CEO of The Anima Centre, with a thirty-year experience on helping organizations 'find their voice', discusses in Chapter 4 'The Soul of the Corporation'. In a superb panorama, Gerald Milward-Oliver presents the ideas of modern thinkers of CSR and comments that for too many CSR is a mere Public Relations (PR) tool and that the PR industry has a visceral disconnection with the moral principles implicit in CSR. He reminds us that the 17th century jurist Edward Coke stated that 'corporations cannot commit treason and be outlawed nor excommunicated, for they have no souls'. He asks whether we can expect a majority of mature corporations to be capable of finding their soul or it is simply misplaced idealism to expect corporations to have a soul at all (understood as the Oxford Shorter English Dictionary which defines the soul as 'the seat of emotions, feelings or sentiments; the emotional part of man's nature; the essential animating part, element or feature of something; the animating principle of the world'). The principle that underlies this chapter is simple – take issues as ethics and CSR deep down into the organization, down into its soul. Understand the soul, feed it – and the organization will be stronger as a result he says. The author also reminds that the Earth Summit in Rio de Janeiro 1992 invited Severn Suzuki, a 12-year old who started the Environmental Children's Organisation in 1989, to address the full plenary session, which was full of high ranking and powerful businessmen. She said to them: 'you teach us how to behave in the world. You teach us not to fight with others; to work things out; to respect others; to clean up our mess; not to hurt other creatures; to share and not to be greedy. Then why do you go out and do the things you tell us not to do'?

Chapter 5 is regarding 'CSR and Public Policy' and is composed by Felix Martín, who is an in-house counsel solicitor who currently works for a leading national food and drinks manufacturing company. The author believes that the promotion of CSR will certainly have a positive though tangential effect on people's attitudes and that a more decisive commitment on the part of the governments to promote a more 'moral', value-driven and less individualistic approach to life will be necessary if CSR is to succeed in delivering sustainability. Felix Martín takes as a starting point the White Paper and subsequent Communication of the EU Commission on CSR, which he considers to represent the most comprehensive attempt of any government body to describe the role of CSR. The EU Commission requires a change of business culture from 'short-term profit maximization' to 'responsible business behaviour', which is the aim of the CSR movement. Felix Martín discusses four ways in which the government action can foster the adoption of CSR practices: by enacting laws that force companies in a particular sector or sectors to change their practices at the risk of financial penalties or imprisonment of the companies' personnel (the 'legislative approach'); by identifying ways in which CSR practices can help address specific issues of concern and interest to a particular company or industry sector; by promoting changes in market behaviour in a particular industrial sector that will lead companies in that sector to adopt CSR practices. The changes mentioned before may also follow from a greater appreciation by the business stakeholders of the importance of CSR practices and their desire to reward companies to adopt such practices by paying more for goods and services or working harder for the same amount of money or receiving lower dividends. The author analyses in detail the 'voluntary approach' to CSR, that is the ways in which governments can bring about the Commission's vision without resorting to further legislation and the 'legislative approach' which is seen by many NGOs as the only way to move the sustainability agenda forward. He believes that one way of managing these two conflicting objectives is to understand that the voluntary approach is a means to smooth out the path for new legislation, rather than of a way for governments to avoid their responsibility as legislators and that the voluntary approach cannot be allowed to obscure or delay the adoption of basic human rights and environmental legislation in developing countries. If the CSR agenda is to succeed, he says, governments must look beyond business ethics to the values that drive society itself. They must make a decisive effort to promote a more 'moral' and less self-centred style of life that will help sweep away unethical and 'unsustainable' market practices.

Change is the epitome of our time. Someone said that today's world is not a continuation of the past, but characterized by discontinuation. Chapter 6 deals with 'CSR in a Changing Corporate World' and has been written by Jerome J. Shestack, who chairs the Litigation Department of Wolf, Block, Schorr and Solis-Cohen LLP law firm, was President of the American Bar Association and is the current Chair of the ABA Center on Human Rights. Jerome Shestack presents a short but interesting history of CSR and finds the main causes of the new thinking on CSR the coming of age of the international human rights standards and the effect of world globalization. The author accurately affirms that in this changing corporate world, globalization places a spotlight on multinational corporate conduct. If globalization's principal achievement is that the rich get richer and the poor get poorer, it will ultimately fail and corporate business will suffer. Jerome Shestack analyses in detail how corporations should handle CSR excursions into this globalized climate. As chair of the Center for Human Rights, Shestack recognizes that in the field of human rights the distinction between business and society has become blurred and is no longer valid and that human rights form an underlying legal foundation for CSR.

'The Triple Bottom Line: Building Shareholder Value' is the title of Chapter 7 written by James E. Roselle, who has been in-house counsel to Bank One Corporation and currently holds the position of Senior Vice President, Deputy General Counsel and Business General Counsel to the Commercial Bank. The author, who has always been attracted by the ethical and social aspects of business, deals with one of the most important aspects of CSR and believes that the financial, social and environmental elements that compose CSR's 'triple bottom line' are of necessity interrelated and must be aligned with the overall corporate goal of sustaining growth and providing value to shareholders. James Roselle considers that the starting points for social responsibility to promote the goals of financial profit, economic growth and asset creation are good corporate governance and financial transparency. An increasing number of companies now recognize the bottom line benefit of CSR and have been willing to invest substantial resources to achieve growth in a socially responsible manner. James Roselle has discovered that in the most successful companies, social responsibility does not exist in isolation from other corporate initiatives. Rather, it forms part of the corporate DNA and is integrated into all business strategies and practices. The author presents and interesting insight on the different CSR's bottom lines and offers a fascinating analysis of whether CSR is a defensive or an offensive strategy, of corporate governance as a precondition of CSR, and socially responsible investing and makes an interesting examination of CSR tracing progress, public disclosing and reporting. He also offers us captivating comments on off shoring and environmental commitments and financial sector initiatives. James Roselle is happy to report that a growing number of public companies consider CSR sufficiently important to establish CSR committees to promote this movement within their corporations.

In Chapter 8, Michael Hopkins and Ivor Hopkins discuss 'Labour Standards and Corporate Social Responsibility: The Need for a Planetary Bargain'. Michael Hopkins is Professor of Corporate and Social Research at Middlesex University Business School and Ivor Hopkins is co-director of MHC International Ltd. The authors outline the elements of what could be a planetary bargain to promote CSR. The two main actors in such a bargain or social agreement would be governments and businesses. They warn that there are many actors on the world stage, and governments are not always the best to represent their own societies, especially in developing countries. Yet, if a planetary bargain is to come about to promote CSR, then the lead will have to come jointly from governments (including international organizations) and business itself. They make an imaginative incursion on the parameters of what each of such main actors could expect from each other in the area of social responsibility and social development. They intelligently discuss the link between a planetary bargain and globalisation before entering into some deal of a planetary bargain and analyse whether the bargain should be voluntary or enter into the legal framework of nations. In their view, although the issue is somewhere between a totally voluntary approach and complete legislation, the exact pointer to be arrived at is through negotiation. One of the key results of such planetary bargain would be to improve social protection for workers around the world and explain the vicissitudes at the international level to include a 'social clause' which has been underway for many decades with the intention to help to promote fair competition between developing countries' exporters by ensuring that those who respect minimum labour standards are not penalized for their efforts to promote human development. However, the 'social clause' is sometimes seen as a disguised form of protectionism – a Trojan horse – which is tantamount to interference in the companies' internal affairs, while they are being asked for reciprocity in social obligations in return for trade concessions and the private sector sees it as yet more restrictions on its ability to provide the best quality of products at the lowest possible price. In conclusion, the stand they take is on the minimalist side of the debate on legislation or not. Clearly – they say – no legislation at all is untenable simply because so much legislation already exists particularly for corporate governance. While full legislation for CSR is also untenable since business could grind to a halt simply in chasing up all the new CSR laws on the statute book, the sensible position for a planetary bargain is sufficient legislation to allow for a level playing field. This legislation must apply to all corporations wherever they are located or it simply will not work. How to enforce even minimalist standards in remote locations from the Dutch Antilles to the Maldives and even China or India is a challenge for the legislators.

In Chapter 9, Marcelle Shoop, Director of Sustainable Development for Kennecott Utah Copper Corporation, addresses one of the CSR's objectives: the environment. The author analyses the historic highlights of environmental degradation and the movements to protect and improve the condition of the biosphere from the Brundtland Commission, the UN Conference on Human Environment and the Stockholm Declaration on the Human Environment 1972, the UN Second Conference and Our Common Future in 1987 that coined the popular definition of 'sustainable development' ('a development that meets the needs of the present without compromising the ability of future generations to meet their own needs'), the UN Conference on Environment and Development in 1992 and the Rio Declaration and Agenda 21 (the 'Earth Summit'), to the World Summit on Sustainable Development in Johannesburg 2002. She vigorously defends that there is growing evidence that engaging in CSR and sustainable environmental practices can create positive value through enhanced reputation, licences to operate, the ability to attract and retain resources – from investment capital to quality employees, saving money, and the ability to identify emerging trends and management risk. Regarding the attraction of investment capital, she highlights the 'Equator principles' adopted by ten leading banks in 2003, a set of a voluntary guidelines to 'manage social and environmental issues' for financing development projects of $50 million or more. It is important to underline the reference that she makes to the CSR characteristics of responsible environmental performance, such a transparency, accountability, reporting and engaging stake-holders (and the efforts of GRI, CERES, AccountAbility AA1000); measuring, setting objectives and targets and continuous improvements (like the action taken by corporations such as ABB, Rio Tinto and Dell); management systems; risk management and opportunity identification; technology, product steward-ship, eco-efficiency and life cycle assessments; and supply chains. The author affirms that environmental stewardship is part of the larger context of conduct-ing business which includes a willingness both to operate transparently and to engage a broad range of stakeholders. It also means actively seeking opportuni-ties for improvement through the use of eco-efficient solutions, by developing new technologies, and by employing life-cycle perspectives in resource and prod-uct stewardship. Marcelle Shoop refers to the challenges of achieving environ-mental sustainability as an objective of CSR. For instance not having a clear business plan to identify a lack of proven or understood business benefits was identified by the World Bank as a barrier for integrating CSR programs for small and medium sized firms, codes of conduct and reporting schemes and challenges also emerge in encouraging the development of new technologies as a means to improve environmental performance. Issues such as general acceptance, cost effectiveness, intellectual property rights and the need for policy frameworks to support the technological advances present potential hurdles for research, devel-opment and use of advanced technologies. The author believes that such a push for improved environmental performance and greater efficiencies will continue and she convincingly declares that business has the opportunity to positively affect the health and prosperity of the Earth's environment.

Human rights, is the third bottom line of CSR. In Chapter 10, Josep Lozano and Maria Prandi discuss 'CSR and Human Rights'. The authors are responsi-ble for the Institute for the Individual, Corporations and Society (IPES) of the ESADE Business School. As they put it, although, on the face of it, human rights and the company seem worlds apart, and, like oil and water, an impossible mix, the reality is proving otherwise. Nowadays companies are among the most deci-sive actors in determining how human rights are put into practice since the income of five TNCs amounts to double the GNP of the 100 poorest countries. The authors give an account of the situation of human rights in the world citing the 2003 reports of Amnesty International and Human Rights Watch, which reveal systematic abuses affecting the right to life and safety of individuals by the state in 71 countries, torture and abuse used in 171 countries (although 134 countries ratified the Convention against Torture) and serious violations of basic freedoms in more than 80 countries. They refer to four basic trends to be iden-tified as catalysers of the new human rights presence in business discourses and practices and at economic forums. First, globalization, which causes economies to resort to internationalization and off shoring, thus spreading productive processes over countries with different levels of human rights protection. Second, the emerging network society in which companies are now perceived not as sim-ply economic actors, but as playing their part along with other social actors in interactions with their equivalents in other fields. Third, information and knowl-edge technologies, which create expectations of greater corporate transparency, while fast-tracking and multiplying content and information on these issues in local and global interactions. Fourth, the emerging risk society by which company reputation, image and identity are coming under scrutiny of certain rising values in a civil society, that is increasingly informed and mobilized on such issues. It is therefore in this context, they say, that our societies are calling on responsible companies to build into their legitimacy, identity and responsibility a respect for human rights. The authors summarize the CSR main initiatives in human rights such as the Global Compact, the Project of the UN Norms on the Responsibility of TNCs, the EU Green Paper on CSR, the OECD Guidelines for Multinational Enterprises, the Ethical Trading Initiative Base Code, the Amnesty International's Human Rights Guidelines for Companies, the Global Sullivan Principles for CSR, the Social Accountability 8000, the SA 8000 nine principles, and the Global Reporting Inactive Guidelines, some of which are annexed at the end of this book. They believe that today the traditional concept by which only states and individuals can be held responsible for abuses of human rights has been called into question – by civil society in general, in political circles and, over the last decade, also by business managers. Indeed, increasing numbers of companies are linking human rights to their CSR strategy upstream as a basis for CSR screening (policy), and downstream as a resource for CSR measurement and evaluation (practice). What is being considered is a new paradigm of company in which respect for minimum international human rights standards has become an issue inextricably linked to the process of building a responsible company.

David Kinley, professor of law and Director of the Castan Center for Human Rights Law in the Monash University of Melbourne, asserts in Chapter 11 on 'Corporate Social Responsibility and International Human Rights Law', that there is a new architecture for human rights protection that is currently emerging. It has been borne of the expansion within international law of the notions of what are the proper and the possible. Thus – slowly from the first wholesale establishment of Inter-Governmental Organizations (IGOs) immediately post-1945, and over the last 20 years – individual, groups, IGOs, NGOs and now corporations, have been admitted into the fold of international law and international human rights law has brokered much of it. The author analyses the third parties at international law showing how non-state actors have a long history of conspicuous presence from the 19th century International Committee of the Red Cross and the first TNCs (the English and Dutch East India companies and the British South Africa company). So, as this new architecture takes shape, the question arises, what have been and will be the consequences for human rights and what will be the effect of expansion at international law of entities capable of bearing human rights responsibilities? In addressing these questions, says the author, it must be stressed that when apportioning human rights responsibilities, we are not dealing with a static quantum burden. Thus it is not simply the case that as additional sites of responsibility are established and encumbered, so the level of the state's liability in respect of human rights protection and promotion is correspondingly reduced. Rather, the human rights burden is both increased in size and to some extent differently composed, as the duty to discharge is shared out across the diffident entities. He examines the precepts upon which this sharing is conducted and how that effects the three categories of human rights duty-holders: states, IGOs and corporations. Historically the human rights responsibilities have been considered to reside solely with the socially-oriented IGOs (UN, ILO, Council of Europe, OAS). while the economic-oriented IGOs (World Bank, IMF, GATT-WTO, OECD and trading blocks NAFTA and APEC) were not considered to have a human rights role. But this is changing. It is clear today that the International Economic Actors (IEAs) have an important role in the promotion and protection of human rights. The first crucial question is 'whether' IEAs ought to be made subject of a duty to protect human rights and the answer is yes because their collective capacity to generate change at all levels of inter- and intra-national relations in social, economic, political, cultural and legal terms, power is immense and manifest, and with it must come responsibilities commensurate with that power and therefore IEAs have a complementary role to play alongside the state. The second question is 'which' rights can IEAs be expected to promote and protect and which cannot be. Kinley believes that 'self-reflexive duty' (mainly prevention of abuses by the TNC itself), which includes the rights to life, liberty, physical integrity, labour rights, health, education, indigenous and environmental rights, constitute core and immediate human rights obligations that TNCs ought to be made subject to, while 'third-party duty' which might potentially stretch across many economic, social and cultural rights might consist a second tier of desirable but not immediately applicable human rights and duties for TNCs. To the third question 'what obligations', the author finds the response in the approach adopted by the UN Human Rights Norms for Corporations, while recognizing that 'states have the primary responsibility' for human rights protection corporations have the obligation to protect human rights 'within their respective spheres of activity and influence'. The bestowal of human rights duties on international economic actors will advance through both international and domestic initiatives. States will likely be the key conduits – being obliged under international law to implement and supervise compliance with such human rights whether at the domestic level (in respect of corporations) or through the relevant inter-governmental organizations forums. Thus, while on the one hand states will see the burden of human rights responsibilities being rightly shared, their own role, far from diminishing, will be increased.

In Chapter 12, Phillip H. Rudolph addresses 'The Tripartite Declaration of Principles Concerning Multinational Enterprises'. Phillip H. Rudolph is a partner of Foley Hoag LLP law firm and a former Vice President at McDonald's Corporation where he served as International General Counsel. The author refers to the Tripartite Declaration (tripartite as informed by the tripartite bodies representative of the ILO, including governments, employees and workers) adopted by the ILO in November 1977 (and later revised in 2002), which primarily addresses the rights at work as the first universally applicable agreement on the subject of TNCs. The Tripartite Declaration provides a set of guidelines broken down into five sections, addressed to ILO member states and TNCs. The first section urges respect for national sovereignty, equality of treatment between TNCs and national enterprises and tripartite cooperation. The second calls on TNCs to generate and expand opportunities for stable and secure employment, use appropriate technologies, and develop structural linkages within the economy of the host country. The third section promotes training and retaining initiatives as well as the promotion of workers. The fourth recommends the provision of favourable wage rates, benefits and work conditions, including maintenance of high standards for occupational safety and health. The fifth section urges parties to respect freedom of association, the right to organize and collective bargaining. The author laments that the Tripartite Declaration is ultimately aspirational and he asserts that the lack of any implementation mechanism, monitoring process, legal mandate or ability to expel egregious violators reduces the effect and reach of the Declaration. That is not to say that the Declaration has had no impact on corporate behaviour. As Phillip Rudolph puts it, while it is true that most of the precepts of the Declaration restate various obligations on governments taken from other sources, the reformulation of some as creating duties on corporations is significant. Given the repeated recitation of this instrument by governments, corporations and labour organisations, it provides, at minimum, strong evidence of a consensus among the three constituencies of the Declaration that corporations have duties towards their employees.

In Chapter 13, Phillip H. Rudolph also discusses 'The Global Sullivan Principles of CSR', which were drafted in 1977 by Reverend Leon H. Sullivan to encourage US companies operating in apartheid-era South Africa to treat their African employees and business partners the same as they would their American counterparts. Based on the principles of non-segregation, fair employment and equal pay for equal work, the Sullivan Principles called for the initiation and development of training programmes, the promotion of non-whites to managerial positions and the improvement of the quality of employees' lives outside the work environment. The Principles included a voluntary code of conduct and a mandatory annual reporting system with accompanying grading procedures that were used to classify firms. In an effort to expand the scope and reach of the Principles beyond South Africa, the Reverend Sullivan created the Global Principles of Social Responsibility which were launched in 1999. According to Phillip Rudolph, the Global Sullivan Principles were designed to work in conjunction with corporations' existing codes of conduct and to apply to every worker, in every industry, in every country. The Principles were created as a code of conduct that could offer a framework to align socially responsible companies and organizations working in disparate industries and cultures so as to promote the common goals of human rights, social justice and economic development. By providing an early example of the effectiveness of leveraging voluntary public commitments by private actors, the Sullivan Principles have helped provide the foundations for many recent initiatives, ranging from the US-based Apparel Industry Partnership (the predecessor to the Fair Labour Association) to the UN Global Compact.

Writing specifically on the Caux Round Table (CRT) Principles, Stephen Young, as the Global Executive Director of the Round Table itself, is well qualified to present the reader with a detailed and enlightening Chapter 14 on the content and objectives of this internationally prominent organization. The author charts the inception of the CRT, delving into the struggle to better the trade situation between international companies and to eliminate harmful xenophobic preoccupations that only served to hinder the progress of global business. He further explains the diverse sources of the philosophy behind the Principles, such as the Japanese vision of 'Kyosei', or rather, the doctrine of 'living and working together for the common good'. In what materializes as a fascinating discussion,

Stephen Young explains how the initial scepticism to codifying ethical principles was overcome in order to finally produce the CRT Principles as they are today. He in turn discusses each of the seven general principles, giving the reader insightful guidance on how a business can establish itself as a socially upright enterprise by following their guidance. The author concludes this chapter by referring to the need for company self-assessment and the hierarchy that must arm itself with the requisite communication to implement ethical principles such as the CRT. When summing up, Stephen Young asserts that the CRT has proved its value in that it has lasted, and is today in en ever stronger position that it was when it originally published its renowned set of Principles.

Hans Corell, presently Ambassador in the Swedish Ministry for Foreign Affairs and former Under-Secretary-General for Legal Affairs and Legal Counsel of the UN for over ten years, addresses 'The Global Compact' in Chapter 15. Hans Corell says that the Compact attempts to achieve two complementary goals. The first is to make the Compact and its principles part of the internal strategy and operation of business and the second is to engage different stakeholders and facilitate cooperation among them. The author indicates that four key mechanisms have been developed to accomplish these goals, namely: dialogue, learning, local networks and project partnerships. The principles upon which the Compact is based are threefold, each based on one of the three documents that have been adopted by states by consensus and thus enjoy universal support, namely: human rights (the Universal Declaration of Human Rights), labour (the ILOs Declaration of Fundamental Principles and Rights at Work) and environment (the Rio Declaration on Environment and Development). Corell refuses the criticism that sometimes is made of the Compact that it attempts to shift the responsibility for the observation of international commitments from government to businesses and stresses that the primary responsibility for the principles rests with governments. With respect to business, the Compact is a voluntary initiative with the purpose of promoting responsible global corporate partnership. He accentuates one of the most important commitments of companies signing the Compact which is to publish in their annual report a description of the ways in which the company is supporting the Global Compact and focuses the nine principles, idea that the author advocated already in 1998 when he was asked to challenge a workshop on the topic 'Is the Business of Human Rights also the Business of Business'. He observes that one question that is often asked is why a company that has already established its own code of conduct should participate in the Compact. The answer is simple, he says such codes are extremely important and companies which have demonstrated leadership and made changes in their policies should be commended. However, he adds that they are typically quite narrow in focus, often leaving out important issues such as human rights and the purpose of the Compact is different because it seeks to add new dimensions to good corporate citizenship by creating a platform to encourage innovation, in particular, through new initiatives and partnerships with civil society and other organizations. Enhancing the role of the lawyer in CSR, Hans Corell points out that sometimes, corporate counsels are concerned that by joining the Compact, companies might be held accountable if they do not meet the standards, which he denies because the Compact is not a legally binding instrument and its principles are aspirational in nature. Business leaders should be brought together to build a movement that is strong enough to support the ideals of the Compact. With his great experience in this area, Hans Corell advises that, a crucial precondition for a successful work within the Compact framework is that the CEO and the board of directors are behind the Compact from whom should emanate the initiative to join the Compact.

The Guidelines for Multinational Enterprises published by the OECD is a basic instrument of the CSR Movement. Chapter 16 deals with 'Promoting Corporate Responsibility and the OECD Guidelines for Multinational Enterprises' and has been written by Donald Johnston, who is the present Secretary of the OECD and a former member of the Canadian Parliament and Cabinet Minister. The author describes a number of the OECD initiatives such as the Guidelines for Multinational Enterprises, the Convention of Combating Bribery of Foreign Public Officials in International Business Transactions and the OECD work on international tax enforcement. The Secretary of the OECD explains that the OECD Guidelines are a government-backed code of conduct for international business, which has been adhered to by 30 OECD member and 8 non-member governments. Observance of the Guidelines recommendations is voluntary for business, but the adhering governments make a binding commitment to promote them among TNCs operating in or from their territories. The OECD Guidelines set out a number of 'principles' for international behaviour, which underpin good corporate citizenship, no matter what may be the local legal framework. The Guidelines are a code of conduct attached to a government-backed mediation procedure that reinforces these market pressures. The author analyses the results of the Guidelines to date and refers to a recent survey, which asked managers of international companies to list influential international benchmarks for corporate behaviour and 22 per cent mentioned the Guidelines without prompting. The success of the Guidelines is evident if we take into consideration some 60,000 web pages referring to the Guidelines and 15 countries using the Guidelines in their export credit and investment guarantee programmes. In addition to the formal adherence, the Guidelines have received official support from business and trade union representatives at the OECD and NGOs have formed a coalition to make use of them. The author enters into the most contentious discussion of voluntary or binding rules and concludes that, having been a practising lawyer and a parliamentarian, his bias had been towards controlling much behaviour through laws and regulations, but he recognizes that his view has changed. Effective pressure for good corporate behaviour, Johnston says, can be exercised not only by legal tribunals but also by the court of public opinion, often finding its expression at shareholders meetings and in consumer action. The Guidelines are a code of conduct attached to government-backed mediation procedure that has been used many times and in a variety of ways, ranging from 'naming and shaming' to highlighting the positive steps taken by companies. Thus, the Guidelines promote appropriate international business conduct by raising the incentives for acting responsibly and by helping companies understand what the appropriate conduct is.

The recent Norms issued by the UN have given rise to a hot debate. Chapter 17 on 'The UN Norms on the Responsibility of Transnational Corporations and other Business Enterprises with regard to Human Rights' aims to provide an overview of the UN initiative and its substantive provisions and to highlight certain problems with regard to the current text. This chapter has been written by Jacob Ragnwaldh, a Senior Associate in the Corporate Accountability and the Litigation and Arbitration practice group of Mannheimer Swartling law firm, and Paola Konopik, an Associate in the Corporate Accountability and the Litigation and Arbitration practice group of the same firm. The authors describe how in 1999 the UN Sub-commission on the Promotion and Protection of Human Rights formed a working group in order to examine the effects on human rights of the activities of TNCs and produced the Norms, which were adopted by the Sub-commission in August 2003. The Norms were subsequently considered at the annual meeting of the UN Commission on Human Rights (UNCHR) in April 2004 and the UNCHR decided neither to approve nor to adopt the Norms but called upon the UN High Commissioner for Human Rights to prepare a report to be submitted to the UNCHR in its annual session in 2005. The proposed Norms have been the subject of a highly polarized debate. Many organization such as Amnesty International, the Ethical Globalisation Initiative and the Prince of Wales Business Leaders Forum, have welcome the Norms as an important tool for business seeking to adhere to human rights. However the Norms have been the object of criticism by business organizations such a the International Organization of Employers, the International Chamber of Commerce, the US Council for International Business and the Confederation of British Industry over the fact that the Norms transfer human rights responsibilities from governments to corporations. Jacob Ragnwaldh and Paola Konopik describe the scope of the Norms and give an overview of the obligations of companies under them and endeavour to set out the most significant aspects of the Norms and problems related thereto such as equal opportunity and non-discrimination, security of persons, workers' rights, consumer protection and environmental protection reparation and refer to the implantation, reporting and monitoring envisaged by the Norms. The authors affirm that the Norms are a work in progress to be reviewed and refined in the years to come even if recognizing the long road ahead and the many questions to be answered to clarify the extent of the responsibility of business for human rights.

Daniel Brennan QC, who is the former Chair of the Bar of England and Wales, has provided a thought-provoking discourse in Chapter 18, which deals with 'Corporate Social Responsibility and Corporate Governance: New ideas and practical applications'. The author explores business in the community with a special reference to the United Kingdom Business in the Community 2003, hailing the beginning of the Corporate Responsibility Index (CRI), and gives an erudite exposé detailing various examples of what might be done to apply CSR in a practical context. He goes on to give a valuable insight into how the CRI works and also dedicates a sizeable part of this contribution to reviewing the Caux Round Table Principles that the reader may find included in the annexes. The author weighs up the pros and cons of the introduction of corporate governance initiatives, specifically indexes that rate companies according to their corporate governance practices. He looks at various past models and discusses their varying degrees of success and gives a prediction of future drives to implement such schemes, with the view of conveying the rationale behind these worldwide efforts culminating in a system that will lend itself to global comparison. Daniel Brennan does not limit his chapter to discussing the implementation of corporate governance initiatives in the US and Europe, but he further describes how necessary such ventures are in developing countries. In summing up, the author concludes by giving an optimistic message to the readers. Whilst recognizing that there will be inevitable difficulties along the way if such major changes are to be successfully adopted, although again referring to the good work of the organisations that he has written about, Daniel Brennan's message is a hopeful one that firmly supports further expansion and implementation of existing CSR practices.

Europe has been one of the pioneer regions on the CSR movement. Chapter 19 deals with the 'European Initiatives' of CSR, written by Jonathan Lux, partner of Ince & Co. law firm, who also chairs the IBA Advisory Panel on Corporate Social Responsibility, Sune Skadegard Thorsen, the owner of the law firm Lawhouse (DK) and Director in Corporate Responsibility Ltd. (UK) and Annemarie Meisling, a Consultant at the same firm. The authors believe that the development of CSR in Europe goes hand in hand with other developments including increasing concerns for our fellow man and an increasing concern for the environment generally. It is therefore unsurprising that European institutions and many of the Member State governments have greeted CSR with enthusiasm. However, there has been considerable debate on how best to promote CSR – namely, whether the European institutions should promote voluntary codes or mandatory regulations. The authors point out that, while the Commission favours a voluntary approach, the Parliament favours a mandatory regime and one can find the same debate at EU Member State level with, for example, some countries having brought in legislation obliging pension funds to report on matters going beyond their financial activities and extending to their social and environmental activities, other Member States have been more cautious in their approach, starting with a network-based dialogue between the various stakeholders creating a multi-facetted development in Europe. The authors make a complete and illustrative description of the main European initiatives in CSR such as the Manifesto of Enterprises Against Social Exclusion in 1995 and the creation of the European Business Network for Social Cohesion which later developed into CSR Europe; the EU Lisbon Summit 2000, which decided that the EU would become by 2010 'the most competitive and dynamic knowledge-based economy in the world, capable of sustainable economic growth with more and better jobs at greater social cohesion'; the Parliament' Code of Conduct, December 1998 and June 2002; the Communication of the EU Commission Concerning CSR, July 2002; the Council Resolution, February 2003; the European Business Campaign on CSR; the European Academy of Business in Society; the Business Leaders Initiative on Human Rights; and the EU Charter of Human Rights. They also refer to the national initiatives to promote CSR, like the Belgian pension fund disclosure and social level laws, the Danish Common Concern Campaign, the Copenhagen Centre and the Business and Human Rights Project, the French mandatory sustainability report and the Study Centre for CSR, the German Round Table on Codes of Conduct and Pension Fund Disclosure, the Norwegian Global Kompakt, the Swedish Partnership for Global Responsibility and the UK Pension Fund Disclosure, the Company Law Review, the Corporate Responsibility Bill and the appointment of a minister for CSR. The authors, however, are dubious that the Lisbon ideal for 2010 will crystallize if the

EU does not intensify its efforts. Finally they propose new attractive ideas such as the adoption of some directives, adopting legislation where companies and investment funds should disclose their impact on the treble bottom line and an EU social labour based on the Belgian and Danish experiences and finally refer to the recent Conference in March 2004 on 'CSR and Corporate Governance: Two Mutually Reinforcing Concepts'.

In Chapter 20, Sune Skadegard Thorsen also addresses 'The European Perspectives' of CSR as a complementary comment on Chapter 19. Sune Skadegard describes and composes the differences of approach of CSR in Europe and in the US. European approaches distinguish themselves from American approaches because they focus on integrating CSR in the way companies do business, whereas the US approach focuses on donation and community involvement. The author explains that in Europe during the 70s and 80s attention was primarily focused on environmental concerns, while the 90s focus expanded to embrace CSR. Sune Skadegard explains to us that a human rights based approach can increase coherence and establish long needed convergence in the field. He analyses the human rights approach by discussing the three bottom lines, the engagement in the developing world on which European companies have been very active in identifying their responsibilities when operating in countries normally under diplomatic pressure for human rights violations. He further deals with the responsibility of the European lawyer (which is especially examined in Chapter 28 and several European cases of companies having adopted proactive attitudes focussing on CSR). It takes the recommendations from the 'CCBE Guide for European Lawyers Advising on Corporate Social Responsibility Issues' (see below) one step further, arguing that company lawyers and leaders can benefit from a proactive approach to their CSR strategy, by integrating Corporate Social Opportunities approaches that can assist corporate clients taking relevant steps beyond compliance thus offering a competitive advantage.

Phillip H. Rudolph writes on the US perspectives in Chapter 21, the 'Central Role of Lawyers in Managing Minimizing and Responding to CSR. A US Perspective'. The author remarks on how jurisdictions outside the US generally rely more heavily on regulatory tools to achieve social and economic goals and, in contrast, in his own country the US social and economic goals are often achievable only through resorting to the courts, so that specific characteristics of the US legal system have combined to make litigation one of the principal tools for achieving social and economic ends. The author analyses the five key drivers for litigation in the US (contingency fees, punitive damages, jury trials in civil suits, the non-embracing 'loser pays' system, and class actions). That is why, according to Phillip Rudolph, the American litigation culture means that clients will increasingly look to their attorneys to develop creative opportunities to advance legitimate CSR goals, where appropriate, through litigation and why the bottom line is that litigation-mania in the US thrusts lawyers into the centre of far more issues than might be the case elsewhere and that will become increasingly central in helping businesses to manage CSR risks and opportunities. He analyses some of the lawsuits asserting claims under the heretofore-obscure Alien Torts Claims Act 1789 and the recent regulatory issues of the Sarbanes–Oxley Act and its implementing regulations. The author believes that an increased awareness in the US in the importance of values and principles – as opposed to simply rules – as drivers of corporate behaviour is leading to regulatory activity that will underscore the importance of building social responsibility into the government structures of US business. Reinier Lock is a lawyer who knows Africa well and is the Chair of the IBA's Section of Energy, Environment and Infrastructure Law. The need to stay current and, indeed, leading edge will drive US companies to 'bake' CSR into their business relationships and lawyers are often the principal drafters of these recipes.

The African perspective constitutes the contents of Chapter 22 and has been written by Reinier Lock under the title 'Africa's Unique Challenge: Linking Economic Growth, Infrastructure Reforms and Corporate responsibilities'. As Reinier Lock says, the new century's fanfare attention to CSR has special poignancy for Africa today. He points out what was made evident at the IBA Regional Conference in Lagos, Nigeria on 'Developing the Law as an Instrument for Social and Commercial Rights, which was attended by 650 lawyers, which Reinier Lock like I had the opportunity to attend and in which he made an outstanding speech. Reinier Lock focuses this chapter basically on the electricity and other infrastructure industries, such as water and transportation in which he is a recognized expert. Citing another speaker in the Lagos Conference and author of a chapter in this book, Isaiah Odeleye, he warns that, unless the legal/regulatory system ensures effective completion in the business sector, and effective regulation to protect it, other aspects of CSR can become meaningless. Lack of competition and inadequate regulation of entities with monopoly or 'market power' can do such fundamental damage to the economy and to all consumers, than other aspects of CSR can be relegated to little more than window dressing. That damage is particularly acute to the infrastructure industries of electricity and water supply. Ironically, however, one of the biggest barriers to economic progress in sectors like electricity and water in many African countries has been the domination of these sectors by governments themselves or by state-owned monopolies (SOM). Many countries have commenced serious 'sector reform' initiatives in power, water and other infrastructure sectors restructuring and privatizing and establishing regulatory regimes independent of government. Hence, the focus in infrastructure areas such as electricity has been on creating economically conducive legal and regulatory frameworks to encourage private sector investment, usually by TNCs that are the focus of typical CSR concerns. The author says that in many African countries, whose power sectors are still dominated by SOMs, the CSR situation is much worse than in the developed countries, because they are run by inefficient entities and labour forces that do not even report to adhere to basic economic principles. Many are inadequately funded for expansion, have antiquated infrastructures, and are incapable of providing adequate and reliable service even to the populations and economic enterprises they serve. In many, corruption within their enterprises or amongst their consumers is rampant. The author describes the three types of major initiatives that are under development in Africa today. The first is the 'private sector reform' or the major review and often overhaul of the industry models for providing basic services such as electricity; the second is some specific CSR exercised by TNCs, and the third comprises some continent wide political initiatives that are very distinctive to Africa. The author pays special attention to the new wave of initiatives in Africa like the New Partnership for Africa Development (NEPAD) designed to unite the continent into an effective economic and trading block and to increase its competitiveness. He expands on three specific initiatives of NEPAD: the African Peer Review Mechanism (APRM), the Infrastructure Initiative (energy, water, transport and ICT) and the Public Private Partnerships (PPP) as well as the initiatives to support transparency and development, the Energy Infrastructure Transparency Initiative (EITI) and the Nigeria Transparency Commitments and Promoting Transparency in the African Oils Sectors (CSIS). Reinier Lock considers that these recent initiatives are tied to the traditional view of most African nations that political human rights have little meaning without economic human rights and that economic development is a key global political issue.

Chapter 23 focuses on 'The Japanese Perspective' and describes how in Japan the recent emphasis on corporate governance has been on compliance systems development and on internal audit. James E. Brumm, who is Executive Vice President and General Counsel of Mitsubishi International Corporation in New York and President of the Mitsubishi International Corporation Foundation, addresses the Japanese CSR development. James Brumm reminds us that Mitsubishi has been one of the pioneers in the CSR movement and refers to the famous three corporate principles that were adopted by Mitsubishi early in the last century: 'Shoki Hoko' or corporate responsibility to society, 'Shoji Komei', integrity and fairness and 'Ritsugyo Boeki', international understanding through trade, which were re-examined and reinterpreted in 2000. After an interesting exposition on the historical background and the development of modern Japanese commercial enterprises, James Brumm explains how over the first fifty years following the end of World War Two, major Japanese companies were characterized by life-time employment, a passive shareholding and a business model on long term gain and market share rather than short term profit and how, with the economic difficulties over the last ten years, that the business model is now in the process of transition with more job mobility, more active shareholding and more attention to the bottom line profit and stock price. He also refers to the pressures from the international NGOs such as the Social Responsibility Investment (SRI) funds. James Brumm affirms that CSR is now a very hot topic in Japan and that the leading companies (Sony, Ricoh, Fuji Xerox, Ashi Beer, IBM Japan, NEC, Mitsubishi and Panasonic) all have a CSR department and a code of conduct that reflects the basic principles of CSR. In fiscal 2003, 650 Japanese companies published environmental or sustainable reports and for fiscal 2004 it is expected that some 900 Japanese companies will publish such reports. However, Brumm recognizes that Japan still lags behind the participation of Western multinationals, probably for language and cultural barriers and therefore only two large Japanese companies participate in the Global Compact. He also enhances the important role that the legal profession plays in the CSR movement in Japan.

Felix Ntrakwah, the senior partner of Ntrakwah & Co. in Accra, Ghana and a former Assistant Registrar General in charge of companies, trademarks and patents in Ghana, deals in Chapter 24 with the 'CSR and Human Rights. The Ghana Experience in the Gold Mining Industry'. Gold has been a major source of wealth in Ghana (the old Gold Coast) and gold mining has provided employment.

THE GLOBAL RESPONSIBILITY OF BUSINESS   21

Areas which were hitherto unknown became accessible because of the gold mining activity, the influx of migrants to the mining communities brings about other commercial activities like trading and other service industries, instead of travelling far away to sell their produce and the farmers in the mining communities have ready markets for their produce. But at the same time, gold mining has brought inadequate housing, prostitution, disorganisation of the family, high cost of living, unemployment of people whose lands have been taken by the mining companies, degradation of the forests, pollution due to the use of cyanide and mercury in the processing of gold, and various diseases like respiratory infection, cholera, malaria and now Aids are prevalent in the mining communities. Felix Ntrakwah offers us an analysis of the Ghana Constitution provisions on human rights in relation to the Mining Minerals Law 1989 and he concludes that it is clear that the private sector including gold mining companies are expected to play a role in society for the purpose of national development. In the past, he says, the general belief was that gold mining companies came to Ghana only to dig for gold for export leaving the poor people poorer that they found them. Gold is a very well known natural resource in Ghana and it is cherished and valued by the village chief as well as the common man. In some areas people still look for gold from the surface of the soil and from the gutter after a heavy rainfall. The expectation is that the mining company that is taking this wealth away must do something for the community. Today CSR has become an important object in all sectors of the economy as it is noted in the Constitution. He analyses the various views on CSR from the community, the TNCs, and even from the 'galamsay' (the small-scale mining company). It is extremely interesting to read some to the interviews and newspaper publications that the author compiles in his chapter. Most of them, the author says, it is the publicity which shows a common trend, which is the periodic support given by one or two gold mining companies to a school, hospital or a village. However, the mining companies do not appear eager to publicize any human rights abuse or the negative effect of their activities. It appears that in spite of all their efforts the mining companies still have a lot to do. Available research shows that there are concerns about open pit drilling, blasting and vehicular movement in some areas. The author recalls that a small scale mining company of which he was a director was prevented from further mining operations unless it showed evidence of discharging its obligations. People carrying offensive weapons blocked access to the mines and dared any manager or worker to enter the mine. This happened because the provision of a school and water that had been promised had delayed even though the mining operations were ongoing. The foreign managers, who were expecting successful results and profits before helping the community, were surprised at the reaction of the community. It was the District Chief Executive who finally had to resolve the problem. The Constitution of Ghana encourages the state to ensure the discharge of CSR. It is therefore important for mining companies to adopt comprehensive CSR policies to be budgeted for and implemented as mining operations begin.

   Chapter 25, entitled 'Codes of Conduct: the History, Variations, Impact and Future of Self-regulation', is written by Phillip H. Rudolph who affirms that much dramatic and positive change has occurred in working conditions throughout global supply chain networks over the past decade, and many of these improvements can be attributed to the increased attention brought about through the variety of multilateral initiatives and the codes of conduct today promulgated by TNCs. The World Bank estimates that there may be as many as 1000 of such codes in existence today. The author says that the factors leading to this proliferation are diverse. Some companies that aspire to leadership in CSR have developed codes as a mechanism for incorporating labour rights, human rights and environmental protection into their business model. Others have developed codes to address a particular legal or reputational issue. Still others have built codes in response to expectations of their business partners. Often, it is a combination of these factors that motivates a company to promulgate a code of conduct governing production and supplier activities. Phillip Rudolph presents an interesting history of the codes of conduct from 1930 to our days and describes the different types of codes of conduct, citing Rhys Jenkins (*Corporate Codes of Conduct: Self Regulation in a Global Economy*, 2001) and the UN which distinguishes five categories of codes: model codes, intergovernmental codes, multi-stakeholder codes, trade association codes and company codes, the advantages and disadvantages of which Rudolph recounts. The advantages are many: supply chain management because codes help rationalize a company's relationships with its vendors; maintaining relationships with business partners; safeguarding brand equity and reputation; effective risk management; production efficiency; managing relations with NGOs and minimizing friction with shareholders; behaving consistently with the company's stated principles and ethics and reducing legal risks. The challenges, however, are also significant such as lack of understanding by many employees (who sometimes jokingly refer to posted codes as 'wallpaper'); the fact that many NGOs are often unfamiliar with the particular circumstances that attain in production facilities in many developing countries; many companies face similar challenges in trying to manage the issues presented by the multiplicity of stakeholders and business drivers and may not elect to sign some of the codes for fear of publicity making an easier target for activists. Despite the range of codes in existence today, some level of standardization among the categories of labour and human rights provisions is common and most codes address some combination of forced labour, child labour, wages, benefits, terms of employment, hours of work, discrimination, abuse, and disciplinary action, freedom of association and collective bargaining, and health and safety. The author concludes that codes of conduct are a means to an end and not the end in itself. Returning to first principles, the Declaration on Human Rights (UNDHR) was adopted by the UN as a yardstick by which to measure the degree of respect for, and compliance with, international human rights standards. Global respect for, and protection of human rights has been and should be the desired end-state. Company codes and voluntary principles evolved as a means to bridging the ever-widening gap between the aspirations of the UNDHR and the post-Cold War explosion of the global economy. But, as the author comments, proliferation of such codes has perhaps distracted the participants in the dialogue, who seem at times to focus more attention on the tools for achieving these goals than on the goals themselves.

Claes Lundblad offers an interesting approach on the legal aspects of the codes in Chapter 26 on 'Some legal dimensions of Codes of Conduct'. Claes Lundblad is a partner of Mannheimer Swartling law firm and heads the firm's

Arbitration and Litigation Practice Group. He recognizes that it may be thought that a discussion of legal issues in relation to ethically based expressions of corporate goodwill is entirely misplaced since codes of conduct are by definition different from legal rules. Their very *raison d'être* is that through their flexible, vague, non-binding and voluntary nature, they complement the strictly binding normative system called law. However, he believes that it is nonetheless apparent that ethical statements may have legal consequences at several levels, which effects may occur irrespective of whether they were intended or not. The author analyses the notion of the codes of conduct, and their originators, contents and addressees and their nature as voluntary commitments. He makes an insightful examination of the codes of conduct issued by companies, either as a complement to the law, as encouraged by law, or as a contractual commitment to codes of conduct required by regulators. He examines the contractual relevance of codes of conduct, including labour contracts, external contracts, contracts with business partners in the supply chain and contracts with investors and financial markets. Particular interest is shown by the author to the analysis of the models originating from intergovernmental organization that the author does with particular attention to the OECD Guidelines. Claes Lundblad predicts that we shall see sooner than later the evolution of more standardized codes of conduct and that more elaborate minimum rules also in that area will evolve. It is to be expected that over the time the voluntary commitments made by companies in respect of ethical behaviour may meet sanctions of a legal nature. The inference to be drawn, according to the author, is that on the one hand companies need to adopt and implement sensible ethical guidelines on CSR issues but that not doing so they should also ensure that what they started as voluntary commitments are not permitted to tavern into an unexpected liability nightmare. To avoid that situation, companies need to take an active and constructive approach to CSR issues. Such a stance is likely to be an effective strategy to avoid the very substantial uncertainties of instruments such as the Draft UN Norms and other international instruments of a similar nature.

In Chapter 27, Jerome J. Shestack discusses the role of the lawyer in CSR under the title 'Social Responsibility and the Lawyer in the 21st Century'. Jerome Shestack opines that for most of its history, the legal profession as a whole has been parochial, insular and self-serving. It became so obsessed with being a service profession to clients, he says, that it became a service profession and nothing else. According to the author, social responsibility has increasingly expanded from its dismal beginnings and the long time disconnect between lawyer and CSR to reach broad areas of social reform and justice beyond legal aid to the needy. Still, for a large portion of the world's lawyers, social responsibility is not a critical element of their practice. Jerome Shestack, who dedicated a great part of his presidency at the American Bar Association to defend lawyers' professionalism against commercialism, makes an important contribution on the role of the lawyer in this movement. He reminds us that 'social responsibility' is not a familiar term in the legal lexicon, but the concept of social responsibility is encompassed in what is known as *pro bono publico*, service for the public good, an exercise that Justice William Brennan described as 'the higher calling of the law', namely the obligation of lawyers to become involved in the overriding concerns of society. The chapter offers an interesting description of how social responsibility has progressed in the legal profession and why it is a vital element of the profession's responsibility. While *pro bono* services have primarily involved legal assistance to the needy, starting in the 1970s, (the author, while Chair of the ABA Section of Individual Rights secured a grant from the Ford Foundation to fund a program to encourage law firms to engage in *pro bono* services), the organized bar in the US increasingly also became involved in other important social issues, such as gender and race diversity, reform of mental health, human rights, environmental protection and civil rights so that the organized bar has proved a significant stimulus for lawyers to become involved in such activities. There are several reasons, according to Shestack, for lawyers, including corporate lawyers, to engage in *pro bono* activities. The first, it is one responsibility simply as a decent human being to help afflicted or vulnerable members of society; second, *pro bono* service offers the opportunity to advance justice; third, lawyers are given privileges by society and often a monopoly status and to give something back to society is only fair; fourth, the profession's desire to be highly regarded can be hardly achieved without contributing their special talents and skills to the public good; and finally, any lawyer engaged in *pro bono* service surely knows the joy and sense of professional fulfilment it brings. Shestack provides a number of examples from the Pro Bono Institute of Georgetown University Law Center and from ACCA, which have identified a number of corporations as having best practices in the *pro bono* field and, as Shestack says, strikingly, in each case, it is the general counsel's leadership that has been the key factor and he gives a number of steps for legal departments to become seriously committed to this movement. The exercise of public responsibility by private sector lawyers, corporate lawyers and bar associations has grown considerably and will continue to grow. Response to this 'higher calling of the law' is recognized as a professional obligation, but unfortunately, all too few lawyers are yet inclined to pursue it. Perhaps, as Shestack hopes, that will change as lawyers realize that their profession will never engender the respect from society that they would like until the lawyers are willing to exercise their talents on behalf of society.

Chapter 28 which deals with 'Lawyers' Responsibility for Advising on CSR' has been written by Jonathan Goldsmith, who is the Secretary General of the Council of Bars and Law Societies of the European Union (CCBE), and was the head of the International Department of the Law Society of England and Wales. The author believes that CSR has increased in recent years as a result of the recognition of the essential contribution of business to social, environmental and human rights progress, and because of pressure from customers, investors, employers, governments, NGOs and public opinion. A growing number of businesses already have CSR as a priority in their agendas. It is the lawyers' role to assist their clients in positioning their business successfully in this new legal landscape. Jonathan Goldsmith describes the CCBE involvement in CSR, which culminated with the publishing of the CCBE Guide for European Lawyers advising on Corporate Social Responsibility Issues, annexed at the end that has the aim of explaining the importance of CSR and its potential impact on clients and why lawyers should advise on CSR. The author agrees with previous contributors in that even voluntary approaches to CSR have a legal context. Laws on misrepresentation or false advertizing frame voluntary company reporting, for example. And voluntary approaches such as companies' codes of conduct can shape the standards or care that are legally expected of businesses. In the workplace, agreements reached through collective bargaining between employees and trade unions can become legally binding thorough incorporation in employment contracts. Jonathan Goldsmith emphasizes that it is the lawyers' role to help their clients in placing their business in the most favourable setting.

In Chapter 29, Richard Taylor and Richard Brophy address 'CSR in Lawyers' Firms'. Richard Taylor, currently of counsel, has been a partner of CMS Cameron McKenna law firm since 1974, and the first chairman of CMS, a transnational legal services organisation, and has represented a number of well known TNCs. Richard Brophy has been the Community Affairs Co-Coordinator at CMS Cameron McKenna since 2003 overseeing its *pro bono*, employee volunteering and chair-table giving schemes. The authors recognize that, notwithstanding that ethical obligations are rooted in the lawyers' entitlement to practise, law firms have tended to avoid any public spousal of CSR in relation to the conduct of their own practices. This is not because law firms are too small, indeed some law firms have thousands of employees, a multiplicity of offices and large turnovers, which make them often larger than some of the clients they serve. Nor is it the reticence of law firms to publicize explicit commitments to CSR. The reason appears to be that law firms feel that they might be constrained with respect to the scope and ambit of their professional work if they were to take or be seen to take particularly moral positions on practices or issues which might be the subject of proceedings involving their clients or generally to hold themselves out of the world as models of ethical behaviour. However, UK lawyers do in fact increasingly carry out a significant number of activities under the overall CSR umbrella. According to a recent Law Society survey, more than half of all solicitors have undertaken *pro bono* work in the course of their careers and some 1,400 barristers volunteer their services through the Bar Pro Bono Unit. Activities carried out by law firms under the CSR banner fall into four broad categories that the authors examine in detail: legal *pro bono* activities, where legal services are provided free of charge to needy individuals or organizations; other *pro bono* activities, where volunteers from the firm assist with deserving causes in other ways; financial support to charitable donations; and internal policies with an ethical dimension, including human rights, risk management, environmental and government policies applied within the firm. The authors develop such categories with ample detail. According to them, the amount of *pro bono* work done by lawyers and law firms will certainly increase in the coming years as the profession responds to the growing interest and involvement in CSR on the part of society generally and also to the desire of those entering the profession to play their part and use their developing expertise and experience for the benefit of others.

In Chapter 30, Isaiah Odeleye, a former Legal Practitioner with the Lagos State Ministry of Justice, who works in Shell Petroleum Development Company of Nigeria Limited as a Legal Company Secretary, discusses 'CSR and the In-house Counsel'. Not without justification, the author concludes that the primary responsibility for CSR in a corporate entity lies with the board of directors of the company. In spite of this, the in-house counsel has a role to play if the milk of human kindness of the company in formulating and implementing its CSR policies is not to turn sour. The in-house counsel, in his capacity as either legal counsel or company secretary, has a key role to play in the CSR issues, but before then, it is necessary for him to have first and foremost the right attitude towards CSR, an ingrained element of modern day business. The author believes that CSR should be part of in-house-counsel's mandate through preventive measures in the memorandum and articles, legal audits, compliance monitoring, formulation CSR policy, legislative proposal, review of company policies, corporate structure, new projects and developments and settlement of company's disputes that he accurately comments on. Isaiah Odeleye expands on the 2002 CSR efforts of the Shell Petroleum Development Company of Nigeria Limited (SPDC) and its activities. The author concludes that in-house counsels have a duty at all times to support the cause of justice and at the same time that clients are entitled to the best of the professional knowledge, skill and judgment which must be thorough and fit for their purpose at all times. We have duty, he says with regard to lawyers, within the scope of our professional duties, ethics and law to ensure that the reputation of our employer or client is deservedly kept spotless. One way of doing it is by playing active roles in CSR issues of our employers or clients.

Michael Hopkins of the Middlesex University Business School addresses Chapter 31, with the 'Criticism of the CSR Movement' which closes the author's contribution to the book. According to Professor Hopkins, CSR is not a new concept, but has rapidly come to prominence in the past few years with hardly a day going past without a new report on CSR by a leading company, international organisation, NGO or journalist. But, he asks, is CSR here to stay or will it disappear into the mists of time as just another fad? This chapter explores the uncertainties around CSR. Michael Hopkins accurately summarizes the main criticisms that are made about CSR which he classifies into seven different statements: lack of definition since everybody seems, as I said at the beginning of this introduction, to have their own concept or notion; CSR is just part of public relations to bamboozle an increasingly sceptical public; CSR is another word for corporate philanthropy and that the contribution that a business directly makes to the welfare of society (or 'the planet') is to be viewed as largely independent of its profitability; CSR is misleading as it diverts from key issues, it is a curse rather than a cure; CSR ignores development economics and its concerns with capitalism, neoliberalism and, anyway, is just a proxy to introduce socialism through the backdoor; the social responsibility of business begins and ends with increasing profits and CSR is an unnecessary distraction; and CSR is a sham because companies cannot be left to self-regulate. To the question whether or not CSR is here to stay or whether it will disappear, Professor Hopkins predicts that it is more likely than the latter view is that CSR will transform into different concepts but not disappear entirely. Since the realm of business in society is so crucial, CSR and its entrails will eventually become embedded in all organisations rather like the concern with the environment right now. Consequently, according to him in the future there will be less talk about CSR simply because it will become just part of routine daily operations

I hope that this book may help the readers, be they businessmen, jurists or anyone else who wants to contribute to a better world through the identification and promotion of human rights. Identifying CSR is not easy. Pascal, in his *Pensées*, said that, '*Si l'on est trop jeune on ne juge pas bien, trop vieux de même. Si on n'y songe pas assez, si on y songe trop, on s'entête et on s'en coiffe. Si on considère son ouvrage incontinent après l'avoir fait on est encore tout prévenu, si trop longtemps après on n'y rentre plus. Ainsi les tableaux vus de trop loin et trop-près. Et il n'y a qu'un point indivisible qui soit le véritable lieu. Les autres sont trop près, trop loin, trop haut ou trop bas. La perspective l'assigne dans l'art de la peinture, mas dans la vérité et la morale, qui l'assignera'?*

I am confident that through its diverse angles, this book will provide the right perspective.

PART II

GENERAL OVERVIEW

Chapter 2

BUSINESS ETHICS

Rosamund Thomas

A. INTRODUCTION TO BUSINESS ETHICS

'Business Ethics' ranges from applications by corporations to list on the new FTSE4Good indexes, to standards of conduct enshrined in a wide variety of corporate 'Codes of Ethics'. In some ways 'Business Ethics', like 'Corporate Social Responsibility' (CSR), is heralded as all-embracing within the business corporation, and at other times, is elusive raising uncertainty as to what it is all about.

For clarity, 'Business Ethics' can be seen as the renewal of earlier business aspirations and practices, which guide the conduct and ethos of the business corporation. From Aristotle in the era of classical philosophy, to attempts in the first half of the twentieth century made by Quaker and other business companies, including Rowntree and Cadbury in Britain,[1] 'ethics' in both business and politics have been put forward as the moral 'motor' by which to drive the enterprise or Government.

But, does 'Business Ethics' concern just morality or does it extend to wider social and environmental responsibility, and corporate governance?

There are many definitions of 'Business Ethics' in the same way that there are numerous different 'Codes of Ethics' and this variety and looseness of terminology, methodology, and 'best practices', can cause confusion.

Therefore, it is helpful in this new Millennium to reconstruct 'Business Ethics' in an understandable manner. 'Business Ethics' comprises:

1. the *values* underlying the business corporation, such as 'integrity'; 'honesty'; 'fairness' and others
2. the corporate '*Code of Ethics*' which goes beyond separate values to become a set of principles that make a clear statement of what the business corporation is willing to do or not to do, like forbidding staff to take bribes or other financial incentives

---

[1] Rosamund Thomas *The British Philosophy of Administration: A Comparison of British and American Ideas 1900–1939* (Ethics International Press Ltd. www.ethicspress.com).

Ramon Mullerat (ed.), Corporate Social Responsibility: The Corporate Governance of the 21st Century, 31–36.
© 2005 *International Bar Association. Printed in the Netherlands.*

3. *Corporate Governance*

Corporate governance is the framework for the policies and procedures which govern the Board of Directors in a business corporation, including non-executive Directors and others who advise the Board.

Corporate governance is a key part of 'Business Ethics' since the morality of the Board and its individual Directors does, or should, underlie these policies and procedures. For example, the remuneration of Directors should reflect the values of 'fairness' and 'honesty'.

Where, then, does the current trend for 'Corporate Social Responsibility' fit? Historically, say during the first half of the twentieth century, British writers on 'Business Ethics', and practitioners, regarded the responsibility of a business company to its local, and the world, community as a key function of 'Business Ethics'. For example, B.S. Rowntree, Oliver Sheldon and Lyndall Urwick, at the Rowntree company, York, and Edward Cadbury, who pioneered the model factory in Birmingham, all subscribed to this idealistic view, but also put their ideas into practice.[2] What, today, we might call 'best practice' and more!

But, 'Business Ethics' as a movement faltered to a large extent in Britain, America, and other countries after the Second World War and became either intrinsic and less overtly stated as a philosophy, Code of Ethics, or set of practices, or became subservient to quantitative methods, including 'cost benefit analysis' which emerged during the 1950s and onwards.

Business Ethics, and Ethics in Government, began to resurface following scandals like Watergate in the United States of America, and others. By the late 1970s/1980s the emphasis focussed again on *morality*, but with the *social* commitments of business corporations being a lesser part. Trust, integrity, and ethical dilemmas, were thought to be subjects which could be taught to business and government leaders, with new courses developing, particularly in the USA post-Watergate, for young students and for practitioners in the professional Schools of Business, Public Policy, and so on.

Of course, some business corporations had continued throughout the twentieth century to set and uphold 'Business Ethics', while others disregarded them. But, in the main, it was not the substance of books or courses on business management after the Second World War until the 1980s and 1990s.

It was nearly a decade later when the modern movement of 'CSR', particularly in Europe, became fashionable – pushed forward by the European Commission[3] and the European Parliament, as well as Scandinavia, Britain and other countries. In reverse to 'Business Ethics', CSR focuses more on the *social, environmental* and *sustainability* issues than on 'morality' – although both the 'Business Ethics' and the 'CSR' movements have converged to an extent – with ever increasing responsibilities being added to both, such as anti-corruption practices; human rights; and even the responsibility of Directors for 'corporate manslaughter'.

Today, given the complexity and rapid development of globalization; the inter-relationships between developing and the developed nations; the growth of

[2]   Rosamund Thomas *The British Philosophy of Administration, ibid.*
[3]   For example, the European Commission's White Paper *Communication from the Commission concerning Corporate Social Responsibility: A Business Contribution to Sustainable Development*, Brussels, 2 July 2002, COM (2002) 347 final.

scientific and technological advances which create new ethical dilemmas, such as genetically modified (GM) foods, both 'Business Ethics' emphasizing the *moral* values, and 'CSR' focussing on *social* and *environmental* performance, are of prime importance.

B. MORAL VALUES

Since this chapter is on 'Business Ethics' more than 'CSR', let us look more closely at values. There are several *types* of values, including economic values (such as 'equity'); political values (like 'democracy'); social values (such as 'equal opportunity'); and moral values. 'Business Ethics' is concerned particularly with moral values, but the other values come into play as necessary.

Most countries have seen the damage which can be caused to their business and government institutions by the breakdown of moral values, particularly 'trust' and 'integrity', but also 'truthfulness', 'openness' and others.

Elsewhere I have defined 'trust' and 'integrity'[4] and I cite them below.

1. 'Trust'

Trust involves *reciprocity*: a relationship between two parties – the one who places his/her trust in another who holds it. The concept of trust is based on a confident belief in, or reliance on, the ability, or character of, the other person. A betrayal of trust damages the relationship which cannot easily, or should not necessarily, be restored, so loss or punishment ensues.

Trust is a *moral* concept but also it may be a *legal* one as, for example, breaches of trust under the law of confidentiality. Honesty, by contrast, is a moral concept, principle or value, which can exist with only one party – the person who sets out to be honest can achieve this status without having to depend on anyone else.

2. 'Integrity'

Integrity means uncompromising adherence to a code of moral values.[5] A person may acquire his/her set of values from diverse sources: the family; the school; the Church; clubs and societies; the country of origin and/or the host country.

These values underpinning integrity belong to the individual and are internalized (that is, *personal* integrity which is a part of his/her sound character, or conscience).

When integrity relates to an organization – whether private or public – the values are those of the collective body (that is, *institutional* integrity). Institutional integrity is based on customs, rules, codes of conduct, and other work policies and practices *external* to the individual, which he/she is expected to adopt.

---

[4]   Rosamund Thomas, 'Public Trust, Integrity and Privatization', *Public Integrity* (USA), Vol. III, No. III, Summer 2001, pp. 242–261.
[5]   See note 4 above and 11 below.

Ideally, personal and institutional integrity should coincide, where relevant. If there is a significant conflict between the personal and institutional values, the employee may consider leaving or resigning from his/her place of work. Similarly, staff recruitment and promotion within a business company should be devised to take account of an applicant's character and attitude towards the corporate objectives and code of conduct. The Co-Operative Bank in England, for example, has made considerable effort to make known to staff its ethical policy and values. As a result it was included in *The Sunday Times 50 Best Companies To Work For, 2001*, with staff not only understanding the bank's culture and values, but also benefiting from them due to high staff satisfaction.[6]

Formal 'whistle blowing' mechanisms within a business corporation through which an employee can first raise his/her concerns in the case of a 'crisis of conscience' or divergence between personal and institutional values, is another method of seeking to reconcile values.

C.   THE CORPORATE 'CODE OF ETHICS'

There are strengths and weaknesses about a corporate 'Code of Ethics'. The strengths of such a Code are:

- the 'Code of Ethics' brings together a business corporation's thinking and practices on values, ethics, and business principles;
- the 'Code of Ethics' is a reminder to Directors and employees alike of their commitment to values and standards;
- the 'Code of Ethics' shows other stakeholders what the business corporation stands for.

Some of the weaknesses of a 'Code of Ethics' are:

- the proliferation of 'Codes of Ethics', most of them varying.
  Professor Michael Hopkins in 2002 published an article 'CSR and Global Business Principles: What a Mess!' in which he reviewed hundreds of Codes of Conduct and principles from around the world. He argues that 'there is a serious need of rationalization if companies are not to become even more confused about what is expected of them ...'. Similarly, he cites an OECD report which identified 182 codes of practice and an ILO report which refers to several hundred.[7]
- the corporate 'Code of Ethics' may be used mainly as a public relations tool, rather than a genuine commitment to ethics, standards and morality;
- the 'Code of Ethics' may be seen by Directors and Managers as having fulfilled their ethical duty, without them practising the spirit and wording of it;
- the corporate 'Code of Ethics' may become a stultifying document, lacking innovation in ethical policies and practices.

---

[6]   *The Partnership Report 2000: Making our Mark*, The Co-operative Bank.
[7]   Professor Michael Hopkins, *CSR and Global Business Principles: What a Mess!*, MCH International, Monthly Feature, September 2002.

To overcome the problem of the proliferation of different 'Codes of Ethics', the *OECD Guidelines for Multinational Enterprises,* revised edition,[8] is hailed by the European Commission, FTSE4Good, and many others, as being an essential set of business principles to form the foundation of any business organization's 'Code of Ethics' or 'CSR' policy. For example, a business corporation's own particular ethical, or moral, values can be added to precede the OECD Guidelines but, if most organizations adopt the OECD Guidelines, a more standard pattern of 'Codes of Ethics' and business principles will result.

The OECD Guidelines, moreover, support the *EU Standards for European Enterprises operating in Developing Countries: towards a Code of Conduct*[9] and vice versa. Furthermore, the OECD Guidelines include corporate governance and respect for human rights and thereby form a co-ordinating bridge between 'Business Ethics' and human and labour rights (e.g. the UN Global Compact and the ILO Declaration of Fundamental Principles and Rights at Work).

D. CORPORATE GOVERNANCE

Corporate governance is, or should be, part of 'Business Ethics', even though it is phrased in factual terms relating to the roles and responsibilities of the Board of Directors in a business corporation.

Matters of remuneration, especially in companies highlighted by the press as having 'fat cats' on their Board, involve moral issues, such as 'greed' and 'self interest'. Companies demonstrating a greater sharing of profits throughout the organization, are more likely to be exhibiting the values of 'fairness' and higher ethical standards.

However, because of specific corporate governance requirements for publicly listed companies, this topic sometimes becomes divorced from mainstream 'Business Ethics'.

E. CONCLUSIONS

Since the Enron scandal in the USA, once again there has been a resurgence of emphasis on the need for 'Business Ethics'.

Leadership from the top in a corporation on 'Business Ethics', and example setting, are key methods of upholding good standards of conduct and morality in any country, and should never be forgotten or overlooked. Directors and Senior Managers take note!

Compliance, regulation, and other enforcement procedures, are not necessarily the most suitable process to uphold ethics in business. Besides leadership, and example in practice from the top down in a business corporation, other effective ways of developing an ethical corporation, based on *motivation* and *understanding*, are:

- regular assessment and, if necessary, modification and development of the ethical policy in a business corporation;

---

[8]   *OECD Guidelines for Multinational Enterprises,* Annual Report, 2001.
[9]   *Report on EU Standards for European Enterprises operating in Developing Countries: towards a European Code of Conduct,* Committee on Development and Co-Operation, Rapporteur: Richard Howitt, 17 December 1998.

- feedback within the business corporation from staff and other stakeholders on the business corporation's ethics and practices. Shell International, for example, uses a website for this purpose;
- establishing a system within the business corporation for keeping abreast with national/European/international developments in 'Business Ethics' and 'Corporate Social Responsibility';
- setting up a 'Business Ethics' and 'CSR' Unit (which may be one and the same) to co-ordinate and implement the business corporation's ethics policy and practices, including reporting to the Board of Directors;
- setting ethical targets[10] to achieve the business corporation's policy;
- training for staff on the corporation's business ethics;
- the establishment of formal whistle-blowing machinery (on a confidential basis) for staff to raise their ethical concerns.

The emphasis placed by some, including the European Commission, on developing measurable indicators by which to assess ethical performance has limited scope. Like enforcement procedures, these methods reduce the moral aspects of 'Business Ethics' to mere tools. Inspiration through leadership, example, and establishing a culture of morality, based on good practices – and training – are more likely to charge the moral motor of the corporation than coercion or quantitative tools.

NOTE

The terms 'ethics' and 'morals/morality' often are used interchangeably. Strictly speaking, ethics differs from morality in that 'conduct may be described as 'moral' when it is maintained or observed as a fact, but, conduct becomes 'ethical' as it rises from fact to ideal'.[11] Since in this book there may be other references to 'moral values' (which, by the above definition, might not be dealing with 'facts' but perhaps 'ideals'), I have not kept strictly to the above definition in this Paper.

---

[10] For a proposal by Rosamund Thomas for 'Eight Ethical Performance Targets' and 'Fourteen Risks to Reputation from Unethical (including illegal) Behaviour', see Developing an Ethical Image: Managing your Reputation via Corporate Branding by R. Thomas in *The Journal of Brand Management* Vol. 6, No. 3, January, 1999, pp. 198–210.
[11] Rosamund Thomas, *The British Philosophy of Administration, op. cit.*, p. 141.

Chapter 3

CSR AND CORPORATE GOVERNANCE

Mark Walsh
John Lowry

A. INTRODUCTION

Ever since Polly Peck, Guinness, Maxwell and BCCI,[1] corporate governance has been an increasing concern for those that direct and manage listed UK and other companies, but the corporate failures and wrongdoing that have come to light since late 2001 have raised the temperature of the international corporate governance debate considerably.[2]

Having already suffered severe stock market losses with the piercing of the new economy bubble in early 2000, the abuses at Enron, Tyco, Global Crossing, Adelphia and WorldCom in the US, and at Ahold, Parmalat, Equitable and now Shell in Europe, have severely impacted investor confidence in the integrity of those charged with the supervision and management of our larger companies. Those responsible have included those that work at or for the companies in question (management and directors), as well as those that deal with and advise them (auditors, banks and law firms).[3] This loss of confidence has had a direct and adverse impact on our capital markets from which we are still attempting to recover.

---

[1]   The abuses identified in these cases went well beyond matters of corporate governance, including criminal conduct such as the appropriation of shareholder and/or employee assets for personal benefit (Polly Peck and Maxwell) and the avoidance of existing securities and bank regulatory requirements (Guinness and BCCI). They resulted in over 23 cases in the English courts alone (including the *MacMillan v. Bishopsgate* and *BCCI* cases) and led directly to at least one corporate governance report (the Cadbury Report is discussed below).

[2]   There continues to be significant disagreement between the leaders of many of the UK's largest companies and those that manage the funds that invest in them. See 'Warring parties set out terms in clubland bash', *Financial Times*, 29 March 2004 at 3, and 'Investors group seeks peace with business', *Financial Times*, 30 March 2004 at 1.

[3]   Many of the abuses that occurred in the US are described in an SEC Staff Report issued under Section 704 of the Sarbanes Oxley Act of 2002, which we sometimes refers to in this chapter as 'Sarbanes Oxley'. See www.sec.gov for a copy of this report. The report identified the roles of senior management at Enron, Adelphia, Tyco and senior and mid level management at WorldCom. It also identified several instances of improper conduct by accountants and lawyers.

Ramon Mullerat (ed.), Corporate Social Responsibility: The Corporate Governance of the 21st Century, 37–60.
© 2005 *International Bar Association. Printed in the Netherlands.*

In this chapter, we first describe the relationship between corporate governance and CSR and the ways in which the corporate governance regimes in the US, the UK and the EU have evolved. We will see that, while the term corporate governance is of comparatively recent origin, laws with corporate governance objectives – passed in response to one crisis or another – have existed for well over a century. With the passage of the Sarbanes Oxley Act in 2002, the US regime is primarily statute and rule based, whereas in the UK and the rest of the EU there is still greater reliance on voluntary or semi-voluntary codes of conduct (i.e. 'soft law'). Secondly, we consider some of the techniques that have been adopted to protect investors and to control and make accountable the key players with corporate governance responsibilities. We conclude by noting that, while progress is being made, there is a need for further harmonization, simplification and more balanced implementation of global corporate governance initiatives and requirements.

B.   RELATIONSHIP BETWEEN CORPORATE GOVERNANCE AND CSR

While the OECD and many national codes of conduct,[4] as well as much academic commentary,[5] use the term 'corporate governance' very broadly to refer to a company's responsibilities to all stakeholders (much in the way the term 'corporate and social responsibility' is used in this book), the term is used by most corporate and securities lawyers[6] to refer more narrowly to the checks and balances adopted by a company to protect the interests of its shareholders. We use the term in its narrower sense in this chapter not only because it allows us to distinguish the subject from what is dealt with in other chapters, but also because it helps us to make an important distinction.

Amongst other things, CSR principles aim to make today's larger public companies responsible members of the community. To ensure that, in addition to complying with the minimum requirements of the law, they conduct their activities in an environmentally sensitive manner, they pay their taxes in full and on time, they respect their employees and pay and treat them fairly wherever they may be based, they source their raw materials from companies that also follow sound labour and environmental practices, and they otherwise act ethically in their dealings with the outside world. Using our narrower definition, corporate

---

4   The OECD's Principles of Corporate Governance refer specifically to the role of stakeholders. The Preamble states that corporate governance involves 'a set of relationships between a company's management, its board, its shareholders and other stakeholders', while Principle II states that the '[t]he corporate governance framework should recognize the rights of stakeholders as established by law and encourage active co-operation between corporations and stakeholders in creating wealth, jobs, and the sustainability of financially sound enterprises'. A majority of EU corporate governance codes at least recognize some degree of interdependency between these constituencies.

5   See e.g. Sheikh and Rees (eds.), *Corporate Governance and Corporate Control* (London, Cavendish, 1995), in which the editors state: 'The modern corporation is perceived as a "caring corporation" which discharges social as well as economic obligations in society' (at 2). Accordingly, they refer to four principal aspects of corporate governance, including responsibilities to 'those making a legitimate demand for accountability'. They refer with approval to other authors who take such a broader view, including Sheridan and Kendall (at 8).

6   See e.g. Sidley Austin Brown & Wood, *Accessing the US Capital Markets* (2004). See also Bostelman, *The Sarbanes Oxley Handbook* (PLI 2004).

governance is more concerned with the enhancement of shareholder value and the protection of shareholder interests. To ensure, through a variety of oversight mechanisms, that management is encouraged to develop the business in the best interests of the shareholders and is not allowed to waste or otherwise divert corporate assets. Arguably the best known definition is that used in the Cadbury Report: 'corporate governance is the system by which companies are directed and controlled'.[7]

CSR principles often emerge over time through effective lobbying by and debates with interest groups and human rights and public interest lawyers[8] (they are still often of a voluntary nature or softer), whereas corporate governance principles are more typically governmentally or shareholder inspired reactions to high profile corporate failures, abuses and other crises (and are more often mandatory) that have harmed the investor community. In some cases, it is hard to distinguish between CSR and corporate governance. Although generally underpinned by detailed statutory provisions, environmental, labour and consumer obligations have more to do with CSR than corporate governance precisely because the largest companies are expected to set a good example for others: to do more than the law requires. Likewise, corporate governance is at times concerned with softer issues such as the promotion of ethical behaviour by directors and managers, but this is usually with the interests of a narrower constituency (the shareholders) in mind.

Whatever merit there is to these distinctions, corporate governance is an increasingly important aspect of CSR. And, as they continue to develop, corporate governance principles will continue to provide the more solid foundations on which broader CSR principles – and business ethics – can be further enhanced.

C. CORPORATE GOVERNANCE IN THE US

1. State Corporate and Securities Laws

In the US, one has to distinguish between federal and state law as applied by distinct federal and state court systems. Traditionally, the laws relating to corporations and the ways in which they raise capital (securities laws) were solely matters of state law: corporate law – or what an English lawyer terms company law – still is. This means that the primary source materials for the rights and duties of directors and shareholders in the US are the state corporation laws and the decisions of the state courts that interpret those laws. Delaware, the home state for many of the largest US companies, has a particularly well established body of corporate law.[9]

---

[7] Report of the Committee on the Financial Aspects of Corporate Governance 1992 is available at www.ecgi.org/codes/country_pages/codes_uk.htm. See para. 2.5.
[8] A good example is the pharmaceutical industry where, quite apart from typical governance issues, the larger companies have been under great pressure to partially surrender patent rights, and agree to pricing levels that do not produce a profit, to ensure key products such as HIV treatments are available to those that cannot otherwise afford them, particularly in developing countries. See the 2003 Corporate Responsibility Report of GlaxoSmithKline plc available at www.gsk.com.
[9] See *General Corporation Law of the State of Delaware*, Del Code Ann. tit. 8. See also F.A. Gevurtz *Corporation Law* (St Paul, Minn, West Group, 2000).

2.   Federal Securities and Other Laws

At different points over the past century, public condemnation of the conduct of
certain US companies – or, more specifically, those that managed them –
prompted the federal government to intervene in these traditional preserves of
state law. This occurred in the late 19th and early 20th Century when the Sherman
and Clayton Acts were adopted in response to the anticompetitive practices of the
trusts that controlled America's rail and communication networks.[10] It occurred in
the 1930s when the federal securities laws (including the Securities Act of 1933
and the Securities Exchange Act of 1934) were adopted in the aftermath of the
1929 stock market crash and the improper behaviour on Wall Street that
contributed to it.[11] And it occurred with the passage of Sarbanes Oxley in 2002
(which is really a series of amendments to the 1934 Act) in the wake of Enron and
the other corporate failures that are referred to in more detail below.[12]

3.   Securities Law Enforcement

The Federal Trade Commission, which had been given – and still has – responsibility for antitrust enforcement, was also given responsibility for federal securities
law enforcement in 1933, but in 1934 these powers were transferred to a newly
established Securities and Exchange Commission.[13] Since that time (and although
each state still has its own securities commission and securities or 'blue sky' laws),
federal oversight of the securities industry has significantly reduced the importance
of the corresponding state enforcement machinery. The SEC has published volu-
minous rules dealing with matters such as the contents of prospectuses, the regulation of broker-dealers (investment firms) and stock exchanges, and the promotion,
structure and fees charged by mutual funds. The SECs detailed disclosure requirements under the federal securities laws are an important corporate governance protection, and many of these SEC rules have significant extraterritorial effect.

While there had been numerous corporate failures prior to that time where
director oversight of management was shown to have been inadequate, it was not
until the collapse of the Penn Central Railroad in 1970 and the publication of
the Penn Central Report in 1972[14] that the SEC became particularly focused on
the roles played by directors and management. In its 1980 Report on Corporate
Accountability,[15] the SEC emphasized the important role played by the board of
directors indicating that at least a majority of the members should be independent and that each board should have independent audit, compensation and
nominating committees.

---

[10] See *Antitrust Laws and Trade Regulation*, 2nd edn., Matthew Bender, 2000. See also the
Robinson–Patman Act of 1936 relating to unfair pricing.
[11] For a discussion of the background to this legislation, see e.g. Johnson and McLaughlin,
Corporate Finance and the Securities Laws, 3rd edn., Aspen, 2004, Chapter 1. See also *Legislative
Histories of the 1933 and 1934 Acts*, published for the Law Librarians Society of Washington DC,
Fred B Rotherman & Co. (1973).
[12] See the House and Senate Reports that preceded *Sarbanes Oxley*, as well as the SECs Report
under Section 704 of that Act, *supra* n. 3.
[13] See Johnson and McLaughlin, *supra* n. 11 at 6.
[14] See SEC Staff Study of the Financial Collapse of the Penn Central Company, CCH Fed Sec L
Rptr, 1972–73 Transfer Binder Par 78,931.
[15] See SEC Staff Study on Corporate Accountability, Committee on Banking, Housing and Urban
Affairs, US Senate, 4 September 1980.

Although the SEC has primary responsibility for securities law enforcement, the state securities commissioners and state attorneys general continue to resist attempts to curtail their influence and, citing SEC failures to effectively use the powers available to it, have been at the forefront of some major recent enforcement initiatives in the US.[16] They have not, however, been a significant contributor to the corporate governance debate, unlike the state courts in Delaware and elsewhere which have.

4.   Stock Exchange Listing Requirements

From the 1980s, there have been a number of other important corporate governance initiatives, which were reflected primarily in amendments to the listing requirements of the New York Stock Exchange and other US exchanges and securities markets. To begin with, following the findings of the SECs 1980 report, these other exchanges and markets amended their listing requirements to require independent audit, compensation and nominating committees. The American Law Institute also published its Principles of Corporate Governance in 1992,[17] but these were controversial and not particularly influential, not least because they attempted to codify corporate governance issues with differing legal and non-legal bases. In 1998, the Blue Ribbon Committee Report on Improving Effectiveness of Audit Committees sponsored by the New York Stock Exchange and NASDAQ was published. This Report, which contained ten recommendations for enhancement of audit committee performance and five guiding principles for audit committee best practices, emphasized independence and financial literacy of audit committee members, as well as quality of financial information. The recommendations were adopted by the SEC in January 2000 and then by the NYSE and NASDAQ through amendments to their listing requirements.[18]

5.   Recent Developments

By early 2000, the SEC was seeking to address conflicts of interest in the accountancy profession, but it did not have other significant corporate governance initiatives in the works; indeed, there was relative complacency about corporate governance issues in the US, particularly as global equity markets were at all time highs. There was a widespread belief, promoted not least by the SEC, that US accounting principles were superior to those used in other countries. To the extent any corporate governance issue was receiving attention, it was the size

---

16   For example, New York State Attorney General Elliot Spitzer has spearheaded recent enforcement actions against investment analysts and mutual fund management companies, notwithstanding the fact that the SEC also has jurisdiction in these areas. Under Chairman Donaldson, the SEC has sought to regain the enforcement initiative and has been allocated significant additional resources by the US Congress to that end.

17   The ALI *Principles of Corporate Governance*, 1992, are available at www.ali.org.

18   See Ira M. Millstein, *Introduction to Report and Recommendations of the Blue Ribbon Committee on Improving the Effectiveness of Audit Committees*, 54 Bus Law 1057 (1999). The Blue Ribbon Report and related listing requirements of the NYSE and NASDAQ are available at www.nyse.com and www.nasd.com, respectively.

of executive compensation packages, but, here again, while there were calls for additional disclosure and the expensing of related costs, there was little pressure for significant reform. The collapse of Enron in late 2001, followed by Global Crossing, Tyco, WorldCom and others in 2002, transformed the corporate governance debate in the US. In an effort to restore investor confidence in the capital markets, President Bush announced 10 principles for reform early in the year and by the end of July he had signed the Sarbanes Oxley Act into law.

Sarbanes Oxley and the SEC rules adopted under that Act represented the most comprehensive reform of the US federal securities laws since the 1930s. They impose significant new responsibilities on chief executive and chief financial officers (i.e. they bring management within the corporate governance net), significantly increase the powers of public company audit committees, provide severe civil and criminal penalties for wrongdoing, and, with the formation of the Public Company Accountants Oversight Board or PCAOB, transform the way in which accountants are supervised and practice. The new requirements, which also required the amendment of US listing standards, apply to non-US companies that file reports with the SEC either because they are listed on a US exchange or because they have completed an SEC registered securities offering. We discuss many of the new requirements later in this chapter.

D.   CORPORATE GOVERNANCE IN THE UK

1.   English Company Law

Corporate governance requirements in the UK have developed in a somewhat similar manner. Just as the duties and rights of US directors and shareholders are to be found in US state corporations statutes and related decisions of US state courts, the duties and rights of directors and shareholders in English companies are found in the Companies Acts (now the Companies Act 1985) and, more importantly, the case law that has interpreted them.[19]

Indeed, the need to have an understanding of overly complex case law developed over 150 years in response to such dated crises as the South Sea bubble, has long been criticized, and is one of the factors that contributed to the as yet unrealized demand for major company law reform in the UK. First considered by the Greene Committee in 1926, the Jenkins Committee in 1962 and the Cohen Committee in 1945, successive UK governments have published numerous reports calling for comprehensive reform of English company law. In 2002, the UK Government published its White Paper, *Modernizing Company Law*,[20] which, as discussed further below, proposes a codification of directors' duties and enhanced company disclosure through an operating and financial review for major listed companies. Most recently, the Companies (Audit, Investigations and Community Enterprise) Act 2004 – what we refer to as the UK's 2004 Act – was adopted. This will come into effect in phases in 2005 and, while not as ambitious

---

[19]   The first Joint Stock Companies Act was passed in 1844, while limited liability was introduced in the Limited Liability Act, 1855. Subsequent legislation, most notably the Companies Act 1948, is the basis on which the companies laws of many commonwealth countries was introduced.

[20]   The White Paper is available at www.dti.gov.uk. See also the Thirteenth Report of the Select Committee on Trade and Industry which is available at www.parliament.the-stationery-office.co.uk.

in scope as Sarbanes Oxley, it places significant additional responsibilities on directors and fundamentally changes the regulatory scheme for accountants.

2.   The Combined Code and the Listing Rules

While legislation and case law are clearly key ingredients of the overall corporate governance package, there is much greater reliance in the UK on non-statutory codes of conduct. Indeed, industry contributions to the corporate governance debate such as the CBIs Principles of Corporate Conduct (1973) and the Institute of Directors' Guidelines for Directors (1985) generally focused on the perceived benefits of self regulation and sought to avoid the imposition of statutory requirements. Until recently, so also did the corporate governance initiatives of shareholders. Reflecting this approach, the primary source of corporate governance responsibilities for UK public companies are contained in the Combined Code of Corporate Governance.[21] Prepared under the auspices of the Financial Reporting Council or FRC, and now part of UK Listing Authority's Listing Rules,[22] the Combined Code is the product of a range of committee reports established in response to some of the more high profile UK corporate failures.

3.   The Reports of the 1990s

The Cadbury Report,[23] published in 1992 and triggered by BCCI and Maxwell, was primarily concerned with the financial aspects of corporate governance. It acknowledged the right of directors to 'be free to drive their companies forward', while at the same time pointing out that the exercise of that freedom must be 'within a framework of effective accountability'.[24] In suggesting the adoption of a code of best practice, it spoke of the need for compliance to be focused on the spirit rather than the letter of its requirements, the fact that this code was based on principles of 'openness, accountability and integrity'[25] and the vital roles played by the board and its individual members. The Greenbury Report[26] in 1995, issued in response to controversial pay packages at the recently privatized utility companies, focused on director's remuneration. Through delegation of compensation questions to an independent committee of the board, it referred to the need to link rewards to performance (by both company and individual) and align the interest of directors and shareholders in promoting the company's progress. While indicating that mistakes had been made, it concluded, however, that UK compensation packages were broadly in line with international standards, and well below US levels. The Hempel Report in 1998, in addition to reviewing the implementation of Cadbury and Greenbury, was focused on the roles of directors, shareholders and auditors in corporate governance, while the

---

[21]   The Combined Code of Corporate Governance, amended as of July 2003, is available at www.fsa.gov.uk/pubs/ukla/lr_comcode2003.pdf.
[22]   The FSAs Listing Rules are available at www.fsa.gov.uk/ukla/2_listinginfo.html.
[23]   *Supra* n. 7.
[24]   Cadbury Report at para. 1.1.
[25]   Cadbury Report at para. 3.2.
[26]   Directors' Remuneration, Report of a Study Group chaired by Sir Richard Greenbury, 1995, is available at www.eccg.org/codes/country_documents/uk/greenbury.pdf.

Turnbull Report in 1999 provided guidance to directors on the implementation of the Combined Code's internal control requirements.[27] Using words that have some relevance today, they said: 'The importance of corporate governance lies in its contribution both to business prosperity and to accountability. In the UK the latter has preoccupied much public debate over the past few years. We would wish to see the balance corrected'.[28] Adopting the Cadbury definition of corporate governance, it reaffirmed the primacy of shareholder interests. 'As the CBI put it … to us, the directors as a board are responsible for relations with stakeholders; but they are accountable to the shareholders'.[29]

4.   Higgs, Smith and More Recent Reforms

The incidence of wrongdoing that occurred – or, should we say, was discovered – in the US from late 2001 onwards, and which resulted in Sarbanes Oxley and related SEC Rules, triggered a further and very comprehensive review of corporate governance requirements in the UK. Although no gross accounting irregularities or fraud were being identified in the UK at the time (and while being willing to attribute this in part to the corporate governance system already in place), the UK Government and industry commentators were keen to ensure that lessons were learned from what was occurring in the US and that potential areas of corporate governance weakness be identified and addressed. More specifically, the UK Government commissioned Derek Higgs (now Sir Derek Higgs) to conduct a review into the role and effectiveness of non-executive directors and Sir Robert Smith to conduct a review of audit committees. Both reports were issued in early 2003, and they lead to the adoption of a series of amendments to the Combined Code as of July that year.[30] At the same time, reports were commissioned into the co-ordination of audit and accounting issues and a review of the regulatory regime for the accounting profession, which reports were issued at the same time as Higgs and Smith.[31] The UK's 2004 Act, which resulted from this process will result in FRC oversight of the accounting profession (different from but with similar objectives as the PCAOB in the US) and increased scrutiny of audited accounts.

5.   Financial Services Law Enforcement

Since the adoption of the Financial Services and Markets Act 2000, primary responsibility for the enforcement of the Listing Rules and other aspects of UK securities regulation has been entrusted to the Financial Services Authority or FSA. However, although the Combined Code is now part of the Listing Rules and the FSA

---

27   Committee on Corporate Governance, Final Report, 1998, is available at www.eccg.org/codes/country_documents/uk/hampel_index.htm. Internal Control – Guidance for Directors on the Combined Code (Turnbull) is available at *http://www.icaew.co.uk/viewer/index.cfm?AUB=TB21_6342*.
28   Hampel Report at para. 1.1.
29   Hampel Report at para. 1.17.
30   The Higgs Review can be located at www.dti.gov.uk/cld/non_exec_review and the Smith Report can be located at http://www.frc.org.uk/images/uploaded/documents/acreport.pdf.
31   See Co-Ordinating Group on Audit and Accounting Issues, Final Report to the Secretary of State for Trade and Industry and the Chancellor of the Exchequer, 29 January 2003, and Review of the Regulatory Regime of the Accountancy Profession, Report to the Secretary of State for Trade and Industry, January 2003.

therefore has a degree of responsibility for ensuring compliance with it, the FSA has no particular input into its contents, and it has tended in practice to disclaim responsibility for reviewing the adequacy of listed company annual compliance statements. Perhaps oddly, the Combined Code is the responsibility of the FRC, which, as indicated, should be viewed as a regulator for the accountancy profession, rather than an enforcer of corporate governance disclosure requirements.

E.   CORPORATE GOVERNANCE IN THE EUROPEAN UNION

With the exception of Luxembourg, there are corporate governance codes in each of the current EU member states (not including the ten countries that have acceded to EU membership in 2004).[32] There are at least 13 in the UK, 4 in Belgium, and 3 in each of France and Germany.

While the legal systems in these countries and the board and other structures that they use vary significantly, there has been an increasing trend toward convergence of corporate governance requirements throughout the EU over the past 10 years, both through implementation of the various EU company law directives, and the adoption of these (usually non-binding) codes of best practice. The objectives behind the codes range from improving companies' performance, competitiveness and access to capital (Portugal, Finland, Greece and Germany) to improving the quality of board (supervisory) oversight (UK, Netherlands, France and Belgium) and improving the quality of information available to the capital markets (Belgium and Italy).

As occurred in the UK and several other member states, Enron and its progeny prompted an EU level review of corporate governance requirements. An EU Group of Company Law Experts, chaired by Jaap Winter, had already been mandated to conduct a review of member state laws with a view to further company law reform, and its remit was expanded to include issues relating to corporate governance. The Winter Report,[33] published in November 2002, concluded that the increasing trend towards convergence of corporate governance requirements in Europe made it unnecessary for EU wide reforms to be implemented, but also made a number of suggestions concerning disclosure for further review by member states.

Since the publication of the Winter Report, the Commission has issued more specific proposals on corporate governance and a directive to combat fraud and malpractice.[34] In the former, it concluded that, while there was no need for an

---

[32]   For a summary of the corporate governance regimes in existence throughout the EU, see Comparative Study of Corporate Governance Codes Relevant to the European Union and its Member States, 2002, which is available at http://europa.eu.int/comm/internal_market/en/company/company/news/corp-gov-codes-rpt_en.htm.

[33]   The Report of the High Level Group of Company Law Experts on a Modern Regulatory Framework for Company Law in Europe, November 2002, is available at http://europa.eu.int/comm/internal_market/en/company/company/modern/consult/report_en.pdf. For a somewhat controversial legislative response to recent corporate governance failures (e.g. Elan Pharmaceuticals plc), see the Irish Companies (Auditing and Accounting Act) 2003, which comes into effect in 2005 and which we refer to as the Irish 2003 Act.

[34]   Communication from the Commission to the Council and the European Parliament, Modernizing Company Law and Enhancing Corporate Governance in the European Union – A Plan to Move Forward, May 2003, is available at http://europa.eu.int/eur-lex/en/com/cnc/2003/com2003_0284en01.pdf. EC Proposed Directive to Combat Fraud and Malpractice, 16 March 2004, is available at http://europa.eu.int/comm/internal_market/auditing/index_en.htm.

EU code of corporate governance, the EU still had an important role to play in the area. More specifically, it proposes to take action 'with respect to a few essential rules [to ensure] adequate co-ordination of [EU] corporate governance codes'.[35] This will include requiring listed companies to include a corporate governance statement in their annual reports, requiring disclosure from institutional investors about their investment and voting policy, strengthening shareholders' rights through access to information and other steps, and changing the law relating to directors to, among other things, confirm the collective nature of board responsibility. The latter, a proposal to combat abuses such as occurred at Ahold and Parmalat, deals with the provision of statutory audits in the EU, including ethical principles to ensure the objectivity and independence of accountants.

F. CORPORATE GOVERNANCE AND DIRECTORS

The corporate governance changes that have recently taken place in the US and the UK significantly impact directors (who were widely perceived to have failed in their oversight functions at the companies we have referred to), particularly members of audit committees. According to recent industry surveys, directors are working harder – and represent better value – than ever. And, while recent reform makes it clear that audit committee members need to be more effective in the future, both the SEC and the Smith Report went to great lengths to confirm that no such committee members should be considered to have assumed greater responsibilities – or potential liability – than other members of the board. The following are some of the more important aspects of corporate governance relevant to directors in both countries, with an emphasis on those aspects that were touched upon as part of the most recent reforms.

1. Directors Duties

At common law, directors of UK companies have a number of duties. These include the need to exercise reasonable care and skill, a duty to act in good faith in what they consider to be in the best interests of the company (sometimes called a duty of loyalty),[36] a duty to use their powers for the purposes for which they were granted and not for improper purposes,[37] a duty not to fetter their future discretion (i.e. how they will vote in the future),[38] and a duty to avoid conflicts of interest and not to personally appropriate corporate opportunities for

---

[35] *Supra* n. 34 at 2. The results of the consultation on the Action Plan were announced on 21 November 2003, and Commissioner Bolkenstein announced on 11 February 2004 that work on these issues would be accelerated through one proposal to amend the 4th and 7th Company Law Directives.

[36] A modern formulation of this duty was provided by Millett LJ (as he then was) in *Bristol & West Building Society v. Mothew* (1998) Ch 1 who observed: 'The distinguishing obligation of a fiduciary is the obligation of loyalty. The principal is entitled to the single-minded loyalty of his beneficiary. This core liability has several facets. A fiduciary must act in good faith; he must not make a profit out of his trust; he must not place himself in a position where his duty and his interest may conflict...'

[37] See *Howard Smith Ltd v. Ampol Petroleum Ltd* (1974) AC 821; PC, and *Extrasure Travel Insurances Ltd v. Scattergood* (2002) All ER (D) 307 (Jul), Ch (D).

[38] *Fulham Football Club Ltd v. Cabra Estates plc* (1992) BCC 863.

themselves.[39] These duties are generally owed to the company and not to the shareholders, although there are exceptions. Under the Companies Act 1985, directors are subject to a range of additional restrictions, including requirements for shareholder approval for matters such as payments for loss of office, employment contracts of more than five years and substantial property transactions.

Following an extensive review of these common law and statutory duties by the Law Commission and the Company Law Review Steering Group, the government proposed in its 2002 White Paper that directors' duties be codified. While generally mirroring the common law and statutory duties referred to above, the seven general principles referred to in Clause 19 of the Companies Bill (and Schedule 2 thereto) go further. In addition to observing a number of specified duties and prohibitions, directors conduct is to be measured by reference to a test with both objective and subjective elements. They will be expected to exercise the care, skill and diligence which would be exercised by a reasonably diligent person with both (i) the knowledge, skill and experience that may reasonably be expected of a director in his or her position; and (ii) any additional knowledge, skill and experience which he or she has.

Under the corporation laws of the US states, directors also have fiduciary and other duties that include a duty of care[40] and a duty of loyalty.[41] These duties, which are generally more subjectively reviewed, are owed to the corporation and its shareholders. Unlike in the UK, directors of US companies are (most notably in Delaware) afforded the protection of the 'business judgment rule' under which courts generally defer to board decisions. This rule, which can be traced to *Percy v. Millaudon*,[42] holds that courts should exercise restraint in holding directors liable for (or otherwise second guessing) business decisions which produce poor results or with which reasonable minds might disagree.[43] The Delaware Supreme Court explained in *Aronson v. Lewis*[44] that the business judgment rule established a gross negligence standard.[45] A classic formulation was delivered by the court in *Miller v. American Telephone & Telegraph* Co:[46]

> The sound business judgment rule ... expresses the unanimous decision of American courts to eschew intervention in corporate decision-making if the judgment of directors and officers is uninfluenced by personal considerations and is exercised in good faith ... Underlying the rule is the assumption that reasonable diligence has been used in reaching the decision which the rule is invoked to justify.[47]

---

[39] Although the precise limits of the corporate opportunities doctrine are still regarded as somewhat uncertain, Professor Prentice describes it as a principle which 'makes it a breach of fiduciary duty by a director to appropriate for his own benefit an economic opportunity which is considered to belong rightly to the company which he serves': see (1974) *MLR* 464. For a paradigm case, see *Cook v. Deeks* (1916) 1 AC 554, PC.

[40] Akin to the modern approach taken in the UK, see above, for example, *Re D'Jan of London Ltd* [1994] 1BCLC 561. See *Francis v. United Jersey Bank* 87 N.J. 15, 432 A2d 814 (1981).

[41] See *Sinclair Oil Corp v. Levien* 280 A.2d 717 (Del. 1971). See also, H. Marsh Jr, 'Are Directors Trustees? Conflict-of-Interest and Corporate Morality' 22 *Bus Law* 35 (1966), as well as the more recent opinion of the Delaware Supreme Court in *Cede & Co. v Technicolor, Inc.*, 634 A.2d (1995).

[42] 8 Mart. (N.S.) 68 (La 1829).

[43] Guvurtz, *supra* n. 8 at 4.1.2.

[44] 473 A.2d 805, 812 (Del. 1984).

[45] See also, *Smith v. Van Gorkom* 488 A.2d 858 (Del. 1985).

[46] 507 F.2d 759 (3d Cir. 1974).

[47] *Ibid* at 762. However, see In re The Walt Disney Company Derivative Litigation, 825 A.2d 275 (Del. Ch. 2003), which reflects an increasingly sceptical attitude towards the decisions of directors of US companies post Enron.

However, judicial review of directors' actions by Delaware courts can be enhanced in certain circumstances, including defending against a change of control or engaging in a sale of control. In those cases, the '*Unocal* standard'[48] or the '*Revlon* test'[49] may be applied. Unlike the business judgment rule, such transactions require the decision of the directors to be tested against a predominantly objective standard[50] very much focused on the primary interests of shareholders. Finally, in transactions involving a conflict of interest, the most exacting standard, namely, 'entire fairness' may apply. Broadly speaking, most US state legislation provides in one form or another a fairness test whereby a conflict transaction entered into by a director will not be void or voidable provided the transaction is proved to be fair. The court is generally concerned with the steps taken by the interested directors to communicate their interest to the company's shareholders and disinterested directors. Thus, the courts have held that fairness requires 'complete candour' by the interested directors in their dealings with the shareholders and any disinterested directors.[51]

2. Audit Committees

Directors are entitled to delegate many of their responsibilities to committees of the board, some of which must be composed either wholly or partially of independent directors. Perhaps the most important of these is the audit committee. Prior to Enron and other recent corporate failures in the US, both the NYSE and NASDAQ required listed companies to have independent audit committees. The UK's Listing Rules had a similar, although less strict, requirement. Notwithstanding these requirements, it became evident that many such committees were either unable to discharge their responsibilities effectively or were not taking responsibility for effective auditor oversight. Both Sarbanes Oxley in the US and the Combined Code in the UK now require that all listed audit committee members be independent, that they be provided with the financial resources to retain independent advice when they feel they need it, that they significantly increase their evaluation of non-audit services being provided by auditors, and that they have increased financial expertise among their members. Sarbanes Oxley requires that all permitted non-audit services be approved by the audit committee, and it requires that each audit committee have what is called an audit committee financial expert, failing which the company must publicly disclose why it does not.[52]

3. Corporate Governance Committees

Corporate governance committees are an established mechanism in both the UK and the US for ensuring that best practices are followed by listed companies. They

---

48   *Unocal v. Mesa Petroleum Co* 493 A.2d 946 (Del. 1985).
49   *Revlon Inc. v. McAndrews & Forbes Holdings Inc.* 506 A.2d 173 (Del. 1985).
50   See further, Gevurtz *supra* n. 9 at 7.3.
51   See, *Fliegler v. Lawrence* 361 A.2d 218 (Del. 1976); *Globe Woolen Co v. Utica Gas & Electric Co* 224 N.Y. 483, 121 N.E. 378 (1918); and *Cookies Food Products Inc v. Lakes Warehouse Inc* 430 N.W. 2d 447 (Iowa 1988). See also, the Del. Gen. Corp Law § 144. See further, J. Lowry and R. Edmunds 'The Corporate Opportunity Doctrine: The Shifting Boundaries of the Duty and its Remedies' (1998) 61 *MLR* 515.
52   The Sarbanes Oxley requirements are discussed in a series of Alerts that are available at www.sidley.com. They include a 11 February 2003 Alert, 'SECs Final Rules on Auditor Independence', and a 2 May 2003 Alert, 'SEC Adopts Final Rule on Listed Company Audit Committees'. See also n. 61 *infra*. For the Smith requirements, see *supra* n. 30.

are responsible for ensuring that the corporate governance requirements described in this chapter are satisfied and, where necessary, for preparing corporate governance compliance statements for inclusion in annual reports. The Combined Code follows a 'comply or explain' methodology, similar to many corporate governance codes in the EU, although the need to explain instances of non-compliance naturally enough fosters a desire by the companies in question to be compliant. Insofar as non-US companies are concerned, the rules of the New York Stock Exchange generally defer to home country requirements, although they also require an explanation as to how those requirements differ from what would be required of a US company subject to its listing requirements. Since 2001, corporate governance committees are taking a much more proactive stance in ensuring the implementation and monitoring of required standards, working together with Disclosure Committees (see below), internal audit and other members of the management team.

4.   Other Board Committees

Both NYSE and NASDAQ listing requirements in the US and the Combined Code require listed companies to have nominating committees. The role of nominating committees has not come under review recently in the US, but the subject was addressed in the Higgs Review, which recommended that they provide support to the board on succession planning.[53]

As reflected by the Greenbury Report and the more recent Tyson Report, *Rewards for Failure*, remuneration of directors and officers has (justifiably or otherwise) been a significant issue in the UK for many years, but in the US (where some truly egregious compensation packages have been allowed) the issue has received comparatively less attention. Nonetheless, US and UK listing requirements both require listed companies to have compensation (remuneration) committees. The focus is increasingly on more adequate disclosure of that compensation, proper accounting for stock options and better linkage between compensation and performance. The role of compensation committees was not addressed in Sarbanes Oxley, while the Higgs Review limited itself to the recommendation that such committees should have delegated responsibility for setting the compensation for all executives officers and directors and the chairman.[54]

5.   Role of the Chairman

The Combined Code has for many years suggested that the roles of Chief Executive and Chairman be separated. This view was reiterated in the Higgs Review, which went on to propose that a Chief Executive should not become Chairman of the same company and that the Chairman should be independent at the time he is appointed.[55] While most listed UK companies separate the roles, some important companies do not and an even greater number continue to

---

[53]   *Supra* n. 29, Chapter 10.
[54]   *Supra* n. 29, Chapter 13.
[55]   *Supra* n. 29, Chapter 5.

permit their chief executives to move up to the role of chairman. No such requirements exist in the US where it has long been the practice for the two roles to be combined, but this is changing. Given the potentially ambiguous status of Chairman, the Higgs Review somewhat controversially proposed that there be a senior independent director to serve as a bridge between the board and the shareholders and this is now part of the Combined Code.[56]

6.   Additional Requirements

The responsibilities of directors of UK and Irish companies have been increased significantly by the UK 2004 Act and the Irish 2003 Act, respectively. The former, in addition to prohibiting charter or other provisions that seek to exempt directors from liability for negligence, default and breaches of duty or trust (although insurance may still be possible), includes a requirement that directors take affirmative action to ensure that the auditors get the information they need to carry out the audit and to certify in the annual report that they have done so. The latter requires directors to certify that they have "used all reasonable endeavours" to secure the company's compliance with its "relevant obligations", which includes "any ... enactments ... that may materially affect the company's financial statements". Significant challenges lie ahead for those required to make these statements.

In the US, required certifications are provided by management, not the directors. However, Sarbanes Oxley includes a number of other requirements of concern to both. For example, in light of the size of the personal loans granted to selected directors and officers at Enron, Tyco, Adelphia and Vivendi and the improper purposes for which these loans were being used, Sarbanes Oxley includes a specific prohibition on the granting, directly or indirectly, of personal loans to directors (and executive officers). And, in response to another Enron specific abuse where directors and officers were selling shares while those invested in Enron pension plans were prohibited from doing so, the Act also generally prohibits directors (and executive officers) from making purchases or sales of a company's equity securities during pension fund blackout periods.[57]

G.   CORPORATE GOVERNANCE AND MANAGEMENT

Recent corporate scandals have resulted in greatly increased focus in the US on the role of management, particularly the chief executive, financial and legal officers. Prior to that time, the responsibilities of these and other senior executives were dealt with primarily in a company's charter documents, its certificate of incorporation and by-laws. These responsibilities are usually drafted in very general terms. One of the problems that Enron identified was that these generalities gave senior management significant latitude to claim they did not know what other officers and employees were doing under their watch. The following are some of the more important reforms that have been implemented to address these and other concerns. It can be seen that these officers now have very significant personal incentives to prevent and root out improper conduct. Unlike the

---

[56]   *Supra* n. 29, Chapter 7.
[57]   These requirements are contained in Sections 402 and 306 of Sarbanes Oxley. They are discussed further below.

US, neither the UK nor other EU member states have introduced similar requirements, but they may ultimately need to address at least some of the issues that have been identified. Meanwhile, of course, the US requirements apply with extraterritorial effect to those that manage UK and other non-US companies that file reports with the SEC.

1.   Certification of Reports and Financial Statements

Sarbanes Oxley now requires CEOs and CFOs to personally certify, amongst other things, as to the accuracy and completeness of company disclosure documents filed with the SEC, the integrity and fairness of its financial statements and the adequacy and effectiveness of internal controls. Severe criminal and civil penalties apply to those that knowingly or willfully make improper certifications.[58]

It is almost impossible for any CEO or CFO of a major public company to have direct personal knowledge of all matters that might need to be disclosed in a public filing. To some extent at least, he or she will be dependent on other employees to bring relevant matters to his or her attention. On the other hand, shareholders are entitled to reasonable assurance that the information made available to them is materially accurate and complete, and are obviously unimpressed when senior management later claim they were unaware of a matter of importance brought to light by others.

2.   Disclosure Committees

One of the ways that CEOs and CFOs now ensure they can make such certifications is by establishing a committee of officers with principal responsibility for gathering the information that is disclosed in a company's public filings. These are not committees of the board, but committees of management that are ideally placed to monitor, strengthen and test the reliability of the disclosure and internal control process. The SEC has specifically endorsed the important role to be played by disclosure committees, although there is no legal requirement that they be established. It appears that most SEC reporting companies have done so.[59]

3.   Forfeiture of Bonuses and Profits

Most CEOs and CFOs are compensated using a formula that is tied significantly to the performance of their companies. Where a company uses improper accounting or other techniques to inflate revenues and profitability, the compensation of these executives is also improperly increased. In addition, where the company's share price is artificially inflated by the use of such techniques, sales of shares by these officers earn them gains they are not entitled to receive. Improper bonuses and profits were made by senior executives at Enron, Global

[58]   The certifications are mandated by Sections 302 and 906 of Sarbanes Oxley. The SEC rules implementing the requirements of Section 302, as well as the Section 906 requirement, are discussed in a 31 August 2002 Alert, 'SEC Adopts Final Rules for CEO and CFO Certification of Annual and Quarterly Reports', available at www.sidley.com/db30/cgi-bin/pubs/securities%20Law%20Alert%20083102.pdf.
[59]   See *Accessing the US Capital Markets, supra* n. 6 at 113, n. 63.

Crossing and WorldCom, amongst others. Under Section 304 of Sarbanes Oxley, CEOs and CFOs are now required to forfeit bonuses and profits from specified securities sales where there has been a financial restatement by the company in question resulting from misconduct. There is no requirement that either officer be personally involved in that misconduct. It is now clear that there was improper booking of oil and gas reserves by Shell over a number of years and, since there have been resulting financial restatements, both the former chief executive and chief financial officers may well be affected by this requirement.

4.   Prohibition against Personal Loans

Under Section 402 of Sarbanes Oxley, executive officers are also subject to a personal loan prohibition of the type applicable to directors and described above. While this prohibitation was implemented in response to the activities of key personnel at Enron and Adelphia, more recent events make it clear that there has been widespread abuse for many years. Indeed, in the report of the Hollinger Special Committee, Conrad Black and David Radler were stated to have operated what it termed a "corporate kleptocracy" (a view they clearly don't share), in which, through personal loan and compensation arrangements, "[t]he aggregate cash taken by [Black, Radler] and their associates represented 95.2% of Hollinger's entire adjusted net income during 1997–2003". Nonetheless, there are a number of important exceptions to the personal loan prohibitation, including a grandfathering of loans in effect on July 30, 2002.

5.   Pension Fund Blackout Restrictions

Under Section 306 of Sarbanes Oxley, executive officers are also generally prohibited from making purchases or sales of company equity securities during pension fund blackout periods. Both the SEC and the Department of Labour have adopted rules to give effect to the new requirements. The prohibition does not apply to all equity securities, but only those acquired in connection with his or her services to the company. The prohibition also does not apply to non-US companies to the same extent as US companies. The term executive officer is more narrowly defined so that it applies only to management employees, the CEO, the CFO and the chief accounting officer. Also, the prohibition only applies if 50 per cent or more of the plan participants are located in the US and the number of affected participants in the US exceeds either 15 per cent of the company's worldwide employees or 50,000.[60]

6.   Codes of Ethics

Under Section 406 of Sarbanes Oxley, affected companies are required to adopt a code of ethics meeting specified requirements that applies to the CEO, the CFO, the principal accounting officer, controller and persons performing similar

---

[60]   See 7 February 2003 Alert, 'Directors and Officers Prohibited from Trading in Issuer Securities During Blackout Periods; Notification Requirements', available at www.sidley.com/db30/cgi-bin/pubs/securities%20Law%20Alert%20020703.pdf.

functions or, if they do not do so, to explain why. The code of ethics must be in writing and must be reasonably designed to deter wrongdoing and promote (i) honest and ethical conduct, including the ethical handling of actual or apparent conflicts of interest between personal and professional relationships; (ii) full, fair, accurate, timely and understandable disclosure in reports and documents filed or submitted to the SEC and in other public communications by the company; (iii) compliance with applicable governmental laws, rules and regulations; (iv) the prompt internal reporting of violations of the code to appropriate persons identified in the code; and (v) accountability for adherence to the code.[61]

7.   Improper Influence on Conduct of Audits

There are often disagreements between a company and its auditors as to how particular transactions or obligations should be classified and reflected in the financial statements. There is often a concern that, with such significant audit (and non-audit) fees at stake, accounting firms are not always able to ensure the right outcome. Acting under Section 303 of Sarbanes Oxley, there is an SEC rule that prohibits officers (and directors), and any person acting under their direction, from exerting improper influence over their auditors. Indeed, the SEC appears to have gone further than the Act by suggesting that some forms of negligent conduct could be prohibited.[62]

8.   Duty on Lawyers to Report Violations

The role of in-house lawyers has come under significantly increased scrutiny both on account of their direct participation in improper activities and their failure to address conduct of other members of management. In the US, lawyers that appear and practice before the SEC (e.g. they prepare or review company filings) are required to report 'up the ladder' to the chief legal officer, the board of directors or an authorized committee of the board evidence of material violations of securities laws, breaches of fiduciary duty and similar violations of which they become aware. While the SEC distinguishes between the responsibilities of 'supervisory' and 'subordinate' lawyers for this purpose, there is generally an affirmative duty to follow up on a reported matter. External lawyers representing such companies are also subject to the new rules.[63]

H.   CORPORATE GOVERNANCE AND SHAREHOLDERS

Corporate governance regimes are usually developed with the primary objective of protecting the rights of shareholders in listed companies, primarily minority

---

[61]   See 31 January 2003 Alert, 'SEC Issues Final Rules on Audit Committee Financial Experts and Codes of Ethics for Senior Financial Officers', available at www.sidley.com/db30/cgi-bin/pubs/securities%20Law%20Alert%20013103.pdf.

[62]   See 27 June 2003 Alert, 'SEC Adopts Rule Forbidding Improper Influence on Conduct of Audits, available at http://www.sidley.com/db30/cgi-bin/pubs/Corporate%20Alert%20062703.pdf.

[63]   See 11 February 2003 Alert, 'SEC Issues Final Rule on Standards of Professional Conduct for Attorneys', available at http://www.sidley.com/db30/cgi-bin/pubs/securities%20Law%20Alert%20021103.pdf.

shareholders with access to limited information. However, if confirmation were needed, recent experiences have shown that these rights have been insufficient to adequately protect their interests. While most of the recent reforms in the US and the UK were certainly designed to give shareholders greater protections (or, put another way, to restore investor confidence in the capital markets), the reforms apply mostly to those responsible for the protection of shareholder interests; directors, management and auditors. The initiatives of arguably greatest importance to shareholders have been disclosure related: how to improve the quality of the financial and other information being provided to them by the companies in which they invest.

1.   Right of Access to Information

Shareholders entitlement to information about the companies in which they invest is generally satisfied through the rules of the UKLA and the FSA in the UK and the even more detailed rules of the SEC in the US; i.e. through the securities laws. Where securities are being offered to the public, this information is included – or, in some jurisdictions, is incorporated by reference – in a prospectus, whereas, on a more ongoing basis, it is contained in annual reports, periodic reports with respect to matters of importance and semi annual and, in the US, quarterly financial reports. In general terms, these documents are required to include all information that is material to investors.[64]

Shareholders may also become entitled to information by company and corporation laws. For example, where directors become involved in a conflict transaction, shareholders are entitled to expect that information about the transaction is either made available to them or to the board. Failure to do so in the UK renders a director liable to an unlimited fine on conviction on indictment under Section 317(7) of the Companies Act 1985. Furthermore, such a contract is voidable, and the company can call upon the director to account for the gains he or she has made. However, a director may obtain immunity against liability for breaches of duty by obtaining an ordinary resolution of the shareholders in general meeting whereby the conflict transaction is ratified.[65] Furthermore, to the extent that article 85 of Table A (a model charter provision annexed to the Act) is adopted, such a director, while being obliged to make disclosure to the board of the 'nature and extent of any material interest', will be relieved of liability to account for any gains made and 'no such arrangements [will] be avoided on the ground of any such interest or benefit'. As the Company Law Review Steering Group has indicated: '[T]he law should only prevent the exploitation of business opportunities where there is a clear case for doing so'.[66]

---

64   Although not a corporate governance case, one of the earlier and better known cases concerning the potential liability of directors and signing officers for material misstatements and omissions in the US is *Escott v. Bar Chris Construction Corp* 283 F Supp 643 (SDNY 1968).

65   *Benson v. Heathron* (1842) 1 Y & CCC 326; *Aberdeen Rly. Co. v. Blaikie* (1854) 1 Macq 461; *North-West Transportation Co. Ltd, v. Beatty* (1887) 12 App. Cas. 589, *per* Sir Richard Baggallay at pp. 593–594; *Regal (Hastings) Ltd. v. Gulliver* (1967) 2 AC 134n (1942) 1 All ER 378. A breach of duty is also ratifiable by obtaining the informed approval of every member who has a right to vote on such a resolution: *Re Duomatic Ltd.* (1969) 2 Ch. 365.

66   *Modern Company Law: Completing The Structure* at paragraph 3.26.

As we have seen, the 'entire fairness' standard by which conflict transactions are assessed in Delaware and elsewhere in the US is also premised on full disclosure or 'complete candour'. The director of a Delaware corporation will be in breach of a fiduciary duty to their shareholders if they misrepresent or omit material information.[67] As the court indicated in *Gerlack v. Gillam*, this is true *whenever* information is being provided.[68] There has been much debate in US courts about when this duty is met, but more recently the emphasis has also been on the disclosure of all 'material' information, a test endorsed by the US Supreme Court in *TSC Industries Inc. v. Northway Inc.*[69] and in the federal securities laws:

> An omitted fact is material if there is a substantial likelihood that a reasonable shareholder would consider it important in deciding how to vote.... It does not require proof of a substantial likelihood that disclosure of the omitted fact would have caused the reasonable investor to change his vote. What the standard does contemplate is a showing of a substantial likelihood that, under all the circumstances, the omitted fact would have assumed actual significance in the deliberations of the reasonable shareholder.[70]

The breadth of the duty stated by the US Supreme Court stands as the antithesis of that which has been seen to be the current position in England. In the US, the duty does not require proof that the actual decision of the shareholders in general meeting would have been different. All that is required is that the omitted fact would have been of relevance.

2. Improved Disclosure

Notwithstanding the extensive disclosure requirements to which English and US companies have been subject for many years, recent events made it clear that the timelines and quality of the information provided needed to be improved. Sarbanes Oxley and related SEC rules include several new disclosure rules. In the EU, a Prospectus Directive with a new detailed disclosure regime for securities offerings was adopted in January 2004 and Transparency Obligations Directive to provide for continuous reporting was adopted in December 2004. These EU initiatives will be followed by complementary – and, in some cases,

---

[67] See *Rosenblatt v. Getty Oil Co* 493 A.2d 929 at 944 (Del. 1985); *Weinberger v. OUP, Inc* 457 A.2d 701 at 710 (Del. 1983); and *Lynch v. Vickers Energy Corp* 383 A.2d 278 at 281 (Del. 1977), discussed below, and re *Anderson, Clayton Shareholder Litig.* 519 A.2d 680 at 689–690 (Del. Ch. 1986). The position in Delaware is in marked contrast to that in England where the traditional view is that the fiduciary duties of directors are owed to the company only, not to the shareholders: *Percival v. Wright* (1902) 2 Ch. 421. However, in certain circumstances a duty may owed to shareholders, see *Coleman v. Myers* (1977) 2 N.Z.L.R. 225; *Allen v. Hyatt* (1914) 30 T.L.R. 444, PC.

[68] 139 A.2d 591 (Del. Ch. 1958) at 593. See also, *Eisenberg v. Chicago Milwaukee Corp.* 537 A.2d 1051 (Del. Ch. 1987). In *Stroud v. Milliken Enterprises Inc.* 552 A.2d 476 at 480 (Del. 1989) the Delaware Supreme Court stressed that a boards 'duty of complete candour to its shareholders to disclose all germane or material information applies as well to matters of corporate governance as to corporate transactions'.

[69] 426 US 438 (1976).

[70] *Ibid* at 440.

entirely new – member state law and rule changes, including most probably mandatory disclosure by UK companies about their use of non-audit services, as envisaged by the 2004 UK Act.

Of course, the ability to digest this additional disclosure will in many cases be limited to sophisticated institutional investors, it being generally recognized that retail investors very often make their investment decisions without any serious assessment of company disclosure documents. Nonetheless, given some of the recent abuses, key areas that have been identified for improved disclosure are the Operating and Financial Review (known as the 'MD&A' in the US) in which investors are expected to receive a meaningful discussion of both historical results and future prospects (to see the company 'through the eyes and ears' of management), and non-routine financial information, such as improved disclosure concerning the use of so called non-GAAP financial measures and pro forma and off balance sheet transactions.[71] There will continue to be a strong focus on the harmonisation of global accounting principles with the adoption of IAS (IFRS) by EU companies in 2005, although the obstacles to progress in this area continue to be significant.

3.   Internal Controls and Disclosure Controls

Another measure adopted as part of the recent reforms in the US was increased scrutiny of the internal controls of public companies. While internal controls have for a long time been subject to review and assessment by outside auditors, corporate failures like Tyco, Adelphia and Hollinger, each of which involved very significant diversion of corporate resources for the benefit of selected directors and officers, make it clear that these controls were not always adequate. Under Sarbanes Oxley, companies must now assess and disclose in their public filings any significant weaknesses and/or changes in internal controls over financial reporting (with auditor attestation of the conclusion), as well as material information concerning a broader category of controls known as disclosure controls and procedures (i.e. the procedure in place to ensure that company disclosure documents are accurate and complete) has been developed by the SEC.[72] The SEC's requirements in this area, which are more complex than Turnbull, have turned out to be the most controversial and costly aspect of Sarbanes Oxley both for US and non-US companies. The FRC has issued guidance concerning the use of Turnbull as an evaluation framework for Sarbanes Oxley internal control requirements, and we can expect a further tightening of internal control requirements by other regulators, including the FSA.[73]

---

[71]   The UK proposals are discussed in the White Paper and the Thirteenth Report of the Select Committee on Trade and Industry, *supra* n. 20. The new US requirements are discussed in a series of Alerts available at www.sidley.com. These include the 10 February 2003 Alert, 'SEC Adopts Disclosure Requirements for Off-Balance Sheet Arrangements and Contractual Obligations', and the 3 February 2003 Alert, 'SEC Adopts Final Rules Regulating Use of Non-GAAP Financial Measures'.

[72]   See 8 August 2003 Alert, 'New SEC Rules – Management Reports on Internal Control over Financial Reporting and Revised Certification Requirements', available at http://www.sidley.com/db30/cgi-bin-pubs/Corporate%20Alert%20080703.pdf.

[73]   FRC, The Turnbull guidance as an evaluation framework for the purposes of Section 404(a) of the Sarbanes Oxley Act, December 16, 2004, is available at *www.frc.org.uk/corporate*. See also 'Companies face test on internal controls', *Financial Times*, 25 May 2004 at 1.

4.   Enhanced Shareholder Activism

The principal institutional fund management groups in both countries have come under increasing pressure to demonstrate their effectiveness as advocates for the retail shareholders they represent. Many such institutional shareholder groups, including Hermes, have corporate governance principles of their own.[74] Indeed, the level of animosity that has developed over the past two years between those that run the largest UK companies and those that manage the funds that invest in them has attracted considerable attention. In 2003 and 2004, institutional investors forced Sir Ian Prosser to stand down as Chairman-elect of Sainsbury, while last year investors succeeded in removing Michael Green as chairman-designate of ITV exerted significant pressure on Jean-Pierre Garnier, the Chief Executive of GSK, in respect of compensation issues. In some large cases, such as Equitable Life in the UK and Hollinger in the US, proceedings have been commenced against former directors, and is to be expected that this trend will continue. Indeed, there has even been a report that a French law will be introduced to allow for US style class action lawsuits.

I.   CORPORATE GOVERNANCE AND THIRD PARTIES

While improved disclosure to shareholders has been a very important theme behind recent reforms, individual investors rely more often on the advice of professional investment advisers and the ratings assigned to the companies in which they invest by the rating agencies, and they rely particularly on the quality and independence of the auditors of those companies in which they invest. The roles played by each of these groups came under increased scrutiny post Enron with the result that the manner in which auditors and investment advisers do business has been significantly changed. Additional responsibilities have also been imposed on the outside law firms used by these companies.

1.   Auditors

Enron and the other major corporate failures in the US revealed the extent to which both auditor quality and independence had been seriously compromised in recent years. Indeed, the activities and collapse of Arthur Andersen resulted in a complete overhaul of the way in which US accounting firms are regulated and the businesses they are permitted to conduct. A key objective behind Sarbanes Oxley was reform of the accounting profession in the US. Related reforms are being implemented in the UK under the auspices of the FRC as a result of the 2004 UK Act.

Among the more important reforms under Sarbanes Oxley, auditors are now prohibited from providing a range of non-audit services to their audit clients, including bookkeeping, management functions, and legal and other services that raise the potential for conflicts of interest. There are also provisions dealing with audit partner rotation, employment of audit firm personnel, and reporting to and

---

[74]   For a selection of such codes, see e.g. www.hermes.co.uk, www.pirc.co.uk and www.napf.co.uk.

communications with company audit committees.[75] Reflecting the findings of the Smith Report, the Combined Code has been amended to require additional scrutiny of non-audit services, and the 2004 UK Act envisages that the use of such services will be subject to mandatory disclosure. The PCAOB in the US and the FRC in the UK are assuming responsibility for the independent regulation of accountants, while a recently proposed EU Directive has called for an audit regulatory committee to co-ordinate oversight activities amongst EU Member States.[76]

2.   Investment Professionals

One of the ways in which the investment banks had for many years generated investor interest in securities offerings they were lead managing was through apparently independent research advice generated by their research departments. This had long been a controversial practice not least because investors were usually much more heavily influenced by the contents of a five page research report than a detailed – often turgid – prospectus. What most retail investors did not realize was that in many cases the writers of this research were being compensated with and under pressure from the bankers leading these transactions to give the companies very favourable coverage. In a number of cases, it also became apparent that the authors of this research were often privately critical of the very companies about which they were writing positive research reports. As a result of enforcement activities undertaken against a number of major US banks, research departments have been fundamentally changed over the past two years.[77] The authors of the research have been separated from the investment banking teams, are separately compensated and are required to personally certify as to their independence in the reports that they write. And the use of so-called deal research, where reports are written and circulated in anticipation of an upcoming offering, has been curtailed significantly.

3.   Rating Agencies

The business of rating corporate and government securities, the rating agency business, is dominated by a small group of companies such as Moody's, Standard & Poor's and Fitch. These companies assign specific graded ratings to debt securities (bonds, commercial paper etc) that reflect their views as to the risk of issuer default. The principal distinctions are between investment and non investment grade debt, although there are sub categories within each. Ratings are one of the primary means by which investors make investment decisions. The recent corporate scandals in the US and Europe have raised serious questions about the effectiveness of the ratings process, just as occurred in the aftermath of the Mexican and Asian crises in the mid 90s. In almost every case, the rating

---

[75]   *Supra* n. 52.
[76]   *Supra* n. 34.
[77]   On 31 October 2003, District Judge Pauley of the Southern District of New York approved a $1.4 billion global settlement of enforcement actions against 10 investment firms and two individuals. See www.sec.gov for links to the relevant SEC enforcement releases.

agencies fundamentally misrated the companies in question because of their inability to properly gauge the debt burdens being assumed. The Senate Committee on Governmental Affairs in the US found that the ratings agencies' 'monitoring and review of [Enron's] finances fell far below the careful efforts one would have expected from organizations whose ratings hold so much importance'.[78] According to the SEC, they 'failed to use the necessary rigor to ensure their analysis of a complex company, such as Enron, was sound'.[79] The SEC is continuing its review of the rating agency business, which, as indicated in a 2003 Concept Release, has included a fundamental review of the overall regulatory regime.

4.   External Lawyers

Some of the transactions that attracted criticism at Enron and other companies were structured by lawyers, and in other cases, lawyers allegedly participated directly in serious abuses. Like in-house lawyers, external lawyers are now subject to a number of additional requirements under Sarbanes Oxley, including an up the ladder reporting requirement of the type discussed above.[80] Unlike, in house lawyers, external lawyers who report issues that are not properly addressed may also need to resign. According to press reports, Akin Gum, a prominent US law firm, did so very recently.

5.   Others

Other third parties that have impacted the corporate governance debate in varying degrees include corporate governance rating systems such as ISS in the US and FTSE ISS in the UK, which rank (in some cases, this effectively means name and shame) companies by reference to published corporate governance criteria, as well as special interest groups seeking to promote board diversity, environmental and other social objectives. Launched in December 2004, the FTSE ISS Corporate Governance Index is the latest in a series of such scoring systems to have been developed post Enron, apparently with the support of those companies that expect to benefit from a positive investor response to their high standards of corporate governance. Last but certainly not least, the SEC made it clear in its settlement with Parmalat that it is prepared to export Sarbanes Oxley-type corporate governance standards to non-US companies (even where they are not subject to Sarbanes Oxley) as part of an overall settlement of antifraud enforcement proceedings.[81]

---

78 Senate Committee on Governmental Affairs, Staff Report, *Financial Oversight of Enron: The SEC and Private Sector Watchdogs*, S. Prt. 107–75 (7 October 2002) at 115.

79 SEC Report on the Role and Function of Credit Rating Agencies in the Operation of the Securities Markets, 24 January 2003 at 32.

80 Section 307 of Sarbanes Oxley and related SEC rules are discussed in the Alert referred to in No. 63 above.

81 SEC v Parmalat Finanziaria, Lit. Rel. No. 18803, 2004 SEC LEXIS 1631. Discussed in 'SEC Settles Enforcement Action Against Parmalat: Settlement continues SEC Trend of Imposing Corporate Governance Reform through Enforcement Actions', available at www.sidley.com/dbt30/cgi-bin/pubs/SECAlertAug0404.pdf.

J.   CONCLUSION

The relationship between a company and its stakeholders differs in the US, on the one hand, and the UK and the rest of the EU, on the other hand, with the interests of shareholders being more clearly paramount in the US. Nonetheless, the broader objectives of the differing corporate governance regimes are clearly similar as reflected in the OECDs Principles of Corporate Governance, the latest version of which was adopted in 2004. The corporate governance matters discussed in this chapter have been focused on the protection of shareholder interests, but the themes – stricter checks and balances on senior management, greater involvement in the supervision of management by directors, avoidance of conflicts of interest and improved disclosure to investors – must inevitably further the interests of those seeking to promote wider CSR objectives. The unilateral imposition of extraterritorial corporate governance requirements, such as those imposed on non-US companies by Sarbanes Oxley and related SEC rules, has complicated what should clearly be a common enterprise. As key constituencies begin to suffer from the effects of this unilateralism, it is to be hoped that the need for and benefits to be derived from greater harmonization of corporate governance initiatives and requirements will be recognized. And notwithstanding the difficulties faced by the American Law Institute and others in the past, it is also to be hoped that further consideration will be given to consolidating corporate governance requirements, which, given the multiplicity of sources from which they are drawn, are unusually difficult for non-lawyer directors and others to source and absorb.[82]

---

[82]   See the remarks of John Thain, CEO of the NYSE, in the *Wall Street Journal* on 28 May 2004 in which he lamented the drop in US listings by non-US companies since the enactment of Sarbanes Oxley. However, see also the remarks attributed to Senator Sarbanes and Congressman Oxley where they responded that industry had been given the opportunity to influence the content of this legislation but, preferring to keep a low profile at the time (unlike many chief executives and chairmen in the UK who responded 'vigorously' to the Higgs Review), had failed to do so.

Chapter 4

THE SOUL OF THE CORPORATION

Gerald Milward-Oliver

Two snapshots. First, in January 2004 the global charity Christian Aid produced a castigating report entitled 'Behind the Mask: the real face of corporate social responsibility'. Backing their argument with case histories of multinational activity in Nigeria, Kenya and India, the charity contends that 'CSR is a completely inadequate response to the sometimes devastating impact that multinational companies can have in an ever more globalized world – and that it is actually used to mask that impact... Business, moreover, has consistently used CSR to block attempts to establish the mandatory international regulation of companies' activities. . . .'

They continue: 'A new industry has grown up to help companies present, implement and monitor what they are doing in the name of CSR. But behind the fine words, is there substance? Does the new language and the emergence of some specialist consultancy firms reflect real change in business practice?'

Second snapshot: a former Chairman of IBM states, 'In the future, a corporation will be judged as much by its social usefulness as by its ability to make a profit'. And a senior UK industrialist agrees: 'It is no longer enough for a company to do what is immediately profitable, expedient or usual; a policy or particular action must also be right, in the sense that it can be convincingly defended before reasonable men'.[1]

Clearly, these are leaders who reflect much current thought. Except that both statements were made more than 30 years ago, when a new management approach was in vogue – the subject of numerous weighty studies and the source of considerable fees for gurus and consultants. It was called corporate social responsibility.

In the 1980s and 1990s, corporate social responsibility lost its way – spurned by the 'me' generation, who preferred individual rewards, who boosted profitability and shareholder returns through re-engineering. Where did all the

---

[1]   Quoted in *Business Survival and Social Change: A Practical Guide to Responsibility and Partnership*, John Hargreaves and Jan Dauman, Associated Business Programmes 1975, p. 7.

Ramon Mullerat (ed.), Corporate Social Responsibility: The Corporate Governance of the 21st Century, 61–75.
© 2005 *International Bar Association. Printed in the Netherlands.*

fine words go about 'social usefulness' when people became as expendable as last years football team shirt? Corporate social responsibility disappeared into the executive woodwork for a generation.

Now CSR is back – and showing signs of becoming absorbed into the mainstream of corporate life, thanks to work handled through the EU, OECD and the International Standards Office, among others. But is the current popularity of CSR going to last? Is it simply a tool of the PR people? How deeply embedded are the *moral* issues that are implicit in the terms corporate social responsibility? How far are corporations questioning their very *souls* when they embrace CSR so enthusiastically?

Sadly there is plenty of evidence to back Christian Aid's scepticism. For example, look at the disconnect that can appear to exist between the statements of individual companies and of their trade associations. . . .

The name of Aretha Franklin is synonymous with soul music. Her best recordings were released in the 1970s by Atlantic Records, *the* soul label. Atlantic is now part of Time Warner. In their 2002 Social Responsibility Report, the parent company states:

> 'In an increasingly global era, being a good corporate citizen is not solely about being philanthropic. It is about how we honour our obligation to share our expertise, technology and human resources with the communities we serve around the world'.

This is the same company whose trade association, the Recording Industry Association of America, sued hundreds of customers, because they bridled against paying as much as $20 for something they could download for free. Almost inevitably, due to the scale of the action taken, lawsuits ended up on the doorsteps of young children and old ladies who had no idea how to turn on a computer, let alone use it to download music titles through peer group software.

The RIAAs approach to file-sharing was intentionally dramatic, in line with statements issued by industry executives. For example:

> 'Internet piracy means lost livelihoods and lost jobs, not just in record companies but across the entire music community. For those who think the 10.9 per cent first half sales fall in 2003 does not speak for itself, look at the other evidence. Artist rosters have been cut, thousands of jobs have been lost, from retailers to sound engineers, from truck drivers to music journalists'. (Jay Berman, IFPI chairman, IFPI Network Newsletter, December 2003).[2]

But in March 2004, a detailed study by Felix Oberholzer and Koleman Strumpf[1] disputed the RIAAs assertions:

> 'We find that file sharing has no statistically significant effect on purchases of the average album. Moreover, the estimates are of rather modest size when compared to the drastic reduction in sales in the music industry.

---

[2]   Quoted in *The Effect of File Sharing on Record Sales – An Empirical Analysis*, Felix Oberholzer Koleman Strumpf, Harvard Business School UNC Chapel Hill, March 2004.

At most, file sharing can explain a tiny fraction of this decline. This result is plausible given that movies, software, and video games are actively downloaded, and yet these industries have continued to grow since the advent of file sharing. While a full explanation for the recent decline in record sales are beyond the scope of this analysis, several plausible candidates exist. These alternative factors include poor macroeconomic conditions, a reduction in the number of album releases, growing competition from other forms of entertainment such as video games and DVDs (video game graphics have improved and the price of DVD players or movies have sharply fallen), a reduction in music variety stemming from the large consolidation in radio along with the rise of independent promoter fees to gain airplay, and possibly a consumer backlash against record industry tactics'.

The role of trade associations is well documented as the means by which individual corporations can distance themselves from unsavoury actions – and we find that, once again, history has a habit of repeating itself.

A century ago, the US motor industry had created a closed shop through their ownership of the Selden Patent – giving them exclusive rights over self-propelled vehicles powered by internal combustion engines. They formed an association to enforce their ownership – in the process keeping cars an expensive toy of the rich. Henry Ford had other ideas. He wanted to reduce the price of a car to the point where ordinary people could afford one. But the other manufacturers, through their association, did not want any more competitors in Detroit – and certainly did not want their cartel to be threatened.

Ford launched his cars – and fought the Selden Patent in Court. The association issued hundreds of lawsuits against Ford customers, accusing them of buying 'unlicensed vehicles'. Public sympathy turned against the bullying tactics of the association, Ford won his case (although it took eight years) – and along the way became the biggest car maker in America.

The UKs Green Alliance questioned the role of trade associations in 2003 in a report entitled 'The Private Life of Public Affairs'. They stated:

'Trade associations, largely unregulated and highly variable in competence and transparency, unwittingly or not play a pivotal role.... They allow companies to air progressive policies in annual reports and the media, whilst distancing their brands from more reactionary views put forward, through trade associations, in the name of the industry as a whole'.

The point was echoed in the same publication by Jonathan Porritt, Director of the Forum for the Future:

'...we are getting a very strong signal now from all sorts of quarters that people are really disgusted by the institutionalized hypocrisy in large companies. They say one thing when they are on their own turf and then license their trade associations or indeed other people in the company to go out and say something completely different as and when it suits them on that occasion'.

Which brings us to another source of unease echoed in the Christian Aid report – the role of the PR industry in setting and implementing CSR strategies and policies. Most PR practitioners want us to believe they are genuinely seeking a productive two-way conversation between their clients and their clients' stakeholders. Of course, many are genuine, succeed – and reap the benefits of their honesty and openness.

But the PR industry itself has a visceral disconnect with the moral principles implicit in CSR. Consider the origins of the industry.

Edward Bernays, the nephew of Sigmund Freud, is regarded by many as the father of public relations. He learnt his trade as part of the US Governments successful campaign of public persuasion that gave President Woodrow Wilson the endorsement to lead his country to war in 1917. Bernays' definitive work, entitled 'Propaganda', was published in 1928.

Life Magazine once included him in a list of the 100 most influential Americans in the 20th century. So it is worth hearing what he has to say:

'The conscious and intelligent manipulation of the organized habits and opinions of the masses is an important element in democratic society...

If we understand the mechanism and motives of the group mind, it is now possible to control and regiment the masses according to our will, without their knowing it'.

Contrast that with some of the language used by the world's biggest PR companies in their own publicity material.

Burson Marsteller describes its work as 'perception management'.

Hill & Knowlton talks of 'managing corporate reputation'. The company also defines its understanding of corporate social responsibility. It is worth citing this in full:

'Today, more than ever, Americans expect companies to conduct themselves in a responsible and ethical manner. Corporate social responsibility (CSR) embodies the idea that companies have an obligation to all of their stakeholders, customers, employees, the communities in which they operate and their shareholders'.

Nothing contentious there – phrasing with which we can all agree. But note what immediately follows:

'Rather than just a burdensome duty, we approach CSR as a potential means of competitive differentiation.

With this approach, corporate responsibility extends beyond mere legal obligations and fiduciary duty to shareholders. CSR becomes an integral component of your company's vision and demonstrates that your company strives to maximize its long-term beneficial contribution to society and minimize any adverse effects of its operations'.

Despite the apparently clear first paragraph, there would not seem to be room in this approach of doing what is right because it is *morally* right. Everything is subservient to the need to manage the corporate reputation above all else. CSR is seen as a PR practitioner's tool – and earns its keep by delivering competitive differentiation. This may not be wrong in itself, but it is all about taking, not about *giving*.

Hill & Knowlton would appear to have a strong understanding of its client base – emphasized by the results of a global poll released in late 2003 by the company called 'Corporate Reputation Watch', covering not only North America but also Europe and Asia.

The poll found that 71 per cent of CEOs cited recruiting and retaining employees as the most important business objective achieved by their own company's CSR initiatives. The survey also found that 'while a vast majority of executives agree that more stringent corporate governance will lead to improved ethical behaviour, only two in 10 strongly agree'. (A more recent report, published by The Conference Board in March 2004, found that only 20 per cent of US respondents cited reputational risk as the most relevant factor when considering greater board scrutiny of ethics programmes (perhaps not surprisingly in that litigious country, legal developments came top of their list of concerns). In the UK, 62 per cent cited reputational risk as the most important, with 46 per cent in continental Western Europe.)

CSR may be a tool in the minds of many corporations, to be used as a means of enhancing the success of the business, rather than as a way of adhering to common standards of moral behaviour. But surely corporate ethics policies cannot be interpreted in the same way? Here again, there is worrying evidence that, for many corporations and individuals, an ethical approach plays – or is perceived to play – second fiddle to the need for corporate success.

In a Business Week poll conducted in mid-January 2002, only one third of respondents felt that big companies followed ethical business practices, and just a quarter thought that those firms were honest in dealing with employees and customers. A similar result was reported in a poll conducted in 14 European countries by the Wall Street Journal Europe and GfK AdHoc Research Worldwide. Only 21 per cent of respondents thought that most CEOs were honest.

David Batstone, author of 'Saving the Corporate Soul'[3] found that 53 per cent of employees in small and large companies said they would be willing to misrepresent corporate financial information if asked to by their bosses. Even more worrying were the results of a Junior Achievement/Harris poll of teenagers aged 13–18, conducted in the US and published in July 2003. Of these future leaders, one third said they would act unethically to get ahead or make more money if there was no chance of getting caught and a further 25 per cent were not sure.

The disconnect between what companies say and do has been highlighted closer to home. I live in what has been described by one eminent architectural writer as 'one of the most atmospheric, best preserved and lively of ancient mill towns'. A two hectare former industrial site right in the heart of the town was purchased in 1998 by Taylor Woodrow, one of the world's largest housebuilders. Detailed local authority planning guidance foresaw a mix of shops, offices, community, education and leisure uses – as well as some residential.

---

[3]   David Batstone, Saving the Corporate Soul & (Who Knows) Maybe Your Own, Jossey-Bass, San Francisco, 2003.

One of the core Business Principles set out by Taylor Woodrow is to 'make a socially responsible contribution' to the communities in which they operate. However, the company resolutely ignored persistent community pressure to adhere to the planning guidance, to the extent that it introduced – and then, as a result of community and local authority pressure, withdrew – three planning applications that would have resulted in a housing estate with peripheral non-residential usage, the most socially *irresponsible* contribution that the townspeople could have wished for.

Public statements by the company of its desire to consult with the community resulted in consistent and realistic responses from a very development-literate community. But most comments disappeared into a black hole because they did not fit Taylor Woodrow's agenda. Six years after the company purchased the site, the battle continued – with the community successfully enlisting the support of the Prince of Wales, whose views on the importance of mixed use sustainable communities have become embedded in government policy.

From a community perspective, there was a gaping hole between the rhetoric of Taylor Woodrow's fine statements and the reality of the work of its people on the ground. This is not to impugn their individual integrity – but to emphasize once again the difficulty that every corporation has when it comes to translating words that have been prepared at a strategic head office level into actions on the ground. Where is the real *soul* of the company reflected – in its words or its deeds?

In a book designed to provide guidance on the use of CSR, these few pages may at first sight appear to be out of character – upsetting the balance provided by my fellow contributors and even questioning the premise that underpins the title. That is not my purpose. A huge amount of valuable and robust work *is* being done to help produce 21st century organizations that are socially responsible organizations, that are ethically driven and, above all, that care. Indeed, in the UK and elsewhere, there remain companies that continue to be driven by ethical approaches inspired by their founders decades ago. But there are serious questions that must be asked about the extent to which CSR is being adopted by corporations as simply another management tool designed to enhance profitability and shareholder return.

We risk being caught in the same trap that we saw more than a decade ago, when vacuous 'mission statements' were being concocted by almost every organization under the sun. Most of those mission statements carried no moral weight – they were the product of advertising agencies, graphic design companies, PR companies. Top executives felt good about their shiny new mission statements, but few of them bothered to delve deep inside the *soul* of the organization to find out what really made it tick. As a result, all too many mission statements have been built on sand – and the fine-sounding words have been abandoned at the first sign of pressure on the share price from hard issues that conflicted with what were seen as the 'soft' and 'fuzzy' words of the mission statement.

The point was made with typical force by Sir Geoffrey Chandler, Founder Chair of the Amnesty International UK Business Group and a former senior executive with the Royal Dutch/Shell Group:

'That the phrase (CSR) is for business a self-inflicted wound seems not to be recognized. It implies that business, uniquely among legal occupations, has no inherent social utility, but requires a sanitizing 'add-on' – something which enables it to 'give back' to society, a sentiment frequently heard on the lips of corporate leaders apparently unaware that this suggests that their core activities are parasitic, which, without appropriate policies and principles relating to the whole of their impact, they may be'.[4]

How can we build something constructive out of this mixed bag of intent and action? Are changes in society setting an agenda that corporations *must* follow if they are to survive in the long-term? Or should we be looking at a completely novel form of enterprise? Can we expect a majority of mature corporations to be capable of finding their soul? Is it simple misplaced idealism to expect corporations to have a soul at all? Should we just accept that – through a mix of market/peer pressure, regulation, self-regulation and conscience – corporations will find their way to meeting society's expectations?

Having spent the past 3,000 words deconstructing the role of CSR through a mix of anecdote, scepticism and even cynicism, let us now endeavour to reconstruct a model that makes sense of corporate social responsibility within an organization that knows itself, its strengths and weaknesses – and that is honest in its desire to conduct a long-term open conversation with its stakeholders.

First, what do we mean by soul? The Oxford Shorter English Dictionary includes these definitions:

'The seat of the emotions, feelings, or sentiments; the emotional part of man's nature. The essential or animating part, element or feature of something. The animating principle of the world'.

But how can a corporation have a soul? In English law, a company is a distinct and separate entity from its owners and the people who run it. It has its own status for taxation, financial and general legal purposes. Over time, it develops its own character that is independent from those that work for it or have dealings with it. But how can this artificial creation – designed to protect a group of individuals from being held personally responsible for the risks attached to doing business – be said to have a soul? The corporation has evolved into the most efficient means of bringing together sources of capital and labour in order to generate profits for the owners. The construct of the organization has effectively taken precedence over the original purpose of the business.

In the process, accounting practice and finance theory have focused on the interests of shareholders in preference to all other groups. The common norm has been that the core purpose of the corporation is to maximize the interests of the recipients of profit, often to the cost of other stakeholders. The genesis of the benefits of self-interest is laid at the door of Adam Smith. But he was well aware of the dangers of an over-emphasis on the interests of one stakeholder over another:

'Our merchants and master-manufacturers complain much of the bad effects of high wages in raising the price, and thereby lessening the sale of

4   *The Curse of Corporate Social Responsibility*, Sir Geoffrey Chandler, New Academy Review Vol. 2 No. 1, Spring 2003.

their goods both at home and abroad. They say nothing concerning the bad effects of high profits. They are silent with regard to the pernicious effects of their own gains. They complain only of those of other people'.[5]

Any company is a collection of individuals, each with his or her own cultural, social and ethical values. Those values may differ between counties. They will certainly differ between countries.

Each individual has his or her own voice. Yet they are all too frequently required to stifle that voice in the name of adherence to 'corporate values' or 'corporate objectives'. What happens when corporations lose contact with the values of the individuals who make the corporation what it is? Most people are decent, honourable individuals. At home, they doubtless lead decent, honourable lives. So why is it, as we saw earlier, that more than half of employees in large and small companies would be willing to misrepresent corporate financial information if asked to do so by a superior?

What happens when the bosses eventually become wholly disconnected? According to calculations made by Business Week, in 1980 CEO compensation in the US was 42 times that of the average worker. By 2000, it was 531 times the average. What level of empathy can CEOs have for their people, *as* people, when they are so far removed from day-to-day reality? Limited liability is a privilege that entails responsibilities. Leaders have to rid themselves of the idea that material success equals entitlement, including entitlement to take whatever actions (ethical or not) are required to achieve further success.

The issue is not complicated. First, there are laws, regulations and conventions. Whatever the effect of an action on shareholder value or customer retention, if it is against the letter and spirit of the law, it should not be taken. But a number of corporations have always taken the viewpoint that that is not enough. Call it the inner voice, the visceral understanding that we all have about what is right and what is wrong. And invariably that inner voice will urge upholding values other than financial.

David Packard (one of the founders of IT company Hewlett-Packard) was convinced that material success was not enough. He and Bill Hewlett developed an ethos that came to be known as 'the HP way' – an ethos that was subsumed into a more conventional business approach when the company merged with Compaq in 2001. Bill Hewlett's son Walter fought long and hard to oppose the merger – and the large-scale redundancies that were promised – in defence of that ethos.

The HP Way was summed up by David Packard in a speech given in 1960, and quoted in a Harvard Business Review article in 1996:

'. . . Many people assume, wrongly, that a company exists simply to make money. While this is an important result of a company's existence, we have to go deeper and find the real reasons for our being . . . You can look around and see people who are interested in money and nothing else, but the

---

5   From *The Wealth of Nations*, Book 1, Chapter 9, p. 76. This and the accompanying points from *Corporate Propaganda: Its Implications for Accounting and Accountability*, David J. Collison, Department of Accountancy and Business Finance, University of Dundee, Scotland.

underlying drives come largely from a desire to do something else: to make a product, to give a service – generally to do something which is of value'.[6]

The principles of corporate behaviour were also set out clearly by the Confederation of British Industry in a report 30 years ago:

'A company should behave like a good citizen in business. The law does not (and cannot) contain or prescribe the whole duty of a citizen. A good citizen takes account of the interests of others besides himself, and tries to exercise an informed and imaginative ethical judgment in deciding what he should and should not do'.[7]

Simply put: with rights come responsibilities – a familiar but all too often ignored point.

An alternative translation of the Swedish word for business (*näringslivet*) is 'nourishment for life'. In this post-Enron world, it is clear that more and more people are listening to their innate need for a more fulfilling working environment – one that delivers more than material necessities. David Batstone made the point succinctly: 'a business will thrive once it aligns the ethos of the company with the values that drive its customers and its own workers'.[8] Paul Dolan, in his story of Fetzer Vineyards (see earlier footnote) echoed that comment, focusing in particular on the need for integrity:

If I lack integrity, it is because I am not acting from what I know to be my own values. I am not whole, I am divided against myself. If a corporation lacks integrity, it is because the corporation is acting from some of its values, but against others. It is expressing the value of its stakeholders in seeking to maximize shareholder value, but suppressing the values of its stakeholders who respect the environment and human rights. In contrast, removing that internal conflict unleashes tremendous creative power. It encourages people to really express what they believe, because the whole organization believes it, too'.[9]

For Paul Dolan and Fetzer, it comes down to a battle for the soul. 'The soul of the business is found in the hearts of its people', he insists. Hans Snook, who made Orange into one of the most successful mobile phone companies worldwide, had similar views. 'There is a new way of running a business', he said. 'It is based on integrity, on believing what you say, and on attempting to deliver it'.

---

6   Quoted in *True to our Roots: Fermenting a Business Revolution*, Paulo Dolan, Bloomberg Press 2003, p. 56. This is the excellent story of how Fetzer Vineyards in California is leading the industry towards sustainable business – preserving the environment, strengthening local communities and enriching the lives of employees, without sacrificing the bottom line. Recommended reading.
7   *The Responsibility of the British Public Company*, Final Report of the Company Affairs Committee, Confederation of British Industry, September 1973, quoted in *Business Survival and Social Change, ibid*, p. 28.
8   *Saving the Corporate Soul, ibid*, p. 239.
9   *True to our Roots, ibid*, p. 114.

Irene Khan, Secretary-General of Amnesty International, addressed this issue in her presentation on Values for Leadership at the 2003 World Economic Forum meeting in Davos.

'Values cannot be a reiteration of platitudes or words invoked without sincerity, for that would make them vacuous. Content-less values are like content-less brands – if we are to be taken seriously then our values must have meaning... If you adopt them you must live by them and be ready to be held accountable for them... The more we live and are known to live by our values, the more trust and confidence we will generate.

How can we integrate these values, this awareness, in a company? It needs to be incorporated into the 'genetic make-up' of the company: companies have to go out and actively earn trust. To be effective, and to be taken seriously, values should not be left in the realm of abstract philosophical concepts, but should be structured in a concrete, normative framework. We need benchmarks to measure and best practices to emulate, because in business what you do not measure, you cannot improve'.[10]

The philosopher Eric Hoffer said that 'the weakness of a soul is proportionate to the number of truths that must be kept from it'. Writer Robert Musil hit the button when he said that there is 'an abiding miscommunication between the intellect and the soul. We do not have too much intellect and too little soul, but too little intellect in matters of soul'. Questions of intellect, soul, even spirituality are all too frequently seen as a complete irrelevance when it comes to running a business. That is fine if you adhere to the sentiments of the 17th-century English jurist Edward Coke, who stated that corporations 'cannot commit treason, nor be outlawed nor excommunicate, for they have no souls'.[11] But a body of evidence is accumulating that demonstrates there are very sound business reasons for finding the soul of the corporation, nurturing it and opening it to the scrutiny of stakeholders.

An investigation of a 'spiritual values-based model' for a corporation was published in 1999 by Milliman and others, called 'Spirit and community at Southwest Airlines'.[12] Southwest was the first truly successful low-cost airline. Founded in 1971 by Rollin King and Herb Kelleher, it began with a simple notion: 'If you get your passengers to their destinations when they want to get there, on time, at the lowest possible fares, and make darn sure they have a good time doing it, people will fly your airline'. In the 33 years since, the airline has consistently recorded profits, while the industry as whole has swung from one financial disaster to another.

---

[10]   World Economic Forum – Annual Meeting 2003 Building Trust, Global Agenda Monitor, p. 48.
[11]   Case of Sutton's Hospital – 10 Report 32, quoted Bartlett's Familiar Quotations, Little Brown, p. 152.
[12]   'Spirit and Community at Southwest Airlines', published in the *Journal of Organizational Change*, Vol. 12, No. 3, 1999, pp. 221–233, MCB University Press. Authors: John Milliman, Jeffrey Ferguson & Bruce Condemi (University of Colorado, US) plus David Trickett (The Jefferson Circle, Fairfax, Virginia, US).

The research concluded:

'Companies that engage not just the minds, but also the hearts and emotions of their employees, will be more profitable. In other words, an organization that earnestly treats its employees as part of its community and emotionally engages them in a company purpose which makes a difference in the world, will obtain a higher level of employee motivation and loyalty – and ultimately higher organizational performance. Southwest Airlines' treatment of its employees as pat of its family and focus on relationships, caring, and emotional expression taps an entirely deeper level of employee spirit, motivation, and satisfaction. In contrast, most companies seek only to engage the workers through pay or through workers' minds and intellect'.

There is no question that ethical business is paying off. A study of UK FTSE 250 companies by the Institute of Business Ethics found that companies performed better on three out of four long-term financial measures if they had a public commitment on ethical conduct.[13]

But that commitment must be part of the corporation's makeup. If not, it will soon be found out. Thanks to the Internet (both email and the Web), stakeholders across the world can scrutinize, exchange experiences, inform others, organize collective responses. Hiding behind theory, process, market forces and other corporate tricks of the trade is no longer possible. It is all out in the open now.

Technological change is one of two factors that have created a seismic shift in the way corporations organize themselves and behave. The other is closely inter-related – the change in attitudes between generations. And both factors add to the pressure for corporations to be more open – and to understand and nurture their soul.

In affluent countries, people increasingly care about the costs that their consumer society are exacting from our world. For example, the polling organization MORI asked 25,000 individuals in 26 countries for their views on corporate citizenship. According to a report from Arthur D. Little,[14] they found that 'more consumers form their impression of a company on the basis of its corporate citizenship practices than do so on brand reputation or financial factors. Almost 60 per cent of those interviewed cited labour practices, business ethics, responsibility to society at large, or environmental impact as factors that influence their views of companies'.

Employees are consumers, too. So corporations need to be aware of the shift in generational expectation and behaviour that also exists within their own workforce, characterized by the weight of evidence that younger employees are increasingly behaving like consumers in the labour market. And they are showing a growing concern over the social and ethical performance of their prospective employers. Increasingly, people are drawn to organizations that inspire, not blind

13 'Ethical business pays off, says study of companies', *Financial Times*, Alison Maitland, 3 April 2003.
14 *The Business Case for Corporate Citizenship*, Arthur D. Little, Sarah Roberts, Justin Keeble and David Brown, 2003.

loyalty, but a deeper belief. The same Arthur D. Little report cited a 1997 Walker Information Survey's finding that 42 per cent of respondents took into account a company's ethics when deciding whether to accept a job. Work completed for Barclays Life in 1999 defined new attitudes amongst those born after 1978, what have been called Generation Y: 'Not for them the surly isolation of the early stage of Generation X (1961–1977), nor the learnt political correctness of the Boomers (1946–1960) – there appears to be a genuine assumption of individuality and tolerance'.[15] They are also the Internet generation. For them, the knowledge economy and ready access to infinite sources of information is a simple matter of fact. They expect to be able to communicate instantly and openly worldwide. There are no national barriers they cannot cross, no Iron Curtain. And, thanks to the power of branding, they expect to be able to be whom they want to be, when and where it suits them. Most of them are apathetic about politics as pursued by the establishment, but they are ready to pursue single-issue politics. Their global reach gives them an unprecedented understanding of the downside to many examples of global branding (environmental degradation, sweatshop production in the poorest countries etc). And their instinctive use of technology for messaging gives them a far greater understanding of the power of networks.

In 1976, former UK Prime Minister James Callaghan noted that 'A lie can be half-way round the world before the truth has got its boots on'. That truism needs to be updated. Trading stakeholders off against each other is no longer possible. Of course, corporations have changed radically in response to technology – and in particular to the fall in costs of telecommunications and computing. They have been forced to better understand their core skills and the value that they add through the goods or services they offer. The growth of the knowledge economy has created the need for corporations to engage with stakeholders, to conduct conversations. Where those conversations are genuinely two-way, they can make the world of difference to the effectiveness of the workplace.

Another consequence of technological change is the creation of new relationships with suppliers, now seen more often as partners. Outsourcing has become one of the mantras of the age, shifting non-core activities to other businesses for whom that activity is core. But this has required the forging of new levels of trust – and there can be a real problem in communicating core corporate values through a value chain that is increasingly outsourced to third party companies whose own corporate values may be informed or coloured by different cultural, religious or ethnic values. That is where the soul of the corporation becomes so important, the software that provides the foundation for everything the corporation does. For some corporate leaders, understanding the issues will be an expectation too far; for others it will provide the touchstone for change that will deliver on stakeholder expectations. One thing is certain, so entrenched is the old way of thinking in many areas (with the focus still firmly on shareholder returns, quarterly results and a

---

[15] Work completed by Research Business International, quoted in 'Tomorrow's Workplace: fulfillment or stress', Michael Moynagh and Richard Worsley, *The Tomorrow Project*, 2001, p. 201.

technical, legalistic mindset) that education is needed, a point made forcibly by Jeffrey Garten, Dean of the Yale School of Management:

'We must rethink the basics of business education… (CEOs) must learn to focus not only on the internal efficiencies of their companies but also on the external relationships and practices – including interaction with governments, international institutions and nongovernmental organizations. Business executives must understand better their overall responsibilities when it comes to the systems, values and culture that drive their global enterprise'.[16]

He adds:

'Today's system for educating business executives does not go far enough to train CEOs to be leaders in society'.[17]

This was borne out in the 'Beyond Grey Pinstripes 2003' global survey of how well business schools are preparing MBAs for social and environmental stewardship. While they found that the issues have become part of the business vernacular, the depth of coverage offered in core MBA course programmes – including accounting, finance, marketing, operations and organizational behaviour – was severely limited. They also found that 'only the most innovative schools have elevated the study of social impact management and environmental management from separate disciplines to the level of sustainability. Sustainability refers to the interrelationship of social, environmental and financial factors – a synthesis often referred to as the triple bottom line'.[18]

Many business leaders will undoubtedly continue to equate talk of the 'soul of the corporation' with fuzzy-headed idealistic issues that have little to do with the grinding task of maintaining market share, competitive differentiation and satisfactory shareholder returns. But they are wrong to do so. They should listen to the new generation of leaders, some of them successfully making their mark as a result of the 'dot com boom', others determined to demonstrate that financial success, ethical business, long-term value and concern for the planet we live on are not mutually exclusive. For the best example of this new way of thinking, read the letter from Google founders Larry Page and Sergey Brin that accompanies their IPO documents, issued in April 2004. It includes the now familiar – and more powerful for its simplicity – commitment to be an ethical business:

'Do not be evil. We believe strongly that in the long term, we will be better served – as shareholders and in all other ways – by a company that does good things for the world even if we forgo some short term gains. This is an important aspect of our culture and is broadly shared within the company'.

---

16 *The Politics of Fortune: a New Agenda for Business Leaders*, Jeffrey E. Garten, Harvard Business School Press, 2002, p. 16.
17 *The Politics of Fortune, ibid*, p. 174.
18 *Beyond Grey Pinstripes 2003*, The Aspen Institute/World Resources Institute.

The principle that underlies this chapter is simple – take issues such as ethics and corporate social responsibility deep down into the organization, down into its soul. Understand the soul, feed it – and the organization will be stronger as a result. For too long, too many business leaders have hidden behind the carapace of process and function. Happy to adopt common-sense solutions at home, they have forgotten how to trust their common-sense at work. They have ignored or forgotten one of the most fundamental of human values – do not do to others what you would not want them to do to you. Thankfully however, there are business leaders who recognize that, if for no other reason than self-interest, the approach adopted by Google, quoted above, makes sense. They accept they must move out of the usual tramlines of thought. They are learning to listen to their intuition, seeking to understand their role in a world that we must all share.

The astronaut Jim Lovell, returning from the moon on the stricken and ill-fated Apollo 13, famously noted how, just by holding up his thumb, he could conceal the earth from his view of space. From the moon's surface, the Earth did indeed seem a small place. The late Carl Sagan picked up on that smallness:

'Look again at that dot. That is here. That is home. That is us ... On it every human being who ever WAS lived out their lives. . . . Think of the rivers of blood spilled by all those generals and emperors so that, in glory and triumph, they could become the momentary masters of a fraction of a dot... There is perhaps no better demonstration of the folly of human conceits than this distant image of our tiny world'.

The need for humanity and a touch of humility was made as forcefully in 1973 by the mathematician and broadcaster Jacob Bronowski in his landmark TV series 'The Ascent of Man'. Visiting Auschwitz concentration camp, where many members of his family perished, he noted that:

'We have to cure ourselves of the itch for absolute knowledge and power. We have to close the distance between the push-button order and the human act. We have to touch people'.[19]

But, as ever, we need to listen most clearly to our children. Severn Suzuki started a club called the Environmental Children's Organization in 1989. In June 1992, she took a stand at the Earth Summit in Rio de Janeiro. They caught the attention of the organizers and Severn was invited to address the full plenary session. Aged just 12 years old, she told the hundreds of adults present (including many heads of corporations and governments) what they needed to hear, but were sometimes too wrapped up in their own processes to listen to. She concluded:

[19]   *The Ascent of Man*, Jacob Bronowski, BBC Books 1973, p. 374.
[20]   Quoted in *The Sacred Balance: Rediscovering our Place in Nature*, David Suzuki with Amanda McConnell, Greystone Books 1997, p. 221.

'You teach us how to behave in the world. You teach us not to fight with others; to work things out; to respect others; to clean up our mess; not to hurt other creatures; to share, not be greedy. Then why do you go out and do the things you tell us not to do?'.[20]

No further comment is needed.

Chapter 5

CORPORATE SOCIAL RESPONSIBILITY AND PUBLIC POLICY

Felix Martin

A. INTRODUCTION: TRANSFORMING BUSINESS CULTURE[1]

a. Sustainability: Legislation v. Trade

This chapter deals with the role of public policy in the promotion of CSR.

I take as my starting-point the White Paper and subsequent Communication of the European Commission (the 'Commission') on CSR because they represent the most comprehensive attempt of any government body to describe the role of CSR in modern industrial society. Washington has not made any significant statements on this topic, notwithstanding active lobbying by the Kenan Institute and others.

The promotion and development of CSR forms an integral part of the Commission's goal of pursuing the economic advancement of the European Union, with the aim of becoming 'the most competitive and dynamic knowledge based economy in the World, capable of (1) *sustainable economic growth* with (2) *more and better jobs* and (3) *greater social cohesion*'.[2] These three objectives reflect specific concerns of a Western industrialized society that remains deeply divided and where unemployment is a current issue.

'Sustainable growth' is industrialized society's equivalent of Brundtland's concept of 'sustainable development', which she defined as 'meeting the needs of the current generation without compromising the ability of future generations to meet their own needs'. Sustainable development is by definition long term. It addresses the great topics of Universal concern identified in Cairo, Rio de Janeiro, Doha, Kyoto and the Millennium Declaration: the relief of poverty, trade liberalization, the protection of human rights and social justice, environmental

---

[1] Unless otherwise indicated, the quotations in this section are taken from the Commission's White Paper on CSR and the Commission's Communication on CSR.
[2] European Council meeting in Lisbon, March 2001.

Ramon Mullerat (ed.), Corporate Social Responsibility: The Corporate Governance of the 21st Century, 77–95.
© 2005 *International Bar Association. Printed in the Netherlands.*

sustainability, technical progress, job creation and the fair distribution of goods. In its Communication on CSR, the Commission referred to those as well as other objectives of particular relevance to the attainment of sustainability in Europe, such as socially responsible restructuring, life-long learning, employee empowerment and improvements in the field of health and safety.

'Social cohesion', the third objective of the Commission's vision, is a key foundation for sustainable growth. It requires bridging the gaps of wealth, culture and background that polarize society.[3] Social cohesion is strengthened by the rule of law, such as the plethora of European social laws adopted by the Commission over the last 15 years. However, too much legislation can shackle the economy and stunt sustainable growth, by imposing unreasonable costs on businesses.[4] Moreover, in an increasingly globalized world, companies can migrate their operations to a different country or region if the cost of implementing legislation becomes too high, thus undermining the local economy even further. All of this will have a negative impact on the 'job creation', which is the second objective mentioned by the Commission.

To achieve the Commission's vision, it is necessary therefore that the correct balance be struck between legislation and the promotion of business. To this end, the Commission wishes to engage the business community in the 'voluntary' pursuit of sustainable growth, under the banner of corporate social responsibility ('CSR') on the basis that 'Business success and *shareholder value* cannot be achieved solely through maximizing short-term profits but instead through market-oriented yet *responsible behaviour*'. Corporate social responsibility must bring about a 'change in business culture, so that sustainability objectives become "an integral part of corporate strategic planning and routine operational performance".

Clare Short highlighted the importance of the role of businesses in the pursuit of sustainability when, as UK Minister for International Development, she noted that the UK foreign development budget of GBP 3.6 billion was but a small fraction of the turnover of the handful of companies that formed the Ethical Trading Initiative, which at the time (2002) totalled GBP 90 billion.[5]

b.   CSR and Shareholder Value

The voluntary engagement of the business community in the CSR movement is predicated on the premise that *shareholder value* is improved through 'responsible behaviour' which, in this context, means behaviour that meets the requirements of sustainability.

CSR can improve shareholder value by:

- Enhancing brand image, acting as a replacement for alternative marketing practices. Wal-Mart, for example, relies heavily for advertising on the CSR activities that its stores carry out in the local communities where they operate. The reputation of Body Shop was built on the ethical sourcing of its products.

---

[3]   By way of illustration, Shell may have to abandon its profitable operations in Nigeria because of the social instability created by differences in wealth, which has led to a rapid spread of crime, rioting and the taking of Shell executives as hostages (Reported in *The Times*, 11 June 2004).

[4]   For example, the cost to companies of implementing the new 'paternity leave' rights, anti discrimination legislation, sick pay rights, etc is estimated at well into the hundreds of millions of pounds a year in the UK alone, and it is partly blamed for the sluggish economic growth, bordering on recession, of Europe over the last few years.

[5]   Rt. Hon. Clare Short MP, Key Note address to the Development Agency Round Table on CSR, January 2002, sponsored by IIED.

- Improving customer satisfaction which translates in repeat business. According to BT, CSR performance accounts for over 25% of the image and reputation driver of customer satisfaction; and 1% improvement in the public perception of BT's CSR activities means a 0.1% increase in customer satisfaction figures.
- Increasing employee satisfaction, which results in the delivery of a better quality service and greater business success.
- Reducing costs, by increasing efficiency through innovation. For example, the adoption of teleconferencing facilities will save travel costs, potentially reducing pollution and leading to more efficient use of employee's time. The introduction of renewable energy sources can result in substantial savings in the long term and have a beneficial effect on the environment.
- Increasing revenue through product differentiation. For example, Costa Coffee, a leading UK coffee retailer, now offers a fair-trade option for tea and coffee in all its stores.
- Creating competitive advantage by raising barriers to entry. However, whilst delivering shareholder value for the implementing company, this can result in market inefficiencies and may require government intervention in the form of financial incentives and training to help other companies overcome such barriers. This is explained further in Section B(d).
- Avoiding the threat of costly litigation and NGO action, that could have a detrimental effect on reputation and therefore on business performance.
- Increasing transparency through corporate governance measures[6] and by requiring disclosures by companies of their sustainability practices. This ensures that shareholders can make informed decisions about their investments although this must be balanced against the additional costs that such measures may impose on businesses.

However, whilst CSR can generate shareholder value, this does not mean that all CSR activities will generate shareholder value to the same extent or for all companies.

Shareholder value depends on factors such as the cost of capital and the level of returns expected, for the industry sector in which the company operates or from companies that share a similar risk-profile. The management priorities of a company in distress or a start-up venture may differ significantly from those of a blue-chip stock in the manufacturing sector. The shareholder value objectives of the owner of a small private business may have little to do with those of a major PLC. There can be, therefore, no uniform definition of 'responsible behaviour' and no definite shareholder value benefit analysis, that is of general applicability to all companies at all times.

A thorough study on the practice of CSR in Italy[7] concluded that the adoption of CSR activities by companies varied by:

a) Size of the enterprise: CSR practice was considerably skewed in favour of large companies. Smaller companies do not have sufficient financial resources or personnel to focus on CSR activities although they may on

---

[6]   I will not deal with corporate governance in any detail in this chapter, as it is sufficiently covered in other chapters of this book.
[7]   Study carried out by the Italian Union of Chambers of Commerce, Industry, Craft and Agriculture in cooperation with Instituto per i Valore d'Impresa under the title 'Models of

occasions undertake them on an ad hoc basis, but without clear strategic purpose; and

b) Sector of the economy in which the enterprise operates:
   • Enterprises belonging to the Agro-industrial, Building and Construction, Manufacturing and ICT macro-sectors, are more attentive to environmental problems associated with production processes and product lifespan.
   • In the Trade and Tourism sector, the main concern is ecological certification and to a lesser extent, improvement of own image through social initiatives.
   • Enterprises producing convenience goods or supply services are primarily concerned with reputation through the development of visible social initiatives. The Credit-Insurance macro-sector, in particular, is a leader in almost all forms of partnership with the community, principally through the sponsorship of social events.

c.   The role of public policy in the promotion of CSR

Based on the foregoing discussion, the role of public policy in promoting the voluntary pursuit of CSR (the "Voluntary Approach") may be defined as the identification of CSR activities that are relevant to each industry sector and making it possible for the greatest number of companies in each sector to take up as many of those activities as possible. This is the basis of the championing approach developed in Section B.

The urgency or importance of the sustainability objectives may in some cases require that specific measures be required from all companies in a given sector or across sectors regardless of shareholder considerations. In such instances, it may be necessary to resort to legislation[8] (the "Legislative Approach"). The Commission has pointed out that the voluntary approach should not be perceived as an abdication by governments of their commitment to sustainability or as a compromise with the interests of business. This theme is taken up in Section C.

Ultimately, however, sustainability is not just about businesses but about society as a whole. Therefore governments must promote the development of a more sustainable society and this is briefly discussed in Section D.

B.   THE 'VOLUNTARY APPROACH'

With the notable exception of wars and revolutions, any process of cultural transformation is by definition slow. It requires gaining the trust and respect of those

---

Corporate Social Responsibility'. It considered the CSR practices across Italy of very small enterprises (1–19 employees), small enterprises (20–49 employees), medium enterprises (50–249 employees) and large enterprises (250+ employees), across nine sectors: Agro industrial, Manufacturing, Building and Construction, Trade and Tourism, Transport, ICT, Credit-Insurance, Services for Enterprises, Services for People. CSR practice was analysed from the point of view of a) area focus (relations with the community, relations with customers and suppliers, environmental measures and employee motivation) and b) and types of CSR instruments used. In addition to the conclusions outlined above, the study also highlighted some differences resulting from differences in legislation or culture.

[8]   In this chapter, the term 'legislation' is used in a broad sense to include statutory instruments, rules, regulations, bye-laws and other forms of normative prescriptions. The term 'government' is also used broadly to include any government agency that is authorised to adopt 'legislation'.

who are most influential in society. Then they must be convinced to become agents of change by accepting the new rules that dictate relationships amongst themselves and with society at large. Others then feel obliged to follow and, provided that the change is not beyond their means, they will follow.

The same process is required to involve businesses in the CSR agenda. Trust and respect is gained by the delivery by governments of a *credible message* on CSR, one that is attractive to companies and society. The agents of change in this case are the big corporations, their leaders and the investor community. The big corporations must become '*champions*' of CSR practice, their leaders must accept the demands of *corporate governance* and the investor community must be encouraged to take up *ethical investment*. The new rules of business inter-action ensure integrity in CSR practice and they are *transparency, co-ordination* and the willingness to *co-operate with SMEs and the social stakeholders* in the pursuit of sustainability objectives. Governments must not only guide and lead this process of transformation, but they must also become participants in it. They must also ensure that CSR activities are properly *aligned with public policy action* so that they can deliver real benefits to society. Finally, in an increasingly global economy, Governments must work with other Governments to deliver a global CSR agenda, and for this they must support the work of *international agencies*.

The rest of this section presents a comprehensive and ambitious framework for government action in promoting the 'voluntary' adoption of CSR practices by businesses.[9]

1. Engaging the Champions

a. Selling the Message

One of the key functions of public policy in the CSR field is to present to businesses the meaning and importance of sustainable growth and development, both for the businesses themselves and for society. This must be done at a general level but also by identifying CSR activities that are of interest and concern to each industry sector and to companies of different sizes within each sector. To this end, Governments are increasingly funding research and holding forums on the benefits of CSR, bringing together researchers, business leaders and political agencies. The UK Government has even appointed a Minister of CSR whose task it is to sell CSR to companies and to actively pursue the broader CSR government agenda.

A forum organized recently by the UK Department of Trade and Industry,[10] which included a large number of industry representatives and consultants, concluded that 'a business with strong corporate social responsibility will often be more successful in generating Economic Value Added'. This is primarily because 'company success depends on balancing multiple priorities and stakeholder interests'.

---

[9]   I have illustrated this section with examples of Government practice from all over the World, taken from various sources, including: *Public Sector Roles in Strengthening Corporate Social Responsibility: A baseline Study* by Tom Fox, Halina Ward and Bruce Howard; The European Commission's Communication on CSR; The Global Compact website; and the DTI website.

[10] Forum for the Future: Sustainability and Business Competitiveness.

Governments can also encourage universities and other teaching institutions to include in their curriculums courses on CSR, as a way to spread the word about CSR to the future leaders of industry. Governments can also work with those same universities as well as with management consultancies that provide CSR advisory services, to better determine the impact of CSR on businesses and society and the ways in which it can be put into practice in different business sectors.

b.   Championing Best Practice

Big companies have extensive personnel resources and the capacity to invest in potentially risky initiatives. They also have a greater appreciation of the benefits of innovation and branding that CSR activities can deliver. Many big companies operate a portfolio of projects, each one with its own profit-and-loss accounts, time-horizons and level of expected returns. This means that these companies can pursue a wider CSR agenda than others. Because they have market power and ample resources, they are in a better position that other companies to experiment by adopting CSR activities (e.g. as a replacement for traditional product marketing) that may deliver benefits to companies in one or more industry sectors. The are also able to run some projects over longer 'time-horizons' or at lower 'returns' than the industry average without significant risk to their competitive position if they think that by doing this they can influence market and societal perceptions of sustainability issues in a way that will deliver value creation for the company. Through these actions they become 'champions' of change.

There are a growing number of corporate initiatives that illustrate this championing attitude. For example, Unilever has decided to source 40 per cent of its primary products in certain channels through fair trade practices. BP has committed itself to implementing a Kyoto-style 10 per cent cut from 1990 levels in its emissions of carbon dioxide. BASF has committed itself to the protection of human rights and the upholding of labour standards by incorporating these issues into the company policy document Values and Principles, 2000. Deloitte Touche Tohmatsu has set up the Multicultural Development Programme to promote the recruitment of black trainee accountants in SA. Costa Coffee, a UK coffee retailer, has decided to charge an extra 10 pence per cup for sustainable development.

Once a big company takes up an activity, it may be easier to convince others to do the same. As the market-leaders change, smaller companies must adapt. The big companies will begin to impose CSR conditions on their suppliers through tendering processes or by incorporating CSR conditions in their contracts. Eventually, this process will alter the boundaries of acceptable business practice in the company's industry sector.

The managers of companies that have adopted a CSR practice must be prepared to explain to their shareholders and the wider stakeholder community the reasons for their decision. This can have a wide impact on public awareness of the importance of sustainability objectives and the need for companies to adopt CSR practices. In this way, these managers become *'leaders of change'*[11] and the championing exercise becomes a *transforming process* for the whole business community.

---

[11]   An example of leadership in this area was the recent declaration of a top HSBC executive that 25% of the value of the brand could be attributed to CSR practice.

Government agencies can, through industry forums and industry research, encourage the adoption of sustainability practices by 'champions', and facilitate benchmarking and the exchange of CSR experience between champions and other companies. They can also endorse the behaviour of 'champions' and those who follow them through award schemes and publicity such as, for example, the EU-Ecolabel, which is awarded to businesses with the highest environmental quality. Finally, Governments can encourage, through corporate governance guidelines, the appointment of non-executives directors with experience in the CSR field and personnel dedicated to the promotion of CSR practice within corporations.

c. Engaging the Financial Community

The personal priorities of *investors* can have a significant effect on company goals. Profit-taking and trading together with quarterly profit announcements, ensure that the company focus is on the short-term maximization of profits rather than long-term growth. This is not good for the companies and it is the type of behaviour that CSR practice is seeking to change.

Ethical indeces like the UK Good4Business and the Novo Mercado in Sao Paolo[12] put sustainability at the core of the investors' agenda. If there is a demand for ethical investments, then these indeces will reward CSR champions and their CSR followers.[13]

Investment Funds, through their research on CSR issues and their client communications can have an important influence on shareholder attitudes. An example of this is the work carried out by Henderson Global Investors, which has been managing sustainability and responsible investment ('sri') since 1977. It seeks to identify companies that could benefit from the global transition to sustainable patters of development ('industries of the future'), and it engages in discussions with these companies and potential investors to encourage the adoption of sri practices.

Notwithstanding the important role of the investment community in the promotion of CSR practices, the fact is that today ethical investment still constitutes a very small, albeit growing, part of the overall investment portfolio. Governments must do more to foster the emergence of ethical investment indeces and funds by giving them publicity, by actively promoting the disclosure of information to investors by companies about their social and environmental practices, and by providing guidelines on ethical investment. They also need to canvass investors and those who can influence investors' decisions. An example of how this can be done is the Just Pensions Project, a two-year scheme funded by the National Lottery Community Fund (UK) and managed by War on Want

---

12   This a listing segment of the Sao Paolo stock market that is dedicated to companies that agree to abide by key corporate governance and disclosure requirements.

13   CSR champions tend to be blue-chip companies and, therefore ethical indeces should be capable of delivering safe long-term returns. However, depending on the investment criteria adopted, these indeces can ignore whole industries that do not represent an ethical concern for some investors (e.g. the tobacco industry for avid smokers) and include others that do (e.g. bio-tech companies working in the Genetic Engineering field). This is one of the reasons why in the US new indeces are emerging that classify companies according to ethical criteria by industry sector, rather than across the whole market. Though this is clearly useful for investors, from a CSR perspectives it can undermine attempts to 'benchmark' best practice across all industries and, thus allows 'unethical' companies to continue to exist.

and Traidcraft Exchange, that encourages pension fund trustees to use their influence in order to persuade pension fund managers to invest in socially responsible enterprises.

d.   Enabling Smaller Companies

The 'championing' approach may raise unrealistic barriers to trade for smaller companies or new market entrants. A classic example is the adoption by retailers of higher quality standards in goods, whilst failing to share with suppliers the associated costs of production. This results in a spiral of poverty down the supply chain. This particular concern has led to the promotion of 'fair trading' practices and has resulted in trade boycotts by consumer groups.

The CSR champions have the *primary* moral responsibility to ensure that their suppliers and stakeholders can participate in and deliver their role in the sustainability agenda. An example of how this can be done is the Ethical Trading Initiative, an alliance of UK retail companies, non-governmental organizations and trade union organizations that is working to improve conditions of employment in the supply chains of corporate members who deliver goods to consumers in Britain.

Governments must enable smaller companies to pursue sustainability objectives by providing tax credits and other financial incentives, such as cheap loans and export-credit guarantee schemes. They can promote the design of appropriate management, measurement and evaluation tools that will help smaller companies to adopt CSR practices, and issue guidelines on the implementation of CSR practice for different sectors. They can also stimulate the development of joint CSR projects between champions and smaller companies.[14] On a broader level, governments must protect and foster competition and take legislative measures to prevent market abuse.

Co-operatives and *not-for-profit organizations* may provide viable alternative business models to limited corporations, with the potential to ensure a better distribution of goods and resources in the community. They may be particularly useful for the development of business activities in the Developing world and may also help to bring together smaller businesses in the common pursuit of sustainable objectives. The UK government, amongst others, is exploring ways to better exploit the benefits of these types of corporate vehicles. It is also encouraging investment in high-risk sustainability projects through Community Development Finance Institutions.

2.   Fostering Integrity

a.   Ensuring Transparency in CSR Practice

Big brand names have the financial where-with-all and experience to actively market their CSR practices, and this may be used as a way to distract public attention from other less ethical practices. For example, the UK leading news retailer may

---

[14]   For example, The Ford Partnership Centre, at the Southampton (UK) Assembly Plant, which was set up in 1999 by Ford Motor Company and Solent Skill Quest, was a result of an initiative by the South East Development Agency (a Government Agency), to attract over 20 employers into new ways of providing skills in the workplace.

promote itself as a company that cares about children's education by delivering free books to schools, whilst showing no interest in the effect that the blatant display of soft-porn materials on its shop-windows may have on children's sexual education. On a similar theme, banks may support glamorous social causes such as art exhibitions, but they may care little about the negative social effects of issuing credit cards to young teenagers. Pharmaceutical companies pursue a wide range of CSR initiatives, but they have shown considerably reluctance to lowering the cost of some essential medicines for distribution in the Developing World.

Therefore, Governments have to foster accountability and transparency in CSR practices, to prevent them from being used as smoke screens by corporations to hide their malpractices. Governments can do this by, for example, actively encouraging companies to disclose their social and environmental policies in their accounts on a voluntary basis, through the application of the principles laid down by the *Global Reporting Initiative*.[15] They can also provide more detailed disclosure guidelines for specific industries.[16]

Governments must also equip consumers with the necessary information (ethical training) so that they can see through the smoke screen of corporate marketing, and devise channels through which consumers can voice their concerns, such as consumer associations, press complaints bureaux, etc. The OECD Guidelines for Multinational Enterprises provide a channel for consumer action, by making it possible for individuals to bring to the attention of the relevant OECD National Point of Contact alleged non-observance of the Guidelines by companies.

b. Co-ordinating CSR Practice

Despite the substantial evidence of convergence, there are still significant disparities amongst the CSR standards adopted by the various corporations even within the same industrial sectors, and the number of companies actively involved in such initiatives is still relatively small. The proliferation of codes of conduct, industry associations, labelling schemes, etc makes it difficult to benchmark CSR practice. Moreover, because of the self-regulating nature of these initiatives, they raise questions about the quality of their verification and monitoring processes, and the associated enforcement mechanisms. Where companies can choose to join or leave voluntary industry associations as they wish, industry associations are unable to enforce compliance with their standards.

Governments have an important role in *coordinating and streamlining* the various CSR instruments available to ensure transparency and effectiveness in CSR practice. They can do this by helping to put together frame-work agreements and model codes of conduct, by designing and promoting quality standards, certification and labelling processes, and by supporting the development of self-regulating industry associations and institutionalising them through charters or other legal instruments. They can also provide non-binding guidelines on CSR practice for different industries.

[15] The adoption of International Accounting Standards 2005 offers a great opportunity to businesses to take up this practice.

[16] The UK Government, for example, has provided extensive environmental disclosure guidelines, and has recently called for voluntary disclosures of revenues paid to Developing countries by extracting industries.

An illustration of this is the Global Code of Ethics for Tourism published by The World Tourism Organisation in 1999 to propose a minimum set of standards for the whole tourism industry. The 'Kimberley Process' involved more than 30 governments, the European Community, the diamond industry, and civil society in the establishment of minimum international standards for national certification schemes relating to trade in rough diamonds, to provide guarantees as to the use to which the proceeds of such trade is put by the governments of the diamond extracting countries. Other examples are the recommendation by the Commission of the Eco-Management and Audit Scheme as a way to achieve continuous improvement in environmental performance, and the EU Multi-Stakeholder Forum on CSR, which seeks to establish a common EU approach and guiding principles on CSR.

c.   Leading by Example

Governments must *lead by example* by assuming CSR standards in their internal operations.[17] They must also be prepared to demand similar standards from businesses with whom they interact. An illustration of this is Proudly South Africa, a company set up by NEDLAD, a South African government agency, to promote South African companies, products and services; it requires companies to demonstrate their commitment to social responsibility as a condition of participating in its promotional activities. The Commission and a number of local and national Governments are increasingly making certain subsidies to enterprises conditional on adherence to certain sustainability objectives.

One area where the Commission and European governments in general have proved reluctant to impose sustainability conditions is public procurement. This may be explained to some extent by the decision of the WTO[18] participation nations not to include environmental and social criteria in the WTO negotiations. However, it also highlights the complexity of prioritising economic and social objectives, which is the same challenge that companies face in implementing CSR practices. The Commission has stated that 'Community policy [on the imposition of CSR criteria on tendering processes] must *balance social and environmental considerations with the value of money for taxpayers and equal access* for all EU suppliers'.

Western governments have acknowledged that Developing nations face particular challenges in eliminating subsidies and other barriers to trade, and have agreed to allow for a gradual process of implementation of the WTO agreements by such nations. However, in addition, they should also accelerate the elimination of subsidies on products, such as textiles and agricultural products, in which (according to the economic model proposed by Ricardo and followed by the IMF and the World Bank) the Developing nations should have a 'competitive advantage'.[19]

---

[17]   A good illustration of this is the UK Government appointment of a 'Green Minister' to champion sustainable development in all its activities. An example taken from the other end of the World is the 1997 Thai Constitution, which introduced legislation to enhance transparency and accountability within the party system.

[18]   The World Trade Organization (WTO) is the only global international organization dealing with the rules of trade between nations. At its heart are the WTO agreements, negotiated and signed by the bulk of the world's trading nations and ratified in their parliaments. The goal is to help producers of goods and services, exporters, and importers conduct their business (www.wto.org).

[19]   The decision by the WTO tribunal to fine the US government for granting illegal subsidies to the US industry must be welcome. Similar fines may be applied against the EU in relation to subsidies granted to the sugar industry, and hopefully more will follow in the future.

The influence of businesses on governments cannot be underestimated. This is especially the case in the Developing World. The turnover of some of the corporate giants exceeds the GDP of some countries. Governments agencies must *avoid conflicts of interests* when courting the goodwill of big corporates that could compromise the interests of sustainable development. They must be prepared to set clear standards of social justice and punish those who breach them. 'Public sector agencies can demonstrate leadership to business in the exemplary way that they themselves engage with stakeholders or promote and uphold respect for fundamental rights. They can demonstrate leadership by carrying out their activities with probity and free from corruption. And they can show leadership in the way that they support transparency about their own activities in relations with external stakeholders'.[20]

3. Working Together

a. *Facilitating Relationships with Stakeholders and NGOs*

Where a 'marketing' agenda drives the pursuit of CSR, then corporates may become involved in activities that have great social visibility but that may fail to deliver relevant benefits to society. Too many initiatives in Africa, for example, have failed because they were skewed in favour of providing technical solutions to problems that required a more human response. The World Bank itself, with its bias in favour of funding large projects, has failed to bring about sustainable growth in local communities, and has contributed to the burden of debt that afflicts many Developing countries.

To address the real priorities of local communities, corporates must work with local stakeholders, such as trade unions, local government representatives, UN agencies, and even with local churches who through their day-to-day dealings with the local community may be in the best position to understand its needs.

Governments must *facilitate* the relationship of corporations with these local stakeholders. They can do this by creating specialist government agencies whose role it is to bring together local stakeholders and the representatives of corporations and to supervize and guide the development of CSR projects. Where the corporations are foreign, these agencies may also assist by providing local information as well as translation services and other practical help. An example of this *facilitating* role is the work of the US Agency for International Development, which funds and promotes projects involving partnerships between local or central government, companies and civil society organisations.

NGOs have an important role to play in helping companies address the needs of local communities in Developing countries as well as supervising the CSR practices of companies in the Developing World. The development of the CSR movement owes a great debt to the activity of NGOs, as it was they who first alerted the international community to the need for more responsible practices in the environmental and human rights arena. However, as CSR practices become a normal part of business practice, NGOs will have to change. Their single-issue focus may have to widen to incorporate a broader CSR agenda and

---

[20] Public Sector Roles in Strengthening Social Responsibility: Taking Stock, by Halina Ward.

they are likely to become more institutionalized, with more transparent corporate structures and a greater ability to engage in constructive communication with the corporate world.[21] Governments must support the work of NGOs by providing financial assistance and by engaging them in social development and environmental projects in such a way as to make them effective contributors to the CSR agenda.

b.   Aligning CSR with Public Policy Objectives

There is a careful balance to be drawn between the spheres of action of government and corporations. Corporations should not take over individual aspects of government action such as education or health provision unless they can ensure that those activities will continue to be funded in the future. Also, the delivery of essential goods and services by private corporations must be properly overseen to prevent abuses and to maintain high standards. The Public/Private Finance Initiative offers a good model of how governments and businesses can work together in the development and provision of public services.

Private initiatives must also be aligned to public policy to ensure that they deliver real benefits to society. An example of how this can be done is the Environmental Covenant, a Dutch policy instrument whereby at least two parties, normally a government agency and the other a representative of a sector of industry, agree on the pursuit of specific environmental targets in mutual dependence. By contrast, without proper co-ordination with government action, private initiatives could do more harm than good. For example, a large consumer goods company recently decided to hand out free condoms in an African country. However, this well-intentioned gesture could backfire by encouraging promiscuity and the further spread of HIV.

Governments can also 'direct' the adoption CSR practice where it meets priority policy objectives. For example, the Ministry of the Environment in Colombia created the Green Markets Programme to encourage the production of 'green' goods and services that may become competitive in the national and international markets.

c.   The Role of International Agencies

Sustainability is a global issue in a world where capital flows freely between countries and people can choose where they wish to live and work. Unless governments agree to align their own public policy objectives, long-term sustainability will fail as a project. International agencies like the UN can play an important role in channelling Governments' foreign policy towards common and meaningful goals. On the other hand, unilateral action such as that of the US in the Iraq conflict or its uncompromising position on the Kyoto Conference can undermine trust between governments and the ability to find common solutions to problems.

---

[21]   This will not be a smooth process, though, as illustrated by the negative reaction from grass-roots supporters generated by the decision of Amnesty International to widen its focus from political prisoners to the protection of human rights internationally.

In the field of CSR, Governments must support the work of International agencies such as the *Global Compact* and the *OECD*. The role of these agencies is extensively covered in other sections of this book. Other UN agencies that also work in the CSR field are the *United Nations Environment Programme (UNEP)*[22] and *The United Nations Industrial Development Organisation (UNIDO)*.[23]

d. Summary of Government Action – the Voluntary Approach

Theme	Government Action
Selling the message	– Promote forums and research on CSR – Appoint CSR ministers and specialist CSR government agencies – Promote teaching of CSR at universities and other teaching institutions
Championing best practice	– Endorse the behaviour of champions through award schemes – Encourage the appointment of CSR officers within companies
Engaging the financial community	– Encourage disclosures by companies of social and environmental performance – Give publicity to ethical funds – Develop non binding guidelines on ethical investment
Enabling smaller companies	– Provide tax credits and other financial incentives – Develop measurement, benchmarking and evaluation tools for CSR practice – Provide training in CSR practice – Issue non binding guidelines for CSR practice in different sectors – Institutionalise and promote the use of alternative forms of company models such as co-operatives and non-for-profit organisations – Develop guidelines to promote competition and prevent market abuse

[22] UNEP engages in discussions with representatives of businesses, large and small, from all parts of the World to promote voluntary initiatives, corporate reporting and environmental management systems and to encourage participation in the Global Compact. It addresses the need for a generally accepted reporting framework through the Global Reporting Initiative and produces the Environmental Management System Training Resource Kit, the Environmental Management System Handbook and the Guide to ISO 14001 for Certification/Registration.

[23] UNIDO promotes cooperation between public and private sector actors to improve the quality, efficiency and competitiveness of small and medium sized enterprises in Developing countries. This is achieved through technology transfers, studies on CSR, encouraging cleaner production and environmental management, etc.

Theme	Government Action
Ensuring transparency in CSR practice	– Encourage the adoption of the principles of the Global Reporting Initiative – Provide ethical training to consumers – Provide channels for consumer complaints and to identify unethical practices by companies – Promote detailed disclosure guidelines for specific industries
Co-ordinating CSR practice	– Develop framework agreements and codes of conduct – Promote quality standards, certification and labelling processes – Institutionalise industry associations – Provide non-binding guidelines on CSR practice for different industries
Leading by example	– Impose CSR conditions on public procurement – Impose CSR conditions for the award of grants or export subsidies – Comply with WTO responsibilities – Avoid conflicts of interests
Facilitating relationships with stakeholders and NGOs	– Work closely with local stakeholders to identify key social needs – Facilitate relationships between corporations and the local stakeholders – Support the work of NGOs
Aligning CSR with public policy objectives	– Promote public/private finance initiatives – Engage in partnership with private entities in the pursuit of societal or environmental objectives
The role of international agencies	– Support the work of international agencies and initiatives in CSR.

C.   THE LEGISLATIVE APPROACH

a.   Introduction

For many NGOs, sustainability is an imperative for today rather than a goal to be achieved some time in the future. To bring this about, they demand new legislation. Why should irresponsible companies get away without being punished?

The truth is that legislation, for all its ills, can have an immediate transforming effect on business's behaviour. Reductions in CO_2 emissions would not have happened without international agreements and legislation. Marks & Spencers would have shut down its French operations without employee consultation, were it not for the extensive employee consultation rights enshrined in the law. Ethical investment would not have taken off but for the decision of the UK government to introduce legislation requiring pension funds to state whether they use ethical criteria in their investment decisions – a number of other European countries have since followed suit. Sweeping corporate governance legislation in the form of the Sarbanes-Oxley legislation has been perceived in the US as the only possible way to beat corporate fraud following the Enron scandal.[24] In the UK new legislation has been passed to enable shareholders of listed companies to vote on the amount that directors of public companies get paid, as a way to beat the 'fat-cat' culture that puts the financial interests of management ahead of those of the company shareholders.

Also, the line between CSR voluntary action and what the law requires is often rather thin. Many of the CSR voluntary activities are underpinned by a strong legislative framework and may follow directly from it. For example, businesses in Europe are increasingly promoting work-life balance initiatives, yet this practice is also a way of implementing the requirements of the Working Week Directive and related legislation. The extensive consultation and compensation rights granted by law to employees, as well as the role afforded by law to trade unions, means that it is in the interest of managers to provide retraining opportunities to redundant employees. Investing in new environmental technology may result in innovation but it may also mitigate the risk of penalties resulting from breaches of environmental laws.

Not surprisingly, therefore, the 'voluntary approach' is perceived by many NGOs as essentially a 'risk management exercise', as a response to the law, rather than as a process that is capable of achieving a 'business culture transformation'. What is required, they argue, is a legislative overhaul that will institutionalize the pursuit of sustainable development. Underpinning this view is also an almost endemic distrust of big business, which they perceive as being manipulative of government, resistant to change and uncommitted to the sustainability agenda.[25]

The two issues considered in the Sections C(b) and C(c) are illustrative of the ongoing debate between the Voluntary and Legislative approaches to CSR. As they apply to the infringement of fundamental human and social rights in Developing Countries by multinational companies, they constitute two aspects of the same problem. Should the protection of such rights be enforced in the country where the company is based or in the country where the wrongdoing took place? The simple answer is in both. The reality is, as we shall see, a little more complex.

---

24 The principles of this legislation are now being taken up by the EU and are instrumental in the International Auditing Standards 200 (fraud).

25 An extreme illustration of this attitude is the views of Deborah Doane of The New Economics Foundation. In an excellent article, 'Beyond Corporate Social Responsibility: Minnows, mammoths and markets', she discusses the weaknesses of the voluntary approach to CSR, and proposes an alternative that she defines as 'social innovation'. The following are extracts from this article: 'Thus far, we have asked the seemingly innocuous 'how can business minimize its negative impacts on society and the environment?' This naturally has resulted in risk-management prescriptions and a defence of the 'voluntary approach' to CSR. . . . A more appropriate question might look like this: what institutions, organizations or actions do we need to deliver a sustainable society . . . Investors themselves should be required to ask this question: does this company meet the aims of a sustainable society?' To answer this question, '. . . it is necessary to have the ability to define alternative behaviours, at all levels within and outside organisations, which might enable different, more sustainable outcomes . . . One could foresee a future whereby big business no longer exists at all. What the ethical minnows have is the ability to innovate: to be closer to the people that produce and consume their products and develop products that serve, rather than drive human need'.

b. Disclosures in Company Accounts

Disclosures by companies of their social and environmental objectives are an essential means to ensure transparency in CSR practice. Although Governments have been actively encouraging voluntary disclosures under the principles of the Global Reporting Initiative, the evidence available shows that such efforts are having relatively little success to date. Moreover, where companies have agreed to disclose information to investors, there is little uniformity in the way that this information is presented making it difficult to compare and limiting its usefulness as an investment tool. US companies have shown even less inclination than their European counter-parts to share information with investors and the recent sweatshop litigation against Nike may do little to change this trend.[26]

Some governments are beginning to pay heed to demands for further legislation in this area.[27] France, for example, has recently imposed some social and environmental disclosure requirements on all listed companies. Belgium has set up a registry of eco-labels and other product certifications, and is forcing companies to disclose specific information on labelling and certification practices. Other countries, like the UK, are considering a 'materiality' based approach though this would, most likely, fail to satisfy the critics of the voluntarist approach.

Yet, the cost to companies of implementing wide-ranging disclosures is considerable. For one, it requires extensive auditing of operations that can be spread out over many countries and errors can result hefty penalties. Also it may result in public demands for businesses to undertake sudden, drastic changes in the way that they conduct their operations, which may not be practical because they ignore the complex reality of doing business in, for example, another country.

Any meaningful legislation in this area must set out some standards against which the disclosures must be made. The legislator must decide whether such standards should apply only to the operations of the company in its own country or also to its operations abroad. The latter requires a clear understanding of the conditions of business that exist in different countries as they apply to different industries. This presents a formidable challenge: hastily drafted legislation is, at best, likely to deal only with some fairly basic issues at a very general level, and may fail to make a difference; at worst, it could impose unrealistic burdens on businesses that could lead to the loss of jobs and much needed investment.

In situations like this, the Voluntary Approach to CSR enables governments to work with businesses to gain an understanding of the issues facing the implementation of CSR practice in different situations and it engages businesses gradually in a culture of greater transparency. Legislation can be introduced in specific instances where the issues at stake are well understood and cannot be compromised, or as a way to punish recalcitrant companies and to establish a level playing field that benefits those companies that have embraced a culture of transparency.

---

[26] Nike was refused protection under the US Constitution First Amendment (protection of freedom of expression) following its publication of statements that it did not source products from manufacturers that used child labour. This may have been the result of an oversight but it has caused no end of damage to Nike's global reputation (though not necessarily to its sales). The case has been recently settled.

[27] Over and above IAS implementation.

c. *Foreign Direct Liability*

Developing countries face the same challenge as Europe in establishing the right balance between trade and legislation though at a more elementary level. In their desire to attract inward investment and trade, they can perceive lack of adequate regulation or enforcement mechanisms, to protect fundamental human and social rights against corporate wrongdoing as a competitive advantage. Many of these countries (backed by the US), for example, have opposed any attempts to include issues of sustainability in the WTO negotiations for fear that it could weaken their negotiating stance.

As a result of this, multinational corporations are increasingly expected to act as 'guardians' of human and social rights in Developing Countries, by ensuring that not only their own business practices in those countries but also those of their suppliers and distributors over whom they may have little or not control, respect those rights. This has been the driver of a great deal of CSR activity to date.

Many NGO are calling on Western governments to hold multinational corporations accountable in their own courts for the action of those corporations in the Developing countries.[28]

A small number of civil court class-actions (mostly NGO funded) have been brought against multinational companies in the UK and in the US (under the 1789 Alien Torts Act (ATCA)[29]) for wrong committed in Developing Countries. These actions are expensive (though UK legal aid has been made available in some cases), present formidable challenges in the gathering of the required evidence and can drag on for years, so they do not represent a very practical form of redress against victims of corporate abuse. To date, for example, all the ATCA cases are still at the procedural stage (i.e. have not been tried on their merits), even though some of them are more than 4 years old.

In addition to those practical challenges, there are legal challenges that any plaintiff would have to overcome even before the action can be considered:

1. In accordance with the rules of conflicts of laws, in order to bring an action in a foreign court, a plaintiff must first demonstrate a link between the defendant company and the country where the courts exercise jurisdiction. The UK cases have all involved UK companies. In the US the courts have been willing to entertain a case against a company whose only presence in the US was an investors relations office of the Company (Cf Unocal case against Total).

2. The plaintiffs must then overcome any objections to the trial on the basis of 'Forum Non Conveniens', that is, that the adequate fora to try the defendant corporation are the courts of the country where the alleged action occurred

---

28 A more detailed exposition of this issue is contained in two publications by Halina Ward that can be found at www.iied.org: 'Legal Issues in Corporate Citizenship' and 'Corporate Accountability in search of a treaty? Some insights from foreign direct liability'.

29 The ATCA gives the US courts the right to hear civil claims by foreign persons for injuries that are caused by actions 'in violation of the law of nations or a treaty of the United States'. The Washington administration has lobbied the US judiciary forcefully to limit the applicability of this Act to its original purpose, which was the protection of foreign diplomats based in the US. The courts seem little inclined to comply with the wishes of the administration.

rather than the UK or the US courts. In the US this doctrine contains an additional element of 'public interest'[30] that does not exist in UK courts.

3. The plaintiffs must also prove a link of causation between the alleged offence and the defendant company. This is often difficult because multinational companies rarely act directly in foreign countries. They tend to set up subsidiaries or act through third party suppliers. They may also restructure in an attempt to hive off potential liabilities. In the UK, the courts have been willing to establish a link of causation on the basis that the head-office had overall responsibility for the abusive practices that the subsidiaries or suppliers had implemented.

The lack of effectiveness of such actions as a means of redress and the uncertainty that the risk of further action or of NGO activism create for multinational companies, suggest that it is in the interest of all parties that there should exist proper legislative and enforcement mechanisms in the countries where the abuse of social and human rights are committed.

It is the responsibility of the International Community to ensure that this be the case and the Voluntary Approach to CSR practice cannot be allowed to cloud this fundamental issue. The sad reality, however, is that International Law offers few tools[31] to the International Community to force recalcitrant governments to adopt the necessary legislative and enforcement measures. Interesting as they might be considerations of reforms of International Law are clearly beyond the scope of this chapter.

D.   TRANSFORMING SOCIETY

Marketing is only effective to the extent that it is successful in identifying and addressing the pervading concerns of the public. Sex, beauty and glamour sell because they tap into people's obsession with self and pleasure.

Many of the benefits of CSR activities are measured in *marketing terms* of improved 'image' and 'reputation' and the resulting positive effect that they have on employee commitment and customer attitudes. The underlying assumption is that employees and customers appreciate the benefits that CSR practices deliver

---

[30]   Cases of this nature can raise sensitive foreign policy issues, and in at least one case (Sarei *et al.* v. Rio Tinto, 221 F. Supp 2D 1116), the US courts dropped the case at the request of the US administration because of the potentially negative foreign policy implications.

[31]   These tools are essentially as follows:

- Unilateral Economic sanctions, such as those imposed by the UK on Zimbabwe or the US on Cuba. These have received wide condemnation from Developing Countries on the basis that they punish the local populations rather than their governments.
- The International Labour Organisation has powers to call on the UN to impose economic sanctions in reaction against very serious abuses by governments of fundamental social rights. However, except in the case of an isolated action against Burma, there is little evidence that it is prepared to use such powers.
- Conventions generally bind only those countries that ratify them so they may not be of much help against countries that do not want to toe the line.
- Traditionally Heads of State benefit from immunity from prosecution whilst they are in office, even if they commit crimes against humanity. Arguably, following the UN action in Bosnia, this rule might no longer apply where crimes against humanity such as genocide is concerned.

for society and would be willing to meet the cost of those practices (by working harder or by paying more for, or buying more of, the company's products).

The issue of sustainability is ultimately much deeper than government and corporations. It goes to the very root of society. Investors are people, shareholders are people, managers are people, and consumers are people. The promotion of CSR will certainly have a positive though tangential effect on society's attitudes towards sustainability, by helping individuals as well as businesses to understand better the importance of developing a more sustainable world. However, businesses can only be expected to go so far, because their interests are tied up with those of their shareholders and owners.

If the CSR agenda is to succeed, Governments must look beyond business ethics to the values that drive society itself. They must then make a decisive effort to promote a more 'moral' and less self-centred style of life that will help sweep away unethical and 'unsustainable' business practices.

Chapter 6

CORPORATE SOCIAL RESPONSIBILITY IN A CHANGING CORPORATE WORLD

Jerome J. Shestack *

One of the terms frequently heard these days in boardrooms and at stockholder meetings is Corporate Social Responsibility (CSR). To some the term is a current fad or buzz word. To others it is a call for conscience by the corporate world. The term has various aliases: community responsibility, good corporate citizenship, corporate social involvement, corporate social conscience. There are also various shadings and nuances. Not surprisingly, CSR has its supporters and its detractors. But whether one supports or derogates it, in this age of globalization, CSR cannot be ignored.

What is CSR?

Broadly speaking, CSR delineates the relationship between business and the larger society. Ramon Mullerat, a foremost exponent of CSR and former president of the Council of the Bars and Law Societies of the European Union, succinctly defined its elements.[1]

'CSR can be defined as a concept whereby companies voluntarily decide to respect and protect the interest of a broad range of stakeholders and to contribute to a cleaner environment and a better society through active interaction with all. CSR is the voluntary commitment by business to manage its role in society in a responsible way. CSR is the commitment of business to contribute to sustainable development working with employees, their families, the local communities in societies at large to improve their quality of life. CSR is cooperation between government, civil society and business'.

Even so defined, CSR has numerous facets. Corporations are besieged by many issues in the name of CSR: stockholder demands, environmental issues, issues of

---

* Jerome J. Shestack is a partner in the Philadelphia law firm of Wolf Block Schorr & Solis-Cohen LLP, and Past President of the American Bar Association and Chair of the ABA Center on Human Rights.
[1] By far, the most comprehensive article on the various aspects of CSR, is R. Mullerat 'Corporate Social Responsibility (A Human Face to the Global Economy)'.

Ramon Mullerat (ed.), Corporate Social Responsibility: The Corporate Governance of the 21st Century, 97–109.
© 2005 *International Bar Association. Printed in the Netherlands.*

sustainability, diversity, labor conditions, ethical investment, philanthropy and others. There is no one agreed upon paradigm.

A.   A SHORT HISTORY

Legal debates over CSR stretch from the 1930s to the twenty-first century. I will dwell here largely on the development of CSR in America, because, both in quantity and size, American corporations have played a dominant role in the capitalist world economy and have influenced corporate development in many nations. Particularly in the age of globalization, there is a fungible quality to multi-national corporations in a capitalistic environment.[2]

A seminal debate about CSR took place in the 1930s between the legal scholars, Adolf A. Berle and E. Merrick Dodd, over the responsibilities owed by corporate managers and directors to their shareholders and other groups directly influenced by the corporation.

Berle put forward an unorthodox theory of the corporate manager's responsibility. Corporate directors had long been held to have some fiduciary duty towards their corporation and shareholders. Nonetheless, statutes and corporate charters generally granted corporate managers and directors broad powers to act according to their discretion in the management of corporations. Berle contended that courts were showing a new willingness to use their equitable powers to force directors to exercise their powers not only for their own benefit, but for 'the ratable benefit of all the shareholders as their interests appears'.

Using a different approach, Professor Dodd of Harvard wanted to give corporate 'business statesmen' leeway to help constituents beyond the shareholder; he proposed that they be treated as agents not of shareholders, but for their corporations.

Unwilling either to abandon the safe harbor of shareholder primacy, or to relinquish prospects for a corporation responsive to all groups it affected, Berle and Dodd reflected tensions that would underlie future debates over CSR. However, both concluded that large corporations had amassed such power in modern America that, if they were not managed in the interest of society, they would soon hold a commanding position over American society. Yet each admitted that there was no clear-cut legal doctrine setting forth just how corporate managers could favor community interest over shareholder wealth.

Following the Berle-Dodd exchange, the debate over CSR essentially lay dormant for nearly twenty years. Beginning in the mid-1950s, there again emerged a social debate over CSR as part of that decade's wider discussion of the corporation's growing power in society and politics.

A leader in the debate, was Peter Drucker, a renowned guru of management technique. Drucker declared the corporation to be the 'representative...

---

[2]   'The variation that occurs between US and other global firms typically is the specificity of their CSR messages with regard to their ultimate goals and objectives'. Thus, 'the structure and conduct of Japanese Firms, as well as the applicable corporate law, are virtually identical to those counterparts in the rest of the world'. J. Snider 'Corporate Social Responsibility in the 21st Century: A view from the World's Most Successful Firms', *Journal of Business Ethics*, December 2003. The German corporate perspective is similar. See Symposium: Corporate Social Responsibilities *84 Cornell Law Rev. 1227*, 1290–1298 (1999).

institution' of modern society and argued that its power over workers and consumers gave it a social and political, as well as an economic, dimension.

Drucker's most dramatic proposal was that managers be freed from their legal subservience to both shareholders and directors. He argued that if the concept of shares was changed from slivers of ownership into mere claims on an enterprise's profits, managers would have greater scope to fulfill political and social roles. He proposed that boards act as a 'maker of policy', with representatives not only of shareholder/investors but also from management, labor, and the communities where the enterprise operated. He believed in the profit motive, but one that had a symbiotic relationship with the corporation's larger social mission.

Initially, Berle's, Dodd's and Drucker's ideas met an apathetic reception. By 1960, however, general discussions over how business statesmen could use their positions to improve society came under pressure because of social unrest, protests over the Vietnam War, and the realities of environmental decline. In the process, the reformers were no longer enamored with finding the 'business statesman', and sought to make the corporation more responsible to other constituencies by instituting greater oversight by directors or shareholders.

The riots that broke out in major American cities beginning in 1965 further pushed business leaders to implement new programs to help resolve, 'the urban problem'. Some large corporations redirected charitable donations to launch programs intended to solve urban ills, to start new employee training programs, and to support minority small businesses.

But there have always been critics of CSR. Opponents focused on the vagueness of the problems that CSR promised to solve, the lack of details concerning how the socially responsible corporation would operate, and the lack of commitment of proponents of CSR for the free market.

These critics argued that business's job was business[3] and it should avoid taking on tasks better performed by charities or government. In 1970, this view received its most forceful statement, in a New York Times Magazine article, written by the era's most prominent free-market economist, Milton Friedman. Friedman's essay entitled 'The Social Responsibilities of Business to Increase Profits'[4] was as attack on CSR, based on both economics and morality. In part, he noted, replacing market mechanisms with political mechanisms to determine how resources should be used, would produce economic inefficiency. But it was also immoral. The 'only social responsibility of business', he argued was 'to increase its profits'. Over the course of the decade many legal scholars and businessmen joined his attack on CSR. From the late 1970s to the mid-1980s, the academic debate over the concept dwindled.

The next external impetus for CSR came with the boom in corporate takeovers during the 1980s. Throughout the world corporations were merging, increasing their power, dominating the international arena and becoming power contenders with government, though without responsibility.

While many deplored the disconnect between corporate power and social needs, and CSR (under a variety of names) became a more frequent discussion

---

3   Often quoted is US President Calvin Coolidge's remark that 'The business of America is business'. To which Sergeant Shriver once commented 'The business of business is America'.
4   *NY Times* 13 September (1970) (Magazine) at 32.

topic in corporate and academic circles, not many corporations acted meaning-fully in pursing CSR. In deed, Friedman's view probably remained the prevail-ing one for most corporations.

But new thinking gained headway in the corporate world during the 1990s and early 21st century as the world itself changed with the end of the cold war and the communication and technology revolutions. Tony Blair, Prime Minister of the United Kingdom, summarized it this way: 'The 21st Century company will be different. Many of the world's best known companies are already redefining traditional perception of the will of the corporation. They are recognizing that every customer is part of the community and its social responsibility is not an optional activity'. Peter F. Drucker opined that the next society's corporation will have the task of balancing the three dimensions of the corporation: as an eco-nomic organization, as a human organization, as an increasingly important social organization.

Expanding the new thinking, advocates of CSR hold that the corporation must focus not just on shareholders, but on 'stakeholders' as well. Stakeholders include customers, employees, vendors and shareholders. And a broader vision of the stakeholder is that it includes the community, government, special interest groups and others affected by the activities of the enterprise. It should be empha-sized, however, that although the vision has become more popular, is still not one adopted by most corporations. I will discuss shortly, just how well the concept has taken hold.

What are the main causes of the new thinking on CSR? They vary, but two stand out: the coming of age of international human rights standards, the effect of globalization. Related to these are other influential developments: the rise of the emboldened shareholder and the scandals that racked the corporate world. Clearly, these developments are intertwined.

B.   HUMAN RIGHTS AND CSR

Human rights form an underlying legal foundation for CSR. Some 60 years ago Archibald McLeish opined that human rights, not communism, would be the true revolutionary movement of the 20th century. He was right. Since World War II, there has been a revolutionary development of international human rights. As Professor Paul Redmond put it, the human rights revolution 'carries the hopes and claims of the most marginal, the dispossessed and weakest on the planet; the satisfaction of their needs is the primary responsibility of national and global institutions, and the ultimate source of their moral legitimacy'.[5] Human rights development and protection are a matter of 'joint global responsibility'.[6]

---

[5]   P. Redmond, 'Transactional Enterprise and Human Rights: Options for Standard Setting and Compliance', 37 *The International Lawyer* 69 (2003). See generally, J. Shestack, 'Globalization of Human Rights Law', *21 Fordham L.Rev.* 558 (1997).

[6]   The initial legal basis for modern human rights is the 1948 Universal Declaration of Human Rights which calls for 'every individual and every organ of society to promote respect for values, rights and freedoms and to secure a universal and effective recognition'. The Declaration was fleshed out by a series of treaties or conventions covering a broad range of human rights. These conventions have been ratified by a majority of the nations in the UN.

Initially, human rights focused on civic and political rights. But the field expanded to include a variety of additional rights. These include conventions on social, economic and cultural rights, worker rights, healthcare and social security. There are also a substantial number of specific human rights conventions, including those dealing with race and women's and children's rights.

The creation of a large body of substantive international human rights law is a tremendous achievement. Law guides conduct, molds attitudes, change practices, shapes morals and provides rooting both for a just world order and the opportunity to improve the general welfare.

Until fairly recently, the conventional wisdom among corporate leaders was that human rights are an issue for governments and NGOs, not for business. Indeed, a principle of non-interference and neutrality as to the host governments was considered the sound course of action. The Swiss model of neutrality, at least, before the revelations of its complicity with Nazi Germany, was considered the ideal. That doctrine, however, was in time, challenged by human rights NGOs, by important elements of the press and by many business leaders as well.

Today, that principle of so-called neutrality is essentially passé. Human rights are high on the global agenda and they are the subject of numerous international treaties which incorporate human rights into the rule of law. An abuser of human rights does more than act antisocially; the abuser violates the law.

By now, it should be axiomatic that CSR must encompass human rights observance. Businesses and corporations are part of the entire society, and human rights focuses on the dignity and worth of the human beings who compose social society. Additionally, human rights form part of international law and corporations are bound by those laws that are applicable to non-state parties. Of course, national laws are also applicable.

Human rights issues impact on many aspects of a corporation's activities both internally and externally. Internally, in a corporation, human rights has a distinct relationship to how a company's employees and business practices are affected. For example, health and safety are covered by human rights treaties that are ratified by most nations. Basic human rights under international law also afford workers the right to have representative organizations of their own for the purpose of collective bargaining. Children are to be protected from exploitation and should not be employed in work harmful to their morals or health or dangerous to their life. A current development lies in the area of environmental crimes and humanitarian law. Here, individuals can be held responsible if specified crimes are committed. There are also other human rights standards, all of which serve to enhance human worth and dignity and have become part of the rule of law.

In the external international area, human rights are often in a state of flux and a satisfactory human rights condition in a country may deteriorate because of an outbreak of civil conflict or some other apocalyptic event. The corporation then has to choose whether to disinvest or risk accusations of collusion with the human rights violators. Very often the corporation may be a supporter of international human rights standards and yet be in a nation where human rights policies are difficult or impossible to implement. However, operating in countries which abuse human rights is a risky business in any case where the company may be at the mercy of the authoritarian government, where the people employed are dissatisfied, and where corruption is generally rampant.

With various international resource companies such as oil and mining, a commitment to human rights may lead to a loss of contracts and economic disadvantage against competitors who have no commitment to human rights. Such companies have choices to make. A study by Shell Corporation in the late 1990s showed that 20 percent; of the corporations decided not to proceed with at least one project because of human rights concerns.

Corporations that choose to work in abusive countries will have to prove that they do not seek to benefit from poor human rights conditions, or else risk adverse publicity, shareholder protests and lawsuits. Among others, non-governmental organizations are quick to identify corporations which are open or complicit accessories to human rights abuse. In recent years, shareholders of a corporation and other stakeholders (e.g., consumers, vendors) have become increasingly articulate about corporate responsibility to observe human rights. For example, corporations operating under apartheid South Africa met with protests, boycotts and calls for disinvestment. Such publicity affects sales and profits and is taken seriously by corporations.

The value of corporate adherence to human rights standards is substantial. As noted, these standards have now been globalized and are highly visible. Public attention is focused on human rights, which includes expectations of realization not only from government but from powerful private interests. Pragmatically, adherence to human rights is likely to enhance corporate recognition, boost the morale of employees, show adherence to a rule of law, and be welcomed by shareholders.

C.   GLOBALIZATION AND CSR

The rise of globalization also affects the exercise of CSR.

When did globalization begin? In a sense, it is not a new term. Indeed globalization is not a destination, but a gradual journey along a road built by the increase in cross-border trade, the flow of capital and the growth of communication technology.

In the current context, I believe that the big bang of the modern globalization era took place on an evening early in November 1989, when the Berlin Wall fell. As with Humpty Dumpy, all of the communist forces could not put that Wall together. Communism became marked for the dust bins of history. The fall of the Wall energized a globalized, capitalist oriented world, not a divided one.

Globalization is characterized by rapid economic integration across national borders, open access to markets, deregulation of cross-border economic activity, free flow of capital and advanced technology. Globalization has resulted in expanded international trade and foreign direct investments and in short-term capital flow following integration of financial markets. Globalization holds the promise of advanced economic welfare worldwide, increased economic opportunity, technology for the underdeveloped nations and dissipation of hostilities in the world.[7]

---

[7]   See E.M. Fox, 'Globalization and Its Challenge for Law and Society', *29 University of Chicago L.J.* 891 (1998).

Globalization raises questions beyond the normal human rights concerns. It includes issues about use of labor, concerns about environmental protection, the need to reduce poverty and the need for sustainable development. Though sustainable development is subject to different definitions, its basic objective is to satisfy daily human needs without jeopardizing the resources on which future generations depend. In that sense, combating poverty and protecting the environment are related objectives. Dealing with those issues is a function of CSR.

In this era of globalization, multi-national corporations can be so powerful with both political and economic strength that they cannot be readily controlled by national governments, particularly governments in developing countries. That power facilitates the ability of multinational corporations to further socially responsible programs if they so choose, but also to be blamed if such programs do not emerge. In short, with power comes responsibility.

The road to globalization has not been smooth, as protestors in Seattle, Washington and Davos, Switzerland and other places have demonstrated. As put by Dean Roger Martin of the Rotman School of Management at the University of Toronto: 'Globalization only heightens public anxiety over corporate conduct. Many people seem to think that corporate virtue declines as international economic activity expands'. Global corporations from advanced countries can enter developing countries and 'average up' by bringing their home country's labor, ethical and environmental practices. But, they may 'average down' when the corporation's policies get in line with lower local practice. Globalization thus places a spotlight on multinational corporate conduct. If globalization's principal achievement is that the rich get richer and the poor get poorer, it will ultimately fail and corporate business will suffer.

D.   WHY SHOULD CORPORATIONS PURSUE CSR?

There are a number of practical reasons for the growing interest by corporations in CSR.

One reason is that in many of the new venues open to multi-national corporations the need for social and economic improvement is huge and compelling. A corporation that fails to respond to those needs risks the hostility of the host country, with a backlash that will be harmful to the corporation.

Another reason for corporations to endorse CSR is that traditional corporate philanthropy has not been as beneficial as expected. Many corporations gave away millions of dollars for good charitable causes. These contributions, more often than not, are unfocused, and respond to desires of executives and employees. Such corporate philanthropy may be market oriented or may be an element of good will and/or good citizenship, but it generally does not convey sufficient social responsibility. Corporate reputation surveys report a great deal of public skepticism about corporate philanthropy. This has caused some, but far from a majority of corporations, to redirect their philanthropy to focus on programs of social or community benefit and to encourage hands-on volunteerism by their employees. But the question still remains whether corporate executives are the ones who should be influencing social values. The answer to this question will depend on how a corporate giving programs is administered and by whom.

Another compelling reason for a pro-active CSR is that, both domestically and internationally, CSR has turned out to be good business. A Hill & Knowlton poll in 2001 showed that 79 percent of the respondents bought goods from companies that they thought were 'good citizens'. Some 71 percent made that a consideration in stock purchases. When asked to name one company believed to be socially responsible 26 percent of Americans were able to name a company. Other polls convey the same results. Additionally, there is a growing recognition that improving social and economic conditions in under-developed countries, can help attract a large untapped consumer market in those countries and be quite profitable for multi-national corporations.[8] This can be an important incentive for CSR.

A telling study is one by the Ford Foundation in 2001. The study dealt with Sears Roebuck's partnering with a non-profit cancer group called The Gilda Club. Sears' annual sales improved by more than 50 percent in areas where such a partnership existed, compared to 16 percent in other cities. An important byproduct was that such programs increased employee satisfaction, which is often translated into customer satisfaction.

Still another consideration is that stakeholders, shareholders and consumers, non-governmental organizations (NGOs), and the general public, have become more emboldened and powerful when expressing their concerns and expectations vis-à-vis companies. Social responsibility and transparency are leading NGO concerns. Consider international NGOs alone – at last count, there were 28,000 worldwide – their visibility and credibility are on the rise. It has been said that NGOs have been called the Fifth Estate in global governance – the true credible source on issues related to the environment and social justice. A recent study found that Amnesty International, the World Wildlife Fund, and Greenpeace outstripped by a margin of nearly two to one the four highest-rated corporations in Europe. Accordingly, many enterprises, in particular the large ones, look for ways to enter into a constructive dialogue with NGOs on socially responsible programs.

Finally a key consideration currently impacting CSR relates to the corporate climate that has developed during the past few years. The recent corporate scandals in the United States, Canada, Britain, France, Italy and other nations, have fueled a skeptical view of corporations. Those corporations with the highest public profiles are the most vulnerable to bad publicity and disaffected consumer reaction. Particularly at a time when corporate scandals over unethical business practices are prevalent, companies are realizing more and more that they must consider not only the demands of shareholders but also the demands of stakeholders and rising public expectations that corporations will accept responsibility for the social impact of their business.

For example, the 2001 corporate leadership report of the Timberland Company made the significant statement that 'it is no longer enough to measure business only by standards of profit, efficiency and market share. We must also ask how business contributes to the standard of social justice, environmental sustainability, and the values by which we chose to live'.

A marketing firm, Cone Inc., reports that in the wake of the Enron and WorldCom scandals, 89 percent of Americans feel that it is more important than

---

[8]   See, A.L. Hammond and C.K. Prahalad, 'Selling to the Poor', *Foreign Policy, May/June, 2004*, p. 30; see also R.C. Martin, 'The Virtue Matrix: Calculating the Return on Corporate Responsibility', *Harvard Business Review on Corporate Responsibility*, p. 83 (2003).

ever for companies to be socially responsible. That view has an international dimension. A Boston College poll on CSR indicated that the majority of 25,000 persons interviewed in 23 countries wanted corporations to contribute to society beyond making a profit.

Some corporations have been slow to grasp this message and have suffered as a result. As Warren Buffett once said: 'It takes 50 years to build a reputation and 5 minutes to ruin it'. Chiquita International received strong criticism from media and labor groups for bad environmental practices in its Latin American operations. After much grief, the company established a partnership with the Rain Forest Alliance and an independent certification of its environmental operations. Nike had its reputation severely damaged when activists charged that it was running sweatshops in Asia. Since then the company has worked hard to manage fair labor conditions in its supply chain. Switzerland-based Nestlé Group has long been a target of human rights activities because of Nestlé's marketing of baby formula over mother's milk in poor countries. In 2002 Nestlé appointed an ombudsman to expose unethical promotional activities. There are many other examples.

Many corporations, however, do grasp the message. Examples of strategic corporate philanthropy with an activist stance on social responsibility are: the anti-hunger programs of General Mills, Grand Metropolitan, Kraft Foods and Sara Lee; AT&T's promotion of food programs for women, infants and children; IBM's support of devices for the handicapped in Japan; Motorola's assistance to health clinics in Hong Kong; and community development corporations by numerous banks to help rundown neighborhoods.

A leading exponent of CSR is Canon, a Japanese technology company. The company's policy is called 'kyosei', a business credo, defined as a spirit of cooperation in which individuals and organizations work together for the common good. Canon takes the cooperative spirit beyond national boundaries and addresses some of the global imbalances in developing countries. Also in Japan, some banks have become leaders in converting bad Third World debt to non-profit economic development activities.

In Taiwan, King Kar, a soft drink maker, mustered a campaign to help victims of a devastating flood in eastern mainland China. Due to the company's initiative, more than 10 percent of Taiwan's 22 million people pledged monthly donations for flood victims. The Taiwan relief campaign has now turned to Somalia and is one of the largest private systems of international relief in the world It bears noting that after languishing in third place in the soft drink market in the late 1980s, thanks to the judicious use of its logo in the above campaigns, the company edged out Pepsi Cola as the number two soft drink maker.[9] Today, one can muster an impressive list of such initiatives.

BHP Billiton, headquartered in Australia and England, has a market capitalization of $59 billion. In a recent interview John C. Fast, the corporation's chief legal counsel, cogently summarized the benefits of CSR:

'Good corporate social responsibility performance is an increasingly important contributor to our licence to operate and grow our businesses.

---

[9] See C. Smith 'The New Corporate Philanthropy', *Harvard Business Review on Corporate Responsibility*, p. 157 (2003).

Companies with a poor track record in these areas will find it increasingly hard to gain regulatory approvals and community support for new developments. The benchmarks provide a degree of assurance to external parties that we are serious about our commitment to corporate social responsibility and have effectively put our policy commitments into practice.

Good corporate social responsibility performance is also increasingly viewed as a good proxy for overall management competency providing an insight for investors into how well we are managing general risk and governance issues'.[10]

In the corporate legal field, some corporate legal departments – with the encouragement of their CEOs – have dramatically, although belatedly, responded to CSR. Recent surveys show that 39 percent of law departments do pro bono work of a socially responsible nature and 46 percent of law departments that don't do pro bono work nonetheless have an interest.

Merck and Co. Inc. has a *pro bono* program which is a preeminent model for a corporate legal department in-house program that qualifies as a contribution to CSR. Their programs reach nearby surroundings but also selected communities world-wide, in cooperation with a variety of international health organizations and human rights NGOs. Starbucks Coffee Company, Abbott Laboratories, Johnson and Johnson, and Pfizer are other companies whose corporate affairs and legal departments have initiated significant social work of benefit to the community. There are many others.

Summarized succinctly, the value of CSR, or more colloquially the value of 'good citizenship', is that it can strengthen a reputation for responsibility, enhance brand recognition, attract better workers, reduce earnings volatility, boost morale, attract investors and stable partners, blunt criticism, and take into consideration the demands of shareholders and stakeholders, including public consumers. These would seem to be compelling reasons for CSR.

D.   HOW SHOULD CORPORATIONS HANDLE CSR EXCURSIONS IN THIS GLOBALIZED CLIMATE?

A whole series of summit conferences and reports have developed standards, guidelines, and codes of conduct addressing the social component of globalization. Among these are the 1995 UN Copenhagen World Summit for Social Development, the UN World Summit on Sustainable Development in Johannesburg in 2002; the ILO's 1998 Declaration on Fundamental Principles and Rights at Work Standards and the OECD 2000 updated study on international trade and core labor standards as The International Organization for Standardization (ISO). NCOs have also developed Amnesty International, Human Rights First and other standards for the CSR area. So have individual companies. There is no dearth of standards and codes waiting to be implemented.[11]

---

[10]   *The Metropolitan Corporate Counsel*, June 2004, p. 63.
[11]   A useful compendium of relevant codes and standards and guidelines is recited in Mullerat fn. 1.

An early appearance of voluntary codes dealing with human rights was in the late 1980s among US-based clothing manufacturers and retailers. With increased societal pressure for enterprise accountability, international firms felt exposed to the bad labor practices of their foreign business partners in the commodity or service chain. In some instances, codes were adopted in direct response to incidents attracting negative publicity in relation to labor, human rights or environmental performance. The higher the public profile of a corporation and its products, the greater its vulnerability to adverse publicity and consumer sentiment.

Codes take several forms. One form is the individual company code, adopted on the firm's own initiative. These were the most numerous, representing 48 percent of codes in an inventory taken by the OECD of codes adopted by corporations based in member countries. The next most numerous group (37 percent of the inventory) were those issued by industry and trade associations in both developed and developing countries, representing a negotiated consensus among member firms in a particular industry. Codes adopted after consultation among those with an interest in a particular industry, such as trade unions and industry associations, comprise 13 percent of the inventory, and codes developed by international organizations represented a mere 2 percent. Finally, there are numerous model agreements, usually developed by NGOs as a framework for individual or industry codes. These existing models and codes present an opportunity for corporations to adopt voluntary CSR initiations in just about every relevant areas.

The essential objectives behind these codes may be summarized as follows:

(1) Reduce absolute poverty by a target date;
(2) Protect the environment;
(3) Attain equitable access to education and primary health care;
(4) Support full fair labor standards, and recognize the right to collective bargaining;
(5) Eliminate forced child labor;
(6) Achieve equality and equity between women and men;
(7) Accelerate development of the least developed countries;
(8) Avoid complicity in human rights abuses; and promote social integration based on enhancement and protection of human rights; and
(9) Increase resources allocated to social development.

However, the mere adoption of code is not a guarantee of their implementation. The efficiency of codes and guidelines largely depends on the seriousness and steadfastness of their implementation by the highest corporate executives.

E.   WHAT HAS GLOBALIZATION ACHIEVED?

So far, it is a mixed bag. There is no doubt that interest in CSR has blossomed considerably since the mid-20th Century.[12] When the Harvard Business School offered its first course in ethics in 1915, there were few takers. Today, more than 95 percent of business schools offer courses in business ethics and CSR, and

---

[12]   See, e.g., *Harvard Business Review on Corporate Responsibility* (2003).

the courses are often mandated. There are more CSR symposia, more learned articles, more conferences and more media attention, more CSR websites than ever before. Business leaders have characterized CSR as 'a competitive necessity'. In fact, there is an impressive list of corporate initiated programs that have benefited society.

One impediment to the blossoming of CSR is that defining CSR is still in flux. Nondiscrimination, free trade, and environment are all CSR issues, but what about nuclear power or pornography, or selling cigarettes to minors. CSR activists themselves are not united on many issues – tariffs, child labor, monopoly power, environmental regulation – to name a few. And despite the evidence cited above, not all are true believers in CSR; many corporations still question what the CSR buys.

A great deal of hypocrisy also exists in this area. Many believe that CSR is a smoke screen behind which anti-social practices continue. Thus, a company may warn children in the United States to shun cigarette smoking, while aggressively promoting smoking in other parts of the world. An oil company may establish a commendable human rights program for its personnel but engage in harmful environmental practices. Such conduct seems to be more of a manipulation of CSR than a commitment to it.

It is customary today for many corporate company websites to trumpet their CSR accomplishments. In fact, however, there is more lip service given to CSR than actual service. A fairly recent survey by the UN Institute of Public Research survey indicated that only 4 out of 10 company boards discuss social and environmental issues and only one-fifth of the organizations have a board member with a visible interest in social issues. At the 2004 World Economic Forum in Davos, Switzerland, of 1,500 delegates, mostly business leaders, only a small percent placed CSR high in measuring corporate success.

There is thus good reason to be cynical about whether CSR will be steadfastedly and comprehensively exercised by most corporations, or whether it merely will result in scattered short-term measures. Professor Friedman's axiom that the business of business is profits, is still powerful.

CSR has undoubtedly been an advantage to some multi-national corporations by enlarging their access to markets, increasing brand recognition, providing inexpensive labor and satisfying shareholders and stakeholders. But globalization has also engendered substantial criticism – that the multi-national corporations have enhanced their power while neglecting the objectives of truly advancing the lot of the under-developed and poverty-stricken nations which they have entered.

This criticism of globalization is not a casual matter. Foreign investment has risen to new heights but only about a third of it goes to developing countries. Developing countries have 80 percent of the world's population but less then 20 percent of global GDP. Only 6 states have larger revenues than the first 6 multinational corporations. The assets of 200 of the world's richest people are more than the combined income of 41 percent of the world's peoples. In some African countries, *per capita* incomes are lower now than they were in 1970. Fully 65 percent of the world's population earn less than $2,000 per year – that is 4 billion people. More than a billion people have to live on less than $1 a day.

What is most distressing is that despite globalization and its benefits, the gap between the rich and the poor is not only huge but is widening. To be sure, there are many reasons for that gap: scarce resources, abysmal education, non-existent technology, rampant corruption, are a few. All of these ills cannot be laid at the doorstep of globalization. But some multi-national corporations exploit and aggravate these conditions, whereas the exercise of CSR can help alleviate them.

Multinational corporations need to address the gap seriously. Multinational corporations like to assert that a rising tide raises all boats. That may be true on a waterway, but it is not true in underdeveloped nations. The sinister side of globalization can cause a serious backlash for multi-national corporations. The failure to make economic and social progress for those most in need – and there are many – tends to destabilize societies and is a threat to world order as well as the business community. Governments are not likely to long indulge a hands-off policy. While some governments have felt diminished power when confronted with the power of multi-national corporations, the national sovereign still has power, influence and sanctions that it can exercise. If globalization fails to meet the expectation of improved economic and social conditions for the more needy of the world's population, sovereign actors will be stimulated to exercise power by national intervention or through inter-governmental coalitions for corporate governance.[13]

In sum, as Ramon Mulleret observed: 'CSR may have entered our national vocabulary, but it has not taken root in our consciousness'. CSR still has a long way to go before it is truly ensconced in the corporate conscience and implemented in its behavior. There is indeed progress, but it travels at a petty pace, when it should be a rapid one.

---

[13] The emphasis here on CSR does not, of course, negate the responsibility of the governments of the wealthy nations to exercise social responsibility such as measures to limit agricultural subsidies and tariffs, ease restrictions on immigrant flow and give more aid to countries based on needs and prospects. That subject, however, is not covered in this article.

PART III

THE MAIN OBJECTIVES OF CORPORATE SOCIAL RESPONSIBILITY

Chapter 7

THE TRIPLE BOTTOM LINE: BUILDING SHAREHOLDER VALUE

James Roselle *

A. CORPORATE CITIZENSHIP

1. Paradigm Shift

In recent years a growing number of public companies have come to recognize that sustainable corporate profit does not result from the single-minded pursuit of financial gain. Rather, sustainable growth and shareholder value are best achieved by working through a broad framework of economic, social, environmental and ethical values and shared objectives that involve constant interaction between the company and its various stakeholders. This paradigm shift, which incorporates financial, social and environmental factors into the company's commitment to growth and sustained profitability, is often referred to as the 'triple bottom line'. This linkage between profit and principles has been described in the following way: 'Without profits, no private company can sustain principles. Without principles, no company deserves profits'.[1]

Skeptics have at various times referred to corporate social responsibility as either 'window-dressing' or 'philanthropy at shareholder's expense', and the lack of consensus about what constitutes corporate social responsibility presents continuing challenges for companies. Financial profit must continue to be the primary and necessary motivation for shareholder companies, because without linkage of corporate actions to enhancing shareholder value the company will fail in its primary mission. Moreover, social responsibility itself will not ensure a

---

* Copyright 2005. All rights reserved. The views expressed in this article are those of the author and do not necessarily reflect the views of any organisation with which the author has been affiliated.

[1] World Economic Forum, 'Values and Value: Communicating the Strategic Importance of Corporate Citizenship to Investors', 2004, p. 21 (Statement of Sir Mark Moody-Stuart, Chairman of Anglo American plc and former Chairman of Shell).

Ramon Mullerat (ed.), Corporate Social Responsibility: The Corporate Governance of the 21st Century, 113–139.
© 2005 *James Roselle. Printed in the Netherlands.*

company's financial success if the company lacks a sound business plan or fails to execute its business plan effectively. Peter Drucker, the well-known management expert, summarized the linkage of corporate actions to financial performance in this way:

> 'The institution's performance of its specific mission is also society's first need and interest. ... Performance of its function is the institution's first social responsibility. Unless it discharges its performance responsibly, it cannot discharge anything else. A bankrupt business is not a desirable employer and is unlikely to be a good neighbor in a community'.[2]

2. Is Social Responsibility a Defensive or Offensive Strategy?

The financial calculus of social responsibility can be computed both in terms of defending the company from adversity and offering the company a means to build competitive advantage. The defensive side of the equation includes the following:

- Preservation of reputation and brand equity
- Reduction of litigation cost and liability arising from environmental or other damage claims
- Avoidance of regulatory fines and penalties
- Avoidance of legislative or regulatory initiatives designed to correct perceived corporate misconduct or indifference to social or environmental issues
- Ability to manage or avoid shareholder proposals related to social or environmental issues that could adversely affect business prospects

Some of the attributes of social responsibility that can be used more offensively include:

- Development of new products to meet emerging social or environmental needs
- Enhanced customer loyalty
- Improved ability to enter new markets and obtain government support for expanded franchise
- Competitive differentiation and enhanced marketing opportunities
- Ability to attract and retain a pool of talented employees

---

[2]   Drucker: *The Essential Drucker*, Harper Business. New York, 2001, p. 58; see also, Ruggie, 'Creating Public Value: Everybody's Business'. Address to Herrhausen Society, Frankfurt, Germany, 15 March 2004: '[T]he expansion in the global rights and reach of firms over the past generation has generated escalating social demands that private enterprise also should create greater public value, beyond traditional forms of compliance and philanthropy. Corporate social responsibility has emerged as the private sector's response to those demands, intended to establish the firm's social license to operate in the new global economic space. ... Thus, corporate social responsibility is not merely a matter of metrics, and not only a business challenge. Far more important, it concerns the changing relationship between business and society, and the recalibration of the respective rights and obligations of different social sectors and actors for meeting social needs. Most fundamentally, it is an issue of governance'.

- Ability to attract merger or acquisition candidates
- Ability to attract investment from a wider range of investment sources[3]

The financial, social and environmental elements that comprise the 'triple bottom line' are of necessity interrelated and must be aligned with the overall corporate goal of sustaining growth and providing value to shareholders. Although certain corporate actions may focus on one of these elements more than the others, the sum of the parts is a balanced response to the company's core constituencies that leads to enhanced 'bottom line' profit and growth.[4]

A number of recent studies have attempted to draw a more direct linkage between social responsibility and bottom line growth. One such study compared the stock market returns of 'visionary' companies with the general market and other comparison companies. The study defined 'visionary' companies as those that are not just motivated by short-term profit, but rather have a long-term vision of the company that incorporates the role of the company in the social and environmental fabric. These companies are guided by a core ideology and sense of purpose that go beyond just making money. Although profit is a necessary condition for existence and a means to an end, it is not the end in itself. The study found that from 1926 to 1990 visionary companies had stock market appreciation on average nearly eight times higher than the valuations of comparison companies.[5]

3.   Business Judgment

The linkage of social responsibility to shareholder value and profitability is necessary in order to provide company directors and management with the legal underpinnings for making decisions that are in the company's long-term best interests. In most jurisdictions directors owe a fiduciary duty to the company and its shareholders that compel the directors to find a reasonable relationship between a proposed action and the long-term interests of the shareholders. Although the directors can take into consideration many factors in making their decisions, they must always put the interests of shareholders first, and are limited in their consideration of the impact of corporate decisions on non-shareholder constituencies.[6]

---

[3]   CCBE: 'Corporate Social Responsibility and the Role of the Legal Profession: A Guide for European Lawyers Advising on Corporate Social Responsibility Issues', September 2003, p. 7 ('CCBE Report').

[4]   See, *Commission on the Private Sector & Development*, 'Unleashing Entrepreneurship: Making Business work for the Poor'. *Report to the Secretary-General of the United Nations* 1 March 2004 ('UN Report'). p. 34: '[Corporate social responsibility] involves being clear about the company's purpose and taking into consideration the needs of all the company's stakeholders–shareholders, customers, employees, business partners, governments, local communities and the public'.

[5]   Collins and Porras, *Built to Last: Successful Habits of Visionary Companies*. Random House, New York, 1995, p. 8; see also, Collins and Porras, *Good to Great: Why Some Companies Make the Leap – and Others Do not*. Harper Collins, New York, 2001.

[6]   See, e.g. *Unocal v. Mesa Petroleum*, 493 A.2d. 946 (Del. 1985) and *Revlon, Inc. v. MacAndrews & Forbes Holdings, Inc.* 506 A.2d 173, 182 (Del. 1986), both of which involved takeover defenses. Unocal held that the directors could consider the impact of a takeover on constituencies other than shareholders, including creditors, customers, employees and the community. In Revlon the court made the following statement: 'A board may have regard for various constituencies . . . provided that there are rationally related benefits accruing to the stockholders'. The court further held that it would not be appropriate to consider non-shareholder interests if corporate control is determined by an auction.

Recent guidelines have encouraged company directors to take a more expansive view of their duties to the company and its shareholders, including consideration of non-shareholder constituencies.[7] In today's environment, taking non-financial risks and opportunities into account is becoming an essential part of overall corporate stewardship, and failure to do so may well be viewed as an abdication of fiduciary responsibility. Some jurisdictions have even enacted so-called 'other constituencies' statutes, which specifically permit directors to consider interests of groups other than shareholders in performing their duties, and some commentators have recommended adoption of such statutes to make clear that directors can consider non-shareholder interests in discharging their duties.[8] However, such statutes could lead to confusion and potentially to litigation involving the extent to which directors can exercise business judgment in considering the interests of non-shareholder groups. On balance it appears preferable to expect directors to take social and environmental issues into consideration in exercising their responsibilities, but recognize that all decisions must ultimately be linked to the best interests of the company's shareholders.

Although social responsibility should be viewed as a key contributor to business growth and profitability, it would be a mistake for social responsibility to be seen only in the context of its contribution to profit. Many socially responsible initiatives cannot be measured on a pure cost-benefit basis, and the studies that have found a linkage between social responsibility and long-term corporate growth have not been able to quantify with any degree of precision the financial benefits of socially responsible initiatives. Perhaps the most effective means for measuring the benefit of social responsibility to the company and its shareholders is to make a holistic analysis of all of the activities of the company that seek to build franchise value, minimize reputation risk and differentiate the company from its competitors. The CEO of Hewlett-Packard summarized this analytic approach in the following way:

'[I]n an economy where intellectual capital is currency, corporate behavior becomes a scorecard by which you are judged—by your customers, your employees, and your shareholders. That scorecard will, of course, include your ability to be a competitive player, but equally important on the scorecard will be:

• Your integrity and your character
• Your ability to transfer value and know-how into local economies in which you do business

---

7   See, e.g. *OECD Principles of Corporate Governance* (2004) at p. 58: 'The board is not only accountable to the company and its shareholders but also has a duty to act in their best interests. In addition, boards are expected to take due regard of, and deal fairly with, other stakeholder interests including those of employees, creditors, customers, suppliers and local communities. Observance of environmental and social standards is relevant in this context'. See also, *The Business Roundtable, Principles of Corporate Governance* (2002) at p. 30: 'Corporations are often said to have obligations to stockholders and to other constituencies, including employees, the communities in which they do business, and government, but these obligations are best viewed as part of the paramount duty to optimize long-term shareholder value'.
8   See, e.g. Olsen and Adams, 'Composing a Balanced and Effective Board to Meet New Governance Mandates', *The Business Lawyer,* Vol. 59, No. 2 (February 2004) at p. 432.

- Your track-record as a socially responsible corporate citizen
- Your ability to sustain and nurture true partnership and ecosystems in which all parties have both social and economic gain[9]

4. Corporate Governance as a Precondition to Social Responsibility

How does social responsibility promote the goals of financial profit, economic growth and asset creation? The starting points must be good corporate governance and financial transparency. Good governance is a key ingredient because without it the company will lack the vision, leadership and accountability to develop sustainable profit in a manner that will appropriately consider the needs of all of the company's constituencies.

At a minimum, corporate governance must ensure that the company has tools required to comply with applicable laws and regulations. These include securities, anti-corruption, taxation and other laws that pertain to the company itself, laws that pertain to the company's relationships with employees, and environmental and other laws that govern the company's conduct with external stakeholders in the communities in which the company does business. Increasingly, however, these minimum standards are insufficient to give the company a competitive advantage or to ensure that social responsibility is a significant contributor to the company's bottom line growth. Rather, the company needs to articulate in a consistent manner how it views its responsibilities and commitments to the people and communities that it seeks to serve.[10]

The following elements are considered to be essential to ensure that corporate governance supports the company's commitment to social responsibility and sustainable growth:

a. Management Commitment to Corporate Purpose and Core Values

The CEO, together with the board of directors, should be able to compose a value or mission statement that will articulate the company's purpose and balance the company's profit motive with its responsibilities to stakeholders and the environment. The value statement may be a formal statement that is publicly available and placed on the company's website, but this formality is not always necessary. The value statement can also be articulated by the CEO in the company's annual report or in periodic communications to employees and other stakeholders. The essential ingredient is for the CEO to be able to deliver a consistent and easy to understand message of corporate purpose that should be aspirational in tone but not over-commit the company to specific social goals. The value statement should enable the board of directors, management and all employees to exercise

---

[9] Chapter 40: 'Carleton S. Fiorina', in *Yaverbaum: Leadership Secrets of the World's Most Successful CEOs*, Dearborn Trade Publishing. Chicago, 2004, p. 98.

[10] See, e.g. *European Commission Green Paper*: 'Promoting a European framework for corporate social responsibility', 2001 (the 'Green Paper'), p. 8: 'Being socially responsible means not only fulfilling legal expectations, but also going beyond compliance and investing 'more' into human capital, the environment and the relations with stakeholders'.

appropriate business judgment to carry out the company's mission through a combination of economic and social decisions that are directly linked to the company's financial success. As an example, the CEO of Merck defined that pharmaceutical company's business success not in terms of profit but in terms of 'victory against disease and help to humankind'.[11] Starbucks, Inc. articulated six core principles for the company, and listed profit last on the list. Yet, Starbucks has grown to more than 6,000 stores and over $3.3 billion in revenues.[12]

A value statement alone, however, is not enough. Prior to the scandal that led to its bankruptcy, Enron had articulated a statement of values that sounded very socially responsible, and the company and its CEO had received high marks for ethics and corporate governance. In retrospect, it appears clear that management did not abide by good ethical standards. Its focus on short-term profits and any means to be able to meet profit expectations led to irresponsible and illegal actions that not only directly led to the company's bankruptcy, but also caused material harm to employees, shareholders, customers and the communities in which the company operated. Even Merck, which has prided itself on its social responsibility record, stumbled recently when it appeared that the company continued to market one of its flagship products, Vioxx, notwithstanding studies that showed a greater risk of stroke and heart attack. The company finally withdrew the product but, as a result of the perception that the company did not act responsibly, it now faces the potential of substantial legal liability to consumers, an erosion of customer confidence, lower stock market value and the risk of employee and management defections.

b.   Board of Directors Oversight

The board of directors or equivalent body should take responsibility for oversight of implementation of economic, social and environmental commitments and should receive regular reports on progress. Large public companies typically set up committees of the board of directors to review and consider various aspects of corporate governance. In addition to audit committees that are usually required by law, many companies have established compensation, nominating, finance, risk and other committees that assist the board in carrying out its responsibilities. A growing number of public companies consider social responsibility to be sufficiently important that they have established a board committee to review the company's philanthropic, community, environmental and other social commitments and inform the full board of the company's progress in meeting its social objectives. The charter of one company's Public Responsibility Committee contains the following purpose statement:

'The Public Responsibility Committee shall review and consider the Company's position and practices on issues in which the financial services industry interacts with the public, such as consumer policies, purchasing from minority owned businesses, philanthropic contributions, privacy, community and neighborhood development, protection of the environment,

---

[11]   Merck 1991 Annual Report.
[12]   See, Monks & Minow, *Corporate Governance*, 3rd edition. Blackwell Publishing, Oxford, 2004, p. 108.

shareholder proposals involving issues of public interest and public responsibility and other similar issues as to which the Company relates to the community at large, and provide guidance to the Company as appropriate'.[13]

Without a committee of the board or similar body that can review all of the company's efforts in meeting social responsibility objectives there is risk that the efforts will not be adequately coordinated or measured. It may also be more difficult to link the various actions to the company's overall strategy and financial capabilities. As an example, the board of directors should consider how much the company can afford to contribute to philanthropic causes and still provide a fair return to the shareholders. A board committee can also serve as a check on the overzealous CEO who may be inclined to have the company make a large donation to the CEOs school in return for having the school named for the CEO.

In addition, the board of directors needs to have a framework for dealing with the marked increase in shareholder resolutions that are linked to social or environmental objectives. The company will be more effective in dealing with shareholder resolutions if it already has in place a framework for evaluating social responsibility actions and a governing body with authority to engage shareholder representatives and outside stakeholders in open discussion of social responsibility proposals and how they may impact the company's business strategy.

c. *Policies and Procedures*

The key document that articulates the company's commitment to corporate citizenship is usually a code of ethics. Following is an excerpt from one company's Code of Conduct:

> 'At _____, nothing is more important to us than our integrity. While it is easy to ask that we each hold ourselves to the highest standard of honesty and fairness, we also realize that you may occasionally have questions about how to handle a particular situation. . . . You can be proud that we enjoy an outstanding reputation in the communities we serve. But reputation is not a static thing. We earn it every day with each action we take'.[14]

Following from the code of conduct, the company should adopt other policies or procedures as necessary to deal with conflicts of interest, reputation risks, charitable giving, employees who wish to serve on charitable or community boards, and other governance matters. In order to be effective, however, the company must ensure that its policies and procedures are supported by the following:

- Quantifiable objectives
- Roles and responsibility for implementation and escalation
- Regular training for affected employees
- Systems and technology to measure compliance
- Legal and compliance oversight
- Independent testing by internal and/or external auditors

13 Bank One Corporation, charter of Public Responsibility Committee.
14 Bank One Corporation, Code of Conduct.

Effective corporate governance and compliance programs are particularly important when the company or its employees are accused of criminal conduct. Sentencing guidelines and regulatory policies will deal more harshly with companies that have not put in place good governance, but will tend to deal more favorably with companies that have put in place corporate governance and compliance procedures that are reasonably designed to prevent improper conduct.

B. THE BUSINESS CASE FOR SOCIAL RESPONSIBILITY

1. Effect of Socially Responsible Investing (SRI)

The growth of SRI has provided both an economic incentive for companies to adopt socially responsible practices and a means to measure comparative investment returns between those companies that meet criteria for social investment funds and those that do not. For example, from May, 1990 to the end of 2004, on a total return basis the Domini 400 Social Index (DSI) increased by 475%, compared with a 401% increase for the S&P 500; the Dow Sustainability Index has increased by 180 per cent since 1993 compared with 125 per cent for the Dow Jones Global Index over the same period.[15] The FTSE4Good and other SRI indexes have generally performed at least as well if not better than non-SRI indexes. Social Responsibility funds and indexes have proliferated around the world and linkages have increased to promote greater consistency of evaluations. Recently, social responsibility investing has even expanded to Africa, with the Johannesburg Securities Exchange SRI Index.[16]

The criteria that SRI funds use inevitably involve a degree of subjectivity as to what elements constitute a socially responsible company. Coca Cola, for example, has demonstrated a commitment to good workplace conditions and environmental safeguards, but has been criticized for using excessive water to manufacture its products. Many tobacco companies and petroleum refiners have also made substantial commitments to social and environmental causes, yet generally are not included in SRI funds because their products are considered to be unhealthy or damage the environment. On balance, SRI evaluations appear to be a positive step in identifying those companies that are viewed as making significant tangible efforts to achieve social responsibility.

Other studies have also demonstrated that enhanced shareholder return is achieved by visionary companies that include social responsibility within their corporate imperatives,[17] and increased shareholder value results from lower risk of environmental or social liability of companies that have embraced social responsibility.[18] Two recent studies in the United States and Europe examined stock market performance of companies that exhibited superior environmental management compared with those regarded as having inferior management of environmental issues (and attempted to neutralize other known investment risk

---

[15] See, www.kld.com; See also, Green Paper, *op. cit.*, p. 9.
[16] See also, *African Institute for Corporate Citizenship Centre for Sustainability Investing*, 'Socially Responsible Investing in South Africa'. 2001.
[17] See, e.g. Hollender and Fenschell, *What Matters Most*, Basic Books, 2004; see also, Hawken, *The Ecology of Commerce: A Declaration of Sustainability*, Harper Collins, New York, 1993.
[18] Earle, 'The Emerging Relationship Between Environmental Performance and Shareholder Wealth', Assabet Group. 2000; see also, www.sustainablemarketing.com.

factors). Both studies found that an index overweighted with companies that practiced better environmental management and underweighted with companies that had inferior environmental management had superior investment returns in the range of 1.8 to 4.4 percentage points per annum, and the degree of performance increased by the degree to which the index was overweighted with better environmentally managed companies.[19]

The proliferation of mutual funds that specialize in ethical investing, as well as organizations that rate companies based on social responsibility factors, is beginning to have a significant impact on corporate priorities and access of companies to the capital markets.[20] In 2003, for example, 95 institutional investors representing over $10 trillion in assets were signatories to a survey request to the FT500 Global Index companies prepared by the Carbon Disclosure Project (CDC). The survey requested disclosure of investment-relevant information relating to risks and opportunities presented by climate change. Based on the responses received, the CDC created a Climate Leadership Index, comprising the 50 'best-in-class' responses.[21]

2. Key Business Factors

The assessment of what determines a company's financial return on socially responsible initiatives is very difficult. Nevertheless, many studies have sought to prove by various methods that socially responsible practices have a measurable impact on financial returns. One study concluded that about one-half of the above-average performance of socially responsible companies can be attributed to their social responsibility, while the other half can be attributed to performance of the industry sector.[22] It is becoming more generally recognized that the extent to which a company's stock market or acquisition value exceeds the book value of its shares depends not just on discounted cash flow models that estimate future financial performance. The value also depends to a large extent on non-financial evaluations of the company's management, perception of the company by its various stakeholders, the company's exposure to litigation and reputation risks and the sustainability of the company's value proposition over time.

Accounting standards applicable to companies are also likely to change in ways that will consider more specifically the financial impact of social and environmental issues. Efforts have been initiated to consider how accounting standards can be updated to improve valuation of intangible assets, including human capital, environmental capital, brand and reputation. Consideration is also being given as to how items such as greenhouse gas emissions should be represented as financial liabilities on company balance sheets, as well as how changes in value of greenhouse gas emissions allowances should be accounted for in income statements.[23]

The business case for social responsibility as a contributor to sustainable growth of business and profits is compelling and has been embraced by a growing number of CEOs. In 2002 the World Economic Forum conducted a survey of over 1,300 companies on global corporate citizenship. When asked to make

---

[19]   Chapter 11: Kiernan, 'Sustainable Development' in Dallas, *Governance and Risk*, McGraw Hill, New York, 2004.
[20]   See, e.g. www.environmentalinvestors.com.
[21]   Carbon Disclosure Project, 'Climate Change and Shareholder Value in 2004' (www.cdproject.net).
[22]   Green Paper; *op.cit.*, p.9.
[23]   Carbon Disclosure Project, *op. cit.*, p. 17.

the business case for social responsibility, CEOs cited the following four factors as being the most significant: (1) managing reputation and brand equity, (2) attracting, motivating and retaining talented employees, (3) protecting the license to operate, and (4) enhancing competitiveness and market positioning.[24]

a. Managing Reputation and Brand Equity

Companies have come to recognize that a large proportion of franchise value cannot be measured by reference only to financial earnings and profits. Rather, goodwill, brand equity and other intangibles constitute a significant percentage of franchise value, ranging by some estimates up to 85 per cent of a company's total market value. Although quarterly earnings may fluctuate, the value that can be ascribed to brand equity tends to be more sustainable and can provide the company with a buffer against the vagaries of short-term financial results. Conversely, damage to shareholder value resulting from reputation damage, perceived irresponsibility in the community or adverse publicity, can far outweigh short-term positive earnings. A recent survey conducted by the World Economic Forum of over 130 member companies found that a majority of member companies believed that 40 per cent or more of their company's market capitalization is represented by brand reputation and 92 per cent perceived brand reputation as important to their company's strategy.[25] British Telecom indicated in a survey conducted by the *Financial Times* that social and environmental performance accounted for more than 25 per cent of overall business and reputation.[26]

Recent scandals in the financial services industry point out the adverse effect on a company's franchise resulting from reputation damage. In 2003, financial firms in the United States paid fines and settlements in excess of $4.2 billion as a result of conflicts involving investment research, improper activities involving mutual fund trading, aiding and abetting Enron, WorldCom and other companies to violate securities laws, and other alleged improprieties. In addition, companies implicated in these scandals must defend lawsuits alleging billions more in civil damages, some have had to enter into agreements with regulatory agencies that in some cases have impaired the ability to do new business, and many have suffered significant decreases in stock market valuations. Asbestos litigation has bankrupted scores of other companies, and many others labor under the cloud of tobacco, toxic waste, product liability or other mega-litigation claims. Litigation related to alleged environmental damage, greenhouse gas emissions, damage to aquafers and other mega-torts are on the increase, and the company's ability to assess financial risk if such claims are successful is becoming ever more difficult.

Many companies have embraced social responsibility as a way to build franchise value and differentiate the company from its competitors. Companies such as The Body Shop and Ben & Jerry's made a conscious decision from their founding to be governed primarily by social and environmental values, and built

---

[24] World Economic Forum, 'Responding to the Leadership Challenge: Findings of a CEO Survey on Global Corporate Citizenship' (www.weforum.org).
[25] World Economic Forum, '2004 Annual Meeting Survey: A Report to World Economic Forum', January 2004 (www.weforum.org).
[26] *What Matters Most, op. cit.*, p. 47.

profitable franchises with strong customer loyalty on social values. However, companies that build brand identity on ethical values also have to be able to deliver both financially and on the core values. The Body Shop, for example, came under sharp criticism in the 1990s from some environmental groups that its commitment not to permit animal testing for its ingredients was inaccurate and that the company had exploited people's idealism for profit. As a result the company lost customer loyalty and its financial results suffered. Rather than abandon its values, the company brought in a new leadership team, reaffirmed its strategic commitment to social and environmental values, established new sustainability reporting, and gradually won back a large number of customers and repaired damage to its financial returns.[27]

From time to time even a commitment to social responsibility will not save the company from reputation damage resulting from faulty products or other factors beyond the company's control. However, companies that have developed a sound social responsibility program may be better able to respond to these challenges and preserve franchise value. The response of Johnson & Johnson to the Tylenol problem is a good example. In 1982, seven people died after ingesting tampered Tylenol. Sales of the product plummeted; the company pulled the product off the market and replaced all bottles with tamper-proof caps. By 1986 the company had regained and increased its market share, but another death occurred from cyanide laced Tylenol. The company again pulled the product and replaced it with caplets that could not be tampered with. In each case, the company had a choice between a defensive response that would minimize profit reduction in the short-term, or a more forceful response that might sacrifice short-term profit but result in product improvement and enhanced consumer safety. In choosing the latter, more positive response, the company regained consumer confidence, rebuilt its market share and substantially enhanced its profits over time.[28]

b.   Attracting, Motivating and Retaining Talented Employees

Employee satisfaction plays a material role in the company's ability to attract and retain talented employees. Companies must be able to provide minimum standards for employees, including a fair wage, safe working environment, consideration of health and welfare benefits, and freedom from harassment and discrimination. But employees are interested not only in fair treatment in accordance with minimum legal requirements; employee loyalty is increased if the company is perceived as responsive to community needs and is viewed as a 'good place to work'. Issues such as the level of compensation for senior executives (including cash compensation, stock options and other 'perks') in relation to compensation for lower level employees, support for training and development that enable employees to advance within the company, and support for participation by employees in outside community and educational programs also play an important part in the overall perception of the company as a preferred employer.

Over time, companies that invest in and demonstrate equitable treatment of their employees can realize significant cost savings related to recruiting new

---

[27]   See, www.thebodyshop.com.
[28]   *Corporate Governance, op. cit.,* p. 59.

workers, facing strikes or other work stoppages, defending lawsuits or claims from unhappy employees, and dealing with possible fraud or other losses that may result from employee disloyalty or unhappiness. An analysis of 'America's Most Admired Companies', as listed in *Fortune* magazine, found that a good corporate reputation increases the length of time that a firm spends earning above-average financial returns and decreases the length of time that it spends earning below-average financial returns.[29]

Many companies look for other ways to go beyond minimum requirements and demonstrate social commitment to the community. For example, in 2003 the US Supreme Court heard argument in a case involving the admissions programs at the University of Michigan, both for the undergraduate school and for the law school.[30] The case involved the extent to which the admissions office of the university could consider race and ethnicity in connection with admissions decisions. Sixty-five leading American businesses filed an amicus brief that supported the Michigan admissions offices. The essential argument of the 65 Leading American Businesses in support of the admissions policies was the following:

'The existence of racial and ethnic diversity in institutions of higher education is vital to *amici's* efforts to hire and maintain a diverse workforce, and to employ individuals of all backgrounds who have been educated and trained in a diverse environment. ... Such a workforce is important to *amici's* continued success in the global marketplace'.[31]

c. *Protecting the License to Operate*

All companies must be able to comply with applicable laws and regulations in order to stay in business. In addition, many types of companies, including public utilities, banks, pharmaceutical companies and others, are viewed as owing special duties to the public, customers or other stakeholders by virtue of their products or services and the implicit or explicit government licensing of their activities.

In the United States, for example, a key imperative of social responsibility for regulated financial institutions is contained in the Community Reinvestment Act.[32] That law was passed in 1977 based on Congressional findings that

(1) regulated financial institutions are required by law to demonstrate that their deposit facilities serve the convenience and needs of the communities in which they are chartered to do business;

(2) the convenience and needs of communities include the need for credit services as well as deposit services; and

---

[29]   Dowling, *Creating Corporate Reputation, Identity, Image, Performance*, Oxford University Press, 2001; see also, Roberts, Keeble and Brown: 'The Business Case for Corporate Citizenship', p. 2.

[30]   *Gratz v. Bollinger*, Slip Op. No. 02-516 (23 June 2003); *Grutter v. Bollinger*, Slip Op. No. 02-241 (23 June 2003).

[31]   *Gratz v. Bollinger and Grutter v. Bollinger*, Brief for Amici Curiae 65 Leading American Businesses in Support of Respondents (18 February 2003).

[32]   12 USC 2901 *et. seq.*

(3) regulated financial institutions have continuing and affirmative obligation to help meet the credit needs of the local communities in which they are chartered.

Implicit in this statement is a determination that if regulated financial institutions are chartered by the government to do business, and as a result enjoy the safety net of deposit insurance, they have an affirmative obligation to serve their communities. On a regular basis each institution's community reinvestment record is evaluated by its primary regulator. Specifically, the bank supervisory agency will:

* Assess the institution's record of meeting the credit needs of its entire community, including low- and moderate-income neighborhoods, consistent with the safe and sound operation of such institution; and
* Take such record into account in its evaluation of an application for a deposit facility by such institution.

A rating is assigned to the bank following the review, and the rating is made public. Ratings may be: 'Outstanding', 'Satisfactory', 'Needs to improve' or 'Substantial noncompliance'. Significantly, a bank's community reinvestment record is subject to review whenever the institution is involved in a proposed merger or acquisition because regulatory agencies are required to consider the commitment of both companies to community investment in determining if the merger will be in the public interest. Community groups are entitled to submit comments and request public hearings to discuss the community investment record of both institutions. Although many banks may be satisfied with a 'satisfactory' rating, those banks that expect to engage in merger-related activities or wish to build closer business relationships with local governmental bodies will find it advantageous to obtain an 'outstanding' rating.

  These procedures have resulted in significant commitments on the part of financial institutions to make increased investments in community projects, including low-income housing, small business loans to minority firms and a wide variety of other community efforts. As an example, in connection with its planned acquisition of Bank One Corporation, JPMorgan pledged $800 billion (7.3 per cent of total combined assets) in loans and investments for poor and minority neighborhoods over the next decade, including $675 billion for home mortgage loans for minority and lower income communities, $90 billion for loans and investments for small-businesses and community-based non-profit organizations, $35 billion for inner-city affordable-housing and community development projects, and other community development commitments. These investment commitments are not charitable contributions, but are made with the expectation that the bank will earn a fair financial return. This total does not include additional amounts that both companies make in charitable or other philanthropic contributions.

  In a global marketplace, the license to operate depends not just on a company's actions in its home jurisdiction, but also in each country in which it seeks to do business. As a result, companies have had to develop more decentralized approaches to social responsibility in order to tailor their actions to the local market while at the same time managing codes of conduct and other policies on a global basis. In each case, the company will have to adopt responses that are consistent with its overall objectives and its ability to earn a fair financial return in the local country.

d.   Enhancing Competitiveness and Market Positioning

An increasing number of companies have adopted social responsibility as a way to create competitive differentiation and open new markets. The Body Shop and Ben & Jerry's are just two examples already discussed. Many studies have demonstrated that customer loyalty is significantly enhanced if the company is considered to be socially responsible. Moreover, the company may have more pricing flexibility because customers will prefer to do business with the socially responsible company even if its prices might be higher than those of competitors who are not considered as responsible. Community groups, local governments and other purchasing or licensing bodies are more likely to favor the socially responsible company with procurement orders, licenses, business concessions or other economic opportunities that will provide the company with enhanced profit potential. It is also increasingly common for companies to scrutinize vendor relationships not just to consider the vendor's financial or operational capability, but also the vendor's commitment to diversity, environmental or other social objectives. In order to be considered as possible vendors, companies are often asked to fill out detailed questionnaires about hiring practices, compliance with anti-bribery and other laws, environmental record and other commitments to social responsibility.

Many public companies historically have made significant contributions to charitable and community organizations. While some companies have made contributions based on a percentage of yearly profits, others have embraced 'strategic philanthropy', by which the company uses its core competencies to make substantial social or environmental investments in ways that also promote the company's products and services. For example, banks have provided financial literacy grants, drug companies have provided free medicine and software companies have provided free software and training to poor communities.

From time to time some shareholders have objected to corporate charitable donations as being inconsistent with the purpose of the company to provide profits to shareholders. Companies have justified charitable contributions as being in the best interests of the company, as can be seen in the response of Johnson & Johnson to a shareholder proposal that the company cease making charitable contributions:

'The charitable contributions of Johnson & Johnson are a powerful reflection of our values and of our responsibility "to the communities in which we live and work and to the world community as well", as articulated in Our Credo. . . . Further, our charitable contributions support our commitment to be "good citizens—support good works and charities", also a fundamental tenet of Our Credo. These contributions support programs that are far-reaching in geographic and substantive scope, from a program that helped in de-worming children in Brazil, to Interchurch Medical Assistance, Inc., which coordinated a relief effort for approximately 300,000 people displaced by a natural disaster in the Congo, to Mobile AIDS Support Services, which assists people living with HIV and AIDS in rural Alabama'.[33]

3.   Linking Social Responsibility to the Profit Motive

Companies have often struggled with the extent to which they should be open about linking social responsibility objectives to profit and corporate self-interest. Many advertisements proclaim the company's good works in social or environmental matters as if the company acted purely for altruistic purposes. In some cases altruism may be the driving force, but more often the company acts out of both a sense of commitment to its stakeholders and a desire to increase brand equity for its products. A recent study found that consumers generally do not object to corporate campaigns that serve society while also helping the company's bottom line.[34] However, if the company is perceived as deceptive or glossing over self-interested motives it can risk undermining its credibility. Particularly if the company has experienced recent social or environmental problems or has a large number of skeptical customers, careful thought should go into the best way to promote the company's commitment to social responsibility and the linkage to the bottom line. Consumers are not likely to react negatively to marketing campaigns that involve social responsibility initiatives if the company is honest about its firm-saving or firm promoting motives.[35]

At the same time, companies must be careful not to over-hype their social responsibility efforts. Products that are labeled as organic, environmentally safe or with other labels that may not have any objective means for determination, can mislead consumers and breed further skepticism about the company's efforts on the part of stakeholders. The safest approach may be to treat social responsibility as a work in progress, in which the company will continue to make efforts to improve its bottom line consistent with its commitment to good citizenship.

C.   TRACKING PROGRESS

One of the necessary but most difficult elements of a social responsibility program is to track progress and success. Begin from the analytical framework that 'if it is not measured it did not happen'. However, performance measurement needs to be flexible, it needs to balance the various interests and constituencies

---

[33]   Johnson & Johnson Notice of Annual Meeting and Proxy Statement, 10 March 2004.
[34]   Forehand and Grier, 'When is Honesty the Best Policy? The Effect of Stated Company Intent on Consumer Skepticism', *Journal of Consumer Psychology*, Vol. 13, No. 3, 2003, pp. 349–356.
[35]   See, 'Learning to Grow Again', Article by Ian Davis, Managing Director, McKinsey in 'The World in 2004'. *The Economist*, December 2003: 'The drive for growth need not be at odds with environmental and other societal concerns. Defensiveness, however, only provides ammunition to the rock-throwers. Business leaders should demonstrate more confidence in their moral position as creators of wealth, opportunity and rising living standards, and work proactively to build trust between their organizations and society at large'.

and it must take into consideration that the linkage to corporate profit and business growth must be tempered by judgment and recognition of the company's core values. The board of directors should have responsibility for oversight of social responsibility commitments, and the company's activities and performance evaluation should be reported to the board on a regular basis.

1.   Public Disclosure

In the United States public companies are required to publicly disclose a large amount of financial and management information in quarterly and annual financial reports.[36] Among other things, Regulation S-K requires management's discussion and analysis of financial condition and results of operations and quantitative and qualitative disclosures about market risk. The Sarbanes-Oxley Act[37] has been a key legislative response to corporate scandals in the United States. Section 302 of Sarbanes-Oxley requires the SEC to issue regulations designed to ensure greater corporate responsibility for financial reports including certification of financial reports by senior officers,[38] Section 404 requires management's assessment about the adequacy and effectiveness of the company's internal controls over financial reporting,[39] and Section 406 requires the SEC to issue regulations to require issuers to make certain disclosures regarding any code of ethics that applies to senior officers of the company.[40] Although the SEC rules do not specifically require public companies in the United States to disclose information about social responsibility efforts (other than code of conduct) or to rate the company's social and community achievements as part of management's discussion of financial condition and results, the sum total of the revised reporting requirements make it incumbent on management to assess and report on any non-financial matters that are likely to have an impact on the company's financial condition or operations.

Many public companies use shareholder letters or other narrative parts of annual reports to highlight the company's commitment to social responsibility, its specific achievements in philanthropy and other efforts to promote social responsibility. Companies have realized the power of social responsibility as a positive message for existing stakeholders as well as a tool to develop new customers and employees and frequently issue press releases that announce new

---

[36]   Regulation S-K: standard instructions for filing forms under the Securities Act of 1933, Securities Exchange Act of 1934 and Energy Policy and Conservation Act of 1975; 17 C.F.R. Part 229.

[37]   P.L. 107-204, 107th Cong., 2nd Sess, 30 July 2002.

[38]   17 C.F.R. Parts 228, 229, 232, 240, 249, 270 and 274; Release Nos. 33-8124, 34-46427, IC-25722. The certification requirement concerning fair presentation of financial information goes beyond presentation in accordance with 'generally accepted accounting principles' and requires 'disclosure of information that is informative and reasonably reflects the underlying transactions and events and the inclusion of any additional disclosure necessary to provide investors with a materially accurate and complete picture of an issuer's financial condition, results of operations and cash flows'.

[39]   17 C.F.R. 229.308; Release No. 33-8238, 68 F.R. 36636.

[40]   17 C.F.R. 229.406; Release No. 33-8177, 68 F.R. 5110.

philanthropic or socially responsible initiatives, or recognition received for achievement as a socially responsible company.[41]

Globally, increasing consideration is being given as to whether public companies should be required to include a statement of the senior officers as to the company's commitment and efforts with respect to social, environmental and community related priorities. Along these lines, the following initiatives are noteworthy:

- OECD Principles of Corporate Governance encourage companies to disclose policies relating to business ethics, the environment and other public policy commitments in addition to commercial objectives.
- The European Commission encourages public companies with at least 500 staff to publish a 'triple bottom line' in their annual reports that measures performance against economic, environmental and social criteria.
- The United Kingdom, France, Sweden, Germany, Netherlands and Switzerland have adopted laws that require pension funds to consider environmental, ethical and social performance of companies in which they consider investing.
- The French Parliament passed legislation in 2001 that requires companies listed on the 'premier marché' (those with the largest capitalizations) to report on environmental and social performance in quarterly and annual financial reports.
- Australia has implemented social responsibility reporting requirements for listed companies; the Financial Services Reform Act of 2001 requires money managers to substantiate claims that they take account of social, environmental and ethical issues.
- In the United Kingdom, a private members' bill was introduced in the House of Commons in 2002 and again in 2003 that would have placed specific reporting and other duties on directors and companies with respect to social, financial and environmental issues. The bill was not acted upon.[42]

2.   Social Responsibility Reporting

An increasing number of companies now issue social responsibility reports on a regular basis in order to discuss and evaluate the company's social responsibility performance. Each company should be free to develop its own goals, timetables and metrics for measuring social responsibility. However, regular reporting of social responsibility both on a global and regional or local basis increases transparency and credibility for the company's objectives. For example, notwithstanding the lack of a legal requirement, a recent survey indicated that about 80 per cent of FTSE-100 companies now provide information about their environmental performance, social impact, or both; and a recent survey of small and medium sized enterprises in the UK found that 61 per cent were involved 'a great deal' or 'a fair amount' in the local community.[43]

---

[41]   See, e.g.: www.csrwire.com.
[42]   See www.parliament.the-stationery-office.co.uk/pa/cm200102/cmbills/145/2002145.pdf; CCBE Report, *op. cit.*, p. 50; and *What Matters Most, op. cit.*, p. 49.
[43]   See www.societyandbusiness.gov.uk.

It is also becoming more common for companies, particularly those that do business in environmentally sensitive industries, to publish environmental performance reports on a regular basis that include quantitative data to measure performance against targets. In some cases the data includes cost accounting, the results may be verified by a third party and the report may include a review of environmental performance of the company's suppliers and outside contractors.[44]

One of the most significant efforts has been to try to encourage convergence of social responsibility reporting by means of consistent guidelines for companies to develop appropriate reporting benchmarks that will promote comparability among companies and industries. As part of this effort the Global Reporting Initiative (GRI) was launched in 1997 in collaboration with the Collaborating Centre of the United Nations Environment Programme. Following consultation with a large number of stakeholders, the GRI issued revised Sustainability Reporting Guidelines in 2002 that provide a framework for companies to provide regular reporting on social responsibility initiatives on a voluntary basis. Among other things, the GRI recommended coordination of social responsibility reporting with financial reporting so that both companies and stakeholders can better understand and measure the extent to which economic, social and environmental performance contributes to competitive advantage.[45] By the end of 2003, GRI reported that 380 organizations around the world—most of them companies—use the GRI Sustainability Reporting Guidelines to report performance.[46]

3. Compensation and Performance Plans

One of the most sensitive tasks for a company's compensation committee is to design compensation programs for senior management and other employees that create the right incentives. The natural inclination is to design compensation programs that create objective measures of performance based on stock market performance, sales targets, percentage of profits or other quantitative measures. The result may be to reward conduct that produces short-term profit but that may not be consistent with the company's core values and long-term objectives.

Companies need to create a 'balanced scorecard' that considers performance related to all aspects of the company's stated objectives, including diversity, recruitment or retention of talented employees, environmental or community commitments. A growing number of companies have designed performance indicators that, in addition to measurement against financial goals, also measure performance against goals related to health, safety, environmental objectives, employee satisfaction and other non-financial criteria in determining overall performance ratings and incentive compensation. These non-financial factors may set specific goals or targets, but should be sufficiently flexible to enable the board of directors to make a qualitative assessment of management's progress in

---

[44]   Joint Study by the OECD Secretariat and EIRIS, 'An Overview of Corporate Environmental Management Practices'. pp. 14–15.

[45]   *Global Reporting Initiative*, 'Sustainability Reporting Guidelines', 2002; see also, *Social Accountability 8000*, which is a set of standards and verification measures for labor conditions developed by Social Accountability International (www.cepaa.org).

[46]   *GRI Annual Review 2003* (www.globalreporting.org).

meeting the company's social responsibility objectives. They should be applied in particular to the CEO, who has leadership responsibility for achieving the company's overall objectives, but they should cascade through the company so that all members of management and other employees understand and buy into them.[47]

D. IS CSR A PUBLIC RELATIONS SMOKESCREEN?

The movement towards corporate social responsibility has not been without criticism. Some critics have made the argument that corporate managers are entrusted with the care of assets belonging to the shareholders, and should not use shareholder funds to support 'feel good' causes.[48] These critics have opposed corporate charitable contributions, as well as other expenditures and investments that do not have a direct and measurable financial benefit to the company. Other critics have found voluntary corporate efforts wholly inadequate to address social and environmental needs. They have asked, for example, how a company that manufactures cigarettes can really embrace social responsibility; or how an oil drilling company can reconcile social responsibility with drilling in the Alaskan tundra.

Many critics have also challenged the notion that there is any consensus as to what constitutes a socially responsible company. Is a company socially responsible if it provides good workplace conditions, yet provides compensation and perks to senior managers far in excess of other workers? Is the company socially responsible if it makes significant philanthropic contributions, but manages to avoid its 'fair share' of taxes that fund schools and hospitals? Companies frequently find that commitments to social responsibility may satisfy some stakeholders but alienate others. Many companies that have made significant efforts at social responsibility have suffered boycotts, loss of customers and financial harm because other groups felt their efforts either were inadequate or were contrary to social or environmental priorities of other stakeholders.

The conflicting social agendas of different stakeholder groups presents perhaps the most difficult management issue for companies that seek to be socially responsible. For example, McDonald's Corporation made a major corporate commitment to social responsibility that included, among other things, issuance of regular social responsibility reports both globally and regionally that meet the GRI standards and a Global Animal Welfare Progress Report. Notwithstanding these efforts, the company has been seriously criticized on the basis that its fast-food products use excessive amounts of water for food preparation and promote obesity in consumers.[49]

Tiffany & Co., the high-end retailer, thought it was doing the right thing when it purchased a newspaper advertisement opposing a mining project in Montana. The CEO stated: 'We... understand that mining must remain an important

---

[47]   'Responding to the Leadership Challenge', *op. cit.*, p. 23.
[48]   'Corporate Social Responsibility: Two faced capitalism', *The Economist*, 22 January 2004.
[49]   See, e.g. www.mcdonalds.com; www.foodfirst.org; Christian Aid, 'Behind the Mask: the real face of corporate social responsibility' (www.christianaid.org.uk).

industry, but like some other businesses benefiting from trade in precious metals, we also believe ... minerals should – and can – be extracted, processed and used in ways that are environmentally and socially responsible'. Although Tiffany was praised by environmental groups, it came under a storm of criticism from labor and land rights groups who accused the company of ignoring 'family wage jobs' and being 'surrogates for extreme green groups'.[50]

These criticisms point out the complexity of the debate and the challenges that companies and their stakeholders face in developing social responsibility initiatives. Companies must recognize that evolving stakeholder issues will present continuing challenges as well as opportunities for companies to demonstrate ongoing commitments to social responsibility consistent with economic and other corporate objectives. Companies also need to balance priorities of various stakeholder groups and may have to weigh the financial and reputational risk or benefit of satisfying certain groups but alienating others. Stakeholder groups need to understand that companies are in business for profit and must be able to balance social commitments with the need to deliver a fair financial return to shareholders. If stakeholders have unrealistic demands and fail to recognize and reward good faith corporate commitments to social responsibility, they risk being excluded from ongoing dialogue with companies and industry groups. Those companies that have been most successful in dealing with conflicting priorities have been those that have actively sought out stakeholder representatives and have engaged in open discussion about the ways in which stakeholder priorities can be reconciled with the company's financial objectives and capabilities.

E.   THE TRIPLE BOTTOM LINE IN OPERATION

1.   Social Responsibility and Economic Development

In recent years there has been growing recognition that corporate social responsibility plays a key role in promoting local, national and global economic development, particularly in less-developed countries.[51] A study prepared for the United Nations estimated that one-fifth of the planet's people live on less than $1 a day. If the managerial, organizational and technological innovation and skills that reside in the private sector can be unleashed to assist local economies, poverty can be reduced and a greater percentage of the world's population will participate in economic development. The World Bank has estimated that corruption can reduce a country's growth rate by 0.5 to 1.0 percentage points a year. Corporate and governmental cooperative efforts to combat corruption have enabled developing countries to increase economic transparency and attract increased foreign investment. Commitments to social responsibility by multinational companies can set an example for good corporate governance and social responsibility that local companies can emulate.

Multinational companies also have much to learn from local companies and local stakeholders as to the social and environmental challenges and issues that

---

[50]   *The Chicago Tribune*, 8 April 2004.
[51]   See, UN Report, *op. cit.*

need to be taken into consideration in order to participate responsibly in the local economy. Recognition of local stakeholder interests can facilitate a growing dialogue in which corporate economic interests can be balanced with local social interests to foster economic development. The recent OECD Principles of Corporate Governance have encouraged this symbiotic relationship.[52]

According to the UN Report, a key dependency for corporate social responsibility efforts is for governments and communities to create an enabling environment that will encourage companies to act in a socially responsible manner and discourage irresponsible behavior. Some of these interdependencies include the following:

- Transparent legal framework and 'rule of law' that provides equivalent treatment for foreign and domestic enterprises
- Independent judicial and administrative system
- Laws that prohibit bribery and corruption
- Government assistance for education, health, training and social infrastructure efforts
- Reasonable tax rates and administration
- Rules that promote market entry and discourage 'informal' markets
- Access to capital markets and financing
- Rules that protect intellectual and other property rights

To the extent that host governments are able to minimize elements of the 'informal economy' that thrive on corruption, lack of transparency and weak institutional environments, they will promote responsible investment by responsible private companies. Moreover, socially responsible companies themselves will benefit by reduction in the number of entities that are able to compete on the basis of unfair and socially irresponsible terms.

The UN Report referred to Costa Rica as a compeling example of how socially responsible investing, coupled with governmental assistance, could unleash economic development. In 1983, the private sector, with support from the government, took the lead in attracting investment through an apolitical non-profit organization, the Costa Rica Investment and Development Organization (CINDE). As a result of these efforts, more than 30 multinational companies, including Intel and other leading companies, have located significant facilities in Costa Rica, employing many thousands of people. Costa Rica has become one of the top 30 software exporters worldwide; it has a 95.5 per cent literacy rate and its foreign direct investment grew tenfold from 1989 to 2002. The government itself has helped by establishing an attractive economic infrastructure to attract investment, including free technical training for more than 127,000 people.[53]

---

[52] *OECD Principles of Corporate Governance* (2004) at p. 46: 'Corporations should recognize that the contributions of stakeholders constitute a valuable resource for building competitive and profitable companies. It is, therefore, in the long-term interest of corporations to foster wealth-creating cooperation among stakeholders. The governance framework should recognize that the interests of the corporation are served by recognizing the interests of stakeholders and their contribution to the long-term success of the corporation'.

[53] UN Report, *op. cit.*, p. 27.

2. Should Corporate Social Responsibility be Mandatory or Voluntary?

It is clear that each company's minimum social responsibility is to comply with applicable laws and regulations. Beyond these minimum standards, much debate has centered on the extent to which social responsibility should be mandated by governments or should rely primarily on voluntary efforts. Companies stress the need for voluntariness and flexibility so that social responsibility can fit within the company's overall objectives and financial capability. Many critics point out that voluntary standards are simply ways for companies to avoid binding regulations that would require adoption of improved standards.

The answer lies between the two extremes. On the one hand, without some government compulsion companies may decline to take any action, and those that do may be placed at a competitive disadvantage with respect to other companies based on cost of goods sold, return on equity or other factors. As can be seen in the United States with respect to the Community Reinvestment Act and in South Africa with the Black Economic Empowerment Act, government can provide a useful structure that will facilitate companies in carrying out socially responsible objectives. Moreover, had it not been for the Foreign Corrupt Practices Act in the United States, which led ultimately to the OECD Anti-bribery Convention and other global efforts to combat corruption, it would not have been possible to reduce bribery and corruption in government procurements and many other parts of the global economy. Corporate efforts alone would have been ineffective in gaining the consensus and commitment to this objective.

On the other hand, companies need to have sufficient flexibility to carry out social responsibility objectives in ways that suit the company's financial capabilities and strategic objectives. Government mandates that provide insufficient room for flexibility can lead to companies deciding to leave the affected market, resulting in adverse effects both on company profits and on community objectives. As can be seen in the Equator Principles and many other voluntary efforts, most companies will, out of self-interest, philanthropic or other motives, develop responses to social and environmental concerns that can result in an appropriate balance between the company's financial objectives and the needs of the community. Continuing efforts at transparency, public disclosure and measurement of results will continue to encourage companies to develop innovative solutions to social and environmental concerns.

Many companies have found it advantageous to join with other companies in the same industry or in different industries to promote social responsibility efforts. In this way the chances of success are increased, movement to the 'lowest common denominator' is avoided and costs can be managed. Many industry specific guidelines have been established by the United Nations, the World Bank, the International Finance Corporation, other international organizations and private industry groups, including the World Business Council on Sustainable Development, the International Business Leaders Forum, and Business for Social Responsibility. These voluntary guidelines may be country specific, industry specific, regional or global in scope. Governments should encourage these cooperative efforts, and should ensure that applicable competition laws do not have the effect of encouraging such efforts.

3.   Social Commitments; the 'Offshoring' Issue

The 'offshoring' issue demonstrates the complexity of balancing a company's financial needs with its social commitments. 'Offshoring' refers to corporate decisions to move jobs from certain higher cost locations in developed countries to lower cost locations, usually in developing countries. The company has a duty to its shareholders to keep costs under control in order to remain competitive in a global marketplace. Moreover, the company can contribute to economic development in poor countries by increasing employment of local workers, improving health care and providing training for development of critical skills. However, offshoring can result in job losses in communities that are adversely affected by the company's decision. Furthermore, if the company does not take steps to implement appropriate working conditions, including reasonable wages, health and welfare benefits, and prevention of abusive practices such as child labor, its efforts could result in harm to the new community.

Among the many companies that have considered social responsibility issues posed by offshoring, British Telecommunications commissioned a study to consider the impact that the offshoring of call centers from the UK to India would have on the company's commitment to social responsibility. The conclusion of the study was that, on balance, offshoring's benefits outweighed the negative impacts. However, the study highlighted two key issues the company should address in order for its offshoring decision to be implemented in a manner consistent with its social responsibility commitment. First, the company should make efforts to assist employees in the UK who would be adversely affected by the offshoring decision. Second, the company should commit to maintain high standards for new employees in India. The study suggested twelve elements of responsible offshoring, including: consultation with affected stakeholders, avoiding involuntary redundancies, retraining of affected employees, training of new employees, investment in the new local community, and sharing of technology and skills to enable local employees to advance.[54] Many other companies that pride themselves on social responsibility have had to balance their commitments to social responsibility with the need to cut costs in order to stay viable and competitive.

4.   Environmental Commitments; Financial Sector Initiatives

The corporate response to environmental challenges is also interesting to observe. Although a number of companies have been operating under a cloud of environmental damage lawsuits and regulatory enforcement actions, a growing number of corporate initiatives are underway to demonstrate private sector leadership in promoting environmental responsibility. Many of these efforts represent responses to the Kyoto Protocol, as well as international, national and local legislative efforts to promote clean water, lower greenhouse gas emissions and other environmental safeguards. For example, the World Economic Forum launched the Global Greenhouse Gas Register to promote greater greenhouse

---

[54]   See: 'Good Migrations? BT, Corporate Social Responsibility and the Geography of Jobs', February 2004 (www.sustainability.com).

gas emission transparency, and many companies have joined the Chicago Climate Exchange, the EPA Climate Leaders program or other voluntary efforts to promote environmental responsibility. In addition, many end-users and financial intermediaries expect to be active in the EU Emissions Trading Scheme, which is scheduled to commence trading in January 2005; investments by companies in the 'clean tech' sector are increasing rapidly; the global carbon market is expanding by double-digits annually; and the non-hydro renewable market is expected to grow faster than any other primary energy source to 2030.[55]

In the financial sector, many of the largest financial institutions have established offices to monitor environmental efforts across the company. Many of the largest institutions are also active in developing, and expect to derive substantial revenues from, new financial products based on environmental initiatives including carbon-, emissions-, renewable energy- and weather-related certificates or indices.

Financial institutions that are active in international project finance have also considered environmental issues related to project finance. At a minimum, environmental problems can affect a borrower's ability to repay its loans as scheduled, thereby resulting in an increase in non-performing loans or loan charge-offs. Beyond that, banks are increasingly concerned with reputation risk that may arise from financing projects that give rise to environmental concerns. In 2003 ten leading banks that engage in project finance announced adoption of voluntary guidelines, called the Equator Principles,[56] that provide a blueprint for managing social and environmental issues related to project finance in developing countries. The number of adopting banks has grown to at least 21 banks in the first year of operation. The Principles are based on policies and guidelines developed by the World Bank and International Finance Corporation.

Banks that adopt the Principles commit to provide loans only to those projects whose sponsors demonstrate their ability and willingness to comply with processes to ensure the projects are developed in a socially responsible manner. A screening process was developed in which each project is categorized as A, B, or C (high, medium or low environmental or social risk). For an A risk and for many B risk projects, the borrower must complete an Environmental Assessment (EA) that addresses the environmental or social issues identified in the categorization process. Such issues may include:

- Sustainable development and use of natural resources
- Protection of health, cultural properties or biodiversity
- Major hazards
- Occupational health and safety
- Involuntary resettlement
- Pollution prevention and waste minimization
- Socioeconomic impacts, and other issues

The EA should result in an Environmental Management Plan. The borrower will be required to comply with the Environmental Management Plan and provide

---

[55]   Carbon Disclosure Project, *op. cit.*
[56]   www.equator-principles.com.

regular reports of compliance. In some cases an independent environmental expert may be appointed. One recent example of the operation of the Equator Principles is the Baku-Tblisi-Ceyhan (TBC) oil pipeline project. Financing for this project in the amount of $3.6 Billion was closed on 3 February 2004. This was the first project treated as Category A under the Equator Principles.

In addition to the Equator Principles, several financial institutions have engaged in dialogue with other NGOs on environmental issues. For example, the Rainforest Action Network, a San Francisco-based environmental group, has lobbied financial institutions to adopt environmental lending practices that will provide loans only to those projects in which sustainable forestry practices can be demonstrated by third-party verification, and avoid funding for logging and other projects located within critical natural habitats unless the borrower demonstrates that it will not significantly degrade or convert the critical natural habitat.[57] The extent to which private financial institutions will continue to provide finance for extractive industries projects will also be influenced by any changes in policy that may result from the World Bank Group's review of its activities in the extractive industries sector.

5.   South Africa—Corporate Assistance for Black Economic Empowerment

South Africa presents a case in point as to how private companies can work with government and other constituencies to develop socially responsible programs, and demonstrates both the benefits and potential abuses of government-sponsored social responsibility efforts. In order to reverse the harm caused by apartheid and increase the effective participation of the majority of South Africans in the economy, the Broad-Based Black Economic Empowerment Bill Act 2003 was signed into law on 6 January 2004 (the 'BEE Act').[58] The BEE Act, together with the Strategy for Broad-Based Black Economic Empowerment and the Code of Good Practice, form a framework in which government will work with private industry groups to promote greater involvement of black people, women and other disadvantaged persons in the South African economy. The BEE Act empowers the Minister of Trade and Industry to issue codes of good practices for various industry sectors that establish targets and scorecards for compliance with black economic empowerment ('BEE').

In order to promote BEE, the government has worked with various industry sectors to develop charters pursuant to which companies commit to take actions to promote BEE goals and agree to be evaluated on the basis of a specific scorecard. Thus far, charters have been adopted for the Financial, Maritime, Mining, and Petroleum and Liquid-Fuels Sectors.[59]

The Financial Charter ('Charter') is instructive as to the implementation of the BEE initiative. The Charter is the result of commitments entered into voluntarily by private sector companies following negotiation between representatives of the South African Government and several stakeholders. Among other things,

---

[57]   www.ran.org.
[58]   Act No. 53 of 2003; www.dti.gov.za.
[59]   www.banking.org.za, www.transport.gov.za, www.dme.gov.za.

it recognizes that 'the financial sector must promote triple bottom line account-ability' and that '[a]ll provisions of the charter are to be achieved in a manner consistent with sound business practice'. The Charter establishes a series of goals with respect to human resource development, procurement policies, enterprise development and ownership, access to financial services, empowerment financing and corporate social investment. The Charter permits a wide degree of flexibility for companies to meet targets in ways best suited to the individual company, and establishes a Charter Council to handle governance issues. Importantly, the Charter also recognizes that the government must ensure a regulatory environment that promotes the empowerment objectives.

Perhaps the most important feature of the Charter is that it establishes a score-card that measures each company's progress with implementation over time. The scorecard assigns grades based on weighted average scores in meeting the targets. Each adopting financial institution is required to report annually to the Charter Council on its progress by means of an independent audit, which is subject to review and approval by the Charter Council. Although compliance with the char-ter is voluntary, the scorecard will affect a company's ability to do business with the government as well as with other firms, since both the government and pri-vate firms will consider the scorecard of each firm with which they consider entering into business arrangements. Companies will receive credit on their own scorecard for doing business with other companies that are either black-owned or have a high scorecard under a BEE charter.

At least in part as a result of the Finance Charter, during 2003, for example, JP Morgan provided financial advisory services that assisted a major gold min-ing company to sell a 10 per cent equity stake. The transaction made the com-pany the leading black-empowered South African gold mining company; it also enabled JP Morgan to be the leading M&A advisor in South Africa. Other ini-tiatives included: support of South African charitable organizations to support aid for education, assistance for persons infected by HIV/AIDS, assistance for the elderly and the disabled, training and secondment programs for emerging black-owned enterprises, and provision of equity research to local black-owned securities firms.

The BEE has come under criticism, however, as being potentially coercive and unreasonably burdensome on the private sector, and for providing benefits to only a small segment of the population. According to some reports, a small num-ber of politically connected individuals have obtained substantial profits from the program while the vast majority of citizens have seen no tangible benefits. The controversy has led to calls for reform of the system to restrict or preclude par-ticipation by government officials, and to refocus the program on entrepreneur-ship rather than simply on the transfer of assets, and limits on the extent to which any one person or family can be "empowered".[60] In addition, some critics have also challenged the BEE as violating principles of the WTO. It remains to be seen whether the BEE will discourage new investment by the private sector or will lead to positive cooperation among companies and the various stakeholders in

[60]   Laurie Goering, 'Critics Say Greed Taints South African Economic Plan', p. 9, Chicago Tribune, December 19, 2004.

South Africa. In principle, the framework represents a rational means for coop-eration between the private sector and government that can result in positive economic results for companies as well as enhanced economic opportunity for citizens of South Africa. However, time will tell whether the framework will ben-efit a large proportion of the citizenry or will simply result in the transfer of assets to a small number of politically connected new black tycoons.

F. CONCLUSION

As can be seen from the above discussion, a growing number of companies now recognize the bottom line benefit of corporate social responsibility and have been willing to invest substantial resources to achieve growth in a socially responsible manner. In the most successful companies, social responsibility does not exist in isolation from other corporate initiatives. Rather, it forms part of the corporate DNA and is integrated into all business strategies and practices.

The key elements in creating a positive 'triple bottom line' are the following:

- Corporate recognition that sustainable profitability, economic growth and future prospects are enhanced by socially responsible policies, investments and programs;
- Management's willingness to track and be held accountable for the com-pany's progress in achieving socially responsible targets on the same basis as other financial results;
- Government recognition of its responsibility to create an enabling environ-ment for private investment through rules that enhance transparency and reward corporate social responsibility; and
- Encouragement of voluntary, flexible and non-coercive partnerships among private sector companies, between private companies and government agen-cies, and between private companies and other stakeholders, that provide flexibility and rewards for companies to meet socially responsible goals by means best suited to the individual company.

In the past, many efforts to achieve corporate social responsibility have been the result of 'push-pull', with companies making decisions based in part on pressure from communities, investor advocates, governments or other constituencies. The future of corporate social responsibility extends beyond the recognition by com-panies that they have a duty to act in a socially responsible manner. Future suc-cess depends on a recognition by all stakeholders that social responsibility is a means to an end and that continuing the dialogue among all stakeholders will lead to improved economic, social and environmental conditions for companies, the local communities in which they do business and the global marketplace.

Chapter 8

LABOUR STANDARDS AND CORPORATE SOCIAL RESPONSIBILITY: THE NEED FOR A PLANETARY BARGAIN*

Michael Hopkins
Ivor Hopkins†

'*Corporate Social Responsibility* is concerned with treating the stakeholders of the firm ethically or in a responsible manner. 'Ethically or responsible' means treating stakeholders in a manner deemed acceptable in civilized societies. Social includes economic responsibility. Stakeholders exist both within a firm and outside. The wider aim of social responsibility is to create higher and higher standards of living, while preserving the profitability of the corporation, for peoples both within and outside the corporation'. (Michael Hopkins)[1]

'Those who engage in social co-operation choose together, in one joint act, the principles which are to assign basic rights and duties and to determine the division of social benefits'. (John Rawls)[2]

A. INTRODUCTION

Corporate Social Responsibility (CSR) is on the 'hotlist' of today's business agenda. Closely linked to this whole discussion is one of the most important stakeholders – that of labour and, more particularly, labour standards.

---

* This paper has been drawn from Michael Hopkins; *The Planetary Bargain: Corporate Social Responsibility Matters*, Earthscan, London, UK, 2003. It was also presented by Ivor Hopkins at a conference organized by the Asian Development Bank, Manila, 2002.
† The former is Professor of Corporate and Social Research at Middlesex University Business School, London, UK and Director, MHC International Ltd., the latter is co-Director of MHC International Ltd – see www.mhcinternational.com.
1   Michael Hopkins: *CSR Matters, op. cit.*
2   John Rawls: *A Theory of Justice*, Oxford University Press, London, 1972, p. 11.

Ramon Mullerat (ed.), Corporate Social Responsibility: The Corporate Governance of the 21st Century, 141–158.
© 2005 *International Bar Association. Printed in the Netherlands.*

In this paper, the elements of what could be in a planetary bargain to promote CSR are outlined. The two main actors in such a bargain are governments and business. There are, of course, many actors on the world stage, and governments are not always the best to represent their own societies especially in some developing countries. Yet, if a planetary bargain is to come about to promote corporate social responsibility then the lead will have to come jointly from governments (including international organizations) and business itself. Therefore, the first two sections in this paper set the parameters of what each could expect from each other. Next is discussed the link between a planetary bargain and globalization before entering into some detail of what a planetary bargain could consist of. Whether a planetary bargain should be voluntary or enter into the legal framework of nations is the final issue covered.

B.   WHAT COULD GOVERNMENTS (AND PEOPLE IN GENERAL) EXPECT FROM BUSINESS IN THE AREA OF SOCIAL RESPONSIBILITY AND SOCIAL DEVELOPMENT?

Before 1991, relatively little literature or research existed in the area of *corporate social responsibility*, particularly outside the United States. Since that date, however, social responsibility has not only entered corporate acceptability but has also blossomed into a large number of activities. Nevertheless, no single objective method has emerged by which corporations might be judged against some sort of international standard although many are trying to do this. Businesses, non-governmental organizations and scholars in Europe, the United States and elsewhere have approached this problem in a variety of ways, but a single set of agreed indicators is still being researched.[3]

Broadly speaking, what can people and governments expect of large transnational companies in the future? A list of items could look something like:

* profitability;
* adherence to an appropriate set of Good Corporate Governance Principles (e.g. OECD Principles of Corporate Governance);
* tax contributions;
* long-term view of investment and profitability;
* environmentally friendly production process;
* socially responsible products;
* code of ethics of company operations;
* comprehensive CSR policy;
* does the company have a social responsibility policy?
* is the policy backed by suitable resources and organization (for example does it perform a social audit)?
* does the company have a management system for social responsibility?
* what is the social responsibility network in the company?
* is there someone to implement the policy?

---

[3]   The Global Reporting Initiative (GRI) has mounted a major effort to develop such indicators – Michael Hopkins was an adviser to the group – see http://globalreporting.org/WorkingGroups/Measurement.

- what social responsibility communications does the company have?
- what social responsibility training does the company have?
- local community support where plants are located;
- philanthropic contributions;
- abstention from corrupt practices;
- refrain from transfer pricing;
- good conditions of work for employees;
- high proportion of workforce in regular protected employment;
- internally flexible labour practices;
- non-discriminatory recruitment and advancement policy;
- skill upgrading programmes conducted either internally or externally;
- labour involved in discussions of structural change, plant relocations and closures through labour-management councils;
- explicit procedures to help employees retrain and relocate in the case of downsizing;
- open accounting procedures for shareholders and disclosure of relevant information for public at large;
- support for social investment funds;
- support to enhance small-scale savings and credit;
- transfer of technology (for example, management skills).

Moves are afoot to bring these ideas into practice. For instance, the UK government has called for a 'new partnership' between the government and the private sector to eliminate world poverty, and has warned companies that they cannot afford to ignore increasing consumer interest in the production of goods.[4] It believes that boycotting retailers who sell products made in Third-World sweatshops is outdated. Work in tandem, the government believes, between the public and private sector, is the main way for poverty to be eliminated.[5] Claire Short, Britain's one-time chief international development minister, called for ethical codes of conduct to govern the relationship between big companies and poor countries. She has pointed out that TNCs have realized that the bulk of economic growth as well as the bulk of population will in future be in developing countries and that they have to be seen to be fair.[6]

Sainsbury's, a supermarket chain in the UK, for instance, has embraced these ideas, and the government has praised its initiatives. The firm has completed four pilot schemes in Africa and Asia to establish a code of ethics for all its own-brand suppliers, and has issued questionnaires to its suppliers that will, eventually, be monitored independently. Sainsbury's says that 'consumers are very interested in ethics now and we get many letters from people saying they shop with us and want to know what our policy is so they can continue to shop with us'.

But what are the limits? Where do state social obligations end and corporate obligations begin? This subject has received an enormous amount of attention – the

---

[4]   According to the Minister for International Development, Claire Short, reported by Sarah Ryle in the *Guardian*, 8 July 1997.
[5]   It is, however, excessively ambitious to believe in the elimination of poverty through any means let alone a combination of private and public sector support. Major inroads can be made but 'eliminate' poverty in the world is difficult if not impossible – see for instance Michael Hopkins: 'CSR, poverty and terror', Monthly Feature, www.mhcinternational.com.
[6]   *Ibid*, footnote 4.

World Bank's 1997 *World Development Report*, for example, was concerned with this question. There is no easy answer, particularly because the relative roles are changing, rapidly in some cases. What is becoming clear is that business is assuming the mantle of social programmes that only in rare cases would it have considered previously. The main difference at the conceptual level, of course, is that government is nationwide. A government is committed to provide old-age pensions applies to all over 65 years of age (say) – but a company's commitment extends only as far as its stakeholders. It is difficult to imagine, for instance, a company located in California being responsible for *all* the pensions of over-65-year-olds in Kansas or Kenya. On the other hand, it is difficult to imagine now that government should be responsible for all telecommunication services as, until recently in Europe at least, it has been.

The authorities at both the United Nations Development Programme, in its 'umbrella programme for engaging the private sector' and its 'Money Matters' initiative, and the World Bank, in its 'Corporate Citizenship' programme, have already started to think how they could engage the private sector more than before. This is because they have seen that public assistance to developing countries has been overwhelmed by the huge private capital flows, at least to the richer developing nations. In parallel with this, the largest donor, the USA, prompted by arch-conservative Senator Helms,[7] withheld its contributions to the United Nations for almost a decade, and still has an uneasy relationship with the UN and international agreements in general.

However, the efforts of the United Nations in humanitarian and human rights has not gone unnoticed in the private sector, as evidenced by the path-breaking personal gift of 1billion US$ by CNN founder Ted Turner. Undoubtedly this will herald an even greater reflection among both wealthy individuals and large private corporations on the sorts of things they can do to promote social responsibility, either through existing organizations or through new ones.

What is considered in Michael Hopkins' book is the need for more social responsibility on the part of enterprises. What was not considered, in any detail, is where it should stop. What are the limits? This will be for the stakeholders of companies to decide in the future. It is especially the case as the nation state itself continues to lose the power to decide on the future of its citizens. This power is being redistributed not only to regional groupings such as the European Union, to smaller regions within a country (for example Scotland and Wales in the UK) and to local communities, but also, even more, and perhaps worryingly given their lack of democracy, to the larger private corporations themselves.

C.   WHAT SHOULD BUSINESSES EXPECT FROM GOVERNMENT IN RETURN FOR GREATER SOCIAL RESPONSIBILITY?

As the balancing part of a planetary social bargain, what can businesses reasonably expect from government, in return for their own best practices in social

---

[7]   Republican Chairman of the Senate's powerful foreign relations committee until replaced by Democrat Joseph Biden in early 2001.

responsibility? Clearly, this will vary from one type of enterprise to another – a financial service company will be less concerned with export quotas on coal than an extractive industry, for instance. And companies will expect different things from international bodies as opposed to national governments. This will also vary from one location to another. Some governments are more liberal than others. Surprisingly, corporations still see themselves as based in one country. Given the concerns about footloose enterprises, it is interesting that corporations still guard some sort of national identity. This will change – for instance, Shell has always had its Dutch and UK components.

Corporations based in Hong Kong face different legislation from those based in Australia, Brazil or the US. There is no global regulator, and companies, although not moving their HQs (in general), do move the locus of their operations to seek the most advantageous conditions. A government that is less 'corporate-friendly' will not lose the HQ of the corporation except in exceptional circumstances (the end of Britain's lease in Hong Kong saw some companies move their HQs). Yet, there will be a convergence toward a set of criteria within which a corporation will operate. What these should be are only partially the subject of international discussion – the WTO, for instance, practically ignores social questions on its agenda although recent globalization protests are leading the WTO to a re-think.

What business should expect from government is a large subject, and so what is done here is simply to list the main concerns of what the private sector could expect from governments in a planetary bargain:

National Level
- stable environment that ensures open markets;
- secure legal framework and fully functioning enforcement institutions;
- non-corrupt, competent, streamlined administrative framework;
- clear investment policy and plans;
- incentives for new (foreign) investment and for domestic investment and savings;
- repatriation of profits and foreign currency;
- flexible labour code;
- democratic practices;
- no forced labour;
- clearly defined rules of operation;
- one-stop information bureau for new and existing investors;
- independent tribunal to adjudicate on disputes;
- fair local banking practices;
- training institutes linked to the needs of the private sector;
- tax incentives for corporations practising CSR policies.

International Level
- fair and open rules for trading;
- independent international body to arbitrate disputes;
- accurate and available information on investment possibilities, impediments to conducting business, and best practices to finance social development.

That dialogue to conclude such a social and planetary bargain has only just begun is illustrated by a meeting held at the UN at the end of 1994 in preparation for the 1995 World Social Summit held in Copenhagen. There, a number of high-ranking UN officials and some senior financial figures (Juan Somavia, then chairperson of the Social Summit and now ILO Director General; James Speth, the then Administrator of UNDP; Marshall Carter, CEO of State Street Bank in Boston; former Citicorp banker Walter Wriston, and so on) sat down to see what common ground could be found between social development professionals and global bankers. The will was there, but the context was missing, according to Carter, who said, 'When we talked about our fiduciary responsibility – to ensure that stockholders are not exposed to undue risk – you could see the development people reaching for their dictionaries'. Since then, the dialogue has blossomed into a series of global events known as Money Matters, in the UNDP and a Money Matters Institute has been formed. Many other global fora have arisen in recent years to address these issues – the ILO Enterprise Forum held in 1996 and again in 1999 attracted over a thousand business and concerned individuals. Following initiatives taken by Marcello Palazzi of the Progressio Foundation in Holland, Habitat organized a meeting where corporations met to discuss their global responsibilities, and both UNDP and UNESCO held similar meetings in 1998.

The United Nations itself launched, in 1999, its 'Global Compact' that seeks the private sector to sign up to a set of nine principles in the areas of labour standards, human rights and environment practices. Several hundred corporations have signed up. Whether this has been to associate themselves with the UN's powerful brand name or means positive action on the CSR front has been subject to intense speculation. It is worth noting, however, that the three areas being covered are only a subset of a full-fledged CSR approach as defined in this book. With the possible exception of labour issues, internal stakeholders are not considered in the Global Compact. Nor is there a concern with verifying the claims of corporations that sign up to the Global Compact. Lack of independent verification is likely to lead to the UN being embarrassed, at the very least, should one of its companies be guilty of poor social responsibility even outside the nine principles. Consequently, although a very useful move toward a planetary bargain, the Global Compact is only a partial response to worldwide global concerns.

What is coming out of all these dialogues and meetings? As Marcello Palazzi said: 'I proposed to UNESCO that we create an "Enterprise Initiative for Cultural and Human Development", a virtual network of business associations and networks that want to do projects together that advance culture and human development'. Little came of that initiative but, undoubtedly, the intense interest in business partnerships will lead to more and more companies adopting socially responsible policies. Certainly, the number of international meetings around topics such as labour standards, business partnerships, corporate citizenship are noticeably increasing. Cynics will say that this is all talk and no action. To an extent this is so but talk will eventually lead to concrete action simply because business will demand this from their international relationships, and as Winston Churchill used to say, albeit in another context, jaw-jaw is better than war-war.

D. PRISONER'S DILEMMA

The strategy to be adopted by government and the private sector should not be one of confrontation, but like the strategy required to solve the prisoner's dilemma, a well-known example from game theory, should be one of compromise. The best solution to the prisoner's dilemma was cooperation between the main actors involved. Lack of cooperation led to high penalties. The analogy is that, should government or enterprises act alone, albeit seemingly in their own best interest, then this would jeopardise their overall position. The compromise for government and the private sector is to develop a voluntary code of practice or social bargain that both observe. Efforts to create such a code do exist and date from the early 1970s, when the United Nations developed a commission on transnational corporations and the OECD developed a set of guidelines for multinational enterprises, and from 1976, when the ILOs world employment conference on basic needs put forward the notion of 'good citizenship'. In the years since, these codes fell hostage to extreme politicization at the international level and interest varied.

More recently, the European Commission, in a white paper[8] has urged a voluntary approach to the implementation of CSR. Curiously, the Commission actually includes the word 'voluntary' in the actual definition of CSR which it defines as 'a concept whereby companies integrate social and environmental concerns in their business operations and in their interaction with their stakeholders *on a voluntary basis*'. This is curious since it rules out an important debate that is currently ongoing about whether CSR should be voluntary or compulsory. My view (see below) is that the issue is somewhere between a totally voluntary approach and complete legislation. The exact pointer to be arrived at through negotiation.

This is also where my metaphor of the prisoner's dilemma falls down, as with all good metaphors they only go so far. The compromise reached[9] was not based on negotiation, since the prisoners were kept in isolation, but on a tacit knowledge that this is the only wholly viable outcome for both prisoners. The actors in the CSR debate are often aware of each other's position. For instance, the EU invited responses on its white paper and received around 250 replies of which about half of the responses came from employers' organizations, business associations and individual enterprises. Trade unions and civil society organizations accounted for another large portion of the responses.

At the national level, the current debate between increased regulation of corporations by the US Government as a result of the various corporate scandals is being carried out among a whole host of institutions. As Alan Blinder noted[10] 'While changes in private sector behaviour will eventually fix many of today's accounting and corporate governance problems, the markets are clamouring for decisive government actions now'. Who in the market and what are the actions are ignored by Blinder who nevertheless noted in they same article the ambivalent attitude toward government intervention when he wrote 'When things go well the markets want to be left alone, but when things start to fall apart they want Washington help'.

---

8   *Commission of the European Communities*: 'Communication from the Commission concerning Corporate Social Responsibility: A business contribution to Sustainable Development', Brussels, 2 July 2002, COM (2002) 347 final, p. 3.
9   We are grateful to an unknown reviewer for pointing this out to us in comments on an earlier version of *The Planetary Bargain*. . . .
10 Alan S. Blinder: 'A time for Government action', *International Herald Tribune*, Monday, 22 July 2002, p. 8.

E.   A PLANETARY BARGAIN AND GLOBALIZATION

1.   What is Meant by Globalisation?

What is the link between CSR and globalization? First, what is meant by global-ization? Essentially, it means that money (financial capital) can move to wherever its owners wish at the flash of a computer button or the click of a mouse. In prac-tice, it also means that the world has become a smaller place because, concomitant with these massive capital flows, have come advances in telecommunications and travel. The use of GSM telephones or the Internet can put the investor in Iceland in direct contact with Wall Street. There is hardly a place on earth where it takes more than a day to travel to from almost any other part. But, of course, it all depends where you start from – as in the old saw, where a person asking for directions in Dublin received the reply, 'Well, I would not start from here'.

Globalization, meaning access to markets, is fine for those with the physical, human and social capital to access them. Those without these attributes, the Bushmen in the Kalahari or nomads in Somalia for instance, find it just about impossible. On the other hand, reductions in telecommunication charges will eventually enable farmers, for instance, in developing countries to communicate directly with the industrialized world thereby enhancing trade and improving living conditions. One of the many problems is that telecommunication charges are often in the hands of public monopolies in developing countries that use these charges as an alternative taxation system. A one minute telephone call, from a small flower grower in Kenya to a buyer in the Netherlands might cost the equivalent of a day's flower harvest. Globalization that enhances internet service and insists on competitive telecommunication charges will help, at the margin at least, lower costs and therefore higher living standards for such producers.

Some readers may reject this flowery example of trade theory in action with-out institutional constraints. But returning to the nomads in Somalia, or at least their descendants, globalization is helping development in one part of Somalia. In the self-proclaimed independent State of Somaliland, in Northern Somalia and a former British protectorate, civil war led to the complete destruction of utilities. Without a public telecommunication monopoly to protect it, Somalilanders use wireless mobile phone technology linked to satellite transmitters to conduct their business. Costs of international calls are fiercely competitive due to the plethora of mobile phone companies operating. Problems exist of course, Somaliland Government Ministers have half a dozen phones on their desk since competing networks do not allow talk across different networks – an example of where a strong Government could enhance actions taken by the private sector. The Government in Somaliland is weak partly through lack of international recognition and partly through historical reasons. A planetary bargain of com-promise between public and corporate sectors could, therefore, also be imple-mented at the local level. Compromise between the fledgling Government in Somaliland (to regulate telecommunications) and the telecommunication private sector to allow cross talk on their networks would be to everyone's advantage. Cross talk would reduce costs of the Government in having so many networks, the market would increase as the population would be able to talk across all networks and the companies would benefit through a larger market.

2. Will Globalization Lead to Lower Wages?

The fear behind increasing globalization is that production will increasingly be allocated to the lowest cost producers, thereby impoverishing the currently richer part of the world. This is known to economists as 'factor price equalization', where the wages of the unskilled in the richer countries fall and those in the poorer countries rise.

But do the wages rise in practice? In many fast-growing developing nations, unskilled wages have risen (at least until the recent Asian crisis) – Malaysia, Thailand, South Korea, Taiwan, Chile, Tunisia, and so on. There, new consumers have been created to replace those supposedly left behind in the richer nations. Their new consumption leads to new exports for the richer nations that themselves have become more efficient, because of the relocation of unskilled jobs to the poorer countries. This is a virtuous circle where all can gain.

However, rapid population growth in other Third World nations and the entry of two monster economies into the global trading system – India and China – mean that the pool of unskilled labour is growing rapidly. Merely relocating production to these countries does not necessarily mean that unskilled wages will rise. Wages normally rise in an open economy to match productivity increases. But even if productivity increases, wages can be kept down in at least two ways: first, employers can simply employ other unskilled workers from the already large labour surplus, or, second, through seeking lower production costs (economists call this rent-seeking), multi-national firms can allow their new investment to float elsewhere, to other low-wage unskilled nations. In these countries, wages should be allowed to rise, along with social benefits, to create the 'virtuous circle'. This can be helped through a voluntary and global bargain between the key actors in the business sector, so that new markets for consumers can be created.

A voluntary bargain can be undermined by rogue companies and one company can always undercut another. However, if a 'bargain' existed to exclude rent-seeking behaviour to the lowest common denominator, it would be in everyone's interest – workers would see their wages rise, company profits would not be undercut by another firm using bargain-basement labour and new consumers would be created. A 'rogue' company that fell out of this bargain could be treated in a number of ways. If the bargain was voluntary, the rogue company might simply chose to ignore it, but it would then be subject to peer pressure. If the bargain was compulsory, who would enforce it? The voluntary solution is preferable, because it means less burden in the cobweb of already complicated rules for doing business. The voluntary solution is less democratic, however, because it allows the company to choose what actions to take with only lip service to its constituents. Basic codes of ethics for international business have been introduced at a rapid rate in recent years, and companies are increasingly observing them.

Thus codes of ethics, as well as the wider issues implied in the 'planetary bargain', are part of globalization. They will ensure that enterprises will employ beggar-thy-neighbour policies less and less. Will the costs of doing business rise? Yes, they will, as the planetary bargain is gradually accepted. But profits will not necessarily fall as new markets are generated from the newly enriched consumers.

A key component of any agreement is that the main private sector companies in the world should participate. This, of course, is difficult because it means private global trading concerns agreeing to work toward better conditions for their workers, wherever they may be. But this is the aim of the UN's Global Compact (see above) and steps are already being made in that direction. Further, with an international agreement between the largest trading concerns to do this, then all gain, because the playing field in which all compete remains level. The competition is then based on new products, services, technology and price, but not upon who manages to exploit their workers the most. Such global Keynesianism (but see below) will stimulate demand for goods in both rich and poor countries.

One of the key results of such a planetary bargain or social agreement will be to improve social protection for workers all round the world. Obviously, the type of social protection devised has to be carefully constructed, so as not to over-burden business with meaningless regulation that leads to inefficiency and increased unemployment. However, social protection that increases workers' pecuniary benefits worldwide through pensions, maternity leave, better pay, and so on is in everyone's interest, because it will stimulate effective demand, con-sumption and consequently increased growth. It is in the interest of private transglobal companies that social protection should rise at the same rate every-where to prevent competitors or rogue countries benefiting from short-term gains through inflicting misery on its people. It is in the interest of nation states, because those who have attempted to improve the lot of its workers will not be undercut by the same rogue countries. Germany has often complained that its high level of social protection gained since 1945 might now have to be disman-tled to compete with the sweat shops of the Third World. The goal, however, must be to move everyone to German levels, rather than to move German levels to those of Somalia, Rwanda or Bangladesh, for instance.

F.   LABOUR CONDITIONS AND TRADE: THE SOCIAL CLAUSE

The idea of relating improved labour conditions to trade is not new. At the inter-national level, this has come under the heading of a *social clause*. Discussions to include this in international agreements have also been underway for many decades.[11] The intention is to help to promote fair competition between devel-oping country exporters, by ensuring that those who respect minimum labour standards are not penalized for their efforts to promote human development.

Progress in including a social clause in effective international agreements has been painfully slow. This is because some developing countries feel that the industrialized countries' concern about working conditions is due above all to their export success, and to the growing pressure for protectionism that has arisen from high unemployment. A social clause is seen as a disguised form of protectionism – a Trojan horse – which is tantamount to interference in their internal affairs, while they are being asked for reciprocity in social obligations in

---

[11]   It has been argued that without such a clause, increased international competition might lead to 'a destructive downward spiral in the conditions of work and life of working people all over the world' (ICFTU – International Confederation of Trade Unions, cited in Van Liemt, 'Minimum Labor Standards: Would a Social Cause Work?' *International Labor Review*, 123, 4 (1989).

return for trade concessions. The private sector sees it as yet more restrictions on its ability to provide the best quality products at the lowest possible prices.

Thus, any negotiation at international level has to be handled carefully – the benefits and costs for both industrialized and developing countries to be clearly spelled out. Something that neither the WTO with its limited staff and research capability, nor ILO, which finds it politically very difficult to support research and analysis of its labour standards, have accomplished to date. And whether the agreement should be voluntary, because it is in everyone's best interest, or regulatory is worthy of further reflection. On this latter point it is worth mentioning that since its establishment in 1919, the ILO has not achieved the passage of any of its conventions and recommendations on labour standards into any form of international law. Many countries have, however, included ILO labour standards into their national laws. There is no international obligation, however, on countries to do so.

Attempts were made to include a linkage between a social clause and trade in the Uruguay Round of GATT that pre-dated the WTO, but was rejected and only faltering attempts have been made in the relatively new WTO. Given the importance of this matter, it is somewhat surprising to see that progress on it at the international level has been so slow. There were no provisions within GATT to ensure pursuing an improved social clause, and the international body, nor are there in its successor the WTO. The ILO, responsible for ensuring the application of labour standards has been slow, even ignored, in its championing of this at the centre of international discussions.

The ILO has, however, been active in producing labour standards through its conventions and recommendations, and at the last count there were 174 conventions and 80 recommendations.[12] Yet it appears to be more active in creating new instruments, thereby spreading itself too thinly, rather than conducting research on the impact and value of its labour standards and in identifying a minimum set of labour standards that could be included in a social clause or a social agreement. For instance, in June 1999 the ILO members adopted convention No. 182 banning the worst forms of child labour. But, as Gijsbert Van Liemt, one of its former analysts, noted:

> 'The ILO Constitution gives no indication of priorities for the application of international labour standards and the wide range of areas covered makes it impossible – particularly in developing countries with their weak administrative machinery – to expect most or even many of them to be implemented'.

The standards generally mentioned, Van Liemt says, are those on freedom of association, the right to organize and bargain collectively, the minimum age for the employment of children, freedom from discrimination in employment, freedom from forced labour and occupational safety and health. Thus the emphasis is on not so much the economic aspects as the legislative. The economic would include such things as social protection, pensions, health insurance,

---

[12]   The ILO's international standards consist of conventions and recommendations. The basic difference between these two forms of labour standard is that a convention is intended to be ratified, like an international treaty; a ratifying state undertakes to discharge certain binding legal obligations and there is regular international supervision of the way in which these obligations are observed. A recommendation, on the other hand, gives rise to no binding obligations, but provides guidelines for national policies and action.

and so on, all of which could stimulate effective demand for new products. But another weakness of ILO policy advice is that it normally raises the cost of labour and hardly ever considers the economic benefits to the institution that has to pay the increased charges implied. This is not a lightly taken point since few would question the desire to implement many, if not all, of ILO social policy. What is not done is to prioritise social policy in terms of what is essential and what is affordable. The core labour standards approach, which has been picked up by the Global Compact, is a step in the direction of prioritising, but on political not on economic grounds.

An OECD study *International Trade and Core Labour Standards*[13] backed up some these statements when it noted[14] that 'there remains a continuing gap between the international recognition of core labour standards and their application. Based on published observations of the ILO Committee of Experts on the Application of Conventions and Recommendations, the OECD study finds *no* indication in recent years of substantial progress overall in reducing non-compliance with respect to freedom of association and the right to collective bargaining among a broad sample of 69 countries that have ratified the two corresponding ILO fundamental conventions'.

The same OECD report noted that the WTO members in their December 1996 Singapore conference rejected the use of labour standards because it saw them as protectionist and in classic UN prose the conference 'recognized' the ILO as the 'competent body to set and deal with core labour standards'. Translation: we do not want to deal with this controversial issue, let the ILO deal with it. Such hiding the problem under the carpet is a legitimate cause of concern to critics of the WTO and at least to some of the active demonstrators known, mistakenly, as anti-globalization protestors.

At the Third WTO Ministerial meeting in Seattle in December 1999 proposals by the US, Canada and the EU to set up a WTO working group on the relationships between appropriate trade, developmental, social and environmental policy choices in the context of adjusting to globalization were rejected!

However, as noted above, there is some light at the end of the tunnel as the ILO, together with the OECD, has moved toward adopting a 'core' set of labour standards. These follow the list applied in much US trade legislation:

- freedom of association;
- the right to organize and bargain collectively;
- the prohibition of forced or compulsory labour;
- a minimum age for the employment of children;
- a guarantee of acceptable working conditions (possibly including a maximum number of hours per week, a weekly rest period, limits to work by young persons, a minimum wage, minimum workplace safety and health standards, and elimination of employment discrimination).

As Stephen Golub remarked, this list blends labour 'rights', such as freedom of association, with regulations on working conditions and wages, which are

[13]   OECD: 'International Trade and Core Labour Standards', Paris, 2000, ISBN: 92-64-18535-6.
[14]   Cited in OECD: 'International Trade and Core Labour Standards', Policy Brief, *OECD Observer*, Paris, October 2000, p. 2.

economic in nature. The OECD/ILOs core list is similar to that of the US, except that the fifth is limited to the elimination of employment discrimination.

The ILOs director-general (DG) in 1997 put his weight and that of his organization behind this core set as, indeed, has the new ILOs new DG, Juan Somavia,[15] but language has been guarded:

> 'although it is up to each member State to decide upon the areas and social priorities which should benefit from the fruits of growth and prosperity generated by globalisation, there is nevertheless a "minimum" programme that each should try to achieve'.

Indeed, a social clause could go further than just trade, and also be linked to public capital flows such as official lending and aid, and to strategic relations such as defence treaties. After all, countries spend billions on their defence industries, largely to prevent the have-nots from obtaining access to that possessed by the haves. Efforts that go into raising living standards through a social clause are likely to have much higher payoffs in terms of peace than is the encouragement of, and therefore the need for, expensive armies.

There have been several other attempts at establishing a social clause at the international level, but these have so far resulted in failure. For example, the European Commission endeavoured to include a social clause with the ACP (African, Caribbean and Pacific) countries that come under its Lomé Convention. But the Convention, signed in 1984, made reference only to respecting human rights, without a follow-up or control mechanism. Similarly, some international commodity agreements contain a social clause – for example, the 1979 Natural Rubber Agreement stated that its members would endeavour to maintain labour standards designed to improve the levels of living in their respective natural rubber sectors – but there is no monitoring or control or legal provision to ensure observance.

Evidence is already accumulating that a planetary bargain or global compact that goes much further than the UN's so-called Global Compact is required. Companies that have already trail-blazed a green path over the past five years in the UK wanted (according to John Elkington, chairman of SustainAbility, in a report published with UNEP) to see dramatic progress in reporting on emissions, spending and social impacts generally. Elkington predicted an explosion of activity over the next few years, even without mandatory requirements, as demands for greater transparency force more companies to report beyond their traditional financial boundaries. Already we see several hundred companies sign up to the UN's Global Compact. However, all of these companies have ignored or skated over the question of a wider ranging global compact than that of the UN and how it could be set into motion. Clearly, more thinking must take place on precisely what kinds of measures should be put into practice, by whom and when. Nonetheless, the UN Global Compact has set into motion a number of working groups to work our some of these issues but, to date, lacks financial resources and in-depth analytical work to progress very far.

---

[15]   The ILO has sponsored a web page to capture developments in this area see: http://oracle02.ilo.org/vpi/welcome.

What, then, could a planetary bargain or global compact contain, and to whom should it be directed? There are three main criteria:

(1) At the international level, there is a case for vigorously pursuing a minimum priority set of labour standards and social protection to include in international agreements in the WTO.
(2) Private companies should be encouraged to work toward a set of minimum working conditions that all will respect. This could be accomplished through such bodies as the UN, ILO, OECD and EU and it is in the private sector's own interest to do this. The leading figures in the major companies in the world should be brought together to thrash out a first agreement.
(3) Individual nations should work actively to agree and to respect a minimum code of ethics for their trade with other nations.

Since the first edition of Michael Hopkins' book, there have been a number of moves to require companies to adhere to a set of global principles – the Global Reporting Initiative, UN Global Compact, AA1000, OECD Corporate Governance Principles etc. Some companies have indicated their willingness to abide by such principles and even to be subject to sanctions for non-compliance. This is because they would be willing to accept a 'level playing field' to which their main competitors would also adhere. Legislation is difficult since implementation of a code by one country would punish those companies headquartered there to the benefit of companies headquartered elsewhere – Cayman Islands, Netherlands Antilles, Panama etc. – where poor levels of corporate governance are legendary. Such a code could not be a once-and-for-all negotiation[16] to produce a global guideline since society changes too fast for this. What is envisaged is a continuing process of dialogue between Governments and enterprises.

Who should represent both sides? In fact such a process has already started in the international organizations, as noted above, at the OECD Corporate Governance fora, World Bank Business Partnership and Corporate Governance discussions, UN Global Compact, UNEP sustainability dimension and Global Reporting Initiative and ILO annual tri-partite conferences of employers, trade unions and Governments.

Who should represent enterprises? This is more problematical. At the ILO, where enterprises have been represented for generations normally by Chambers of Commerce, rarely do the large corporations show up. The UN Global Compact has had more success, and ILO is represented, but the agenda to date has been limited to only a few stakeholders as noted above. Nevertheless, enterprises are active in a variety of NGO settings such as Business for Social Responsibility (BSR), the European Business Network (EBNSC), the World Business Council for Sustainable Development (WBCSD) or the International Chamber of Commerce (ICC). Yet, in each case the agenda is different and concepts are vague.

---

[16] We are grateful to Masaru Ishida of the ILO for his insightful comments on this point in his review of the first edition of this book – see M. Ishida in *Books, International Labour Review*, Vol. 138 (1999), No. 4, pp. 468–471.

What about other stakeholder groups such as the trade unions, consumers, non-unionized workers, distributors, retailers, suppliers, shareholders, and so on? To date, no one body has involved all these groups as well as Governments and Enterprises. The nearest organization is the ILO but there debates are intensely political and the ILO has found it nearly impossible to implement even one specific area of corporate social responsibility that of a core set of labour standards.

G. SHOULD THE PLANETARY BARGAIN TO PROMOTE CSR BE VOLUNTARY OR COMPULSORY?

There is currently much discussion on this point. The scandals in the USA have led congress to advance legislation on some aspects of CSR – the corporate governance part. On 24 July , 2002, both the house and senate agreed on a broad overhaul of corporate fraud, accounting and securities laws aimed at curbing the abuses that shook Wall Street. They also prohibited Wall Street investment firms from retaliating against research analysts who criticize clients of the firm; bar companies from extending unusual loans to executives; prohibit accounting firms from offering nine types of consulting services to public companies they also audit; and prevent officials from facing judgements related to securities fraud violations from using bankruptcy court to escape liability.

In the UK legislation is already a little more stringent than the USA and a Minister of CSR has been appointed by the Government but, to date, there has been little or no action. The inaction has led a coalition of NGOs, known as CORE, to demand the UK parliament for legislation around CSR. Predictably, according to Janus,[17] the UK's business association the CBI (Confederation of British Industries) stated 'we believe that CSR should remain market-driven. We do not support a mandatory approach and believe that a one-size fits all policy is just not possible'.

The EU, as noted previously, believes in a voluntary approach to CSR. While one of the EUs most active members, France, has devised legislation calling for all large companies to produce social reports on an annual basis by the year 2004. On the other hand, Adrian Henriques has wisely noted[18] that the most common reason given for why new legislation would set CSR back is because of the 'lowest common denominator argument' and he continues 'if there were legislation on CSR, then companies would deliver what the law requires, but never more'.

A bargain of a much harsher nature than envisaged here was mooted by Adam Smith in his *Wealth of Nations*. According to one interpretation, by Bernard Avishai writing in the *Harvard Business Review*, Smith's writings set forth a compact by which entrepreneurs were bound. 'In being so constrained, they owed the government their support only as far as it furthered their companies' commerce. It was unreasonable for government to interfere with supply and demand in any market, including the poor law'. But, as Avishai noted, this contract or bargain underestimated how explosive unemployment could be. Consequently, by the end of the nineteenth century, democratic radicals had pressed successfully for

[17]   Janus, 'Comment' in *Ethical Corporation Magazine*, July 2002.
[18]   Guest Column, *Ethical Corporation Magazine*, March 2002.

ending child labour, shortening the work day, increasing public schooling and establishing some form of unemployment insurance. Arguably, this new social contract or bargain eventually led to the downfall of communism.

It was the exploitation of labour, the foundation of Karl Marx's theories in *Das Kapital*, that eventually led to the Leninist worker revolution and the communist state. Marx argued that workers would rise up against capital as they saw their level of living stagnate compared with that of the owners of capital. The Soviet Union turned (without permission!) into Marx's experimental laboratory. But the success of the market system in allowing workers to become stakeholders in private capital, through the rise and increasing power of the trade union movement, led eventually to market capitalism growing stronger rather than collapsing. Indeed, the strength of the market economies, and the wealth created therein, led eventually to the collapse of Marx's experimental state, the Soviet Union, as it proved hopelessly inefficient at delivering to its workers a decent standard of living.

'Substitution of altruism for self interest on the part of business enterprises is not called for in resolving environmental problems – indeed an attempt at such substitution might have mischievous consequences', wrote Jerome Rothenburg in 1974. This seems excessively naïve now, after nearly two and a half decades of consciousness-raising and campaigns against polluting industry. However, Rothenburg *is* correct to say that self-interest is not simply 'to be left intact, it is to be relied upon'. He says that it is the responsibility of the public sector to enact policies that elicit socially responsible behaviour from firms that are following self-interest. The task for governments is to induce firms to act in ways that are socially desirable in the aggregate. This is so not only for governments, but also the informed public, NGOs (non-governmental organizations), campaigners, associations and the like.

In practice, evidence is already accumulating that businesses are taking it upon themselves to act socially responsibly, and this is much ahead of any legislation either proposed or even dreamed of. Many companies, such as BP, Co-op Bank, Shell, BT, ABB etc. believe that their existing behaviour exceeds most existing standards and, of course, wish to bring other companies, especially their competitors, up to the same level. They welcome the shaming and naming of rogue companies thereby encouraging limited legislation. On the other hand, Janus[19] observes that few companies have a sophisticated approach to CSR – or even any approach at all! He continues 'were legislation to be introduced now, most companies would not be able to comply'.

Thus, businesses need prodding to ensure CSR is on their agenda. As Samuel Brittan of the *Financial Times* remarked, 'It is doubtful whether managers have the knowledge to take into account the second and third order effects of their actions on national (or international for that matter) well-being'. This knowledge problem is 'often overlooked by so-called ethical economists', he says. And while a simple profit-maximization model provides 'subsidiary performance indicators for decentralized managers within a corporation', this does not apply to the much 'vaguer stakeholder objectives'.

How will a planetary bargain come about? Pressure is now being put by many consumers, employees, campaigners and shareholders on enterprises to become

[19] *Op. cit.*

socially responsible, which they are actually doing. It would be nice to imagine, as proposed above, a planetary bargain that arises from all the major companies in the world sitting around a table and horse trading to come up eventually with a final document. Anti-trust provisions will not allow this but stakeholder pressure will be society's 'invisible hand', guiding, suggesting, protesting, campaigning and regulating the wilder excesses that will create the planetary bargain. It will not occur by itself without vigorous actions or attempts to document and suggest alternative ways of conducting business. The socially responsible 'invisible hand' will have to be guided by the millions of concerned people who care about such things. Given that more and more enterprises see that such a course is in their long-term interest, the ground is fertile for this guidance to take place.

So, a planetary voluntary bargain is already on its way. Even as far back as 1976, both the OECD and the ILO produced guidelines for the conduct of international business by transnational enterprises. The ILO report stated that 'This Declaration sets out principles in the fields of employment, training, conditions of work and life and industrial relations which governments, employers' and workers' organizations and multinational enterprises are recommended to observe on a *voluntary* basis'. The Caux principles provide a philosophical set of principles encompassing business and environmental issues as did the original Global Sullivan Principles of Corporate Social Responsibility[20] developed in the 1970s. And the CEP has developed an overseas labour-auditing process. As its executive director, Alice Tepper Marlin, says:

'CEP has set universal standards for labour conditions, getting companies to say they will only contract with those who comply...companies almost certainly will begin implementing this'.

The CEP, now known as Social Accountability International (SAI) has called this 'Social Accountability 8000 (SA 8000)', and it takes as its core nine ILO conventions (on such topics as forced and bonded labour, freedom of association, home work, and so on, as well as the Universal Declaration of Human Rights and the UN Convention on the Rights of the Child.[21]

The ILO's labour standards, the area in which one would imagine such work would have been carried out, have never applied to business, because employers' organizations carry one-fourth of the vote on the ILO's governing body. Historically, employers' organizations have been against any standards set by the ILO for business, even though ILO standards are not followed up by any legislative body. But times are changing, and businesses, especially in the industrialized countries, are starting to realise that social responsibility pays, and that they have nothing to fear from reasonable standards of conduct.

What, therefore, are the pluses and minuses for CSR regulation?

Pluses from legislation:
- It would help to avoid excesses of exploitation of labour, bribery, and corruption
- Companies would know what is expected of them thereby promoting a level playing field

[20] See www.globalsullivanprinciples.org.
[21] See www.cepaa.org.

- Many aspects of CSR behaviour are good for business (reputation, human resources, branding, easier to locate in new communities etc.) and legislation could help to improve profitability, growth and sustainability
- Some areas, such as downsizing, could help to re-address the balance between companies and their employees
- Rogue companies would be penalized because of their lower standards
- The wider community would benefit as companies reach out to address some of the key issues of under-development around the world

Minuses from legislation:
- Additional bureaucracy and therefore costs of observance would rise
- Costs of operation could rise above those required for continued profitability and sustainability
- Critics already argue that the CSR of companies is simply to make a profit, and legislation would increase the vocalization of these concerns

In conclusion, the stand taken here is on the minimalist side of the debate on legislation or not. Clearly, no legislation at all is untenable simply because so much legislation already exists particularly for corporate governance. While full legislation for CSR, whatever that would mean, is also untenable since business could grind to a halt simply in chasing up all the new CSR laws on the statute book. Thus the sensible position for a planetary bargain is sufficient legislation to allow for a level playing field. This legislation must apply to all corporations wherever they are located or it simply will not work. How to enforce even minimalist standards in remote locations from the Dutch Antilles to the Maldives and even in China or India is a challenge for the legislators.

Chapter 9

CORPORATE SOCIAL RESPONSIBILITY AND THE ENVIRONMENT – OUR COMMON FUTURE

Marcelle Shoop

A. INTRODUCTION

Today's global landscape – its natural environment and resources, its societies, its economies, its sustainability – is changing more quickly and being altered more significantly than at any other time in human history.

In 1987, the *World Commission on Environment and Development* (the '*Brundtland Commission*') recognized the pitfalls the world would encounter through overpopulation, unchecked resource consumption, degradation of habitat, loss of biodiversity, and continued poverty. But along with citing those dangers in its report, *Our Common Future*, the Commission determined that changing the course of environmental deterioration could not be accomplished in isolation from economic development and social concerns. The lack of economic development evidenced by poverty creates its own type of environmental stress, as 'those who are poor and hungry will often destroy their immediate environment in order to survive'.[1] Conversely, economic development driven to meet the rising living standards of the affluent adversely affects the environment by its demands on resources and resulting pollution.[2] Accordingly, the *Brundtland Commission* encouraged societies to pursue environmentally sustainable economic development to eradicate poverty while seeking to meet the needs of both the present and future generations.

To successfully achieve the global goals of sustainable development and environmental protection, businesses must play a key role.[3] After all, as noted in

---

[1] *Report of the World Commission on Development and the Environment, Our Common Future*, 1987, ch. 1, ¶8 (1987), at 40 (hereinafter 'Our Common Future').
[2] *Id.*
[3] See *Agenda 21, Strengthening The Role of Business and Industry*, ch. 30 (1992); see also, *Johannesburg Declaration on Sustainable Development*, ¶¶27, 29 (2002).

Ramon Mullerat (ed.), Corporate Social Responsibility: The Corporate Governance of the 21st Century, 159–182.
© 2005 *International Bar Association. Printed in the Netherlands.*

Our Common Future, 'Industry extracts materials from the natural resource base and inserts both products and pollution into the human environment. It has the power to enhance or degrade the environment; it invariably does both'.[4] The pathway to enhancement rather than degradation lies in sustainable environmental performance.

En route to sustainability socially responsible businesses recognize the necessity to operate in an environmentally responsible manner and accept that environmental stewardship is part of the larger context of conducting business. This acceptance includes a willingness both to operate transparently and to engage a broad range of stakeholders. It also means actively seeking opportunities for improvement through the use of eco-efficient solutions, by developing new technologies, by employing life-cycle perspectives in resource and product stewardship, and by positively addressing biological diversity.

These aspects of environmental stewardship as features of corporate social responsibility are explored further in this chapter.

B.   ENVIRONMENTAL PROTECTION – HISTORIC HIGHLIGHTS

1.   Environmental Protection through Command and Control

World history of environmental degradation and the movements to protect and improve the condition of the biosphere provide context for concerns expressed by the *Brundtland Commission*. Given the volumes of excellent works documenting the evolving relationship of humans and their environment, the following discussion is only a small window into that history.

Ideologies emphasizing nature as distinct from humankind, full of resources to be exploited to serve the needs of humans,[5] have been blamed for the destruction of ecosystems and over-consumption of resources by an elite world minority. Early environmentalism tried to arrest this lack of control through 'conservation', which called for wiser and less wasteful use of resources – but use nonetheless.[6] At the same time, a more protective 'preservation' movement emerged arguing that nature was valuable in and of itself. While such early 'environmental' efforts were important in shaping initial constraints on growth, they did not eliminate mounting damage to the environment.

Eventually, the rampant economic growth of the industrialized world between 1945 and 1973, and the resulting environmental impacts, created its own backlash in environmentalism.[7] Reports of Ohio's burning Cayhouga River, unhealthy levels of air pollution in major cities across the globe, a cellulose plant

---

[4]   *Id.* at ch. 8, ¶ 3, 207.
[5]   See *Joseph Petulla, American Environmental History: The Exploitation And Conservation of Natural Resources*, 217–35 (1977); see also Paul S. Weiland, *Amending the National Environmental Policy Act: Federal Environmental Protection in The Twenty-First Century*, 12 J. Land Use & Envtl. L. 275 (Spring 1997).
[6]   *Id.*
[7]   J.R. McNeill, *Something New Under The Sun – An Environmental History of The Twentieth Century World*, ch. 11, 337, W.W. Norton & Company, Inc., New York, NY (2000).

on the banks of Lake Baikal in western Siberia, the energy crisis in 1973,[8] and the discovery of toxic chemicals at Love Canal near Buffalo, New York, in the late 1970s were just a few of the episodes stimulating the environmental movement.

In the 1960s and 1970s environmentalism as a social movement gained significant momentum worldwide.[9] In 1962, Rachel Carson, once a government biologist, published *Silent Spring*. This writing that condemned the reckless use of pesticides such as DDT and their damaging effects on birds is often credited with raising general environmental consciousness.[10] The resulting controversy rocketed Carson, her book, and its message to the forefront of people's awareness as she appeared on national television and the book was eventually published in seven languages.[11] In 1966, the Council of Europe announced '[t]hat the year 1970, would be European Conservation Year (ECY)'.[12] The purpose was to 'raise environmental awareness and thereby "to encourage all Europeans to care for, work for, and enjoy a high quality environment"'. The year 1970 also saw the first Earth Day. Founders proclaimed 'Planet Earth is facing a grave crisis which only the people of Earth can resolve, and the delicate balances of nature, essential for our survival, can only be saved through a global effort, involving all of us....'[13]

This era of environmentalism ushered in the 'command and control' approach to environmental degradation. Globally, it culminated in the enactment of numerous laws designed to control pollution and waste and to protect natural resources and wildlife.

These traditional regulatory systems are not the primary drivers for socially responsible business behaviour. However, they will continue to play a role in environmental performance, particularly to the extent they create level playing fields and provide incentives to internalize the external costs of environmental impacts.

2.   International Cooperative Efforts

In the early 1970s, international concern for the planet's health led to a meeting that arguably would signal the developed world's determination to reverse decades of environmental degradation and to set a course to provide for future generations. In 1972, world leaders gathered in Stockholm for the *United Nations Conference on the Human Environment*. That meeting resulted in agreement 'on an urgent need to respond to the problem of environmental

8   The oil production restrictions imposed by the Organization of Petroleum Exporting Countries (OPEC) in 1973 played a significant role in shaping energy conservation efforts and focusing on the environmental impacts of oil production. McNeill, *supra* note 13, at 301–05.
9   McNeill, *supra* at note 13, chs. 11–12; see also Stacy J. Silveira, *The American Environmental Movement: Surviving Through Diversity*, 28 B.C. Envtl. Aff. L. Rev. 497 (2001).
10 Rachel Carson, *Silent Spring*, Houghton Mifflin Company, Boston, MA (1962).
11 McNeill, *supra* at note 13, 339.
12 John Sheail, *An Environmental History of Twentieth-Century Britain*, 146, Palgrave, Houndsmills, Basingstoke, Hampshire, UK (2002).
13 *UN Earth Day Proclamation*, 1971, at http://www.themesh.com/un.html.

deterioration'.[14] Following a second Conference on the Human Environment in 1982, the United Nations established the World Commission on Environment and Development. Chaired by Norwegian Prime Minister Gro Harlem Brundtland, the Commission in 1987 published *Our Common Future*, a sweeping treatise that coined the popular definition of 'sustainable development'.[15]

The *Brundtland* report was the catalyst for the first Earth Summit, the *United Nations Conference on Environment and Development* in 1992. International leaders gathered in Rio de Janeiro concluded that 'protection of the environment and social and economic development are fundamental to sustainable development'.[16] The *Rio Declaration* reaffirmed the *1972 Stockholm Declaration on the Human Environment*, with a goal of developing international agreements that respect the interests of all people while protecting the 'integrity of the global environmental and developmental system'.[17]

The *Rio Declaration* was supported by *Agenda 21*, a comprehensive plan of action for a global partnership for achieving sustainable development. Its major components address social and economic dimensions, conservation and resource management, roles of major groups, and the means to implement the Agenda. During the Earth Summit, agreement was reached on two other historic accords of environmental significance. One of these, the Convention on Biological Diversity, 'links traditional conservation efforts to the economic goal of using biological resources sustainably and equitably'.[18] Under the Convention, governments are to develop national biodiversity strategies and action plans, utilizing monitoring, designation of protected areas, rehabilitation, restoration, control of non-native species, and public outreach.[19]

The United Nations Framework Convention on Climate Change, also agreed to at the Earth Summit in 1992, has an ultimate objective of stabilizing concentrations of greenhouse gases[20] in the atmosphere at 'levels that would prevent 'dangerous' human interference with the climate system'.[21] This agreement was expanded on in 1997 by the Kyoto Protocol, which was designed to refine how the objectives of the Framework Convention would be achieved. The Kyoto Protocol set differing levels of greenhouse reduction targets and deadlines for industrialized countries (Annex 1) and requires the parties to implement domestic policies and measures to achieve the targets. The overall target for Annex 1 signatories is to achieve a 5 percent reduction from 1990 levels by 2008–2012.[22]

---

[14]   *Johannesburg Declaration, supra* note 3, at ¶ 8.
[15]   Sustainable development is 'development that meets the needs of the present without compromising the ability of future generations to meet their own needs'. *Our Common Future, supra* note 4, at ch. 2, ¶ 1, 52.
[16]   *Johannesburg Declaration, supra* note 3, at ¶ 8.
[17]   *United Nations, Rio Declaration on Environment And Development* (1992).
[18]   *Secretariat of The Convention on Biological Diversity, How The Convention on Biological Diversity Promotes Nature And Human Well-Being*, 8 (1999).
[19]   *Id.* at 9.
[20]   Greenhouse gases include: Carbon dioxide (CO_2), Methane (CH_4), Nitrous oxide (N_2O), Hydrofluorocarbons (HFCs), Perfluorocarbons (PFCs), and Sulphur hexafluoride (SF_6).
[21]   *United Nations Climate Change Secretariat, A Guide to the Climate Change Convention Process*, Preliminary 2nd ed., Bonn (2002).
[22]   UNFCC *Caring for Climate, Climate Change Secretariat, A Guide to the Climate Change Convention and the Kyoto Protocol*, Bonn (2003).

Ten years following the Earth Summit, the World Summit on Sustainable Development convened in Johannesburg, South Africa in September 2002. The purpose of the Johannesburg Summit, often referred to as Rio+10, was to review the level of progress that had been achieved on commitments made in 1992 at the Earth Summit. The Johannesburg Declaration on Sustainable Development, consisting of 37 principles, reaffirmed the commitment to sustainable development through the Johannesburg Plan of Implementation.[23] To realize the goals of sustainable development, the implementation plan commits to concrete actions and measures to '[p]romote the integration of the three components of sustainable development – economic development, social development and environmental protection – as interdependent and mutually reinforcing pillars'.[24]

C. CSR AND ENVIRONMENTAL PERFORMANCE

The shift toward sustainability and greater environmental responsibility relies on proactive environmental stewardship and self-regulation rather than the traditional command and control approach.[25] Environmental responsibility for business as noted in *Agenda 21* is:

'[the] responsible and ethical management of products and processes from the point of view of health, safety and environmental aspects. Towards this end, business and industry should increase self-regulation, guided by appropriate codes, charters and initiatives integrated into all elements of business planning and decision-making, and fostering openness and dialogue with employees and the public'.[26]

Presumably, this proactive stewardship approach driven from within a business means that organizations will implement consistently high environmental standards regardless of the region in which they are doing business, even if not required by the laws of the region.

1. Business Case for Environmental Responsibility

Some argue that corporate social responsibility runs counter to the very foundation of a market economy and the role of profits within it and is bad for business and the environment.[27] Conversely, in the context of environmental sustainability, it can be argued that the future is not adequately accounted for in

---

[23] Also referred to as the Plan of Implementation of World Summit on Sustainable Development.

[24] *World Summit on Sustainable Development, Plan of Implementation*, ch. I, ¶2 (2002), at http://www.un.org/esa/sustdev/documents/docs.htm (hereinafter *Johannesburg Plan Of Implementation*).

[25] See *Agenda 21, supra* note 3, at ch. 30; see also *Guide to the Global Compact: A Practical Understanding Of the Vision and Nine Principles*, 58, at (Essential Readings) (hereinafter *Global Compact Guide*), http://www.unglobalcompact.org/Portal/Default.asp.

[26] *Id.*

[27] See Charles O. Holliday, JR. *et al.,Walking The Talk, The Business Case for Sustainable Development* ch. 4, Greenleaf Publishing, Sheffield, UK (2002).

the marketplace.[28] If environmental responsibility were not incorporated into the market, presumably the market would continue to take a free ride on the environment – potentially leading to the 'tragedy of the commons'.[29] The theory being that an individual or entity has no motivation to protect the common natural resources while attempting to maximize short-term self-interests, absent other controls. Concerns such as over-fishing, over-grazing, and de-forestation are a few examples where this economic theory could play out. Yet policies, laws, regulations and social conscience all seeking to avoid that tragedy do play a role in the marketplace.

There is growing evidence that engaging in corporate social responsibility and sustainable environmental practices can create positive value through enhanced reputation, license to operate, and the ability to attract and retain resources – from investment capital to quality employees. Other value may result from cost savings associated with environmental improvements such as reduced production inputs, the ability to identify emerging trends and to manage risk and competitive advantage.

In a global marketplace, quality reputation is a vital asset. Companies with good reputations for identifying and managing their environmental impacts responsibly will find it easier to obtain approvals to do business in new regions and to expand existing operations. A good reputation can also directly affect financial results by avoiding boycotts and poor sales. Polls have shown that a growing percentage of consumers consider corporate social responsibility when purchasing a product or speak out negatively against it to others as a response to a company's irresponsible behavior.[30]

The ability to attract investment capital is critical for many businesses and some investors are looking more closely at environmental risk factors. As of September 2004, twenty-eight banks had adopted the *Equator Principles,* a set of voluntary guidelines to 'manage social and environmental issues' for financing development projects of $50 million or more. The Equator Principles are based on policies and guidelines of the World Bank and its private sector investment firm, the International Finance Corporation (IFC). Under the Equator Principles, the banks will lend only to 'those projects whose sponsors can demonstrate ... their ability and willingness to comply with comprehensive processes aimed at ensuring that projects are developed in a socially responsible manner and according to sound environmental management practices'.[31]

Many businesses have discovered that environmental responsibility can save money and create value. Some of these financial aspects are easy to quantify. Eliminating the use of certain chemicals in the workplace or changing processes can eliminate waste and significantly reduce disposal costs. Improving energy

---

[28]   Robert M. Solow, 'Sustainability: An Economist's Perspective', *Economics of The Environment, Selected Readings,* ch. 5 at 131, 134, 4th ed., edited by Robert N. Stavins, Harvard University, W.W. Norton & Company, New York, NY (2000) (hereinafter *Economics of the Environment*).

[29]   *Id.* at 135; see also Garret Hardin, 'The Tragedy of the Commons', *Economics of the Environment, supra* note 28, ch. 2 at 9.

[30]   See *Surveys Find Many Consumers Hold Companies Responsible For Their Actions,* referencing survey sponsored by Pricewaterhouse Coopers and Reputation Institute, (1999) at http://www.pwcglobal.com; see other polls listed in *Walking the Talk, supra* note 27 at 110.

[31]   See *Leading Banks Adopt Equator Principles,* at http://equatorprinciples.ifc.org.

efficiency can reduce energy costs. Reducing spills and releases can avoid cleanup costs. Other aspects of environmental responsibility are harder to quantify, such as technological improvements, with value realized only in the long-term.

Environmentally responsible companies have the opportunity in some locations to qualify for less regulatory intervention or special incentives. For example, the US EPA's National Environmental Performance Track is a voluntary program in which applicants must have an externally audited environmental management system, a history of sustained legal compliance, a commitment to improved environmental performance with specific measurable targets, and a public outreach program including environmental reporting.[32] The program offers incentives such as designating a qualified facility as a low priority for enforcement inspection purposes and allowing discretionary consideration in penalty assessment activities for good faith efforts to comply.[33] The incentives are designed to (i) recognize and reward environmental accomplishments; (ii) encourage facilities to perform beyond basic compliance; (iii) allow members to operate more efficiently; and (iv) demonstrate that innovation is integral to EPA's evolving regulatory framework.[34]

Still, the nature of publicly owned corporations and the pressures from investment analysts and markets that place significant emphasis on short-term economic performance can create a tension when environmentally responsible behavior manifests itself in longer-term performance rather than short-term value creation. In a recent survey of European fund managers, analysts and relations officers, 78 percent thought that effective management of environmental and social risk added to long-term market value, while only 32 percent believed such issues affected short-term market value.[35] Just as significant, the recent Global CEO Survey found that 71 percent of CEOs responded that they would consider foregoing short-term profitability in exchange for long-term shareholder value.[36]

The marketplace is changing and there are many investors and funds that are examining environmental performance as part of their investment criteria, and investors are being encouraged to consider the longer time horizons in this

[32]   US Environmental Protection Agency, National Environmental Performance Track Program Guide, 5–6 (2003), available at http://www.epa.gov/performancetrack/programguide.pdf (March. 2003).

[33]   US Environmental Protection Agency, National Environmental Performance Track Frequently Asked Questions, at http://www.epa.gov/performancetrack/faq.htm (last updated 26 February 2004). Pending and Future Incentives appear to offer even more enticement to apply. Reduced frequency of maximum available control technology (MACT) reporting, increased hazardous waste storage timeframes, and reduced reporting and monitoring under the 1996 discharge monitoring report (DMR) program or fast-track new source review NSR) permitting are a few of the future incentives proposed by EPA. Id. An applicant is informed of the incentives for which it is eligible when accepted into the program. National Environmental Performance Track Program Guide, supra note 32, at 9.

[34]   US Environmental Protection Agency, National Performance Track Program Regulatory and Administrative Incentives, at http://www.epa.gov/performancetrack/benefits/regadmin.htm.

[35]   See The Global Compact Financial Section, Who Cares Wins, Connecting Financial Markets to a Changing World – Recommendations By the Financial Industry to Better Integrate Environmental, Social and Governance Issues in Analysis, Asset Management and Securities Brokerage, 11 June 2004, at http://www.innovestgroup.com (referencing the CSR Europe, Deloitte, Euronext: Investing in Responsible Business. The 2003 survey of European fund managers, financial analysts and investor relations officers).

[36]   Pricewaterhouse Coopers, 6th Annual Global CEO Survey (2003), at http://www.pwcglobal.com.

analysis.[37] Although the less obvious tangible and the intangible aspects of environmental performance can be difficult to quantify, the belief is that companies that perform well environmentally and socially are generally better managed overall.[38]

2. Standards for Corporate Governance and Social Responsibility – Voluntary Compacts, Codes, Principles, and Commitments

Better overall management stems from clearly articulating and instituting core values that define expected corporate behavior and provide the framework within an organization for the business to achieve responsible environmental performance.[39] However, those values and underlying principles need to be consistently reinforced and implemented through systems and management commitment to achieve results. Many companies also express their commitment to governance principles and corporate social responsibility by endorsing one or more voluntary codes.[40]

The last decade has seen the development of numerous voluntary codes of conduct, guidelines, principles, charters and standards, all designed to guide corporate behavior in the direction of improving social and environmental performance. While many address environmental performance, there also are industry-specific codes,[41] and many codes that contain sustainability principles applicable to all aspects of corporate social responsibility and the environment.

Examples of environmental principles contained in voluntary codes are illustrated by such internationally recognized guidelines as the *United Nations Global*

---

[37]   See *Calvert Funds*, at http://www.calvert.com/sri_6545.html (2 Octber 2003); see also *The Global Compact Financial Section, supra* note 35.

[38]   See Dow Jones Sustainability Index, *Sustainability Investment*, at http://www.sustainability-indexes.com/htmle/sustainability/sustinvestment.html (2003) ('The concept of corporate sustainability is attractive to investors because it aims to increase long-term shareholder value. Since corporate sustainability performance can now be financially quantified, they now have an investable corporate sustainability concept....'); see also *The Global Compact Financial Section, supra* note 35; *The United Nations Environment Programme Finance Initiative (UNEP FI) Asset Management Working Group (AMWG), The Materiality of Social, Environmental and Corporate Governance Issues to Equity Pricing: 11 Sector Studies by Brokerage House Analysts* (2004) at http://www.unglobalcompact.org/Portal/Default.asp (June 2004).

[39]   See Jeffrey Hollender & Stephen Fenichell, *What Matters Most, How a Small Group of Pioneers is Teaching Social Responsibility to big Business, and Why big Business is Listening* (2004).

[40]   Enhancing corporate environmental responsibility and accountability through voluntary initiatives, codes of conduct, and reporting and verification is advocated by *Agenda 21* and the *Johannesburg Plan of Implementation*: This would include actions at all levels to:

(a)   Encourage industry to improve social and environmental performance through voluntary initiatives, including environmental management systems, codes of conduct, certification and public reporting on environmental and social issues, taking into account such initiatives as the International Organization for Standardization standards and Global Reporting Initiative guidelines on sustainability reporting, bearing in mind principle 11 of the Rio Declaration on Environment and Development....

Johannesburg Plan of Implementation, supra note 24, at ch. III, ¶ 18.

[41]   See *International Mining & Metals Council Sustainable Development Principles 2003*, at http://www.icmm.com/icmm_principles.php.

Compact (Global Compact),[42] the *International Chamber of Commerce (ICC) Business Charter for Sustainable Development*,[43] the *Organisation for Economic Co-operation and Development (OECD) Guidelines for Multinational Enterprises*,[44] and the *Coalition for Environmentally Responsible Economies (CERES) Principles*.[45]

More than 1700 businesses, organizations and countries have signaled their endorsement of the *Global Compact*, a set of ten principles intended to 'advance responsible corporate citizenship so that business can be part of the solution to the challenges of globalization'.[46] The *Global Compact* highlights three primary environmental principles:

- adopting a precautionary approach to environmental challenges, (i.e., risk management);
- pursuing initiatives to promote greater environmental responsibility; and,
- encouraging development and diffusing environmentally beneficial technologies.[47]

The *ICC Business Charter for Sustainable Development* is a set of 16 principles for environmental management developed in 1991. In addition to environmental principles consistent with those in the *Global Compact*, the ICC charter calls for:

- establishing environmental management as one of the highest corporate priorities;
- integrating management systems, educating employees to work in an environmentally responsible manner, using environmentally sound product and operational design;
- minimizing waste, reducing the life cycle environmental impacts of products and services; and
- engaging customers and the public.[48]

The *OECD Guidelines for Multinational Enterprises* cover a broad range of responsible business conduct, including principles to protect the environment, public health and safety, and generally to conduct activities in a manner contributing to the wider goal of sustainable development.[49] The OECD environmental guidelines are consistent with the *Global Compact* and the *ICC*

---

[42]   The *United Nations Global Compact (Global Compact)* is a set of ten principles that world business leaders are encouraged to embrace voluntarily, covering labor, human rights, and the environment. See *The United Nations Global Compact* (2003), at http://www.unglobalcompact.org (last visited 12 July 2004) (hereinafter '*Global Compact*').

[43]   See *The Business Charter For Sustainable Development*, at http://www.iccwbo.org/home/environment_and_energy/charter.asp.

[44]   See *Organization For Economic Co-Operation and Development, Guidelines for Multinational Enterprises* (2000), at http://www.oecd.org.

[45]   See http://www.ceres.org.

[46]   *The Global Compact, Corporate Citizenship in the World Economy*, (Brochure), January 2003, at http//:www.unglobalcompact.org.

[47]   Principles 7, 8 and 9 specifically concern socially responsible approaches to the environment. *Id.*

[48]   See *Business Charter, supra* note 43.

[49]   *Id.* The principles cover human rights, information disclosure, anti-corruption, taxation, labor relations, environment and consumer protection.

environmental principles, with an emphasis on collecting measurable information and disclosing environmental performance.

The *CERES Principles* developed by a coalition of investment funds, analysts, environmental organizations, and public interest groups contain ten points of environmental conduct. These *Principles* are endorsed by over 70 companies that have specifically committed to continuous environmental improvement.[50] By adopting the *CERES Principles*, companies acknowledge that they '[h]ave a responsibility for the environment, and must conduct all aspects of their business as responsible stewards of the environment by operating in a manner that protects the Earth'.[51]

Whether driven by voluntary codes, self-motivated corporate values, or legally imposed requirements, several broad themes emerge as a basis for what constitutes socially responsible and sustainable environmental performance:

- Operating with *Transparency*, being *Accountable* and *Engaging with Stakeholders*, and *Reporting* on Performance
- *Measuring* Environmental Performance, Setting *Objectives and Targets*, and Seeking *Continuous Improvement*
- Implementing good *Management Systems*
- *Managing Risk* by assessing and mitigating environmental risk
- Seeking improved *Technology* to reduce environmental impacts
- Engaging in *Product Stewardship* by understanding the *life cycle* environmental impacts of products and services throughout the value chain, and seeking to improve performance and reduce impacts through *eco-efficient* solutions
- Working with *suppliers* to address upstream environmental impacts
- Adopting considered approaches to *biological diversity*

These characteristic behaviors are best implemented as part of the larger business planning context and as part of an integrated business decision-making process that not only considers the environmental implications but social and economic aspects as well.

3.   CSR Characteristics of Responsible Environmental Performance

a.   *Transparency, Accountability, Engaging Stakeholders and Reporting Performance*

While the criteria for financial accountability and transparency, especially for publicly traded companies, have been evolving for decades, similar concepts for reporting on the details of environmental performance are of relatively recent vintage and are generally still voluntary. However, efforts are underway to impose

---

[50]   See http://www.ceres.org.
[51]   See *id.*

new requirements or clarify existing requirements for reporting on environmental performance and emerging trends in the context of materiality. The proposed UK regulations on company Operating and Financial Reviews (OFR) will require a publicly available narrative report on a company's objectives, strategies, and key drivers aimed at risk identification and management. Potentially, this could include information on environmental matters as well as information about employees, communities and social issues to the extent the information is relevant for an understanding of the business and the future outlook.[52] The OFR is intended to '[i]mprove transparency and accountability by providing shareholders with better and more relevant information on the business, its performance in the past and its prospects for the future'.[53]

The idea of voluntarily reporting details of environmental performance to the public, in addition to required regulatory reporting, started to gain traction in the 1990s. For example, signatories to the Minerals Council of Australia Code for Environmental Management began preparing publicly available environmental performance reports in 1996.[54] The Global Reporting Initiative (GRI),[55] CERES Environmental Principles, AccountAbility AA1000 Assurance Standard,[56] and similar sustainability reporting and assurance guidelines began to surface in the late 1990s.

The GRI Guidelines, developed using a multi-stakeholder process, are designed as a reporting framework on social, environmental, and economic performance.[57] Reporting guidelines such as those developed by GRI provide organizations with direction about the type of information to report – indicators of sustainability. The Guidelines contain specific reportable content criteria to promote balance in reporting and comparability of reports.[58] Of the 50 core indicators, 16 concern environmental matters,[59] while 19 out of the 47 'additional' indicators also address environmental issues.[60] Indicators are defined as a 'measure of performance, either qualitative or quantitative'.[61] The environmental indicators cover matters such as material inputs, energy and water use, air emissions,

---

[52] UK Department of Trade and Industry, Draft Regulations on the Operating and Financial Review and Directors' Report: A Consultative Document, at Section 1.2, 7 (2004).

[53] Id. Section 3.31, 22.

[54] Australian Minerals Industry, Code For Environmental Management, Signatory Values (1996, rev'd 2000), at http://www.minerals.org.au.

[55] Established in 1997 through a partnership between the Coalition for Environmentally Responsible Economies (CERES) and the UN Environment Program (UNEP), with the 'goal of enhancing the quality, rigour, and utility of sustainability reporting'. Global Reporting Initiative, preface to Sustainability Reporting Guidelines (2002), at http://www.globalreporting.org/guidelines/2002/gri_2002_guidelines.pdf (hereinafter 'Gri Guidelines').

[56] The AccountAbility, AA1000 Assurance Standard, developed by AccountAbility, is intended to cover a full range of corporate responsibility reporting and associated performance. 'AccountAbility is an international, not-for-profit, professional institute dedicated to the promotion of social, ethical and overall organizational accountability....'AccountAbility, About US (2003), at http://www.accountability.org.uk.

[57] GRI Guidelines, supra note 55, at 8 (using the GRI Guidelines).

[58] Id.

[59] Core indicators are those 'relevant to most reporting organizations and of interest to most stakeholders.' Id. pt. C, at 35, 49–51(Report Content).

[60] Additional indicators are those that may represent leading practice, but are used by few; provide information of interest to the reporter's stakeholders; or are worthy of further consideration as a future core indicator. Id.

[61] Id. pt. D, at 62 (Glossary and Annexes).

effluents and waste, impacts on biodiversity and habitat, and environmental impacts of products and services.[62] There is still debate whether these types of indicators are meaningful gauges of environmental performance or improvement and whether they can lead to a positive impact on the environment.

While more than 500 organizations worldwide were using the GRI Guidelines as of August 2004,[63] the level of resources required for reporting can present a barrier for some companies. Engaging stakeholders to determine what information they want to know, developing systems to collect relevant data, and devoting financial and human resources to prepare the reports are no small undertakings. Recognizing these challenges, the WBCSD has made some important observations:[64]

- Companies should strike a balance between what stakeholders want to know and what is practical and feasible to report
- A long lead-time is necessary to develop data-gathering systems
- The cost of gathering data will be lower if it is already being collected for a specific business purpose
- Flexibility in reporting standards is critical

Sharing environmental performance details with the public at large, outside normal regulatory reporting, is a trend that runs counter to many businesses and the legal profession representing business. Fear of liability and increased attention on company performance are not unfounded, particularly given the outcome of a lawsuit filed against Nike, Inc.[65] The lawsuit alleged that the company's communications concerning conditions in overseas factories constituted negligent misrepresentation and intentional or reckless misrepresentation, unfair business practices, and false advertising under California laws.[66] The California Supreme Court, without ruling on liability, found that although Nike's communications concerned issues of public importance, they were nonetheless unprotected commercial speech and subject to limitations to preclude deception.[67] Following a decision by the US Supreme Court declining to rule on the free speech issues, Nike ultimately settled the lawsuit out of court.[68]

Advocates of sustainability reporting have been concerned that the lawsuit would have a chilling effect on sustainability reporting. Recognizing that the trend and requirements for environmental reporting will continue to grow, businesses may be able to diminish their concerns about reporting by ensuring adequate systems are in place and resources are available to collect and verify the data and information reported.

---

[62]   *Id.* pt. C, at 35, 49–51(Report Content).
[63]   See *Global Reporting Initiative, New Database Launched as GRI Reaches 500 Mark* (10 August 2004), at http://www.globalreporting.org/news/updates/article.asp?ArticleID=338.
[64]   WBCSD, *Sustainable Development Reporting: Striking the Balance*, 10 (2002), at http://www.wbcsd.ch (hereinafter 'Striking the Balance').
[65]   See *Nike, Inc. v. Kasky*, 539 US 654 (2003).
[66]   Respondent's Brief at 10, *Nike Inc. v. Kasky*, 539 US 654 (2003) (No. 02-575).
[67]   *Kasky v. Nike, Inc.*, 45 P. 3d 243, 247 (Cal. 2000).
[68]   Nike, *supra* note 65.

Ultimately, it might be possible that the act of reporting on environmental performance and raising attention to the details of that performance might very well be an impetus for continued environmental improvement.

b. Engaging Stakeholders

Part of being transparent and accountable is sharing information with, and listening to, stakeholders. A stakeholder can be a person, group or entity directly or indirectly affected by the organization and its activities, or those with a direct interest, involvement, or investment in an organization. Among many of the possible categories of stakeholders are shareholders and employees, contractors, suppliers, customers, regulators, elected officials, local communities, and neighbors.

The AA1000 Assurance Standard calls for adopting organizations to agree to the 'practice of "inclusivity"'.[69] This practice requires the organization to identify and understand its social, environmental, and economic performance and the associated views of stakeholders; to consider and coherently respond to the aspirations and needs of its stakeholders in its policies and practices; and to provide an account to stakeholders for its decisions, actions, and impacts.[70]

Similarly, GRI guidelines on transparency and inclusivity call for an explanation of the organization's approach for determining who the stakeholders are that the organization engages; what engagement methods are used; what information is learned from stakeholders; and what is done with that information.[71]

Engaging communities and neighbors is particularly important where operational activities can have a significant impact locally. A good example of this is the Diavik Diamond Mines in the Northwest Territories of Canada. The company started production in 2003 following two years of construction and eight years working with surrounding communities and Aboriginal groups to plan the project.[72] Regular community meetings allowed Diavik to develop a shared vision of the future and with the 'help of elders, traditional knowledge was incorporated into the project'.[73] This process led Diavik to enter into an Environmental Agreement with local Aboriginal groups and federal and territorial governments.[74] The agreement formalizes Diavik's environmental protection commitments and provides transparency and oversight to local communities. The agreement also established the Environmental Monitoring Advisory Board (EMAB) for the Diavik Diamond Mine. The EMAB, made up of representatives of parties to the Environmental Agreement, has a mandate to make

---

[69] *AccountAbility, AA1000 Assurance Standards*, 11–13 (2003) (specifically principles 1 (Materiality), 2 (Completeness), and 3 (Responsiveness).
[70] *Id.* at 11.
[71] *GRI Guidelines, supra* note 55, at 24–25, 42.
[72] RIO TINTO, *Rio Tinto's Contribution in the Rio Decade* (2002) (positive action case studies – relationships, the key to planning), at http://www.riotinto.com (positive action case studies – relationships, the key to planning).
[73] *Id.*
[74] Diavik Diamond Mines Inc., *Sustainable Development Report*, 2003, Environmental Stewardship – Commitments, at 35, at http://www.diavik.ca/.

recommendations concerning effectiveness of the management, mitigation and monitoring plans implemented by Diavik and to identify when additional monitoring is required to make sure that the predictions of environmental effects are accurate.[75]

c. Setting Objectives and Targets, Measuring Performance and Providing for Continuous Improvement

Reporting on environmental performance requires an organization to measure performance with some aspect of comparability. As noted above, working with stakeholders and understanding their interests can guide what environmental indicators an organization measures and reports. Additionally, reporting criteria such as GRI or CERES include environmental indicators that can be used as a guide.

To report on performance there must be measurable objectives and targets. Reporting against those targets can be a way to achieve and show improvements in environmental performance. A few examples of publicly reported environmental improvement targets include:

- DuPont has committed to 'drive toward zero waste generation at the source ... giving priority to those that present the greatest potential risk to health or the environment.'[76]
- Rio Tinto, an international mining and metals company, has established efficiency targets based on per tonne of product produced. These include reductions between 2003 and 2008 of (i) ten percent in fresh water withdrawn; (ii) five percent in energy used; and, (iii) four percent in total greenhouse gas emissions.[77]
- Dell computers has a goal to 'provide product end-of-life management solutions that reduce environmental impact', with a target to 'increase product take-back by 50 percent' by fiscal year 2005. In designing for the environment, Dell has identified a number of targets, including eliminating 'halogenated flame retardants in desktop computer, portable computer, and server chassis plastic parts by year-end 2004'.[78]

When a target is not achieved, it is important that the report explain why, and what will be done to continue efforts to meet the target. The importance of setting stretch targets that are difficult to achieve should not be avoided for fear of not meeting the target. Stretch targets can be used to drive continuous improvement as long as progress is being made toward achieving the targets.

---

[75]   *Id.* Environmental Monitoring Advisory Board at 37.
[76]   *The Dupont Commitment*, at http://www1.dupont.com/NASApp/dupontglobal/corp/index.jsp.
[77]   Rio Tinto, *Social and Environment Review Highlights*, 3 (2003), at http://www.riotinto.com/library/reports/PDFs/2003_socEnvReview.pdf.
[78]   Dell, *Dell Sustainability Report*, Dell Fiscal Year 2004 in Review 60 (2004), at http://www.dell.com/downloads/global/corporate/environ/2004Report.pdf.

d. Management Systems

Corporate accountability relies on appropriate internal control and assurance programs as part of an overall corporate governance program. Adequate corporate governance systems are necessary to assure oversight and review of environmental performance at the highest levels of the organization. An environmental management system (EMS) will not substitute for the need for high level reviews, 'strategic environmental thinking or rigorous governance'.[79] However, an EMS can be the cornerstone for many environmental programs and can operate as part of a broader framework of an overall internal control and assurance program.

An EMS imposes discipline on the process of managing environmental issues. Two internationally recognized environmental management systems include: (1) the International Standards Organization (ISO) 14001 standards; and (2) the European Eco-management and Audit Scheme (EMAS).

ISO 14001 is a way of defining, documenting, applying, and auditing good business practices to environmental aspects of the business. An ISO 14001 EMS includes: (1) upper management commitment to compliance; (2) pollution prevention and continuous improvement; (3) ongoing management participation identifying significant environmental issues; (4) legal and other requirements; (5) establishing measurable environmental objectives and programs to achieve objectives measuring, monitoring and auditing environmental performance; and (6) implementing corrective and preventive action.

ISO 14001 does not contain substantive or prescriptive requirements, but provides flexibility in order to be relevant to numerous types of organizations. In simple terms, it comes down to a system for: (1) saying what you are going to do (procedures); (2) doing it (implementation); and (3) being able to demonstrate that you did it (records, audits).

EMAS is a voluntary 'environmental management scheme' initiated for industrial operations in 1995 and expanded in 2001 for use by any type of business operating in the European Union and the European Economic Area.[80] The intent of EMAS is to encourage 'continuous evaluation and improvements in the environmental performance' of a participating organization.[81] EMAS components include (1) a verified environmental review to identify environmental aspects; (2) an environmental management system; (3) environmental auditing; and (4) a publicly available environmental statement on environmental performance.[82]

The EMAS program imposes more substantive, specific requirements than does ISO 14001, and requires environmental performance information to be made public.[83] However, because of the overlap with ISO 14001, EMAS has

---

[79] See Richard MacLean, *Lessons From Enron – Examining the Parallels to Environmental Governance*, *Corp. Strategy Today*, Issue V / VI, June 2002, at 31.

[80] *Eco-management and Audit Scheme, Frequently Asked Questions*, at http://europa.eu.int/comm/environment/emas/tools/faq_en.htm#top (hereinafter *EMAS Questions*)

[81] *Id.*

[82] *Id.*; see also *Eco-Management and Audit Scheme, What is Environmental Management?* at http://europa.eu.int/comm/environment/emas/about/enviro_en.htm.

[83] For more detail on differences between EMAS and ISO 14001, see *EMAS Questions supra* note 80.

made it easier for organizations using the ISO 14001 EMS to adapt the program to meet EMAS requirements.[84]

Implementing an environmental management system does not necessarily guarantee compliance or better environmental performance. However, the infrastructure required to meet the various EMS standards establishes a mechanism to ensure more comprehensive training and understanding of environmental requirements for employees and a formal process for senior management review. Moreover, an EMS should lead to the identification of improvement opportunities, both with respect to enhanced compliance and reduced environmental impact.

e. Risk Management and Opportunity Identification

Risk management as an essential characteristic of environmentally responsible corporate behavior can be approached from two perspectives. In one context, risk management focuses on assessing and managing risk to human health or the environment from ongoing or proposed activities.[85] In a broader context, risk management also focuses on assessing and managing risk to the business associated with environmental issues.

Risk has been characterized as a '[c]ontinuum where unknown exposures become recognized, the associated uncertainty is analyzed and understood and the risks are measured and appropriately managed'.[86] Risk management entails a systematic approach for identifying and evaluating risks within some framework that takes into account the likelihood and consequences of the risk and mitigating the risk appropriately. Managing risk goes hand-in-hand with making good business decisions to ensure long-term value to shareholders. Failing to plan for, and manage, risk can adversely affect the worth or viability of the corporation. Such failings can also leave officers and directors open to shareholder derivative lawsuits.

(i) Assessing and Managing Risk to the Environment

Assessing and managing risk to the environment and human health and safety is a feature of socially and environmentally responsible corporate conduct.[87] Identifying and assessing potential environmental and human health impacts of

---

[84] *Id.*

[85] The concept of risk management is inherent in Principle 7 of the Global Compact that 'Businesses should support a precautionary approach to environmental challenges'. Principle 7 promotes a 'systematic approach to *risk assessment* (hazard identification, hazard characterizsation, appraisal of exposure and risk characterization), *risk management* and *risk communication*'. *WBCSD, Global Compact: A Primer On The Principles* – Raising the Bar, ch. 1 at 32, Greenleaf Publishing, Sheffield, UK (2004); see also *OECD Guidelines, supra* note 44, at ch. V, ¶4 ('Consistent with the scientific and technical understanding of the risks, where there are threats of serious damage to the environment, taking also into account human health and safety, not use the lack of full scientific certainty as a reason for postponing cost-effective measures to prevent or minimize such damage'.)

[86] Donna Herrmann Sandidge, *Defining Environmental Risks and 'Uncertainty' Under the Sarbanes-Oxley Act of 2002, Corp. Strategy Today*, Issue IX 2004, at 49.

[87] Risk has been defined as 'The potential for realization of unwanted, adverse consequences to human life, health, property, or the environment; estimation of risk is usually based on the expected value of the conditional probability of the event occurring times the consequence of the event given that it has occurred.' Society for Risk Analysis http://sra.org/resources_glossary_p-r.php.

a proposed or ongoing activity, project or product requires an understanding of the baseline environmental conditions and the realm of influence of a particular activity or organization.[88]

The 'Guide To The Global Compact' identifies several 'useful tools to gather information on the potential issues and impacts associated with technological, process, planning and managerial changes'.[89] These include:

- an *environmental risk assessment* to establish the potential for unintended environmental damage alongside other risks
- a *life cycle assessment* (LCA) to explore the opportunities for more environmentally benign inputs and outputs in product and process development
- an *environmental impact assessment* to ensure that impacts of development projects are within acceptable levels, and
- a *strategic environmental assessment* to ensure that impacts of policies and plans are taken into account and mitigated.[90]

(ii) Assessing, Managing and Disclosing Risk of Environmental Issues to the Business

There is increasing pressure on businesses to disclose more information on how they identify and manage environmental risk and the implications on the short- and long-term value of the company.[91] The requirement to disclose material environmental exposures and emerging trends is not new under Sarbanes Oxley, but the law does oblige '[c]ompanies to implement a systematic and demonstrable process that is rigorous enough to reasonably uncover and report material risks that may be present, as well as what measures are in place to mitigate these risks.'[92]

Implementing a risk management system to address impacts to human health and the environment resulting from a particular company's activities should be a component of a broader overall risk management strategy that also manages risk to the business associated with environmental issues. The latter in turn can be part of a larger risk management system sometimes referred to as 'enterprise risk management' (ERM). ERM is a systematic process of identifying, measuring, prioritizing and managing insurable and non-insurable risks across the entire enterprise.[93] This broad risk management approach is intended to consider not just the traditional financial and hazard risks that are easily predictable and typically insurable. ERM also sets out to address operational and strategic risks, with the objective to identify and then manage risks in a fashion that protects assets and resources, while creating opportunities and the ability to realize value.[94]

---

[88]   See '*Guide To The Global Compact*', (A Practical Understanding of the Vision and Nine Principles) at 54, http://www.unglobalcompact.org.

[89]   *Id.*

[90]   *Id.*

[91]   See *Striking the Balance*, *supra* note 64, at 9.

[92]   Donna Herrmann Sandidge, *supra* note 86.

[93]   *Id.* at 49.

[94]   *Id.*

The potential risks and impacts that climate change could pose to businesses is a significant focus of risk management today. Some companies are analyzing these potential risks by evaluating a range of financial ramifications that might result from policy changes, taxes associated with greenhouse emissions, higher fuel and energy prices, changes in consumption patterns, reputational impacts and missed opportunities, as well as impacts to operations or markets from severe or changing weather conditions. Some businesses, such as oil companies, auto manufacturers, or coal producers, also are assessing long-term risk to their businesses associated with the use phase of their products' lifecycle impacts. For such products, the greenhouse gas impacts from the use or consumption phases can be significantly greater than the impacts associated with the extraction, production or manufacture of such products.

While many companies might be considering these types of risks, investment fund managers have openly questioned the extent to which they are adequately advising investors about them. The Investor Network on Climate Risk coordinated proxy resolutions in 2004 at a number of companies seeking more disclosure concerning their response to the business risks and opportunities associated with climate change, as well as efforts to quantify and reduce their greenhouse gas emissions.[95] In April 2004, 13 pension funds working with CERES called on the US Securities Exchange Commission (SEC) to require companies to disclose risks associated with climate change.[96] A recent report commissioned by the United Nations Environmental Programme Financial Initiative to look at materiality of social, environmental and governance issues in equity financing recommended that financial regulations and standards be clarified to require disclosure of these issues when they are material.[97]

The push for disclosure and risk analysis is not entirely concerned with negative impacts. Understanding and managing risks related to emerging environmental trends also creates opportunities. The issue is to identify and then manage those opportunities. In the context of climate change many of these opportunities are related to technology innovations and changing markets. Hybrid automobile engines, hydrogen fuel cells, and energy efficient motors are just a few of these new opportunities.

f. Technology

'[T]he concept of sustainable development does imply limits—not absolute limits but limitations imposed by the present state of technology and social organization on environmental resources and by the ability of the biosphere to absorb the effects of human activities. But technology and social organization can be both managed and improved to make way for a new era of economic growth. ...'[98]

---

[95]   The purpose of INCR, launched in November 2003 at the Institutional Investor Summit on Climate Risk, is to promote better understanding of the risks of climate change among institutional investors. INCR encourages companies in which its members like invest to address material risks and opportunities to their businesses associated with climate change and a shift to a lower carbon economy. See http://www.incr.com/.

[96]   See http://ceres.org/.

[97]   *United Nations Environment Programme Finance Initiative, supra* note 38.

[98]   *Our Common Future, supra* note 4, at 24.

This 'eco-efficient' concept of sustainable development is not solely about quantitative growth. Rather, the concept emphasizes qualitative development that utilizes technology, efficiencies and knowledge to achieve sustainable societies.

'Delinking' economic growth from environmental degradation through efficiency improvements and technological advancements is critical for sustainability, reducing pollution and waste and reducing resource consumption.[99] Environmentally friendly technologies:

'[A]re less polluting, use all resources in a more sustainable manner, recycle more of their wastes and products, and handle residual wastes in a more acceptable manner than the technologies for which they were substitutes. Environmentally sound technologies are not just individual technologies, but total systems which include know-how, procedures, goods and services, and equipment as well as organizational and managerial processes'.[100]

Environmentally friendly technologies also include 'process and product technologies' that generate low or no waste for the prevention of pollution, and 'end of the pipe' technologies for treatment of pollution after it has been generated.[101]

The *Johannesburg Plan of Implementation* urges increases in eco-efficiency through technology transfer and collaborative efforts to develop technologies.[102] Climate change concerns are behind major cooperative research and technology development programs. Recognizing the long-term implications of climate change, collaborative programs are pursuing new technologies to supply power to an ever-increasing demand for world energy that can contribute to reductions in long-term greenhouse emissions. The Global Energy Technology Strategy Program (GTSP),[103] the Futuregen Project,[104] and Coal21[105] are three research

[99] Principle 9 of the UN Global Compact provides that: 'Businesses should encourage the development and diffusion of environmentally friendly technologies'. See *Global Compact, supra* note 42.

[100] Chapters 34, 34.1, 34.2, 34.3, *Agenda* 21, *supra* note 3; See also *Global Compact Guide supra* note 25, at 64.

[101] *Id.*

[102] *Johannesburg Plan of Implementation, supra* note 24, ch. III ¶ 15, ('(f) Increase eco-efficiency, with financial support from all sources, where mutually agreed, for capacity-building, technology transfer and exchange of technology with developing countries and countries with economies in transition, in cooperation with relevant international organizations'.).

[103] GTSP has adopted an integrated approach to explore the scientific, economic, regulatory and social aspects of climate change, while aligning 'new or existing technologies to mitigate negative consequences'. See http://www.pnl.gov/gtsp/index.stm. Research and development is being conducted in focus areas including 'carbon capture and disposal, biotechnology, hydrogen and transportation systems, renewables, nuclear, and energy intensity'. See http://www.pnl.gov/gtsp/about/about.stm. Sponsored by a number of public, private and government organizations, with a steering committee of international experts, research is being conducted by scientists from Battelle and the Department of Energy's Pacific Northwest National Laboratory (PNNL), as well as the Joint Global Change Research Institute, which is a partnership between PNNL and the University of Maryland. See http://www.pnl.gov/gtsp/sponsors.stm, http://www.pnl.gov/gtsp/steering.stm.

[104] FutureGen is the Integrated Sequestration and Hydrogen Research Initiative, being developed by a US government and industry research project to design and construct a nearly zero emissions coal-fired power and hydrogen production plant, utilizing carbon sequestration. FuturGen, *A Sequestration And Hydrogen Research Initiative* (2004), at http://fossil.energy.gov/programs/powersystems/futuregen/futuregen_factsheet.pdf.

[105] In Australia, COAL21, launched in March 2004, is a collaborative effort among governments, coal producers and the electrical utility industry looking at new technologies to reduce greenhouse

and technology programs wherein governments, industry and NGOs are working together to develop clean power generation technology. These efforts are pursuing technological advances to reduce power generation emissions to near zero, utilizing carbon capture and disposal methods. The programs also are studying other alternative fuel benefits, such as hydrogen production, and looking at renewables and energy intensity improvements.

Today, organizations find themselves in a position where they can make choices to harness evolving technologies that not only safeguard the environment and minimize the depletion of natural resources, but which also open the way for new business opportunities and sustaining resources for future generations.

g. Product Stewardship – Eco-Efficiency, Life Cycle Assessments, and Extended Producer Responsibility

Product stewardship involves understanding and managing the impacts that products and services can have on the environment or human health within a broad sphere of influence up and down the value chain. Product stewardship is not only environmentally responsible, it also can play a key role in competitive positioning in the market place, as well as identifying and improving environmental impacts arising throughout the supply chain.

The US EPA defines Product Stewardship as a 'principle that directs all those involved in the life cycle of a product to take responsibility for reducing the health and environmental impacts that result from the production, use, and disposal of the product. ... The product stewardship approach provides incentives to manufacturers to consider the entire life-cycle impacts of a product and its packaging – energy and materials consumption, air and water emissions, the amount of toxics in the product, worker safety, and waste disposal – in product design, and to take increasing responsibility for the end-of-life management of the products they produce'.[106]

Product stewardship integrates concepts of eco-efficiency, life cycle assessments and supply chain responsibility with the active engagement of customers, suppliers, regulators and other relevant stakeholders. Localized operational impacts from production are only one component of a comprehensive product stewardship approach. Placing the emphasis on environmental impacts of products or services from development, production, transport, use and disposal leads to greater opportunities to improve and create a net positive impact on the environment.

(i) Eco-Efficiency
According to the World Business Council on Sustainable Development (WBCSD), eco-efficiency is achieved 'by the delivery of competitively priced goods and services that satisfy human needs and bring quality of life, while

gas emissions from coal-fired electric generating plants. The effort focuses on technologies that hold potential to significantly reduce, even achieve near zero emissions, increase coal efficiency and facilitate hydrogen production. *Coal21, Reducing Greenhouse Gas Emissions Arising from the Use of Coal In Electricity Generation: A plan of action for Australia-Overview*, at http://www.coal21.com.au/overview.php.

[106] *Product Stewardship Institute, What is Product Stewardship? (2004)*, at http://www.productstewardship.us/whatisproductstewardship.html.

progressively reducing ecological impacts and resource intensity throughout the life cycle, to a level at least in line with the Earth's estimated carrying capacity'.[107] The notion of 'eco-efficiency' as a management tool links financial and environmental performance in such a way that value is created at the same time impacts to the environment are reduced.[108]

Three objectives of eco-efficiency identified by the WBCSD are:

- Reducing the consumption of resources, including minimizing the use of energy, materials, water, and land, enhancing recyclability and product durability and closing material loops;
- Reducing the impact on nature, including minimizing air emission, water discharges, waste disposal, and the dispersion of toxic substances as well as fostering the sustainable use of renewable resources;
- Increasing product or service value; this means providing more benefits to customers through improving the functionality and flexibility of products as well as providing additional services (such as maintenance, upgrading, and exchange services).[109]

Eco-efficiency improvements allow for continued qualitative growth, thereby contributing significantly to the transition to sustainable development.

(ii) Life Cycle Assessments

Understanding the life cycle impacts associated with the production, use and disposal of a product or service is an important feature in a proactive product stewardship program. A product's life cycle is the series of stages it goes through from the time the raw materials are removed from the ground to its final disposition at end-of-life.[110] A life cycle assessment, as characterized by the international ISO 14040 series on Life Cycle Assessment standards,[111] examines the inputs and outputs of each process in the product system from cradle to grave, or any part of the process as defined in the scope. This analysis identifies all the environmental impacts within the defined scope, such as energy and resource consumption, waste and pollution, greenhouse gases and global warming potential, acidification potential and smog.

While life cycle assessments are not an exact science, they have many useful purposes, including identifying where in the process or value chain environmental improvements can be made. A company may be able to use the life cycle assessment to identify stages within the production or service phase where impacts can be reduced through process changes, technology advances, materials input and transportation substitutions, to uncover tradeoffs for environmental improvement.

---

[107]   Striking ther *Balance, supra* note 64.
[108]   *Id.*; see also *Five Winds International, The Role of Eco-Efficiency: Global Challenges and Opportunities in the 21st Century* (2000) (Part 1: Overview and Analysis Prepared for The Eco-Efficiency Working Group Sustainability Project Policy Research Initiative (Canadian Federal Government)).
[109]   *Walking The Talk, supra* note 27, at 87.
[110]   See ISO Standard 14040.
[111]   The series was developed by international experts on Life Cycle Assessment from more than 50 countries during a period of more than ten years.

(iii) Extended Producer Responsibility (EPR)

Extended Producer Responsibility (EPR) is an area of growing importance for environmental and product stewardship. Driven by laws, policies, and, in some cases, voluntary endeavors, EPR reflects the view that responsibility for a product goes beyond the production gate and extends to some degree into and beyond the marketplace. EPR includes an effort to reduce and eliminate waste from packaging, electronics, cars, large appliances, and other products by shifting the end-of-life responsibility back to the manufacturer in line with the 'polluter pays' principle.[112]

End-of-life management requirements influence product design and encourage application of 'Design for the Environment' (DfE) principles, a systematic approach for reducing environmental impacts through product design. Integrated Product Policy (IPP) focuses on the product along the life cycle value chain, not just end of life. Emphasis along the value chain translates into more opportunities to lessen the overall environmental impacts of a product from materials input, waste generated in the production and use phase, or end-of-life disposition.[113]

h. Supply Chains

Addressing the environmental impacts inherent in supply chains is also a component in an overall environmental stewardship program for a business's products or services. When looking at the entire life cycle, the impacts associated with inputs may have as much or more of an influence on the overall environmental impacts of a product or service as the production phase. Influencing the supply chain by working with suppliers and requiring suppliers to meet certain environmental standards is another way that organizations can potentially reduce the overall environmental impact.

The supply chain has received significant attention in the areas of labor, health and safety concerns, particularly in the garment and agricultural fields. Increasing emphasis on the environmental performance of suppliers is being influenced by downstream customers as seen in programs adopted by corporations such as Starbucks, and Sony.

Starbucks has initiated a Preferred Provider program where applicants must detail their environmental and social measures to produce coffee in a sustainable fashion. Preferred Providers agree to abide by principles known as the Conservation Principles for Coffee Production.[114] Starbucks purchases certified organic, certified shade-grown, and certified fair trade coffees as part of its overall product line.[115] Starbucks supplier programs include providing financial support to farmers to grow coffee in traditional shade-grown style that is protective of rain forest canopy, certified by Conservation International.[116]

---

[112] See Brady *et al, Extended Producer Responsibility, Integrated Product Policy and Market Development: Lessons from Europe and the US,* Five Winds International (2003) at http://fivewinds.com.
[113] *Id.*
[114] See *What Matters Most, supra* note 39, at 118.
[115] *Starbucks Corp.,* Corporate Social Responsibility 2003 Annual Report (2003), 'Coffee CSR 2003' Certified Coffees 31, at http://www.starbucks.com/aboutus/csrannualreport.asp.
[116] *Id.*

Sony has an extensive 'green' procurement program for suppliers.[117] Its Green Partner Standards for environmental management systems was introduced in 2001, and in 2002 Sony issued the 'Management regulations for environment-related substances to be controlled which are included in parts and materials.'[118] These regulations ban or require reduced levels of identified substances in parts and materials, including certain heavy metals, chlorinated organic compounds, brominated organic compounds and other miscellaneous substances such as polyvinyl chlorides and asbestos.[119] As of mid-2003, Sony indicated it would only do business with suppliers that qualified as Green Partners.[120]

i. Biodiversity

Avoiding continuing loss of biodiversity is seen as critical to eradicating poverty and ensuring sustainable ecosystem management. It is estimated that '40 percent of the global economy is based on biological products and processes'.[121] The direct and indirect relationships between biodiversity and commerce are extensive. The livelihoods of millions are tied to businesses such as forestry, fishing, agriculture, pharmaceuticals or tourism, all of which rely extensively on biodiversity use.[122]

Many of the behaviors of an environmentally responsible business (e.g., risk management or product stewardship) can be utilized to minimize or avoid negative impacts to biological resources. However, prospects abound to make positive impacts to biological diversity. Large amounts of land or other habitat is physically owned, managed, operated or affected by many businesses, particularly those in the agricultural industries, or the extractive industries of mining, oil and gas development. These offer significant opportunities for companies to preserve biodiversity, limit habitat fragmentation, and enhance the biological knowledge base.[123]

Developing strategies to address impacts on biodiversity, seeking opportunities to contribute to biodiversity projects, and employing considered approaches to biological resources are important aspects for corporate social responsibility and environmental sustainability.

---

[117] See *Sony Corp., Corporate Social Responsibility: Sony and the People*, at http://www.sony.net/ SonyInfo/Environment/people/supplier/index.html.

[118] See *Sony Corp., Procurement and Purchasing: Green Procurement*, at http://www.sony.net/ SonyInfo/procurementinfo/procurement/en-procurement_green.html.

[119] *Sony Corp., Management regulations for environment-related substances to be controlled which are included in parts and materials* (2004), SS-00259 3rd Edition, 2004 at http://www.sony.net/SonyInfo/procurementinfo/procurement/ss00259/ss259_excerpts_e.pdf.

[120] *Id. supra* note 118.

[121] *World Summit on Sustainable Development, A Framework for Action on Biodiversity and Ecosystem Management,* Water, Energy, Health, Agriculture and Biodiversity (WEHAB) Working Group 7 (2002).

[122] *Id.*

[123] For example, several international companies – Anglo America, British Petroleum, Premier Oil, Rio Tinto, Total, and Vodafone – have partnered with the United Nations Environment Program (UNEP) and the World Conservation Monitoring Centre (WCMC) '*to create a comprehensive knowledgebase on global biodiversity able to support national and international policy development and decision making.*' UNEP/WCMC, Project PROTEUS, at http://www.unep-wcmc.org/.

D.   CHALLENGES

Challenges of moving toward environmental sustainability as an objective of corporate social responsibility will continue to unfold. The World Business Council on Sustainable Development notes that the opportunities and the challenges of corporate social responsibility are in the implementation phase.[124]

Not having a clear business case can add to the challenges of implementation. In a recent report prepared for World Bank, lack of proven or understood business benefits was identified as an important barrier to integrating corporate social responsibility programs for small and medium supply firms.[125] Many suppliers did not believe that the purported benefits outweighed the cost of implementing corporate social responsibility, especially given the buyers' seemingly contradictory demands on prices, quantities and deliveries.[126] With some exceptions, suppliers claimed that implementing corporate social responsibility did not translate into long-term customer relations and could be a disadvantage when the playing field is not even.[127]

Other challenges to implementing corporate social responsibility stem from the trend toward international codes and reporting schemes. Standardizing these codes might assist in avoiding confusion and the general overload from the myriad of existing codes. However, standards must be flexible enough to address local conditions and site-specific issues or risk hampering the acceptance of corporate social responsibility and reporting. To the extent the public, governments or investors use reported information to make performance judgments or decisions, a 'one-size-fits-all' approach could lead to misunderstandings or incorrect conclusions or improper comparisons. Additionally, given the resources required to collect and report on environmental performance, balancing '[w]hat stakeholders find interesting to know, what they have the right to know, what can be put to meaningful use in companies, and the cost of producing the information', is an important consideration in assessing the business case.[128]

Challenges also emerge in encouraging the development of new technologies to improve environmental performance. Issues such as general acceptance, cost-effectiveness, intellectual property rights and the need for policy frameworks to support the technological advances all present potential hurdles for research, development and use of advanced technologies.[129]

Despite such challenges, the push for improved environmental performance and greater efficiencies will continue and business has the opportunity to positively affect the health and prosperity of the Earth's environment.

---

[124]   See WBCSD, *Annual Review, Reconciling the Public and Private Agendas*, (2003).
[125]   Helle Bank Jørgensen & Peder Michael Pruzan-Jørgensen, Pricewaterhousecoopers (Denmark) et al., *Strengthening Implementation of Corporate Social Responsibility in Global Supply Chains*, Report Prepared for Corporate Social Responsibility (CSR) Practice in the Investment Climate Department of the World Bank Group (2003).
[126]   *Id.* at 28.
[127]   *Id.*
[128]   *Id. supra* note 124.
[129]   *Id. supra* note 124.

Chapter 10

CORPORATE SOCIAL RESPONSIBILITY AND HUMAN RIGHTS

Josep M. Lozano
María Prandi

On the face of it, human rights and the company seem worlds apart, and like oil and water, an impossible mix. But reality is proving otherwise. Every day brings more tangible and visible evidence of how closely human rights and today's enterprises are linked, the key perspective being corporate social responsibility (CSR). Until recently, human rights were mostly thought to inhabit the domain of rights and duties of states, never (compliance with the law apart) the corporate domain. Although currently gaining ground in theoretical debates and in the practice of some companies, the issue is not really a new one. The mid-1970s had seen a dawning realization of how company power was extending beyond economic to political, cultural and social areas. Since then, the continuous evolution of company activities and power seem to have radically restructured the equilibrium of their relations with the State and society.[1] Nowadays, companies are among the most decisive actors in determining how human rights are put into practice.[2]

Several working documents of the UN Commission on Human Rights and the UN Sub-Commission on the Promotion and Protection of Human Rights[3] as well as Security Council resolutions[4] establish a close relationship between the activities of some companies and human rights abuses. These documents stress the fact that companies have very often applied the so called 'downward harmonization', which basically entails the selective adoption of the employment and environmental legislation offering the lowest international social, environmental

---

[1]   The income of five transnational companies amounts to double the Gross Domestic Product (GNP) of the 100 poorest countries.
[2]   Felipe Gómez Isa, 'Las empresas transnacionales y los derechos humanos' in *Boletín de Estudios Económicos*, Vol. LV, No. 170, August 2000, p. 333.
[3]   See <http://www.unhchr.ch/data.htm>.
[4]   See <http://www.un.org/Docs/sc/>.

Ramon Mullerat (ed.), Corporate Social Responsibility: The Corporate Governance of the 21st Century, 183–203.
© 2005 *International Bar Association. Printed in the Netherlands.*

and human rights standards. The documents also point out that while companies may contribute to development by creating jobs, paying taxes and transferring technology, they may also instigate structural violence, poor working conditions and destruction of ecosystems, and in so doing effectively become barriers to sustainable development of the least favoured nations. As a result, the above documents offer substantial input into the timeless debate around company contributions to the right to development.

Today, the traditional concept by which only states and individuals can be held responsible for abuses of human rights is clearly being called into question - by civil society in general, in political circles and, over the last decade, also by some business managers. Indeed, increasing numbers of companies are linking human rights to their CSR strategy *upstream* as a basis for CSR screening (policy), and *downstream* as a resource for CSR measurement and evaluation (practice). What is being considered today is a new paradigm of company in which respect for minimum international human rights standards has become an issue inextricably linked to the process of building a responsible company.

Social, political and economic actors no longer view companies as mere suppliers of products and services but as new social, economic and environmental actors in a globalized economy where production processes are being closely examined. Nowadays, the question goes beyond environmental and social quality concerns (CSR matters) and includes human rights issues. Organizations formerly operating within a legal framework are now aware of a new frame of reference instigated by citizens and consumers. These days, society's relationship with companies and their 'authorization' to act is under constant review, and currently extends to whether they violate human rights within their area of influence. In effect, companies are being required to build their legitimacy and identity on the basis of respect for human rights, increasingly seen an integral part of responsible 21st-century businesses and business leadership.

The crucial issue here, however, is not only where human rights fit into CSR strategies, but how this is happening, and what present and future challenges to expect. As we will see later, the process seems to start from within, when companies begin to question why and how they should be managing this new field within its CSR strategy. Looking at this issue, we too have identified some questions, questions that we will attempt to work through during the course of this article.

- What is the general human rights context within which companies are operating? In other words, what are the real trends on the human rights agenda internationally, and what are the new challenges facing their protection and promotion?
- In this context, why are human rights being included on company agendas today? What are the main initiatives linking companies with protection of human rights, turning it into the core value of company CSR?
- But we should also ask: just what kind of human rights are we talking about in the company context? And what is the area of influence of companies in the field of human rights?
- Finally, what are the issues still to be addressed on international and corporate agendas that link human rights to the business field?

A.   HUMAN RIGHTS IN THE WORLD

Before going on, we will try to get a clearer view of the situation of human rights today. Being aware of current trends and debates and starting to think them through will help decide what issues affect or might have a bearing on the international context within which companies operate. For far from being isolated from world events, corporate responsibility is deeply affected by a whole range of other trends.

Whereas until recently, the debate on globalization had held centre stage in most discourses on the new challenges to the protection and promotion of human rights. But by 2003 and 2004, the atrocities of 11th September 2001 in New York and 11th March 2004 in Madrid were making the international struggle against terrorism its most visible *leitmotiv*. This is confirmed by an analysis of reports from the various human rights organizations (Amnesty International[5] and Human Rights Watch[6]) and international or intergovernmental organizations (European Union[7] and United Nations, in the latter, reports of the 59th session of the United Nations Commission on Human Rights[8]). All show that the world situation on human rights issues in 2003 was still marked by the international agenda imposed after the 11 September 2001 attacks. In many countries, anti-terrorist legislation, practices and policies were seen to be threatening serious violations of civil and political rights. This and other threats to economic, social and cultural rights (ESCR) were borne out by resolutions of the United Nations Commission on Human Rights.[9] Otherwise, 2003 also saw violations of basic freedoms, an increase in the practice of torture, deterioration in prison conditions, lack of procedural guarantees and hardening of policies for granting refugee and asylum status.[10] Analyses and prospects were not much more encouraging as regards ESCR.

More specifically, the 2003 reports of Amnesty International and Human Rights Watch reveal systematic and generalized abuses affecting the right to life and safety of the individual by actions or omissions of the State in 71 countries. Torture and abuse were used in 117 countries (although 134 countries ratified the Convention against Torture) and there were serious violations of basic freedoms in more than 80 countries. Groups most affected here were defenders of human rights and media workers. Moreover, abuses were often committed in a context of impunity.[11] The European Commission[12] pinpointed many worrying human rights situations worldwide, and the Swedish and Greek presidencies respectively identified a total of 32 countries, mainly in Asia. Of particular relevance during the 59th session of the United Nations Commission on Human

---

5   Amnesty International, *Report 2003*, Amnesty International Publications, London, 2003.
6   Human Rights Watch, *World Report,* New York, 2003.
7   Council of the European Union, *European Union Annual Report on Human Rights 2003*, Brussels, 13 October 2003.
8   Geneva, 17 March–25 April 2003. See <http://www.unhchr.ch>.
9   Resolutions E/CN.4/RES/2003/37 and E/CN.4/RES/2003/68.
10 School of Peace Culture, *Alert 2004! Report on Conflicts, Human Rights and Peace-building,* School of Peace Culture, Barcelona, 2004. See <http://pangea.org/unescopau>.
11 *Ibid.*
12 Council of the European Union, *Annual Report on Human Rights of the European Union 2003*, Brussels, 13 October 2003. See <http://europa.eu.int/comm/europeaid/projects/eidhr/documents_en.htm>.

Rights were reports by Special Rapporteurs and resolutions on serious human rights situations in 19 countries[13] as well as presidential statements on 3 further countries.[14]

In conclusion, 2003 saw the consolidation of post-11S legislative trends towards restricting basic freedoms and extending controls over movements of displaced people, refugees and asylum seekers (above all in developed countries). However, in spite of this deterioration in the promotion and protection of human rights at national level, the United Nations continued to adopt new legal instruments for protection against these abuses in international scenarios[15]. In Africa, America and Arab League countries there were important initiatives for human rights protection, for instance the coming into operation of the African Court on Human and Peoples' Rights. On 23 April, the 60th session of the United Nations Commission on Human Rights closed[16] in Geneva in the presence of the new High Commissioner, L. Arbour. The main challenge signalled by many human rights organizations during the period had been met: that among other important issues addressed, some measures be adopted to protect the human rights put in jeopardy by anti-terrorism measures.

B.   HUMAN RIGHTS ON THE CSR AGENDA

Four basic trends can be identified as catalysers of the new human rights presence in business discourses and practices and at top-level economic forums.[17] First, the controversial process of economic globalization. In an unequal world, globalization causes economies to resort increasingly to internationalization and off-shoring, thus spreading productive processes over countries with very different levels of human rights protection. Second, the emerging network society. Under its rules, companies are perceived as not simply economic actors, but as playing their part along with other social actors in interactions with their equivalents in other fields. Third, information and knowledge technologies, which create expectations of greater corporate transparency, while fast-tracking and multiplying content and information on these issues in local and global interactions. Fourth, the emerging risk society, by which company reputation, image and identity are coming under the scrutiny of certain rising values in a civil society that is increasingly informed and mobilized on such issues. One of a company's main assets, on a par with other more tangible assets like product quality and technological innovation, is its reputation. For example, a report of the International Business Leaders Forum[18] has concluded that the risk to companies being associated with human rights violations grew consistently in the eighties but above all in the nineties. It is

---

13   Afghanistan, Belarus, Bosnia and Herzegovina and Ex-Yugoslavia, Burundi, Cambodia, Chad, Cuba, the Democratic Republic of Congo, Haiti, Iraq, Myanmar, occupied Territories including Palestine, the Democratic People's Republic of Korea, Liberia, Sierra Leone, Turkmenistan, Somalia and the Sudan.

14   Colombia, Haiti and Timor-Leste.

15   For example, the adoption of the International Convention on the Protection of the Rights of all Migrant Workers and their Families.

16   Geneva, 17 March–23 April 2004. See <http://www.unhchr.ch>.

17   See the G8 agendas at <http://www.g8.gc.ca/> and those of the World Economic Forum <http://www.weforum.org/>.

18   See <http://www.iblf.org>.

therefore in this context that our societies are calling on responsible companies to build into their legitimacy, identity and responsibility a respect for human rights.

C. CORPORATE SOCIAL RESPONSIBILITY AND HUMAN RIGHTS: MAIN INITIATIVES

Beyond initiatives put forward by international organizations in the 80s and the 90s (such as the Declaration on Fundamental Principles and Rights at Work (ILO), the Tripartite Declaration of principles concerning Multinational Enterprises and Social Policies (ILO) and the WHO/UNICEF International Code on Marketing of Breastmilk Substitutes) all aimed at giving companies guidance on the incorporation of human rights criteria into their strategies it ought to be stressed that in recent years, new proposals on these same issues have been consolidating in international, business and third sector circles. Guided by the type of instruments featured in the report of the European Commission, *Mapping Instruments for Corporate Social Responsibility*, we briefly highlight below the most significant instruments in this area, including guidelines and statements of principles, and systems of accreditation and accountability.

Initiatives analysed come from the United Nations Global Compact[19] (henceforth the Global Compact), Draft Norms on the Responsibilities of Transnational Corporations and other Business Enterprises in Regard to Human Rights[20] (UN Norms), the European Union Green Paper on Corporate Social Responsibility[21] (Green Paper), the OECD Guidelines for Multinational Enterprises[22] (OECD Guidelines), the Ethical Trading Initiative Base Code[23] (ETI Code), Amnesty International's Human Rights Guidelines for Companies[24] (AI Guidelines), Global Sullivan Principles for Corporate Social Responsibility (Sullivan Principles), Social Accountability 8000[25] (SA8000) and the guidelines of the Global Reporting Initiative[26] (GRI Guidelines).

1. United Nations Global Compact[27]

The current Secretary General of the United Nations, Kofi Annan, declared in 1998 that he 'was building a more solid relationship with the business community. Thriving markets and human security go hand in hand: without one we will not have the other'.[28] Later, on 31 January 1999 at the World Economic Forum

---

19   See <http://www.unglobalcompact.org>.
20   See <http://www.unhchr.ch>.
21   Commission of the European Community, *Green Book. To foster a European Framework for the Social Responsibility of Companies*, COM(2001)366 end, 18.7.2001. See <www.europa.eu.int/comm/employment_social/soc-dial/csr/csr_index.htm>.
22   See <http://www.oecd.org/daf/investment/guidelines/>
23   See <http://www.eti.org.uk>.
24   See <http://www.amnesty.org.uk/business/pubs/hrgc.html>.
25   See <http://www.cepaa.org>.
26   See <http://www.globalreporting.org>.
27   *Ibid.*
28   Department of Public Information of the United Nations, DPI/1820/Rev.1 June 1998.

at Davos Kofi Annan launched the so-called 'Global Compact', an agreement between the United Nations and the world business community, for the respect and promotion of human rights.

Global Compact urges the business community to respect a series of principles divided into nine sections, inspired by existing international instruments. This new instrument considers as basic respect for rights contained in the Universal Declaration of Human Rights (UDHR) but adds that companies must embrace the other international instruments of human rights, and suggests those that might 'inspire' the private sector in their work to act in the protection and promotion of human rights[29] for example the International Labour Organization's Declaration on Fundamental Principles and Rights at Work and the Rio Declaration on Environment and Development. After a round of consultations to evaluate the possibility of incorporating a tenth principle concerning corruption, the Office of Global Compact suggested to the Secretary General of United Nations, K. Annan, the inclusion of this tenth criterion in the summit of 24 June 2004. Global Compact thus includes expectations of society which recognize that companies have responsibility for the impact of their activities. This is a series of voluntary recommendations requiring an effort of cooperation between the different institutions of society that the United Nations has qualified as an open model due to the flexibility and the invitation to shared learning that it implies. Here, company and stakeholder submissions are shared openly and publicly in the Learning Forum.

The nine principles are:

Human Rights
• Principle 1: Businesses should support and respect the protection of internationally proclaimed human rights within their sphere of influence; and
• Principle 2: make sure that they are not complicit in human rights abuses.

Labour Standards
• Principle 3: Businesses should uphold the freedom of association and the effective recognition of the right to collective bargaining;
• Principle 4: the elimination of all forms of forced and compulsory labour;
• Principle 5: the effective abolition of child labour; and
• Principle 6: eliminate discrimination in respect of employment and occupation.

Environment
• Principle 7: Businesses should support a precautionary approach to environmental challenges;
• Principle 8: undertake initiatives to promote greater environmental responsibility;
• Principle 9: encourage the development and diffusion of environmentally friendly technologies; and
• Principle 10: Business should work against corruption in all its forms, including extortion and bribery.

---

[29] OHCHR, *Business and Human Rights: A Progress Report*, Geneva, 2000. See <http://www.unhchr.ch/business.htm>.

Global Compact therefore invites companies to (1) support and respect the internationally proclaimed protection of human rights within their sphere of influence, and adds that (2) they must ensure that they are not complicit to human rights abuse, an issue that carries a lot of weight as far as the United Nations' position is concerned. In any event, Global Compact is not a performance or assessment tool. It does not provide a seal of approval.

According to the report *Business and Human Rights: A Progress Report*[30] that examines progress in the field of the Global Compact, companies who support this initiative must:

- Respect local and international laws principles on human rights spans both legal frameworks.
- Satisfy consumer concerns, given recent allegations about activities violating economic, social and cultural rights like labour rights.
- Promote the rule of law.
- Build community goodwill.
- Select partners, suppliers or subcontract companies according to their respect for human rights.
- Explore human rights situations in the countries where they invest so as not to interfere with international or European sanction policies.
- Introduce and effectively apply social responsibility measures on human rights.

Finally, Global Compact suggests that companies should follow a series of practical steps for the integration of human rights into their corporate strategy:

- Identify issues relating to human rights that a company can and must confront. This will vary considerably depending on the sector and the country in which they operate.[31] The analysis of the impact of business activities on human rights and their relationships must help to define the corresponding policy and its implementation.
- Carry out a policy based on international instruments.
- Define mechanisms for implementation.
- Dialogue/Collaboration: For many companies, this is the first step and consists of starting from a consensus between the different actors involved, facilitating transparency in the process.
- Train own and foreign staff on corporate principles on human rights issues.
- Develop internal and specialist capacity on human rights, devoting human resources to promotion and surveillance of this issue at company premises.
- Involve company partners in respect for human rights contents in corporate politics, establishing fluent communications.
- Establish a mechanism of internal audit on the issue.
- Establish mechanisms for independent verification and above all public communication of the results.

---

[30]   *Ibid.*
[31]   It can be seen that while most companies focus on employment questions, mining and textile companies need other more complex approaches.

Recent years have seen the development of numerous initiatives for partnership between the business sector and various United Nations agencies. But what is new in Global Compact is that it calls on the business sector to become directly involved in the implementation of human rights globally, and to actively convert human rights into a framework of reference for their actions. Proof of the enthusiasm generated by this initiative in the business field is the recent launching of a series of national platforms (in Spain, France, Egypt, Japan, etc.) that attempt to offset criticisms made by the third sector on the lack of guarantees on monitoring of commitments by certain companies.

2. United Nations Norms on the Responsibility of Transnational Corporations[32]

The second United Nations initiative originated in its Sub-Commission on the Prevention of Discrimination and Protection of Minorities (now Sub-Commission on the Promotion and Protection of Human Rights) that in 1998[33] established a Working Group of 5 experts on working methods and activities of transnational corporations.[34]

This Sub-Commission decided to establish for a three-year period a working group with five members with the following mandate:[35]

- To identify and examine the effects of working methods and activities of transnational corporations on the enjoyment of economic, social and cultural rights, and the right to development, as well civil and political rights;
- To examine, receive and gather information, including any working document prepared by a member of the Sub-Commission, on effects of the working methods and activities of transnational corporations on the enjoyment of economic, social and cultural rights and the right to development, as well as of civil and political rights;
- To analyse the compatibility of the various international human rights instruments with the various investment agreements, regional as well as international, including, in particular the Multilateral Agreement on Investment;
- To make recommendations and proposals relating to methods of work and activities of transnational corporations in order to ensure that such methods and activities are in keeping with the economic and social objectives of the countries in which they operate, and to promote the enjoyment of

---

[32] See <http://www.umn.edu/humanrts/links/businessresponsabilitycomm-2002.html>.

[33] Sub-Commission on Prevention of Discrimination and Protection of Minorities of the European Economic and Social Committee of the United Nations, *The relationship between enjoyment of economic, social and cultural rights and the right to development, and the working methods and activities of transnational companies*, Resolution 1998/8 of 20 August 1998, E/CN.4/Sub.2/RES/1998/8.

[34] Mr El-Hadji Guisse (Africa), Mr Zhong Shukong (Asia), Mr Asbjorn Eide (Western European and other States), Mr Paulo Sérgio Pinheiro (Latin America), Ms Antoanella Iulia Motoc (Eastern Europe).

[35] *Ibid.*

economic, social and cultural rights and the right to development as well as of civil and political rights;

- To prepare each year a list of countries and transnational corporations indicating, in United States dollars, their gross national product or financial turnover, respectively; and
- To consider the scope of the obligation of the States to regulate the activities of transnational corporations, where their activities have or are likely to have a significant impact on the enjoyment of economic, social and cultural rights and the right to development, as well as of civil and political rights of all persons within their jurisdiction.

Although the mandate did not specify as an issue for debate the creation of an instrument to regulate the activities of transnational corporations, one of the proposals that was discussed at the first session in Geneva in August 1999 was the text 'Principles on the conduct of companies with regard to human rights'. This was prepared by David Weissbrodt (University of Minnesota), an expert in the field, whose main proposal was the establishment of a code aimed at company regulation.[36] The voluntary or compulsory nature of this proposal became the object of a fierce debate between supporters of a binding regulation (some NGOs with consultative status) and the defenders of a simple declaration of principles.

Finally on 13 August 2003, the Sub-Commission unanimously adopted the Draft Norms on the Responsibilities of Transnational Corporations and other Business Enterprises in regard to Human Rights that were included on the agenda for discussion in the 60th session of the United Nations Human Rights Committee in 2004. However it seems that the proposal was adjourned in the expectation of a new report of the United Nations High Commissioner for Human Rights, to be reconsidered in the 61st session.

Main criteria established by the norms:

- Corporations shall ensure that they have no negative impact on the enjoyment of human rights in its widest sense.
- Corporations shall establish internal mechanisms that ensure compliance with human rights.
- Corporations shall submit to independent monitoring.
- Corporations shall ensure non-discriminatory practices.
- Corporations shall not benefit from contexts where International Humanitarian Right is violated.
- Corporations shall respect labour rights.
- Corporations shall maintain fair marketing practices.
- Corporations shall respect the environment and contribute to sustainable development.

---

[36] Sub-Commission on the Prevention of Discrimination and Protection of Minorities of the Economic and Social Committee of the United Nations, *Principles Relating to the Human Rights Conduct of Companies*, working document of Mr David Weissbrodt, E/CN.4/Sub.2/2000/WG.2/WP.1 of 25 May 2000, pp. 11–13.

- These criteria shall be applicable to contractors, sub-contractors and suppliers.
- Corporations shall provide prompt, effective and adequate reparation to persons, entities and communities.

3.   European Union Green Paper on Corporate Social Responsibility[37]

Corporate Social Responsibility (CSR) and its linking with human rights has gradually become part of the agenda of the European Union (EU). The European Parliament (EP) began to examine the subject in the late 1990s, but it was not until 2001 that the Commission published its Green Paper on CSR[38] and July 2002 when they completed their strategy with a Communication[39] on the subject.

The first initiative on the social responsibility of European companies in the EP took place in the nineties. At the end of 1998, the EP discussed a resolution on creating a code of conduct for European companies who operated in SDS (Still in Development States). The EP had over the years supported the need for development and monitoring of codes of conduct addressed at the business sector. In December 1996, the Annual Report on Human Rights called for the creation of a code for European companies operating in third countries to force them to respect human rights (including civil, social, economic and environmental rights) with the inclusion of control and sanction mechanisms.

In December 1997, the EP approved a report on offshoring and direct foreign investments in third countries, in which the need was reiterated for the creation of a code of conduct devoted to European companies based in human rights. It is recommended that companies undertake to respect in their activities the requirements that figure on the list in the Official Journal of the EC as guarantees of human rights.

Finally, the 'Resolution on EU standards for European enterprises operating in developing countries: towards a European code of conduct' of the EP (A4-0508/98), a proposal by Richard Howitt was approved in January 1999. If we refer to the contents of the resolution, we note the strong appeal to the Commission for (1) the establishment of a code of conduct; (2) the creation of the independent and impartial 'European Monitoring Platform' to which formal complaints could be made; (3) as a temporary measure, the EP would designate specialist *rapporteurs* and hold public sessions of the EP with the presence of observers; (4) the inclusion of the Declaration of the ILO on labour principles and rights (1998) in EU agreements with third countries;

---

[37]   Commission of the European Community, *Green Paper on Promoting a European Framework for Corporate Social Responsibility*, Brussels, 18.7.2001 (COM (2001) 366 end) pp. 14–16. See <http://www.europa.eu.int/comm/employment_social/soc-dial/csr/csr_index.htm>.
[38]   *Ibid.*
[39]   Commission of the European Community, *Communication from the Commission concerning Corporate Social Responsibility: a Business Contribution to Sustainable Development*, COM (2002) 347 – end, 2 July 2002.

(5) the proposal of incentives for companies to comply with international standards and facilities for access to EU funding and (6) the possibility of acquiring a 'social label'.

Some years later, after the subject had matured sufficiently within the European Union, the Green Paper on promoting a European framework for Corporate Social Responsibility[40] addressed this issue in terms of the role that could be played by companies that decide voluntarily to contribute to a better society. The paper is a direct contribution to the goal of making the EU the most competitive and dynamic knowledge-based economy in the world, capable of sustainable economic growth with more and better jobs and greater social cohesion (March 2000 Lisbon European Council). The Green Paper also makes clear, however, that codes of conduct do not substitute for national and international laws, but can complement them.

Regarding human rights, the Green Paper argues that CSR is closely linked to human rights, above all in international activities and supply chains. The Paper also mentions the environment and sustainable development in its references to human rights, implying a broad interpretation of corporate human rights that includes what have been defined as 'third generation rights'. There is a growing conviction, it asserts, that the impact of company activities on the rights of employees and local communities goes beyond the field of labour rights as such. The EU also argues for the need for information and training in this field, both within and outside the company. Finally, it highlights the need for gradual and continuous improvement in levels of protection for human rights, including proactive action to promote human rights in the corporate arena.

4.   OECD Guidelines for Multinational Enterprises[41]

The OECD Guidelines are voluntary recommendations addressed by governments to multinational enterprises operating in or from adhering countries. These Guidelines form part of the OECD Declaration on International Investment and Multinational Enterprises adopted in 1976 to facilitate direct investment in its Member States. They provide voluntary principles and standards for responsible business conduct, forming the first multilateral initiative taken by several governments in the corporate human rights field. The 2000 Review of the Guidelines recommends observance of the Guidelines by enterprises wherever they operate, even outside the OECD area.

Areas dealt with in the Guidelines:

* Labour and industrial relations,
* Human rights and environment,
* Information disclosure,
* Competition, taxation,
* Science and technology.

[40]   *Ibid.*
[41]   See <http://www.oecd.org/daf/investment/guidelines/>.

The Guidelines aim to encourage positive contributions to corporate economic, environmental and social progress, and to minimize difficulties that might arise due to their incorporation. They are intended to create a common international framework of reference to complement corporate initiatives in the field. This has involved the creation of an implementation system sustained by three core concepts: National Contact Points, the OECD Committee on International Investment and Multination Enterprises (CIME) and the advisory Committees to the OECD of business and labour federations.

It should be noted that the Guidelines were reviewed in 2000 to adjust them to the new challenges presented by globalization, incorporating additional references to certain human rights. This updating of the original 1976 provisions (in a text already revised in 1979, 1982, 1984 and 1991) introduced recommendations relating to the elimination of child labour and forced labour, as well as recommendations on human rights in general, corruption, consumer rights and the need for transparency.

5.   Ethical Trading Initiative Base Code[42]

The Ethical Trading Initiative (ETI) is an 'alliance of mainly retail or consumer goods' companies, NGOs and trade unions operating in the UK, whose aim is to improve labour conditions in the global supply chains which produce goods for the UK market'.[43] The ETI Base Code and the accompanying Principles of Implementation contains nine clauses which reflect the most relevant international standards with respect to labour practices. The aim of the ETI is to identify, develop and encourage good practice in the implementation of labour rights. The Principles of Implementation set out general principles for the implementation of the Base Code.

The Base Code refers to the following circumstances:

* Employment is freely chosen,
* Freedom of association and the right to collective bargaining are respected,
* Working conditions are safe and hygienic,
* Child labour shall not be used,
* Fair living wages are paid,
* Working hours are not excessive,
* No discrimination is practised,
* Regular employment is provided, and
* No harsh or Inhumane treatment is allowed.

Thus, this initiative binds companies strictly to compliance with labour rights.

---

[42]   See <http://www.ethicaltrade.org>.
[43]   *Ibid.*

6.   Amnesty International's Human Rights Guidelines for Companies[44]

Amnesty International argues in its guidelines that corporations have the responsibility to contribute to the proactive promotion and protection of human rights. Companies, they say, must oversee the rights of their employees. Further, they have the moral and legal responsibility to use their influence in promoting respect for human rights wherever they operate. Here Amnesty International tells companies must go beyond specifying policies and practices on staff and safety systems. They must not stand aside if they could pressurize governments or armed groups who are committing violations of human rights within their areas of influence.

The guidelines refer to the following criteria on human rights:

- Community rights,
- Labour rights,
- Right to non-discriminatory treatment,
- Right to freedom from slavery,
- Health and security,
- Freedom of association and right to collective bargaining, and
- Equitable employment conditions.

These guidelines offer companies a basic framework for developing human rights policies in a wider sense and provide a checklist of principles based on internationally accepted human rights standards that are embodied in a range of UN conventions and protocols.

7.   Global Sullivan Principles for Corporate Social Responsibility[45]

In 1977 the Reverend Leon Sullivan launched the Sullivan Principles with the aim 'to persuade US companies with investments in South African to treat their African employees the same as they would their American counterparts'.[46] These principles were then re-launched in 1999 as the Global Sullivan Principles for Corporate Social Responsibility and they are supposed to be applicable to companies operating in any part of the world.

The Global Sullivan Principles refer to the support for:[47]

- Universal human rights,
- Equal opportunities,
- Respect for freedom of association,

---

[44]   See <http://www.amnesty.org.uk/business/pubs.shtml#guidelines>.
[45]   See <http://www.globalsullivanprinciples.org>.
[46]   *Ibid.*
[47]   *Ibid.*

- Levels of employee compensation,
- Training,
- Health and safety,
- Sustainable development,
- Fair competition, and
- Working in partnership to improve quality of life.

According to the organization, a company adhering to the Principles is expected to provide information which demonstrates its commitment to them. The Principles have been endorsed and implemented by companies, business organizations, business councils, non-governmental organizations, local authorities, etc. To date (April 2004), around 100 companies have expressed their commitment with the Principles worldwide.

8.   Social Accountability 8000[48]

Social Accountability International (SAI), a non-profit organization based in New York (known until recently as the Council on Economic Priorities Accreditation Agency), addressed the growing concern about labour conditions around the world by developing in 1998 a standard for workplace conditions (Social Accountability 8000), as well as a system for independently verifying factories compliance. As the organization states, 'SA8000 is promoted as a voluntary, universal standard for companies interested in auditing and certifying labour practices in their facilities and those of their suppliers and vendors. It is designed for independent third party certification'.[49] SA8000 certifies compliance through independent auditors. On human rights, SA 8000 refers to labour rights and envisages the following nine principles based on international human rights norms such as the International Labour Organisation conventions, the United Nations Convention on the Rights of the Child and the Universal Declaration of Human Rights.
   SA8000 nine principles:

- Child labour,
- Forced labour,
- Health and safety,
- Compensation,
- Working hours,
- Discrimination, and
- Free association and collective bargaining.

This proposal, which allows companies themselves to manage implementation of labour rights, includes both negative rights (prohibition of forced labour, for example) and positive rights (stating for example that companies must ensure a living wage).

---

[48]   See <http://www.cepaa.org>.
[49]   *Ibid.*

9.   Global Reporting Initiative Guidelines[50]

The Global Reporting Initiative (GRI), with headquarters in Amsterdam, is 'a multi-stakeholder process and independent institution whose mission is to develop and disseminate globally applicable Sustainability Reporting Guidelines'.[51] The GRI voluntary Guidelines released in 2000 and aimed to help organizations to report on the economic, environmental, and social dimensions of their activities, products, and services were reviewed in 2002[52] after a wide multi-stakeholder and consulting process. These currently form the main international frame of reference for CSR reporting and incorporate parameters based on human rights.

This initiative was set up in 1997 by the Coalition for Environmentally Responsible Economies (CERES) but in 2002 the GRI became independent. Nowadays it is an official collaborating organization of the United Nations Environment Programme (UNEP) and works in cooperation with the Global Compact. Nevertheless, the GRI also incorporates the active participation of a wide range of stakeholders such as corporations, governments, non-governmental organizations, consultancies, accountancy organizations, business associations, rating organizations, universities, and research institutes which contribute to the ongoing development of the GRI materials. In fact, a series of additional instruments has been developed to facilitate reporting; for example, technical protocols, sector supplements and issue guidance documents. To date, more than 400 organizations all over the world have published reports that adopt part or all of the Guidelines. Nonetheless, one of the most frequent criticisms of this system is that the GRI does not assess the conformity of reports or certify compliance regarding the Guidelines.

In the section devoted to social reporting, the GRI uses several human rights indicators based on a series of international human rights instruments. For example, the Tripartite Declaration of Principles relating to Multinational Enterprises and Social Policies (ILO) and the OECD Guidelines for Multinational Enterprises.

Social indicators are based on the following labour rights and other human rights:

Labour practices and decent work:
- Employment
- Labour/management relations
- Health and safety
- Training and education
- Diversity and opportunity

Human rights:
- Strategy and management
- Non-discrimination
- Freedom of association and collective bargaining

---

[50]   *Ibid.*
[51]   *Ibid.*
[52]   A fresh revision is expected in 2005.

- Child labour
- Forced and compulsory labour
- Disciplinary practices (additional indicator)
- Security practices (additional indicator)
- Indigenous rights (additional indicator)

This reporting initiative emphasizes that 'an organization's contribution in the area of labour practices should not be simply to protect and respect basic rights; it should also be to enhance the quality of the working environment and value of the relationship to the worker (...). Human rights indicators under human rights help assess how a reporting organization helps maintain and respect the basic rights of a human being'.[53] Unlike other initiatives, the GRI also includes a reference in its section on group rights to the rights of indigenous peoples.

10.   Corporate Initiatives

If initiatives taken from the company side are examined we find that, in practice, increasing numbers of these are citing human rights in their corporate codes of conduct or triple bottom line reporting as universal values governing their actions. Others, without making explicit mention of human rights, incorporate them in both policy and practice.[54] Also significant over the last ten years is how quickly human rights are being embraced by companies. This growing response to a new and changing scenario has sometimes been very high-profile, in the wake of the numerous scandals, trials and campaigns implicating some companies and their *anything goes strategies*. At other times it has been a discrete process of gradually impregnating corporate business strategies elsewhere.

In this first, reactive – phase, largely during the eighties and nineties, companies began referring to human rights in their corporate codes in reaction to surveillance by certain organizations and media, denouncing examples of poor company management, mainly in transnationals in the textile and mining sectors. Here, a growing number of European companies and several key economic sectors mainly in OECD countries began constructing their human rights responsibilities by adopting a code of conduct or statement of principles.[55]

According to a survey carried out by the Ashridge Center for Business and Society on the 500 most important companies in the world (*Fortune*), the following human rights appear in their statements of principles, codes of principles or corporate strategy.

---

[53]   *Ibid.*
[54]   Mikael K. Addo, 'Human Rights and Transnational Corporations: An Introduction' in Mikael K. Addo (ed.), *Human Rights and the Responsibility of Transnational Corporations*, Kluwer Law International, London, 1999, pp. 28–29.
[55]   OECD (1998) Trade Directorate, *Codes of Corporate Conduct: An Inventory*, OECD, TD/TC/WP(98)74/End.

Discrimination based on race, sex, language or political or religious grounds	94%
Occupational safety and health at work	92%
Rights of local communities	66%
Right of people to protect and respect their cultural identity	58%
Right of association and trades union rights	38%
Prohibition of child labour	34%
Prohibition of forced labour	30%
Reference to UN international human rights instruments	16%

Source: Based on Andrew Wilson, Chris Gribben, *Business Responses to Human Rights,* Ashridge Center for Business and Society, April 2000, p. 15.

Later, a growing number of companies became involved, not just developing a discourse on their web pages but actually putting into practice specific human rights policies.[56] During this second-proactive-phase, more and more companies have been adopting corporate policies on human rights,[57] diagnosing risks in human rights terms and introducing appropriate mechanisms, methodologies and internal and external assessment systems. So it should come as no surprise that during the current more mature phase companies are moving from words to deeds and starting to create new instruments for management. By creating new challenges, methodologies and systems of assessment for organizations to manage, this development will undoubtedly be one of the keystones in company image and reputation and company legitimacy of the future.

Here, the Ashridge Center for Business and Society also stated that:

44% of companies recognized that their codes make some reference to human rights (above all European companies and those in the mining sector)

60% of companies had someone responsible for human rights management (a department or person assumes this responsibility)

60% of companies had someone or a department responsible for human rights management

36% of companies say they have at some time decided not to proceed with a foreign investment because of concerns over human rights issues although many of these decisions are not viewed as human rights decisions but are considered simply as business decisions.

19% of companies recognized having disinvested from a particular country because of concerns about human rights issues (above all in the USA)

Source: Andrew Wilson, Chris Gribben, Business Responses to Human Rights, Ashridge Center for Business and Society, April 2000, pp. 2–3.

[56]   Christopher L. Avery, *Business and Human Rights in a time of Change,* Amnesty International UK, London, 2000.

[57]   Peter Frankental and Frances House, *Human Rights, Is It Any of Your Business?* Amnesty International UK and The Prince of Wales Business Leaders Forum, London, 2000.

After analysing these initiatives from different fields it can be said to be empirically proven that human rights are indeed on the agendas of companies, international bodies and the third sector.

However, this process is not free from debate and there are currently many and diverse debates on the matter (not only on the legal vs voluntary issue[58]) which basically focus on following questions: (1) What human rights should the company take into account? Are we talking about labour rights alone or about the impact of companies on a wider range of human rights; and (2) What is the area of influence of companies on human rights? Which stakeholders do companies consider in their human rights strategy, and consequently what is the scope and what are the limits of their responsibility?

To help explore the terms of this debate we first analysed the type of human rights mentioned by some of the main CSR initiatives analysed above. The attached table gives a summary of which human rights the different CSR initiatives linked to the corporate field.

Here we can decide whether the various instruments refer to respect for human rights in their widest sense, including first, second and third generation rights, or whether they are limited to the labour and environmental rights traditionally linked to corporate CSR. It was also thought appropriate to give cases where the initiative refers to international human rights instruments, since it was felt that these should be the main reference points for corporate human rights strategy.

Main instruments on CSR and human rights.

Initiatives/references to:	Human rights	Labour rights	Environmental rights	Reference to international instruments
Instruments for promotion				
Global Compact	√	√	√	√
UN Norms	√	√	√	√
Green Paper	√	√	√	√
OECD Guidelines	√	√	√	√
ETI Code		√		√
AI Guidelines	√	√		√
Sullivan Principles	√	√	√	
Accreditation systems				
SA8000	√	√		√
Accountability and reporting systems				
GRI Guidelines	√	√	√	√

Source: Own figures from European Commission, Directorate – General for Employment and Social Affairs, *Mapping Instruments for Corporate Social Responsibility*, European Commission, Luxembourg, 2003.

---

[58] Rory Sullivan (ed.), *Business and Human Rights. Dilemmas and Solutions*, Greenleaf Publishing, Sheffield, 2003, pp. 22–32.

As the table shows, most CSR instruments analysed include as valid parameters for promotion, certification and/or reporting a wide range of human rights, not limited to labour rights. Such CSR instruments include what has been called the universal, indivisible and inherent nature of human rights, thus linking companies to international standards of first, second and third generation human rights in their area of influence and their daily *praxis*. Judging from our analysis, there are no 'first-class' and 'second-class' human rights in Corporate Social Responsibility. However, initiatives do place special emphasis on labour rights and rights relating to the protection of the environment. This takes us back to the proposal of the Green Paper on promoting a European framework for Corporate Social Responsibility, which argues that there is a growing conviction that company activities have an impact on the rights of its employees and local communities that goes beyond the labour rights field.

As regards how to define the area of influence of the company on human rights areas and the scope and limitations of corporate responsibility, it is salient to remember the focus proposed by the Global Compact. This invites companies not only to respect the international protection of human rights in their area of influence, but also to ensure that they are not complicit in human rights abuses. It is common these days to assume that direct responsibility (in respect for human rights in a company's area of influence, including suppliers, customers and partners) goes hand in hand with a broader indirect responsibility, regarding company complicity in human rights abuses committed by other actors (dictatorships, armed groups, etc.), and in which it plays a negative or positive role.

The area of influence any company over human rights will be strongly influenced by the type of relationships it establishes, and with which of its stakeholders. Stakeholder theory presents a systematic view of the relationships a company establishes with its environment, in other words with each individual or group of individuals who can affect or be affected by its objectives or activities. It therefore gives a face to the groups for whose human rights the company is responsible. Using this perspective, a company assumes its responsibilities and evaluates the consequences of its actions in the social sphere. Seen from the stakeholder viewpoint, company decision-making is achieved by evaluating economic and social effects, but also human rights effects on its stakeholders. The main effect of this approach is that the company determines the scope of its human rights responsibility by taking the people affected as the central axis of its human rights strategy.

D.   THE COMPANY AND HUMAN RIGHTS: PENDING AGENDA ISSUES

In the introduction we talked about a new scenario, where new responsibilities are emerging, due to constant reconfiguration of relationships of power between civil society, the State and the company. The latter is not considered to be a mere economic actor but a social actor who interacts with others, and through its very existence shapes our *modus vivendi* and *modus operandi*, crucially determining individual enjoyment and use of human rights. In this context, if we read the preamble of the United Nations Universal Declaration of Human Rights (UDHR) about moral aspects of the system for international protection of human rights, we read:

> 'The General Assembly proclaims this Universal Declaration of Human Rights as a common standard of achievement for all peoples and all nations, to the end that every individual and every **organ of society**, keeping this Declaration constantly in mind, shall strive by teaching and education to promote respect for these rights and freedoms and by progressive measures, national and international, to secure their universal and effective recognition and observance, both among the peoples of Member States themselves and among the peoples of territories under their jurisdiction'. (bold added).

This text argues that both companies, as authentic economic and social organs of present-day societies, and individuals jointly with States and nations, are invited to respect and ensure respect for the principles proclaimed in the UDHR. Although the UDHR is not in itself legally binding, it represents a universal commitment to the defence of the basic rights of the individual. Apart from this, Article 30 of the UDHR states that 'Nothing in this Declaration may be interpreted as implying for any State, group or person any right to engage in any activity or to perform any act aimed at the destruction of any of the rights and freedoms set forth herein'.

Today, the Gordian Knot still waiting to be undone is, beyond how to manage human rights in the company, how to measure business management in terms of human rights. In this sense, companies have recourse to creating indicators to help them evaluate their compliance with human rights and to correct inappropriate practices and processes. The Human Rights Compliance Assessment of the Danish Center for Human Rights[59] is an instrument that tries to bring human rights into corporate management through a specific database on policies, practices and indicators of assessment.

Seen from this perspective, CSR and human rights policy may be on the way to becoming a definitive part of overall business strategy, included in corporate strategy and decision-making. Today the challenges of international competitiveness demand that companies not only know how to manage crises of reputation in the media, but also gain comparative advantage through their human rights record.

No less important in this process is its spin-off: the establishment of new relationships, new collaborations with the third sector, involving co-responsibility for and 'co-construction' of projects. During this construction, in which company managers engage in constant internal-external interaction, dialogues with stakeholders are indispensable. We are looking, then, at a challenge to capacity for participation and commitment. A challenge which will end in the conclusion that without respect for human rights, CSR could not exist. Although respect for human rights might be seen as an integral part of responsible 21st-century businesses and business leadership, we must bear in mind that this is a complex issue, presently under construction. And like other process under construction, it suffers all the contradictions and difficulties common to all creative processes.

[59]   See <http://www.humanrightsbusiness.org/>.

BIBLIOGRAPHY

Mikael K. Addo (ed.), *Human Rights and the Responsibility of Transnational Corporations*, Kluwer Law International, London, 1999.

Amnesty International, *Report 2003*, Amnesty International Publications, London, 2003.

Christopher L. Avery, *Business and Human Rights in a time of Change*, Amnesty International UK, London, 2000.

Commission of the European Community, *Green Paper on Promoting a European Framework for Corporate Social Responsibility*, Brussels, 18.7.2001 (COM (2001) 366 end).

Council of the European Union, *Annual Report on human rights of the European Union 2003*, Brussels, 13 October 2003.

Department of Public Information of the United Nations, DPI/1820/Rev.1 June 1998.

European Commission, Directorate – General for Employment and Social Affairs, *Mapping Instruments for Corporate Social Responsibility*, European Commission, Luxembourg, 2003.

Human Rights Watch, *World Report*, New York, 2003.

Peter Frankental, Frances House, *Human Rights, is it any of your Business?* Amnesty International UK and The Prince of Wales Business Leaders Forum, London, 2000.

Felipe Gómez Isa, 'Las empresas transnacionales y los derechos humanos' in *Boletín de Estudios Económicos*, Vol. LV, No. 170, August 2000.

OECD, Management of Small business, *Codes of Corporate: An Inventory*, OECD, TD/TC/WP(98)74/End, 1998.

OHCHR, *Business and Human Rights: A Progress Report*, Geneva, 2000.

School of Peace Culture, *Alert 2004! Report on Conflicts, Human Rights and Peacebuilding*, School of Peace Culture, Barcelona, 2004.

Sub-Commission on Prevention of Discrimination and Protection of Minorities of the Economic and Social Committee of the United Nations, *The relationship between enjoyment of economic, social and cultural rights and the right to development, and the working methods and activities of transnational companies*, Resolution 1998/8, 20 August 1998, E/CN.4/Sub.2/RES/1998/8.

Sub-Commission on Prevention of Discriminations and Protection of Minorities of the Economic and Social Committee of the United Nations, *Principles relating to the conduct of companies on human rights issues*, working document of Mr David Weissbrodt, *Principles relating to the conduct of companies on human rights issues*, working document of Mr David Weissbrodt, E/CN.4/Sub.2/ 2000/WG.2/ WP.1 25 May 2000.

Rory Sullivan (ed), *Business and Human Rights. Dilemmas and Solutions*, Greenleaf Publishing, Sheffield, 2003.

Andrew Wilson, Chris Gribben, *Business Responses to Human Rights*, Ashridge Center for Business and Society, April 2000.

Chapter 11

CORPORATE SOCIAL RESPONSIBILITY AND INTERNATIONAL HUMAN RIGHTS LAW*

David Kinley†

A. INTRODUCTION

There is a new architecture for human rights protection that is currently emerging. It has been borne of the expansion within international law of the notions of what are the proper and possible subjects at international law and what are the proper and possible objects. Thus – slowly from the first, wholesale establishment of inter-governmental organizations (IGOs) immediately post-1945, and more quickly over the last 20 years or so – individuals, groups, inter-governmental organizations, non-governmental organizations (NGOs) and now even possibly corporations, have been admitted in one form or other into the fold of international law. What is especially significant about this development in the present context, is that so much of it has been brokered by international human rights law.

The emergence of this new architecture has flowed directly from the primacy in international law that is now afforded to the two great globalizing enterprises of economic liberalisation on the one hand, and human rights standardization (or universalization) on the other. For alongside the separate, though related matter of the legitimacy of military intervention, the legitimacy of interventions based on economic or humanitarian rationales are equally questioned in international law.

B. THIRD PARTIES AT INTERNATIONAL LAW

In the arena of international relations – if less so, or not at all, in international law – non-state actors have a long history of conspicuous presence and impact.

---

* This chapter is based on a paper presented to the *Culture and Technologies in Asia: The Paradigm Shifts,* Monash University Research Unit on Culture and Technologies in Asia Conference held in Mumbai, India, 9–13 February 2004.
† Professor of Human Rights Law, University of Sydney, Australia.

Ramon Mullerat (ed.), Corporate Social Responsibility: The Corporate Governance of the 21st Century, 205–214.

For example, in the 19th century: International Committee of the Red Cross, and the first transnational corporations (TNCs) of the English and Dutch East India companies and the British South Africa company; and the International Labour Organization (ILO) and Permanent Court of International Justice in the early 20th century. Orthodoxy held however that states were the only significant actors on the international law stage – hence *inter-national*. The mushrooming of international bodies after WWII – not just under the UN's broad auspices, but also the Organization of American States, the Council of Europe, and the EEC/EU, as well as NATO & the Warsaw Pact, GATT and the World Bank and the IMF – began to challenge that, such that speaking parts were also found for these inter-governmental organizations. And as some of them (especially in the field of human rights) spawned international legal regimes that targeted individuals and groups – bestowing on them rights and some responsibilities, so the cast grew. And latterly auditioning has progressed in respect of NGOs, especially international NGOs and TNCs.

All this has resulted in reformulations, redefinitions and re-labeling of international law concepts and terms. The 'subject/object dichotomy' in international law as well as the term 'international' itself have become unfashionable, and are now often replaced by the more chic, and more accurate terminology of 'participants' and 'transnational' (or 'supranational'), respectively. In legal terms then, states retain the principal roles, but they now share the stage. Indeed, this much has been recognized at least since the earliest days of the UN itself, in that the UN Charter (1945) expressly stipulates the separate human rights responsibilities of the States Parties (in Art. 56) and the UN and all its agencies (in Art. 55), and the Preamble to the UN's seminal human rights instrument – the Universal Declaration on Human Rights (1948) – proclaims that 'every *individual* and every *organ of society* ... shall strive to promote respect for these rights and freedoms and by progressive measures, national and international, to secure their universal and effective recognition and observance ...'

Certainly, these developments reflect the *real politik* of the international sphere, but they have posed problems for international law, especially in respect of enforcement, and further, especially in terms of enforcement of international human rights standards, and regarding IGOs as well as states. For IGOs, it has concerned those organs *not* traditionally included in the field of human rights – i.e. the economically oriented International Financial Institutions (IFIs) – which is understandable, as well as the socially oriented institutions of the ILO and the UN. In relation also, to corporations international law is unclear as to the status or for some, even the fact of their legal personality, quite apart from the next step of arguing that human rights responsibilities be placed on their shoulders. The best approach to this problem, it is argued, is to take the view that whatever result of any claimed extension of international legal personality, it is not a matter of 'one size fits all' – thus '[j]ust as is the case with international organizations, the international legal personality of corporations differs from that of states'.[1] Already, corporations do have duties at international law (e.g. under treaties covering civil liability for environmental damage through oil pollution or other hazardous

---

[1]   Nicola Jägers, *Corporate Human Rights Obligations: In Search of Accountability* (2002), p. 34.

materials), and rights, for instance, regarding access to dispute settlement mechanisms (e.g. under NAFTA), so are according to the qualifying criteria of some, clearly legal personalities in public international law.

To be sure, the human rights responsibilities of all these non-state actors vary, as do any relevant mechanisms for enforcement, but the foundations are there to be built on, and thereby to establish a parallel, complementary sector of non-state actor responsibilities for human rights protection.

C.   CONSEQUENCES FOR HUMAN RIGHTS?

So, as this new architecture takes shape, the question arises: what have been, and will be, the consequences for human rights protection and promotion? Or, to put it another way, what will be the effect of expansion at international law of the categories of entities capable of bearing human rights responsibilities?

In addressing these questions, it must be stressed at the outset that when apportioning human rights responsibilities, we are not dealing with a static quantum of burden. Thus, it is not simply the case that as additional sites of responsibility are established, so the level of the state's liability in respect of human rights protection and promotion is correspondingly reduced. Rather, the human rights burden is both increased in size and to some extent differently composed, as the duty to discharge is shared out across the different entities. My aim then, at this point, is briefly to examine the precepts upon which this sharing is conducted, and how, broadly, that affects three particular categories of human rights duty-holders – namely, states; IGOs and corporations.

1.   States

Certainly, the shifts in perspective and terminology in international law indicated above, signified the end of the states' monopoly of the stage in formal terms. Still, the fundamental role of the state as the key instrument by which international law finds its domestic voice (which remains, unquestionably, its most important voice) has been preserved. In terms of the implications this has in respect of human rights responsibilities, states are generally ambivalent. For on the one hand they are at best wary, and at worst antagonist towards the prospect of IGOs such as the UN having the authority to challenge their sovereign jurisdictional claims on the grounds, essentially, that human rights require better protection than that being afforded by the state. On the other hand, states may not be at all displeased at the prospect of others, including corporations (and even certain sacrificial individuals, in respect of international criminal law), having to bear some of the responsibility for the task of protecting human rights.

In fact, there is and will be a likely increase in the state's responsibility emanating from the fact that the parameters of the state's human rights responsibility are drawn wider than merely the state ensuring that its own organs do not transgress. This is because international human rights law typically charges the state with the responsibility to ensure that it polices all human rights transgressions within its jurisdiction, no matter the legal character of the perpetrator, the responsibility is held to cover both actions by state and non-state organs alike. The fact that the state now does more policy-making and policing than direct service provision, may indeed more ably equip it to meet its jurisdictional obligations under international human rights law.

2. IGOs

Historically, the human rights responsibilities have been considered to reside wholly and solely with the socially-oriented IGOs, that is, typically, the UN and the ILO, and those IGOs whose broad mandates have allowed them to develop social or human rights agendas – for example, the Council of Europe, Organization of American States, Organization of African Unity (now African Union). The economically-oriented IGOs such as the World Bank and the IMF, the GATT/WTO, the OECD, and trading blocs such as the EU, NAFTA, and APEC, were not considered to have any human rights role. This is changing, in part due to the forces outlined above, but also, in the case of the EU in particular, because as the organization becomes more powerful and more intrusive, its economic bounds are weakened and its purposes become porous to such social concerns as human rights protection.

In an important respect, of course, the human rights role provided to and played by the social IGOs such as the UN has been key to the whole movement of broadening the base of human rights duty-bearers. But the ongoing nature of the movement has yielded other, less obvious, effects. Thus, for example, the UN's mounting focus on how human rights responsibilities might be spread to encompass both its economic cousins in the IGO family and corporations. In the last five years, for example, the UN has been involved in at least four major initiatives in this regard, alongside a steady stream of high level rhetoric and less formal negotiations, discussions and meetings between the UN and the various agents of economic globalisation (including, of course, the states). These vary in nature, form, status, import and potential. They are: the UN Global Compact (a largely rhetorical mechanism for engagement between business and the UN); a policy initiative of the former UN High Commissioner for Human Rights to raise the issue of business responsibilities for human rights as an important matter for discussion between states and the UN human rights committees and a 1999 policy established by UNCTAD (the UN Commission on Trade and Development) on the Social Responsibility of TNCs; and finally (and potentially most significantly) the UN's *Norms on the Responsibilities of TNCs and Other Business Enterprises in Regard to Human Rights* which after several years of largely unnoticed toil by a working group of a UN sub-committee, have received spotlight treatment at both the 2004 and 2005 annual Commission on human rights meeting in Geneva. These Norms would directly bind states and possibly also corporations to ensure that they respect the treaty provisions 'within their respective spheres of influence'.

There are also a number of other initiatives undertaken by other IGOs that reflect these human rights concerns – specifically, the ILOs revised *Tripartite Declaration of Principles Concerning Multinational Enterprises and Social Policy* (2000) and the OECD's *Guidelines for MNCs* (2000).

The debate surrounding the potential for the World Trade Organization (WTO) to take on human rights responsibilities is not so much concerned about what new instruments might be established as it is about the interpretation and application of the existing ones. The GATT/WTO legal regime already harbors a number of putatively human rights-based principles, including (a) the principle of non-discrimination (between trading nations), (b) the GATT Article XX exceptions to unfettered trade, which significantly include when it is necessary to protect human health (see, for example the WTO's French Asbestos case),[2] and (c), perhaps most tellingly, the conspicuously well-protected intellectual property rights under the Agreement on Trade-Related Aspects of Intellectual Property Rights (TRIPs). This is telling because as no less than George Soros puts it:

'The WTO opened up a Pandora's box when it became involved in intellectual property rights. If IP rights are a fit subject for the WTO, why not labour rights, or human rights?'[3]

This point bears dwelling upon. For, whatever the merits of a wider human rights remit for the WTO (and I return to this debate in the final section), it simply cannot be said that human rights are improper concerns in trade debates and are alien to WTO thinking. The manner in which intellectual property rights are protected under TRIPs demonstrates both their importance to trade and, on the part of the WTO, a significant degree of comfort with rights protection of this particular kind. For not only does the TRIPs agreement break the mould of WTO treaties dealing only with the rights and obligations of states (it expressly provides for the rights of individuals (and corporations)), the whole intellectual property regime self-consciously operates as a trade barrier, rather trade liberalizer. The very objection that is often raised against any suggestion that human rights generally ought to be incorporated into trade law is permitted in respect of intellectual property rights. The push to build upon and expand these human rights dimensions in trade law will certainly increase in the near future.

Finally, the campaigns to have the World Bank (alongside the regional development banks in Asia, America and Europe) and the IMF take seriously the human rights impact of their economic aid and development policies have at times foundered on rocks of the minimalist interpretation of the Articles of Agreement of both institutions which arguably forbid them to pursue policies that have any political (or social) purposes or effects. This has been so, despite at times the colorfulness of the debates (such as that of former Bank Chief Economist and top Clinton adviser), Joe Stiglitz's attack on the IMF in particular for what he considers to be wilful blindness over its unavoidable and often considerable, *non*-economic footprint).[4]

In point of fact, the IMF is certainly more intransigent on this point than the World Bank, due in part to the Funds untrammeled focus on the major economic levers of a state in need – inflation and monetary policy, fiscal management and

---

[2]   WTO Appellate Body Report, *European Communities – Measures Affecting Asbestos and Asbestos-containing Products,* WTO DOC, WT/DS135/AB/R (12 March 2001).

[3]   Quoted by P. Alston, 'Resisting the Merger and Acquisition of Human Rights by Trade Law: A Reply to Petersmann', (2002) 13(4) *European Journal of International Law* 815, 818.

[4]   *Globalization and its Discontents* (2003).

public sector debt. The Bank's more micro-economic, development-project oriented agenda has perhaps allowed it at least to entertain the idea of the relevance of human rights to its actions. So, whilst it is a long way from embracing a human rights approach in its policy-making processes, or even from developing a specific human rights policy, it is at least apparently prepared to concede the impact its actions have on human rights. The Bank's President, Jim Wolfensohn, is adamant that the Bank 'is already engaged in human rights' and that it is, in fact, 'one of the major protectors and developers of programs which ... give rights to people, starting with reducing poverty and the desire to give people the chance for a better life'.[5] What is remarkable about this statement is not so much that it is so stridently put, but the fact that such stridency is necessary to state the obvious. It is little exaggeration to say that the Bank's key strategic and operating principles – as guided now by the Millennium Development Goals – are designed so as to promote the respect and protection of some of the most basic human rights; namely, the rights to self-determination, to life and an adequate standard of living, to participate in public affairs, to education and the freedom of expression, to work and to health and to a clean and safe environment. It is just that the economists who fill the Bank's offices in Washington DC are neither conversant nor comfortable with articulating these aims in human rights terms. Such schizophrenia may not sit easily with the Bank; but it is now, increasingly, expected of it.

3.   Corporations

In many respects, some of the most significant developments regarding the human rights responsibilities of corporations at international law are coming through a number of the initiatives detailed above, albeit by way of indirect regulation. For even when their provisions concern the behavior of corporations, these instruments are, or would be, directly binding on states at international law; the corporation being itself then directly responsible to the state(s) within whose jurisdiction it operates.[6]

Outside these initiatives, the vast bulk of the legal regulation of corporations in terms of human rights is performed by domestic legislation and law; though, by virtue of the extraterritorial dimensions of some of these (most notably the USA's *Alien Torts Claims Act* and reforms to the common law notion of *forum non conveniens*), they might be vested with some 'international' element, even if short of constituting part of international law proper.

D.   INTERNATIONAL ECONOMIC ACTORS AND HUMAN RIGHTS

Lumping all the international economic actors (IEAs) together – that is, the international financial institutions of the IMF and the World Bank (together with

---

5   World Bank seminar entitled, 'Human Rights and Sustainable Development. What Role for the Bank?' 2 May 2002, Washington DC.
6   See further D. Kinley and J. Tadala 'From Talk to Walk: The Emergence of Human Rights Responsibilities For Corporations at International Law' (2004) 4 *Virginia Journal of International Law*, 931, 960–61.

the regional development banks of Asia, Africa and the Americas), the WTO and other economic or quasi-economic IGOs and TNCs – I turn now to review the current position as well as consider what are the prospects for the greater involvement of IEAs in the protection and promotion of human rights.

Simplistic arguments on the matter of IEAs roles in human rights protection are just that, and therefore have little use beyond their undoubted, but still limited, rhetorical impact. To say blandly that the 'business of business is business', or that international trade has nothing to do with human rights (or equally the doublespeak claim that free trade is all about the alleviation of poverty (and therefore by implication all about protecting human rights), or even that economic theorising and policy-making is severable from its social impacts is to defy reality and deny fact. But it is little better to assert that corporations should replace the profit motive with a human rights motive, or that all IEAs should be made responsible for the protection of all human rights recognized under international law equally, and that they be expected to bear the duties to protect those rights under international law in much the same way as do states.

4.   Whether?

All that said, there remains the crucial question of *whether* IEAs as a group or in their individual sub-groups, ought be made subject to a duty to protect human rights. Albeit, obviously, to varying degrees and in different formats, my answer is: yes they should. Their collective capacity to generate change at all levels of inter- and intra-national relations in social, economic, political, cultural and legal terms power is as considerable as it is obvious, and with it must come responsibilities commensurate with such power. To the extent then that the various actions of IEAs impact upon human rights – and the impact is diverse and substantial – means must be established to articulate their responsibility for the results of their actions and mechanisms devised to regulate and enforce such responsibility. Both the human rights impact and the need for responses to it are especially significant in developing countries, where, either through design or incapacity, the state's record of protection and promotion of human rights is poor. For as the impact of TNCs and the WTO is heightened in Developing Countries (DCs) and Least Developing Countries (LDCs) and as it is in the developing world alone that the aid and development agencies operate, the potential for IEAs to do good and bad is often very great indeed. This is not to say that the DC and LDC governments ought to be in some way relieved of their human rights obligations at international law – and it should be noted here that as a combined group, the 120 DC and LDC states have a better ratification record than the 75 economically developed states across the UN's six principal human rights instruments (even accepting that implementation is another matter altogether) – but rather that IEAs can have a important complementary or supporting role to play alongside the state.

In any event, the pressure on IEAs to recognize, respect and protect human rights is growing across many fronts – political, community, legal and even economic (for instance the argument that human rights friendly corporations, following in the footsteps of environmentally-friendly corporations, can thereby gain a competitive edge). The prospect of being the 'Enron of human rights'[7] is not an appealing one for any TNC; the chiding that the IMF and World Bank receive over their reluctance to acknowledge the impact of its activities on human rights – both in positive and negative ways; and the persistent questioning of the WTO's ambiguous and sometimes hypocritical relationship with human rights are all significant features of the general movement. The particular role of international law is also instrumental in providing the vehicle by which human rights responsibilities might be mediated on the international plane, and by providing a backdrop to the development of domestic legal initiatives.

5. Which?

The matter of the interrelationship between IEAs and states on human rights responsibilities is a crucial one. This is because the argument that IEAs, to vary-ing degrees, can be expected to protect and promote human rights, is subject to a pair of key qualifications. These are: (i) that the human rights that IEAs ought to be obliged to protection and promotion cannot be the same, either in breadth or form, as those that states are mandated to protect, and (ii) that whatever the catalogue of rights, the manner of the obligation imposed on IEAs cannot be the same as that for states.

The question of 'which rights?', is one that has exercised the minds of a number of commentators, nearly all of whom focus on establishing some sort of framework within which to classify those rights that can and should be protected by IEAs and those which cannot or need not be. Thus, for example, adaptations to the classic 'three Ps' formulation for states obligations – to *prevent* human rights abuses, to *provide* human rights protection, and to *promote* human rights – is one way forward. In this respect, and regarding TNCs, Tadaki and I have, else-where, made a distinction between what we call a 'self-reflexive duty' (mainly prevention of human rights abuses by the TNC itself) and a 'third-party duty' (mainly aiding protection and promotion of human rights by others (principally the state)).[8] The former category (which includes the rights to life, liberty and physical integrity, labor rights, health, education, indigenous and environmental rights directly related to the enterprise) constitute core and immediate human rights obligations that TNCs ought to be made subject to; the latter category, which might potentially stretch across many economic, social and cultural rights and a number of related civil and political rights (e.g. right to privacy, freedom of speech and thought, and fair trial) might comprise a second tier of desirable, but not immediately applicable human rights duties for TNCs.

With some adaptations, similar frameworks might be used in respect of determining the appropriate rights duties of the World Bank, the IMF and even the WTO.

---

[7]   Elliot Schrage 'Emerging Threat: Human Rights Claims' 81(8) (Aug. 2003) Harvard Business Review, Forethought, Memorandum.

[8]   D. Kinley & J. Tadaki, 'From Talk to Walk: The Emergence of Human Rights Responsibilities for Corporations at International Law', (2004) 44 *Virginia Journal of International Law* 931.

6.   What?

The parallel question of 'what obligation?' closely follows from the above in that the nature of the obligation must be commensurate with the type of rights required to be protected. The key, once again, appears to lie in the framework one adopts to determine the question. It is clearly inappropriate to use the formulation adopted in many international human rights instruments to bind signatory states – namely, that they must ensure, by whatever means are appropriate, the rights covered in the instrument to all within their jurisdiction and to protect their human rights from threats that emanate from public or private entities. The approach adopted in the UN's Human Rights Norms for Corporations provides one model for addressing this problem. The Norms, whilst recognising that 'states have the primary responsibility' for human rights protection, stipulate that corporations and other business enterprises have the obligation to protect human rights *'within their respective spheres of activity and influence'*, which obligation would – in any *legal* sense – be mediated through state regulation rather than constitute a new, free-standing obligation placed directly on corporations.

Beyond the axiomatic assertion that IEAs are not states, and are therefore not to be treated as states are treated at international law, the twin qualifications of the 'which' human rights and 'what' obligations, arise, in fact, out of concerns as to capacity and legitimacy. As regards capacity, for instance, by virtue of their very economic rationales, IEAs generally speaking possess neither the expertise in, nor the understanding of, human rights to be able to devise policies and pursue effective programs in their protection. Thus, the almost overwhelming incidence of economists in the World Bank and IMF (the 'prizing of economists' as Darrow puts it) does not lend itself easily to the breeding of a human rights-conversant culture.[9]

In respect of corporations, the tentative conclusions that my colleagues and I are able to draw from our empirical research with TNCs is that by and large they are not at all aware of the nature and scope of what constitutes human rights and how their activities affect them.[10] For most, relevant human rights (if they are recognized as human rights at all) are equated to labor and other workplace rights. The place of human rights within the context of corporate social responsibility (CSR) is for many an unrealized, and unsettling notion; and in any case for many their conception of CSR (whether with or without human rights) is based on their philanthropic activities, which can be very varied indeed. Overall, it can be fairly said that an appreciation of human rights concerns, beyond an awareness of their rhetorical use, is almost absent throughout corporate ranks. Typically, where such expertise does reside it is often in only one person (or exceptionally a small team), whose position hovers somewhere between community relations and ensuring legal compliance; in fact, interestingly, most appear to operate within the Legal Counsel's sphere of responsibility.

The capacity of the WTO in its current form to take on board human rights concerns is also something of an unknown quantity. Certainly, human rights arguments are being raised before – and being unpredictably handled – by the

---

[9]   M. Darrow, Between Light and Shadow: The World Bank, *The IMF and International Human Rights Law* (2003), p. 199.

[10]   See <www.law.monash.edu.au/castancentre/projects/mchr>

Dispute Settlement Mechanism. It is true that should it be so required greater human rights expertise could be imported onto the Panels that hear these cases. But what is perhaps of greater significance in this regard is the question of how colored will be the WTOs understanding of human rights when they are brought within its fold. Might, for instance, the WTOs importation of human rights elevate the particular and contentious 'right to trade' to the status of a human rights alongside the rights to health, adequate standard of living, education, non-discrimination etc.

Furthermore, beyond these questions as to the capacities of IEAs (at least as they stand at present) to embrace human rights responsibilities, there lies the complex question of the legitimacy of bestowing such responsibilities. I am not here referring to legitimacy in the sense of whether or not IEAs should have human rights duties (they should have, in some form), but rather in the sense of the legitimacy of IEAs to fulfil certain human rights duties – that is, those duties that might be considered to be at the outer reaches of an IEAs 'sphere of influence'. Thus, one might ask, in situations where there is an absence of an effective means to protect human rights – especially, for example, in a country where the state simply has not provided such – *and* the IEA is able to provide assistance, ought it do so? The scope here is enormous – for example, should a powerful mining TNC lobby a human rights-neglecting state in which it operates for improvements in its free speech laws or the reform of policies that discriminate against women or ethnic minorities? It will certainly already engage with the government on matters of its tax liabilities and royalty payments, and maybe even on labor and workplace health and safety laws, so why not other matters that relate directly or indirectly to its business interests also? And in light of the ambivalence of the World Bank over its human rights role, together with its relative lack of human rights knowledge, can we safely urge it to go further in its insistence on 'good governance' standards being met by recipient countries to actively push for religious freedoms, fairer elections, the relaxing of barriers to freedoms of association and movement and for speech to be made freer? There are no easy answers to these questions, and I do not have a clear idea of how they can be answered adequately, but they are matters that will have to be addressed.

E.   CONCLUSION

A new architecture of human rights responsibilities within international law is already established and its progress from drawing board to reality is under way. The bestowal of human rights duties on IEAs will continue to advance through both international and domestic initiatives. States, what is more, will likely be the key conduits – being obliged under international law to implement and supervise compliance with such human rights whether at the domestic level (in respect of corporations) or through the relevant IGO forums (in respect of, for example, the WTO, World Bank and IMF). Thus, while on the one hand states will see the burden of human rights responsibilities being rightly shared, their own role, far from diminishing will be increased. This ought to be as much a matter of concern for IEAs as it is for states, and as much a concern in developing states as in developed ones.

PART IV

WORLDWIDE INITIATIVES ON CORPORATE SOCIAL RESPONSIBILITY

Chapter 12

THE TRIPARTITE DECLARATION OF PRINCIPLES CONCERNING MULTINATIONAL ENTERPRISES*

Phillip H. Rudolph

The Tripartite Declaration of Principles concerning Multinational Enterprises ('MNEs') was adopted by the Governing Body of the International Labour Organization ('ILO') in November 1977. The Tripartite Declaration is the first universally applicable agreement on the subject of MNE behavior.[1] Its drafting was informed by the tripartite body of representatives to the ILO, including governments, employers, and workers, as well as by the work of the Organization for Economic Cooperation and Development (OECD),[2] which originally adopted Guidelines for Multinational Enterprises in 1976 (and later revised them in 2000).[3]

According to the ILO, MNEs, governments, employers' organizations, and workers' organizations are 'recommended to observe on a voluntary basis' the guidelines of the Tripartite Declaration, which primarily addresses the rights of labor. A multinational enterprise is broadly defined under the Declaration to include 'enterprises, whether they are of public, mixed or private ownership, which own or control production, distribution, services or other facilities outside the country in which they are based'. The Tripartite Declaration further states that 'this Declaration does not require a precise legal definition of multinational enterprises; [rather, the foregoing definition] is designed to facilitate the

*   Written by Phillip H. Rudolph, Partner, Foley Hoag LLP. The author would like to acknowledge and express his gratitude to Sarah Altschuller and Susan Rohol for their excellent assistance with and contribution to these materials.
1   *Tripartite Declaration of Principles Concerning Multinational Enterprises and Social Policy*, ILO, 204th Sess., O.B. Vol. LXI, Series A, No. 1, ILO Doc. 28197701 (1978), available at http://www.ilo.org/public/english/employment/multi/decl.htm (last visited 17 June 2004).
2   *Id.* See also, Surya Deva, 'Human Rights Violations by Multinational Corporations and International Law: Where from Here'? 19 *Conn. J. Int'l L.* 1, 11–12 (2003).
3   *OECD Declaration and Decisions on International Investment and Multinational Enterprises*, 21 June 1976, 15 I.L.M. 967, available at http://www.oecd.org/document/53/0,2340, en_2649_34887_1933 109_1_1_1_1,00.html (last modified 27 June 2000).

Ramon Mullerat (ed.), Corporate Social Responsibility: The Corporate Governance of the 21st Century, 217–219.
© 2005 *International Bar Association. Printed in the Netherlands.*

understanding of the Declaration.'[4] The ultimate vision behind the drafting of the Declaration was that 'adherence to the Declaration by all concerned would contribute to a climate more conducive to economic growth and social development'.[5]

The Tripartite Declaration provides a set of guidelines and challenges, broken down into five major sections, to ILO member states and MNEs. The first section specifically urges respect for national sovereignty, equality of treatment between MNEs and national enterprises, and tripartite consultation and cooperation. The second section calls on MNEs to generate and expand opportunities for stable and secure employment, use appropriate technologies, and develop structural linkages within the economy of the host country. The third section promotes training and retraining initiatives as well as the promotion of workers in all occupational categories. The fourth section recommends the provision of favorable wage rates, benefits, and work conditions, including maintenance of high standards for occupational safety and health. The fifth section urges parties to respect freedom of association, the right to organize, and collective bargaining in all matters related to industrial relations.[6] The Tripartite Declaration also makes specific reference to human rights, providing that all of the parties concerned 'should respect the Universal Declaration of Human Rights and the corresponding International Covenants adopted by the General Assembly'.[7]

A number of ILO Conventions and Recommendations reinforce the rights and obligations of MNEs as articulated in the Tripartite Declaration. The text of the Declaration was also further revised in March 2000 to incorporate the ILO Declaration on Fundamental Principles and Rights at Work.[8] The new revisions call upon governments, workers, employers, and MNEs to contribute to the realization of this Declaration and to ratify the minimum age and child labor Conventions and corresponding Recommendations.[9] Under the procedures of the Tripartite Declaration, complaints concerning a multinational corporation's noncompliance with the code's provisions should first be raised with the corporation itself and the host government. If the dispute fails to be resolved at the first level, the host government or a labor union may invoke review by the ILO's

---

[4] *Tripartite Declaration of Principles Concerning Multinational Enterprises and Social Policy*, ILO, 204th Sess., O.B. Vol. LXI, Series A, No. 1, ILO Doc. 28197701 (1978), available at http://www.ilo.org/public/english/employment/multi/decl.htm (last visited 17 June 2004).

[5] *Id.*

[6] *Id.*

[7] *Id.* at para. 8. (referring to the International Covenant on Civil and Political Rights ('ICCPR'), adopted 16 December 1966, entered into force 23 March 1976, 999 UNTS 171, reprinted in 6 ILM 368 (1967); and the International Covenant on Economic, Social and Cultural Rights ('ICESCR'), adopted 16 December 1966, entered into force 3 January 1976, G.A. Res. 2200A (XXI), UN Doc. A/6316 (1966), 993 UNTS 3, reprinted in 6 ILM 360 (1967).

[8] See *Report of the Subcommittee on Multinational Enterprises*, GB279/12 (November 2000), available at http://www.ilo.org/public/english/standards/relm/gb/docs/gb279/pdf/gb-12.pdf (last visited 17 June 2004).

[9] See Minimum Age Convention 138, entered into force 19 June 1976, and Worst Forms of Child Labor Convention 182, entered into force 19 November 2000, available at http://www.ilo.org/public/english/standards/norm/whatare/fundam/childpri.htm. See also general commentary on the History of the Tripartite Declarations from the International Labor Organization, at http://www.ilo.org/public/english/employment/multi/history.htm (last modified 9 April 2003).

Tripartite Subcommittee on Multinational Enterprises, assuming the case satisfies the jurisdictional threshold.[10]

The Declaration's guidelines, like all of the ILO's standards, are ultimately aspirational. The lack of any implementation mechanism, monitoring process, legal mandate, or even the ability of the ILO to expel egregious violators reduces the effect and reach of the Declaration. It essentially relies on public pressure to motivate offending members to alter their behavior. That is not to say the Declaration has had no impact on corporate behavior. While it is true that most of the precepts of the Declaration restate various obligations on governments taken from other sources, the reformulation of some as creating duties on corporations is significant. Given the repeated recitation of this instrument by governments, corporations, and labor organizations, it provides, at minimum, strong evidence of a consensus among the three constituencies of the Declaration that corporations have duties toward their employees.[11]

---

[10]   Christopher R. Coxson, 'The 1998 ILO Declaration on Fundamental Principles and Rights at Work: Promoting Labor Law Reforms Through the ILO as an Alternative to Imposing Coercive Trade Sanctions,' *17 Dick J. Int'l L.* 469, 481 (1999).
[11]   Steven R. Ratner, 'Corporations and Human Rights: A Theory of Legal Responsibility', *111 Yale L. J.* 443, 487 (2001).

Chapter 13

THE GLOBAL SULLIVAN PRINCIPLES OF CORPORATE SOCIAL RESPONSIBILITY*

Phillip H. Rudolph

The original Sullivan Principles were drafted in 1977 by Reverend Leon H. Sullivan to encourage US companies operating in apartheid-era South Africa to treat their African employees and business partners the same as they would their American counterparts.[1] Reverend Sullivan drafted the Principles in an effort put pressure on those doing business with the Government of South Africa to promote racial equality and to improve the quality of life of non-white populations in South Africa. This effort followed his unsuccessful efforts as a member of the Board of Directors of the General Motors Corporation to convince the company to divest from the country.[2]

Based on the fundamental principles of non-segregation, fair employment practices, and equal pay for equal work, the Sullivan Principles called for the initiation and development of training programs, the promotion of non-whites to managerial positions, and improvement of the quality of employees' lives outside the work environment.[3] The Sullivan Principles included both a voluntary code

---

* Authored by Phillip H. Rudolph, Partner, Foley Hoag LLP. The author would like to acknowledge and express his gratitude to Sarah Altschuller and Susan Rohol for their excellent assistance with and contribution to these materials.

[1] For more information on the original Sullivan Principles, see *The Global Sullivan Principles of Social Responsibility*, Corporate Social Responsibility News and Resources, at http://www.mallenbaker.net/csr/CSRfiles/Sullivan.html (last updated 13 June 2004).

[2] See Henry J. Richardson, 'Reverend Leon Sullivan's Principles, Race, and International Law: A Comment', 15 *Temp. Int'l & Comp. L. J.* 55, 56–58 (2001).

[3] The original six principles sought:

1. Non-segregation of the races in all eating, comfort and work facilities.
2. Equal and fair employment practices for all employees.
3. Equal pay for all employees doing equal or comparable work for the same period of time.
4. Initiation and development of training programs that will prepare in substantial numbers Blacks, and other non-whites for supervisory, administrative, clerical and technical jobs.
5. Increasing the number of Blacks and other non-whites in management and supervisory positions.

Ramon Mullerat (ed.), Corporate Social Responsibility: The Corporate Governance of the 21st Century, 221–224.
© 2005 *International Bar Association. Printed in the Netherlands.*

of conduct and a mandatory annual reporting system, with accompanying grading procedures that were used to classify firms.[4] The Principles were amended over the years to prescribe a minimum wage that would be above a 'living wage', to require recognition of black trade unions, and to encourage South African companies to follow equal rights principles.

Between 1977 and 1982, the number of firms that adopted the principles increased from twelve to almost 150.[5] During this time, corporate executives in South Africa began investing in the lives of black South Africans by offering scholarships, increasing the number of non-white supervisors and managers at their companies, and providing funding for health, education, and housing projects.[6] In 1987, however, Reverend Sullivan abandoned the Principles and decided to call instead for total divestment of multinationals from South Africa.[7] Even though the original Principles did not end apartheid within the time frame set by Reverend Sullivan, they have been lauded as one of the most effective efforts to end discrimination against blacks in South Africa, and are recognized as having contributed to the dismantling of apartheid.[8]

In an effort to expand the scope and reach of his efforts beyond South Africa, the Reverend Sullivan created the Global Sullivan Principles of Social Responsibility in 1997; the Principles were officially launched in 1999.[9] These new Principles rest upon two structural devices: (1) a list of core standards and pledges, and (2) transparency disclosures relevant to the standards of participating firms.[10] At their launch, Reverend Sullivan described the objectives of the Principles as being to 'encourage companies to support economic, social, and political justice wherever they do business'.[11]

6. Improving the quality of employees' lives outside the work environment in such areas as housing, transportation, schooling, recreation and health facilities.

See John Christopher Anderson, 'Respecting Human Rights: Multinational Corporations Strike Out', 2 U. Pa. J. Lab. & Emp. L. 463, 477 (2000).

[4] See Rev. Leon Sullivan. 'Agents for Change: The Mobilization of Multinational Companies in South Africa', 15 Law & Pol'y Int'l Bus. 427 (1983). For an assessment of the evolution of the principles, see generally D. Reid Weedon, Jr., 57 Business & Society Rev. 56 (1986).

[5] John Christopher Anderson, 'Respecting Human Rights: Multinational Corporations Strike Out', 2 U. Pa. J. Lab. & Emp. L. 463, 478 (2000).

[6] David Hess & Thomas W. Dunfee, 'Fighting Corruption: A Principled Approach; The C2 Principles (Combating Corruption)', 33 Cornell Int'l L.J. 593, 617–18 (2000). See also Jorge F. Perez-Lopez, 'Promoting International Respect for Worker Rights Through Business Codes of Conduct', 17 Fordham Int'l L. J. 43 (1993).

[7] David Hess & Thomas W. Dunfee, 'Fighting Corruption: A Principled Approach; The C2 Principles (Combating Corruption)', 33 Cornell Int'l L. J 593, 616–18 (2000).

[8] Henry J. Richardson, 'Reverend Leon Sullivan's Principles, Race, and International Law: A Comment', 15 Temp. Int'l & Comp. L. J. 55, 58 (2001). But see, Adelle Blackett, 'Global Governance, Legal Pluralism and the Decentered State: A Labor Law Critique of Codes of Corporate Conduct', Ind. J. Global Legal Stud. 401, fn. 21 (2001) for discussion of the limited ability of self-regulatory devices to secure labor rights absent other regulatory and enforcement measures. See also Karen Paul, 'The Inadequacy of Sullivan Reporting', 57 Business & Society Rev. 61 (1986).

[9] The Global Sullivan Principles of Social Responsibility, Corporate Social Responsibility News and Resources, at http://www.mallenbaker.net/csr/CSRfiles/Sullivan.html (last updated 13 June 2004).

[10] Henry Drummonds, 'Transnational Small and Emerging Business in a World of Nikes and Microsofts', 4 J. Small & Emerging Bus. L. 249, 281 (2000).

[11] 'The Global Sullivan Principles of Corporate Social Responsibility', MallenBaker.Net, available at http://www.mallenbaker.net/csr/CSRfiles/Sullivan.html (last checked 10 June 2004). See also David D. Caron, 'The Structure and Pathologies of Local Selective Procurement Ordinances', 21 Berkeley J. Int'l. L. 159, 164, fn. 9 (2003).

The Global Sullivan Principles were developed with the input of several multinational enterprise (MNEs) and include broad directives on labor, business ethics and environmental practices of MNEs and their business partners. The pledges and principles include: (1) express support for universal human rights; (2) promotion of equal opportunity for employees; (3) respect for employees' freedom of association; (4) compensation enabling employees to meet their basic needs and improve their skills; (5) provision of a safe and healthy workplace; (6) promotion of fair competition; and (7) cooperation with governments and communities to improve employees' quality of life, training, and opportunities.[12] In endorsing the Principles, companies agree to develop and implement policies, procedures, training, and internal reporting structures to ensure commitment to the Principles throughout their organizations. Endorsers of the Global Sullivan Principles also agree to be transparent in their implementation of the principles and to provide information that demonstrates publicly their commitment to the principles.[13]

Built on a vision of aspiration and inclusion, the Global Sullivan Principles were designed to work in conjunction with corporations' existing codes of conduct and to apply to every worker, in every industry, in every country. The Principles were created as a code of conduct that could offer a framework to align socially responsible companies and organizations working in disparate industries and cultures so as to promote the common goals of human rights, social justice, and economic development. United Nations Secretary General Kofi Annan has voiced the UN's support for the Principles, stating that 'enlightened business leaders recognize that their reputations, and even their bottom lines, are intimately tied to good corporate citizenship'.[14] Hundreds of manufacturers, service businesses, professional service firms, business associations, governments, and non-profit organizations have officially endorsed the Global Sullivan Principles. General Motors, Royal Dutch/Shell, Chevron, Colgate-Palmolive, Sunoco, and Sodexho are just some of the large multinational enterprises among the hundreds of endorsers.[15]

Since their drafting in 1977, the original Sullivan Principles have served as the inspiration for the drafters of other corporate social responsibility principles including the CERES (the Coalition for Environmentally Responsible Economies) Principles, which offer guidelines by which corporations may pursue and implement environmentally sound policies. The CERES Principles (originally known as the Valdez Principles) focus on sustainable use of natural resources; waste minimization and recycling; the wise use of energy; the marketing of safe products and

---

[12] Henry Drummonds, 'Transnational Small and Emerging Business in a World of Nikes and Microsofts', 4 *J. Small & Emerging Bus. L.* 249, 281, fn. 112 (2000). See also *Global Sullivan Principles Draw Support from Companies at United Nations Launch*, 17 Hum. Resources Rep. (BNA) 1283 (1999).

[13] Philip Berkowitz, 'Extraterritorial Application of US Employment Laws', *American Law Institute—American Bar Association Continuing Legal Education: Complying With The Labor and Employment Laws of The Nafta Countries*, 165, 172–73, (2003).

[14] *Id.*

[15] A complete list of manufacturers, service business, non profit organizations, and business associations that officially endorse the principles as of 9 October 2002 is available at http://globalsullivanprinciples.org/Endorser_list_Oct9.PDF.

services; and protection of the biosphere.[16] Organized in 1988 by the Board of Directors of the Social Investment Forum, an association of socially responsible investment firms and public pension funds, working together with leading environmentalists, the CERES Principles have been endorsed by over 70 companies, including Polaroid, Timberland, Ben & Jerry's, as well as General Motors, Bank of America, IT&T Industries, and Sunoco.[17] Indeed, by providing an early example of the effectiveness of leveraging voluntary public commitments by private actors, the Sullivan Principles have helped provide the foundation for many recent initiatives, ranging from the US-based Apparel Industry Partnership (the predecessor to the Fair Labor Association) to the UN Global Compact.

[16]   Brad Lehrman, The Social Investment Forum, in *The Social Investment Almanac* 12, 13 (Peter D. Kinder, *et al.* eds., 1992). See generally Elizabeth Glass Geltman & Andrew E. Skroback, Environmental Activism and the Ethical Investor, *22 J. Corp. L.* 465, 470–75 (1997); Valerie Ann Zondorak, A New Face in Corporate Environmental Responsibility: The Valdez Principles, 18 B.C. *Envtl. Aff. L. Rev.* 457 (1991).
[17]   For more information about CERES see http://www.ceres.org/about/main.htm.

Chapter 14

THE CAUX ROUND TABLE PRINCIPLES FOR BUSINESS: DECISION-MAKING MATRIX FOR A MORE MORAL CAPITALISM

Stephen B. Young

Ideals and values, if they are important enough, can effect social action. Mind imposes itself on the world through will. With this understanding, the Caux Round Table Principles for Business were published in 1994 to improve global business culture.

The Caux Round Table first gathered in 1986. That year, Frits Philips, then head of The Philips Company, the firm founded by his family in The Netherlands making light bulbs and consumer electronics, invited Japanese, European, and American colleagues to confront the divisive xenophobias then rampant in the automotive and consumer electronic industries. It was the time of Japanese manufacturing triumphs. Philips sought through dialogue to temper the angry passions seeking to keep Japanese companies out of Europe and America and European and American companies out of Japan. Philips was joined in this effort by Olivier Giscard d'Estaing, vice-chairman of Insead, the prestigious business school in France.

At that first meeting of what was to become the Caux Round Table, Philips' guests conceded that xenophobia, with its appeals to prejudice, ugly emotions, and racism, was no basis for global business. If the Japanese made better products for a lower price than did the Europeans and Americans, they should reap the reward of that commercial success. Conversely, European and American companies should not be excluded by acts of politics from selling in Japan's domestic markets. Business should just be business, the group concluded, and to the winner on the merits of fair competition should justly go the spoils.

Participants found the collegiality of Caux contagious and returned once a year to reaffirm their sensibility about the international professionalism of business. Leadership of the group then shifted to Ryuzaburo Kaku, chairman of Canon,

Ramon Mullerat (ed.), Corporate Social Responsibility: The Corporate Governance of the 21st Century, 225–234.
© 2005 *International Bar Association. Printed in the Netherlands.*

Inc. To his colleagues on the Caux Round Table, Kaku claimed that he had dramatically improved Canon's financial prospects by following a strategic vision he called *Kyosei*. Roughly translated, *Kyosei* means 'living and working together for the common good'. It is a vision of moral capitalism, a form of stewardship sensitivity, derived from Japanese cultural insights.

In 1991, Kaku came to Minnesota to present his approach to business management using the principle of *Kyosei*. American business leaders there were arguing about their own American analogue to *Kyosei*. Some called it 'business ethics', others called it 'stakeholder theory', and still others spoke of 'sustainability'.

Kaku received a warm reception from some Minneapolis business leaders. The Minnesota Center for Corporate Responsibility was then writing down guidelines for business managers reflecting the stakeholder concept of business ethics. Invited to Caux, Switzerland, for the 1992 global dialogue of the Caux Round Table, two Minnesota business leaders brought with them these proposed Minnesota principles for ethical and socially responsible business. They challenged members of that year's Round Table to write global guidelines for companies.

Though initially skeptical of the American legalistic fixation that rules of conduct be written down, Kaku was up to the challenge of drafting guidelines for global business. The Caux Round Table participants set about blending the Minnesota principles of stewardship with regard to stakeholder concerns with second, Kaku's vision of *Kyosei* and, third, with Pope John Paul II's principle of human dignity. America, Japan, and Europe each contributed a moral vision to the final statement of global business principles. What resulted was historic – the first global code of conduct for capitalists written by senior capitalists from different moral traditions.

The Caux Round Table Principles – now most frequently called the CRT Principles – contain an introduction, a preamble, seven General Principles, and six sets of stakeholder principles, which are guidelines for a company's responsibility toward its customers, employees, owners and investors, suppliers, competitors, and communities.

THE PREAMBLE

The Preamble to the CRT Principles for Business states, 'Law and market forces are necessary but insufficient guides for conduct'. And '... we affirm the necessity for moral values in business decision-making'. The CRT Principles are a call to stewardship in business, finance, and commerce. They recognize the intangible moral responsibilities that come with possessing economic power. They are a guide for the implementation of moral capitalism.

THE GENERAL PRINCIPLES

The Seven General Principles:

1. The responsibilities of businesses: beyond shareholders toward stakeholders.
2. The economic and social impact of business: toward innovation, justice, and world community.
3. Business behavior: beyond the letter of law toward a spirit of trust.

4. Respect for rules.
5. Support for multilateral trade.
6. Respect for the environment.
7. Avoidance of illicit operations.

By following these Principles, a business can establish its credentials as a socially responsible enterprise.

1. The Stakeholder Ethic

The CRT Principles forthrightly embrace the stakeholder ethic, finding it compatible with both *Kyosei* and human dignity. The Preamble to the Principles states that '... respect for the dignity and interests of stakeholders [is] fundamental'. Most of the seven General Principles for business provide guidance for consideration of stakeholder interests.

General Principle No. 1 makes the case for stakeholder sensitivity: 'The value of a business to society is the wealth and employment it creates and the marketable products and services it provides to consumers at a reasonable price commensurate with quality. To create such value, a business must maintain its own economic health and viability, but survival is not a sufficient goal'. 'Businesses have a role to play in improving the lives of all their customers, employees and shareholders by sharing with them the wealth they have created. Suppliers and competitors as well should expect businesses to honor their obligations in a spirit of honesty and fairness. As responsible citizens of the local, national, regional and global communities in which they operate, businesses share a part in shaping the future of those communities'.

In specific implementation of the general injunction contained in General Principle No. 1, the entire contents of Section 3 of the CRT Principles for Business is devoted to the six stakeholder groups – customers, employees, owners and investors, suppliers, competitors, and communities. Furthermore, General Principle No. 2 focuses multinational corporations on the obligation to consider the needs of stakeholders in poor and developing countries.

And, General Principle No. 6 holds that the environment is really a stakeholder as well so that responsible businesses need to promote sustainable development and prevent the wasteful use of natural resources. The command of General Principle No. 2 that businesses must innovate in technology and production methods as part of their social responsibility guides business to increasingly sustainable use of the world's natural environment. Pollution of the environment and heedless use of its resources were largely created by technology, production methods, and economic growth; these trends can be reversed in time by the very same forces that created them.

General Principle No. 3 ties it all together: businesses must conduct themselves with sincerity, candor, truthfulness, and transparency. And they must keep their promises. Enron failed to do this; so did the tobacco companies in their advertising about the dangers of nicotine addiction, Arthur Andersen in certain of its audits, and Wall Street investment firms in the advice provided to many of their trusted clients.

2.   General Principle No. 1

The Responsibilities of Businesses: Beyond Shareholders toward Stakeholders

The value of a business to society is the wealth and employment it creates and the marketable products and services it provides to consumers at a reasonable price commensurate with quality. To create such value, a business must maintain its own economic health and viability, but survival is not a sufficient goal.

Businesses have a role to play in improving the lives of all their customers, employees, and shareholders by sharing with them the wealth they have created. Suppliers and competitors as well should expect businesses to honor their obligations in a spirit of honesty and fairness. As responsible citizens of the local, national, regional, and global communities in which they operate, businesses share a part in shaping the future of those communities.

This General Principle defines the social office of private enterprise. It is to create wealth and employment and to produce products and services at a reasonable price commensurate with quality. All business activity, and all business judgments, must keep this role in mind. To deviate from the role is to lose the right way of doing business. From the perspective of the CRT Principles, a business, therefore, is a social status with duties and responsibilities to the common good. It does more than make money for its owners and investors. This logic would apply as well to an individual who dedicates his or her capital to profitable enterprise. The CRT Principles apply to 'business' not just to corporations.

General Principle No. 1 creates a duty to reduce poverty by increasing wealth and employment where conditions permit. The business approach to poverty reduction is doing more business. Subsidy of the poor and the funding of social capital expenditures are primarily the responsibility of government and public charities to which businesses contribute through taxes and charitable contributions. General Principle No. 1 also affirms that a business must maintain its own economic health and viability – business is not to be subsidized, but must pay its own way – to create more and more wealth for society.

3.   General Principle No. 2

The Economic and Social Impact of Business: Toward Innovation, Justice, and World Community

Businesses established in foreign countries to develop, produce, or sell should also contribute to the social advancement of those countries by creating productive employment and helping to raise the purchasing power of their citizens. Businesses also should contribute to human rights, education, welfare, and vitalization of the countries in which they operate.

Businesses should contribute to economic and social development not only in the countries in which they operate, but also in the world community at large, through effective and prudent use of resources, free and fair competition, and emphasis upon innovation in technology, production methods, marketing, and communications.

The responsibility of business to build better lives for people throughout the global community is reinforced in General Principle No. 2, which says that businesses should 'contribute to the economic and social development . . . in the world community at large'.

The CRT Principles acknowledge the power of multinational corporations to improve conditions in countries where they do business, calling on such companies to 'contribute to the social advancement of such countries by creating productive employment and helping to raise the purchasing power of their citizens'. Businesses, the CRT Principles assert, should also contribute to human rights, education, welfare, and vitalization of the countries in which they operate.

4.   General Principle No. 3

Business Behavior: Beyond the Letter of Law toward a Spirit of Trust

While accepting the legitimacy of trade secrets, businesses should recognize that sincerity, candor, truthfulness, the keeping of promises, and transparency contribute not only to their own credibility and stability but also to the smoothness and efficiency of business transactions, particularly on the international level.

This General Principle calls for acting according to the standards of trust that moral capitalism requires and rewards. This General Principle ties the CRT Principles for Business to the foundations of a moral capitalism. By acting with 'sincerity, candor, truthfulness, and transparency' and by the 'keeping of promises', businesses build social capital necessary for robust and sustainable economic growth. General Principle No. 3 calls for character in decision making, not just grudging compliance with the least requirements set by local laws and regulations.

5.   General Principle No. 4

Respect for Rules

To avoid trade frictions and to promote freer trade, equal conditions for competition, and fair and equitable treatment for all participants, businesses should respect international and domestic rules. In addition, they should recognize that some behavior, although legal, may still have adverse consequences.

This General Principle on respect for rules provided another foundation for moral capitalism. Not every person in business likes to run the risk of failure. Those who fear genuine free markets are often disposed to go beyond the bounds of legitimate market competition to avail themselves of some external force or power with which to get their way with customers, workers, investors, or suppliers. Legal privileges (monopolies, licenses, rights to trade) can, and corruption and insider relationships do, interfere with ordinary market forces to turn such forces against ethical outcomes. By insisting on respect for rules, General Principle No. 4 would keep all those who seek to profit from market activity within the bounds of legitimate competition.

This self-restraint is most important for a moral form of capitalism, for those without money or access to political power have little by which they can protect themselves from imperious, overbearing players. Power abuse converts moral capitalism into brute capitalism.

Finally, General Principle No. 4 points to a range of business decisions that, although strictly legal, are immoral or unfair. In the spirit of *Kyosei* and with respect for human dignity, this General Principle demands that businesses refrain from making such decisions.

6.   General Principle No. 5

Support for Multilateral Trade

Businesses should support the multilateral trade systems of the GATT/World Trade Organization and similar international agreements. They should cooperate in efforts to promote the progressive and judicious liberalization of trade and to relax those domestic measures that unreasonably hinder global commerce, while giving due respect to national policy objectives.

This General Principle adds its voice to the other parts of the CRT Principles for Business that encourage investment and trade with poor, developing, and emerging-market nations. By implication, the Principle calls on domestic firms to broaden the scope of their purchases and sales to embrace a global business community.

7.   General Principle No. 6

Respect for the Environment

A business should protect and, where possible, improve the environment, promote sustainable development, and prevent the wasteful use of natural resources.

This General Principle states in comprehensive fashion the obligations of a business to be mindful of the needs of our global environment. A business should, under this General Principle, protect and, where possible, improve the environment, promote sustainable development, and prevent the wasteful use of natural resources.

8.   General Principle No. 7

Avoidance of Illicit Operations

A business should not participate in or condone bribery, money laundering, or other corrupt practices: indeed, it should seek cooperation with others to eliminate them. It should not trade in arms or other materials used for terrorist activities, drug traffic, or other organized crime.

This final General Principle reinforces the requirement of moral capitalism that businesses must avoid illicit and corrupt transactions in order to sustain the cultural framework supporting moral capitalism. This rejection of illicit means is one important way in which companies and individuals can contribute to the formation and growth of constructive social capital.

9.   From Aspiration to Action

Giving people mental constructs like the CRT Principles for Business to apply in their calculations of how best to gain business advantage will impact their behavior. The teaching of norms, although it is no guarantee that students will apply their lessons well, nonetheless is where we must start in improving levels of corporate social responsibility throughout the global business community.

Idealists, however, are often dismissed by self-proclaimed realists or 'practical people' as being excessively naïve in that their aspirations for humanity go beyond the apparent scope of the possible. Nowhere is this skepticism more vibrant than in business. Ideals and morality are often spoken of as virtual antimatter to the behaviors allegedly needed to maximize profits. So the CRT has faced a serious problem of changing business behaviors: publishing principles does little to get them implemented.

The CRT understands that morality works in the business corporation through hierarchy, moving from vague but lofty ideals down through principles and standards, to objectives, and then to action. Consider Chart 1 below illustrating the flow of ideals into accomplishments.

At the highest level of this roadmap for implementation of high business ideals, a map directing our principles, our standards, our management benchmarks, and our decisions, we find our best ideals, our highest aspirations, and our vision of the common good. Setting these values and ideals in place for a corporation or a business is the responsibility of its owners, its board of directors, and its top managers.

These governing ideals could be taken from religion, but they don't have to be found only there. People responsible for an enterprise could agree among themselves on a common goal, arriving at that end from different religious starting points. In just such a fashion did the CRT Principles for Business themselves arise from a blending of Roman Catholic teachings and American Protestant and secular traditions of stewardship with Japanese Buddhist and Shinto perspectives.

At the next level below our ideals, the socially responsible business should place a set of principles, like the CRT Principles for Business, or the ten principles of the United Nations' Global Compact.

Flowing down toward more objectivity and specificity, we next find standards and guidelines such as the self-assessment and implementation management process invented by the CRT and called 'ARCTURUS'.

At the level of stakeholder engagement, a company seeking to meet its proper responsibilities under a moral capitalism would apply to its decision making the considerations listed for each of the six stakeholder groups in Section 3 of the CRT Principles for Business.

Moral Capitalism

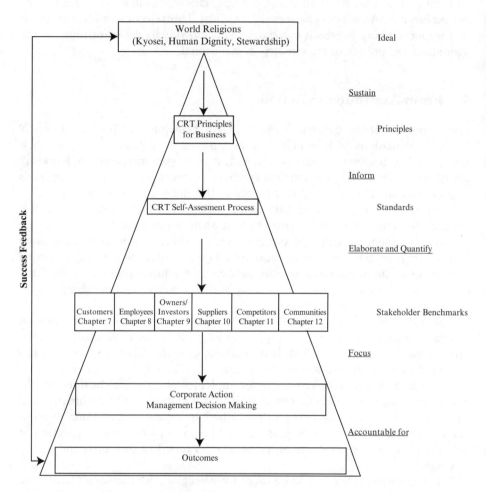

Chart 1. Represents the value-action system of moral capitalism.

Then we come down to the most challenging level of all: management performance. At this level, the devil is truly in the details. Judgment and intellectual effort are required to square-up the demands of daily decision-making with the company's standards, principles, and ideals.

Below the action level we find outcomes, which can be measured to see how much progress toward our goals and ideals we are making. In a successful company, its accomplishments will reflect its ideals.

10.   Arcturus: The CRT's Self-Assessment and Improvement Process

Principles do not self-execute. Leaders must invoke them to set goals for managers, and managers, in turn, must be aware of the deeper purposes behind

Chart 2. Assessment framework – criteria matrix

Category	1. Fundamental Duties	2. Customers	3. Employees	4. Owners/ Investors	5. Supplies/ Partners	6. Competitors	7. Communities
1. Responsibilities of business	Criterion 1.1	Criterion 1.2	Criterion 1.3	Criterion 1.4	Criterion 1.5	Criterion 1.6	Criterion 1.7
2. Economic and social impact of business	Criterion 2.1	Criterion 2.2	Criterion 2.3	Criterion 2.4	Criterion 2.5	Criterion 2.6	Criterion 2.7
3. Business behavior	Criterion 3.1	Criterion 3.2	Criterion 3.3	Criterion 3.4	Criterion 3.5	Criterion 3.6	Criterion 3.7
4. Respect for rules	Criterion 4.1	Criterion 4.2	Criterion 4.3	Criterion 4.4	Criterion 4.5	Criterion 4.6	Criterion 4.7
5. Support for multilateral trade	Criterion 5.1	Criterion 5.2	Criterion 5.3	Criterion 5.4	Criterion 5.5	Criterion 5.6	Criterion 5.7
6. Respect for the environment	Criterion 6.1	Criterion 6.2	Criterion 6.3	Criterion 6.4	Criterion 6.5	Criterion 6.6	Criterion 6.7
7. Avoidance of Illicit operations	Criterion 7.1	Criterion 7.2	Criterion 7.3	Criterion 7.4	Criterion 7.5	Criterion 7.6	Criterion 7.7

the tasks set before them and their subordinates. The Caux Round Table has, therefore, borrowed a page from business: management by objective. The CRT Principles for Business have been converted into management objectives suitable for executives in companies large and small. Corporate boards of directors, chief executive officers, and line managers all can now more easily and reliably become successful stewards of sustainable business value. Results of operations can be monitored against strategic and tactical risk profiles and for positive or negative contributions to various value drivers in the zones of capital factors, conversion of capital into product or services, the quality and price point of product and services, and customer satisfaction and loyalty.

Where risks or negative detractions from value are detected, changes can be made to improve enterprise results, lower risks, and enhance overall value. Improvement flows from present results to assessment, reflection, action, and better results in a continuous process. Implementing a comprehensive improvement process will bring a company more and more into effective alignment with the CRT Principles for Business and the practices of moral capitalism.

Business people are goal oriented; give them goals and incentives, and progress comes along without a second thought. This Caux Round Table self-assessment and improvement process evaluates companies on forty-nine areas drawn from the CRT Principles for Business as they impact the six stakeholder constituencies. Chart 2 presents the complete measurement matrix of the forty-nine significant zones of value enhancement and risk possibility. Each cell in the matrix demands management attention for complete stewardship of the business.

Inquiry by senior management as to whether the company has a policy for success in each cell, how each policy has been translated into goals, and what results have been achieved in reaching for those goals will provide a 360-degree survey of the corporation or the enterprise. The concerns of every stakeholder will be addressed, and fidelity to each of the CRTs recommended seven General Principles will be assessed. Shortfalls will emerge for management attention; risks will press themselves on management for reduction. Acting on its self-assessment will make the company more profitable and more socially responsible.

CONCLUSION

In the ten years since their publication, the CRT Principles for Business have remained the *only* set of principles for corporate social responsibility proposed by business leaders. The CRT Principles for Business also remain the most comprehensive principles available for business decision making, thanks to the thoroughness of their consideration of stakeholder concerns. And, finally, the CRT Principles for Business perhaps deserve special consideration for their unique ability to expressly link vertically universal ideals with the very practical decisions that regularly and systematically challenge the intellectual and ethical resources of business managers.

Chapter 15

THE GLOBAL COMPACT

Hans Corell

A. THE BEGINNING

At the World Economic Forum in Davos on 31 January 1999, United Nations Secretary-General Kofi Annan advocated the Global Compact. As a point of departure, he proposed nine universal principles in the areas of human rights, labour and environment. Referring to these principles, he asked business leaders to contribute to a sustainable and inclusive global market. The actual launch of the Compact took place in July 2000.

Much has happened since then, and today the Compact encompasses several hundred companies and business organizations, both national and international, from all regions of the world. It also includes international trade unions or union bodies, civil society entities at the global level, business schools and UN agencies. In this context, it is also important to note that it also includes CSR organizations.

B. THE PURPOSE

The purpose of the Compact is to convince the actors on the global markets that they should rally around shared values. In order to achieve more sustainable and inclusive global markets special attention should be paid to the world's poorest people.

The Compact attempts to achieve two goals that are complementary. The first, which is of particular interest to all lawyers advising business, is to make the Compact and its principles *part of the internal strategy and operations of business*. The second goal is to engage different stakeholders and facilitate cooperation among them, in particular, when there are common problems that must be solved.

Within the Compact four key mechanisms have been developed to accomplish these goals, namely: dialogue, learning, local networks and project partnerships.

Ramon Mullerat (ed.), Corporate Social Responsibility: The Corporate Governance of the 21st Century, 235–242.
© 2005 *International Bar Association. Printed in the Netherlands.*

C.   THE PRINCIPLES

The principles upon which the Global Compact is based are taken from the areas of human rights, labour and the environment. These principles are derived from three documents that have been adopted by states by consensus and thus enjoy universal support, namely:

- The Universal Declaration of Human Rights[1]
- The International Labour Organization's Declaration on Fundamental Principles and Rights at Work[2]
- The Rio Declaration on Environment and Development[3]

The Global Compact asks companies to embrace, support and enact, within their sphere of influence, a set of core values within these three areas. The principles are as follows:

Human Rights[4]
- *Principle 1*: Businesses should support and respect the protection of internationally proclaimed human rights; and
- *Principle 2*: make sure that they are not complicit in human rights abuses.

Labour Standards[5]
- *Principle 3*: Businesses should uphold the freedom of association and the effective recognition of the right to collective bargaining;
- *Principle 4*: the elimination of all forms of forced and compulsory labour;
- *Principle 5*: the effective abolition of child labour; and
- *Principle 6*: the elimination of discrimination in respect of employment and occupation.

Environment[6]
- *Principle 7*: Businesses should support a precautionary approach to environmental challenges;
- *Principle 8*: undertake initiatives to promote greater environmental responsibility; and
- *Principle 9*: encourage the development and diffusion of environmentally friendly technologies.

For the purposes of the present brief overview, it is not necessary, nor is it possible, to go into detail about the contents of the principles. In subdivision J, reference is made to material that contains extensive explanations of what these principles represent and the reasons why they are included in the Compact.

1   http://www.un.org/Overview/rights.html.
2   http://www.ilo.org/dyn/declaris/DECLARATIONWEB.INDEXPAGE.
3   http://www.un.org/esa/sustdev/documents/agenda21/index.htm.
4   http://www.unglobalCompact.org/content/AboutTheGC/TheNinePrinciples/humanrights.htm.
5   http://www.unglobalCompact.org/content/AboutTheGC/TheNinePrinciples/labour.htm.
6   http://www.unglobalCompact.org/content/AboutTheGC/TheNinePrinciples/environment.htm.

D.   THE ACTORS

The purpose of the Compact is to involve all actors concerned. First and foremost, governments are concerned, since they are the ones who define and adopt the principles on which the Compact is founded. Next comes business, since the purpose of the Compact is to influence business. Another obvious actor is labour, since labour is the focus of several of the principles and is engaged in the process of global production. Civil society and the United Nations itself are other important actors.

1.   Governments

The Global Compact is sometimes criticized for attempting to shift the responsibility for the observation of international commitments from governments to business. It is therefore important to stress at the outset that the primary responsibility for the principles rests with governments. First, governments provide the necessary legitimacy and universality to the principles of the Compact. All of the underlying documents have been adopted under the auspices of intergovernmental organizations. Consequently, implementation of the principles must be based on and take place within the standard legal framework at the national level. Hence, it is for governments to support the implementation of the Compact at the global and national levels.

As the system has developed, governments seek to support the Compact at the national level, in particular, in the formation of networks. They are also encouraged to establish policies to advance the purposes of the Compact. At the global level, governments engage with the Secretary-General to develop the Compact and to engage other actors in the work.

2.   Business

With respect to business, it is important to stress that the Compact is a voluntary initiative with the purpose of promoting responsible global corporate citizenship. One of the fundamental ideas is that business leaders should be brought together to build a movement that is strong enough to support the ideals of the Compact. *Therefore, a crucial precondition for a successful work within the Compact framework is that the Chief Executive Officer, and the Board of Directors are behind the Compact.* It is from them that the initiative to join the Compact must emanate.

In the words of the Global Compact Office, the company that has committed itself to the Compact and is principles:

* Must set in motion changes to business operations so that the Global Compact and its principles become part of strategy, culture and day-to-day operations;
* Is expected to publicly advocate the Global Compact and its principles via communications vehicles such as press releases, speeches, etc.; and

- Is expected to publish in its annual report or similar document a description of the ways in which it is supporting the Global Compact and all its nine principles.

To this author, the last item is of particular interest, since this was an idea that he advocated already in June 1998 when he was asked to challenge a Workshop on the topic 'Is the Business of Human Rights also the Business of Business'.[7]

3.   Labour

As it appears, internationally recognized labour standards, including the fundamental rights are part of the nine principles of the Compact. These standards are developed in a process in which business and labour play critical and central roles. However, labour plays a role that is different from those of business and other elements of civil society. This is the reason why labour is treated as a separate actor in the Compact. Of particular interest is here that labour has a distinct role in ILOs supervisory procedures designed to ensure that agreed labour standards are implemented at the national level. Furthermore, it is important in this context to refer to the practice of solving issues of interest to the Compact through collective bargaining agreements. This is common practice in many counties and is now also expanding at the global level. A number of framework agreements have been concluded between major companies and the international trade union bodies.

4.   Civil Society

Important actors in the Global Compact are also organizations from the civil society. They provide valuable assistance by lending credibility and social legitimacy to the efforts, and they can often help by solving problems and explaining the Compact's operations in more general contexts. These organizations participate both in the dialogue and as project partners. However, equally important is their advocating the nine principles to larger audiences and challenging business both locally and at the global level to take a stand on the issues that the Compact is concerned with.

5.   Others

There are also institutions with expertise in the areas of human rights, labour and the environment that can contribute to the activities of the Compact. Many such institutions have also made important contributions. Academic institutions and think tanks are among the participants, and there is an Academic Network that plays a catalytic role in the Compact's operation by preparing business case studies and commentaries on examples, and by undertaking research on global corporate citizenship.

---

[7]   http://www.un.org/law/counsel/english/address_06_26_98.pdf.

E. HOW DOES ONE PARTICIPATE?

First, reference should be made to the extensive information on participation in the Global Compact which is available on the Compact's website.[8] The information is directed not only to business but also to non-governmental organizations and other non-business participants.

With respect to substance, as previously said, the Compact and its principles must be translated into business strategies and operations. Obviously, the responsibility for this activity rests with each participating company. But in order to further advance the goals of the Compact the actors are encouraged to work together through dialogue, learning and projects at all levels.

1. Dialogue

The Global Compact Office stresses that dialogue is central in order to achieve mutual understanding and joint efforts among business, labour and non-governmental organizations in solving key challenges of globalization. The Office maintains that in this effort to influence policy-making and the behavior of all stakeholders the outcome is threefold: products that can engender changes in policy frameworks, encompassing both incentive structures and regulatory mechanisms; products that can influence the actual behaviour of participants; and collective action by like-minded actors working together.

2. Learning

The Compact's Learning Forum has three specific goals: to identify critical knowledge gaps and to disseminate information; to communicate good practices and cutting-edge knowledge to participants; and to foster accountability and transparency through its web portal that should both facilitate dialogue and enable web links to relevant public documents. An important ingredient is the sharing of experiences in the form of presentations, examples or case studies both at meetings and on the Compact's website.

3. Projects

As already emphasized, an important goal of the Compact is to provide opportunities for the poor. A means to this end are Partnership Projects. The Compact's website is therefore open to participating companies, labour and civil society organizations who want to share such experiences with others. In case there are UN organizations with relevant operational capacities and competencies, the Compact Office offers support by facilitating access to them.

4. Networks

An important element in the work of the Global Compact is the development of networks at the regional, national and local levels. Of particular interest is that

---

[8] http://www.unglobalcompact.org/Portal/Default.asp.

many local networks exist, some of them similar to what has been developed at the global level. This activity is greatly encouraged and supported by the Global Compact Office.

F.   THE ADMINISTRATION OF THE GLOBAL COMPACT

As mentioned, the Global Compact was launched at the initiative of the Secretary-General of the United Nations. To administer the initiative, a Global Compact Office was established at the UN Headquarters. It is financed by governments and is working within the framework of the United Nations and in accordance with its goals.

The Compact is furthermore supported by four UN core agencies, namely the Office of the High Commissioner for Human Rights, the International Labour Organization, the United Nations Environment Programme and the United Nations Development Fund. However, this does not mean that other UN agencies are excluded from participation. To provide strategic advice to the Secretary-General there is also an Advisory Council, composed of personalities from business, labour, civil society and academia. Further information about the administration of the Compact appears on its website.

G.   THE GLOBAL COMPACT AND CSR

One question that is often asked is why a company that has already established its own code of conduct should participate in the Global Compact. The answer is very simple: such codes are extremely important. And companies that have demonstrated leadership and made changes in their policies should be commended. However, such codes are typically quite narrow in focus, often leaving out important issues such as human rights. The purpose of the Global Compact is however different: it seeks to add new dimensions to good corporate citizenship by creating a platform – based on universally accepted principles – to encourage innovation, in particular, through new initiatives and partnerships with civil society and other organizations.

So, basically, the Global Compact is a voluntary corporate citizenship initiative with two main objectives: to mainstream the nine principles in business activities around the world and to catalyze actions in support of United Nations goals.

The obvious conclusion is that those who advise companies and, in particular, transnational companies must have a clear understanding of these interrelationships and that the business community has an important role to play here.

H.   THE GLOBAL COMPACT AND CORRUPTION

Already at the outset, questions were raised regarding the need for a principle-based approach to fighting corruption within the framework of the Global Compact. This issue was revived after the signing of the United Nations Convention against Corruption in Merida, Mexico on 9 December 2003.[9]

---

[9]   http://www.unodc.org/unodc/en/corruption.html.

Against this background the Secretary-General started in January 2004 consultations with participating companies to solicit their views regarding a potential introduction of a tenth principle against corruption.[10] A formal letter was sent to all participants seeking their views. The Secretary-General stressed that the adoption of such a principle would only occur if there was broad-based support, and that such an addition would be exceptional in nature. The consultation process concluded on 7 May 2004.[11]

Based on the results of the consultation process, the Secretary-General formally proposed to a Global Compact Leaders Summit, held in New York on 24 June 2004, the following principle against corruption:

'Business should work against corruption in all its forms, including extortion and bribery'.

With the Secretary-General's announcement to the summit, this principle, the tenth principle, was adopted.[12]

I. THE ROLE OF THE LAWYER

Needless to say lawers, and in particular those who serve as corporate counsel, have an important role to play in relation to the Compact. One can take human rights as a point of departure even if the argument could be made equally for labour and environment. Lawyers also have a special responsibility in society. It is of particular importance that they are familiar with the international obligations that their country has undertaken at the international level, i.e. vis-à-vis other states, and contribute to the fulfillment of such obligations.

Naturally, a corporate counsel's main responsibility is to his or her client. But the two responsibilities may not necessarily conflict. On the contrary! The matters that the Compact focuses on are often given prominent attention in the media and public discussion. Ultimately, companies will be assessed by public opinion. And, as we know, in the public debate the agenda is often set by non-governmental organizations. It is therefore important that companies are proactive in the fields that the Compact encompasses also in their own interest.

It is said that corporate lawyers are concerned that by joining the Global Compact, companies might be held accountable if they do not meet the standards. I do not believe that this is so, since the Compact is not a legally binding instrument. Rather, the principles are aspirational in nature. We should also remember that human rights protection is an obligation mainly for governments vis-à-vis their citizens and those who reside in their countries.

---

10 http://www.unglogalCompact.org/Portal/?NavigationTarget=/roles/portal_user/dialogue/Dialogue/nf/nf/transparency.

11 http://www.ungloablCompact.org/irj/servlet/prt/prtroot/com.sapportals.km.docs/ungc_html_content/NewsDocs/result%20consultation.doc.

12 In his closing remarks at the Summit, the Secretary-General said: 'Today we added a tenth principle to the Compact, to combat corruption. The extensive consultation that you went through to arrive at this amendment not only showed that an overwhelming majority of participants wanted to strengthen the Compact in this way; it also was an exemplary deliberative process. As a result, the Compact is now better positioned to address one of the most pernicious obstacles to growth and development, and to cooperate more intensively with groups such as Transparency International'.

This focus on governments has resulted in a debate where some argue that a transnational company cannot raise human rights issues because that would have detrimental effects on the possibilities of the company to do business in the country in question. This is of course an argument that cannot be swept aside completely. But there are ways to address this dilemma also. We should remember that there are multinational companies that have been severely criticized, and probably also suffered economically, because of lack of observation of human rights, labour and environmental standards.

Another concern expressed by corporate lawyers is that companies might be held liable for the behaviour of their contractors and subcontractors. In my view this is not so, at least not because of the Global Compact. Furthermore, and more importantly, there should be means of dealing also with this problem. In particular, one could stipulate in the contracts (where appropriate also with reference to subcontractors) standards that the companies engaged must honour. Indeed, more and more companies are considering their supply chains in the broadest sense, and asking their business partners to uphold similar principles.

J.   MATERIAL AVAILABLE

As already mentioned, there is a very useful website to assist all interested.[13] It is strongly recommended that corporate lawyers and other interested visit this website, which contains extensive material which is constantly updated. Also, in case the need arises to present the matter e.g. at a board meeting there is even a PowerPoint presentation that can be used for the purpose.

---

[13]   See note 8.

Chapter 16

PROMOTING CORPORATE RESPONSIBILITY: THE OECD GUIDELINES FOR MULTINATIONAL ENTERPRISES

Donald J. Johnston

A. CORPORATE RESPONSIBILITY AND THE INTERNATIONAL ECONOMY

International investment by multinational enterprises is at the heart of the current debate on globalization. The Monterrey Conference and the Johannesburg Summit in 2002 called attention to the importance of responsible international business for spreading the benefits of globalization more widely. The 2003 G8 Summit Declaration underscored the importance of 'fostering growth and promoting a responsible market economy'. The Declaration explicitly cites the OECD Guidelines for Multinational Enterprises and commits the G8 to work with interested countries to create an environment in which 'business can act responsibly'.

Thirty-eight governments – from the 30 OECD members and from 8 non-members[1] – have adhered to the OECD Guidelines for Multinational Enterprises, a government-backed code of conduct for international business. Today they are exploring how the Guidelines can best contribute to improving the functioning of the global economy and to promoting corporate responsibility. The Guidelines are recommendations by the 38 governments on business conduct covering such areas as human rights, labour relations, environment, combating corruption and consumer protection. Observance of these recommendations is voluntary for business, but the adhering governments make a binding commitment to promote them among multinational enterprises operating in or from their territories. In making this commitment, governments aim to 'to strengthen the basis of mutual confidence between enterprises and the societies

---

[1] The eight countries are Argentina, Brazil, Chile, Estonia, Israel, Latvia, Lithuania and Slovenia.

Ramon Mullerat (ed.), Corporate Social Responsibility: The Corporate Governance of the 21st Century, 243–250.
© 2005 *International Bar Association. Printed in the Netherlands.*

in which they operate, to help improve the foreign investment climate and to enhance the contribution to sustainable development made by multinational enterprises'.[2]

The OECD's view is that the primary contribution of business – its core responsibility – is the conduct of business itself. The role of business in society is to develop investments so as to yield adequate returns to the suppliers of capital. In so doing, companies create jobs and produce goods and services that consumers want to buy.

However, corporate responsibility goes beyond this core function. Companies are expected to obey the various laws that are applicable to them and, as a practical matter, must often respond to societal expectations that are not written down in law books. Many multinational enterprises have tens of thousands of employees and hundreds of products. They straddle dozens of legal, regulatory and cultural environments. Because of this, compliance with law and with societal expectations expressed through other, less formal channels is often a formidable challenge.

Many companies have invested heavily in trying to meet this challenge. Indeed, the development of business tools such as codes of conduct and related management and reporting systems has been one of the major trends in international business over the last 25 years. OECD research[3] shows that thousands of enterprises on at least four continents have participated in this trend. It also suggests that there are significant variations – by country and by sector of operation – in the issues companies choose to deal with and in their approaches to these issues. Examples of such divergences can be seen in Figures 1 and 2. Figure 1 shows that nearly all of the top 100 multinational enterprises publish policy statements on environment and health and safety while fewer than half deal publicly with the issue of corruption. Figure 2 reveals large sectoral variations in the propensity of companies to publish policy statements on corruption. While such variations reflect the diversity of companies' individual business environments, they also reflect other differences such as the state of development of agreed norms for conduct in different issue areas and sectors. Understanding these differences and encouraging convergence toward good practice are among the main objectives of the OECD Guidelines.

Of course, there is an ongoing debate about the effectiveness of voluntary initiatives. Some parties believe that they represent the business sector's contribution to the goal of building effective standards of international business conduct. This voluntary approach offers the flexibility needed to adapt to and learn from regional, sectoral and individual business circumstances. Others view these efforts as little more than public relations ploys and would favour replacing them with binding rules involving sanctions and other enforcement mechanisms. Only these, they feel, will give the standards enough 'teeth' to influence corporate behaviour in a meaningful way. I will return to this point.

The OECD member governments believe that these initiatives are helping to improve the functioning of the global economy, as examples of their application

[2]   Preface of the OECD Guidelines for Multinational Enterprises.
[3]   *Corporate Responsibility: Private Initiatives and Public Goals*, OECD, Paris, 2001.

(number of companies in top-100 list making statements)

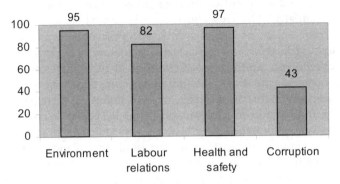

Figure 1. Policy statements by issue area.

Source: 2003 Annual Report on the OECD Guidelines.

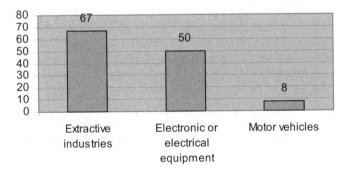

Figure 2. Anti-corruption statements by sector of activity.

Source: 2003 Annual Report on the OECD Guidelines.

have shown. Private initiatives allow businesses and societies to 'feel their way forward' in the many areas where standards on acceptable management practices for business are not yet firmly established. For example, OECD research suggests that the published policies of OECD-based companies with outsourcing operations have tended to converge with respect to the core labour standards they ask their suppliers to observe. Nearly all companies with publicly-available outsourcing policies now mention all core labour standards, whereas few covered all core standards in the late 1990s.[4] However, the research also suggests that most companies – 118 out of a sample of 147 companies operating in sectors where core labour standards are a strategic concern – do not publish their outsourcing policies. Thus, while there is evidence of significant progress in this area, there is

---

4   The core labour standards are set forth in the International Labour Organization's *Declaration on Fundamental Principles and Rights at Work*. They include freedom of association, elimination of all forms of forced or compulsory labour, effective abolition of child labour, the elimination of discrimination with respect of employment and occupation. For a detailed discussion of these standards, see *International Trade and Core Labour Standards*, OECD, Paris, 2000.

also evidence suggesting that many companies operating in sensitive sectors could do more to contribute to broader efforts to enhance compliance with core labour standards. The Guidelines provide several channels through which companies, trade unions and NGOs work with governments to promote further progress. As described below, these channels include: (1) discussions between adhering governments and other stakeholders of individual company conduct in specific business situations (including specific companies' approaches to respecting workers' rights to freedom of association or to managing the risk of employing child or forced labour); and (2) analysis and discussion of generic corporate responsibility issues.

At the same time, it would be naïve to think that a meaningful system of global norms could exist without binding regulation and formal deterrence. For the time being, much regulation and law enforcement is very much anchored in national economic systems. Future international regulation in some areas could emerge from gradual convergence and coordination of national practices. The OECD has taken steps to encourage this. The OECD Convention on Combating Bribery of Foreign Public Officials in International Business Transactions – which obliges signatories to enact laws and criminal sanctions against bribery of foreign public officials – is an important example. Another example can be found in OECD work on international tax enforcement. I would caution, however, against exaggerating the degree to which formal law enforcement can or should solve all the world's problems. I return to this idea in my conclusions. Moreover, many of these initiatives are not quite as 'voluntary' as they might seem. Webster's dictionary defines 'voluntary' as 'acting or done with no external compulsion or persuasion'. If one accepts this definition, then many private initiatives are not really voluntary – they are private responses (built into management systems and other business practices) that are driven by powerful financial, legal or regulatory pressures created by the broader society in which businesses operate. For example, environmental regulation in the European Union provides incentives for adopting certain environmental management practices. The US Federal Sentencing Guidelines provide another example of this deliberate coordination of public and private efforts. The Sentencing Guidelines provide powerful legal incentives (in the form of the possibility of more lenient sentences) for companies to adopt management systems that would allow them to show that they have made credible efforts to prevent violations of law by their employees.

Thus, the idea that there is a stark difference between binding and 'soft' initiatives is not a valid one. In fact, these initiatives are integral parts of broader systems for influencing business conduct. The challenge is to promote a workable mix of public and private initiatives and to get all actors in the broader system – both public and private – to take up their responsibilities. Private initiatives by companies are part of this broader effort, but companies cannot, by themselves, create workable norms for conduct for the global economy. Indeed, the Guidelines recognize that business should not be asked to take on other actors' – especially governments' – responsibilities. If they are to build effective systems for promoting appropriate business conduct, governments and private sector actors must act in partnerships underpinned by an appropriate allocation of roles and responsibilities for each.

The OECD Guidelines for Multinational Enterprises, which I will describe below, are one of the most concrete examples in the OECD of how successful private-public partnerships can be used to help make the global economy work better.

B. THE OECD GUIDELINES FOR MULTINATIONAL ENTERPRISES

The OECD Guidelines for Multinational Enterprises seek to encourage and reinforce the private initiatives for corporate responsibility that are described above. They express the shared views of 38 adhering governments on ethical business conduct.

Key features of the Guidelines are:[5]

- They contain voluntary recommendations to multinational enterprises in all major areas of business ethics.
- Adhering governments sign a binding commitment to promote them among multinational enterprises operating in or from their territories. Thus, the Guidelines represent a unique combination of voluntary and binding elements.
- The most visible sign of adhering governments' commitment to the Guidelines is their participation in the instrument's distinctive follow-up mechanisms. These include the operations of National Contact Points (NCP), which are government offices charged with promoting the Guidelines and handling enquiries in the national context.
- One of the NCPs' responsibilities is to consider 'specific instances'. Under this procedure, NCPs act as referees in multi-stakeholder discussions of specific company behaviour in specific business situations. In effect, this creates a case based approach to the problem of building behavioural norms for appropriate international business conduct.
- The Guidelines are part of a broader and balanced instrument of rights and commitments – the OECD Declaration on International Investment and Multinational Enterprises. In addition to the Guidelines, the Declaration provides guidance for governments in the areas of national treatment, avoiding imposing conflicting requirements on international investors and investment incentives and disincentives.[6]

The 38 governments that adhere to the Guidelines represent countries that are the source of most of the world's foreign direct investment and are home to most major multinational enterprises (97 out of UNCTAD's top 100 multinational enterprises are covered by the Guidelines). Although the Guidelines have been in existence since 1976, they were significantly revised in June 2000. After four

---

5   For fuller information on the Guidelines, see www.oecd.org/daf/investment/guidelines/.
6   For fuller information on the OECD Declaration, see www.oecd.org/daf/investment/instruments/.

years of implementation under the revised procedures, it is fair to ask what kind of impact the Guidelines have had to date.

1.   Results to Date

The 2000 review of the Guidelines and subsequent work by adhering governments have strengthened the instrument and raised its profile. There is growing evidence that the Guidelines are becoming an important international tool for corporate responsibility. The Guidelines have been translated into at least 24 languages. A recent survey asked managers of international companies to list influential international benchmarks for corporate behaviour – 22 per cent of them mentioned the Guidelines without prompting. Some 60,000 web pages refer to the Guidelines. Fifteen countries use the Guidelines in their export credit and investment guarantee programmes. In addition to the formal adherence by 38 governments, the Guidelines have received official support from business and trade union representatives at the OECD. NGOs have formed a coalition to make use of them.

The implementation procedures are being actively used, tested and refined. As of June 2003, 64 specific instances had been considered.[7] Some of these deal with company conduct in OECD countries, but most look at business conduct in non-OECD countries and cover issues that go to the heart of the current debate on globalization. For example:

- *Zambian copper mining.* The Canadian NCP has looked into the resettlement plans of a company operating in Zambia's copper belt. As a result of this consideration, the company agreed to postpone its resettlement plans for one year to allow time to rethink the plans – both the company and the NGO coalition (involving a Canadian and Zambian NGO) that were parties to this specific instance agreed that the procedure made a useful contribution to reducing tensions.
- *Korean suppliers in a Guatemalan export processing zone.* The Korean NCP has looked into a Korean company's respect of freedom of association – a core labour standard – in an export processing zone in Guatemala. The Korean NCP encouraged the company to inform the Guatemalan workers of their rights and to respect these rights. The company responded by issuing a manual in comic book form illustrating workers' rights under Guatemalan law.
- *Swedish business service provision in Ghana's gold sector.* The Swedish NCP looked at two Swedish companies' involvement (as business service providers) in Ghana's gold sector. The NCP collected information from on-site visits, from the Swedish embassy and from Ghanaian NGOs. It concluded that, while there are significant environmental and social problems in Ghana's gold sector, the two companies could not be held responsible for these problems because they were too far removed from them.

---

[7]   *2003 Annual Report on the OECD Guidelines for Multinational Enterprises: Focus on Enhancing the Role of Business in the Fight Against Corruption*, OECD, Paris, 2003.

These are just a few of the many specific instances that have been considered by NCPs so far. Some of the positive developments that have been noted from these and other experiences include:

- *Using the embassy networks as an accountability mechanism.* It is now becoming common practice for NCPs to use embassies (as well as employees from overseas development assistance programmes) as sources of information for consideration of 'specific instances' (e.g. see Swedish case above). In 2003, five adhering countries now feature the Guidelines as part of the training material given to embassy personnel before they take up their posts.
- *Giving a voice to trade unions and civil society actors from the non-OECD area.* Many of the specific instances have been brought by trade unions and NGOs from the non-OECD area working in partnership with OECD-based actors. The Guidelines strengthen these non-OECD actors by providing an international forum in which they can voice their concerns and by allowing them to gain experience with international institutions and procedures.
- *A way for governments to engage with companies on issues of business ethics at a lower standard of 'proof' than that required by formal legal proceedings.* A number of actors, including the UN Expert Panel on the illegal exploitation of natural resources in the Democratic Republic of Congo, have noted that the Guidelines allow governments to engage with companies with greater flexibility than that permitted by legal proceedings.
- *A tool for companies.* Trade unions and NGOs have been attracted to the specific instances procedure for some time. But companies are now starting to realize that it can be a useful tool for them as well. Business recently asked the Guidelines institutions to assist them in dealing with bribe solicitation and ways of responding to this request are currently being explored. In addition, the specific instances procedures can help provide concrete guidance to companies – it can reassure them (as in the Swedish case described above) while sometimes also helping them to identify shortcomings.

Guidelines implementation – which includes an annual Corporate Responsibility Roundtable organized in conjunction with the annual meeting of NCPs – also provides an opportunity for business, trade unions and NGOs to share their views on major corporate responsibility issues (e.g. responsible supply chain management, business' contribution to the fight against corruption). Among other things, this allows them to influence NCPs thinking on high profile issues. The summaries of these discussions, published in the annual reports on the Guidelines, provide a public record of the views of governments, business, trade unions and NGOs on these issues.

2. Ongoing Challenges

While their overall visibility has grown, more needs to be done to raise public awareness of the Guidelines and to demonstrate that they can make a vital contribution to the global economy. A number of priority areas for future work have been identified:

Transparency and effectiveness of NCPs. The NCPs are focusing on enhancing the transparency and effectiveness of their operations. They are sharing their experiences through a regular annual meeting in order to ensure that the specific instances are considered in a fair way. One of the main outstanding issues is the disclosure of information at the various stages of the 'specific instances' process.

Parallel legal procedures. Surveys of NCPs show that specific instances are often conducted in parallel with consideration of related matters under legal or administrative procedures. NCPs have started to explore under what circumstances the Guidelines procedures can make positive contributions over and above those made by other procedures.

Enhancing the contribution of business in weak governance zones. The OECD is working on providing terms of reference for conducting business with integrity in countries with very weak governance. This work will draw on the OECDs integrity package, which includes the Guidelines as well as the OECD Anti-Bribery Convention and Recommendations, the Corporate Governance Principles and Guidelines on Avoiding Conflict of Interest in the Public Service.

Partnerships with other international organizations. The Guidelines are one of several global corporate responsibility initiatives. The OECD is building partnerships with other international organizations – in particular with the United Nations, the World Bank and the Global Reporting Initiative (GRI). The GRI has issued a map of how the GRI indicators can be used by companies to report on their performance relative to the Guidelines' recommendations. The OECD Investment Committee will be working with the UN Global Compact on follow-up to the UN Expert Panel's Report on Illegal Exploitation of the Democratic Republic of Congo.

C.   CONCLUSIONS

Having been a practicing lawyer and a parliamentarian, my bias has been towards controlling much behavior through laws and regulations – a rules-based system, if you like. My view has changed. The OECD Guidelines for Multinational Enterprises (like the OECD Principles of Corporate Governance) set out a number of 'principles' for international behavior which underpin good corporate citizenship, no matter what may be the local legal framework. Effective pressure for good corporate behavior can be exercised not only by legal tribunals with lawyers debating whether a rule has been breached, but also by the court of public opinion, often finding its expression at shareholders meetings and in consumer action. The Guidelines are a code of conduct attached to a government-backed mediation procedure that reinforces these market pressures. This procedure has been used many times and in a variety of ways, ranging from 'naming and shaming' to highlighting the positive steps taken by companies. It also provides a mechanism through which governments help businesses explore what ethical conduct means in situations where this is far from obvious. Thus, the Guidelines promote appropriate international business conduct by raising the incentives for acting responsibly and by helping companies understand what appropriate conduct is.

Chapter 17

THE UN NORMS ON THE RESPONSIBILITIES OF TRANSNATIONAL CORPORATIONS AND OTHER BUSINESS ENTERPRISES WITH REGARD TO HUMAN RIGHTS

Jakob Ragnwaldh
Paola Konopik

The last few years have seen growing concern over the effects of globalization. Liberalization of trade, large-scale privatization and the diffusion of information technology have contributed to the creation of multinational corporate groups of unprecedented might. Indeed, corporations are often seen as the main beneficiaries of the global economy. As multinationals continue to have dramatic impact on individuals, communities and nations, increasing attention has been drawn upon the status of corporations in the international community. Particular focus has been placed upon the relevance of human rights within the business community as a result of the implication of certain corporate bodies in human rights abuses.[1]

It was in response to this concern that the United Nations began to pay greater attention to the impact of corporate operations on human rights. In the 70s, 80s and 90s, unsuccessful attempts had been made within the United Nations to adopt human rights standards for businesses.[2] In 1999, however, the United Nations Sub-Commission on the Promotion and Protection of Human Rights

---

[1] *Human Rights Principles and Responsibilities for Transnational Corporations and Other Business Enterprises, Introduction,* UN Doc. E/CN.4/Sub.2/2002/XX/Add.1 (2002).

[2] See e.g. the *Draft United Nations Code of Conduct for Transnational Corporations,* UN Doc. E/1990/94. See also Sarah Joseph, *An Overview of the Human Rights Accountability of Multinational Enterprises,* pp. 83–85, published in *Liability of Multinational Corporations Under International Law,* edited by M.T. Kamminga and S. Zia-Zarafi, Kluwer Law International, The Hague, 2000.

Ramon Mullerat (ed.), Corporate Social Responsibility: The Corporate Governance of the 21st Century, 251–262.
© 2005 *International Bar Association. Printed in the Netherlands.*

(the 'Sub-Commission')[3] formed a working group in order to examine the effects on human rights of the activities of transnational corporations.[4] This working group produced the *UN Norms on the Responsibilities of Transnational Corporations and Other Business Enterprises with Regard to Human Rights* (the 'Norms') [5] and a Commentary on the Norms,[6] which were unanimously adopted by the Sub-Commission in August 2003.[7]

The Norms were subsequently considered at the annual meeting of the United Nations Commission on Human Rights (the 'UNCHR')[8] on 20 April 2004. The UNCHR decided neither to approve nor to adopt the Norms, emphasizing that the Norms currently constitute a draft proposal only, without any legal standing. However, the UNCHR called upon the United Nations High Commissioner for Human Rights to prepare a report on the scope and legal status of existing initiatives and standards relating to corporate human rights responsibilities, including the Norms. The report, which is to be prepared in consultation with 'all relevant stakeholders', is to be submitted to the UNCHR at its annual session in 2005, in order to allow the UNCHR to identify options for strengthening standards on corporate human rights responsibilities.[9]

The proposed Norms have been the subject of a highly polarized debate. Many organizations, such as Amnesty International, the Ethical Globalization Initiative and the Prince of Wales Business Leaders Forum, have welcomed the Norms as an important tool for businesses seeking to adhere to human rights. Several multinational corporations have also taken the initiative to 'road-test' the Norms in their operations.[10]

However, the Norms have also been the subject of much criticism. Business organizations, such as the International Organization of Employers, the International Chamber of Commerce, the United States Council for International Business and the Confederation of British Industry have opposed the Norms. Such organizations have complained about being excluded from the drafting process and have expressed concern over the fact that the Norms transfer human rights responsibilities from governments to corporate entities.

The aim of this paper is to provide an overview of the scope of the Norms and its substantive provisions and to highlight certain problems with regard to the

---

3   The Sub-Commission is the main subsidiary body of the United Nations Commission on Human Rights, and is composed of 26 human rights experts acting in their personal capacity. See http://www.unhchr.ch/html/menu2/2/sc.htm.
4   Resolution 1998/8, 20 August 1998. This five member working group was headed by Law Professor David Weissbrodt.
5   *Norms on the Responsibilities of Transnational Corporations and Other Business Enterprises with Regard to Human Rights*, UN Doc. E/CN.4/Sub.2/2003/12/Rev.2 (2003), available at: http://www.1umn.edu/humanrts/links/norms-Aug2003.html.
6   *Commentary on the Norms on the Responsibilities of Transnational Corporations and Other Business Enterprises with Regard to Human Rights*, UN Doc. E/CN.4/Sub.2/2003/38/Rev.2 (2003) (the 'Commentary'). Available at: http://www1.umn.edu/humanrts/links/commentary-Aug2003.html.
7   Resolution 2003/16, 13 August 2003.
8   The UNCHR is an intergovernmental organ within the United Nations, consisting of representatives of 53 governments. See http://www.unhchr.ch/html/menu2/2/chr.htm
9   Decision 2004/116, 22 April 2004.
10   A group of seven multinationals consisting of ABB, Barclays, MTV Europe, National Grid Transco, Novartis, Novo Nordisk and the Body Shop International have formed the Business Leaders Initiative on Human Rights, to help further integrate human rights in business practices. An interim report on the results of this tentative application of the Norms will be published in 2005. Information is available at: http://www.bhrseminar.org/2003%20Seminar/pressrelease.pdf.

current text. The paper will also discuss the contribution of the Norms towards the development of increasing accountability for corporations.

A. BUSINESSES COVERED BY THE NORMS

The Norms apply to 'transnational corporations and other business enterprises'.

A transnational corporation is defined as an 'economic entity operating in more than one country or a cluster of economic entities operating in two or more countries – whatever their legal form, whether in their home country or country of activity, and whether taken individually or collectively'.[11]

The term 'other business enterprise' includes 'any business entity, regardless of the international or domestic nature of its activities, including a transnational corporation, contractor, subcontractor, supplier, licensee or distributor; the corporate, partnership, or other legal form used to establish the business entity; and the nature of the ownership of the entity'. Moreover, it is provided that the Norms are 'presumed to apply, as a matter of practice, if the business enterprise has any relation with a transnational corporation, the impact of its activities is not entirely local, or the activities involve violations of the right to security'.[12]

Based on this definition, it is not entirely clear which businesses fall under the scope of the Norms. This is especially true for entities not qualifying as transnational corporations. Although the Norms have been interpreted as encompassing purely domestic enterprises,[13] this does not necessarily follow from the definition of 'other business enterprise'. The first part of the definition includes virtually every business, including purely domestic businesses. However, the definition goes on to formulate a presumption for the application of the Norms in cases where the business enterprise has some form of international activity or relation with a transnational corporation. The obvious question is why the drafters included such a presumption when the first part of the definition provides for the application of the Norms to any business entity, regardless of its international or domestic activity. In conclusion, the definition is ambiguous and appears to be subject to broad interpretation.[14]

B. THE SCOPE OF THE NORMS

The Norms affirm that States shall bear the primary responsibility of promoting and ensuring respect for human rights. However, as organs of society, companies, as well as their officers and other persons working for them, also have human rights obligations and responsibilities under the Norms. Corporate human rights obligations are, however, secondary to those of States, and limited to their 'respective spheres of activity and influence'. Within this sphere of activity and

---

[11] The Norms, para. 20.
[12] The Norms, para. 21.
[13] See e.g. Amnesty International's booklet, *The UN Human Rights Norms For Business: Towards Legal Accountability* (2004) p. 8.
[14] In the following, and for the sake of simplicity, the terms 'corporations', 'companies' or 'businesses' will be used instead of 'transnational corporations and other business enterprises'.

influence, businesses have the obligation to 'promote, secure the fulfilment of, respect, ensure respect of and protect human rights recognized in international as well as national law'.[15] This is a key feature of the Norms. The extent to which corporate entities have obligations under international law is highly contentious. It is therefore unfortunate that the Commentary provides little guidance on this issue.

Although it is difficult to delineate the exact scope of corporate human rights responsibilities under the Norms, such responsibilities are undoubtedly far-reaching. The Commentary affirms that a corporation shall ensure (i) that it is not complicit in any human rights abuses, (ii) that it does not benefit from such abuses, and (iii) that it shall refrain from activities that would undermine governmental efforts to promote and ensure respect for human rights. Furthermore, the Commentary explains that companies shall use their influence in order to help promote and ensure respect for human rights. This has been interpreted as requiring, inter alia, that a corporation make efforts to influence a host government where violations of human rights are occurring, even in circumstances where such violations are not in any way connected with the corporation's activities.[16]

In current international law, the human rights obligations of private actors are framed in essentially negative terms. This means that individuals and corporations have a duty to refrain from violating the human rights of others. It is doubtful if and to what extent such obligations can be extended, insofar as they relate to private entities. Governments, on the other hand, have extensive 'positive duties' to promote, protect and fulfil the respect for human rights in their territories. These affirmative obligations are difficult to transpose onto corporations. If positive obligations are to be imposed upon companies, certain limitation language would more than likely be required. For instance the Norms might limit the 'sphere of activity and influence' with respect to the positive duties imposed on corporations. The Human Rights & Business Project of the Danish Institute for Human Rights suggests that companies should have positive human rights duties in four situations; (i) in relation to their workers, (ii) in relation to anyone residing on their land, (iii) when their products are used in violation of human rights, and (iv) in situations where a company in fact replaces the government.[17] The affirmative duties imposed on corporations under the Norms would benefit from a similar limitation.

---

[15]   The Norms, the preamble and para. 1.

[16]   In this respect, Sune Skadegard Thorsen has commented that 'if national violations of human rights law are discovered, companies will be expected to bring this up with governments for open discussion'. Mr Skadegard Thorsen points to the freedom of association in China as an obvious example. See Sune Skadegard Thorsen, *CSR Europe Q&A session: United Nations Norms on the Responsibility of Transnational Companies*, p. 13, available at: http://www.csreurope.org/whatwedo/ Themes/Businessandhumanrights/unnorms/ See also, Sir Geoffrey Chandler: 'there is understanding that the very presence of a company in a country ruled by an oppressive regime represents complicity if it is silent in the midst of human rights violations'. Sir Geoffrey Chandler, *The slow march to corporate accountability*, Ethical Corporation, 3 May 2004.

[17]   *Defining the Scope of Business Responsibility for Human Rights Abroad*, The Human Rights & Business Project of the Danish Institute for Human Rights, available at: http://www.human rightsbusiness.org/resp_6.htm.

C.   OVERVIEW OF THE OBLIGATIONS OF COMPANIES UNDER THE NORMS

The Norms are based on the *Universal Declaration of Human Rights* (1948) and other international treaties and conventions, such as the *International Covenant on Economic, Social and Cultural Rights* (1966) and the *International Covenant on Civil and Political Rights* (1966).

The approach of the Norms is to identify the rights and international instruments relevant to the conduct of business. Many provisions of both the Norms and the Commentary refer to a number of international conventions. The vast majority of these international instruments have been written to apply to governments. Although international instruments may be helpful when interpreting corporate obligations, their application to private actors is often far from evident. Consequently, such extensive references to international instruments may render it a difficult task for a corporation to determine in specific instances whether or not it is in compliance with the requirements of the Norms. Instead of simply incorporating these international instruments by reference, it would be far more beneficial for the Norms to set out in detail how the relevant international instruments are to be applied by companies in a business context.

One of the most interesting features of the Norms is that they have been drafted with the aim of producing a truly normative document. The document contains 19 substantive provisions and includes provisions regarding implementation, monitoring and reparation. This feature distinguishes the Norms from other guidelines, such as the United Nations Global Compact principles.[18] We have endeavoured to set out below the most significant aspects of the Norms and some of the problems related thereto.

1.   Equal Opportunity and Non-discrimination

Paragraph 2 of the Norms sets forth the fundamental human rights principles of non-discriminatory treatment and the right to equal opportunity. Corporations must not discriminate on the basis of the status of the individual unrelated to the requirements of the job to be performed, i.e. on the grounds of race, colour, sex, language, religion, political opinion, national or social origin, indigenous status, disability or age. The Commentary provides further examples such as health and marital status, capacity to bear children, pregnancy and sexual orientation. Given that neither of these lists is exhaustive, it is clear that the Norms contain extensive non-discrimination guarantees.

2.   Security of Persons

Paragraph 3 provides that corporations must not engage in or benefit from international crimes or violations of humanitarian law, such as crimes against humanity, genocide, torture, forced disappearance, forced or compulsory labour

---

[18]   Available at www.unglobalcompact.org/content/AboutTheGC/TheNinePrinciples/thenine.htm.

or hostage taking. These are well-defined, grave breaches of human rights and few would argue that corporations should not be required to comply with international criminal law in the conduct of their operations.

Further, pursuant to paragraph 4, companies are required to ensure that any security arrangements must observe international human rights norms, national laws and the professional standards of the country in which they operate. As a consequence, businesses must not hire security forces, which are known to be violators of human rights. Moreover, companies should examine security personnel prior to their employment and ensure that security forces are adequately trained and follow applicable international standards. The applicability of human rights obligations to the use of corporate security forces has attracted much attention over time[19] and the imposition of human rights obligations in such circumstances can be justified on the grounds that the use of such forces involves corporations performing a function that is typical of governments.

3.   Workers' Rights

Five substantive provisions of the Norms (paragraphs 5 to 9) are devoted to workers' rights. The Norms prohibit forced labour and child labour. Moreover, corporations are required to provide a safe and healthy working environment and to respect the freedom of association and the right to collective bargaining. Paragraph 8 demands that businesses provide workers with remuneration ensuring 'an adequate standard of living for them and their families'. The remuneration shall take 'due account of their needs for adequate living conditions with a view towards progressive improvement'.[20] The Commentary explains that the remuneration shall be 'freely agreed upon or fixed by national laws or regulations (whichever is higher)'. It appears the Norms would allow a corporation to pay minimum wages under the laws of the host country as long as such remuneration is sufficient to meet the basic needs of workers and their families. While the aim of the clause may be clear, commentators have highlighted the practical difficulty in determining a level of salary, which will ensure 'adequate living conditions'.[21] In this respect, the issue of adequate remuneration is a point that would merit further refinement.

4.   Consumer Protection

Paragraph 13 deals with consumer protection and requires companies to ensure that all goods and services provided are safe for their intended and reasonably

---

[19]   Among previous initiatives with respect to corporate use of security forces are the *UN Code of Conduct for Law Enforcement Officials*, adopted by General Assembly resolution 34/16 of 17 December 1979 and the *US-UK Voluntary Principles on Security and Human Rights*, adopted in 2000.

[20]   The term adequate standard of living also appears in Article 11 of the *International Covenant on Economic, Social and Cultural Rights* (1966), which states that each and every individual has the right to an adequate standard of living, including adequate food, clothing and housing.

[21]   Mallen Baker, *Analysis: Raising the heat on business over human rights*, Ethical Corporation, 18 August 2003. See also Sir Geoffrey Chandler, *Letters to the Editor: UN Sub-Commission's draft Norms on the Responsibilities of Transnational Corporations*, Ethical Corporation, 2 September 2003.

foreseeable uses. Moreover, paragraph 11 provides that businesses shall 'seek to ensure' that their goods and services are not used to abuse human rights.[22] The Norms do not provide any guidance on the extent of this latter obligation. Interpreting paragraph 11 in a broad sense could lead to very onerous obligations being placed on corporations. Certain questions must be asked in this respect: What measures are reasonable to demand of a company seeking to comply with this provision? To what extent must a company foresee potential uses of the goods or services provided by it? What is the extent of the company's obligations after the product has been placed on the market and purchased or acquired by violators of human rights? It may be necessary to limit a company's responsibility in this regard to human rights abuses which the company could reasonably have foreseen.

5. Environmental Protection

Paragraph 14 requires compliance with national laws and regulations as well as national and international practices, objectives and standards on the preservation of the environment. Moreover, businesses shall conduct their activities in a manner so as to contribute to the goal of sustainable development. One must assume that there is an implicit disclaimer on the balancing of environmental and economic interests in the assessment of a company's environmental performance under the Norms. Otherwise, it may be questionable whether some business activities, such as the extraction of fossil fuel, would at all be compatible with the Norms and the goal of sustainable development set out therein.

6. Reparation

One of the potentially most burdensome features of the Norms is the provision on damages contained in paragraph 18. This provision obliges corporations to 'provide prompt, effective and adequate reparation to those persons, entities and communities that have been adversely affected by failures to comply with these Norms through, among others, reparations, restitution, compensation and rehabilitation for any damage done or property taken'. The scope of this provision is very broad, insofar as any violation of the Norms may result in a company having to pay damages. As a result, it is fundamentally important for businesses to be able to foresee what constitutes a breach of the Norms. However, as discussed above, many of the Norms' provisions are ambiguously worded and as a result there is likely to be much uncertainty in determining when a company will be required to pay damages for a breach of the Norms. The issue of foreseeability will more than likely be taken into account by the business community when deciding whether or not to embrace the Norms.

---

[22] The requirement is stricter with respect to businesses supplying military, security or police products or services, which shall take 'stringent measures' to prevent such products or services from being used to commit human rights or humanitarian law violations. See the Commentary, para. 3(a).

D. THE IMPLEMENTATION, REPORTING AND MONITORING ENVISAGED BY THE NORMS

The Norms call upon States to 'establish and reinforce the necessary legal and administrative framework for ensuring that the Norms and other relevant national and international laws are implemented by corporations'. In this context, the Commentary suggests that governments should use the Norms as a 'model for legislation or administrative provisions'.[23]

1. Implementation

Paragraph 15 requires businesses to implement internal rules of operation in compliance with the Norms. Pursuant to the Commentary, corporations shall provide training to employees and shall make the internal rules available in the language of all relevant stakeholders. Corporations shall also 'apply and incorporate these Norms in their contracts and other dealings'. The Commentary further states that corporations shall ensure that they only do business with natural or legal persons adhering to the Norms or substantially similar standards. In this manner, companies must seek to influence the human rights behaviour of their business partners. If the business partner, however, persists in breaching the Norms, the company must cease any further business dealings.

Another interesting feature of the Norms is that corporations are required to assess the human rights impact of any major initiative or project before pursuing it, and to make available the results of the study to relevant stakeholders, whose comments shall be considered.[24]

2. Reporting

Companies are required to periodically report on their implementation of the Norms to all stakeholders and to the United Nations. Reporting is a key provision of the Norms, offering a practical means of improving compliance with corporate human rights obligations. There have already been examples of governments imposing mandatory corporate social responsibility reporting in national legislation[25] and it has been suggested that widespread reporting requirements could limit the need for further regulation with respect to corporate human rights obligations.[26]

---

[23] The Norms, para. 17.

[24] The Commentary, para. 16(i).

[25] For example, the French and Australian Parliaments have passed resolutions requiring manda-tory disclosure of social and environmental issues in companies' annual reports. See *CSR Corporate Social Responsibility and the Role of the Legal Profession, A Guide for European Lawyers Advising on Corporate Social Responsibility Issues*, CCBE, September 2003, p. 5.

[26] See Sir Geoffrey Chandler, *supra*, note 16.

3.   Monitoring

With respect to monitoring, paragraph 16 provides that companies shall be subject to periodic monitoring by the United Nations and other international or national mechanisms already in existence or yet to be created. The monitoring process shall be transparent and shall allow for complaints from stakeholders.

In its decision adopting the Norms, the Sub-Commission proposed that the working group should operate as a forum for dialogue between stakeholders and businesses. The working group was to receive information from stakeholders on corporate activities affecting human rights and invite the corporation concerned to comment on the information.[27] The UNCHR, however, rejected this idea and declared that the Sub-Commission should not perform any monitoring function in respect of corporate compliance with the Norms.[28]

E.   THE NORMS – A HELPFUL TOOL FOR COMPANIES?

It is now proposed to address the question as to whether the Norms are a helpful tool for companies seeking to assess their human rights obligations. It is contended that, apart from listing those international conventions which are instrumental in interpreting corporate obligations, the Norms, as they are currently drafted, offer little assistance to corporations in identifying their human rights obligations.

In the course of the above examination of the various provisions of the Norms, we have highlighted some of the difficulties which we envisage arising in relation to the corporate human rights obligations stipulated by the Norms. Such difficulties include the need to limit the scope of positive duties imposed on corporate entities, the determination of adequate remuneration and the extensive obligation to pay reparation.

From the point of view of companies seeking to identify their human rights obligations however, the principal criticism of the Norms must be in respect of their general nature and potential for broad interpretation. Certain provisions of the Norms are saved from such critique insofar as they contain obligations in respect of which there is a broad consensus in the international community. The content and scope of the prohibition on forced labour and the other provisions involving international criminal law are more readily identifiable as a result of the consensus regarding their content. In relation to the majority of the obligations set out in the Norms, there is, however, no such consensus. For example, there is no general international consensus as to the scope of the obligation upon corporations to pay adequate remuneration or to contribute to the right to development. In such circumstances, neither the Norms nor the Commentary provide sufficient guidance as to the scope of business responsibility and as a result, the content of many of the provisions of the Norms may be subject to wide interpretation. In particular, in such situations where there is no broad consensus as to the content of a particular obligation, the Norms may be required to define

---

[27]   *supra*, note 7.
[28]   *supra*, note 9.

more precisely the scope of the obligations being imposed upon corporations and in particular establish a clear minimum standard which corporations must meet.

Finally, it should be stated that the general wording of the Norms and the potential for broad interpretation will also have a detrimental effect on corporations' ability to insure against the potential costs of failing to comply with the Norms. A stable and regulated business environment is necessary for successful corporate operations and insuring against potential future costs is an important tool for a company seeking to create such an environment. In this context, it will be important for companies to be able to insure against any potential costs arising by operation of the Norms. In order to assess such future costs for the purpose of insurance, it is essential that corporations are able to foresee, with a sufficient degree of certainty, what their human rights obligations are under the Norms. This may be an important factor in determining whether companies decide to endorse the Norms.

F. THE NORMS AND INCREASING CORPORATE ACCOUNTABILITY

Since World War II, international human rights law has evolved towards conferring rights and imposing obligations on individuals. It is debatable as to what extent this also holds true for corporate entities.[29] However, it appears consistent with the current development that corporations will face increasing obligations under international human rights law. Among the most difficult tasks is defining the scope of business responsibility in the field of human rights. In this respect, the development and application of non-binding guidelines and standards for corporate behaviour plays an important role, giving more precision to corporate human rights obligations. Established corporate standards and practices, although non-binding, are an important factor in the current development of minimum standards and increasingly binding obligations for corporations in the field of human rights. Parallel with this development, there is also a movement towards greater national accountability, through implementation of international instruments and the adoption of national legislation regarding, inter alia, reporting requirements with respect to social and environmental performance.

Apart from legal accountability, there is also a large degree of external pressure being exerted upon companies to respect human rights and to commit to corporate social responsibility. Increasing public exposure and growing consumer awareness will undoubtedly lead to more pronounced negative effects for corporate human rights violators in the future. Inadequate human rights risk

---

[29] See Beth Stephens: *Corporate Liability for Violations of International Human Rights Law*, 114 Harv. L. Rev., pp. 2025, 2030–31 (2001). See also Andrew Clapham, *The Question of Jurisdiction Under International Criminal Law Over Legal Persons: Lessons from the Rome Conference on an International Criminal Court*, pp. 139–195, published in *Liability of Multinational Corporations Under International Law*, edited by M.T. Kamminga and S. Zia-Zarafi, Kluwer Law International, The Hague 2000; International Council on Human Rights Policy: *Beyond Voluntarism: Human Rights and the Developing International Legal Obligations of Companies*, February 2002, pp. 55–57. See also the Human Rights & Business Project of the Danish Institute for Human Rights, *supra*, note 17.

management may jeopardize brand value and limit a company's ability to compete in the market as well as its access to capital and qualified personnel. It may also subject a company to claims for damages. Business cannot afford to ignore human rights issues. A growing number of companies acknowledge their responsibility for human rights, but business leaders must also accept that increasingly binding regulations may eventually be required in order to bring corporate performance into line with the values of society.

The Norms have been described as an attempt by the United Nations to provide guidance to companies in respect of what human rights obligations they should fulfil.[30] It appears that the Norms were also drafted with the purpose of being somewhat controversial so as to fuel the debate on the scope of corporate obligations.[31] Indeed, the Norms have triggered broad debate and attracted the attention of the business world. However, as discussed in this article, many problems remain to be solved.

At its annual meeting in 2004, the UNCHR confirmed the importance and priority of corporate responsibility with regard to human rights. Significantly, both developed and developing countries endorsed the decision of the UNCHR.[32] The Norms therefore remain on the UNCHR agenda. The future of the project will, to a great extent, depend on the new High Commissioner Louise Arbour, who will be in charge of drafting the report commissioned by the UNCHR.[33] UNCHR, in its decision, specifically asks that 'all stakeholders' be consulted when preparing the report.[34] This request may be in response to the criticism from the business community that it was virtually excluded from the drafting process. It is imperative that companies are involved in defining corporate human rights responsibilities and the development of standards. Projects such as the Business Leaders Initiative on Human Rights' road testing of the Norms are important to identify realistic standards and determine what is reasonable to expect from businesses.

G. CONCLUSION

The Norms are on the UNCHRs agenda and the UNCHR has confirmed the priority it accords to the question of the responsibilities of transnational corporations with regard to human rights. Even though the current version of the Norms is unlikely to be adopted at the annual meeting of the UNCHR in 2005,

---

[30] *U professor helps draft new human rights standards*; University News Service, 4 September 2003. Available at: http://www1.umn.edu/umnnews/Feature_Stories/U_professor_helps_draft_new_human_rights_standards.html.

[31] Bernadette Hearne, *Proposed UN Norms on human rights: Is business opposition justified?*, Ethical Corporation, 22 March 2004.

[32] *Supra*, note 9. The decision of the UNCHR was adopted by consensus. The drafting was made by the UK government on behalf of Australia, Belgium, the Czech Republic, Ethiopia, Ghana, Hungary, Ireland, Japan, Mexico, Norway, South Africa and Sweden. See Bernadette Hearne, *Analysis: Proposed UN Norms on human rights shelved in favor of more study*, Ethical Corporation, 3 May 2004. The cooperation of developed and developing countries is significant as previous attempts to adopt corporate human rights norms within the United Nations have failed, in part, due to conflicting north/south differences of opinion. See also Sarah Joseph, *supra* note 2.

[33] UN Press Release GA/10231.

[34] *Supra*, note 9.

we should expect to see a revised proposal in the future. As indicated by the Sub-Commission, the Norms are a work in progress, to be reviewed and refined in the years to come. We are currently in the process of clarifying the extent of the responsibility of businesses for human rights. The Norms are a reflection of this development, and, at the very least, serve to remind us of the long road ahead and the many questions that remain to be answered.

Chapter 18

CORPORATE SOCIAL RESPONSIBILITY AND CORPORATE GOVERNANCE: NEW IDEAS AND PRACTICAL APPLICATIONS

Daniel Brennan

A. WHAT HAPPENS NEXT?

The value and need for principles of corporate social responsibility and corporate governance are becoming well established. The contents of the other chapters of this book amply illustrate that. We are therefore now at a stage when the corporate world and the community in which it operates want practical and innovative applications of these principles. What follows is a set of examples of what can be done:

- to assess whether a company is operating with social responsibility
- to consider international initiatives to improve the levels of such responsibility
- to introduce new ways in which corporate governance standards (which go hand in hand with corporate social responsibility) can be tested and reviewed objectively.

The examples are not exhaustive but they do indicate that we are now into the next stage of applying the established principles.

B. ASSESSING CRS STANDARDS

1. Business in the Community

The latest initiative is significant. In the United Kingdom Business in the Community began its Corporate Responsibility Index in 2003 and on 14 March

Ramon Mullerat (ed.), Corporate Social Responsibility: The Corporate Governance of the 21st Century, 263–276.
© 2005 *International Bar Association. Printed in the Netherlands.*

2004 139 participating companies met in London to be congratulated by the UK Department of Trade and Industry – for being one of the Companies That Count – by deciding to measure and control their impact on the society and environment in which they operate. The Corporate Responsibility Index (CRI) measures the impact businesses have on the staff they employ, the society in which they operate, and on the environment. It is designed to help managers improve their performance with consumers and investors.

Business in the Community, who devised the CRI, emphasize its strategic and financial importance to every business. The management of risks, transparency of systems, and corporate ethics upon which a business operates are central features. The proportion of people in the UK saying corporate responsibility is very important in their purchasing has risen from 24 per cent in 1997 to 38 per cent in 2003. Research published by the Co-operative Bank, as part of the Ethical Purchasing Index, shows that the total value of ethical consumption in Britain is now almost £20 billion. Sales of ethical goods grew 13 per cent in 2002, at a time when the British economy grew 1.7 per cent.

The CRI is a way in which all large businesses can report on their ethical and environmental performance. It is a tool and not a complete system. But it is an effective tool.

2.   How the CRI Works

It is a voluntary self assessment survey that provides an annual benchmark of how companies manage, measure and report their corporate responsibility. Business in the Community defines corporate responsibility as 'a company's positive impact on society and the environment, through its operations, products or services and through its interaction with key stakeholders such as employees, customers, investors, communities and suppliers'.

The Index is open to all companies in the FTSE 100, FTSE 250 and the Dow Jones Sustainability Index and to Business in the Community member firms that have a significant economic presence in the UK but not listed in the there. In 2004 500 companies were invited to take part. Of these, 139 companies completed the Index – 14 per cent more than in the first year. Importantly the 139 comprise most of the largest companies operating in the UK.

The CRI has issued companies with a web based tool developed by Business in the Community, and is protected by a password to each company, allowing participants to complete the survey on-line and to load the information that supports their submissions.

The Index model is based on a framework of four components now shown graphically.

Corporate strategy	⇨	Integration	⇨	Management	⇨	Performance and impact
				• Community • Environment • Marketplace • Workplace		

The corporate strategy section looks at how the nature of the business and its activities influences the company's values, how these tie in to strategy and how they are addressed through its management, development of policies, and responsibilities held at a senior level in the company.

The integration section looks at how companies organize, manage and integrate corporate responsibilities throughout their operations.

This integration is assessed in the management section which reviews processes for managing different stakeholder relationships. This section involves the key issues for a business and it monitors its policies, objectives and targets. The four management areas include community, environment, the market place, and the workplace.

The performance and impact section involves a company's performance across a range of social and environmental areas. There are a total of six impact areas. All companies make mandatory reports on two environmental impacts: global warming (or energy and transport together) and waste management.

In addition, companies are asked to select two social impacts drawn from product safety, occupational health and safety, human rights and the supply chain, diversity in the workplace, and community investment and an additional two self- selected impact areas material to the business.

The survey is scored with each of the four main sections being equally weighted at 22.5 per cent of the marks. A further mark is a warded for the level of assurance provided by a participant with a maximum of 10 per cent. In addition each of the four components in the management section is equally weighted and each of the social environmental impacts also equally weighted.

This is a self assessment process and each company is responsible for signing off its own Index results by its chief executive or through the board member dealing with corporate responsibility.

A number of levels of assurance are provided in the Index process. To underpin the integrity of the Index, Business in the Community has worked through a validation process, including checks throughout key stages in the collection, analysis, aggregation and presentation of data.

The Index process has been independently assured by Arthur D. Little, the Management Consultancy.

3. Caux Round Table

On an international scale the Caux Round Table (CRT) Principles for Business, and most recently their Principles for Government, represent the views of business leaders from Europe, Japan and the United States who are committed to energizing the role of business and industry as a vital force for innovative global change.

The Round Table was founded in 1986 by Frederik Philips, former President of Philips Electronics, and Olivier Giscard D'Estaing, Vice Chairman of INSEAD, as a means of reducing escalating trade tensions. It is concerned with the development of constructive economic and social relations as between parties and countries. At the urging of Ryuzaburo Kaku, Chairman of Canon Inc., the Round Table has focused attention on the importance of global corporate responsibility in reducing social and economic goods towards peace and stability.

The CRT believes that the world business community will play an important role in improving economic and social conditions. Its principles aim to express a gold standard against which business behaviour can be measured. It involves a process that identifies shared values, reconciles differing values, and fosters a shared perspective on business behaviour acceptable to, and respected by all.

The principles are rooted in two basic ethical ideals: kyosei and human dignity. The Japanese concept of kyosei means living and working together for the common good enabling co-operation and mutual prosperity to co-exist with healthy and fair competition. Human dignity refers to the sacredness or value of each person as an end, not simply as a means to the fulfillment of others purposes or even majority prescription.

Business behaviour can affect relationships among nations and peoples and so affect the prosperity and wellbeing of us all. Business is often the first contact between nations and by the way in which it causes social and economic changes, has a significant impact on the level of confidence or fear felt by people worldwide. The CRT places its primary emphasis on putting one's own house in order, and in seeking to establish what is right rather than who is right.

The business principles are now set out.

Section 1:   Preamble

The mobility of employment, capital, products and technology is making business increasingly global in its transactions and its effects. Law and market forces are necessary but insufficient guides for conduct. Responsibility for the policies and actions of business and respect for the dignity and interests of its stakeholders are fundamental.

Shared values, including a commitment to shared prosperity, are as important for a global community as for communities of smaller scale. For these reasons, and because business can be a powerful agent of positive social change, we offer the following principles as a foundation for dialogue and action by business leaders in search of business responsibility. In so doing, we affirm the necessity for moral values in economic decision-making. Without them, stable business relationships and a sustainable world community are impossible.

Section 2:   General Principles

Principle 1.   The responsibilities of corporations: beyond shareholders towards stakeholders

The value of a business to society is the wealth and employment it creates and the marketable products and services it provides to consumers at a reasonable price commensurate with quality. To create such value, a business must maintain its own economic health and vitality, but survival is not a sufficient goal.

Businesses have a role to play in improving the lives of all of their customers, employees and shareholders by sharing with them the wealth it has created. Suppliers and competitors as well should expect businesses to honour their obligations in a spirit of honesty and fairness. As responsible citizens of the local, national, regional and global communities in which they operate, businesses share a part in shaping the future of those communities.

Principle 2. The economic and social impact of corporations: towards innovation, justice and world community

Businessess established in foreign countries to develop, produce or sell should also contribute to the social advancement of those countries by creating productive employment and helping to raise the purchasing power of their citizens. Business should also contribute to human rights, education, welfare and vitalization of the countries in which they operate.

Businesses should contribute to economic and social development not only in the countries in which they operate but also in the world community at large, through effective and prudent use of resources, free and fair competition, and emphasis on innovation in technology, production methods, marketing and communications.

Principle 3. Corporate behaviour: beyond the letter of law towards a spirit of trust

While accepting the legitimacy of trade secrets, businesses should recognize that sincerity, candour, truthfulness, the keeping of promises, and transparency contribute not only to their own credibility and stability but also to the smoothness and efficiency of business transactions, particularly on the international level.

Principle 4. Respect for rules: beyond trade friction towards co-operation

To avoid trade frictions and promote freer trade, equal conditions for competition, and fair and equitable treatment for all participants, businesses should respect international and domestic rules. In addition, they should recognize that some behaviour, although legal, may still have adverse consequences.

Principle 5. Support for multilateral trade: beyond isolation towards world community

Businesses should support the multilateral trade system of the World Trade Organization and similar international agreements. They should co-operate in efforts to promote the progressive and judicious liberalization of trade and to relax those domestic measures that unreasonably hinder global commerce, while giving due respect to national policy objectives.

Principle 6. Respect for the environment: beyond protection towards enhancement

A business should protect, and, where possible, improve the environment, promote sustainable development , and prevent the wasteful use of natural resources.

Principle 7. Avoidance of illicit operations: beyond profit towards peace

A corporation should not participate in or condone bribery, money-laundering and other corrupt practices: indeed, it should seek co-operation with others to eliminate them. It should not trade in arms or materials used for terrorist activities, drug traffic or other organized crime.

Section 3: Stakeholder Principles

Customers: We believe in treating all customers with dignity, irrespective of whether they purchase our products and services directly or otherwise acquire them in the market. We therefore have a responsibility to:

- Provide our customers with the highest-quality products and services consistent with their requirements

- Treat our customers fairly in all aspects of our business transactions, including a high level of service and remedies for customer dissatisfaction
- Make every effort to ensure that the health and safety of our customers, as well as the quality of their environment, will be sustained or enhanced by our products or services
- Assure respect for human dignity in products offered, marketing and advertising
- Respect the integrity of the culture of our customers

Employees: We believe in the dignity of every employee and in taking employee interests seriously. We therefore have a responsibility to:

- Provide jobs and compensation that improve workers' living conditions
- Provide working conditions that respect employees' health and dignity
- Be honest in communications with employees and open in sharing information, limited only by legal and competitive constraints
- Listen to and, where possible, act on employee suggestions, ideas, requests and complaints
- Engage in good-faith negotiations when conflict arises
- Avoid discriminatory practices and guarantee equal treatment and opportunity in areas such as gender, age, race and religion
- Promote in the business itself the employment of differently abled people in places of work where they can be genuinely useful
- Protect employees from avoidable injury and illness in the workplace
- Be sensitive to the serious unemployment problems frequently associated with business decisions, and work with governments, employee groups, other agencies and each other in addressing these dislocations

Owners/investors: We believe in honouring the trust our investors place in us. We therefore have a responsibility to:

- Apply professional and diligent management in order to secure a fair and competitive return on our owners' investment
- Disclose relevant information to owners/investors subject only to legal and competitive constraints
- Conserve, protect and increase the owners'/investors' assets
- Respect owners'/investors' requests, suggestions, complaints, and formal resolutions

Suppliers: Our relationship with suppliers and subcontractors must be based on mutual respect. We therefore have a responsibility to:

- Seek fairness and truthfulness in all our activities including pricing, licensing and rights to sell
- Ensure that our business activities are free from coercion and unnecessary litigation
- Foster long-term stability in the supplier relationship in return for value, quality, competitiveness and reliability

- Share information with suppliers and integrate them into our planning processes
- Pay suppliers on time and in accordance with agreed terms of trade
- Seek, encourage and prefer suppliers and subcontractors whose employment practices respect human dignity

Competitors: We believe that fair economic competition is one of the basic requirements for increasing the wealth of nations and ultimately for making possible the just distribution of goods and services. We therefore have a responsibility to:

- Foster open markets for trade and investment
- Promote competitive behaviour that is socially and environmentally beneficial and demonstrates mutual respect among competitors
- Refrain from either seeking or participating in questionable payments or favours to secure competitive advantages
- Respect both tangible and intellectual property right
- Refuse to acquire commercial information by dishonest or unethical means, such as industrial espionage

Communities: We believe that as global corporate citizens we can contribute to such forces of reform and human rights as are at work in the communities in which we operate. We therefore have a responsibility in those communities to:

- Respect human rights and democratic institutions, and promote them wherever practical
- Recognize government's legitimate obligation to the society at large and support public policies and practices that promote human development through harmonious relations between business and other segments of society
- Collaborate with those forces in the community dedicated to raising standards of health, education, economic wellbeing and workplace safety
- Promote and stimulate sustainable development and play a lead role in preserving the physical environment and conserving the Earth's resources
- Support peace, security, diversity and social integration
- Respect the integrity of local cultures
- Be a good citizen through charitable donations, educational and cultural contributions, and employee participation in community and civic affairs

4.   The Self-Assessment and Improvement Process

The CRT principles represent a stakeholder-based, and cross cultural statement of business values. The CRT has developed a managerial tool, that puts them into practice, called Self-Assessment and Improvement Process (SAIP). This is designed to assist company workers at every level to undertake an organizational self appraisal process. It has already been successfully beta tested in the

United States, Japan and Germany. It works up through different levels of company involvement as now set out:

Phase I: Awareness
Who. CEO or COO, acting individually
What. 'Impromptu survey' using Summary Criteria
Required Time. 30 minutes
Focus. Approach
Outcomes. Systematic speculation ('check the box') about company status, attention to issues or corporate ethics and corporate social responsibility.

Phase II: Preliminary Assessment
Who. Senor Management Team
What. A 'pro forma evaluation' using Summary Criteria[1]
Required Time. 30 minutes
Focus. Approach, Deployment
Outcomes. An initial, evidence-based evaluation of company efforts, including a preliminary score and a first-pass identification of improvement opportunities.

Phase III: Improvement
Who. 'Full Implementation Team' (cross-functional, cross-employee group, etc.
What. A full systematic written response to either the Summary or 'long form' criteria[2]
Required Time. 3 to 12 months
Focus. Approach. Development, Results
Outcomes. A comprehensive, fact-based evaluation.[3]

- A score based on these efforts
- An identification of improvement opportunities
- An action plan for improvement incorporating data about relevant best-practices

The primary result is the enhancement of company performance that accrues from the action plan implementation.

---

[1]   The assessment is 'pro forma' insofar as (1) it considers only two of three potential performance dimensions (*Approach and development,* but not *results*), and (2) evidence is collected to support the assessment – for example, documented policies and practices – nut not detailed data about company decisions and actions. (See n. 3 below).

[2]   Companies can tailor the implementation to meet their needs. For example, a firm may utilize the more specific, 'long form' criteria for a stakeholder, to facilitate the detailed examination of a vital relationship. Also, a firm may adapt or modify specific benchmarks, to focus them on unique company concerns.

[3]   A fact-based evaluation transcends an evidence-based evaluation in that both *relevant evidence* is gathered (e.g. documented policies/practices) and *additional data* on company performance is collected (e.g. data about decisions and actions to assess whether they in fact conform with written policies/practices).

Phase IV: World Class Performance

Actions undertaken in the foregoing levels culminates in world class performance. It is characterized by two types of *continuous improvement*: (1) ongoing, incremental efforts in areas previously targeted for improvement, and (2) new improvement initiatives in areas which to date have gone unaddressed. It may also entail *broadened deployment* of the improvement effort, e.g., to divisions or entities within the firm heretofore uninvolved in assessment and improvement activities. At this stage, the company's performance typically, would receive *recognition* from external organizations, and it would be viewed as a *role model* by other companies.

The SAIP can be tailored both as to time and depth in relation to company size, and to accommodate the learning curve of how best to use the SAIP.

As the process is a self-assessment, it acts as a diagnosis of all the critical value drivers supporting a company's sustainable profitability in an ethical and socially responsible manner. The analysis of assessment results permits senior management to set appropriate benchmarks for future improvement of company performance. The process can be employed as the above chart shows in four different levels of complexity – on an initial level of intuitive executive assessment through three levels of increasing complexity and more rigorous documentation. The SAIP is the subject of a significant academic paper by Professor Kenneth Goodpaster *et al* 'Stakeholder thinking – Beyond Paradox to Practicality' JCC7 Autumn 2002 Greenleaf Publishing pp. 93–111.

The CRT Principles are thus applied through the SAIP system:

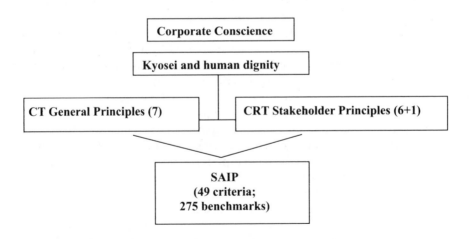

C. INTERNATIONAL INITIATIVES

1. The World Economic Forum has carried out two important initiatives recently.

In January 2004 the WEF's Corporate Citizenship Initiative released results of a survey of CEOs and CFOs of a number of companies focusing on the communication of corporate citizenship to investors and financial institutions.

70 per cent of the respondents expected increased interest in environmental social and governance (ESG) issues by mainstream investors in the future.

ESG issues were also highlighted by the respondents in terms of problems of definition, making and measuring the business case, quality and quantity of information, skills and competence, and different time objectives.

But the message was positive and so the WEF Global Corporate Citizenship Initiative, in association with AccountAbility, is now investigating how to develop ESG in mainstream investment policies and practices. The initiative involves of a series of international round tables with major players such as pension funds, asset management companies and regulators. Results were published in a WEF – AccountAbility Report in October 2004.

2. The UN Global Compact in 2004 produced a major report 'Who Cares Wins'. It sets out recommendations by the financial sector better to integrate ESG issues in analysis, asset management and securities brokerage. This involved 20 of the world's leading financial institutions. Its conclusions are:

- *Analysts* are asked to better incorporate environmental, social and governance (ESG) factors in their research where appropriate and to further develop the necessary investment know-how, models and tools in a creative and thoughtful way. Based on the existing know-how in especially exposed industries, the scope should be expanded to include other sectors and asset classes. Because of their importance for sustainable development, emerging markets should receive particular consideration and environmental, social and governance criteria should be adapted to the specific situation in these markets. Academic institutions, business schools and other research organizations are invited to support the efforts of financial analysts by contributing high-level research and thinking.
- *Financial institutions* should commit to integrating environmental, social and governance processes. This must be supported by a strong commitment at the Board and senior management level. The formulation of long-term goals, the introduction of organizational learning and change processes, appropriate training and incentive systems for analysts are crucial in achieving the goal of a better integration of these issues.
- *Companies* are asked to take a leadership role by implementing environmental, social and corporate governance principles and policies and to provide information and reports on related performance in a more consistent and standardized format. They should identify and communicate key challenges and value drivers and prioritize environmental, social and governance issues accordingly. We believe that this information is best conveyed to financial markets through normal investor relation communication channels and encourage, when relevant, an explicit mention in the annual report of companies. Concerning the outcomes of financial research in this field, companies should accept positive as well as critical results.
- *Investors* are urged to explicitly request and reward research that includes environmental, social and governance aspects and to reward well-managed companies. Asset managers are asked to integrate research on such aspects in

investment decisions and to encourage brokers and companies to provide better research and information. Both investors and asset managers should develop and communicate proxy voting strategies on ESG issues as this will support analysts and fund managers in producing relevant research and services.

– *Pension fund trustees* and their *selection consultants* are encouraged to consider environmental, social and governance issue in the formulation of investment mandates and the selection of investment managers, taking into account their fiduciary obligations to participants and beneficiaries.

– *Governments* and *multilateral agencies* are asked to proactively consider the investment of their pension funds according to the principles of sustainable development, taking into account their fiduciary obligations to participants and beneficiaries.

– *Consultants and financial advisers* should help create a greater and more stable demand for research in this area by combining research on environmental, social and governance aspects with industry level research and sharing their experience with financial market actors and companies in order to improve their reporting on these issues.

– *Regulators* are invited to shape legal frameworks in a predictable and transparent way as this will support integration in financial analysis. Regulatory frameworks should require a minimum degree of disclosure and accountability on environmental, social and governance issues from companies, as this will support financial analysis. The formulation of specific standards should on the other hand, rely on market-driven voluntary initiatives. We encourage *financial analysts* to participate more actively in ongoing voluntary initiatives, such as the Global Reporting Initiative, and help shape a reporting framework that responds to their needs.

– *Stock exchanges* are invited to include environmental, social and governance criteria in listing particulars for companies as this will ensure a minimum degree of disclosure across all listed companies. As a first step, stock exchanges could communicate to listed companies the growing importance of environmental, social and governance issues. Similarly, *other self-regulatory organizations* (e.g. NASD, FSA), professional credential-granting organizations (e.g. AIMR, EFFAS), *accounting standard-setting bodies* (e.g. FASB, IASB), *public accounting entities*, and *rating agencies and index providers* should all establish consistent standards and frameworks in relation to environmental, social and governance factors.

– *Non-Governmental Organisation* (NGOs) can also contribute to better transparency by providing objective information on companies to the public and the financial community.

This is a major report and it represents the views of senior executives of financial institutions and companies which are signatories to the Global Compact. Whilst establishing the link between ESG issues and investment decisions, this report seeks to contribute to better integration of the factors and investment decisions which ultimately support the implementation of the Global Compact principles throughout the business world.

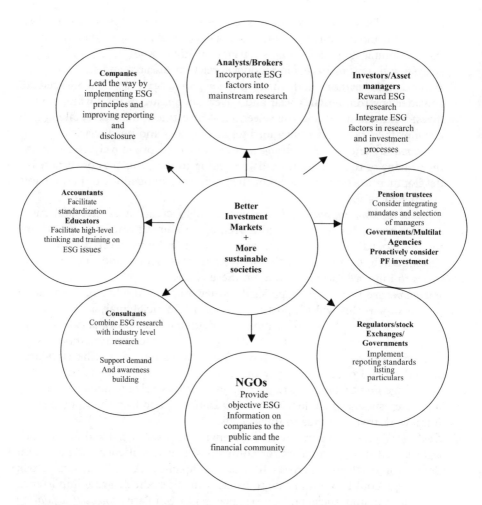

Graphical summary of key recommendations of "Who Cares Win"
Overall goals:
– Stronger and more resilient financial markets
– Contribution to sustainable development
– Awareness and mutual understanding of involved stakeholders
– Improved trust in financial institutions

D.   CORPORATE GOVERNANCE INITIATIVES

1. Many investors and executives would welcome an index that rates companies according to their corporate governance practices. But there are significant, but not insoluble, tecnical problems with such an initiative.

Standard & Poors introduced a model in America several years ago. It operated on a voluntary basis but has not thus far become generally accepted.

However a representative of the Association of British Insurers has described the benefit – 'an index gives you a thumbnail sketch of the company and shows you how it is improving over time'.

Many investors would welcome such a corporate governance index. Both the Investment Management Association and the National Association of Pension Funds in the UK have given cautious approval to the theory.

FTSE, led by its Director Mark Makepeace, in December 2004 launched a Corporate Governance Index. This was in partnership with Institution of Shareholder Services, a provider of proxy voting and corporate governance services in the US and abroad.

FTSE and ISS have identified five areas for comparison: board composition and independence; executive and director compensation; company ownership; audit independence, and take over defences and shareholder rights.

They want to make global comparisons. They seek to achieve correct weighting for regions because of difference in practices and cultural emphases between countries.

It is likely that this new FTSE Index will target the US and Europe and then develop into other markets.

2. It is essential that corporate governance standards are introduced in the economies of developing countries. The fact that badly managed companies may make significant profits in the volatile markets of the developing world is no indication of long-term economic strength. Asia provides evidence of common aims for corporate governance in an established and in a new economy. It is highly significant that the Tokyo Stock Exchange published for the first time its own 'Principles of Corporate Governance for Listed Companies' in the summer of 2004. In China the China Securities Regulatory Commission have also recently added to their Register of Expected Requirements from Listed Companies to complement the Code of Corporate Governance which they issued several years ago.

It is clearly in the interests of the economies of the developing world to introduce systems for evaluating corporate governance standards in companies either by weightings or an index,used by stock exchanges and investors, or both.

3. That such systems can work is demonstrated by the introduction of the Novo Mercado in Brazil. It is a segment of the market of the Sao Paulo Stock Exchange. Companies listed in the segment have strict CG controls including abiding by US and international accounting standards and maintaining a free float of at least 25 per cent. An arbitration panel has been created to settle shareholder disputes. Investors such as Merrill Lynch put NM companies at the top of their rankings for CG. The reason for the creation of the NM is to allow companies who want to abide by international best practice to differentiate themselves from the main Brazilian listed rankings. It is also expected that their adherence to the NM listing rules will allow those companies to attract quality domestic and international investors and ultimately lower their cost of capital.

The system of the Novo Mercado is only slowly being accepted, but it is working and provides a model for what can be achieved in the developing world.

E.   CONCLUSION

The variety of initiatives outlined in this chapter shows the determination by many to work for progressive change to implement CSR and CG. Bodies such as

Business in the Community and the Caux Round Table, or international bodies under the umbrella of the United Nations or World Economic Forum, and proposed stock exchange indices and national governments wishing to achieve good corporate governance all represent a new sense of purpose. We now have innovative and practical applications of established principle. There may be pitfalls on the way ahead. But we have started on the right path to put principle into practice.

PART V

REGIONAL PERSPECTIVES

Chapter 19

THE EUROPEAN INITIATIVES

Jonathan Lux
Sune Skadegard Thorsen
Annemarie Meisling

A. EUROPE AND CSR

The development of Corporate Social Responsibility (CSR) in Europe goes hand in hand with other developments including increasing concerns for our fellow man and the environment generally. It is, therefore, unsurprising that European institutions and many of the member state governments have greeted CSR with some enthusiasm. However, there has been considerable debate on how best to promote CSR – namely, whether the European institutions should promote voluntary codes or mandatory regulations.

The CSR movement in Europe gained momentum in the mid-1980s with human rights activists starting to pressure companies to act in a responsible manner and abandon the exploitation of workers in third-world countries especially the use of child labour. It took some ten years before the significance of these issues came to be recognized at the European Union (EU) level and it was only from the mid-1990s that the European institutions started to engage in the debate.

The present chapter describes the characteristics of the European CSR movement, focussing primarily on the legislative measures at the EU institutional level with some examples of initiatives taken in the member states and European networks.

The first nine sections outline the development of CSR in Europe from the mid-1990s in chronological order. Sections J–M describe a number of voluntary network initiatives and section N gives some examples of relevant initiatives in EU member states. Finally, the legislative measures to promote CSR in Europe are discussed in a wider context in section O.

Ramon Mullerat (ed.), Corporate Social Responsibility: The Corporate Governance of the 21st Century, 279–298.
© 2005 *International Bar Association. Printed in the Netherlands.*

B.   MAIN INITIATIVES

Both the European Parliament and the Commission are working to develop policies to stimulate CSR throughout the EU. The main difference in the approach between the two revolves around whether the EU measures should be voluntary or mandatory. The Commission favours a voluntary approach whereas the Parliament favours a mandatory regime. One can find the same schism or debate at EU member state level with, for example, some countries having brought in legislation obliging pension funds and listed companies to report on matters going beyond their financial activities and extending to their social and environmental impact. Other member states, on the other hand, have been more cautious in approach, starting with a network-based dialogue between the various stakeholders. There is something to be said for each approach and the two approaches have served to create a multi-faceted development in Europe. The basis of discussions has often been codes of conduct on human rights and good corporate governance from which other aspects of CSR have evolved.

At an institutional level, the main initiatives have been the Commission Green Paper on CSR and the establishment of a multi-stakeholder forum. The United Kingdom and France have so far taken the lead, adopting several kinds of legislation on CSR and company reporting at the national level.

C.   MANIFESTO OF ENTERPRISES AGAINST SOCIAL EXCLUSION

The CSR movement at a European institutional level began in 1995, when the then President of the European Commission, Jaques Delors launched a 'Manifesto of Enterprises Against Social Exclusion'.[1] The manifesto appeared as a voluntary initiative taken by the corporate sector, to express their willingness to prevent and combat social exclusion and enhance their social responsibility. One of the ways decided upon was the creation of a European network – the European Business Network for Social Cohesion (EBNSC), which later developed into CSR Europe.[2] The manifesto was officially signed by the member states at a conference in London on 11 and 12 of May 1995. It is still used by a range of large enterprises, national business organizations and governments as a point of departure for business involvement on social cohesion. The manifesto contains a declaration and guidelines, proposing possible avenues for action, for interested businesses to adapt and extend in line with their individual concerns.

CSR Europe has taken the manifesto further and helps companies to achieve profitability, sustainable growth and human progress by placing CSR in the mainstream of business practice. CSR Europe offers business managers learning, benchmarking and capacity building opportunities as well as facilitating a broader stakeholder dialogue.

[1]   See www.csreurope.org/aboutus/socialexclusion_page393.aspx.
[2]   See www.csreurope.org.

D.   EU LISBON SUMMIT, MARCH 2000

An extraordinary European Council meeting of heads of state and government was held in Lisbon on 23 and 24 March 2000. The aim of this 'Summit' meeting was to promote measures to strengthen employment, economic reform and social cohesion in the new 'knowledge-based economy'. Whilst the manifesto had engendered certain worthwhile changes in business practice, it was not until the Lisbon Summit that CSR was pushed to the top of the EU political agenda. At the Lisbon Summit, the European leaders integrated CSR into the strategic goal of the EU to become, by the year 2010, 'the most competitive and dynamic knowledge-based economy in the world, capable of sustainable economic growth with more and better jobs and greater social cohesion'.[3] As is recorded in the Council Conclusions, companies are expressly required to act from a 'corporate sense of social responsibility regarding best practices on lifelong learning, work organization, equal opportunities and social inclusion and sustainable development'.[4]

E.   EU COMMISSION'S GREEN PAPER ON PROMOTING A EUROPEAN FRAMEWORK FOR CSR, 2001

In continuation of the steps taken at the Lisbon Summit, and in line with the sustainable development strategy for Europe agreed at the European Council meeting in Gothenburg in 2001, the Commission published a Green Paper in July 2001[5] on a European framework for CSR.

The Green Paper aims to foster a debate on CSR, the role of the EU in developing CSR and the creation of partnerships amongst stakeholders, in which all actors have an active role to play. This CSR initiative by the Commission is not an attempt to shift public responsibilities to the private sector; rather, the intention is to complement the activities of public and local authorities.

The Green Paper sets out how the Commission views the concept of corporate social responsibility in the EU context. The Commission starts by conceptualizing CSR, placing it in the 'triple-bottom line' context of people, planet and profit. This is an appropriate starting point, as the triple-bottom line is a globally acknowledged concept when it comes to tackling sustainable development issues at the corporate level.

The Commission defines CSR as: '[A] concept, whereby companies integrate social and environmental concerns in their business operations and in their interaction with their stakeholders on a voluntary basis. Being socially responsible means not only fulfilling legal expectations, but also going beyond legal compliance and investing "more" into human capital, the environment and the relations to stakeholder.[5] The experience [has been] that going beyond legal compliance can contribute to a company's competitiveness'.[6]

---

3   Lisbon European Council: Presidency Conclusions 29/13/2000 NR: 100/1/0.
4   Article 39 in the Council Conclusions at www.europa.eu.int/comm/off/index_en.htm.
5   European Commission 'Promoting a European Framework for Corporate Social Responsibility'. Green Paper. Employment and Social Affairs, July 2001. See www.europa.eu.int/comm/ employment_social/soc-dial/csr/greenpaper.htm.
6   Commission Green Paper p. 8. www.europa.eu.int/comm/employment_social/soc-dial/csr/ greenpaper.htm.

The Commission treats 'legal expectations' as those deriving not only from national law but also from international law: 'By stating their social responsibility and voluntarily taking on commitments which go beyond common regulatory and conventional requirements, which they would have to respect in any case, companies endeavour to raise the standards of social development, environmental protection and respect of fundamental rights'.[7]

The Commission's goal is to complement and add value to existing CSR activities by 'providing an overall European framework, aiming at promoting quality and coherence of CSR practices [... and] supporting best practical approaches to cost-effective evaluation'.[8]

The Commission appears to treat all voluntary initiatives on the 'triple-bottom line', extending beyond compliance with legal obligations, as CSR initiatives. In other words, the Commission presupposes that companies will observe national and international legislation, including the international human rights covenants. However, this may be an over-optimistic assessment. Most European companies may comply with national legislation but many may still be violating provisions of international law, such as freedom of association and collective bargaining, the right to equal opportunities on the labour market, the right to privacy etc. This notwithstanding, the Commission's approach may be helpful in that it stresses that companies should not only aim to comply with national and international legislation. The Commission's expectation is that there should be something more to company activities than compliance with legal obligations if they wish to present themselves as responsible businesses in the wider context.

The authors' paper used different terminology to describe performance by companies, which extends beyond compliance with legal obligations – namely, corporate social opportunity. All companies should fulfill the responsibilities defined by law, both national and international. This would create the necessary foundation for moving into the sphere, which the Commission has focused on – a sphere of proactive engagement.[9]

According to the Commission, CSR has two dimensions, internal and external.

- The internal dimension covers the responsibility towards employees, including their health and safety, reasonable working hours, diversity in the recruitment process and due consultation of employees, when considering structural changes in the company, such as down-sizing or restructuring. Another part of the internal dimension is the responsible management of environmental impacts and efficient use of natural resources. In other words, the internal dimension covers core labour rights and environmental responsibility.
- The external dimension of course extends beyond the 'walls' of the company to the local community and other stakeholders such as business suppliers, customers, public authorities and NGOs. One factor is that

---

[7]   Commission Green Paper p. 4. www.europa.eu.int/comm/employment_social/soc-dial/csr/greenpaper.htm.

[8]   Commission Green Paper p. 7. www.europa.eu.int/comm/employment_social/soc-dial/csr/greenpaper.htm.

[9]   See Ramon Mullerat (ed.), Corporate Social Responsibility: The Corporate Governance of the 21st Century, 2005 Kluwer Law International. Chapter 20 by Skadegard Thorsen and Meisling.

companies working closely with business partners in supply chains, can both reduce costs and increase quality. Thus, building a good relationship with one's suppliers 'may result in fair prices, terms and expectations along with quality and reliable delivery'.[10]

Outsourcing is becoming increasingly popular but companies should remember that they still have responsibilities towards their new suppliers as well as their staff. In the external dimension of CSR, human rights play a central role. Companies must consider this when setting up business operations in countries where human rights violations occur and should also consider the impact on their global supply chain.

Now, some talk simply of 'Corporate Responsibilities' to encompass the whole of the company's relationship to sustainable development. In other words, this would encompass economic, environmental and social responsibilities.

The Commission's focus on human rights is very relevant. Multinational companies face human rights challenges including matters such as child labour, working conditions, relations with governments, where human rights violations are prevalent. In short, a human rights policy is indispensable. However, it is to be noted that human rights are equally relevant in the 'internal dimension'.[11] The bottom line for all issues mentioned by the Commission under its description of the internal dimension is basic human rights: health and safety of workers, reasonable working hours together with maximum working hours, diversity in the recruitment process in accordance with non-discrimination and equal opportunities principles together with due consultation of employees when considering structural changes in the company, including down-sizing or restructuring.

Many only take note of only human rights when discussing CSR in relation to operations in third-world areas but this is a mistake. The large number of cases pending in the European Court of Human Rights provides ample evidence that human rights are under threat all over the world, including our own backyard. To focus simply on human rights abuses in third-world countries is mistaken and suggests double-standards; indeed, it is reminiscent of 'old empire'.

The Commission stresses the importance of codes of conduct in the CSR field. However, the Commission discourages companies from developing such codes themselves but, rather, promotes the use of established international standards, such as the Universal Declaration of Human Rights, the International Labour Organization's (ILO) Declaration on Fundamental Principles and Rights at Work and the OECD Guidelines.[12] It is felt that making use of the established international framework will increase the possibility for companies to speak with one voice towards their supply chain and thereby put pressure on them to respect human rights, etc.

---

[10]   See Commission Green Paper p. 13. www.europa.eu.int/comm/employment_social/soc-dial/csr/greenpaper.htm.
[11]   See Ramon Mullerat (ed.), Corporate Social Responsibility: The Corporate Governance of the 21st Century, 2005 Kluwer Law International. Chapter 20 by Skadegard Thorsen and Meisling.
[12]   Since the publishing of the Green Paper the UN Norms for Transnational Companies have been developed.

The Commission also recommends that CSR activities be integrated into the management of the company, rather than simply being an 'add-on' to the core activities[13] of the business. Further, ongoing verification and assessment is necessary together with CSR reporting. The reporting should be transparent and linked to international standards such as the SA8000[14] and be verified by independent third parties.

If CSR is to be more than simply a marketing exercise then it is crucial that it be an integrated part of the daily management of a company. It should be supported by the senior management and used in their strategic planning process. If the company is to derive competitive advantage and take corporate social leadership, it is vital that it addresses CSR in a serious manner.[15]

Throughout its paper the Commission argues the business case for companies engaging in CSR; the so-called 'win–win scenario'. Thus, there is a value for companies in having a healthy and motivated workforce as well as to reduce energy and waste disposal bills (achieved by managing the environmental impact of the enterprise in a responsible way) just as there is a value for the environment and society at large. Focussing on voluntary efforts and the 'win–win' outcome helps the Commission avoid the far more difficult issues which would arise if it were decided to legislate in this area – e.g. for mandatory minimum standards.

The Commission's initiative in drafting this Green Paper has been well received and more than 250 organizations – businesses and various other institutions – have responded to the Green Paper. The overall consensus from this exercise is that the business community favours a voluntary approach to CSR; that CSR should be market-driven and that legislation should not be imposed. However, the unions and civil society organizations emphasize that voluntary initiative may not be sufficient to protect workers' and citizens' rights. In general, stakeholders agree that there must be transparency in terms of company practices together with comprehensive and reliable information.

The Commission's Communication published in 2002 takes account of these comments and proposes further steps for EU action – see section G.

F.   COUNCIL RESOLUTION, DECEMBER 2001

The EU Council has expressed its support for the Commission's CSR initiative in its resolution of December 2001.[16] This resolution records, in positive terms, that CSR contributes to attaining the objectives laid down by the European Council in Lisbon, Nice and Gothenburg for the EU to become the most competitive and dynamic knowledge-based economy.

---

[13]   See Commission Green Paper p. 15. www.europa.eu.int/comm/employment_social/soc-dial/csr/greenpaper.htm.

[14]   SA8000 is a standard for assessing labour conditions in global manufacturing operations. The Council on Economic Priorities Accreditation Agency establishes it.

[15]   See Ramon Mullerat (ed.), Corporate Social Responsibility: The Corporate Governance of the 21st Century, 2005 Kluwer Law International. Chapter 20 by Skadegard Thorsen and Meisling.

[16]   Council Resolution of 3 December 2001 can be found in the Official Journal of the European Union (OJC 86, 10 April 2002).

G. EUROPEAN PARLIAMENT'S CODE OF CONDUCT, DECEMBER 1998 AND JUNE 2002

The European Parliament was one of the first institutional players to engage in the development of CSR. Already in 1996, the Parliament published a report on human rights calling for a code of conduct for European companies operating in third-world countries. In 1997, the Parliament once again called for a code and in July 1998 the Parliament published a report together with a European code of conduct covering the activities of Trans-National Corporations (TNCs) operating in developing countries.[17]

In its report, the Parliament takes CSR engagement one-step further than the Commission and calls for the establishment of a European framework setting a legal basis for companies' operations worldwide. In other words, the Parliament proposes a code, which would set out minimum applicable standards such as the ILO Declaration, the OECD Guidelines, the UN Declarations and the two UN Covenants.

It may be said that the UN has taken up the EU Parliament's suggestion in that the UN norms on transnational companies with regard to human rights[18] in many ways reflect the demands of the Parliament. However, the norms are not legally binding (see chapter 17).

By way of criticism, it may be said that the EU Parliament is focussing only on the human rights abuses occurring in the developing countries. Of course, it is said that the human rights abuses occurring in these parts of the world are more severe than the abuses occurring in the western world. However, it is clear from the many cases pending before the European Court of Human Rights that there are also numerous examples of human rights violations in the western world. Companies that focus simply on challenges in the developing world, run the risk of setting double standards, not acknowledging the challenges for economical developed countries; challenges that have increased dramatically with the staging of 'The War on Terrorism'.

By way of reaction to the Commission's Green Paper, the EU Parliament in its resolution of 2002[19] called for mandatory triple-bottom line reporting by companies on their social and environmental performance, including annual equal opportunity plans. The Parliament also called for the creation of an EU multi-stakeholder CSR platform and the mainstreaming of CSR in all areas within the competence of the Parliament, including regional and social funds.

---

[17] European Parliament: 'European criteria for companies operating in developing countries LDCs: towards a European code of conduct', INI/1998/2075. See also A4-0508/98-Howitt and A4-0198/98-Fassa.

[18] UN Norms on the Responsibilities of Transnational Corporations and Other Business Enterprises with Regard to Human Rights, UN Doc. E/CN.4/Sub.2/2003/12/Rev.2 (2003). Adopted in 13 August 2003, by UN Sub-Commission on the Promotion and Protection of Human Rights resolution 2003/16, UN Doc. E/CN.4/Sub.2/2003/L.11 at 52 (2003).

[19] European Parliament resolution on the Commission Green Paper on Promoting a European framework for Corporate Social Responsibility (COM(2001)366 – C5-0161/2002-2002/2069(COS)).

H.   COMMUNICATION OF THE EU COMMISSION CONCERNING CSR, JULY 2002

While the Green Paper was a discussion on CSR, the 'European Communication on Corporate Social Responsibility: A Business Contribution to Sustainable Development',[20] is an EU strategy to promote CSR in Europe. Unlike the Green Paper, it sets out a set of actions to be taken.

In the communication, the Commission underlines that the principles of community action shall be:

- voluntary;
- transparent;
- adding value;
- taking a triple-bottom line approach;
- based on existing international agreements and instruments.

It will be noted that the Commission now refers to the existing international agreements. However, the Commission continues to lay stress on the voluntary basis of the initiative. If international law were to be used to define CSR, it would lead to the setting of minimum standards for corporate behaviour. However, that could end up by driving a wedge between the industries themselves, their various stakeholders and the politicians. Stressing the voluntary nature of the initiative is therefore necessary to promote the engagement of the most important stakeholders in the exercise – the companies themselves.

As regards concrete initiatives on CSR, the Commission will inter alia:

- establish a 'multi-stakeholder forum';
- facilitate and develop user friendly CSR tools for Small and Medium Size Enterprises (SMEs);
- increase the knowledge on CSR and promote the development of CSR management skills;
- maintain CSR in all community policies.

The foregoing are important initiatives; especially the multi-stakeholder forum. The mainstreaming of CSR in all community policies is likely to have positive consequences for the future development of CSR in Europe.

The aim of the multi-stakeholder forum was to exchange experiences on best practices. The participants in the forum were to establish a common EU approach and identify areas where additional action could be needed at the European level.[21] The list of participants included stakeholders such as: European organizations representing both employers and employees, consumer organizations, civil society as well as professional associations and business networks. The forum had

---

20   European Commission Communication from the Commission concerning Corporate Social Responsibility: A Business Contribution to Sustainable Development, 'Brussels, 2nd July 2002 Com (2002) 347 Final'. See www.europa.eu.int/comm/employment_social/soc-dial/csr/csr_index.htm.
21   Commission Communication paper p. 22. www.europa.eu.int/comm/employment_social/soc-dial/csr/csr_index.htm.

two plenary meetings a year together with periodic theme-based round tables. A steering group was responsible for the daily management of the forum. The final report of the forum was made available in autumn 2004.[22]

Further CSR principles are to be integrated into EU policies where appropriate. The communication outlines the relevance of CSR in the fields of employment and social policies, enterprises, environmental issues, consumers, public procurement, external relations including development policies and trade. The Commission underscores the fact that 'CSR practices contribute to the objectives of EU policies, in particular sustainable development, by supplementing existing policy tools such as trade and development'.[23] See section O for further details of the progress of additional Commission initiatives.

I.   COUNCIL RESOLUTION, FEBRUARY 2003

As was the case with the Green Paper, the EU Council has supported the initiatives spelt out by the Commission in its communication, especially the establishment of the multi-stakeholder forum on CSR.[24] In its resolution of 6 February 2003, the Council has encouraged the Commission to continue to ensure transparency and efficiency in the work of the multi-stakeholder forum and to take into account also the commitments agreed at the World Summit on Sustainable Development in Johannesburg. As in its previous resolution, the Council has called upon member states to promote CSR at national level, especially by encouraging and establishing partnerships.

J.   EUROPEAN BUSINESS CAMPAIGN ON CSR

CSR is not only being promoted at EU institutional level. The EU Social Fund, CSR Europe, the Copenhagen Centre, the International Business Leaders Forum and various other partners have joined together following the Lisbon Summit in 2000 to launch a major campaign to promote corporate social responsibility.[25] The goal was to mobilize 500,000 business partners to integrate CSR into their business management by 2005.

The European Business Campaign on CSR is a business contribution to the goals formulated at the Lisbon Summit and developed by the Commission. The CSR campaign organizes conferences all over Europe and every fourth year they arrange an 'Olympics', rewarding achievements in the field of CSR.

Two of the important initiatives taken by the campaign are the:

- Social Responsible Investment (SRI) Compass;[26] and the
- Small and Medium Size Enterprises-key (SME-key).

---

22   *Ibid.*
23   Commission Communication paper p. 24. www.europa.eu.int/comm/employment_social/ soc-dial/csr/csr_index.htm.
24   Council Resolution of 6 February 2003 on Corporate Social Responsibility. Official Journal of the European Union (2003/C 39/02)
25   www.csrcampaign.org.
26   www.sricompass.org.

The SRI Compass is an online resource featuring all existing green and ethical investment funds and indices in Europe. It provides stakeholders with an overview of the size, growth and dimensions of the SRI market and offers companies concrete evidence and information on SRIs financial benefits in terms of attracting investors for green and ethical funds. CSR Europe manages the SRI Compass.

The SME-key[27] is a web based support portal, which helps small and medium size companies to evaluate and strengthen their activities in the CSR field. The SME-key has three objectives. It (i) outlines the business case for social responsibility; (ii) provides a step-by-step guide to help companies evaluate their activities; and (iii) offers a database of case studies and social reports.

Companies are supposed to report on their triple-bottom line. As part of its social responsibility, the company has to consider various stakeholders including employees, customers, community, business partners, public authorities and NGOs. The database comprises around 60 companies at present.

The initiative is interesting as it addresses small and medium sized companies, which normally have only limited resources to invest in CSR. However, the SME-key does not distinguish between compliance with legal obligations, on the one hand, and proactive initiatives, on the other. It is obvious from the Commission's definition of CSR that compliance with national and international legal obligations and going beyond such obligations are two different things. This may be difficult for companies using the SME-key to recognize this difference.

The main difficulty arises if a company tries to use the SME-key as a means of risk management. Following the key is not a guarantee that the company complies with international standards. National legislation may vary but international regulation applies equally to all companies. It would improve the SME-key if it set out a regime to ensure, as a minimum, that companies comply with international regulations.

K.   EUROPEAN ACADEMY OF BUSINESS IN SOCIETY

Many stakeholders including the European Commission, government officials and the companies concerned have been asking for research, education and training in the field of CSR. The European Academy of Business in Society (EABIS)[28] present a serious response to this demand. EABIS is another part of the European CSR campaign, as mentioned above. EABIS is an alliance between Europe's leading business schools and more than a dozen multinational companies and focusses exclusively on research and training.

EABIS carries out research, education and training on sustainable development by integrating the business experiences with academic tradition. By this approach, the academy aims to drive CSR into the mainstream of business practice, theory and education and to become not only a European centre of excellence, but also a worldwide reference point for CSR.

The aim is to be achieved by interdisciplinary research, engaging top universities in CSR education and training for business and academics in the field.

---

[27]   www.smekey.org.
[28]   www.eabis.org.

L. BUSINESS LEADERS INITIATIVE ON HUMAN RIGHTS (BLIHR)

As with the European Business Campaign on CSR, the BLIHR is a business initiative to strengthen CSR. BLIHR can be differentiated from the campaign in terms of its focus on human rights and its membership, which comprises exclusively multinational companies and not NGOs or academic networks. Mary Robinson is the honorary chair. The BLIHR has set a voluntary, three-year programme designed to integrate human rights into business decision-making and to empower and strengthen existing initiatives. The work programme consists of three to four working groups a year and a commitment to report annually on progress.

The key areas BLIHR intends to address are:

- limits of responsibility;
- guarding against complicity in human rights abuses;
- considering whether regulation is appropriate;
- considering how the UN norms on transnational companies can contribute to the CSR work of companies.

One of the important projects to be developed by the BLIHR is a toolkit for business, which intends to offer practical support to companies in implementing the principles of the Universal Declaration on Human Rights. The first tool in the toolbox is a human rights matrix, which maps out the business relevance and importance of the various elements in the UN norms. It outlines what are regarded as 'essential' rights, giving rise to minimum obligations; second, matters which are to be 'expected' of business but not to be treated as mandatory; and, third, matters which are to be regarded as 'desirable' on the part of business, but to be implemented on a voluntary basis.[29]

One of the arguments for mapping out the corporate human rights landscape is explained by Mary Robinson in these words: 'In my travels as a UN High Commissioner for Human Rights to over 80 countries I found that business leaders were interested in engaging on human rights questions and were increasingly aware that they had been dealing with human rights issues for years using different labels. [...] But what I also found was, that business leaders were unsure about where their responsibilities for human rights begin and end'.[30] The matrix is the first attempt to map out the beginning and end and the territory in between.

This initiative is expected to develop key learning points for companies in relation to CSR. Taking in human rights both from compliance and proactive angles will enable the participants via mandatory reporting to share their learning with a wider circle of companies. A prerequisite for the participating companies is to understand the breadth of human rights and this in itself brings an awareness of the usefulness of the universally agreed principles.

The matrix is a useful tool in helping business to prioritize the rights depending on the business sector and the countries in which the particular company

---

[29]   See www.blihr.org.
[30]   BLIHR 'BLIHR Report 1: Building understanding', BLIHR. London and Amsterdam, 2003.

may be engaged. The weakness of the tool lies in the fact that it does not adequately reflect the full range of rights: a challenge for the UN norms themselves.

M.   EU CHARTER OF FUNDAMENTAL RIGHTS

The EU Charter of Fundamental Rights[31] is the key document setting out the underlying values of the EU.

This European Charter may, in the future, have a bigger impact than at present on the European CSR movement. The Charter is legally binding upon the EU institutions and the member states only when applying community law. However, as part of the move to establish an EU-wide constitution, it can be expected that the Charter will be inscribed into one of the coming treaties and thereby become legally binding upon member states in all respects. This would have an important secondary effect. The Charter faithfully reflects the rights and freedoms contained in the International Bill of Human Rights. Accordingly, in the process of adopting the EU Charter, the vast majority of the European population will become acquainted with the content of international human rights and this will eliminate one of the key difficulties in way of adopting a rights based approach to CSR; namely, the widespread lack of knowledge of the scope and content of human rights.

The Charter is mainly addressed to the actions of community institutions, but companies will also have to take note of it as many of its provisions may affect business. The provisions which business will have to take into account as and when the Charter is inscribed in the Treaty are:

- *labour rights*: slave, forced or compulsory labour; child labour; freedom of association/collective bargaining; non-discrimination/equal opportunities; fair and just working conditions; workers right to information and consultation within the undertaking;
- right to work and protection against unfair dismissal;
- right to life;
- *development rights*: right to education, to health, and social security;
- right to hold opinions and freedom of expression, thought, conscience and religion;
- right to a family life;
- right to privacy and protection of personal data;
- cultural, religious and linguistic diversity;
- right to peaceful assembly;
- freedom to conduct business;
- informed consent to medical/biological trials;
- intellectual property rights and the right to enjoy technological development;
- the rights of the elderly;
- integration of persons with disabilities;
- environmental protection;
- consumer protection.

---

[31]   Charter of Fundamental Rights of the European Union. Official Journal of the European Communities, 2000 (2000/C 364/01).

Compared with the European Convention on Human Rights (ECHR) the EU Charter is wider in scope regarding economic, social and cultural rights as well as more extensive equality rights. As regards the relationship between the Charter and ECHR, it is stated in article 52 of the Charter that 'insofar as this Charter contains rights which correspond to rights guaranteed by the [ECHR] the meaning and scope of those rights shall be the same as those laid down by the said Convention'. The issue of which rights in the Charter correspond to those in the ECHR is set out in the explanatory memorandum commissioned by the Presidium,[32] and not in the charter.

N. OTHER NATIONAL INITIATIVES TO PROMOTE CSR IN EUROPE

1. BELGIUM – Pension Fund Disclosure – Social Label Law

In 2001, the Belgian Council of Ministers adopted a regulation requiring pension funds to reveal whether they apply ethical, environmental and social performance criteria in deciding which companies to invest in and, if so, what those criteria may be.[33]

a. Social Label Law

The Social Label Law was adopted by the Belgian Parliament in February 2002 and is the first of its kind in the world. Its purpose is to allow both domestic and foreign companies to apply for a 'social label' which certifies that the product in question has been produced in accordance with the ILOs eight core conventions covering, freedom of association, the right to collective bargaining, abolition of forced labour, elimination of child labour and equal opportunity and treatment in the workplace, respectively.

The law creates a committee of 16 members, comprising representatives of the employer's federation, NGOs, trade unions, consumer's organizations and public officials. Companies applying for a 'social label' must undergo a social audit and these audits will be reviewed and assessed by the Committee.

Italy and Denmark have seen similar legislation in drafts and the European Parliament has indicated an intention to move in such direction.

The social label is important as it gives consumers an option to choose for themselves – namely, whether they will opt for products with the label and

---

[32] Articles where the meaning is the same as the corresponding Articles of the ECHR, but the scope wider. Art. 9: The scope is extended to other forms of marriage, Art. 12(1): The scope is extended to EU level. Art. 14(1): The scope is extended to cover vocational and continuing training. Art. 14(3) regarding the rights of parents, Art. 47(2) and (3): The limitation to the determination of civil rights and obligations or criminal charges does not apply as regards Union law and its implementation. Art. 50: The scope is expanded to EU level between the Courts of the member states. Finally, citizens of Europe may not be considered as aliens in the scope of the application of Community law, because of the prohibition of any discrimination on grounds of nationality. The limitations in ECHR Art. 16 do not apply to them in this context. Convention document CHARTE 4473/00.

[33] www.europa.eu.int/comm/employment_social/soc-dial/csr/country/belgium.htm.

thereby support companies with a good CSR profile. At present, it is almost impossible for the consumer to know how the goods have been produced. It will be interesting to see whether European consumers are willing to pay a little extra for goods carrying the social label.[34]

There are further hurdles, which the Social Label Law must surmount. It has been argued that the law constitutes a technical hindrance to trade. The law has therefore been under review by the WTO and European Commission to investigate whether it violates trade policies and distorts competition.[35] The universality of the human rights in question should outweigh the suggested distortion to trade and competition; it would be absurd to talk in terms of human rights distorting competition. However, a real concern with the Social Label Law is that it focuses on the traditional core labour rights only; in other words, a company could obtain the social label notwithstanding that it blatantly violates other human rights.

2.   DENMARK – Our Common Concern Campaign – The Copenhagen Centre – The Business and Human Rights Project

In 1994, the Danish Minister of Social Affairs launched 'Our Common Concern Campaign' with the objective of putting CSR onto the agenda of Danish businesses.

The campaign has extended into a variety of initiatives, including the Copenhagen Centre and the development of the 'social index'. The initiative focusses only on the creation of an inclusive labour market by establishing various partnerships and initiatives to assist companies in hiring and training minority or otherwise socially excluded groups.

a.   The Copenhagen Centre

The Copenhagen Centre[36] is an autonomous international research institution designed to contribute to the creation of inclusive labour markets by promoting voluntary partnerships amongst business, government and civil society. The partnership initiative offers practical training and advice for business leaders in the development of partnerships.[37] Recently, the strategic focus has shifted towards good corporate governance and globalization. The links between corporate governance, globalization and CSR have to be developed further and it will be interesting to see how the Centre will add to the discourse.

---

[34]   A European-wide poll conducted by CSR Europe has analyzed the willingness of European citizens to pay extra for ethically produced goods. See Confederation of Danish Trade Unions (LO) 'Consumers can make a difference' LO Newsletter, p. 28.

[35]   See Susan Ariel Aaronsen & James Reeves, 'The European Response to Public Demands for Global Corporate Responsibility', National Policy Association, 2002, p. 46.

[36]   www.copenhagencentre.org.

[37]   This initiative builds on the experience and expertise of three partner organizations: The Copenhagen Centre, University of Cambridge Programme for Industry and The Prince of Wales International Business Leaders Forum – all of which are not-for-profit institutions with educational objectives.

b.   *The Business and Human Rights Project*

The Business and Human Rights Project was set up as a joint enterprise by the Confederation of Danish Industries (DI), the Danish Industrialisation Fund (IFU) and the Danish Institute for Human Rights (DIHR) and was subsequently supported by the Danish Government.[38]

The Business and Human Rights Project strives to combine the academic expertise on human rights with the practical knowledge of the business community. The DIHR, a national human rights and research institution, has charge of the Project but representatives from IFU and DI also participate in the steering committee.[39] The steering committee meets every three months to discuss the research and ensure that the project continues to meet the needs of the business community.

The project aims to help companies achieve concrete human rights standards and help them to maintain those standards through training and advisory services. The project has developed a Human Rights Compliance Assessment (HRCA) tool based on more than 80 international human rights instruments and treaties. A short version of the HRCA was made available as a web based computer program, which will enable companies to assess their own business practices. The tool was launched in autumn 2004.

It will be interesting to see whether companies will use the HRCA. With over 1,000 indicators in the full tool, there is a real risk that companies will find it too complex. However continuous dialogue with stakeholders, including business, have been completed to ensure that the HRCA will be user-friendly.

The focus of the HRCA is human rights challenges in the developing world. It could be argued that HRCA should also include human rights abuses in the western world to avoid any suggestion of an 'us and them' approach. If the HRCA can be used, independently of geographic location it will become an important and useful tool in the assessment of companies and could be used in the companies' risk management processes.

3.   FRANCE – Mandatory Sustainability Reporting – French Study Centre for CSR

a.   *Mandatory Sustainability Reporting*

As of May 2001, France became the first country to require publicly listed companies to describe the social, environmental and financial consequences of their activities in their annual reports – a so-called triple-bottom line reporting. The French Parliament passed the New Economic Regulations Law requiring mandatory disclosure of social and environmental issues in companies' annual reports and accounts.[40] It requires all companies listed on the 'premier marché' (those with the largest capitalizations) to report against a template of social and environmental indicators, including those related to human resources,

---

[38]   www.humanrightsbusiness.org.
[39]   The project was initially funded by the two organizations but the Danish government through its Development Aid organization, Danida, took over funding of the project.
[40]   See www.occes.asso.fr/fr/comm/nre.html.

community issues and engagement, labour standards and key health, safety and environmental standards.[41]

b.   French Study Centre for CSR

The Observatoire sur la Responsabilité Sociétale des Entreprises (ORSE) set up in 2000, by business partners, is a network designed to study and promote corporate social responsibility and socially responsible investment in France and foreign countries.[42] ORSE collects, analyzes and advertises information on CSR as well as it facilitate the CSR work of its members, by information on best practices, relevant networks, CSR instruments and tools. ORSE gathers together 70 actors, including major French corporations, fund managers and their professional organizations, banks and insures, trade unions, professional organizations and non-governmental organizations.

4.   GERMANY – Round Table on Code of Conduct – Pension Fund Disclosure

a.   Rugmark

In the early days, German consumers were concerned that rugs, and later soccer balls, were made using child labour. This resulted in the certification label 'Rugmark'. 'Rugs certified with this label cost 1 per cent more and, this money goes to schools for the children of the workers producing the rugs. These children get an education and an opportunity to gain greater skills and higher wages'.[43]

b.   Round Table on Code of Conduct

In Germany, a network of representatives of the government, private sector, trade unions and non-governmental organizations has been established to improve the implementation of labour standards in developing countries through voluntary codes of conduct. The multi-stakeholder Round Table on Codes of Conduct[44] seeks to develop a common understanding of how voluntary codes of conduct can be introduced and applied effectively, transparently and in a spirit of participation. It is however, not a priority of the Round Table to develop its own code of conduct.

As with the BLIHR project the thematic content of the Round Table is the Universal Declaration of Human Rights, together with international human rights conventions, the ILO Declaration on Fundamental Principles and Rights at Work 1998, and the UN Secretary-General's Global Compact Initiative.

c.   Pension Fund Disclosure

The German government passed legislation in 2001 requiring pension funds to declare whether and how they integrate social and environmental factors

[41]   Halina Ward, 'Legal Issues in Corporate Citizenship', IIED Publication, 2003.
[42]   See www.orse.org/gb/home/index.html.
[43]   Susan Ariel Aaronsen & James Reeves 'The European Response to Public Demands for Global Corporate Responsibility', National Policy Association, 2002, p. 18.
[44]   www.coc-runder-tisch.de/index2_engl.htm.

into their investments decisions. The initiative is similar to the Belgian and British schemes.

5.   NORWAY – Global KOMpakt

a.   KOMpakt

The Norwegian KOMpakt is not to be confused with the UN Global Compact. The KOMpakt is a consultative body on human rights and Norwegian economic involvement abroad, established by the government.[45] Among the participants are organizations representing the employers and employees, NGOs and business. The purpose is to enhance understanding among the relevant Norwegian constituencies for the interface between business and human rights in the context of globalization.

Besides the plenary meetings and seminars, KOMpakt has established three thematic working groups. These focus on the normative and norm-creating challenges to the promotion of human rights in general, the business dimensions of the human rights engagement and the political perspectives of the initiative. All the working groups report to the plenary.

6.   SWEDEN – Swedish Partnership for Global Responsibility

Some of the largest Swedish firms have been known for their social and environmental responsibility, such as Volvo, a carmaker, Ikea, a furniture retailer and Hennes and Mauritz, a retailer of clothes. However, the government did not inspire social responsibility in Sweden before 2002,[46] until it actively took part in the debate.

a.   Swedish Partnership for Global Responsibility[47]

The initiative of a Swedish Partnership for Global Responsibility was taken by a group of ministers in 2002 with the purpose of promoting constructive cooperation between the government, business sector and other sectors of society.

The partnership initiative was launched by an open letter to Swedish companies. In the letter, the government encouraged Swedish companies to publicly support the OECD Guidelines and the UN Global Compact. Further, the companies were encouraged to report, once a year, on concrete measures taken to implement the OECD and UN guidelines. The initiatives are published on the governments website and reported to the OECD.

As part of the partnership the government has meetings with the Swedish business environment on how (i) the government can best support the companies that want to take global responsibility, (ii) they can encourage companies to get involved and (iii) the partnership be enhanced. Further, the government is arranging seminars on various topics and disseminating information on CSR developments relevant to Swedish companies.

---

[45]   Norwegian Ministry of Foreign Affairs 'The Consultative Body for Human Rights and Norwegian Economic Involvements Abroad: Kompakt'. Published December 1998.

[46]   Susan Ariel Aaronsen & James Reeves, 'The European Response to Public Demands for Global Corporate Responsibility', National Policy Association, 2002, p. 48.

[47]   www.utrikes.regeringen.se/inenglish/policy/global_responsibility/index.htm.

Private-Public-Partnerships (PPP) are increasingly being developed all over Europe. There are different kinds of partnerships. Many of them are related to public investments, where the project is 'privatized', meaning that a public company is driven like a private company on market conditions. Another kind of partnership is related to very concrete projects, which normally can be described as minimalist, where the government helps or facilitates CSR initiatives taken by companies. The Swedish initiative resembles the latter.

Some new types of partnerships are broader and the state makes an agreement with a company, on the condition that some minimum human rights standards are observed. An example is the European Cotonou agreement. Some companies also pose conditions to state parties regarding human rights, due to the risk of being associated with the state, if the state is charged with human rights violations. BP has recently developed such approach with the assistance of Amnesty International.

7.   UNITED KINGDOM – UK Pension Fund Disclosure – UK Company Law Review – The UK Corporate Responsibility Bill – Minister for Corporate Social Responsibility

a.   UK Pension Fund Disclosure[48]

In 1999, the UK Parliament approved the Pensions Disclosure Regulation. The Regulation amended the 1995 Pensions Act, requiring all trustees of UK occupational pension funds to disclose, 'the extent (if any) to which social, environmental or ethical considerations are taken into consideration in the selection, retention and realization of investments'.[49] The Occupational Pension Schemes [Investment] Regulations came into effect on 3 July 2000.

b.   Minister for Corporate Social Responsibility[50]

In 2000, the promotion of CSR became an official policy strategy of the UK government. Prime Minister Tony Blair appointed a Minister for CSR, within the Department of Trade and Industry, to provide a strategic focus and leadership on CSR issues across departments of the UK government. The ministry for corporate social responsibility was the first of its kind. It is obvious that the government found that it had an important role to play in the development of CSR and promotion of best practices.

c.   The UK Corporate Responsibility Bill[51]

The UK Corporate Responsibility Bill, originally introduced in the House of Commons by Labour backbenchers in June 2003, is a Bill requiring companies

---

48   www.hmso.gov.uk/sr/sr1996/Nisr_19960584_en_1.htm.
49   Amendment 3, in the Occupational Pension Schemes (Investment, and Assignment, Forfeiture, Bankruptcy, etc.) Amendment Regulations 1999. See www.legislation.hmso.gov.uk/si/si1999/19991849.htm.
50   www.societyandbusiness.gov.uk.
51   www.parliament.the-stationery-office.co.uk/pa/cm200102/cmbills/145/2002145.htm.

to produce and publish reports on environmental, social, economic and financial matters. Companies registered in the UK and companies operating within the UK will all be subject to the Act. The companies are also to disclose how they assess their financial, environmental and social impact.

The proposed Act expands directors' duties and liabilities as a means to ensure compliance. It also imposes on the companies a duty to consult with affected stakeholders, before embarking upon a major project. The Bill was never approved.

d. Operating and Financial Reviews[52, 53]

The UK government has also been reviewing company law in relation to CSR objectives. In 2001, it launched an independent review, which was published in July and includes proposals to improve corporate accountability and transparency. As a response to the recommendation the UK Government published a white paper on 'Modernising Company Law' in 2002 (Cm5553). The process was taken one step further in May 2004 when the British Government announced a consultation on a draft regulation suggesting that quoted UK companies listed on the London, New York and Nasdaq stock exchanges will have to include social and environmental performance in Operating and Financial Reviews (OFR).

The draft regulation gives directors the discretion to decide that social and environmental information is not relevant to their company's OFR. However, if the company decides that it is not relevant they must make an explicit statement to that effect.

There is no doubt that the UK is a leading force in Europe in the CSR field. The above examples are only a small part of the CSR initiatives. What is especially interesting in the UK is that the government has initiated various enabling initiatives such as the Pensions Act, but also that the Government is prompted by an opposition that has drafted the Corporate Responsibility Bill. The companies have in general accepted the government policy and tried to gain a competitive advantage from the disclosure of their CSR initiatives.

O. DISCUSSION ON LEGISLATIVE MEASURES TO PROMOTE CSR IN EUROPE

The Lisbon Summit was the starting point for a number of interesting initiatives, among other the European Commission Green Paper and Communication on CSR, which started a serious CSR process at the EU level, state level and in the civil society. However, will the European Union reach its goal in 2010 of being 'the most competitive and dynamic knowledge-based economy in the world, capable of sustainable economic growth with more and better jobs and greater social cohesion'[54] through present efforts on CSR? The authors are dubious, if the EU does not intensify the effort.

---

[52] http://www.icfconsulting.com/Publications/Perspectives-2004/uk-ofr.asp.
[53] www.dti.gov.uk/cld/review.htm. See also www.dti.gov.uk/companiesbill.
[54] See the Council Conclusions at www.europa.eu.int/comm/off/index_en.htm.

The developments at the European Institutional level had a good start and most of the Commission initiatives: The 'multi-stakeholder forum', the user friendly CSR tools for SMEs as well as the promotion of CSR management skills have been carried out. However, the Commission is a long way from integrating CSR into all policies at the European level, as intended. Even in obvious policy areas, such as the company law, CSR has not been effectively implemented. In the 'Communication from the Commission to the Council and the European Parliament', regarding 'Modernising Company Law and Enhancing Corporate Governance in the European Union – A Plan to Move Forward' there is not a single word about CSR, although corporate governance is a relevant tool for integrating CSR.

In many ways, it seems as though the CSR policy development has been stalled with the multi-stake-holder forum. The forum is important and interesting, but also a slow initiator. The question remains how the EU can take the process beyond the multi-stakeholder forum? What legislative measures, if any, are needed? Is it possible for the EU and the Governments to take the process a step further and still respect the voluntary nature of the CSR process, which the business world seems to prefer and which is one of the principles in the EU CSR framework?

One could look to the experience from the member states in the search for answers. Several of the member states, like France and the UK have enacted legislation on CSR, which preserve a voluntary element. EU could consider adopting directives along the same lines and the following will give some examples.

EU could adopt legislation where the companies and investment funds should disclose their impact on the trible-bottom line. Such an initiative would respect the voluntary nature of CSR, but at the same time enable companies to compete on their CSR strategies.

Another initiative could be to improve transparency in company law and auditing. Such initiative could prevent economic scandals and corruption. Further it would be fruitful for the CSR development if CSR is integrated into corporate governance strategies and thinking. The EU has initiated discussions on the integration and held a conference, but no concrete initiatives were launched. The Conference held in March 2004 was named 'Corporate Social Responsibility and Corporate Governance: Two Mutually Reinforcing Concepts'.

Yet again, the EU could be the initiator of a social label based on the experiences from Belgium and Denmark. Only if the social labels are harmonised can the consumers gain from the initiative. Once again, a harmonization will give the companies a competitive advantage if engaging in CSR.

Initiatives regarding sustainable economic growth could enable the EU to take an important step closer to its Lisbon goals of being the most competitive and dynamic knowledge-based economy in the world.

Chapter 20

A EUROPEAN PERSPECTIVE

Sune Skadegard Thorsen
Annemarie Meisling

A. THE EUROPEAN PERSPECTIVE

The concept of establishing responsibilities for European companies within society beyond the mere purpose of creating profit has been increasing in the past 25–30 years. During the 70s and 80s attention was primarily focused on environmental concerns. However, in the 90s, focus expanded to embrace Corporate Social Responsibility (CSR). In Europe, companies have drafted codes of conducts governing own ethical behaviour, suppliers' behaviour or even industry behaviour as such. Governments have started to pass legislation on social and environmental reporting on top of traditional economic demands.

At present it is possible to talk of a particular European discourse on CSR, that rests on the triple bottom line, has evolved around the companies' engagement in the economic developing world, is based on international agreements and which is voluntary. European approaches distinguish themselves from American approaches. In general, the former focuses on integrating CSR in the way companies do business, whereas the latter focus on donation and community involvement schemes.

With few exceptions, lawyers have not until recently engaged in the debate on and development of CSR. In many countries lawyers have been sceptical of the development and concerned that unforeseeable costs would arise from CSR commitments not least in relation to litigation risks. However, lawyers have started opening their minds to CSR, both not only seeing the value for society but also looking at an opportunity for delivering services. Thus, lawyers increasingly participate in the promotion and development of the field.

As one of the first steps in this direction, the Council of the Bars and Law Societies of the European Union (CCBE) in 2003, published a Guide for European Lawyers advising on corporate social responsibility issues (Guide). The 2003 edition has been updated by a 2004 edition, reflecting developments in 2003–2004 and explicating various issues in relation to CSR such as client-attorney privilege and corruption.

Ramon Mullerat (ed.), Corporate Social Responsibility: The Corporate Governance of the 21st Century, 299–310.
© 2005 *International Bar Association. Printed in the Netherlands.*

This chapter comments on European CSR development and argues that an 'human rights' based approach can increase coherence and establish long needed convergence in the field. It takes the recommendations from the Guide one step further, arguing that company lawyers and leaders can benefit from a proactive approach to their CSR strategy, by integrating Corporate Social Opportunities (CSO). The CSO approach can assist corporate clients taking relevant steps beyond compliance thus offering a competitive advantage.

1. 'Human Rights'-Based Approach to the CSR Development in Europe

a. Triple Bottom Line

Despite small nuances concerning the way various CSR terms conform into the European discourse, the following concepts appear to gain consensus amongst leading actors in the field as well as the European Commission, the European Parliament, and many governments around Europe. The main concept behind the CSR is Sustainable Development. Sustainable Development for business is defined or made operational through the triple bottom line, popularly described by the three Ps; *People, Planet, Profit,* breaking down the components needed when describing how business can assist in contributing to sustainable development.

Companies are compelled to find sustainable solutions for their relation to *human beings* (CSR, hereunder the relationship to employees, suppliers, customers, local communities and other stakeholders), to the *external environment* (including biodiversity and animal welfare), and to the *economy* (including the economy of the community).

The chapter will not go into detail with the triple bottom line, which is described in Chapter 7, but merely touch upon the advantages of a rights based approach to the 'people' bottom line.

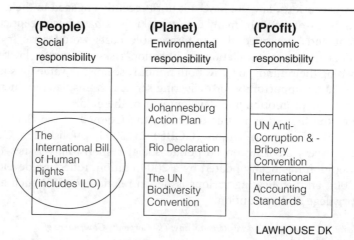

Framing Corporate Responsibilities

(People) Social responsibility	**(Planet)** Environmental responsibility	**(Profit)** Economic responsibility
The International Bill of Human Rights (includes ILO)	Johannesburg Action Plan	UN Anti-Corruption & - Bribery Convention
	Rio Declaration	
	The UN Biodiversity Convention	International Accounting Standards

LAWHOUSE DK

Figure 1. The triple bottom line.

The advantages of framing the triple bottom line by international instruments are higher objectivity and materiality and that the instruments are globally accepted as universal values. 'Corporate ethics' as any ethical position will depend on the individual, proposing the values.

The discussion on the universality of the International Bill of Human Rights[1] forming the basis the 'people' bottom line also occurs in business circles. It is hard to disregard the fact that the Universal Declaration of Human Rights and the two covenants that followed in the mid-sixties, are the only values accepted and recognized by all the nations in this world. As such human rights are, so far, the only relatively well-defined values that can claim status as an international reference for responsible corporate behaviour.

The International Bill of Human Rights is primarily intended to bind governments, however, several of the rights are of immediate and direct relevance to business. These are primarily:

- Labour rights: Slave, forced or compulsory labour; child labour; freedom of association/collective bargaining; non-discrimination/equal opportunities; rest, leisure and holidays; minimum wages; health and safety
- Right to work, i.e. protection against unjustified dismissals and technical/ vocational guidance and training
- Right to life
- Development rights: Right to education; to health; to adequate food and fair distribution of food; to clothing; to housing; to social security; to enjoy technological development
- Right to hold opinions and freedom of expression, thought, conscience and religion
- Right to a family life
- Right to privacy, e.g. surveillance, personal information, drug testing
- Minority rights to culture, religious practise and language, and cultural rights (indigenous peoples)
- Right to peaceful assembly
- Right to take part in political life
- Informed consent to medical/biological trials
- Intellectual property rights and the right to enjoy technological development.

The goal of the CSR movement is to ensure that corporations display good corporate governance ensuring the implementation of these core values into their daily operations. Since the triple bottom line has an international legal frame, lawyers have an important role to play on advising the boards and management on the interpretation of the conventions and the scope of the duties. It can be difficult for non-lawyers to estimate the scope of the obligations, when companies declare that they commit themselves to respect, protect, fulfil and promote Human Rights.

---

[1]   The criticism has been that human rights are not 'truly' universal, but merely a product of western values. However, the Vienna Declaration, 1993, with the support of the vast majority of states in UN declared the International Bill of Human Rights as universal in addition to describing the rights as indivisible, interdependent and interrelated.

The European Charter for Fundamental Rights may in the future add momentum to the European rights based CSR movement. With the constitutional process in the European Union (EU) it is expected that the Charter will become part of such a treaty and thereby become legally binding upon member states in all aspects. The Charter mainly addresses the actions of the governments, but companies will have to take it into consideration as many of its provisions affect business. Further the EU will be obliged to ensure the rights enshrined in whatever legal acts are passed. The Charter covers the rights contained in the International Bill of Human Rights. The Charter, however, elaborates further on a few rights and even expands its coverage beyond the International Bill by adding specific provisions on:

- Protection in the event of unjustified dismissals
- Integration of persons with disabilities
- Workers' rights to information and consultation within the undertaking
- Consumer protection
- The rights of the elderly
- Environmental protection, and
- Rights of access to placement services.

b.   Engagement in the Developing World

European companies have been very keen to identify their responsibilities when operating in countries normally under diplomatic pressure for human rights violations. Companies have mainly concentrated on negative obligations, e.g. the company should merely refrain from participating in state violations or the company should speak up against such violations; the agenda appears to focus only on countries where gross violations occur.

This approach is reflected in several of the more interesting initiatives in recent years: Amnesty International (AI) in collaboration with International Business Leaders Forum issued in 2002, a global risk map of human rights violations, where the organizations would plot in presence of transnational businesses. The map clearly emphasized countries from Africa, Asia, South America and the former Soviet Union. Not a single country from the economic developed part of the world was included.

Similar the FTSE4good index requires from the companies that participate in the index that they have policies and strategies to address human rights concerns; however only if they operate in certain countries that according to the American 'Freedom House' index have a troublesome score. Both this index and the AI mapping appear to focus primarily on civil and political rights. The Business and Human Rights project at the Danish Institute for Human Rights, which is primarily occupied by defining human rights indicators for business, was construed as a project defining human rights considerations for Danish businesses operating abroad.

Drawing from many years experience working internationally with human rights, the authors propose, that the business and human rights agenda is not pursued as an 'us and them' approach. Many European companies and governments tend merely to focus on the supply chain management system and business in

THE EUROPEAN PERSPECTIVES 303

the economic developing countries, when developing a CSR strategy. However, ample evidence from the European Court of Human Rights and other human rights institutions show that human rights should be a concern for any business no matter where it operates. Companies in the economic developed world are in constant danger of violating the right to privacy – through extensive registration of information on customers or increased surveillance – the right to non-discrimination – be it for women, minorities or disabled – and many other core rights. Human rights will be under constant pressure all around the globe and companies should not take a Euro centric approach.

An 'us and them' approach will also make it difficult to find support for corporate social responsibility on a global scale. Finally it is an expression of intolerable double standards that the economic developed countries start raising demands on principles, that they do not acknowledge or implement fully themselves.

c. International Agreements

There is a growing trend, mainly dominated by academics, to elaborate binding international regulation on companies, with the focus on multinationals. This trend has been fuelled by entrepreneurial lawyers who have revived the use of 300-year-old legislation, the American Aliens Torts Claims Act, for the purpose of suing American based companies for violations of human rights. Similar cases have been initiated in other primarily common-law jurisdictions.

The tendency is closely linked to WTO developments focusing on the perceived negative aspects of globalization, hereunder the rising social gaps both within and in between states. The UN Draft Norms on the Responsibilities of Transnational Corporations and other Business Enterprises with regard to Human Rights (the Draft Norms) presented by the UN Sub-Commission on the Promotion and Protection of Human Rights is of major importance in this respect of Chapter 14. The principles are based on international norms – however both hard and soft law. Among the various external codes available today, this is the most comprehensive document, covering the breadth of corporate responsibilities from anti-trust, over corruption and environment to basic human rights. It provides for a useful template against which companies can assess the coverage of the initiatives and in relation to a few labour rights the depth and appropriateness of such initiatives.

However, by introducing liability for companies for violating the principles, the Draft Norms 'fell between to chairs' – between a document facilitating business on range of awareness with specific learning points and binding legislation to which the companies can be held responsible. It is obvious that more work has to be deployed to make the principles fully instrumental to business in either direction. However, the decision as to whether the Draft Norms aim at becoming binding regulation with attached liability or a facilitating document has to be made as such a decision will heavily influence the wording of such a document. If the former prevails the Draft Norms will probably have to undergo lengthy discussions and major changes. Presently the UN Human Rights Commission have referred the Draft Norms to the Office of the High Commissioner for Human Rights, which will have to submit a report to the Commission taking into consideration all existing codes and norms in spring 2005 following stakeholder meetings with business, governments and civil society.

The concept of binding non-state parties to international agreements present a lot of challenges, though the International Labour Organisation (ILO) has successfully established so-called tripartite conventions on the human rights defined as core labour rights. The conventions are agreed between States, employer and worker representatives. Another great challenge will be monitoring and enforcing the principles. Issues of piercing the corporate veil and *forum non conveniens* will also play a role. However, the new UN anti-corruption convention and the Rome Statute offer interesting mechanisms to be considered.[2]

d.   Voluntary Codes of Conduct

Most European enterprises stress the voluntary nature of CSR.[3] Companies, business associations, NGOs (Non-Governmental Organizations), unions and various international organizations are issuing a plethora of codes of conduct as tools to address the social dimension of companies' relations to their stakeholders, primarily their supply chain partners. There is a great risk in the mantra deployed by most actors that 'no-one-size-fits-all'. It is true that different sectors and different states act in a variety of circumstances that cannot be immediately compared. However, when we are referring to basic human rights principles these should pertain to any action no matter where or under what circumstance it is carried out. The basic human rights define only the very minimum of human dignity and existence. There is plenty of room for any business to focus CSR efforts on issues that are of more special importance to that specific branch or sector. But all minimum standards should be observed when operating. As such the basic human rights could successfully be implemented as part of any company's compliance programmes.

2.   The Responsibilities of the European Lawyer

The Guide for European Lawyers Advising on CSR encourages European lawyers to increase their knowledge on CSR and consider it as part of their legal profession. It argues that the lawyer, as the only professional, 'has a ready access to EU board rooms, and enjoys legal privilege.'[4] It is stated in the Guide that:

'CSR should be part of company policies and integrated into strategies and decision-making. In this regard, the lawyer has a number of boardroom responsibilities.

- The lawyer should make the company management aware that CSR is an issue, which they will have to deal with.
- As lawyers are specialist advisers to corporations this will reflect on their responsibilities when acting as a member of, or secretary to, the Board of

2   See 'Contemporary Directions for Business on Human Rights' by Skadegard Thorsen and Meisling, Sept 2004. www.lawhouse.dk
3   See the Synthesis of Consultation on Green Paper on CSR, in the European Commission's 'Corporate Social Responsibility – A business contribution to sustainable development, p. 5. European Commission July 2002.
4   CSR, Corporate Social Responsibility and the Role of the Legal Profession. A Guide for European Lawyers advising on Corporate Social Responsibility Issues. Council of the Bars and Law Societies of the European Union. p.8 2003.

Directors. CSR must be considered as an area where negligence may very well result in losses of a considerable size for the involved company. If the issues leading to the loss were treated during a board meeting and the lawyer did not respond adequately, due to ignorance, this may lead to liability.'

Apart from these responsibilities, the in-house lawyer has to be aware of a number of challenges on the human rights agenda. There is a risk that if a company's problems, in relation to human rights become public news and it is not handled appropriately, stakeholders will become disappointed and may react by:

- Not seeking or seizing employment in the company
- Not investing or withdrawing investment in company shares
- Not purchasing the products or services from the company
- Refraining from co-operation with the company
- Influencing other stakeholders to act as described above.

Since human rights is within the legal field, it will be expected of the lawyer to inform the board on these problems. The only way a lawyer is able to ward off such risks is, in cooperation with the managers, to adopt a carefully prepared and clear approach on human rights. The approach has to be implemented and communicated in intelligible ways. There is considerable enhanced corporate reputation to be gained through recognizing that a company will be most successful, also financially, when it presents and adheres to a strong, socially responsible profile based on human rights.

It is also expected from the lawyer to be aware of the cases being tried in a number of countries' courts, with allegations that multinational corporations, in some cases through their business partners, have contributed to human rights violations through their global operations.

Recent years' massive exposures of human rights violations by companies and the awareness of the potential financial risk involved by not fulfilling stakeholder expectations entail that corporate management no longer is in a position to claim to be acting in good faith by referring to a 'Business Judgment Rule'. Liability for negligent or willful behaviour causing shareholder loss is incorporated into most legal systems in the world. The lawyer should be expected to inform the company of these changes in due time.

3. Compliance vs. Opportunity (CSO)

The duties and responsibilities of the lawyer, as described above, are related to the compliance side of the CSR agenda. It is risk management rather than opportunity enhancing considerations. The following will be dealing with the proactive side of the CSR. The CCBE Guide mentions that there exists a proactive approach, but does not describe it.

In the proactive approach the companies go beyond the compliance side and use their CSR strategy to brand themselves and create a competitive edge. This can only be done by passing the line of compliance and adopting a proactive approach.

Taking a proactive approach, means choosing some values or rights that the company actively promotes, beyond what they are obliged to do. Experience from

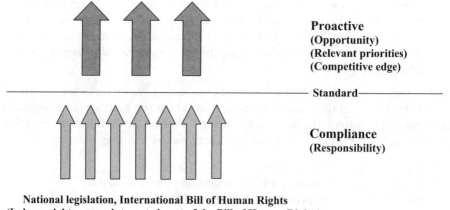

Proactive
(Opportunity)
(Relevant priorities)
(Competitive edge)

——————————————————————————————— Standard———————————

Compliance
(Responsibility)

National legislation, International Bill of Human Rights
(Labour rights are an integrated part of the Bill of Human Rights)

Figure 2. CSO.

companies adopting this approach has shown that it can be valuable to formulate the proactive strategies in line with the International Bill of Human Rights since:

- There is a general support of international human rights as contributing to sustainable development,
- Human rights are globally recognized and accepted,
- Human rights provide a good basis for making values operational,
- Most NGOs addressing the problematic parts of globalization base their arguments on human rights issues and understanding.

Not many companies have yet integrated a proactive approach, but those who have, can brand themselves on their CSR strategies in ways that are not possible for the companies only working with the compliance side. The stakeholders are no longer impressed by a company in compliance of what, by now, should be expected.

When choosing a proactive strategy it is important that the values are relevant to the specific sector. It will be expected to the food industry to have a strategy regarding the right to food, for the pharmaceutical industry to pay specific attention on the right to health, etc. An illustrative example would be the proliferation of McDonalds HIV/AIDS campaign in Africa. Despite the very positive aspects of high initiative, the company was open for criticism for diverting attention from McDonalds impact on the right to food; a challenge the company is addressing.

The external funding should be an integrated part of the proactive approach. Many European Companies sponsor or donate to various purposes locally or abroad, without having an overall strategy, except from creating a good image. However, there is a risk that random activities, such as supporting elderly in a region or giving funding to a festival, can seem as though the company is trying to divert the attention from the core activities of the company. It may create beneficial synergies important that funds are streamlined into supporting the proactive goals that are defined in line with the core activities of the company.

In the following two cases of companies having adopted proactive approaches focussing on Corporate Social Opportunities will be explored.

a. Case: Novo Nordisk – International Pharmaceutical Company

Novo Nordisk (NN) is a focussed health care company and world leader within the diabetes and insulin delivery systems. NN market its products in more than 180 countries around the world.

Regarding CSR NN supports a proactive strategy, creating a competitive edge on the CSOs. It is committed to the triple bottom line and supports the Universal Declaration on Human Rights. The commitments are integrated in the organization and they use five different follow-up methods to provide ongoing systematic and validated documentation of their performance: Financial follow-up and reporting, Environmental and Social Reporting, Organisational Audit, Facilitations, Succession Management. Further, NN was among the first companies in Europe to join the Global Compact.

NN argues that it supports the Universal Declaration because it operates in a series of human rights violating countries and human rights standards can inform and guide the company in its socially responsible initiatives.

Initially NN has chosen to be proactive on two main human rights areas, which are in the core of their activities: the right to health, including access to health, and equal opportunities and diversity.

Right to Health and Access to Health

Pharmaceutical companies exist by improving their customers' right to health and spend millions in research and development on life prolonging medicine. However, pharmaceutical companies, like NN, face a dilemma, since they on the one hand have to protect the patents and maintain a sustainable profit to carry out research and production in the future, but on the other hand must realize that people in large parts of the world are denied access to health, since facilities are not available or the medicine can not be afforded.

NN chose to address the problems of global health in a proactive manner through the Leadership in Education and Access to Health Programme (LEAD).[5] With the LEAD programme NN lays the groundwork for making

WHO priorities	Novo Nordisk response
1. Development of National health care Strategies	National Diabetes Programme
2. Building national Healthcare capacity	World Partner Programme
3. Best possible pricing	Best possible pricing in LDC
4. Additional funding	World Diabetes Foundation

[5]   See Novo Nordisk Sustainability Report 2003 under 'Global Health Strategy': can be downloaded at www.novonordisk.com/sustainability.

long-term strategic decisions and for assisting and funding projects in various economic developing countries, all rooted in a business model for ensuring access to health. LEAD is modelled on the four priorities of WHO for improving access to healthcare in the economic developing world.

Re. 1. The national Diabetes Programme is a programme where NN, through its global network of affiliates, supports governments to develop national strategies to fight diabetes.

Re. 2. In the World Partner Programme, established in 2002, NN conducts fact-finding analysis in developing countries, initially six of the poorest countries in the world. The model points out, what is needed in order for a country's diabetes care system to function optimally and effectively. It looks for ways to improve diabetes care in the developing world while remaining a viable and profitable business. After the fact-finding analysis NN establishes partnerships with patient organisations, ministries of health and other stakeholders to implement reasonable diabetes programme.

Re. 3. In 2001 NN decided to offer insulin products to the public health systems in the 49 least developed countries (LDC) at prices not to exceed 20 per cent of the average price in the industrialized countries.

Re. 4. The World Diabetes Foundation with an endowment of 67 million Euros is a fund for sustainable, innovative and helpful programmes to improve care for people with diabetes in the developing world. The programmes have to include elements of education, training, awareness raising and capacity building.

The proactive approach gives NN a competitive advantage because it is able to expand into the economic developing world in a responsible way, while contributing to sustainable development, expanding its market shares and enhancing its image.

Equal Opportunities

As mentioned above, it is very important when a company brands itself as responsible, that it is not implementing double standards by focussing their CSR strategies in the economic developing world only. NN is also proactive in this field and addresses equal opportunities and diversity management in all affiliates. This approach also increases the image of the company, while ensuring that NN is able to attract and retain the most competent employees.

To ensure that all employees enjoy equal opportunities in all the affiliates in 68 countries, NN has developed corporate guidelines. NN aims to secure equal opportunities in:

- Recruitment, terms of employment, in promotion and termination,
- Ensuring that no distinction, exclusion or preference is practised in relation to, and
- Equal treatment regardless of – gender, sexual orientation, age, disability, marital status, religious beliefs, creed, colour, race or ethnic origin, or political orientation.[6]

---

[6]   See Definitions of Equal Opportunity at Novo Nordisk Equal Opportunity Toolbox at http://eotoolbox.novonordisk.com.

b. Case: Sonofon – National Based Mobile Telephone Company

Sonofon is a medium size Danish company with a turnover of more than 537 mio. Euro and a workforce of 1,300 employees. Sonofon offers telecoms with a special emphasis on flexible, useful and simple solutions. The company was incorporated in 1991 and has enjoyed continuous growth over the past ten years. Today Sonofon is the second largest telco in Denmark with more than a million mobile subscribers.[7]

Like other socially responsible companies Sonofon is member of Global Compact and will report against the Global Reporting Initiative. What is interesting about Sonofon, in a CSR context, is that it is a medium size company without presence in other countries than Denmark, but nevertheless it has adopted a proactive human rights approach to its CSR strategy. The motivation was enhanced by the existing company values being 'challenging, attentive and simple'. Further it wanted to base its CSR strategy on values that would also be relevant in a distant future with possible mergers, expansions or outsourcing.

In relation to compliance Sonofon reports to the triple bottom line and considers carefully what responsibilities it has under the three bottom lines, besides the rights of the worker and national legislation. Identified issues were discussed with the board of directors and executives.

For proactive approaches Sonofon has defined the right to privacy, the freedom of expression and information and the right to take part in the technological development as most relevant priorities for a mobile telephone company (telco).

Right to Privacy

It is part of the daily tasks of a telco to wield sensitive data. As a responsible company Sonofon has to handle the customers' technological footprints respecting the privacy of the individual. Telco companies in Denmark face a dilemma because the customers have a right to privacy, but on the other hand companies has to keep information on the customers in five years in case of complaints. Due to mandatory registration, Sonofon has information on the customers' whereabouts, the length of their conversations and their contact net. Written data will likewise be stored. This puts an obligation on the company to develop guidelines on how to handle best, such data.

While responsible handling of data relates to compliance Sonofon has decided to take their initiative one step further. As part of the CSO agenda Sonofon has chosen to reject the offers they have had on resale of information. According to the law Sonofon could sell such information to buyers who wanted to market various goods to Sonofon customers. However, Sonofon has chosen to value the right to privacy of its customers higher than the possible economic gain.

Freedom of Speech and Information

There are hardly any places left where a mobile phone cannot reach a signal. Telco companies have always been working proactively with this right, widening

---

[7]   Information on Sonofon's Strategies on Corporate Social Responsibility can be found at www.sonofon.dk under 'About Sonofon' and 'CSR'.

the possibility of people to speak on their way. The freedom of receiving information has been increased with the expansion of the mobile phone, since users can receive all sorts of information on their portables.

However, Sonofon is also aware that increased opportunities require some rules of the game that it should inform its customers about. This is e.g. not to use the mobile camera to take pictures in degrading situations and to be considerate when using the mobile phone i.e. recommending customers to turn off the phone in certain situations.

Right to Take Part in the Technological Development
Sonofon has been enhancing the technological development in Denmark by a continuous development of the mobile network and its applications. Further it uses donations ensuring that as many as possible become 'technological winners', including people with disabilities. As a way to promote its message it has launched a competition on 'how to create a larger understanding of the technological development'.

D. CONCLUSION

The CSR development in Europe has increased within the last decade, however, without much participation of lawyers. Lawyers have unique competences and opportunities advising on CSR since they master the methodologies and are trained to undertake interpretation of the international conventions, which frame the development. Lawyers also have ready access to the EU boardrooms and enjoy the client-attorney privilege that will be of importance considering the sensitive areas under the agenda.

European lawyers could and should engage more actively in the development, not only to ensure compliance and avoid big losses for companies, but also to increase corporate social opportunities adopting proactive approaches. Experience shows that companies adopting such an approach gain competitive advantages. Framing the proactive approach in a human rights context will enhance such gains.

Chapter 21

THE CENTRAL ROLE OF LAWYERS IN MANAGING, MINIMIZING, AND RESPONDING TO SOCIAL RESPONSIBILITY RISKS – A US PERSPECTIVE

Phillip H. Rudolph*

A. INTRODUCTION

As social responsibility becomes an increasingly central aspect of day-to-day business for companies large and small, lawyers should and must become active participants in the CSR dialogue. This is true in all parts of the world, but may be uniquely true in the United States, where specific characteristics of our justice system have thrust legal professionals – or have invited such professionals to thrust themselves – into the center of issues as to which lawyers outside of the United States might normally watch from the sidelines.

Jurisdictions outside of the United States generally rely more heavily on regulatory tools to achieve social and economic goals. Lawyers are certainly important to the formation, evaluation, and assessment of these tools, but there is little about the world of regulation that drives lawyer involvement in every aspect of social, economic and political life. In contrast in the United States, for reasons spelled out below, social and economic goals are often achievable, or perceived to be achievable, only through resort to the courts. Indeed, specific characteristics of the US legal system have combined to make litigation one of the principal tools for achieving social and economic ends.[1]

---

*   Phillip H. Rudolph is Partner of Foley Hoag LLP.

[1]   Though certainly creating unparalleled mechanisms for the achievement of social goals, and opening courthouse doors to people whose legitimate concerns might otherwise go unanswered, the litigation culture in the United States also creates opportunities for tremendous abuse by opportunistic individuals who may be less interested in redressing wrongs than in lining their own pockets. The tensions between these extremes create challenges for social activists and businesses alike, and underscore the importance of sophisticated legal involvement in the social responsibility dialog.

Ramon Mullerat (ed.), Corporate Social Responsibility: The Corporate Governance of the 21st Century, 311–319.
© 2005 *International Bar Association. Printed in the Netherlands.*

This phenomenon is quite relevant to CSR practitioner. The American litigation culture means that clients will increasingly look to their attorneys to develop creative opportunities to advance legitimate social responsibility goals, where appropriate, through litigation. For example, whether one views this as good or bad, the evolution of the once-obscure Alien Tort Claims Statute, discussed later, as a tool to redress international human rights abuses is a compelling example of the creative use of the US legal system in this manner. But on the flip side of this same coin, the American tendency to over-rely on courts to resolve problems that they might not be best suited to address means that US clients will need to rely more heavily on their lawyers to defend their interests against what might be thought of as overaggressive use of the court. More often than not, one person's 'creative' litigation will be another person's 'abusive' litigation. This chapter does not attempt to pass judgment one way or the other. The bottom line, however, is that litigation-mania in the United States thrusts lawyers into the center of far more issues than might be the case elsewhere.

Litigation aside, however, lawyers are central to the CSR dialog in the United States for two other more traditional and less controversial reasons. First of all, regulatory schemes governing corporate conduct generally result in the legitimate reliance by regulated companies on legal counsel. Although – for reasons that will be discussed later in this chapter – the United States is certainly not leading the pack in terms of CSR-type regulation, the post-Enron wave of regulatory activity has put increasing pressure on companies to build substantive and effective ethics and social responsibility programs. These regulations, in turn, beget lawyers.

Second, even if we were to somehow throw away the regulators and the courts, companies must, as part of doing business, interact with other companies. Increasingly, the role of traditional commercial lawyers demands an ability to evaluate and consider the relevance of a company's social and environmental performance in helping clients make decisions regarding mergers, acquisitions, partnerships, supply chain relationships, and the entire gamut of commercial relationships that exist among and between businesses. This is the bread and butter of commercial lawyering. CSR is fast becoming just another critical component of the diligence and dealmaking process.

This chapter will address each of these factors in somewhat greater depth. The bulk of the discussion, however, will focus on litigation, because it is the litigation culture in the United States that underscores the importance and relevance of US lawyers in the overall CSR dialogue.

B. LITIGATION ISSUES

Litigation has become a combination of popular sports and popular entertainment in the United States. The cable television station – Court TV – televises judicial hearings and trials, and its commentators have become national figures. Countless celebrity judges convene televised hearings through the medium of 'People's Court' and similar shows to address and resolve petty disputes between publicity-hungry Americans. US television is also filled with fictional shows dramatizing the activities of lawyers, judges, and the legal system generally. And whether art is imitating life or vice versa, the American legal system has produced an endless litigation maelstrom that is, to date, without peer anywhere else in the world. There are five key drivers of this phenomenon:

- First, in United States, unlike most others jurisdictions, contingency fees – *i.e.* fees paid out of a percentage of whatever a lawyer is able to recover for his or her clients – are a favored approach to enabling those who might not otherwise have the financial ability to pay for a lawyer to do so.[2] As a result, lawsuits that might otherwise not be brought in the absence of such a tool may be filed with impunity. Not all of these lawsuits are meritorious. But, combined with the additional factors discussed below, contingency fees reduce the disincentives for clients and lawyers to pursue (and perhaps also reduce their capacity to identify) even arguably frivolous lawsuits. What this means is that the courthouses of the United States are filled to capacity with a hodge-podge of meritorious and not so meritorious cases, and capable lawyers are necessary to assist the courts in determining which are which.
- Second, the United States essentially fathered the concept of exemplary, or punitive, damages – again premised on no-doubt lofty goals and ideals aimed at punishing corporate wrongdoers for particularly heinous or egregious activities. But this innovation has mutated and grown somewhat out of control. Many legal observers around the world believe that the case that highlights the dangers of the punitive damage tool was that in which a woman who spilled a cup of coffee on her own lap was able, through her lawyers, to persuade a jury to award her several *million* dollars in punitive damages against the company that sold her the coffee (a beverage which, in its normal usage, is supposed to be served hot).[3]

  In large measure as a consequence of this and countless similar examples, punitive damages are the subject of great debate within the United States. Again, it is not the intention of this chapter to opine one way or the other. Good or bad, a consequence of the size of such damages and the willingness of juries to award them (*see* below) is that people who might not otherwise have suffered actual damages of a scope that would justify a lawsuit are far more willing to bring one where they can seek punitive damages and hope to win the jackpot. This is particularly so if their lawyer is working on a contingency fee basis.
- Third, the US legal system allows for – indeed requires – juries at the request of any party to a civil lawsuit. Although criminal juries are internationally recognized as critical tools for providing justice for the accused, civil juries are somewhat unique to the United States. Such juries are, at best, unpredictable. At their worst, they have evolved into instruments for the redistribution of wealth in American society. No entity in Western civilization has become so readily enamored of the David vs. Goliath story than

---

[2] The United Kingdom has also opened the door to these sorts of payment schemes. The UK also has a Legal Aid system that pays the costs of indigent litigants. Because of the absence of several other of the catalyzing factors discussed herein, neither of these devices has, *as yet,* produced the flood of litigation that characterizes the US legal system.

[3] This case was later settled for a much smaller, though not publicly disclosed, sum.

have civil juries, which replay the tale with regularity in courthouses across America. Think again of hot coffee.

It should thus come as no surprise that virtually every civil complaint filed in the United States is accompanied by a request for a jury trial. It should similarly come as no surprise that most corporate defendants, regardless of how strong their case might be on the merits, will try to avoid having their case actually go to a jury, either through seeking early summary resolution by the trial judge on legal issues, or through the expedient of settlement. Again, because civil juries are, at best, unpredictable, a plaintiff with a weak case has less reason to avoid the courts than he or she might have if his or her case was to be presented to a judge for final adjudication.

- Fourth, unlike most other civilized countries, the United States has not embraced a 'loser pays' system. A litigant who loses a lawsuit outside of the United States expects to pay the other side's costs. This is a very effective mechanism for screening out frivolous or weak lawsuits in jurisdictions outside of the United States. But this rule is not in place within the United States. Instead, a US litigant who loses a lawsuit picks up his toys and goes home. Perhaps he sues his lawyers.

- The fifth factor that helps contribute to the litigation culture in the United States is the class action lawsuit. This mechanism was created to enable victims of mass torts and similar such omnibus wrongdoing to bring lawsuits as a class where doing so as individuals would not be worth the time and money. The class action lawsuit has become a valuable tool for remedying harms occasioned upon large groups of people. It is an important way to empower individuals who might otherwise not be able to do so to seek justice and redress wrongs.

Unfortunately, the class action remedy has also become an effective tool for certain lawyers to garner extraordinary legal fees in instances in which the actual plaintiffs recover very little. This is yet another example of a well meaning instrument whose use has been subverted in too many cases. For this reason, the application of these well-intentioned class action tools has been the subject of much criticism, discussion, and debate within the US legal community. Suggestions to amend the relevant rules are constantly being proposed, with an eye towards protecting the people intended to benefit by the class action mechanisms. But for now, this somewhat flawed tool has further contributed to the America's burgeoning litigation culture.

In short, plaintiffs – particularly those whose attorneys are working on a contingency fee basis – have very little disincentive *not* to bring lawsuits since, under the absolute worst-case scenario (they lose), they pay neither the costs for their own lawyers nor the costs of their successful opponents. On the other hand, they have every incentive to bring a lawsuit, since juries can be unpredictable, and potential punitive damages can be astronomical.

These five seemingly unrelated and independently rational, indeed enlightened, elements of the US legal system therefore combine, like a perfect storm, to create a giant metaphorical Petri dish for the uncontrollable proliferation of lawyers and lawsuits. The law schools in the States are filled to bursting with eager young lawyers-in-waiting. And the courts are straining at the seams to administer lawsuits that are mocked, though slowly gaining a foothold, outside of the United States.

Why is this relevant to CSR? Quite simply, in contrast to most other parts of the world, because the US system fosters the use of litigation as an almost populist tool for the achievement of social and economic ends, many of the key CSR issues facing companies and their stakeholders are beginning to be played out in the courtrooms of the United States. A few examples will illustrate:

- At least two dozen federal lawsuits asserting claims under the heretofore obscure Alien Tort Claims Act (enacted by the first Congress in 1789),[4] presently are pending against corporations for alleged human rights abuses perpetrated by the governments of countries in which these corporations either do business or source goods.[5] This statute was enacted by the very first Congress of the United States to provide protections in the United States courts principally to victims of piracy on the high seas and to ambassadors attacked on foreign soil. It was effectively rediscovered in the 1980s after lying fallow for almost 200 years, and has been used to seek redress for alleged international law violations of multinational corporations and their local partners or vendors.

  The US Supreme Court recently upheld the viability of the ATCA, though the degree to which that law can be used to see redress of claims against corporations remains uncertain. But, regardless, American lawyers have other nascent tools – among them the Torture Victim Protection Act[6] and the UN-sponsored Convention Against Corruption[7] – by which they might try to hold multinationals accountable in US courts for workplace and human rights abuses perpetrated in developing countries.

- Within the past few years, claims brought under the Federal RICO statute[8] have been asserted in class action lawsuits against American multinationals for alleged workplace abuses occurring in production facilities in the United States' territory of Saipan. RICO was enacted by the US Congress originally to target organized crime activity, but has been used by lawyers to support an array of federal lawsuits never contemplated by Congress. Millions of dollars in settlements have been paid by corporate defendants to resolve the Saipan lawsuits.[9]

- In 2003, the California Supreme Court held that statements made by Nike in defense of critics' attacks on workplace practices in facilities making Nike footwear were not entitled to full free speech protections. The court thus ruled that Nike could be sued by a gentleman named Mark Kasky, on behalf of the citizens of the State of California, on the theory that its statements

4 Alien Tort Claims Act (ATCA), 28 USC § 1350 (2004).
5 See, e.g., *Doe, et al. v. Unocal Corporation, et al.*, 110 F.Supp.2d 1294 (C.D. Cal. 2000), aff'd in part, rev'd in part, 2002 WL 31063976 (9th Cir. 18 September 2002), rehearing en banc granted, vacated by 2003 WL 359787 (9th Cir. 14 February 2003).
6 The Torture Victim Protection Act (TVPA), 28 USC § 1350, note (2004).
7 United Nations Convention Against Corruption, *opened for signature* 9 December 2003, available at http://www.unodc.org/unodc/en/convention_corruption_merida.html.
8 Racketeering Influenced and Corrupt Organizations Act (RICO), 18 USC §§ 1961–1968 (2004).
9 *Doe v. The Gap Inc.*, No. 99–329 (C.D. Cal. filed 13 January 1999); *Union of Needletrades Industrial and Textile Employees v. The Gap*, No. 300474 (Cal. Sup. Ct. filed 23 Sept. 1999); *Doe v. Advanced Textile Corp.*, 214 F.3d 1058 (9th Cir. 2000). For more information on the lawsuits and settlement, see http://www.globalexchange.org/campaigns/sweatshops/saipan/.

were fraudulent under California law.[10] The United States Supreme Court opted not to rule on a challenge to that decision, and Nike subsequently settled the case before the California court had the chance to consider whether the challenged statements were true or not. Though the importance of consumer protection must not be minimized, it has been noted, even by Mr Kasky's lawyer, that the ability to bring such a costly and high profile lawsuit could have the serious potential to inhibit speech by corporations discussing important social issues, even where such speech might be proven after a full trial on the merits to have been completely legitimate.

- An NGO called Earthrights International has recently published a 'how-to' manual described as 'an information and education tool for individuals and/or organizations contemplating litigation as a remedy for human rights or environmental harms in United States courts.'[11] This down-loadable manual is 'directed toward non-lawyers who want to learn about this type of litigation, and possibly participate in a lawsuit.'[12]

Quite simply, over the past several years, there has been ever-growing volume, both in quantity and in decibels, of affected corporate stakeholders, including but not limited to labor groups, environmental interests, socially responsible investor groups, non-governmental organizations, governments, suppliers, communities, and others. This volume is heightened still further by the evolving tools – most notably the Internet – that are readily available to enable them to spread their messages. In the United States, this means 'here come the lawyers.' Stakeholders have become increasingly sophisticated and are increasingly aware of the effective use of tools of leverage and persuasion. As the example of Earthrights International makes clear, the legal system (particularly in the US) offers up an incredibly usable and effective toolbox for these groups. Stated bluntly:

> [t]he days of flying under the radar screen are gone. There are a lot of watchdog groups out there taking a look at what you are doing, your code of conduct, business partners and suppliers. That list of websites grows each month and these NGOs, unions and activist groups are all sharing information. And they are putting corporations in their crosshairs.

Conduct Unbecoming, Corporate Legal Times, October 2002.

C.   REGULATORY ISSUES

Both in-house and outside lawyers in the United States have been preoccupied with the Sarbanes-Oxley Act, its implementing regulations, new NYSE and

---

[10]   *Kasky v. Nike, Inc.*, 27 Cal. 4th 939 (Cal. 2002), *cert. dismissed, Nike, Inc. v. Kasky*, 539 US 654 (2003).
[11]   Earthrights International, Earthrights Litigation Manual (2003), available at http://www. earthrights.org/legalmanual/litigationmanual.pdf (last visited 13 June 2004).
[12]   *Id.*

Nasdaq listing rules, and all other regulatory detritus of the spate of corporate scandals that rocked the US and world markets as the curtains opened on the new Millennium. This regulatory horn of plenty – precipitated by a distinctly American tendency to focus on rules rather than values to drive behavior – itself might be characterized, at least in the short run, as the 'US Lawyer Full Employment Act.' Stated in the form of an axiom (Axiom #1), 'where there are rules, there are lawyers.' The lawyers' jobs are, respectively, to help their clients understand and comply with the rules, and the sue companies for violating the rules (Axiom #2 – where there are lawyers, there are lawsuits).

This is relevant to CSR because there is at least a dawning realization on the part of some businesses and some lawyers that a way to avoid the pitfalls of Enron and WorldCom (and Parmalat) is to build organizations in which behaviors are driven by values and principles rather than simply by rules. Stated somewhat simplistically, increasing numbers of business leaders are becoming savvy to the notion that one should not have to consult a guidebook to understand the fundamental difference between right and wrong. In fairness, many business leaders have known this for some time, and did not need the lessons of Enron to clue them in. Others are learning. Still others have much to learn.

This recent regulatory cornucopia in the United States also suggests – at least between the lines – a growing recognition by lawmakers that business organizations with strong, well-developed, and effectively communicated values and principles possess an ethos that enables employees from the top to the bottom to make difficult decisions in situations in which rules might not offer clear guidance. In fact, there are explicit threads of this notion running through Sarbanes-Oxley and the newly revised US Sentencing Guidelines – emphasizing the need for company ethics programs to be 'effective' and suggesting if not stating outright that simple, check-the-box approaches to such programs may not be meet that standard.[13]

As American companies evolve towards a greater emphasis on values and principles – even if, or perhaps particularly since such evolution is driven by regulation – US lawyers should and will play an ever-important role in helping their clients meet these heightened or at least different expectations.

D. BUSINESS ISSUES

Even setting aside the litigation and regulatory drivers of US-lawyer involvement in CSR, CSR presents abundant opportunities for strategic, thoughtful, and forward-looking lawyers to assist their American clients, as well as their international clients with business interests in the United States. The day to day

---

[13] For example, recent amendments to the United States Sentencing Guidelines were explicitly intended to 'promote an *organizational culture* [within companies] that encourages a commitment to compliance with the law.' US Sentencing Commission, Proposed Amendments to Sentencing Guidelines 58 (13 January 2004), page 60 (emphasis added). The amendments are contained in U.S.S.G. Section 8 B2.1. A copy of the Commission's Report is available at www.ussc.gov/2004guid/rfJan04.pdf. Notably, the specific purpose for these amendments was 'to *reflect the emphasis on ethics and values* incorporated into recent legislative and regulatory reforms [e.g. Sarbanes-Oxley]....' *Id.* (emphasis added).

commercial activities of most US businesses require companies to interface with an array of stakeholder as to whom lawyers play an on-going and critical role. These stakeholders include business partners, suppliers, customers, licensees and licensors, and even merger candidates. As CSR becomes increasingly imbedded in the cultures and values of companies and each of these stakeholders (and others), traditional business relationships will incorporate social, environmental, and ethical components to a greater and greater extent.

Lawyers typically represent the front lines in the development of documents and tools intended to embed these expectations into commercial relationships. More and more deals are requiring, as part of the due diligence process, an assessment of CSR-related activities and risks. Many companies expect their business partners to undertake activities designed to minimize the CSR risks associated with the particular venture in which the companies are involved, and attorneys are increasingly being relied upon to make this happen. CSR audits and program development are becoming part of doing business in a global environment, and legal involvement can help protect the integrity of such efforts.

Although this is by no means US-specific (indeed, a far fuller discussion of the world-wide commercial law aspects of CSR can be found both in Chapters 21 and 26 of this treatise), the sheer volume of commercial activity occurring within and relating to US-based multinationals requires US lawyers to have a complete understanding of the CSR 'portfolio' of their clients. Though US lawyers have come to embrace governance as an inseparable part of providing commercial guidance and representation to their clients, they are still at the early stages of fully realizing the importance, indeed the centrality, of social responsibility as a component of doing business in America in the new millennium. As their clients' understanding continues to grow, US lawyers will become key players in helping to define commercial expectations surrounding the social responsibilities of US businesses.

E.   CONCLUSION

Like swallows to Capistrano or pilgrims to Lourdes (or, some may say, coals to Newcastle), American lawyers can always be relied upon to 'be there' in great quantity and with unerring consistency. But in fairness to US lawyers, legal and other systems governing business operations in the United States, and the nature of the issues and stakeholders impacted by the activities of US companies overseas, compel the involvement of good, strategic legal minds to help companies assess the implications – legal and otherwise – of their activities. As corporate social responsibility becomes increasingly central to the day-to-day business activities of US-based multinationals, US lawyers will become increasingly central in helping businesses manage CSR risks and opportunities.

Forward-looking, business-minded in-house lawyers are typically best suited to this role, because they understand as no outside lawyer can the unique drivers of their clients' businesses. But outside attorneys with appropriate experience and perspective working with companies, governments, NGOs, and other stakeholders can and will become increasingly a part of the CSR activities of US businesses. Regardless, however, of whether they sit within the corporate headquarters or service their clients from a private outside practice, US lawyers are critical members of the corporate social responsibility dialog for several reasons. For one thing, the litigation climate in the United States will increasingly demand this. Moreover, an increased awareness in the United States of the importance of values and principles – as opposed to simply rules – as drivers of corporate behavior is leading to regulatory activity that will underscore the importance of building social responsibility into the governance structures of US businesses. Finally, the need to stay current and, indeed, leading edge will drive US companies to bake CSR into their business relationships, and lawyers are often the principle drafters of these recipes.

Chapter 22

AFRICA'S UNIQUE CHALLENGE: LINKING ECONOMIC GROWTH, INFRASTRUCTURE REFORMS AND CORPORATE RESPONSIBILITIES

Reinier Lock

The new century's fanfare attention to corporate social responsibility (CSR) has special poignance for Africa today. It is linked to far older and deeper emotional perceptions emanating from colonial rule and even pre-colonial exploitation (such as Belgian kings' devastating exploitation of the Congo's national and human resources in the 19th century). These historical perceptions strengthen the intensity of the focus on CSR; but they could also undermine its rationality.

Nowhere was this intensity more evident than while participating in the IBA's recent outstanding conference on law and social responsibility, attended by some 650 lawyers, in Lagos, Nigeria.[1] The deep concern about CSR, and over broader themes relating to human rights and development, was palpable and admirable.

But in the dialogue emanating from the audience, a more disturbing theme was evident – a tendency to blame it all on large, usually multinational, corporations; and to ignore the massive failures of governments and of their democratic accountability. These failures have plagued all too many African countries, most since the wave of independence from colonial rule in the 1960s and 1970s. Too many autocratic or unaccountable governments have plundered their nations' resources, with devastating effects on their economies and on the human rights of their citizens

Oversimplification of the CSR challenge – to blame it all on multinational corporations – is, of course, exacerbated in the arena on which this article will focus – electricity and other infrastructure industries, such as water and transportation.

---

[1]   International Bar Association Regional Conference. 'Developing the Law as an Instrument for Social and Economic Rights', Lagos, Nigeria, 5–8 April 2004 (hereinafter 'Lagos conference').

Ramon Mullerat (ed.), Corporate Social Responsibility: The Corporate Governance of the 21st Century, 321–335.
© 2005 *International Bar Association. Printed in the Netherlands.*

A. CSR FAILURES IN ENERGY

There are perhaps no more currently publicized and notorious failures of CSR, and of the overall accountability of corporations, even to their own employees, than the exposures of destructive trading practices in a surprising number of the major US energy companies. These abuses were led, of course, by Enron – but followed also by other major multinational energy giants, primarily in electricity, such as AES, Calpine and CMS. All had had major international operations. They had been in the forefront of the 'gold rush' of US and European energy companies into the international energy development arena in the mid-1990s. They had had good records in social responsibility, e.g. AES' tree planting initiatives to offset global warming.

However, driven largely by corporate scandals relating to market manipulation, deceptive accounting, and simple failures to report on time to shareholders, Enron essentially imploded and its stock value plummeted to almost zero. Most of its leadership has faced, or is now facing, serious criminal and civil liability.

Other once revered market players, such as AES and CMS, came close to the same fate – losing most of their market value, much of it over exposure of deceptive trading practices.[2] These practices affected only a small part of their overall operations but devastated their company stock values (often by losing over 90 percent of their value).

B. THE REAL DAMAGE

However, while the collapses or virtual collapses of these corporations did damage their operations and market ratings, the direct damage to the energy sectors of the countries in which they operated was less evident. In many cases, governments had already moved to limit their own exposures by canceling deals with overseas independent power produced (IPP) companies. In some cases, such as Indonesia, governments simply reneged on arrangements because of collapses of their own currencies and the inability to repatriate dollars to foreign developers. In short, the nexus between the market trading practices of Enron and other IPP companies in the US, and their overseas electricity operations, was less direct or clear.

The primary devastation was exacted upon the companies themselves, their shareholders (who lost most of their investments) and their employees (who lost their jobs). While exposing a corporate culture, and the laws that govern it, that is far from perfect, the market system had exacted its own devastating (and, as to employees, by no means fair) punishment.

Probably the biggest damage to developing country economies caused by this market devastation came not from the collapse of some highly publicized IPP projects, such as Enron's infamous Dahbol project in India, but from the drying up of what had once been a flood, or promised flood, of foreign private investment. This investment was, and still is, crucial to meet the expansion needs of very capital intensive infrastructure industries, such as power and water.

---

[2] 'Round trip trading', essentially trading with oneself to inflate stock prices, was a practice that caught many of them.

Both these industries are critical foundations for sustained economic growth and human welfare. Some African countries, even today, provide electricity and clean water to only small minorities of their population. In too many countries, development of both basic services has been grossly neglected. Where provided at all, typically by government/state-owned monopoly entities ('SOMs'), they have generally been provided inefficiently, and often with great waste of scarce resources, especially capital.

C.   REPAIRING CORPORATE ACCOUNTABILITY

The corporate practices that have caught the headlines over the past two years, especially in the energy industry but also in industries as basic as food (Parmalat and Martha Stewart!) in fact relate to a quite narrow area in the broad spectrum of CSR – essentially the stock trading, accounting and reporting practices of major corporations. Much of the emphasis of lawmakers in the US and EU is therefore upon tightening existing, already complex and quite sophisticated, securities laws; upon governance, disclosure, corporate accounting and reporting practices; and the attendant legal and ethical regimes. The renowned Sarbanes-Oxley legislation in the US, for example, deals only with the relatively narrow area of how US corporations are to be governed (internally) and how they are to report to their shareholders and to the US Securities and Exchange Commission (SEC). Much of the focus now of US Boards of Directors, the ultimate decision makers in corporate governance, is upon transparency of accounting and adequacy of reporting.[3]

D.   THE BROAD FOCUS OF CSR

As pointed out by one of the leading human rights experts at the Lagos conference, Ramon Mullerat, (then co-Chairman of the IBA's Human Rights Institute), the concept of CSR is far broader than, and hence distinguishable from, this narrow concept of corporate accountability. The latter focuses on the effectiveness of existing governance and disclosure systems of major corporations – the current focus in the US and Europe.

CSR embraces the broad concept of companies voluntarily deciding to respect and protect much broader interests than those of their corporate shareholders – or even their employees. However, as noted at the Lagos Conference by Mr I. Odeleye (a leading Nigerian lawyer and Company Secretary of Shell, Nigeria), there is no universally precise definition of CSR. It embraces a wide range of 'often competing or conflicting environmental economic, human and societal imperatives'. This entails the corporation developing its own policy to pursue and balance these imperatives in areas such as community development

---

[3]   The author witnessed the intensity of this focus while serving on the Board of a statewide cooperative transmission company in the US.

and involvement, personnel policy, business relations, environmental protection, supplier relations and human rights.[4]

While corporations are typically subject to domestic laws in most of these areas, e.g. labor and environmental laws, the notion of CSR is to create a corporate conscience and culture that develops a cohesive social commitment that transcends and enhances such specific legal requirements, often on a transnational level. A good example is the impressive effort of some of the mining companies, such as Rio Tinto, to develop sustainable development policies for the communities in which their mining operations might deplete natural resources, and might cause environmental damage and potential social and economic disruption.[5]

Mr Odeleye draws a critical connection between CSR as a corporation's policy and the corporation's practical need to strike an appropriate balance 'under law and regulation in an atmosphere of fair competition' between its economic needs to make a profit for its shareholders and its taking account of the often competing needs of other stakeholders.[6]

E.   THE CHALLENGE OF ECONOMIC REGULATION

The essence of this piece of wisdom from Mr Odeleye is that, unless the legal/regulatory system ensures effective competition in the business sector, and effective regulation to protect it, other aspects of CSR can become essentially meaningless. Lack of competition and inadequate regulation of entities with monopoly or 'market power' can do such fundamental damage to the economy, and to all consumers, that other aspects of CSR can be relegated to little more than window dressing.

That damage is particularly acute in the infrastructure industries that are this writer's specialization – such as electricity and water supply. Inefficiency in these areas has enormous economic, social, developmental and even health costs, especially for developing countries. It undermines economic human rights in a fundamental way; and that renders most other human rights far less meaningful.

The provision of adequate service in these infrastructure areas is therefore the focus of this chapter. Because so many of Africa's economies have such basic challenges, and most an urgent need to develop these infrastructure industries, one of the best building blocks for their development, and for economic human rights, is the creation of legal and regulatory regimes that impose the necessary economic discipline to garner investments needed for capital-intensive sectors like electricity. Creating such regimes is a critical foundation for the basic infrastructure development that underlies economic progress; and CSR in the typical sense can only be meaningfully developed as this progress takes root.

---

[4]   See generally, papers of Messrs Mullerat and Odeleye at Lagos conference.
[5]   See Marcelle F. Shoop and Preston S. Chiaro, *Sustainable Development and Mining: Oxymoron or Opportunity*, 49 Rocky Mt. Min. L. Inst., Ch. 11 (2003) (hereinafter 'Shoop and Chiaro').
[6]   Odeleye paper at 2.

F. THE FURTHER CHALLENGE: STATE-OWNED MONOPOLIES

Hence, CSR has often played a low-key role in confronting this infrastructure challenge. Only recently has it reached a high level of profile under recent Africa-wide initiatives (see below).

Ironically, however, one of the biggest barriers to economic progress in sectors such as electricity and water in many African countries has been the domination of these sectors by governments themselves – or, more precisely, by stated-owned monopolies ('SOMs'). These are often overseen directly by governments or by government-appointed boards. Seldom have these enterprises been run on anything approaching sound business principles. Too often, they have been driven by conflicting and often irrational social priorities. Too often, they have been victims of rampant inefficiency and, sometimes, outright corruption.

Moreover, most have been plagued by two massive myths. First, for years governments argued that, because they were State-owned, they would naturally act in the public interest and in consumers' interests. Second, they argued that direct government oversight would provide effective regulation.

It has now been recognized in most developing countries, and strongly advocated by the international funding agencies (IFAs) such as the World Bank, that neither is typically the case. Moreover, many African countries have massive development needs for new infrastructure, with huge capital needs governments simply cannot handle, even with IFA support. Hence, there has been a strong drive to reverse the legacy of infrastructure sectors dominated by SOMs.

Many African countries have commenced serious 'sector reform' initiatives in power, water and other infrastructure sectors – restructuring and privatizing or commercializing State-owned enterprises. Many are establishing regulatory regimes independent of government and have adopted policies to encourage at least some form of private sector enterprise and investment. Hence, two basic movements are at the core of this reform – encouraging private sector participation (PSP) or at least business-oriented State enterprises; and creating independent professional regulators.

These initiatives are not without hurdles – predictable resistance from those in governments, labor unions and SOMs themselves. Each constituency fights to protect the old myths (e.g. that they best serve the 'public interest') and to defend bloated employment rights. They often argue that one simply cannot leave to private sector ownership industries viewed as so basic to essential human needs. (So, of course, is food; and food is best provided in competitive private markets).

In most African countries today, this critical conversion of infrastructure sectors – from economically unaccountable and inefficient bureaucracies to business-oriented and effectively regulated (and sometimes restructured) industries – has either only recently occurred (i.e. within the last decade); or is just underway (the conversion process typically takes years); or is still under consideration.

In many countries, governments are still reluctant to fully achieve the 'two separations' urged by the World Bank and other IFAs – separation of the business entity from the State; and separation of the sector's regulation from the SOM entities and from government itself, i.e. the creation of truly independent, professionally focused regulation.

Much of the challenge in implementing restructuring initiatives, the author has found, lies in these areas. In the SOM context, the 'bright lines' between Government, the regulator and the regulated entity, blurred for decades, are not achieved overnight. They often take a series of painstaking efforts to restructure the sector into business units and to set up independent regulatory institutions. This often involves major restructuring of the industry itself and of legal and regulatory framework for the sector; and it requires a massive capacity building exercise at both the corporate and regulatory levels.

The only legitimate argument for some level of ongoing government involvement – the 'natural monopoly' aspects of some parts of these industries – is best dealt with by sector-specific independent regulation or by effective competition authorities or, usually, by some combination of the two. In many African countries today, these regulatory and competition law institutions are very new or not yet formed. Fully functioning independent regulatory entities are a recent creation and, in many countries, their legitimacy and effectiveness are yet to be proven.

However, progress over the last decade has been considerable. Many African countries have embarked upon impressive sector reform programs of national systems and, in areas such as electricity, where there are great economies of scale and scope in trading, made impressive advances in establishing regional trading and even regional regulatory arrangements.[7]

G.   STATE-OWNED MONOPOLIES AND CSR

Hence, the focus in infrastructure areas such as electricity has been on creating economically conducive legal and regulatory frameworks to encourage private sector investment, usually by the very large international private companies that are the focus of typical CSR concerns. Perhaps ironically too, some of the worst culprits for social and economic irresponsibility have been the large state-owned enterprises themselves; and their potential savior has often been some greater level of involvement by those very international private companies.

While this may seem to turn the typical focus of CSR on its head, in fact it is doing no more than recognize a reality that is pervasive in some economies – that the State-owned and parastatal enterprises that are prevalent in many African economies face many of the same CSR challenges that confront private sector companies, but perhaps in a different way. They face some distinctive challenges because of their special historical role in these economies. Many of these are distinctive to their specific countries. As noted above, the World Bank and other IFAs have developed some general principles for power sector and other infrastructure 'reform' – but most of the challenge lies in effective implementation of these principles in specific situations.

---

[7]   Two of Africa's largest regional organizations, SADC and ECOWAS, have over the last decade established regional electricity trading structures ('power pools'), and regional organizations of electricity regulators which have made significant progress in the regional oversight of electricity trading.

Moreover, even once the functioning independent regulatory entity discussed above is in place, there is no assurance that CSR will automatically follow. The serious affront to CSR in the US electricity sector, noted above, exposed serious failures in the array of developed complex laws in both the economic regulatory and corporate securities areas, and in the regulatory agencies that oversee them, regimes that had been in place for about 70 years.

The US electricity sector, dominated by privately owned but economically regulated corporations – saw serious failures of economic regulation itself at both the State and federal levels. Consumers suffered from such failures through much higher tariffs. This led to fiascos such as California's electricity crises over the last five years – and even to conceptually indefensible episodes of direct government intervention such as Governor Gray Davis' in California.

In many African countries, whose power sectors are still dominated by SOMs, the CSR situation is often worse. As noted above, many are run by inefficient entities and labor forces that do not even purport to adhere to basic economic principles. Many are inadequately funded for expansion, have antiquated infrastructures, and are incapable of providing adequate and reliable service even to the populations and economic enterprises they do serve. In many, corruption within their enterprises or amongst their consumers (who routinely steal or do not pay for electricity) is rampant.

Hence, in these countries, CSR has an additional crucial challenge that really precedes effective adherence to traditional CSR – the conversion of the SOM structure into an economically efficient and accountable enterprise capable of providing adequate basic service – the essential foundation for making CSR meaningful to their consumers or populaces. The challenge of establishing a climate of effective CSR therefore requires a further dimensional advance to overlay the evolution of these new structures.

H.   AFRICA's NEW EMPHASIS ON CSR

In Africa today, there are three types of major initiatives that are under development to tackle the special challenge facing Africa's infrastructure industries. The first is the major review and, often, overhaul of the industry models for providing basic services such as electricity – the 'sector reform' movement described above. While global in dimension, it has distinctive features and, as noted, important international dimensions under Africa's regional arrangements.

The second initiative is some specific CSR exercises by major multinational corporations – again with global scope but special challenges in Africa. The third comprises some continent wide political initiatives that are very distinctive to Africa. These will be described below.

I.   CORPORATE CSR – A CASE STUDY IN MINING

One of the best examples of multinational corporations addressing CSR issues in the context of major industry-specific human rights concerns comes from an industry not typically viewed as infrastructural, but closely associated with developing economies – mining.

As with many developments in the electricity and water areas (e.g. dams that serve both hydropower and water provision purposes and that raise environmental, ecological and human settlement issues), mining raises major CSR issues.

Because mining operations have such an immediately dramatic effect on local communities and their environment, several mining companies have taken the lead in developing a 'sustainable development' approach to the enterprise. As noted in the Plan of Implementation of the World Summit on Sustainable Development held in Johannesburg, RSA in 2002 (hereinafter 'Johannesburg Plan') '[minerals] are essential for modern living'.[8]

The challenge in this context, then, is to incorporate CSR into the ongoing business model for future development and to get the buy-in of relevant stakeholders, i.e. to go beyond ephemeral philanthropy. The goal is to integrate economic, social and environmental considerations into business actions/decisions that will lead to sustainable development.[9]

The crucial cementing element is governance – the systems, policies, regulations and procedures that marshal these elements into an orderly decisional process.[10] A major emphasis of Johannesburg Plan implementation in mining focuses on full participation of stakeholders, such as indigenous communities, in the life cycle of mining operations and post-closure rehabilitation, and in promoting transparency and accountability.[11] Greater emphasis is also placed on renewable energy, cleaner fuel and energy efficiency technologies in mining operations, which are often energy-intensive.[12]

A number of major multinational initiatives, both continent-wide and country-specific, are underway to achieve these goals.[13] Many of these rely on voluntary initiatives, standards, codes and guidelines by the principal actors in the industry, notably most of the major international mining companies. These initiatives raise challenging legal issues as to the long-term effect of such codes (e.g. whether they will ultimately be effective; or conversely, whether they will broaden beyond voluntary adherence into enforceable rules of law).[14]

However, these legal concerns have apparently not hindered a recent aggressive agenda by some mining companies to convert social and environmental responsibility initiatives from 'socially acceptable policies' into good business practices that confer long-term competitive advantages over rivals. For example, Rio Tinto, one of the most aggressive players in this new arena, turned in its best economic performances in its history in 2001 and 2002, remarkable in the context of a global economic downturn in these years.[15]

---

8   Shoop and Chiaro at II-3. This article describes the issues and initiatives underway in this area; and case studies of actions of some of the major mining industry players.
9   *Id.* at II-4.
10 *Id.*
11 *Id.* at II-6.
12 *Id.* at II-7.
13 For an excellent overview, see Shoop and Chiaro at II-7–II-24.
14 *Id.* at II-24.
15 *Id.* at II-29. The article provides an interesting case study of Rio Tinto's comparative 'best practices' dynamic amongst its 80 operations and a series of specific case studies from Rio Tinto operations. *Id.* at II-31–II-35.

Underlying this social responsibility, then, is economic common sense. Competitive advantages arise from long-term cost savings such as recycling and waste management improve; and from attracting more private investors (e.g. from major pension and other financial management funds that increasingly rate companies in terms of sustainable investment policies). The product is new guidelines, led by the World Bank and other IFIs and now widely adopted by private banks, under the so-called Equator Principles.[16]

Perhaps because mining is so obviously destructive of finite natural resources (i.e. its products get used up and its operations often have stark environmental impacts), and because its operations often involve major global companies whose units can readily share experiences, the mining industry has taken a lead over energy in CSR. Its experiences in this arena should be carefully examined by the energy industries, especially the battered international 'IPP' industry, many of whose companies are still suffering from the effects of 'Enronitis'.

J.   CSR IN AFRICA'S NEW POLITICAL ARENA

The dawn of the 21st century has seen a wave of new initiatives in Africa – continent wide, regional and country-specific – designed to reverse negative legacies in Africa's past and to create a climate for sustained economic growth and political democracy. At the helm of this movement, operating under the broad auspices of the African Heads of State,[17] is the New Partnership for Africa's Development – the so-called NEPAD process – a development framework that emphasizes partnership at several levels.

At NEPAD's heart are the goal of sustainable development and a series of initiatives designed to unite the continent into an effective economic and trading bloc and to increase its competitiveness – especially in the strained world of scarce development capital that is so crucial to infrastructure development and economic growth.

The two central pillars of NEPAD are its commitment to democracy and good political governance; and to good economic and corporate governance. While the core of CSR might lie in the latter, as noted above, in Africa, especially with so many of its infrastructure industries with massive State involvement, the two are closely linked. Failures in political governance can readily undermine the best efforts in CSR. That is why Africa's initiative to link them so closely through a variety of major specific programs[18] is so farsighted and critical.

The challenge, already well recognized in Africa, will be effective implementation of these programs. Two that have special significant to infrastructure will be examined below, the others just noted.

---

[16]   *Id.* at II-30–II-31.
[17]   Operating under the auspices of the African Union (AU), the overarching regional organization for all of Africa (replacing the Organization of African Unity – the OAU).
[18]   These were set forth in detail in a major NEPAD policy agenda, titled 'NEPAD at Work: Summary of NEPAD Action Plans, July 2002'. (Hereinafter 'NEPAD Blueprint'). The document sets forth a wide range of specific initiatives to comprise the Short Term Action Plan and agenda strategies for developing a Medium/Long Term Action Plan.

First, however, it is useful to briefly examine the broad coverage envisaged for NEPAD:

- Democracy and good political governance. This envisages a series of specific commitments relating to the rule of law, separation of government powers, individual political rights and freedoms, and equality of opportunity. A series of specific measures to support democratic processes and good governance and to protect human rights comprise NEPAD's 'action plan' in this arena.[19]
- Economic and corporate governance. NEPAD has developed eight internationally approved 'prioritized and approved codes and standards' to serve as a baseline for each country to promote market efficiency, curb waste, consolidate democracy, and 'encourage private financial flows'.[20] These relate to monetary and financial policies; fiscal and budgetary transparency; public debt management; accounting and auditing standards; banking supervision principles – and corporate governance. Specific transparency codes are also developed for financial management of payment systems; anti-money laundering; and principles for securities and insurance supervision and regulation.

To supplement these policy pillars for development, the NEPAD agenda calls for a series of measures to encourage socio-economic development, such as better education and training in areas such as ICT (information control technology) and HIV/AIDS.

K.   SPECIFIC NEPAD INITIATIVES

Three specific initiatives of NEPAD are of special significance to infrastructure development:

1.   African Peer Review Mechanism (APRM)

Targeted as one of the first concrete initiatives of NEPAD, the APRM is a self-monitoring mechanism, to be acceded to by all Member States, to ensure compliance with agreed political economic and corporate governance values, codes and standards. The goal is to foster policies, standards and practices by African governments that lead to political stability, economic growth, sustainable development and economic integration between countries, relying heavily on transparency and comparison to encourage best practices.

Detailed processes are established for the direction and management of the APRM by a panel of distinguished experts, supported by the NEPAD Secretariat to develop the data base and carry out the analytical work for the peer review process.[21] For each country, a program of staged reviews, analysis and, most

---

[19]   NEPAD Blueprint at 4–5.
[20]   *Id.* at 6.
[21]   *Id.* at 8–9.

crucial, interactive dialogues on the findings and recommendations of Peer Review Team with the subject government is envisaged. A process for the government to show 'a demonstrable will to rectify the identified shortcomings' and to receive assistance from other governments in doing so; or to face possible sanctions if they stonewall the process, is set forth in detail.[22]

As of writing, the APRM process was well underway. While it is a process directed in the first instance at governments, it has obvious implications for the parastatal infrastructure corporations owned by governments, for their regulators, and for the private sector entities that operate in these sectors.

Wisely, the AU has seen the APRM process as a crucial building block for progress in other areas, including sector governance of the infrastructure areas and the development of 'public private partnerships' (PPPs) in the area.[23] The process is already advocated and emphasized by those in the lead of economic reforms in African countries such as Nigeria's Finance Minister, Dr Ngozi Okonjo-Iweala.[24]

2. Infrastructure Initiative

One of the most emphasized NEPAD initiatives relates to infrastructure – energy, water, transport and ICT. The blueprint document focuses on the 'infrastructure gap' and the development of regional infrastructure as critical to economic growth.[25] It notes the overall problems in these sectors – of inadequate service and financing, inefficient management and operation; and advocates the acceleration of sector reform initiatives and regulatory frameworks to confront these problems.

NEPAD sees its role, building on initiatives by governments, IFAs and private entities in these sectors, as encouraging sector reforms and harmonizing regulatory systems between countries, encouraging 'pooling' of initiatives to develop large scale regional projects, and facilitating the sharing of 'best practices'.

A major underlying objective is 'strengthening...of sector governance arrangements that are rule-based, predictable, transparent and participatory' – all to create 'the enabling environment for enhancing competitiveness and stepping up the flow of investments' in these sectors.[26]

A specific focus of the Short Term Action Plan has been the identification and 'fast-tracking' of projects that could contribute to regional infrastructure provision and integration but have been stalled for years for political reasons or inadequate investment profiles and inadequate policy, regulatory and institutional frameworks. These have been highlighted by NGOs in developed countries, e.g. on Wall Street by the US-based Corporate Council on Africa.

The Blueprint then examines the issues and specific institutions distinctive to each sector (e.g. the African Energy Commission as to energy).[27]

---

22 *Id.* at 10–12.
23 See below.
24 See, e.g., Presentation at Center for Strategic and International Studies Conference, Wash. D.C., March 10, 2004.
25 NEPAD Blueprint at 42–48.
26 *Id.* at 43.

3. The PPP Initiative

The Blueprint focuses on PPPs as one of the best ways to foster development, especially in the infrastructure areas, in order to bypass the operating problems and investment deficiencies of SOM enterprises. It notes how Africa seriously lags other regions in this area; and notes causes such as inadequate legal and regulatory frameworks for PPPs, lack of technical/management skills for PPPs, bad risk profiles, limited infrastructure and undersized markets.[28]

Governments, the Blueprint asserts, will have to improve the business climate by needed reforms in legal and regulatory frameworks and drafting new laws and model codes for PPPs; and in assisting in the development of regulatory bodies.[29]

L.   SPECIFIC INITIATIVES TO SUPPORT TRANSPARENCY AND DEVELOPMENT

The NEPAD process has spawned numerous supportive initiatives, both in Africa and in developed countries in Europe and North America. Three merit special mention, necessarily brief for space reasons. Each opens up new issues and areas of endeavor which are in their early stages. Each has the potential for major policy initiatives in the transparency area of CSR.

1.   The EITI[30]

Championed by the UK Prime Minister, Tony Blair, and other international leaders, the EITI is designed to focus on the need for accounting and other forms of transparency in oil-producing regions, such as Nigeria and the other countries of Central/West Africa that have exploitable oil and gas deposits. The EITI is very specifically focused on problems peculiar to that industry, such as accounting for oil revenue flows, oil revenue disposal and audits of the sector's financial operations.

2.   Nigeria's Transparency Commitments

Led by its new Finance Minister, Nigeria is playing a leading role in supporting the EITI and other initiatives to promote transparency, corporate accountability and CSR, especially in Nigeria's giant energy companies that play such a dominant role in its economy.[31]

---

[27]   *Id.* at 43–48.
[28]   *Id.* at 49. A stunning figure is that Africa accounted for only US $14 billion of investments in PPPs compared to US $237 billion for Latin America and the Caribbean region in the 1990–1998 period.
[29]   *Id.*
[30]   The Extractive Industries Transparency Initiative.
[31]   The Nigerian National Petroleum Corporation (NNPC) and the National Electric Power Authority (NEPA).

The Government of Nigeria has developed two domestic institutions – the National EITI Stakeholders Workgroup and a new office in the Finance Ministry. The goal is to develop a framework to monitor oil and gas revenues, undertake analyses, conduct audits, analyze joint venture agreements and monitor revenue collections in the complex area of business operations in the oil and gas sector; and to strengthen the country's regulatory and collections apparatus. Underlying the initiative is the need to gain government control over revenue accountability for parastatal corporations whose economic and CSR performances are critical to the country's future.

3. 'Promoting Transparency in the African Oil Sector' (CSIS)[32]

In parallel with, and interacting with Nigeria's EITI initiative, the CSIS, a US-based NGO, conducted an analytical exercise by a multi-stakeholder Task Force to examine the transparency issues related to the oil and gas sectors in West and Central Africa and to develop recommendations for US policy towards the region. The Report contains depth analysis and a series of recommendations which space does not permit be detailed here. However, the underlying theme of the Report is clear – the need for the US and the IFAs to develop mechanisms and policies to encourage transparency in the sector and in specific projects such as the Chad-Cameroon Pipeline.

Each of these three supportive initiatives is ongoing and has produced useful information and perspectives on the focus of this chapter – the challenge of introducing effective mechanisms for CSR into Africa's energy infrastructure industries. Each presents a useful case study that may merit further review.

M. CONCLUSION

The challenge of implementing CSR in many African countries is compounded in the infrastructure sectors, which are so critical to economic human rights, by the need to fundamentally reform these sectors themselves and to redefine the appropriate role of governments in them. In this area, CSR has deep and complex dimensions.

Also unique to Africa is the massive dimension of underdevelopment in base infrastructure services to populations in all too many countries – requiring massive investments to turn this around.

The dream of the 1980s and 1990s, shared by many developing countries, was that foreign private investment would move in to fill much of that void. This would allow the World Bank and other IFAs to move out of funding capital intensive physical infrastructure and to focus on broader social investments, e.g. in health care and education.

---

[32] Report of the Center for Strategic and International Studies (CSIS), *Task Force on Rising US Energy Stakes in Africa*, March 2004.

With the collapse of that dream over the last several years, the World Bank and other IFAs have been forced back into addressing infrastructure more frontally. Countless initiatives are underway to address this challenge; but none have yet produced a 'magic bullet' solution – because there is not one.

What will be needed is a well-coordinated, deliberate and visionary level of co-operation between private (often international) corporate interests, governments and the (often State-owned) providers of basic infrastructure services and, to the extent they can assist this process, the IFAs and other NGOs. For all the rhetoric, the current reality is a far cry from achieving this. It will require some focused, difficult and time-consuming steps to get there.

First, the whole concept of CSC and its concomitant building block – transparency – needs to be broadened and applied where it will have most impact – to governments and their parastatals; to private enterprises, whether domestic or foreign; and even to the IFAs themselves.[33] Without full government support and complicity in advancing CSC in many African countries, the concept becomes meaningless – and a joke when bribery of government officials becomes a sine qua non to doing effective business.[34]

What may be needed, then, as a legal antecedent to the complex of legal arrangements that typically underlie infrastructure projects, is a clear framework agreement that embodies all the necessary basic commitments – and provides a legal basis for their enforcement against any of the parties.

Easily stated, this is not easy to achieve, as the ongoing efforts of IFAs such as the IMF to discipline the macroeconomic policies of major countries such as Argentina and Brazil demonstrate. There is perhaps no entity that has the ultimate leverage over desperate or reluctant governments to fully discipline them; and the ultimate weapon of the IFAs – withholding funds – is self-limiting, declining in potence as loans are disbursed.

What is encouraging in Africa is how far the need to address these challenges has permeated not only many national governments, but also its regional organizations such as ECOWAS and SADC; and most recently the Africa-wide initiatives under the auspices of the African Union.

This has led to exciting new development initiatives in Africa such as an effort in many countries to create regimes that will effectively support 'rural electrification', a 'bottom up' business model for both rural and urban electricity development by local communities. Organizations, such as the US-based National Rural Electric Cooperative Association (NRECA), which spawned massive electrification advances in countries such as Bangladesh and Bolivia, are now starting to focus on Africa, encouraged by regional and international organizations.

Most recent, and perhaps most exciting for this topic, are major Africa-wide initiatives under the NEPAD process. These include efforts to enhance development of major regional infrastructure projects (such as the potentially gigantic Inga hydropower project on the Congo River) and the Africa Peer Review

---

[33] There had been slow but steady recognition of its own CSR faults by the World Bank e.g., in the environmental area following the Arun project scandal in Nepal.

[34] The need of US corporations to comply with the US Foreign Corrupt Practices Act has long been a point of contention between US and other countries' corporations – potentially undermining the goal of a 'level playing field' that IFA competitive procurement practices try to achieve.

Mechanism to obtain government transparency commitments, both discussed above.

These recent initiatives are tied to the traditional view of most African and other developing nations that *political* human rights have little meaning without *economic* human rights; and that economic development is a key global political issue between developed and Group of 77 nations. These initiatives create an interesting new dynamic that is of special relevance to the topic of CSR.

While these initiatives are still in the early stages of conceptualization, and concerns have emerged as to their implementation, it is important to note that they are spearheaded by Africa's two superpowers – Nigeria and South Africa.

Each has recently emerged, in very different circumstances, from decades of autocratic and, in many respects, corrupt and inefficient rule. Both are still fledgling democracies in their own rights; and both face economic and human crises (e.g. AIDs in RSA; ethnic violence in Nigeria) that threaten them on an ongoing basis and restrain their enormous potentials for economic growth. Yet each has taken a strong lead in both internal infrastructure and CSR reforms, and in the Africa-wide initiatives to create, and successfully combine, economic progress and CSR. Many other African countries have already sensed the challenge – not to be outdone by their giant neighbors!

Chapter 23

THE JAPANESE PERSPECTIVE

James Brumm

A. HISTORICAL BACKGROUND

Japan, while being an island country that has gone through periods of isolation, has also over the past two thousand years been deeply affected by outside influences. The earliest and one of the most powerful was from China, which over a long period of history deeply influenced Japan religiously, culturally, legally, governmentally and philosophically, not to mention giving Japan the basis for a written language. Buddhism, Confucianism and Chinese principles of law and government were absorbed and integrated into the Japanese society. However, Japan was not a *tabula rasa*, and with each new idea Japan integrated it into its existing society and transformed it to make it uniquely Japanese.

Western ideas first began to penetrate Japan in the 16th century when Spanish, Portuguese and Dutch explorers and missionaries began to visit Japan. In 1603 Japan closed itself off to the world and was isolated for some 250 years until the 1850s when it was forced to open up to the outside world. The next 100 years was a period of adjustment, at times painful and violent, with absorption of western ideas and a transformation of those ideas into a uniquely Japanese approach. With the arrival of the black ships of Commodore Perry in 1853, Japan had to struggle with how to maintain its independence in the face of threats from the imperialist powers of the western world. Along with building up a strong military, 'the new government set to modernizing the social and political organization of the country on the principles of modern capitalism'.[1] As in the past, there was not an outright adoption of foreign concepts but instead an attempt to 'adopt the material civilization of Europe and to harmonize it with Oriental morality. . . . "Western techniques, Oriental morality" '.[2]

The second major period of significant foreign influence on Japan in the last 150 years was the US occupation of Japan following Japan's defeat in World War II.

---

[1] Yoshiyuki Noda, translated by Anthony H. Angelo, *Introduction to Japanese Law*, Tokyo: University of Tokyo Press, 1976, p. 42.
[2] *Ibid*, pp. 60–61.

Ramon Mullerat (ed.), Corporate Social Responsibility: The Corporate Governance of the 21st Century, 337–346.
© 2005 *International Bar Association. Printed in the Netherlands.*

A new Constitution was imposed on the nation by the US, as were a number of new laws. New concepts of freedom and civil and human rights were introduced and a model was established for a parliamentary democracy based on capitalism. Again, Japan adapted these influences to suit its own culture and long held beliefs. Japan recovered rapidly from the devastation of the war and, as is well known, has developed into one of the largest and most powerful economies today, even despite its economic troubles over the past decade. Many of today's major multinational commercial enterprises and major financial institutions in the world are Japanese. They have been quite successful and compete on equal standing with western multinationals and financial institutions and the names of many of them are household words – Sony, Panasonic, Toyota, Mitsubishi. As successful multinationals, Japanese companies have been met with the same challenges western multinationals have been met with and have faced the challenge of developing and applying concepts of corporate social responsibility (CSR). As we will see, the Japanese corporate world has reacted to this movement and has developed its unique approach to CSR.

B. DEVELOPMENT OF MODERN JAPANESE COMMERCIAL ENTERPRISES

Japanese companies, as modern commercial enterprises, began being formed in the 1870s. During the period of reception of western law concepts beginning after the Meiji Restoration in 1868, Japan adopted a civil code based on the French Civil Code in 1890 and a commercial code based principally upon the French Commercial Code in 1891. The Commercial Code was amended and expanded in 1899 with substantial revisions based on German legal influence.[3] With the US occupation of Japan following World War II, as mentioned above, there was the increased influence of US legal concepts and a Constitution and a number of laws were adopted based on US legal approaches.

While many companies grew independently during the period following the 1870s, several companies grew into large industrial combines such as Mitsui, Mitsubishi, Yasuda and Sumitomo and dominated the Japanese economic scene until World War II. These combines were dissolved at the end of World War II under the American occupation. On top of the European civil law base, a US drafted constitution was adopted and a number of US based laws, such as an antimonopoly law and a securities law, were enacted. In the period following World War II, after some initial economic difficulties, the Japanese economy grew rapidly. Along side the rebirth of the old industrial-financial combines of Mitsui, Mitsubishi and Sumitomo in a new form (commonly referred to as 'keiretsu'[4]), new companies particularly in the automotive field, such as Toyota and Nissan, and in the consumer electronics field, such as Sony, Toshiba and Matsushita (Panasonic), became worldwide business organizations.

---

[3]   *Ibid*, pp. 41–53.
[4]   'A horizontal keiretsu is a group of very large companies with common ties to a powerful bank, united by shared stockholdings, trading relations, and so on'. Kenichi Miyashita and David W. Russell, *Keiretsu: Inside the Hidden Japanese Conglomerates*, New York: McGraw-Hill, Inc., 1994, p. 7.

Over the first fifty years following the end of World War II, major Japanese companies have been characterized by life-time employment, a passive shareholding and a business model based on long term gain and market share rather than short term profit. Particularly with the economic difficulties the Japanese economy has encountered over the last ten years, that business model is now in the process of transition with more job mobility, more active shareholding and more attention to bottom line profit and stock price. In addition, overseas capital markets have become more important following the expansion to overseas commercial markets and investor relations has become important on a worldwide basis. Also, foreign shareholding of Japanese publicly traded companies has increased significantly. For example, in the case of Mitsubishi Corporation, shareholding by foreign companies and individuals went from 5.3 percent in 1993, to 11.4 percent in 1998, and at 19.7 percent in 2003 and to 31 percent in 2004.[5] In addition, the Nikkei Shimbun reported that as the end of fiscal 2003 (31 March 2004), foreign shareholding of Japanese companies was at the all time high of 21.8 percent while the holding of stock in Japanese companies by Japanese banks had dropped to an all time low of 5.9 percent.[6] These trends, together with the decline in cross-shareholding by the various keiretsu in Japan and the increased direct foreign investment in Japan,[7] signify a very different dynamic in stock ownership and one result is to subject publicly held Japanese companies to greater pressure to conform to international standards of corporate governance and CSR.

C. CSR AND CORPORATE GOVERNANCE ISSUES IN JAPAN

In the same way that corporate scandals in the US, such as Enron, WorldCom and Tyco, have increased calls for better corporate governance, scandals in the Japanese corporate world have had the same result. Not only has there been domestic pressure but also large foreign institutional investors such as the California Public Employees' Retirement System (CalPERS) have actively sought to influence and improve corporate governance in Japan. In 2003 CalPERS announced it would invest $200 million in a Japanese turnaround fund aimed at revitalizing Japanese companies. However, CalPERS emphasized that they would 'take a conciliatory, not combative approach' at corporate governance in Japan recognizing the difference in corporate and social culture.[8]

Alongside the calls for better corporate governance has been a movement to bring environmental and social responsibility to Japanese companies. This has been initiated by individual North American and international NGO environmental campaigns and has been aimed against Japanese company overseas resource projects, import activities and development and purchasing policies.

---

[5] Mitsubishi Corporation 2003 Annual Report, p. 57 and Mitsubishi Corporation 2004 Annual Report, p. 53.

[6] Nikkei Shimbun, 18 June 2004, at p. 1.

[7] E.g. Renault/Nissan, DaimlerChrysler/Mitsubishi Motors, the buyout of the Long Term Credit Bank of Japan by Ripplewood and its reconstitution as the Shinsei Bank applying western lending practices instead of traditional Japanese lending practices.

[8] New York Times, 14 April 2003, p. 7; as supplemented by a telephone conversation with Ted White, Manager, Corporate Governance Unit, CalPERS.

Recently, with the growth of NGOs in Japan, often as branches of international NGOs, pressure has increased and has brought Japanese companies into direct contact with local NGOs. Pressure has also been generated from increased scrutiny by Socially Responsible Investment (SRI) funds. Although most SRIs are in Europe and the US, there are now SRIs in Japan as well. The result of all of this has been not only overseas pressure to apply CSR principles to Japanese companies but also an extensive debate within Japan on what is CSR and how it should be applied. Again, as with the history of previous external influences, Japan is developing CSR in its own unique way.

1. Antecedents to CSR

CSR is indeed a very hot topic in corporate, government, public policy and academic circles in Japan today. However, the roots are much deeper. With a rapid transition from a feudal and agrarian based society to a modern industrial capitalist society in the short period from 1868 to the early twentieth century, many cultural and ethical traits of the highly structured pre-industrial society were incorporated in the new commercial activities. For example, the origins of Sumitomo's corporate philosophy go back 350 years to Masatomo Sumitomo who wrote the Monjuin Shiigaki consisting of five articles on the conduct of business and how to live a good life. Based on these precepts, in 1891 the following articles were prescribed as Sumitomo's operating principles:

> '1. Sumitomo shall achieve strength and prosperity by placing prime importance on integrity and sound management in the conduct of its business
> 2. Sumitomo shall manage its activities with foresight and flexibility in order to cope effectively with the changing times. Under no circumstances, however, shall it pursue easy gains or act imprudently'.[9]

The Mitsubishi group of companies, a family led group of companies between 1870 and 1945, addressed the issue of social responsibility and ethics formally in 1920. Its founder Yataro Iwasaki had encountered social injustice early in his life and was once jailed for protesting against unfair governmental treatment. However, under his guidance and vision, his successors from the Iwasaki family studied abroad – Yanosuke in New York City, Hiyasa at the University of Pennsylvania and Koyata at Cambridge and Mitsubishi acquired a world view early on and a familiarity with western ideas. They became the second, third and fourth leaders of Mitsubishi.[10] In 1920 at a branch managers' conference of Mitsubishi Trading Company, the overseas sales and purchasing arm of the Mitsubishi Group, Koyata Iwasaki told the management:

> 'If others try to compete with you by unfair means, fight them with fairness. If others try to trick you, face them with honesty. If they try to use nepotism and influence to get the better of you, treat them with kindness

---

9   www.sumitomocorp.co.jp/english/company_e/governance/index.shtml.
10 Yasuo Mishima, translated by Emiko Yamaguchi, The Mitsubishi: Its Challenge and Strategy, London: JAI Press Ltd, 1989, pp. 2–5, 113–115, 117, 159.

and conscientiousness. As far as I know, the unfair and unjust have never won the final victory in history'.[11]

Based on this speech the three corporate principles of Mitsubishi were adopted. They are:

1. 'Shoki Hoko' – Corporate Responsibility to Society
2. 'Shoji Komei' – Integrity and Fairness
3. 'Ritsugyo Boeki' – International Understanding through Trade

These three principles have been the basis for business activities by Mitsubishi Corporation and other companies in what is referred to as the Mitsubishi Group. While the explicit adoption of such basic principles was not so common in late nineteenth and early twentieth century Japan, in general terms Japanese companies have looked at themselves as more than simply a company that is driven by profit. For a long period of time the focus has been primarily on their own employees. In fact some have asserted that Japanese companies are run for the benefit of their inside management and their employees rather than the shareholders, although this is changing. The shift to raise capital through capital markets, domestically and overseas, instead of bank lending, the recognition of the importance of company and product brand and company reputation and the increased concern over the stock price and how it is affected by external events has caused Japanese company focus to move from inner-directed to increasingly outer directed externalities.

This is not to say that Japanese companies have not had breaches of ethics, scandals and even violations of law or have not disregarded environmental and social standards. However, they have learned not only what is expected of them domestically but also internationally in terms of corporate citizenship and realize for many reasons including competitive advantage in an increasingly difficult global market that CSR and corporate governance are critical issues.

As an example of the recent development of CSR in Japanese companies based on the earlier ethical principles adopted at the formation of the companies, Mitsubishi Corporation established a Global Environmental Issues Committee in 1989, set up an Environmental Department in 1990 (now the Office of Environmental and Social Responsibility), formulated Standards of Conduct in 1992, adopted an Environmental Charter in 1996, had its environmental management system accredited under ISO 14001 in 1998, constituted a Code of Conduct in 2000, was listed on the FTSE4Good index in 2002 and the Dow Jones Sustainability Index in 2003 and formed a CSR Task Force in 2003.[12] Not all of this was achieved without external pressure and Mitsubishi Corporation itself was the target of a campaign on the tropical rainforests in the 1990s and an environmental campaign against the expansion of a salt project in Mexico between 1995 and 2000. It also observed the developments of corporate governance, CSR and SRI worldwide and how both foreign and Japanese multinational corporations dealt with these issues in reaction to corporate governance failures or to the increasing expectations of companies in regard to environmental and social responsibilities.

11   *Ibid*, p. 154.
12   Mitsubishi Corporation Sustainability Report, 2003.

In addition, although the original three principles continued to guide Mitsubishi Corporation over the years, in light of modern corporate social responsibility concepts the three principles were reexamined and were reinterpreted in 2000 to mean:

Corporate Responsibility to Society – Strive to enrich society, both materially and spiritually, while contributing towards the preservation of the global environment

Integrity and Fairness – Maintain principles of transparency and openness, conducting business with integrity and fairness

International Understanding through Trade – Expand business, based on an all-encompassing global perspective.

2. Current CSR Issues

As mentioned above, CSR is now a very hot topic in Japan. Among the leading companies involved in CSR, are Sony, Ricoh, Fuji Xerox, Asahi Beer, IBM Japan, NEC, Mitsubishi Corporation and Panasonic. All of these companies have a CSR department or task force and have a code of conduct that reflects the basic principles of CSR.

The Keidanren (the Japanese Chamber of Commerce and Industry) has formed a working group to tackle CSR and revised their charter of corporate behavior. In addition, the Ministry of Economy, Trade and Industry (METI) has started a working group with the cooperation of the Japanese Standards Association to develop CSR standards in Japan.[13] They are now working to give their views to international organizations such as the ISO that are working to develop CSR standards. Together, the Keidanren, METI and the eight company working group intend to release in 2004 a concrete CSR agenda for Japan.[14]

In addition, CSR has been given wide coverage by the press and the Nikkei Shimbun (the Japanese equivalent of the Wall Street Journal or the Financial Times) has organized conferences on CSR and has established a CSR Project. In December 2003, Nikkei organized a symposium on 'Cause Branding' dealing with CSR issues. The speakers were senior management representatives from NTT Docomo, Mitsubishi Corporation and Fuji Xerox and the symposium was moderated by a scholar on CSR from Hitotsubashi University. It received significant coverage (four pages) in the Nikkei Shimbun.[15] On 27 April 2004 Nikkei Shimbun sponsored another symposium with senior management representatives from Tokio Marine and Fuji Xerox as well as a university professor speaking, followed by a panel discussion with panelists representing government, academia, the legal profession and industry. The Nikkei Shimbun devoted a five-page section in the paper to the symposium in which a number of prominent

---

[13]   The eight members were Ricoh, Sony, Panasonic, NEC, Shiseido, Omron, Ito-Yokado and Mitsubishi Corporation.
[14]   UNIDO Asia Pacific News 2003 Tokyo Meeting November 2003, 12 December 2003, p. 4.
[15]   Nikkei Shimbun, 25 December 2003.

companies took ads to show their dedication to CSR. The next Nikkei CSR Project symposium was to be held on 18 June 2004 on SRI.[16]

a. *Corporate Sustainability Reports*

Another indication of how CSR is developing in Japan is through the number of companies issuing sustainability reports and the development and sophistication of the content of those reports. In fiscal 2003, environmental or sustainability reports were published by 650 Japanese companies. For fiscal 2004, it is expected that some 900 Japanese companies will publish reports.

Originally such reports started out primarily as Environmental Reports. As an example, in 1999 Mitsubishi Corporation published its first Environmental Report. It was 21 pages and all but two pages focused on the environment, with the other two pages being on social contribution activities. In 2001 the report was entitled 'Environmental Sustainability Report' and while the emphasis was still heavily on environmental issues, the report expanded to 29 pages and included a section on Corporate Citizenship, breaking those citizenship activities down into education, social welfare, culture and art, environment and global communication.

In 2002 Mitsubishi Corporation published a 'Sustainability Report' and incorporated a section on its philosophy and principles (the three corporate principles, the Standards of Conduct and the Environmental Charter) and sections on improving workplace conditions and on stakeholder relations. However, the more substantive change came with the 2003 Sustainability Report. It expanded to 45 pages and the emphasis shifted to CSR with environment being one of three components of CSR – an environment report, an economic report and a social report. The social report increased the coverage of employee relations and issues as well as stakeholder relations. More importantly, the Sustainability Report incorporated a section on corporate governance and compliance. This latter development is consistent with the development in Japan of associating corporate governance with CSR.

In addition, the 2003 Mitsubishi Corporation Annual Report opens with a page devoted to the Three Corporate Principles and the President's Letter to *Stakeholders* (no longer a letter to *shareholders*) devotes an entire section to Corporate Social Responsibility and Governance. Also included in the Annual Report is a 10-page section entitled Governance and Corporate Social Responsibility. Thus, beyond the Sustainability Report itself, the same subjects of CSR and Governance have been elevated to a prominent position in the Annual Report.

b. *International Activities*

While Japanese companies in many cases have embraced CSR in Japan and are applying it as individual companies, it is my impression that their participation in international CSR activities lags behind the participation of western multinationals. Often it is necessary to overcome language and culture barriers to explain

[16] Nikkei Shimbun, 24 May 2004, pp. 26–30.

why an environmental or social issue, especially one that has currency in Western Europe or North America and that does not always have an analogy to Japanese society or that does not embrace the same values as those found in Japan, is important to a Japanese multinational and to human society at large. As a result, for example, there are only two large Japanese companies participating in the UN Global Compact. Membership in organizations such as Business for Social Responsibility and the World Business Council for Sustainable Development by Japanese companies is disproportionately small. In the financial sector, the Japanese Bank for International Cooperation (JBIC), Japan's major export credit agency, 'published in April 2002 its 'Guidelines for Environmental and Social Considerations' to filter new lending projects'.[17] However, of the twenty-five banking institutions that have announced adherence to the international Equator Principles for environmentally responsible lending, only one of those is a Japanese bank.[18] On the other hand, in the achievement of ISO 14,001 environmental management system accreditation Japanese companies have excelled with 9,467 Japanese companies out of a total of accredited 40,970 companies worldwide.[19]

c. Role of the Legal Profession in Japan on CSR/Corporate Governance

In terms of corporate governance issues, the Japanese legal profession is active, particularly in how to implement the recent changes in the Commercial Code that allow for the option of a committee-type governance structure as well as counseling companies and their management on governance issues and increasing shareholder litigation. In the case of Mitsubishi Corporation, in 1995 new directors were given a two-day seminar on director responsibilities that included a significant portion devoted to director legal responsibilities and director liability. Outside lawyers specializing in corporate governance issues were brought in to give lectures on this subject. In July 2001 a Governance Committee was established to advise the Board on governance issues and in addition to the four board members there were two University scholars and one outside lawyer on the Committee. Particularly as governance and compliance issues are rule based and involve legal issues, I would expect to see outside lawyers increase their role in developing the corporate response to governance.

In addition to outside lawyers, the legal departments of major Japanese companies play an active role and as in the case of Mitsubishi Corporation there is an elaborate compliance structure with heavy involvement by the legal department.

On the other hand, with pure CSR, I have not as yet seen significant involvement by outside lawyers other than when advice is needed on some specific legal issue related to the practical application of some particular principle. At Mitsubishi Corporation the CSR Task Force has a member from the legal department, but he is only one of 18 members from corporate and business

[17] Ibid.
[18] See www.equator-principles.com.
[19] Arif Zaman, Made in Japan: Converging Trends in Corporate Responsibility and Corporate Governance, Report of Research Findings, July 2003, The Royal Institute of International Affairs, p. 17.

departments. As CSR is still primarily value-based application of responsibilities above and beyond legal requirements, that will probably still be the general trend. However, as Japanese companies become more active in the international arena on CSR and subscribe to codes of conduct such as the UN Global Compact or the Equator Principles, I would think there will be a greater role for both in-house legal staff and outside lawyers in analyzing the obligations to be undertaken by the companies, interpreting the codes, dealing with the conflicts with legal obligations undertaken commercially as well as drafting provisions on CSR obligations in project documents, commercial contracts and supply chain relationships.

D.   DEFINITIONS OF CSR AND EVOLUTION OF CSR IN JAPAN

The definition of CSR is still in the process of development and there are many definitions both western and Japanese. Some definitions are quite broad and general such as:

'Operating a business in a manner that meets or exceeds the ethical, legal, commercial and public expectations that society has of business'.[20]

In the UK and the US much of CSR focuses on the environment and human rights issues. For example,

'A concept whereby companies integrate social and environmental concerns in their business operations and in their interaction with their stakeholders on a voluntary basis'.[21]

Contrast these definitions with the definition of CSR by Mitsubishi Corporation:

'Corporate Social Responsibility means that a corporation pays close heed to relationships with all its stakeholders, and always acts with an awareness of these relationships, in ways that are concrete and practical'.[22]

Another definition used by Mitsubishi Corporation has been 'a concept whereby companies integrate social and environmental concerns into their interaction with their stakeholders on a voluntary basis (including compliance, governance, accountability, transparency and sustainability)'.

As Arif Zaman points out in his study on CSR in Japan, a key driver for CSR is customer relationships. He specifically notes:

'Brand consciousness is important in the mind of the Japanese consumer. Consumers associate product quality, safety and reliability with the reputation of the company that produces it'.[23]

Because of the many issues domestically in Japan on corporate governance and the concerns of domestic stakeholders, especially customers and employees

---

[20]   Business for Social Responsibility.
[21]   2001 Green Paper of the Commission of the European Communities.
[22]   Mitsubishi Sustainability Report 2003, p. 43.
[23]   Zaman, *Ibid.* p. 13.

being at the center, combined with the international pressures on Japanese multi-nationals that focus on different issues such as their impact on the environment and social issues – particularly with natural resource project development – CSR and SRI are complex issues being debated.

An interesting point is how CSR is related to corporate governance issues in Japan. As has been stated in the western context:

> 'Although CSR is related to and overlaps in some respects with the concepts of corporate governance and ethics, it is nevertheless distinct. . . . governance programs tend to be internally focused and, generally retain a heavy rules-based flavor. In contrast CSR tends to be more values-based and externally focused'.[24]

In Japan, in contrast, it is my impression that CSR and corporate governance are dealt with as two aspects of the same issue – how do corporations behave responsibly to society and the various stakeholders. In Japan, the recent emphasis on corporate governance has been on compliance systems development and on internal audit. Perhaps in some ways this is due to the fact that boards of directors are largely staffed by inside directors and corporate governance is carried out by executive officers. If and when boards become more independent, corporate governance may be handled in a different way. Still I think it will continue to be looked at as part of CSR, i.e. how does a company deal with its external stakeholders and how does it build and protect its reputation.

---

[24]   Danette Wineberg and Phillip H. Randolph, 'Corporate Social Responsibility: What Every In-House Counsel Should Know', *ACC Docket*, May 2004, p. 72.

Chapter 24

CORPORATE SOCIAL RESPONSIBILITY AND HUMAN RIGHTS – THE GHANA EXPERIENCE IN THE GOLD MINING INDUSTRY

Felix Ntrakwah

A. INTRODUCTION

A gold mining company began mining near a village which is very close to my village. In no time some men in the village started complaining about the disappearance or misconduct of their wives. Divorce rate began to rise and there were violent protests by some of the men and the youth. Their main complaint was that money had been put in the hands of the employees of the mining company majority of whom were recruited from outside the village. They contended that the display of wealth resulted in some women leaving their husbands in search for the employees of the mining company. It took the intervention of the District Chief Executive (the Government's representative in the District) before the violent protests stopped. In the end, additional youth from the village were employed.

Did the mining company abuse the fundamental human rights of the men of the village by putting money in the hands of the employees who snatched their wives? Was it the corporate social responsibility of the mining company to ensure that the wives of such men remained faithful? I am unable to answer. However, these and many more questions which would normally not feature on the agenda of a gold mining company outline some of the real issues on the ground where there is a gold mining activity in Ghana. Under these circumstances Human Rights and Corporate Social Responsibility (CSR) can assume various dimensions and meanings. I do not therefore intend to attempt definitions. What the stakeholders say will be our guide.

Ramon Mullerat (ed.), Corporate Social Responsibility: The Corporate Governance of the 21st Century, 347–362.
© 2005 *International Bar Association. Printed in the Netherlands.*

B. HISTORY

Gold mining in the Gold Coast (the former name of Ghana) started many years ago. The gold rush in the nineteenth century saw the commencement of industrial gold mining mostly by foreign companies. In the 1950s the Government of Ghana bought the equity shares of some mining companies.

Since then the State became directly involved in the ownership and operation of some gold mining companies through statutes that led to the establishment of the State Gold Mining Corporation. The state has divested its interest in some of the companies under the State Gold Mining Corporation. Many of the companies operating now are substantially privately owned.

There are now companies like Ashanti Goldfields Company Limited (Ashanti) a nineteenth century company which recently merged with Anglogold and is now known as Anglogold Ashanti, Bogoso Gold Limited, Newmont and others as well as small scale mining companies.

C. APPLICABLE LAWS

The gold mining industry in Ghana is regulated by various statutes including the following:

- Minerals and Mining Law, 1986 (PNDCL 153), as amended by the Minerals and Mining (Amendment) Act 1994 Act 475
- Minerals Commission Act 1993 (ACT 450)
- Small Scale Gold Mining Law 1989 (PNDCL 218)
- Mercury Law 1989 (PNDCL 217)
- Environmental Protection Agency ACT 1994, ACT 490
- Precious Minerals Marketing Corporation Law, 1989 (PNDCL 219)
- Mining Regulations, 1970 (L.I. 665) as amended by L.I. 689, Explosive Regulations, 1970, Minerals (Royalties) Regulations, 1987.

D. ADVANTAGES AND DISADVANTAGES OF GOLD MINING IN GHANA

Gold has been a major source of foreign exchange for Ghana. Gold mining has provided and continues to provide employment. Areas which were hitherto unknown became accessible because of the gold mining activity. The influx of migrants to the mining communities brings about other commercial activities like trading and other service industries. Instead of travelling far away to sell their produce the farmers in the mining communities have ready markets for their produce.

It is common knowledge supported by various studies that gold mining in Ghana also has its bad side. Since this paper is not about the advantages and disadvantages of gold mining in Ghana I will just enumerate some of the disadvantages. These are: inadequate housing, prostitution, disorganization of the family, high cost of living with the attendant social problems, unemployment of people whose lands have been taken by the mining companies, degradation of the forest, pollution of the atmosphere, water pollution, chemical pollution due to the use of cyanide and mercury in processing gold. It is widely known that various diseases like respiratory infection, cholera, malaria and now HIV/Aids are prevalent in the mining communities.

In the past, in a typical mining settlement there was discrimination in terms of the conditions of service and emoluments of the white executive and the Ghanaian counterpart. Junior members of staff lived in crowded and dirty compounds whereas the senior officers lived in large bungalows. For some of the mining companies better housing facilities are still required.

E. HUMAN RIGHTS AND CONSTITUTION

From the foregoing observations, there is no doubt that gold mining in Ghana raises complex issues of human rights and corporate social responsibility. Ghana has elaborate provisions on human rights in the 1992 Constitution (the Constitution).

For further discussions on human rights and corporate social responsibility let us now consider the relevant provisions of the Constitution in relation to the Mining and Minerals law 1989 (PNDCL 153). We must therefore note the key words used in the Constitution.

It is provided in article 18 of the Constitution as follows:

'18　(1)　every person has the right to own property either alone or in association with others.
　　(2)　No person shall be subjected to interference with the privacy of his home, property, correspondence or communication except in accordance with law and as may be necessary in a free and demo-cratic society for public safety or the economic well-being of the country, for the protection of health or morals, for the prevention of disorder or crime or for the protection of the rights or free-doms of others'.

Article 20 of the Constitution makes provision for compulsory acquisition of property. The relevant clauses are (2) and (3) which we quote below:

　(2)　Compulsory acquisition of property by the State shall only be made under a law which makes provision for:-
　　i.　The prompt payment of fair and adequate compensation; and
　　ii.　A right of access to the High Court by any person who has an interest in or right over the property whether direct or on appeal from any other authority for the determination of his interest or right and the amount of compensation to which he is entitled.
　(3)　Where a compulsory acquisition or possession of land effected by the State in accordance with clause (1) of this article involves displacement of any inhabitants, the State shall resettle the displaced inhabitants on suitable alternative land with due regard for their economic well-being and social and cultural values.

As regards the compulsory acquisition of property the key words and phrases which should make everybody comfortable are:

    a. 'prompt payment of fair and adequate compensation'
    b. 'right of access to the High Court'
    c. 'the state shall resettle the displaced inhabitants on suitable alternative land'.

Article 24 of the Constitution deals with economic rights in the following words:

'24(1) Every person has the right to work under satisfactory, safe and healthy conditions, and shall receive equal pay for equal work without distinction of any kind'.

Article 36 of the Constitution which is part of the directive principles of State policy provides that:

(1)   the State shall take all necessary action to ensure that the national economy is managed in such a manner as to maximise the rate of economic development and to secure the maximum welfare, freedom and happiness of every person in Ghana and to provide adequate means of livelihood and suitable employment and public assistance to the needy.

(2)   The State shall in particular, take all necessary steps to establish a sound and healthy economy whose underlying principles shall include:

    a. The guarantee of a fair and realistic remuneration for production and productivity in order to encourage continued production and higher productivity;

    b. Affording ample opportunity for individual initiative and creativity in economic activities and fostering an enabling environment for a pronounced role of the private sector in the economy;

    c. Ensuring that individuals and the private sector bear their fair share of social and national responsibilities to contribute to the overall development of the country.

I must remark that the Constitution does not define 'social and national responsibilities'. However, it is clear that the private sector including gold mining companies are expected to play a role in the society for the purpose of national development.

We now consider some sections of PNDCL 153 on property acquisition. Section 2 of PNDCL 153 empowers the Government to acquire land or authorize its occupation and use in order to secure the development or utilization of a mineral resource. Section 70(1) to 72 which deal with mineral rights are also quoted below:

70. (1) The holder of a mineral right shall exercise his rights under this law subject to such limitations relating to surface rights as the Secretary may prescribe.

     (2) The rights conferred by a mineral right shall be exercised in a manner consistent with the reasonable and proper conduct of the operations concerned so as to affect as little as possible the interest

of any lawful occupier of the land in respect of which such rights are exercised.

(3) The lawful occupier of any land within an area subject to a mineral right shall retain the right to graze livestock upon or to cultivate the surface of such land in so far as grazing or cultivation does not interfere with the mineral operations in the area.

(4) In the case of mining area, the owner or lawful occupier of the land within the mining area shall not erect any building or structure thereon without the consent of the holder of the mining lease, or if such consent is unreasonably withheld, without the consent of the Secretary.

71. (1) The owner or occupier of any land subject to a mineral right may apply to the holder of the right for compensation for any disturbance of the rights of such owner and for any damage done to the surface of the land, buildings, works or improvements or to livestock, crops or trees in the area of such mineral operations.

(2) An application for compensation under subsection (1) of this section shall be copied to the Secretary and the Land Valuation Board.

(3) The amount of compensation payable under subsection (1) of this section shall, subject to the approval of the Land Valuation Board, be determined by agreement between the parties concerned and if the parities are unable to reach an agreement as to the amount of compensation, the matter shall be referred to the Secretary who shall in consultation with the Land Valuation Board determine the compensation payable.

72. The holder of a mineral right shall in the exercise of his rights under the licence or lease have due regard to the effect of the mineral operations on the environment and shall take such steps as may be necessary to prevent pollution of the environment as a result of such mineral operations'.

Even though subsections (1) and (2) of section 70 recognize that mineral rights are subject to limitations, it appears that as between the holder of a mineral right and the lawful owner or occupier of the land the holder of the mineral right is more powerful if not superior. The occupier or owner of the land may have acquired the land by customary gift from a family. The land may even have been purchased and registered. None of these land owners enjoys the protection of the law in the same way as the holder of the mineral rights whose operations are not to be interfered with.

It is conceded that this is not the law that should list the constitutional and civil rights of the individual or their protection. However, the provision that the owner or lawful occupier of the land may apply to the holder of the mineral right for compensation suggests that the lawful owner or occupier is already at a disadvantage. Gold mining activities take place mostly in the rural areas where the inhabitants are mostly illiterates and barely survive on subsistence farming. Besides, there are instances where the mineral right is transferred to another company thus making it difficult for the occupier or lawful owner to determine who to deal with.

Nobody can acquire mineral right except through the State Agency, Minerals Commission. A mining lease is subject to ratification by Parliament as provided in Article 268 of the Constitution. Under section 8(1) of PNDCL 153 the State acquires 10 per cent shares of a mining company free of charge and may even acquire additional 20 per cent by agreement with the holder of the mineral right. Section 68(1) of 153 also vests the immovable assets of the holder of the mining lease in the Republic upon the termination of the mining lease. In effect it is the State that takes away the individual's surface rights whenever mineral right is given to another person in an area with existing surface rights. I will describe this as compulsory acquisition of surface rights.

PNDCL 153 does not provide for prompt payment of fair and adequate compensation as required by the Constitution. The situation is not made any better by merely copying an application addressed to the holder of mineral right to the Land Valuation Board. By the time an agreement is reached on the amount of compensation, whatever is on the land may already have been destroyed thus making it even difficult for eventual valuation by the Land Valuation Board. Meanwhile, the owner or lawful occupier of the land is prohibited from interfering with mining operations. There is no express provision in PNDCL 153 compelling the holder of mineral right to pay compensation. Consequently an application is subject to acceptance or approval and therefore the holder of the mineral right can reject an individual's application or even refuse to acknowledge receipt. Indeed, in my view, to the extent that sections 2 and 71 of PNDCL 153 do not provide for prompt payment of fair and adequate compensation they can be said to be inconsistent with the Constitution. The Supreme Court should be interested in determining whether a law that enables the compulsory acquisition of the individual's property by the State whilst leaving the individual to his fate should continue in force. It is regrettable that the key words used in the Constitution are conspicuously absent from PNDCL 153.

Section 72 of PNDCL 153 merely enjoins the holder of mineral right to take steps to have due regard for the environment and to prevent pollution. Furthermore, it is to be noted that the law is silent on compensation for pollution which is associated with gold mining activities. As the law stands it places the occupier or lawful owner of the land at the mercy of the holder of mineral right. PNDCL 153 contemplates the abuse of human rights and yet does very little for the protection of such rights. The present position of the law can create unnecessary tension between the occupier or lawful owner of the land, inhabitants of the mining community and the innocent holder of mineral right who equally requires protection and clear guidelines.

Other laws like the Environmental Protection Agency Act 1994 (ACT 490) deal with the environment. Any person undertaking any gold mining or investment activity that involves the environment is required to submit an environmental impact assessment plan to the Environmental Protection Agency. Mining companies are also required to provide their plans for resolving problems that crop up regarding the environment. All these do not go far enough in dealing with the social issues that arise from gold mining activities. The State agencies that should check the activities of the mining companies as regards the environment are limited in resources. According to Act 490 the sources of finance of the Environmental Protection Agency includes gifts. The question is whether the

Agency can or should accept a gift from a gold mining company whose activities it supervizes. In fact a lot therefore depends on the ability, fellow feeling and conscience of the owners and operators of the gold mining companies.

F. CORPORATE SOCIAL RESPONSIBILITY

In the past the general belief was that gold mining companies came to Ghana only to dig for gold for export leaving the people poorer than they found them. Gold is a very well known natural resource in Ghana. It is cherished and valued by the village chief as well as the common man. In some areas people still look for gold from the surface of the soil and from the gutter after a heavy rainfall. The expectation is that the mining company that is taking this wealth away must do something for the community. In the past very little attention was paid to this expectation. Those who appreciated the expectation hardly saw it as corporate social responsibility owed to the community.

However, in modern times because of Ghana's association with the international community, concerns expressed by shareholders and the awareness created in civil society by the media and non-governmental organizations, corporate social responsibility has become an important subject in all sectors of the economy as we have just noted from the Constitution.

Apart from the major foreign mining companies there were in the past small scale miners whose activities were largely described as illegal since they either had no mining lease or operated in the concessions of the big foreign mining companies. This type of small scale mining was popularly known as 'galamsay'. I am told that this word is a corruption of the words 'get the mineral or gold and sell'. With the coming into force of the Small Scale Gold Mining Law 1989 (PNDCL 218) small scale mining is legalized but reserved for Ghanaians who lawfully acquire mineral rights. Notwithstanding the legalization of small scale mining 'galamsay' still continues.

The operators of gold mines who should be concerned about human rights and corporate social responsibility are not only the multinationals but also the small scale mining companies, the providers of the mines support services and the 'galamsay miners'. Therefore in order to appreciate corporate social responsibility in the gold mining industry we have to look at it from various perspectives.

G. VARIOUS VIEWS OF CORPORATE SOCIAL RESPONSIBILITY

1. The Community

I will now attempt to state what the inhabitants of the areas where gold mining activities take place mean by corporate social responsibility of a mining company:

'We are poor people sitting on a non-renewable natural resource called gold which we inherited from our forefathers. We do not have the means to exploit our resources. Government has by law assumed ownership of the gold. Any attempt by us to mine gold even in our own compound without a licence from the government is considered illegal. We breathe fresh air and our environment is clean. We organize communal labour to improve our surroundings. Our women are faithful. Our land is rich so we do not travel far away to farm or hunt for animals. We produce cocoa and other cash crops for a living. We eat fresh fruits and vegetables. We drink from the small river that is protected by trees. What we look forward to is an improvement in our lives. Therefore remember us as you undertake your mining activities. Lead us not into further poverty or disease but help us improve our living standards. We do in particular need good drinking water, good roads, good schools, a new chief's palace, a clinic and the employment of both men and women. We need our forest for further farming activities and for hunting. We must also conserve part of the forest and the environment for posterity'.

2.   Multinationals

I can also imagine the multinational or a big mining company arguing about social responsibility in these terms:

'We have borrowed to supplement the contributions of our shareholders. We owe it a duty to show profits at the end of the year and also pay dividends. We started this business with 10 per cent shares to the Government free of charge. Government may by agreement acquire a further 20 per cent shares. We pay royalties of between 3 per cent to 12 per cent which the government is supposed to use to develop the community. The gold we export is going to add to the foreign exchange earned by the country. We also pay our taxes. All these contributions should help the government provide the amenities the community is looking forward to. The construction of roads and major projects should be the responsibility of the government. We contribute in various ways to the community. Out of our profits we will do more to help the society including the creation of jobs, building of schools and the provision of medical supplies'.

3.   Small Scale

The small scale gold mining company begins with limited resources. The usual promise to the community is that;

'We will build a new school for you when we find gold. We can do more when we make profit'.

4.   Galamsay

What will the 'galamsay' miner say about corporate social responsibility? The method of mining itself is illegal. Indeed there have been reports of 'Galamsay' miners digging under school buildings and very close to railway tracks in search of gold and diamonds. Perhaps the 'galamsay' miner will ask 'what do you people mean by corporate social responsibility? I just want gold'.

H. SITUATION ON THE GROUND

A lot can be said about the corporate social responsibility being discharged by some companies like Ashanti. In addition to various assistance to the community and the country including health and education, Ashanti has contributed to the development of football by building a football stadium in Obuasi where it operates. The company has a strong football team called 'Goldfields' as well as a training school for footballers. However, the fact that for many years the roads in Obuasi were virtually impassable coupled with the dust and dirt in Obuasi must have confused a lot of people as to the real meaning of corporate social responsibility. Perhaps this is a clear example of the confusion in the minds of some inhabitants of the mining communities regarding State responsibility and corporate social responsibility. It is on record that the mining companies organize annual safety week to promote safety awareness. Some of the companies take occupational safety seriously and ensure the protection of their employees by supplying their safety needs.

I. NEWSPAPER PUBLICATIONS

I must confess that after I had written my paper up to this point I decided to find out more on what is currently considered by the mining companies themselves as social responsibility. And here I make reference to the electronic and print media.

1. Ghana Television reported on 23 February 2004 that Bogoso Gold Limited had invested USD35,000,000.00 in gold mining. The report said the company would use part of its dividends to assist the communities within which it operates. The big show of the day was the donation of medical supplies including laboratories, beds and mattresses to hospitals within its catchment area through a non-governmental organization (NGO) called Project Care. The news item was followed by an enumeration of the problems in the area of operation of the company, notably tuberculosis, maternal mortality, HIV, typhoid and others.

2. In a report on the statement made by Dr Sam Jonah, Chief Executive of 'Ashanti' regarding the merger between Anglogold and Ashanti the 'Ghanaian Chronicle' wrote the following on 24 February 2004.

   'Talking about the achievements of 'Ashanti', he said, they were instrumental in fashioning out new and successful partnerships with stakeholders including government and local communities.

   'For example, 'Ashanti' financed the rural electrification project for 36 communities in and around Obuasi and partly financed the construction of an eye clinic in collaboration with the Bryant Mission.

   'Ashanti' also supports HIV/AIDS counselling projects in Tanzania. Other projects in Bibiani in Ghana, Siguiri in Guinea and Geita in

Tanzania also stand testimony to this. He stated that Ashanti's trail-blazing activities manifest themselves even more in what they have shown to the world they can achieve with the empowerment of nationals, be it in Guinea, Ghana, Zimbabwe or Tanzania to work in and manage our operations.

'We are proud of our efforts and success in empowering local people in the countries in which we operate'

3. The Daily Graphic wrote on 3 March 2004 as follows:

'Newmont, the world's leading gold producer, says it intends to engage about 800 people in its two mining sites when it begins mining operations in the country next year.

The Manager, West Africa Newmont Ghana Gold, Mr Bill Zisch, made this known at a dinner with a cross-section of journalists in Accra last Friday. Mr Zisch indicated that the company had obtained its Environmental Impact Assessment certificate and was optimistic that it would use the best practices in ensuring an environmental friendly atmosphere in its area of operations.

He said the company had developed a nursery plantation to ensure the development and sustainability of reclaimed lands.

'In this regard, our community relationship with our stakeholders is to ensure collaboration efforts of all to ensure a sustainable relationship',

4. Ghana Television reported on 8 March 2004 that AGC Bibiani Limited had donated computers to a school and uniforms and scholarships to some students. Officials of the company were seen and heard promising the company's willingness to assist communities in its catchment area.

5. The 'Daily Graphic' also filed the following report: on 13 March 2004 'GOLD Fields Ghana Limited, a mining company, has decided to invest an additional $200 million in the mining sector. The additional investment is in response to the congenial business climate prevailing in the country. Already, the company, which began operation in the country in 1993, has invested $500 million in the Ghanaian economy. Mr Ian Cockerill, the President and Chief Executive of Gold Fields Ghana Limited, made this known when he led a seven-member delegation from the company to pay courtesy call on President J.A. Kufour at the Castle, Osu yesterday. Mr Cockerill said it was no coincidence that two world leading gold mining companies were investing in the Ghanaian economy. He said Ghana provided a good environment corporate investment and indicated that his company had enjoyed investing in the country and being part of the business community. He said the prevailing investment climate was a credit to the government's Golden age of Business declaration. President Kufour said the success story of Gold Fields was what all Ghanaians wanted to hear. He said it was important for all interested groups to co-operate to attract more investment. He said he was happy that the company was a good corporate citizen'.

J. INTERVIEWS

'The Mirror' carried a full page report on 13 March 2004 on an interview by one A. E. A. Damoah conducted with seven persons with their pictures in the Prestea Bogoso area. It is not known who commissioned or sponsored this publication with the title 'DEVELOPMENT CONCERNS IN MINING COMMUNITIES – Impression from Prestea Bogoso'. However being of interest, it is reproduced below in full:

Michael Appiagyei, Headmaster of Prestea Goldfields Schools

The school came from the bowels of the mines and has continued to receive assistance from it. The Bogoso Mines has provided the school with 14 classroom blocks with toilet facilities. In addition, the school has been provided with sporting equipment. For instance, four sets of jerseys were donated from the just-ended games, two for primary and two for the junior secondary school. However, the schools need further improvement, especially more classrooms to make teaching and learning more effective in the delivery of quality education. The Goldfields Schools Complex is made up of kindergarten, primary and junior secondary schools with a total enrolment of 2.116. Our relationship with the mines has improved and we are looking forward to further fruitful collaboration. Initially, there was the fear that surface mining was going to escalate the incidence of diseases in the catchment area, but this has not been the case. We are planning to start a senior secondary school programme in the near future and hope the company will support us.

James Okeh Bossman, Farmer Bogoso-Dumasi

It is true that the company has assisted a number of farmers in the provisions of inputs and seed money for land preparation, which we appreciate, but the money is rather small. After the planting, farmers need resources to maintain the farm within the first three years. Cost of labour in our locality is high because most youths prefer to engage in small scale mining rather than farming. On infrastructural development, we need to emphasize that the company has not done badly though much needs to be done. The company has continued to provide us with tanker services, but they are not adequate. In addition, communities in the catchment area need to be assisted to construct public places of convenience. We would also appeal to the Wassa West District Assembly to assist schools with inadequate furniture because some children carry their chairs to school.

Eunice Amihere, Assembly member, Bola Side Electoral Area, Prestea

'As far as development activities are concerned, the Bogoso Gold Limited is not doing badly. A new labour office and a post office have been constructed by the company, and in addition, a police station is under construction. I also remember the company assisted a number of schools, churches and individuals with quantities of roofing sheets to rehabilitate their structures. Through the Alternative Livelihood Programme introduced by the company, some farmers have been assisted with farming inputs. Some people in the locality are of the view that the opening of the underground mines is likely to result in the employment of more people, which, in consequence, will improve their purchasing power. The electoral area needs places of convenience and accessibility should also be improved. Though the Minerals Commission has provided some communities with pipe-borne water, the supply is still inadequate. Poor drainage is another area, which need some attention. Most gutters in the area are choked. One major problem is the dependency syndrome that has been perpetuated since mining activities started.

George Andoh, Farmer, Dumasi

We are mainly farmers cultivating cash crops such a oil palm, citrus and food crops such as cassava, maize and vegetables including tomatoes and beans. Land for agricultural production is available but the yield is still low. We therefore need assistance in the form of supply of agro-chemical, seedling and credit facilities. So the communities appreciate the efforts of Bogoso Gold Limited within the last three years where a number of farmers have been assisted with agro-chemical, oil palm seedlings and ¢500,000.00 for land preparation. As a beneficiary I have the conviction that if the package continues many farmers in the community are likely to improve their income levels. In consequence, the people would be able to contribute to development activities. However, relative to demand, the number of beneficiaries is small. I would therefore appeal to the company to do something about it. Again, the amount given for land preparation should be increased. The company has done well in the provision of social infrastructure. For instance, it has constructed a number of schools in the catchment area including Dumasi. Second, the community continues to enjoy water through tanker services. However, the provision of permanent water facility is likely to solve inadequacy in supply. In the educational sector, we would suggest the institution of a scholarship scheme to cater for needy students. It is refreshing that the company has started employing some youth in the area to improve the local economy. Indeed, the presence of the company is timely and reassuring, so we are expecting that it will continue to contribute towards the development of the catchment area.

Augustina Amina, Unit Committee Chairman, Ankobra

Though initially, the Ankobra community was apprehensive about the activities of Bogoso Mines, following a series of consultations, and a demonstration by the company to improve development activities, the relationship has been cordial. Within the last few years, we have witnessed some improvement in infrastructural development. For instance, the construction of a market as promised has been completed. A new labour office and a post office have also been completed while a police station is under construction. All this is laudable but there is more room for improvement. This community has no reliable water supply because the existing boreholes produce hard water. Inhabitants have to walk about half a kilometre to the barrier to fetch water. The company has started work on a gravity system to improve the situation, but the construction work has been slow. We acknowledge that some of the youth in this community have been offered employment at the mines, but the number is small. Moreover, attachment of students' to the mines has also been of benefit to us.

Isaac Adjei-Mensah, Administrative and Human Resource of Manager, Bogoso Gold Ltd.

Our catchment community with a population of over 20,000 is considered a major stakeholder, so efforts are being made to improve the cordial relationship existing between us. This has been evident in three main areas, namely infrastructure development, the introduction of Alternative Livelihood Programme and consultation. On infrastructure development, the company has spent about ¢6.7 billion within the past four years on the construction of schools, potable water, sporting activities and road rehabilitation. Specific projects include the construction of a six-class room and the provision of hand-dug well for Dumasi. The Bogoso Gold Limited is the only major supplier of employment in the Bogoso area apart from traditional agricultural activity. The company is injecting about ¢13.200 million per annum in direct employees salaries and ¢720 million in other services and community projects in the areas. The company envisages that with expansion of Boundaye mines in 2005/6, more job opportunities are likely to increase. The company currently has a regular workforce of 584 and temporary staff of 166, making a total of 750.

James Oppong, Chief Farmer, Bogoso-Dumasi

Despite the surge of mining activities, farming is still an important activity in this area. However, income levels are still below expectation. I believe this is one of the major reasons why in 2001, the company decided to assist a number of farmers to cultivate cash crops, especially oil palm and citrus. The package of assistance consist of 180 seedlings, two bags of fertilizers, agro-chemicals and spraying machines, cutlasses, Wellington boots and a loan of ¢500,000.00 for land preparation. A total of 21 farmers in Dumasi benefited from the package in 2001–02 farming season. Last year, we were asked to form a co-operative union, and thus the Dumasi Muti-purpose Area Co-operative Oil Palm Union was established with about 100 members. We appreciate the desire of the company to employ as many youths as possible from the locality. For instance, recently 30 youths have been employed as permanent workers. We are also aware the company cannot employ all the people so we appreciate the Alternative Livelihood concept which seeks to encourage others to go into farming and other ventures such as fish-pond and grasscutter rearing. However, the assistance package should be improved. We cannot deny the contribution of the company in infrastructure development such as building of classroom blocks, supply of sporting equipment, but we would ask for more. One major problem facing us is lack of decent accommodation for teachers in the area. We would also expect the district assembly to come out with a programme to assist communities in the area under the poverty reduction programme'.

K.   PUBLIC CONCERNS

From the foregoing reports one thing becomes obvious; this is the publicity given to the donations given by the gold mining companies. The publicity shows a common trend, which is the periodic support given by one or two companies to a school, hospital or a village. Some companies are known to have contributed to the HIV/AIDS campaign. However, the mining companies themselves do not appear eager to publicize any human rights abuse or the negative effects of their activities. It is the research reports of others and the occasional display of resentment by the inhabitants of the mining communities that bring attention to any human rights abuse or apparent neglect in the discharge of corporate social responsibility by some mining companies.

It appears that in spite of all their efforts the mining companies still have a lot to do. Available research shows that there are concerns about open pit drilling, blasting and vehicular movement in some areas. The issues of pollution caused by cyanide and mercury to rivers and the outbreak of diseases like malaria HIV/AIDS are matters of public concern. Some civil society organizations condemn mining in the forest reserves. An example is a letter addressed to the president of the Wold Bank Group dated July 2003 bearing the names of 102 persons including foreigners. Part of this letter reads as follows:

'Some Local communities in villages surrounding the reserves have begun to question the logic of allowing surface mining where they have long been prevented from farming or harvesting wood in the reserves. They have therefore vowed to resist any attempt to conduct surface mining in the forests, expressing heightened concern about the detrimental legacy of surface gold mining in villages like Atuabo, Damang, Teberebie, Kyekyewire, Abekoase, Bibiani, Prestea, Hemang-Prestea, and Sansu, to name but a few. The Aboduabo Farmers Association submitted a petition to the World Bank's, Ghana office in February 2003 asking the Bank to encourage the government to rescind mining licenses in the Tano-Suraw Reserve. Several other communities have also expressed their commitment to resist mining in the Bonsa and Supuma Forest Reserves'.

L.   SOURCES OF FUNDING CORPORATE SOCIAL RESPONSIBILITY

How is a company to fund its corporate social responsibility? Should the cost of corporate social responsibility be considered as operational cost? Should corporate social responsibility be funded out of stated capital (investment made by the shareholders?) or profits only? There may be various views on this subject but to the mining communities or society at large, the source does not matter so long as it is legal. All limited liability companies in Ghana are governed by the Companies Code 1963, ACT 179. It is provided in Section 202(1) of the Companies Code that:

'Notwithstanding subsection (3) of section 137 of this Code or any provision in the company's Regulations the directors of a company with shares shall not, without the approval of an ordinary resolution of the company.

(c)   make voluntary contributions to any charitable or other funds, other than pension funds for the benefit of employees of the company, of any amounts the aggregate of which will, in any financial year of the company, exceed £1,000 or 2 per cent of the income surplus of the company at the end of the immediately preceding financial year, whichever is the greater'.

This provision of the Code is obviously intended to control the board of directors with respect to what may be given out. If contributing to the electrification of villages, giving computers to schools or beds to hospitals is considered a donation then Section 202(1)(c) of the Code appears to be a limitation on the board of directors of a mining company. It means the board of directors of a company without a positive income surplus should not give more than £1,000.00 in any year. In the case of a company with positive income surplus only a maximum of 2 per cent of such surplus can be given in a particular year. I must however add that any mining company that hides behind this provision of the code and feel constrained will have itself to blame since shareholders' resolution can be planned for and obtained.

This Code was passed in 1961 and at a time when the debate on corporate social responsibility had not taken the global dimension it has taken today. The Code is in the process of being amended and it is hoped that this section will be one of those to be affected.

M. CONCLUSION

As lawyers you may have the opportunity at one time or the other to advise clients who go into the gold mining industry in Ghana. What must be noted is that the argument about discharging corporate social responsibility only out of profits is unimpressive if not unacceptable to the inhabitants of the mining communities. To them if the 'galamsay' miner using pickaxe and shovel can easily find gold then once mining operations begin they expect to see evidence of improvement in their quality of life, especially when pollution of the environment starts showing.

I do recall that a small scale mining company of which I was a director was prevented from further mining operations unless it showed evidence of discharging its corporate social responsibility. People carrying offensive weapons blocked access to the mines and dared any manager or worker to enter the mine. This happened because the provision of a school and water that had been promised had delayed even though mining operations were ongoing. The foreign managers who were expecting very successful results and profit before helping the community were surprised at the reaction of the community. It was the District Chief Executive who finally resolved the problem. The mining communities can otherwise be very cooperative. They show understanding when approached on matters of corporate social responsibility instead of the mining companies determining their needs without consultation. The reports reproduced in this paper demonstrate the different ways in which corporate social responsibility can be discharged. Gold mining companies should therefore be seen to be pro-active in order to avoid conflict with the communities in which they operate. The exercise of mineral right strictly as legal right without a human face is not the best and can lead to avoidable conflict.

There is a school of thought that the payment of taxes and royalties which is sometimes used as evidence of corporate social responsibility is rather a legal obligation which is not considered by some mining communities as being of direct benefit to them. The Constitution of Ghana encourages the state to ensure the discharge of corporate social responsibility. It is therefore important for the mining companies to adopt comprehensive corporate social responsibility policies to be budgeted for and implemented as mining operations begin.

PART VI

CODES OF CONDUCT

Chapter 25

THE HISTORY, VARIATIONS, IMPACT AND FUTURE OF SELF-REGULATION

Phillip H. Rudolph*

A. INTRODUCTION

The past several years have experienced a proliferation of Codes of Conduct promulgated by multinational corporations and their business partners. The factors leading to this proliferation are as diverse as the particular codes themselves. Some companies or organizations that aspire to leadership in the area of corporate social responsibility ('CSR') have developed codes as a mechanism for incorporating labor rights, human rights, and environmental protection into their business model. Others have developed codes to address a particular legal or reputational issue. Still others have built codes of conduct in response to expectations of their business partners. Often, it is a combination of these factors, and others too plentiful to recount, that motivate a company to promulgate a code of conduct governing production and supplier activities. Whatever the catalyst, the World Bank now estimates that there may be as many as 1000 such codes in existence today, developed voluntarily by transnational companies in response to myriad business pressures.[1] This proliferation, in turn, has been fed by an ever-more active, effective and efficient group of corporate stakeholders – particularly nongovernmental organizations ('NGOs') and socially responsible investor organizations ('SRIs') – that increasingly seek to hold corporations accountable not merely for their own activities, but for those of their supply chain partners as well.

Despite this recent explosion, codes designed to address corporate activity have existed in some form or another for several years. This chapter will examine the historical development of these codes, discuss different types of codes, evaluate

---

* Phillip H. Rudolph is Partner of Foley Hoag LLP. The author would like to acknowledge and express his gratitude to his colleague Jonas Monast for his excellent assistance with and contribution to this chapter.
1 Gare Smith & Dan Feldman. *Company Codes of Conduct and International Standards: An Analytical Comparison Part I of II,* World Bank, USA, 2003, 2.

Ramon Mullerat (ed.), Corporate Social Responsibility: The Corporate Governance of the 21st Century, 365–384.

the drivers behind the recent flurry of activity in the area, and assess the impact on the broader human- and labor-rights goals for which these codes have been created.

B.   A BRIEF HISTORY OF CODES OF CONDUCT

Modern day business codes of conduct might be traced back to at least as early as the 1930s. During that decade, for example, the International Chamber of Commerce developed model codes relating to advertising practices, followed by codes on marketing and direct marketing.[2] The 1930s also saw General Robert Wood Johnson, founder of Johnson and Johnson, advocate 'a new industrial phi- losophy', making clear his belief, and that of his company, that a corporation's responsibility extends to all of its stakeholders, including its customers, employ- ees, the community, and stockholders.[3] The Johnson and Johnson Credo, embodying General Johnson's commitment to corporate responsibility, was published in 1943 and remains in effect today.[4] Similarly, in 1934, Mitsubishi Trading Company developed its 'Three Corporate Principles', including corporate responsibility to society, integrity and fairness, and international understanding through trade.[5]

However, the development of codes of conduct aimed at promoting socially responsible behavior by business enterprises can really be traced to the adoption of the Universal Declaration of Human Rights ('UDHR') in 1948.[6] Born in the wake of World War Two and in response to the atrocities perpetrated before and during that conflict, the intent and purpose of the UDHR was to secure 'the uni- versal and effective recognition and observance' of clearly delineated human rights standards.[7] One of the first products of the newly-created United Nations, and adopted unanimously by its members, this document reflects a global embrace of the notion that human rights should be respected and protected everywhere:

> [T]his Universal Declaration of Human Rights [is] a common standard of achievement for all peoples and all nations, to the end that every individual and *every organ of society*, keeping this Declaration constantly in mind, shall strive by teaching and education to promote respect for these rights and freedoms and by progressive measures, national and international, to secure their universal and effective recognition and observance, both among the

---

[2]   Jill Murray. *Corporate Codes of Conduct and Labour Standards.* International Labor Organization, Bureau of Workers' Activities. Available at http://www.itcilo.it/actrav/actrav-english/telearn/ global/ilo/guide/jill.htm.

[3]   Deborah Leipziger *The Corporate Responsibility Code Book*, Greenleaf Publishing Ltd., United Kingdom, 2003, 341–342.

[4]   *Id.* at 342. See Johnson & Johnson website: http://www.jnj.com/our_company/our_credo/ index.htm;jsessionid=SYPGFMWCB342GCQPCB3SZOYKB2IIWNSC.

[5]   Mitsubishi Corporation, *Corporate Citizenship: Environmental and Social Sustainability*, http://www.mitsubishicorp.com/en/csr/ess/ess01.html.

[6]   United Nations Universal Declaration of Human Rights, *Adopted and proclaimed by General Assembly Resolution 217 A(III) of 10 December 1948.*

[7]   *Id.*, at Preamble.

peoples of Member States themselves and among the peoples of territories under their jurisdiction.[8]

The reference to 'every organ of society' is broadly recognized today as including multinational corporations, although few such entities existed at the time the UDHR was adopted.

The post-World War Two environment witnessed the early evolution of transnational business enterprises and of financial activities somewhat less defined by political borders than they had previously been – a phenomenon now referred to as 'globalization'. Although the Cold War served as something of a constraint, the foundations for the current global economy were built during this period. It was also during this Cold War period that international standards of corporate governance began to germinate. These were initially manifested in wholly voluntary, government-sponsored initiatives such as OECD's 1976 *Guidelines for Multinational Enterprises*,[9] and the ILO's 1977 *Tripartite Declaration of Principles Concerning Multinational Enterprises and Social Policy*.[10] They found voice as well in the 1977 *Sullivan Principles for South Africa*.[11] Developed by Reverend Leon Sullivan, these were aspirational principles aimed at companies doing business, or considering doing business, in apartheid South Africa. Reverend Sullivan's voluntary principles were unique in that they were privately initiated. They represent an early step in the evolution of private initiatives aimed at filling real or perceived holes in governmental efforts to achieve the human rights goals of the UDHR.[12]

With the foundations for cross-border economic enterprises already in existence, the end of the Cold War witnessed an explosive growth in transnational businesses and in a truly global economy. This in turn resulted in expanded outsourcing of production by transnational enterprises to less-developed, low wage and lightly regulated venues. And an outgrowth of this phenomenon was what human, labor, and environmental activists have characterized as a global 'race to the bottom' for plunging wages in labor-intensive, low-tech industries. These developments transcended the practical ability of national governments to impose constraints on real or perceived abuses, insofar as individual nations could regulate activities within their borders but were less equipped to regulate international activities and, for their own parochial reasons, were often unwilling in any event to do so. Consequently, other organizations and groups attempted to fill the void.

---

[8] *Id.* (italics provided).
[9] Organisation for Economic Co-Operation and Development, *The OECD Guidelines for Multinational Enterprises*, 2000.
[10] *ILO Tripartite Declaration of Principles Concerning Multinational Enterprises and Social Policy*, 16 November 1977, reprinted in (1978) 17 ILM 422. The ILO Declaration contains 'detailed provisions concerning equality of opportunity and treatment, security of employment, wages, benefits and conditions of work, safety and health, freedom of association, and the right to organize and collective bargaining.' *Id.*
[11] See *Global Sullivan Principles of Social Responsibility*, http://globalsullivanprinciples.org/new_page_4.htm.
[12] Citations to and explanations of the UDHR can be found on the websites of a number of companies dedicated to corporate social responsibility, such as British Petroleum (http://www.bp.com/subsection.do?categoryId=2011558&contentId=2016955), Reebok (http://www.reebok.com/Static/global/initiatives/rights/understanding/universal.html), and Timberland (http://www.timberland.com/timberlandserve/content.jsp?pageName=timberlandserve_inform_global).

Corporate scandals involving high-profile defense industry contractors in the 1980s, as well as the enactment in 1991 of the US Federal Sentencing Guidelines,[13] which provided for leniency in sentencing for corporations having a program 'to prevent and detect violations of the law', have also been credited with providing stimuli for the development of corporate codes of conduct.[14] For example, the US Federal Sentencing Guidelines detail seven criteria against which such corporate programs are to be judged, including 'the existence of standards or codes of conduct, training or other communication regarding the standards, and the designation of a high-level individual to oversee compliance'.[15]

In the meantime, the economic disparities between developed and developing countries in the 1990s, and the inability or unwillingness of national governments to address the consequences, led to the development of global business principles by an expanding array of entities that included intergovernmental organizations such as the UN,[16] private organizations,[17] and NGOs.[18] During this same period, NGOs and SRIs – who concluded that some form of 'self-regulation' by companies was necessary – became more sophisticated in their approaches to influencing the activities of transnational companies. Effective use by these groups of the media and, later, of the internet, produced high-profile campaigns commencing in the late 1990s targeting the labor, human rights and environmental practices of well-known multinational companies.[19]

---

[13]   2002 Federal Sentencing Guidelines, *Recommended Conditions of Probation – Organizations, 2002*, §D1.4.

[14]   See *ILO, Corporate Codes of Conduct;* see also European Institute for Business Ethics, What Can We Learn from the US Federal Sentencing Guidelines for Organizational Ethics?, available at http://www.itcilo.it/actrav/actrav-english/telearn/global/ilo/code/whatcan.htm#Abstract.

[15]   The types of Codes produced as a result of the Sentencing Guidelines generally focused up internal corporate ethics and behaviors, and were less directed at the external impacts of corporate activities. Also, these 'codes' or standards of business conduct guided the behavior of company employees but did not, as a general matter, impose requirements or expectations on suppliers or business partners.

[16]   E.g. the *United Nations Global Compact* (2000) (aimed at fostering partnerships between corporations, the UN and NGOs through soliciting acceptance by corporations of nine core principles promoting sustainability, human rights, and labor rights), the *ILO Declaration of Fundamental Principles and Rights at Work* (1998) followed by an updated *Tripartite Declaration of Principles* (2000); *Report of the United Nations Conference on Environment and Development* (Rio Declaration) (1992) (setting forth principles on environmental stewardship).

[17]   E.g., *Fair Labor Ass'n Code of Conduct* (1998) (consortium of apparel and footwear companies with a common code of conduct and monitoring system); *Global Sullivan Principles* (1999) (partnership of global companies embracing eight aspirational principles on human rights, labor rights, fair competition, and community development).

[18]   E.g., *Workers Rights Consortium* (2000) (developed and organized by US colleges and universities to inspect and verify conditions in factories producing logo-ed apparel); *Global Reporting Initiative* (1997) (launched by the Coalition for Environmentally Responsible Economies ('CERES') to develop a multistakeholder process for reporting social and environmental performance by companies); *Social Accountability 8000* (comprehensive code of conduct developed by Social Accountability International, embracing ILO conventions, UDHR, and similar initiatives).

[19]   As one commentator has noted, 'The days of flying under the radar screen are gone. There are a lot of watchdog groups out there taking a look at what you are doing, your code of conduct, business partners and suppliers. That list of websites grows each month and these NGOs, unions and activist groups are all sharing information. And they are putting corporations in their crosshairs'. *Conduct Unbecoming,* Corporate Legal Times, October 2002.

These developments caused transnational corporations to sit up and take notice. In very little time, in response to increasing stakeholder pressure, companies everywhere began to promulgate codes defining human rights, labor rights, environmental, social, and ethical requirements for themselves and their suppliers. These codes typically have complemented national legislation, and embrace to varying extents many of the principles enunciated in the intergovernmental, private, and NGO-driven initiatives discussed earlier. What began as a somewhat precocious undertaking by privately-held Levi Strauss in 1991[20] became, by the end of the decade, a prerequisite for doing business in a global environment. The era of code proliferation had arrived.

C.   TYPES OF CODES

As mentioned above, there are now at least 1,000 codes of conduct in existence, promulgated by a wide array of players from the private sector, the public sector, and governmental and intergovernmental entities. These codes represent a fairly broad spectrum of approaches for addressing corporate behavior. Despite the range of approaches found in the various codes, there is much overlap in their goals and objectives. In an attempt to simplify the discussion of the various types of codes of conduct, this chapter will address the different codes under the five general categories identified by the UN: model codes, intergovernmental codes, multi-stakeholder codes, trade association codes, and company codes.[21] These boundaries tend to overlap a bit, but are generally helpful in discussing the variety of codes being considered by companies.

1.   Model Codes

Numerous model codes have been developed by intergovernmental organizations or NGOs. These codes are voluntary guidelines, typically aspirational and nonbinding, and are intended to provide examples of best practices or general operating standards in the areas of human rights, labor rights, and environmental protection. For example, the UN Global Compact sets forth ten principles to guide company operations, but it is not intended to 'police,' enforce or measure the behavior or actions of companies. Rather, the Global Compact relies on public accountability, transparency and the enlightened self-interest of companies, labor and civil society to initiate and share substantive action in pursuing the Global Compact's goals.[22] Similarly, the Global Sullivan Principles are intended to provide companies with guidance as to how and why they should align their internal policies to uphold generally recognized labor rights and standards for

---

[20] One of the first companies to establish a comprehensive code of conduct defining expectations for its overseas suppliers was Levi Strauss & Co., with its 1991 Terms of Engagement for Foreign Business Partners. Interestingly, Levi Strauss took a leadership role on this issue notwithstanding that it is a privately held company, and thus was not subject to the types of shareholder pressures that have motivated other transnational companies today to enact similar codes.

[21] Rhys Jenkins, *Corporate Codes of Conduct: Self Regulation in a Global Economy*, United Nations Research Institute for Social Development, 2001, 20.

[22] The Global Compact, *UN What is the Global Compact?*, UN.

ethical business dealings.[23] There is no independent verification associated with these codes, and companies adopting either one must, for all intents and purposes, 'self-monitor' their compliance with the expectations delineated therein.[24]

Another example of such an effort is the Caux Round Table Principles for Business, which 'aim[] to express a world standard against which business behavior can be measured'.[25] The Caux Round Table Principles – promulgated by the Caux Round Table, an international network of business leaders founded in 1986 – recognize that business behavior should be driven by more than simply internal pressures, and attempt to define the responsibilities of businesses to their stakeholders, employees, owners and investors, suppliers, competitors, and communities.[26] Similar to the Sullivan Principles and the Global Compact, there is no monitoring mechanism and the principles are quite general in nature.

Nongovernmental organizations also have developed a plethora of model codes targeted at specific industries. For example, the Sustainable Agriculture Network and the Rainforest Alliance have cooperatively developed the Better Banana Project. Recognizing that 'the banana industry is an economic pillar in many tropical countries', these two NGOs put together these criteria aimed at decreasing the negative ecological impacts of banana plantations.[27] As of 2000, at least two multinational banana companies, Chiquita and Reybancorp, had signed on to the program. Other examples of NGO-develop model codes include the Fair Trade Labelling Organization's Fair Trade Standards for Hired Labour,[28] and the Rainforest Alliance's Generic Coffee Standards.[29]

---

[23]   Global Sullivan Principles of Social Responsibility. http://globalsullivanprinciples.org/principles.htm. Examples of the Principles' include

Express[ing] support for universal human rights …

Promot[ing] equal opportunity for [] employees at all levels of the company with respect to issues such as color, race, gender, age, ethnicity or religious beliefs, and operate without unacceptable worker treatment such as the exploitation of children, physical punishment, female abuse, involuntary servitude, or other forms of abuse. [and]

Respect[ing] employees' voluntary freedom of association.

Id.

[24]   Although the Global Compact is a nonbinding commitment, member companies may face negative repercussions for perceived noncompliance. On 14 April 2004, for example, presidents of four labor unions, including the United Steelworkers of America and the Canadian Labour Congress, officially requested that the United Nations review Nike's affiliation with the Global Compact due to Nike's alleged failure to abide by its principles governing freedom of association. CSR Wire, Press Release from: United Steelworkers of America, 28 April 2004, http://www.csrwire.com/print.cgi?sfArticleId=2680; SocialFunds.com, http://www.social funds.com/news/article.cgi/1411.html.

[25]   *Caux Round Table Principles for Business*, Caux Round Table, available at http://www.cauxround-table.org/principles.html (last visited 18 April 2004). An example of these principles includes:

Businesses established in foreign countries to develop, produce or sell should also contribute to the social advancement of those countries by creating productive employment and helping to raise the purchasing power of their citizens. Businesses should also contribute to human rights, education, welfare, and vitalization of the countries in which they operate.

Id. at Principle 2.

[26]   See www.cauxroundtable.org.

[27]   Rainforest Alliance, Conservation Programs, available at http://www.rainforest-alliance.org/programs/cap/program-description2.html.

[28]   Fairtrade Labelling Organizations International, *Generic Fairtrade Standards for Hired Labour*, 2003, http://www.fairtrade.net/pdf/hl/english/sportsballs.pdf.

[29]   See http://www.rainforest-alliance.org/programs/cap/get-certified.html.

The Council on Economic Priorities (now called Social Accountability International) took the concept of a model code one step further by developing an auditing and certification scheme on labor and social issues. Entitled Social Accountability 8000 ('SA8000'), this program is based on the core ILO conventions and related international human rights instruments, including the Universal Declaration of Human Rights and the UN Convention on the Rights of the Child. The goal of SA8000 is to create a common standard for companies to employ to guarantee the basic rights of workers.[30]

Although these model codes are not intended to create mechanisms with which to hold companies directly liable in any legal sense, model codes help identify and define common standards to which companies are felt to be accountable, and lawyers helping companies address CSR-related issues should be aware of these developments. Regardless of whether or not a company could face legal liability for non-compliance with general CSR model codes of conduct, these codes could be and increasingly are the source of campaigns by NGOs and other key stakeholders. Disregard for the principles could lead, at minimum, to public relations and reputational risks.[31] Notably, though not surprisingly, companies that make an effort to comply with their voluntary commitments are often recognized by NGOs for such leadership.[32]

2. Intergovernmental Codes

Intergovernmental codes are negotiated at the international level and are agreed to or adopted by sovereign governments.[33] As mentioned above (see notes 9 and 10), early examples include the OECD's Guidelines for Multinational Enterprises and the ILO's Tripartite Declaration of Principles Concerning Multinational Enterprises and Social Policy. A more recent effort can be found in the ILO's Declaration on Fundamental Principles and Rights at Work, embodying the four main principles of the core ILO conventions, including: (a) freedom of association and the right to collective bargaining; (b) the elimination of forced and compulsory labor; (c) the abolition of child labor; and (d) the elimination of discrimination in the workplace.[34]

The OECD Guidelines were updated in 2000 to include recommendations calling for the elimination of child labor and forced labor, thus incorporating all

---

[30] Teresa Fabian. *Social Accountability 8000 (SA8000) – the first auditable, global standard for ethical sourcing driven by CEPAA*, Council on Economic Priorities, January 1998, http://www.citinv.it/associazioni/CNMS/archivio/lavoro/Presentazione_SA8000.html.

[31] For example, Global Witness issued a press release on 30 March 2004 criticizing many diamond jewelry retailers for failure to comply with promises to self-regulate to ensure human rights protections, and specifically criticized the World Diamond Council for failure to adequately monitor self-regulation compliance. *Broken Vows: Diamond Jewellery Retailers Fall Short on Conflict Diamond Pledge*, Global Witness, 2004.

[32] Global Witness' report on diamond jewelry retailers recognizes that Tiffany & Co. 'stood out because it outlined its policies to back up the warranty in detail and described how it has strengthened its sourcing procedures and control over its supply chain to prevent dealing in conflict diamonds'. *Broken Vows, Exposing the 'Loupe' Holes in the Diamond Industry's Efforts to Prevent the Trade in Conflict Diamonds*, Global Witness, 2004, p. 3.

[33] Rhys Jenkins, *Corporate Codes of Conduct: Self Regulation in a Global Economy*, United Nations Research Institute for Social Development, 2001, 20.

[34] *ILO Declaration on Fundamental Principles and Rights at Work*, International Labor Organization http://www.ilo.org/dyn/declaris/DECLARATIONWEB.INDEXPAGE.

of the ILO's core labor standards.[35] This update also resulted in the inclusion of new provisions on the environment, combating corruption, and consumer protection.[36] Implementation provisions were revised to help the National Contact Points (the persons and entities designated to handle inquiries regarding the Guidelines for the participating governments) carry out their duties. The OECD also added provisions to promote transparency, accountability, and best practice compliance.[37]

Although these OECD Guidelines are non-binding tools to help multinationals 'operate in harmony with government policies and with societal expectations',[38] they could well evolve into a more prescriptive set of principles governing the conduct of business in OECD member states.[39] This would not be unprecedented. The OECD's Anti-Bribery Convention, which includes a monitoring mechanism to evaluate compliance, demonstrates the willingness of OECD member states to build legal mechanisms to enforce the organization's otherwise non-binding initiatives.

Other intergovernmental efforts also are beginning to gain some measure of traction. For example, in 2001, the European Commission published a paper calling for a common CSR framework that is integrated into existing efforts such as the Global Compact, the OECD Guidelines, and the ILO Principles.[40] The paper also calls for EU companies to integrate social responsibility into their existing management structure. Following multi-stakeholder dialogue throughout the EU, the Commission is expected to issue a white paper late in 2004 setting forth recommendations for EU-wide expectations of businesses on CSR issues.[41]

Finally, in August 2003, the United Nations Sub-Commission on the Promotion and Protection of Human Rights issued a document entitled 'UN Norms on the Responsibilities of Transnational Corporations and Other Business Enterprises with Regard to Human Rights'.[42] Intended to 'codify' binding human rights standards under international law, the Norms called for member states to implement legal mechanisms to enforce the standards set forth therein, and for UN monitoring and enforcement of corporate compliance. The Norms, which were sharply criticized by business organizations, reflected a move by the United Nation Sub-Commission in the direction of regulation (and punishment) of multinationals with respect to human rights issues. Almost certainly

---

[35]   OECD, OECD Guidelines for Multinational Enterprises, 2000, 5.
[36]   Id. at 22–25.
[37]   Id. at 6.
[38]   OECD. OECD Guidelines for Multinational Enterprises, About, http://www.oecd.org/about/0, 2337,en_2649_34889_1_1_1_1_1,00.html.
[39]   United States Council for International Business. Corporate Codes of Conduct: A Review of Recent Initiatives, 1999, http://www.uscib.org/index.asp?documentID=1357.
[40]   European Commission Directorate General for Employment and Social Affairs, Promoting a European Framework for Corporate Social Responsibility: Green Paper, 2001.
[41]   Before these activities by the EU, the European Parliament in 1999 adopted a resolution calling for the development of a model code of conduct for EU companies. That effort has, for the present, been subsumed by the European Commission's own activities in the CSR realm.
[42]   Norms on the Responsibilities of Transnational Corporations and Other Business Enterprises with Regard to Human Rights, UN Sub-Commission on the Promotion and Protection of Human Rights, 55th Sess. Agenda Item 4, at 1, UN Doc. E/CN.4/Sub.2/2003/12/Rev.2 (2003). http://www.unhchr.ch/ Huridocda/Huridoca.nsf/0/64155e7e8141b38cc1256d63002c55e8?Opendocument.

in no small part due to the international business community's vocal opposition, the Norms were withdrawn in April 2004 and have been referred to a new task force for further consideration.[43] Notwithstanding their tabling, the Norms reflect the increasing momentum towards an enforceable international standard for the operations of multinational corporations.

3. Multi-Stakeholder Codes

Multi-stakeholder codes are generally developed through negotiations among businesses, NGOs, trade unions, and/or governmental representatives. Multi-stakeholder dialogues have a greater likelihood of leading to a standardized approach to corporate codes, drastically simplifying the obligations of vendors who supply goods to more than one company. Additionally, the pooling of resources and the common interest in ensuring compliance with and effectiveness of such codes makes it more likely that effective monitoring and internal quality controls will be implemented.

The multi-stakeholder approach is exemplified in the UK's Ethical Trading Initiative ('ETI') Base Code.[44] Through ETI, an alliance of companies, NGOs, and trade unions work together to promote corporate responsibility through the implementation of codes of conduct. ETI receives support from the UK Department for International Development and the Department for Trade and Industry. Using the ILO's core labor conventions, the ETI Base Code addresses the following nine areas: the free choice of employment, freedom of association and the right to collective bargaining, safe and hygienic working conditions, child labor, a living wage, working hours, non-discrimination, the provision of regular employment and the absence of harsh or inhumane treatment. ETI members are expected to incorporate the Base Code into their business practices, ensure that their suppliers meet standards for performance and transparency, and allow monitoring and independent verification.[45]

While ETI is a broad effort aimed at many different industries utilizing diverse supply chains for goods and services, many multi-stakeholder codes are aimed at specific industry sectors. For example, the Fair Labor Association, brought to life as the Apparel Industry Partnership under former US President Clinton, represents an example of a cooperative effort between government officials, businesses, NGOs, and labor unions to address human rights and labor concerns primarily in the footwear and apparel sectors.[46] FLA member companies agree to comply with the organization's standards regarding working conditions, and are subject to periodic independent monitoring to ensure continued compliance. Another industry-specific multi-stakeholder code is the Forest Stewardship Council's

---

[43]   *United Nations Press Release: Action on Draft Resolutions on the Report of the Sub-Commission on the Promotion and Protection of Human Rights, United Nations,* 20 April 2004.

[44]   Ethical Trading Initiative. http://www.ethicaltrade.org/.

[45]   Ethical Trading Initiative, The Base Code, http://www.ethicaltrade.org/Z/lib/base/code_en.shtml; Ethical Trading Initiative, The Base Code: Principles of Incorporation, http://www.ethicaltrade.org/Z/lib/base/poi_en.shtml.

[46]   Fair Labor Organization. http://www.fairlabor.org; US Department of Labor. Apparel Industry Partnership's Agreement. 14 April 1997. http://www.itcilo.it/actrav/actrav-english/telearn/global/ilo/guide/apparell.htm.

(FSC) code for forestry operations, providing a set of standards for sustainable management of timber.[47] Harvesters who demonstrate compliance with these standards can market their wood products as certified, and may use the FSC trademark logo.

4. Trade Association Codes

Trade associations provide an example of interest groups that have developed codes of conduct aimed at their particular industrial sectors. The British Toy and Hobby Association Code and the Kenya Flower Council Code, both developed by trade associations, are intended to guide the activities of all association members. Yet another trade association undertaking can be found in the initiative of the World Diamond Council to establish a warranty system aimed at preventing the purchase and sale of 'conflict diamonds'.[48] Additional examples of trade union-like codes include the International Chamber of Commerce's Business Charter for Sustainable Development[49] and the Rules of Conduct on Extortion and Bribery in International Business Transactions.[50] And though not explicitly a trade association initiative, the 'Equator Principles', based on the policies and guidelines of the World Bank and International Finance Corporation (IFC), establish social and environmental screens for use by financial institutions in evaluating project finance ventures.[51]

The UK Banana Industry Code of Best Practice,[52] whose signatories include Bristol Fruit Sales, Del Monte, Fyffes, Geest Bananas, J.P. Fruit Distributors Ltd., Keelings, M.W. Mack, and S.H. Pratt, helps illustrate the problems and challenges that may arise with codes developed solely by trade unions or individual companies. This code was developed to respond to criticisms of social and environmental practices of the banana industry. Although its underlying goal is the development and implementation of banana industry procedures that 'protect the environment and workers' rights and conditions', the UK Banana Industry Code has been subjected to criticism by NGOs and others due to its lack of procedures for independent, impartial verification. This, in turn, has resulted in some controversy over whether the industry is complying with its commitments.[53]

---

[47]   *Forest Stewardship Council United States: Standards & Policies*, http://www.fscus.org/standards_criteria/.

[48]   See, e.g., World Diamond Council, www.worlddiamondcouncil.com/home.html.

[49]   International Chamber of Commerce, *Business Charter for Sustainable Development*, http://www.iccwbo.org/home/environment_and_energy/sdcharter/charter/principles/principles.asp.

[50]   International Chamber of Commerce, *Extortion and Bribery in International Business Transactions*, 1999, http://www.iccwbo.org/home/statements_rules/rules/1999/briberydoc99.asp.

[51]   *The Equator Principles: A Framework for Financial Institutions to Manage Environmental and Social Issues in Project Financing*, http://www.equator-principles.com/.

[52]   UK Banana Group, *The UK Banana Industry Code of Best Practice*, http://www.bananalink.org.uk/future/future_5.htm#ukbg; http://www.bananalink.org.uk/documents/Banana_Group_Code.doc.

[53]   See, e.g. Banana Link, http://www.bananalink.org.uk/.

5. Company Codes

Company codes differ significantly by sector and even by company within each sector.[54] These may include: (1) compliance codes, with directive statements providing guidance as to appropriate conduct for management and/or subcontractors; (2) corporate credos, providing broad general statements of corporate commitments to ethical and responsible conduct; or (3) management philosophy statements, enunciating the company's or the CEOs methods of conducting business.[55]

Larger companies tend to adopt formal codes of conduct, and typically have more resources to invest in compliance programs. For example, codes of conduct have been adopted by companies focused on such diverse industries as footwear,[56] apparel,[57] personal care products,[58] oil and gas,[59] retail food,[60] toys,[61] and electronics and computers,[62] among others. Companies with significant licensing businesses (e.g., The Walt Disney Company[63]) also rely heavily on codes to manage and monitor the activities of vendors. These codes run the gamut in terms of specificity, scope, and enforcement.

The UN has found that companies with direct contact with the consuming public tend to be farther along in the development and adoption of codes of conduct.[64] Those companies in sectors supplying consumer goods and well known-brand names are especially likely to be the leaders in the development and adoption of codes of conduct. This almost certainly flows out of their daily proximity to their consumers, and the importance of goodwill as a significant asset of consumer brands.[65]

---

[54] For a detailed comparison of specific code provisions in the apparel, footwear, light manufacturing, agribusiness, tourism and extractive industries, see Smith and Feldman, *Company Codes of Conduct and International Standards: An Analytical Comparison*, The World Bank Group, Corporate Social Responsibility Practice, Oct. 2003 (Vol. 1) & Mar. 2004 (Vol. 2).

[55] ILO, Bureau for Workers' Activities, *Corporate Codes of Conduct*, available at http://www.itcilo.it/english/.

[56] See, e.g. Nike. Code of Conduct. http://www.nike.com/nikebiz/nikebiz.jhtml?page=25&cat=code; Reebok. A *Guide to the Implementation of the Reebok Human Rights Production Standards*, http://www.reebok.com/Static/global/initiatives/rights/pdf/ ReebokHR_Guide.pdf.

[57] See, e.g. Timberland, *Code of Conduct*, http://www.timberland.com/corp/english_feb02.pdf; Gap Inc. *Our Code of Vendor Compliance*. http://www.gapinc.com/social_resp/ifpr/op&p.htm.

[58] See, *e.g.* The Gillette Company, *Corporate Social Responsibility*, 4–7, http://gillette.com/community/Corporate_Social_Responsibility_Report_2004.pdf; The Body Shop. Code of Conduct for Suppliers. Nov. 2001. http://www.thebodyshop.com/web/tbsgl/images/tbs_supplier_code_of_conduct.pdf.

[59] British Petroleum, http://www.bp.com/genericsection.do?categoryId=931&contentId=2016995; Royal Dutch/Shell Group. http://www.shell.com/home/Framework?siteId=royal-en&FC2=/royal-en/html/iwgen/environment_and_society/commitment_policies_standards/ zzz_lhn.html&FC3=/royal-en/html/iwgen/environment_and_society/commitment_policies_standards/dir_policies_standards.html.

[60] Starbucks, *Supplier Code of Conduct*, http://www.starbucks.com/aboutus/supplier_code.asp; McDonald's, *Codes of Conduct for Suppliers*, 2000.

[61] Mattel, *Global Manufacturing Principles*, http://www.mattel.com/about_us/Corp_Responsibility/cr_global.asp.

[62] Honeywell, *Code of Business Conduct*, http://www.honeywell.com/sites/docs/doc113a400-fb726b959d-3e3e4447ab3472a0c2a5e5fdc1e6517d.pdf.

[63] The Walt Disney Company, *Code of Conduct for Manufacturers*, http://disney.go.com/corporate/compliance/code.html.

[64] Rhys Jenkins, *Corporate Codes of Conduct: Self Regulation in a Global Economy*. United Nations Research Institute for Social Development, 2001, 8.

[65] *Environics Int'l Ltd., Millennium Poll On Corporate Social Responsibility Executive Briefing* (1999). See also *Cone/Roper, Cause Related Trends Report* (1999), (American consumers and employees

D.   ADVANTAGES AND CHALLENGES

At a practical level, this abundance of codes, principles and norms creates both advantages and challenges for companies. These advantages and challenges, in turn, impact different constituencies and stakeholders. The following evaluation considers these implications from the perspective of some of the key stakeholders.

1.   Advantages

a.   *Supply Chain Management*

Codes and compliance programs help rationalize a company's relationships with its vendors, and help assure that the entire supply chain of a company adheres to consistent, well-defined and principled ethical standards. Similarly, such programs define clear criteria for the selection and retention of company suppliers, as well as for termination of vendors that fail to live up to company expectations.

b.   *Maintaining Relationships with Business Partners*

Just as a company would seek to assure that the vendors and suppliers with whom it does business comply with defined standards of human rights, so too do the business partners with whom the company does business wish to assure that the company is similarly committed. A failure of the company or its vendors in the human rights arena can well have an effect both upstream and downstream. Hence, for example, the failure on the part of factories producing Kathy Lee Gifford's line of clothing in the late 1990s to effectively manage their human- and labor-rights risks damaged the reputation not only of the Kathy Lee brand, but also that of its licensing partner, Wal-Mart.

c.   *Safeguarding Brand Equity and Reputation*

Negative news stories about human and labor rights abuses by vendors of multinational companies can have and have had devastating and lasting impacts on companies and their reputations, regardless of the underlying merits of the allegations. For example, high profile stories in the late 1990s alleging unfair labor practices at factories producing products for Nike and for Wal-Mart were followed by a noticeable reduction in the share value of those companies. And despite remedial efforts, both companies – fairly or not – continue to bear the stigma associated with the reporting of human rights and labor rights abuses allegedly occurring several years earlier in their suppliers' facilities.

---

support cause-related activities of corporations, and companies see benefits to brand reputation, image and bottom line by engaging in such activities).

d. Effective Risk Management

Well-crafted and substantive company codes incorporate clear processes for defining expectations, monitoring against those expectations, and implementing corrective measures as and when necessary. These in turn (i) minimize (though they do not eliminate) the risk of serious code violations by company vendors and business partners; (ii) provide explicit mechanisms for addressing violations when and if they arise; and (iii) provide a foundation of credibility when dealing with affected stakeholders in the event of violations.

e. Production Efficiency

By establishing clear-cut guidance, codes of conduct generate a degree of certainty and predictability that enhances suppliers' ability to produce goods efficiently. Such programs also strive to ensure working environments that promote retention, minimize turnover, and thereby cut down on employee training time and sub-optimal utilization of production facilities.

f. Managing Relations with NGOs

The array and number of organizations that have taken an active interest in global human rights, labor rights, and environmental issues is extraordinary. Whether human rights organizations, student groups, environmental groups, labor interests, religious organizations, socially responsible investor groups, or customers, companies must increasingly devote serious attention to anticipating issues of concern and creating programs to address those concerns, even if it is not possible to perfectly satisfy everyone's expectations. The activities, sophistication and credibility of stakeholders have grown dramatically over the course of the past decade, and this trend seems destined to continue unabated. Although the existence of codes of conduct will not, by itself, assure that companies will have smooth or pain-free relationships with their stakeholders, the absence of such codes will almost guarantee less-than-optimal relationships with them.

g. Minimizing Friction with Shareholders

Assets in professionally managed, socially screened investment portfolios increased 36 percent between 1999 and 2001.[66] In 2003 in the United States alone, $2.16 trillion (or one out of every nine dollars under professional management in the United States) was being invested through use of some form of an SRI screen.[67] CSR-screened portfolios grew in value seven percent from 2001, while the broader universe of all professionally managed portfolios fell four percent during the same period.[68] In 2003, 310 proxy resolutions on social issues were filed, representing an increase of 15 percent from 2001.[69] Like all

---

[66] Sarah Roberts *et al.*, *The Business Case for Corporate Citizenship*, Arthur D. Little, Inc., 2003, 5.
[67] Social Investment Forum, 2003 Report on Socially Responsible Investing Trends in the United States.
[68] *Id.*
[69] *Id.*

stakeholders, shareholders can vote with their feet, and can (and have) abandoned companies that they believe have failed to develop effective tools, including codes and compliance programs, to address human rights, labor rights, and environmental issues.

h.   Behaving Consistently with the Company's Stated Principles and Ethics

An ethics program that purports to define the company's values and behaviors to its employees and internal constituents will lack credibility and force if those ethical principles are not applied with equal force to the company's vendors and other business partners. Moreover, employees who try to operate consistently with the company's prescribed ethical principles will experience countless ethical dilemmas if forced to deal with vendors and business partners as to whom those principles are not applied. Codes of conduct provide mechanisms for companies to enunciate clearly their values, principles, and expectations to those with whom they do business around the globe, and help harmonize the internal and external expectations of the company.

i.   Reducing Legal Risk

Increasingly, courts are being invited to evaluate and remedy alleged workplace abuses that implicate human and labor rights issues. A well-known example of such litigation is the civil lawsuit against Unocal filed in California state and federal courts alleging that the company and it local subsidiary knowingly participated in human and labor rights abuses, including forced labor, forced relocation, rape, torture, and murder, in the course of constructing a pipeline in Burma.[70] Similarly, in March 2004, a US federal court ruled that two Chevron Texaco subsidiaries could be tried for the acts of their Nigeria-based subsidiary, due to the subsidiary's alleged complicity in human rights abuses committed by the Nigerian military.[71] These cases are just a few of a growing number of lawsuits being asserted for alleged misconduct by companies or their vendors at facilities around the world (including in the United States).

Other human rights and labor rights cases recently or presently before US courts include:

- A criminal action against Tyson Foods for alleged labor rights abuses in the United States;[72]
- A suit under the US Alien Tort Claims Act against Union Carbide for alleged violations of international law leading to the chemical explosion at one of its plants in Bhopal, India;[73]

---

[70]   *Doe, et al., v. Unocal Corporation, et al.*, 110 F.Supp.2d 1294 (C.D. Cal. 2000), aff'd in part, rev'd in part, 2002 WL 31063976 (9th Cir. 18 September 2002), rehearing en banc granted, vacated by 2003 WL 359787 (9th Cir. 14 February 2003).

[71]   *Bowoto, et al., v. Chevron Texaco Corp.*, No. C99-2506 (N.D. Cal. filed 27 May 1999); see also *Bowoto v. Chevron Texaco Corp.*, Order Denying Defendants' Motion for Summary Judgment on Phase I, Order No. C 99-2506 SI (23 March 2004).

[72]   *Trollinger v. Tyson Foods, Inc.*, 2004 WL 1207016 (6th Cir. 2004).

[73]   *Bano, et al. v. Union Carbide Corp.*, 273 F.3d 120 (2nd Cir. 2001).

- Class action suits alleging human rights violations by global brand name apparel producers in connection with production facilities in Saipan.[74]

In addition, the past few years have also seen an increasing number of lawsuits initiated outside the United States for alleged human rights, labor rights and environmental malfeasance by multinationals or their subsidiaries or affiliates.[75]

Regardless of whether the plaintiffs ultimately prevail, such cases result in immeasurable damage to the goodwill of the companies involved, as well as diverting financial and management resources. Although litigation cannot always be avoided, the enactment and enforcement of thorough and substantive codes of conduct can help companies identify and address potential human rights and labor rights issues in a proactive manner, and thereby reduce both the likelihood of something occurring that would give rise to legal exposure, and the potential scope of that exposure should something go wrong.

2. Stakeholder Challenges

As might be expected, the proliferation of codes and standards also creates some unique and vexing challenges for companies trying to build meaningful social and environmental protections into their global operations. Although these challenges do not militate against enactment of company codes, they do underscore the importance of companies recognizing that codes are merely means to an end, and do not represent the end itself. Meaningful CSR leadership by companies requires far more than the mere adoption of codes of conduct. Specifically, CSR activities are ultimately aimed at addressing and, if possible, optimizing a company's positive impacts and minimizing a company's negative impacts on its stakeholders. Without more, codes may not achieve these objectives. The discussion below focuses on some key stakeholders, and addresses whether codes do or can accomplish these objectives.

a. Vendor Employees

Although worker education is a critical component of effective codes, this seemingly straightforward element has led to some difficult challenges for multinational companies and their suppliers.[76] A common provision in most codes of conduct is a requirement that the codes be posted in the facilities in which products are being made, so that factory employees can readily see the code and understand their rights thereunder. While sound in theory, this step by itself has proven to be an ineffective means for informing workers of their rights. When codes first started becoming popular in the mid to late nineties, it was not

---

[74] *Doe v. The Gap Inc.*, No. 99-329 (C.D. Cal. filed 13 January 1999); *Union of Needletrades Industrial and Textile Employees v. The Gap*, No. 300474 (Cal. Sup. Ct. filed 23 September 1999); *Doe v. Advanced Textile Corp.*, 214 F.3d 1058 (9th Cir. 2000). For more information on the lawsuits and settlement, see http://www.globalexchange.org/campaigns/sweatshops/saipan/.

[75] *Lubbe v. Cape plc*, 4 All ER 268 (2000), 2 Lloyd's Rep 383 (2000); *Ngcobo v. Thor Chemicals Holdings Ltd.*, The Times 10 November 1995, CA 9 October 1995.

[76] Though focused on factory labor, this discussion has equal applicability to agricultural workers.

uncommon to find codes posted in English in facilities in which the English language was unintelligible. Companies, with the help of NGOs, quickly recognized that this was doing workers no good whatsoever. The solution was only marginally better – posting of codes in the native language of the workers. This approach had the benefit of practicality, since the native language was at least theoretically recognizable to the workers (at least in its spoken form). Unfortunately, many factory workers are illiterate and cannot read the posted codes.

Add to this the fact that most such facilities are, in fact, producing goods for more than one customer. What this means is that each company for whom production is being undertaken will require that a copy of its code be posted in a conspicuous location at each facility. Typically there is a wall in a fairly prominent spot at the facility (often near where the workers enter and exit the facility at the beginning and end of their shifts), which is literally covered with the codes of the many companies for whom the factory is producing goods. Compliance monitors jokingly refer to such posted codes as 'wallpaper'.

In practical terms, even when the workers can understand the individual codes, it is extremely difficult to make sense of the multitude of codes posted on the wall, most of which are similar but few of which are identical. If one goal of codes is to enable workers to understand their rights, the proliferation of codes and the mechanisms most companies employ to convey their contents to workers are not well designed, at least standing alone, to achieve that end.[77]

b. Factory Management and Owners

The multiplicity of codes and code expectations creates similar challenges for factory management – even those managers with a sincere desire to meet their customers' code expectations. For while factories typically employ a single group of workers, many produce goods for an array of different customers, each of whom has prescribed subtly (or not-so-subtly) different expectations for their production facilities. One company's code might permit voluntary overtime, so long as workers do not work more than 72 hours per week. Another company's code might impose an absolute prohibition on workers working more than 60 hours per week. If production is taking place for both companies at the same time – often the rule rather than the exception – conflicts such as this pose tremendous challenges for factory management.

On top of this, companies regularly send monitors into facilities to monitor compliance with their codes of conduct, which results at times in a steady and unbroken parade of auditors passing through vendor facilities, auditing against similar yet rarely-identical standards, and demanding the time and attention of factory management. The degree of disruption and dislocation associated with these activities can be significant, and contributes to resistance by factory management of the CSR initiatives of their customers.

---

[77] Some companies have laudable worker education programs. Timberland, for example, has worked with Verité, an independent, non-profit social auditing and research organization, to provide workers with opportunities to learn about their basic labor rights, including the Timberland Code of Conduct, as well as computer skills, mathematics, remedial English, sewing, cooking, music, dance and interpersonal communication skills. Julia Lloyd, *China Life Skills Program Expanded*, Spring/Summer 2003, http://www.verite.org/news/frameset.htm.

c. NGOs and SRIs

Most NGOs and SRIs legitimately strive for continuous improvement in workplace conditions, but Western-based organizations are often unfamiliar with the particular circumstances that attain in production facilities in developing countries. Although consistency of approach is certainly in the interest of their constituencies, the differences among the many codes of conduct present an opportunity for NGOs and SRIs to drive movement towards greater and greater compliance expectations, even where those expectations might be unrealistic. In other words, they may recognize that on paper some companies impose higher standards of compliance than others, and might – often with imperfect understanding of the reasons behind these differences – use them to press for higher standards by those companies that have embraced what might be viewed as lesser standards – even if legitimate practical challenges inhibit the latter company's ability to meet these heightened expectations. The result is something that might be viewed as a code of conduct arms race towards increasingly lofty compliance expectations, even where those expectations might exceed a company's practical ability to accommodate them. As a consequence, companies might embrace code standards that they know they cannot yet achieve, if only to buy temporary peace from their stakeholders. This, in turn, can feed a broader skepticism and cynicism about the bona fides of a company's CSR efforts.[78]

d. Companies

As described above, numerous companies in many different industrial sectors have adopted a vast array of codes of conduct. The differences are a result of myriad factors, including the focus and interest of the board of directors, the corporation's history and culture, pressure from external groups or business partners, or developments within the industry. The approach to codes also depends on who within the company is involved in developing, implementing and monitoring compliance with the company's program. As the ILO reports:

> The near-universal inclusion of general counsel in the deliberations and drafting of US ethics codes suggests that many US companies believe their codes require the same careful drafting used in legal documents....

> In contrast to the US pattern, only 35 percent of the European companies consulted their general counsel when drafting their codes. They are more likely to discuss issues related to the code with employee representatives (55 percent). This procedure, meanwhile, is used by very few US companies (13 percent). Although the prevalence of codes among survey participants is lower in Europe than in the United States or Canada, there may be an effort among those companies that do have them to use ethics statements to develop uniform standards in harmony with European Union directives on employee rights and corporate social responsibility. European companies also used consultants more often when drafting their codes.

---

[78] A solution to this dilemma is the establishment by the company and its stakeholders of a meaningful and substantive program of engagement, so that challenges of this type can be reduced or eliminated.

Canadian companies were most likely to involve the CEO and senior executives from major departments, and least likely to involve employee representatives. Employee representatives did not participate in code deliberations with any of the responding companies.[79]

Although approaches to the creation and adoption of codes of conduct may differ, many companies face a series of similar challenges in trying to manage the issues presented by the multiplicity of codes and standards, and the multiplicity of stakeholders and business drivers. Simply defining what should go into a company's own code of conduct depends upon a clear understanding of the various pressure points throughout the supply, production, distribution, and sales chains. In addition, companies must be aware of the variety of voluntary initiatives discussed above – ranging from the UN Global Compact to the ILO principles to SA 8000 to the Global Sullivan Principles, and to many gradations of more focused or industry-specific standards as well – each of which is supported and advocated by different groups of company stakeholders, and many of which cannot simply be embraced by companies in toto.

For example, while the UN Global Compact is laudable at a macro level, many companies might be unwilling or unable as a practical matter to embrace every one of the ten principles enunciated therein. Some companies, for example, may be willing to respect freedom of association where permitted by law but cannot, as a practical matter and consistent with the expectations of some company stakeholders, 'uphold the freedom of association and the effective recognition of the right to collective bargaining' where such rights do not exist as a matter of law.

Other companies – including very socially responsible companies – may elect not to sign on to the Compact for fear that publicly joining the Compact might, ironically, make them a bigger and easier target for activists than would remaining on the sidelines. There is some sense in which the challenge that Nike faced (see footnote 24, *supra*) dramatically underscores this concern. On the other hand, a failure to join the Compact may itself have some stigmatizing effect with certain company stakeholders.

E.   STANDARDIZATION AND HARMONIZATION

Despite the range of codes in existence today, some level of standardization among the categories of labor and human rights provisions is common. Given the solid foundation of the UDHR and the global acceptance of the ILO principles, most codes address some combination of the following issues: forced labor; child labor; wages, benefits, and terms of employment; hours of work; discrimination; harassment, abuse, and disciplinary action; freedom of association and collective bargaining; and health and safety.[80] According to the earlier-referenced World Bank study, 'the greatest point of conformity on every code of conduct

---

[79]   ILO. *Corporate Codes of Conduct and Labour Standards*. International Labour Organization, Bureau of Workers' Activities, Available at http://www.itcilo.it/actrav/actrav-english/telearn/global/ilo/code/main.htm.

[80]   Gare Smith & Dan Feldman, *Company Codes of Conduct and International Standards: An Analytical Comparison Part I of II*, World Bank, USA, 2004, 6–11.

examined was the prohibition against the use of forced labor. Every firm and non-corporate code prohibited its use'.[81] The same prohibition is also found in codes addressing the agricultural sector, although less conformity on the issue is found among the extractive industries.[82] Another example of an emerging trend in many sectors is the establishment of a minimum working age for children. Depending on the sector, this may range from 14 or 15 (in the light manufacturing and apparel industries) to a general prohibition against hiring minors, as is common in the extractive industries.

As referenced earlier, among the more challenging issues companies are faced with in creating and assuring compliance with codes revolves around the related concepts of freedom of association and collective bargaining. While these rights are, at least in theory, globally accepted international norms (and therefore are expected by NGOs to be 'adopted' in company codes of conduct), there are many jurisdictions that either explicitly or implicitly forbid either. Many companies attempt to finesse this challenge by adopting code language that promises not to interfere with freedom of association and the right to collective bargaining where such rights exist. Other companies are beginning to develop more creative approaches to addressing this challenge. Reebok's code, for example, strives to 'ensure that workers are represented on safety committees, and they are allowed to elect worker representatives. Reebok also mandates a system for resolving workplace disputes'.[83] These standards are applied by Reebok regardless of whether local law permits freedom of association or collective bargaining rights.

In contrast to code provisions that derive from the UDHR and the ILO principles, code of conduct provisions regarding environmental performance and protection tend to be somewhat more variable, and differ depending on the affected industrial sectors. Notwithstanding this, it is not uncommon for companies either to rely primarily on a general policy statement regarding environmental protection in the their codes or to rely on environmental management systems based on the standards set out in the International Organization for Standardization's ISO 14000 certification program.[84]

F.   FUTURE OF CODES

Much dramatic and positive change has occurred in working conditions throughout global supply chain networks over the past decade, and many of these improvements can be attributed to the increased focus and attention brought about both through the variety of multilateral initiatives discussed earlier and through the adoption of codes of conduct by countless transnational businesses. But it must be recognized and remembered that codes of conduct are a means

---

[81]   *Id.* at 6.
[82]   Gare Smith & Dan Feldman. *Company Codes of Conduct and International Standards: An Analytical Comparison Part II of II.* World Bank, USA, 2004, 5.
[83]   *Id.* at 10. Reebok, *A Guide to the Implementation of the Reebok Human Rights Production Standards,* http://www.reebok.com/Static/global/initiatives/rights/pdf/ReebokHR_Guide.pdf.
[84]   See, e.g., New Balance Athletic Shoe, Inc. *Supplier Code of Conduct,* http://newbalance.com/loc/en/resources/PDFs/SupplierCodeofConduct.pdf'; International Organization for Standardization, *Environmental Management: The ISO Family of International Standards,* http://www.iso.ch/iso/en/prods-services/otherpubs/iso14000/index.html.

to an end. They are not the end in itself. Returning to first principles, the UDHR was adopted by the United Nations as a yardstick by which to measure the degree of respect for, and compliance with, international human rights standards. Global respect for, and protection of, human rights is, has been, and should be the desired end-state. Company codes and voluntary global principles evolved as a means of bridging the ever-widening gap between the aspirations of the UDHR and the post-Cold War explosion of the global economy. But the proliferation of such codes and principles in the past decade has perhaps distracted the participants in the dialogue, who seem at times to focus more attention on the tools for achieving these goals than on the goals themselves.

Codes are a necessary step in the gradual evolution towards the achievement by transnational supply chains of global human rights, labor rights, environmental, social, and ethical objectives. But the dialogue must continue to evolve beyond mere codes (and their equally limited counterpart, compliance monitoring) and focus more on systemic mechanisms for promoting these objectives.

Transnational companies must play an ever-increasing role in setting high expectations for their global vendor base and in working with that base to meet these objectives. Corporate stakeholders will put increasing pressures on transnationals to promote and achieve these goals, so corporations will have strong incentives to do so, or perhaps more accurately, strong disincentives to fail. Success, however, will depend upon the formation or strengthening of more strategic, long-term relationships between corporations (purchasers) and their vendors and suppliers – relationships in which the achievement of human rights, labor rights, and environmental goals redound to the mutual benefit of both, and in which each supplier recognizes that the 'social' and 'environmental' qualities of the products it makes are as central to its success as product quality itself – indeed is part and parcel of product quality.

Chapter 26

SOME LEGAL DIMENSIONS OF CORPORATE CODES OF CONDUCT

Claes Lundblad

A. INTRODUCTION

In the last decades of the 20th century companies gradually came to appreciate the need for ethical guidelines as an important tool for the conduct of their business. The notion of companies having a corporate social responsibility (CSR) gained ground. Arguably the adoption and implementation of a Code of Conduct has today become a *'standard operating procedure in global business operations'*[1]

The driving factors behind that development are several. One important background factor was no doubt the growing realization, based on the devastating experiences of the Second World War and the globalization of commerce in the post war era, that it is necessary for business to develop and maintain sustainable ethical standards. The idea that corporate entities can and should be bearers of moral obligations gradually evolved. Over time the notion that 'the business of business is business' became more controversial. At least large portions of the public in reasonably developed countries, have come to expect that companies should conduct their business so as to comply with ethical standards prevalent in the rest of society. Another factor contributing to the increased interest in human rights issues may be found in the rapid dissemination of information in an era of sophisticated and widely accessible information technology. As has been often pointed out, the financial might of large industrial concerns has increased tremendously in the last decades of the 20th century. In 1999 it was observed that out of the 100 largest economies in the world half were nations and the other half were companies. The role of the media in raising ethical issues in commercial life is apparent. In the 'old days' it was thought that the duty of corporate management was, almost exclusively, to look after the interests of the shareholders.

---

[1]   See Elliot J. Schrage: *Promoting International Worker Rights trough Private Voluntary Initiatives: Public Relations or Public Policy* (Report to the US Department of Trade, University of Iowa, January 2004) p. 3.

Ramon Mullerat (ed.), Corporate Social Responsibility: The Corporate Governance of the 21st Century, 385–399.
© 2005 *International Bar Association. Printed in the Netherlands.*

That view has been largely abandoned. Societies impose additional obligations on business enterprises. The public expects companies to behave in an ethically responsible way. Thus corporate management is more and more called upon to meet the ethical expectations of society at large. There is now a growing appreciation that, in addition to the interest of the shareholders to attain a profit on their investment, companies must also take into account the interests of other groups. These groups are often referred to as *stakeholders*. Whilst that concept, whose origins have been traced to the 1960s,[2] does not have a well defined meaning it is often said to include a variety of groups typically affected by the way companies conduct their businesses. Thus, into the stakeholder category fall shareholders, employees, customers, business partners, non-governmental organizations (NGOs) as well as the societies in which the company operates.[3]

The ethical statements that companies make have different objectives. They take many forms and they have many names *e.g. ethical guidelines, codes of ethics, mission statements, corporate credos or codes of conduct.*[4] As will be discussed below it is as yet difficult to discern a clear pattern as to the contents of ethical statements. A uniform standard is yet to be achieved. However, as will also be addressed, some elements are common. I will in this paper use the name *Code of Conduct* to cover all the different forms of corporate ethical statements.

This paper will discuss some legal dimensions of Codes of Conduct. For that discussion it is appropriate to make two initial observations.

A discussion of legal issues in relation to Codes of Conduct (or for that matter any other expression of will) is best conducted in relation to one or more defined legal systems, be it national law or international law at large. A general discussion of legal issues without such link easily becomes overly abstract. Yet this paper largely falls into that category. The nature of the subject is such that a discussion of the legal aspects of Codes of Conduct, which are typically adapted to the businesses of multinational enterprises, will have to take into account the laws of several jurisdictions. I do not purport to cover a large number of different legal systems. Nor will I discuss international law in any detail. My intent is rather to point to some possible problem areas without the ambition of providing clear solutions. The answers to the questions raised will have to be sought to some (minor) extent in international law but, more importantly, in the national systems wherein the companies conduct their business.

It may be thought that a discussion of legal issues in relation to ethically based expressions of corporate good will is entirely misplaced. Codes of Conduct are by definition different from formal legal rules. Their very *raison d'être*, it may be argued, is that through their flexible, vague, non-binding and voluntary nature they complement the strictly binding normative system called law. That is no doubt correct. However, it is nonetheless apparent that ethical statements may have legal consequences at several levels. Such effects may occur irrespective of

2   See Lynn Sharp Paine: *Value Shift*, McGraw Hill, New York, N.Y. 2003 ('Paine').
3   An example of a wide definition is contained in Article 22 of the UN Norms on the Responsibilities of Transnational Corporations and Other Business Enterprises with Regard to Human Rights (UN Doc E/CN.H/Sub 2/2003/38/Rev., 2 (2003) (the 'Draft UN Norms').
4   For a study of the subject see Patrick E. Murphy: *Eighty Exemplary Ethics Statements*. University of Notre Dame Press, Notre Dame, Indiana, 1998.

whether they were intended or not. The basic message of this paper is to point to the importance of careful reflection of what should go into the Code of Conduct and what should not. In that context the possible legal effects of Codes of Conduct should be considered.

B.   CODES OF CONDUCT – WHAT ARE THEY?

For the following discussion on legal issues it may be convenient briefly to reiterate some typical features of Codes of Conduct.

The mushrooming prevalence of Codes of Conduct has been referred to above. Very few large multinational enterprises would today lack a Code of Conduct. The corporate scandals of the early years of this century and the resulting legislative measures have undoubtedly played an important role in this development.[5]

1.   A Definition

One of the most comprehensive studies on the subject was published by the OECD in 2001, *Corporate Responsibility: Private Initiatives and Public Goals (OECD 2001)*.[6] In that study the OECD defines a Code of Conduct as

'commitments voluntarily made by companies, associations or other entities, which put forward standards and principles for the conduct of business activities in the marketplace'.

According to the OECD, the definition so drafted includes self-imposed obligations and negotiated instruments. But it does not cover rules applicable to corporate governance. The reason for that is no doubt that the corporate governance area primarily deals with the *internal* relations between those directly interested in the company, viz. its shareholders, management, board and employees.

A definition is of course designed so as to suit the needs of its originator. The question is whether the definition is suitable from the point of view of fruitful analysis. It is submitted that for purposes of discussing of the legal dimensions of ethical statements corporate governance may be highly relevant, especially since it has been the focus of the debate over responsible corporate conduct in the last few years. Important legislative measures adopted in the post-Enron era at what must be unprecedented speed concern primarily the internal corporate governance issues. Moreover, the traditional Codes of Conduct encompassed by the OECD definition often contain provisions focusing on the shareholders' legitimate interest in receiving a reasonable profit on their investment. Thus the borderline between traditional CSR issues and traditional governance issues is not clear cut. This paper will to some extent discuss the legal issues on the basis of

---

5   A background description of this development may be found in Paine: pp. 1–8.
6   This paper draws substantially on the factual findings of that report (the 'OECD Report').

Codes of Conduct in that broader perspective. It follows that the limiting words in the OECD definition '... *in the marketplace* ...' should be left out.[7]

2.   The Originators

As appears from the OECD definition, the issuers of Codes of Conduct may be individual companies. In fact Codes of Conduct of that type appear to be the most common kind. Other important issuers are industry organizations, partnerships of stakeholders (mostly NGOs and trade unions) and intergovernmental organizations.[8] Model codes originating from intergovernmental organizations are becoming increasingly important. A prominent example is the *OECD Guidelines for Multinational Enterprises* revised in 2000 and the currently much debated *draft UN Norms* adopted by a sub-committee of the UN Commission on Human Rights in 2003.

3.   The Contents and the Addressees

Codes of Conduct issued by companies do not follow a particular pattern. They take many forms. Unsurprisingly there is no one-size-fits-all. There is great diversity based on the size of the company, its geographical location(s) and its commercial focus. Some codes are single issue instruments whereas others cover a wide range of issues. The language used is sometimes precise and commitment-like. In many other cases the language used is vague and rather sweeping. Some codes contain specific rules on implementation, monitoring, reporting and sanctions. More often these aspects, or some of them, are not dealt with at all or else dealt with in a non-committing manner. Also the cultural background of the originator plays a role in the selection of most important issues.

Main areas typically covered by Codes of Conduct are labour relations, environmental protection and – especially for European companies – protection of human rights in the broader sense. Other frequent main areas are consumer protection, anti-corruption, competition and information disclosure. These areas in turn are often broken down in sub-areas. This appears to be particularly common in the two most important main areas, labour relations and environment.

---

[7]   In this context it is worth noting that the definition laid down in the US Sarbanes-Oxley Act of 2002. Under Section 406 of that act a 'Code of Ethics' is defined as

such standards as are reasonably necessary to promote
  1. honest and ethical conduct, including the ethical handling of actual or apparent conflicts of interest between personal and professional relationships
  2. full, fair, accurate, timely and understandable disclosure in the periodic reports required to be filed by the issuer
  3. compliance with applicable governmental rules and regulations

It would appear that this language probably does not cover CSR issues but falls squarely into the corporate governance area.

[8]   In the OECD Report 246 Codes of Conduct were studied for structure and content. Out of these 48% were codes issued by companies, 37% by business organizations, 13% by 'partnerships of stakeholders' and 2% by inter-governmental organizations.

There are five principal audiences towards whom the corporate commitments are directed in the typical Code of Conduct: the employees, the customers, the business partners, the public and the national governments. Some codes, as mentioned, also address commitments to shareholders, and a few even discuss competition issues.

4. Codes as Voluntary Commitments

Under the OECD definition Codes are characterized by the fact that they are voluntary or self-imposed. Usually this results from the fact that the company itself chooses to issue a set of rules. No doubt corporate leaders of many companies take the trouble of adopting and implementing ethical guidelines because they believe that by so doing they promote the over all interests of their company. In some cases, however, it may be questioned how voluntary the measure is. The adoption of a Code of Conduct sometimes results from outside pressure. One source of such pressure is governments. Companies may be forced to respond to governmental pressure by adopting ethical guidelines in an attempt to deflect or soften the threat of legislation. Other Codes of Conduct result from agreements made with bodies such as trade unions or market places where the company's shares are traded. The voluntary character of such instruments may of course be called into question. As will appear from the discussion below the context of the ethical commitments may be relevant in assessing the legal aspects thereof.

C. DO CODES OF CONDUCT HAVE LEGAL DIMENSIONS?

The brief answer to the question is clearly in the affirmative. In several ways. Some of these dimensions will be discussed in the following. Before doing so, however, it is pertinent to point out that, of course, Codes of Conduct are only one way in which ethical issues are becoming relevant to corporate conduct. As the development of the last few decades has demonstrated, several tools are gradually evolving as a legal means of enforcing human rights and other 'ethical' issues. Among these are the emerging rights of action under different national laws. Such actions do not seem to have been based on Codes of Conduct but rather on national laws with extra-territorial application. As examples of this may be mentioned the very controversial attempts made in recent years to apply the US Alien Torts Statute of 1789. That statute has in been invoked in a number of lawsuits before the US Courts against companies for alleged violations of human rights outside the United States. Other examples may be found in national statutes in Belgium and France. It appears, however, that Belgium is now in the process of limiting the right to restrict the hitherto universal competence of the Belgian Courts to plaintiffs of Belgian nationality or residence.

The increasing interest in human rights issues has resulted in interest also being directed to Codes of Conduct as a possible basis for action against companies.

For purposes of analysing the legal relevance of ethical statements it is worthwhile to distinguish Codes of Conduct by their source of origin as different issuers typically have different objectives. It is unsurprising that ethically coloured guidelines issued by stakeholder groups and, even more so, by inter-governmental bodies often have a more far reaching and 'binding' appearance than do self imposed standards issued by the companies themselves or by their organizations. In the following, Codes of Conduct issued by companies will be discussed. In addition, some problems in relation to the important OECD Guidelines will also be dealt with.

D.   CODES OF CONDUCT ISSUED BY COMPANIES

It can be safely assumed that the typical corporate originator of a Code of Conduct does not intend to incur legally binding obligations as a result thereof. The intent to be bound is usually a decisive factor when Courts or other bodies administering justice are asked to determine legal issues relative to different forms of expression of will. Yet legal relevance may be attributed to Codes of Conduct notwithstanding lack of such intent. These may be indirect or they may be direct. I will start with the indirect aspect because of its more general nature.

1.   General Relevance

a.   Codes of Conduct as a Complement to the Law

There are many reasons why companies may wish to raise (or be seen to raise) their ethical standards. Some sceptics suggest that corporate Codes of Conduct are rarely meant to bring about actual change in the way companies do business. The purpose, it is suggested, is quite different. Thus companies are sometimes suspected of using such instruments as public relations ploys intended to patch up a tainted reputation or to create an impression of high ethical standards. Corporate management is said to be interested only in paying lip service to eth-ical behaviour, which for non-commercial reasons has become fashionable. In the real world, so the argument goes, the adoption of a code does little to affect actual behaviour.

It must be assumed that there are several companies whose published ethical standards are there to dress up windows with attractive curtains hiding squalid interiors. Yet many companies have a very different attitude. They truly believe that ethical behaviour pays in more than one way.[9] One is the purely financial side.[10] Another is the management of legal risk.

Multinational companies are supposed to comply with the laws of several sys-tems, national and international. Different rules usually apply in the different jurisdictions where the company conducts its business. Companies, some say, are

---

[9]   For a thorough discussion of the subject see Paine in Chapter 2.

[10]   The UK Institute of Business Ethics found (as reported at www.ibe.org.uk) that there is strong evidence that large UK companies who have adopted a code of ethics financially outperform those companies who say that they do not have a code. This, it is suggested, confirms prior stud-ies made in the US.

also subject to international law requirements.[11] The legal systems to which companies are subject are invariably more or less patchy. They do not explicitly set forth *all* the rules that the company has to observe. To ensure compliance with the law companies are often well advised to create a system of ethical guidelines, which, if transformed into actual behaviour, reduce the risk of violation of the law. The Code of Conduct can serve as an important complement to the legal rules. The risk of legal action against the company can thereby be reduced both in the criminal field and in the civil field.

A common Code of Conduct rule is that the employees of the company have a duty to follow the law. It may be considered superfluous to include in ethical guidelines a rule, which applies, by definition. It should be pointed out that in some cultures the law is not seen as the norm to be followed but rather the norm which, if considered to be inconvenient, should be appropriately circumvented. In such cultures a statement of 'the obvious' may serve a purpose. That view may be relevant in respect of legal rules, which carry a sanction if not complied with. But some legal rules are not of that nature. Some do not stipulate any sanction for the transgressor. To increase the likelihood of compliance also with that kind of legal rules an ethical standard of this type may be relevant. Moreover, if the Code of Conduct gains contractual relevance the commitment to comply with the law becomes a contractual duty carrying sanctions under civil law in addition to any criminal law sanctions. The full legal effects of a compliance-with-law-undertaking in a Code of Conduct to comply with the law is yet unclear and remains to be explored.

Reduction of legal risk is an important task for companies. Some commercial risk can be covered by insurance. Some legal risk cannot or only at an exorbitant price. A Code of Conduct properly designed, monitored and sanctioned can serve to reduce legal risk.

---

[11] The extent to which corporate entities may be subjects of rights and obligations under international law is highly controversial. The traditional view is that international law is a concern only for states. The principal purpose of international law is to regulate state to state relations. Since the last world war, however, the notion has evolved that individuals as well as companies do have rights and obligations under international law. The responsibility of individuals under international *criminal law* is well known. In addition illustrative examples of how *civil rights* are bestowed on companies and on individuals are the African Charter on Human and People's Rights (1981), the American Convention on Human Rights (1969) and the European Convention for the Protection of Human Rights and Fundamental Freedoms (1950). Other examples are the right of private investors to bring action against states under the World Bank sponsored Washington Convention on the Settlements of Investment disputes between States and Nationals of Other States (1965) as well as under the investment protection provisions and dispute resolution mechanisms contained in the more than 2000 bilateral and multilateral investment treaties now in existence.

The extent to which companies also have *obligations* under international law is much more uncertain. In current international law there seems to be very scant support for such a proposition (For a different view see, for example, a paper published in 2002 by the International Council on Human Rights Policy: *Beyond Voluntarism, Human rights and the developing international legal obligations of companies.*) In this context it is worth noting that the Draft UN Norms argue that business enterprises are 'obligated to respect generally recognized responsibilities and norms contained in United Nations Treaties and other international instruments ...' The draft also seeks to impose (in Article 18) a far reaching obligation for companies to pay 'prompt, effective and adequate reparation to 'those persons, entities and communities that have been adversely affected by [violations of the norms]. The authors of the Draft UN Norms appear to be seeking to create an international instrument which substantially differs from the current position under international law.

b.   Codes of Conduct Encouraged by Law

In the wake of the corporate scandals of the last few years' legislators have gradually come to realize that law enforcement may be greatly enhanced through the existence and implementation of Codes of Conduct. A good example is the US Sarbanes-Oxley Act of 2002. That statute is generally designed to enhance corporate governance in companies under the supervision of the Securities and Exchange Commission. The law imposes upon the leading officers of such companies a duty to disclose the existence of a Code of Conduct (or in the language of the act a 'Code of Ethics') applicable to certain leading officers. If not, the company is required to explain why. In addition, changes in or exceptions to the code must be disclosed. The 'comply or explain' technique chosen by the US legislator is an interesting example of how soft rules of ethics in effect become very similar to 'hard' legal rules.[12] It may be assumed that the method of implementation embodied in Sarbanes-Oxley will continue to serve as a pattern for rule makers.

Another example of public promotion of Codes of Conduct may be found in the US Federal Sentencing Guidelines. Under these principles the existence of a Code of Conduct may be taken into account when the Courts determine the severity of punishment for certain corporate crimes.

c.   Contractual commitment to Codes of Conduct Required by Regulators

Another method for imposing upon companies' standards that are not required by law is for regulatory bodies to require companies to commit to such standards by contract. An example of this is the imposition of corporate governance rules under listing contracts, viz. contracts between a market place (typically a stock exchange) and the individual company desiring to have its shares listed in that market. The requirement may take the form of a minimum model code. A case in point is a recent proposal for Codes of Conduct to be adopted by the Stockholm Stock Exchange.[13] As a result of that proposal it is not unlikely that publicly traded companies must, by way of a contractual commitment, adopt a Code of Conduct with specific features.

2.   Specific Relevance

The following sections discuss briefly some situations wherein the contents of Codes of Conduct may become relevant as legal obligations of the issuing company.

---

[12]   The technique was not invented by the US legislator. It has older origins and has been used at least over the last decade in a number of corporate governance codes.

[13]   The Committee entrusted with this task was appointed by the Swedish Government in the wake of perceived corporate governance aberrations among companies publicly traded on the Stockholm Stock Exchange. The Committee submitted a Draft Standard Code of Conduct in April 2004. The draft model code focuses on corporate governance issues. The draft, however, requires companies also to adopt a Code of Conduct addressing CSR-issues at large. It is proposed that the Standard Code be incorporated into the Listing Contract of the Swedish Stock Exchange.

a. *Contractual relevance of Codes of Conduct*

(i) *Labour Contracts*

Codes of Conduct often impose upon the employees of the issuing company a duty to observe the guidelines laid down in the code. Often the wording is vague and rather aspirational. In other instances the language is more stringent and clearly intended to bring obligations upon the employees. This is particularly so when the Code of Conduct itself contains sanctions which may be imposed by the company on its employees in cases of non-observance of the code. The nature of those sanctions vary. Sometimes penalties in the form of monetary sanctions against the employee are provided for. More often the sanction issue is left open for the company to decide on a case-by-case basis.

How then is it that the Code of Conduct can legally be made part of the individual employment contract? It is useful to consider that aspect from the point of view of the *obligations* thereby imposed by the company on the individual employee. A different aspect is whether the Code of Conduct may also create *rights* for the employee in relation to his employer.

Sometimes the obligations laid down in the Code of Conduct are such that the code does not add anything new. The same obligations follow already from the general duties of any employee. This of course is the case where the behaviour is directly prohibited/prescribed by the national law governing the employment contract. It may also follow from the general civil law duties of the employee towards his employer, e.g. from the duty of loyalty to which an employee is subject under many national laws. Obligations contained in a Code of Conduct, which do not follow from the general statutory duties or from the general principles applying to the employment contract, can become part of the individual employment contract in more than one way. One possibility is that the individual employment contract makes a direct reference to the Code of Conduct thereby incorporating the code as part of the contract. Another possibility is that the Code of Conduct has been negotiated between the company and the relevant trade unions thereby in effect giving the Code of Conduct the status of a collective agreement, which under national law usually is binding upon the individual employee without direct incorporation into his employment contract. In instances where the Code of Conduct has not been so dealt with it may be difficult for the employer to impose Code of Conduct duties on the employees. It is doubtful whether any national law stipulates that the guidelines laid down in a Code of Conduct are legally binding on the individual employee merely because the company has chosen to adopt a Code of Conduct.

Turning next to the other facet: Does the Code of Conduct create *rights* for the employee to enforce against his employer in case of transgression by the company? The picture is not entirely clear. It is not inconceivable that an employee might contend e.g. that the existence and content of a Code of Conduct adopted by his employer and publicly described was in fact an important basis for him to seek employment with that particular employer. The employee may contend that the Code of Conduct has become a part of his employment contract and that if the employer then violates the principles to which he has proclaimed to adhere an issue may arise as to whether or not the employer has also violated the employment contract. It appears that issues of that kind have arisen before the

US Courts. It is as yet unclear to what extent those actions have attained their purpose. It would appear not to be inconceivable that such an action may succeed.

(ii)   External Contracts

It is not unusual that Codes of Conduct contain language to the effect that external parties with whom the company does business must ensure that the company will respect its principles laid down in the code. Sometimes the code stipulates that the company will incorporate all or part of the Code of Conduct into the external contracts, made by the company. In other instances the company makes external representations to the effect that third parties should grant the company preferential treatment precisely because the company has undertaken to observe certain ethically coloured business principles. An example of this is companies claiming to have made ethical abstentions from certain types of business thereby becoming eligible for ethical investment fund money or listing on certain trading lists. The range within which a Code of Conduct may come into play is broad. Some of these will be discussed here.

(a) *Contracts with business partners in the supply chain.*   Some Codes of Conduct clearly have the objective to influence the behaviour of their trading partners in the supply chain. This applies particularly to partners up the chain. Suppliers of goods and services are often required to make specific commitments in respect of labour relations, the environment and human rights. Codes of Conduct frequently stipulate that failure by the supplier to observe such rules may subject him to different types of sanctions, ultimately the discontinuation of business relations. Some Codes of Conduct provide that, failing corrective action, the company will terminate also existing supply contracts.

Again the question of the legal relevance of conduct rules such as those mentioned above is somewhat unclear. It is submitted that the mere inclusion of a provision of that kind in a Code of Conduct will not ordinarily suffice to make it legally effective. It appears unlikely that Courts will consider that extra-contractual provisions, such as those included in a Code of Conduct, by themselves constitute a sufficient basis for a purchaser to impose sanctions against his supplier because the supplier has violated principles contained in the Code of Conduct of the purchaser. For that to happen the conduct of the supplier would materially have to violate the terms of the individual supply contract (or applicable national or international criminal law). The purchaser's Code of Conduct will therefore become legally relevant only if considered to be incorporated in the commercial contract. For such incorporation to occur it is not sufficient for the purchasing company to make public that it has adopted a Code of Conduct. The Code of Conduct would have to be made public so that it constitutes an equivalent of a general condition of trade. (In this context it is interesting to note that the Draft UN Norms stipulate that companies are to make the norms part of their external business contracts.) It is yet to be seen whether and in what circumstances the Courts will be sympathetic to a suggestion that – without direct or indirect incorporation - the terms of a Code of Conduct should be considered applicable to the individual business contract. If indeed that route is taken it is not far fetched to assume that, in the event of the company itself deviating from it own code, also the supplier may be entitled to invoke the Code of Conduct against the company. It is not inconceivable that a supplier may argue that, when concluding the business contract, he knew that his customer had adopted a certain Code of Conduct and that therefore he assumed that he was doing business with someone anxious to maintain high ethical standards. If that assumption turns out to be wrong, the supplier might argue that he is entitled to terminate his contract or else impose contractual sanctions.[14] As will be apparent, the idea of a Code of Conduct with ethically based principles often phrased in aspirational language being mixed into commercial contracts (whose provisions are especially designed to permit the test of legal analysis) is prone to create contractual havoc. Rights and obligations ambiguously stated are very likely to form the basis of legal conflict in contractual relations.

(b) Contracts with investors and financial markets. From a modest start it appears that a growing amount of investors' money is going to companies professing to adhere to certain ethical standards or business principles. Ethical investment funds undertake, in relation to their investors, not to invest in certain types of companies, for instance those dealing with merchandise considered to be questionable from an ethical point of view. Weapons, tobacco and alcohol are well known examples. In other instances ethical funds shun investment in companies whose production methods are considered unacceptable, e.g. because the production chain is seen to include child labour or otherwise sub-standard working conditions. Some indexes specialize in shares of companies, which fulfil certain ethical minimum standards. Examples of this are the FTSE4Good list and the Dow Jones Sustainability Index. Assume then that a company desires to attract ethical investment money by issuing a Code of Conduct designed to convey the message that the company adheres to high ethical standards and hence qualifies for that kind of funding. Assume further that, having received such funding, the company substantially fails to live up to those principles. Can the deviation from the Code of Conduct be used by investors as a basis, for instance, for a compensation claim or other legally enforceable sanction? To the extent that the behaviour of the company also violates a contractual undertaking (for instance under a listing contract with a particular market place) the possibility of legal sanction is apparent (e.g. in the form of delisting at the initiative of the relevant stock exchange). The situation is more complex outside the classical contractual area. If as a result of the company's deviation from its proclaimed ethical principles a corporate scandal results and if that scandal substantially reduces the market price at which the shares in the company are traded a disgruntled investor might in some jurisdictions have a basis for a claim against the company to compensate him for his loss. It appears not to be at all inconceivable that for instance such a company may be held liable to its shareholders for being in breach of a covenant made in relation to its potential investors as a means to attract new money. To determine the extent of the company's commitment the contents of the Code of Conduct may be highly relevant.

---

[14] A purchaser may have perfectly valid commercial reasons for that view. There are many examples of companies having incurred substantial damage (economic and non-economic) as a result of media focus on real or perceived human rights violations having occurred in the supply chain of the company. The mere suggestion that goods were produced in sweat shops, or by the use of forced labour or child labour can cause very severe damage. As is well known the sales of goods legislation typically does not address that type of 'defect' in the supply but focuses rather on the quality of the goods, the time of delivery etc.

Codes of Conduct, dealing with corporate governance issues are becoming increasingly important. Some such codes deal exclusively with corporate governance. Others focus primarily on classical CSR issues but also address some corporate governance issues. A third category deals equally with both corporate governance issues and CSR-issues. As regards Codes of Conduct dealing with corporate governance issues the rules of conduct can be made legally binding in several ways. One possibility is direct legislation requiring the company to adopt a minimum model code and to comply with it. Another possibility is, as above indicated, the adoption and compliance with a model code to be included as part of a listing contract between the company and a market place at which the shares in the company are publicly traded.

3.   Marketing Relevance

A Code of Conduct may be used by a company as a marketing tool for its products. High ethical principles may, particularly in respect of consumer goods retailing, be a powerful argument to convince the consumer to select a certain product. The assertion that a supplier uses only environmentally friendly production methods of foodstuffs or washing agents is an example of this. Claims that third world textile production does not involve child labour or sweat shops are common. The list can be made long. What then if it appears that the claim to ethical production turns out to be wrong and contrary to the picture conveyed by the published Code of Conduct of the producer. Does that mean that the producer is misleading the market by making false statements about his business methods? And if so can the misleading statements be attacked by the consumer by legal means, e.g. by applying to the court for an order prohibiting the practise? This situation is similar that which happened in the well known case *Kasky v Nike*. That case, amicably settled before final resolution, did not result in a clear answer. The US Supreme Court, before which the case was eventually brought, did not decide whether CSR claims made by Nike could form a basis for a false marketing claim against it. (In the lower courts the case had turned on whether or not the statements made by Nike were protected under the freedom of speech rules of the US Constitution.) But the Kasky case is a good illustration of how a Code of Conduct may well gain legal relevance beyond what was originally conceived by the issuing company. It is to be expected that further attempts in that direction will be made by individual consumers, consumer groups or by public agencies for consumer protection. In jurisdictions allowing class actions in some form the risk should be apparent.[15]

4.   Standards of Care

It is not uncommon for Codes of Conduct to contain specific statements on various aspects of the production process. One such aspect is safety. It may be safety

---

[15]   Class actions or, as they are sometimes called, 'group actions' appear to be gaining increased popularity also outside the United States. One example of this is Sweden where, under recently enacted legislation, a group action may be brought not only by a group of consumers but also by private organizations set up to advance consumer interests or by public agencies entrusted with consumer protection.

for workers engaged in the production process. It may also be safety for the consumer. If for such company it should happen that the production process or the products should cause damage the issue typically arises as to whether or not the company has observed a proper standard of care. Ordinarily the standard of care is objective. The question arises, however, whether a company, that has made behavioural statements in a Code of Conduct, should be required to live up to a standard of care consistent with those statements even if they imply a standard that is higher than the objective standard. It is not inconceivable that the Courts (or for that matter arbitral tribunals in case of contractual disputes) would require such a higher standard from someone professing to observe such a standard, especially if it is thought that the higher standard was proclaimed in order for the company to obtain commercial benefits.[16]

5. Instructions to Corporate Organs

A different aspect of a Code of Conduct is to consider whether, after adoption by the appropriate company organs, the guidelines embodied therein also constitute an instruction binding upon the management in the sense that legal sanctions can be extracted e.g. from a Managing Director who acts in contravention of the code and who thereby causes economic damage to the company. The answer to that issue appears to be largely unsettled so far as the CSR motivated instructions are concerned. The corporate governance issues are different. The rules on that subject have often an appearance of direct instructions to company organs as to how they should deal with certain internal issues, e.g. remuneration programs to managers, the nomination process for certain officers of the company, or the contents of the periodic accounts. In many cases there can be little doubt that the officers concerned are duty bound to follow such instructions. It may well be that the same principle is applied to CSR-programs.

E. MODEL CODES ORIGINATING FROM INTERGOVERNMENTAL ORGANIZATIONS – THE OECD EXAMPLE

Model Codes of Conduct have in some cases been generated by intergovernmental organizations. Arguably the most advanced model to date is that laid down in *OECD Guidelines*. As is well known the code constituted by those guidelines is a part of a wider set of rules, *The OECD Declaration on International Investment and Multinational Enterprises*. Given the importance of the OECD Guidelines some legal aspects of those rules will be addressed below.

---

[16] A somewhat odd example of how different standards may be applied to the ethically conscious compared to those more indifferent to the issues is the following. In the last few years a number of Swedish companies have chosen to participate in the Global Compact project launched by the Secretary General of the UN, Mr Kofi Annan, in 1999 and supported by several governments. Some of these companies have declared their support *inter alia* by statements in their Codes of Conduct. In 2004 a Swedish Public Agencies (The Equal Opportunities Ombudsman and the Ombudsman for ethnical discrimination) decided to order those companies to make a special report on compliance with Swedish Law on non-discrimination.

It is often pointed out the OECD Guidelines are voluntary by their very nature. Companies are encouraged voluntarily to adhere to those rules. Some do, some do not. There are no formal legal sanctions, which can be extracted from those companies who, in spite of having proclaimed their commitments to the guidelines, do not comply with the rules. Such is the public picture. In reality the situation is somewhat different.

In view of the standing of the OECD and its guidelines it would be very precarious for serious multinationals to be seen as having violated the OECD Guidelines. The fact that compliance with the guidelines cannot be enforced in a court of law does not mean that they are without sanction. For most major companies the media picture of their business is vital for their long-term survival. It is these days trivial to point out that adverse publicity may erode the company's tangible and intangible assets in a very short time. To their 'stakeholders' Arthur Andersen and Enron are painful examples of this. Hence, a serious allegation that a multinational company violates human rights anywhere in the world is something companies do not take lightly. The non-regulated sanctions imposed by the Court of Public Opinion can be infinitely more costly, also in economic terms, than any compensatory judgment given by a Court of law applying well established principles of the law of damages after a controlled procedure with due process safeguards.

Under the OECD system a National Contact Point ('NCP') is to be set up by each member state government. The NCP may be an individual or an organ of the state. If a complaint is made against a company for guideline violation it is the task of the NCP to determine whether or not to open a case. If the NCP so decides 'proceedings' will start. The purpose of that exercise is to achieve a settlement between the complainant and the company. If that turns out not to be possible the NCP may issue a statement in respect of the complaint. Such a statement by the NCP may contain criticism of the company concerned e.g. for human rights violations.

The system as designed by the OECD Guidelines raises a number of important issues both in respect of procedure and substantive content.

The procedural side is this.

In view of the potential adverse impact of a statement made by a NCP accusing a company of serious violation of the OECD Guidelines it would appear that the guidelines should also embody that some basic principles as to how the procedure before the NCP should be conducted. A host of questions arises. Is it necessary that the complainant have an identifiable substantive interest in the matter for the NCP to open a case? Is the company entitled to be heard and answer serious allegations made against it? Are the complainant and the company allowed to invoke evidence in support of their respective positions as to the facts? Is oral argument permissible? What settlements should the NCP strive for? And what if more than one complainant appears and those complainants have different and conflicting views as to the relevant facts or as to the contents of a desirable settlement with the company? The OECD Guidelines provide no answer to these (and other) fundamental issues. It is for the NCP to take a decision on those matters. Although the OECD through a joint body, MIME, apparently strives for a common approach to basic principles it is unclear what the result thereof will be. Substantial experience is as yet lacking. The NCPs are bodies set up by member governments. It follows that in carrying out their functions they act as administrators of public power the exercise of which may have a very substantial impact on private economic interests. In the light thereof it is troubling that the OECD Guidelines do not address these important issues in sufficient detail.

As the analysis shows also the implementation of 'voluntary' guidelines may have dramatic effects for the individual. It is hardly acceptable that the existing lacunae in the rules are left open. It is submitted that in civilized society the exercise of public power must be conducted in forms satisfying basic 'due process' principles. The desire not to adopt a legalistic approach to guideline implementation may result in procedures that are unacceptable to the enterprises whose voluntary commitment to the guidelines is the very core of the system. To avoid that outcome, some measure of 'legalism' – paradoxically a somewhat suspect concept in this context – needs to be introduced into the OECD system. At the very lease, notions of fundamental fairness and due process should be scrupulously observed.

F.   CONCLUDING REMARKS

The enormous increase in the number of Codes of Conduct observed in recent years and the public focus on such instruments suggests that we shall sooner rather than later see the evolution of more standardized Codes of Conduct, at least to the extent that certain minimum criteria will evolve. That is already happening on the corporate governance side. On the CSR side the picture is more diverse. The reason for the more advanced state of uniformity for corporate governance rules is most probably that the corporate scandals of recent years have predominantly focused on such issues. The result has been legislative and other measures towards model rules. The emergence of the Sarbanes–Oxley Act and the regulatory measures undertaken by the Securities and Exchange Commission in relation to the act has no doubt played an important role. If – or rather when – similar incidents occur on the CSR side it may well be that more elaborate minimum rules also in that area will evolve. It is not inconceivable that the next major ethical corporate scandal will appear on the CSR side. It is to be expected that over time the voluntary commitments made by companies in respect of ethical behaviour may meet sanctions of a legal nature. This paper has pointed in some directions. There are no doubt others. The inference to be drawn is that, on the one hand companies need to adopt and implement sensible ethical guidelines on CSR issues but that, in so doing, they should also ensure that what started as voluntary commitments are not permitted to turn into an unexpected liability nightmare. To avoid that situation companies need to take an active and constructive approach to CSR issues. Such a stance is likely to be an effective strategy to avoid the very substantial uncertainties of instruments such as the Draft UN Norms and other international instruments of similar nature.

PART VII

LAWYERS AND CORPORATE
SOCIAL RESPONSIBILITY

Chapter 27

SOCIAL RESPONSIBILITY AND THE LAWYER IN THE 21ST CENTURY

*Jerome J. Shestack**

To discuss social responsibility and 'the lawyer' in the 21st Century is a daunting endeavor. What is commonly understood is that lawyers serve clients. But there is no universal consensus on such aspects as public service, ethical standards, educational requirements, philosophies or influence.

The phrase social responsibility calls for a commitment to help advance a more humane society, improve the general welfare and alleviate the conditions of the needy in the many areas requiring help. But that commitment itself has many variations.

In the legal lexicon 'social responsibility' is not a familiar term, but the concept and values of social responsibility are encompassed in what is known as '*Pro Bono Publico*' – service for the public good. *Pro bono* service refers to that portion of a lawyer's work which has a public aim. It is an exercise of what Justice William J. Brennan described as 'the higher calling of the law' – namely, the obligation of lawyers to become involved in the overriding concerns of society.[1]

The discussion here will cover how social responsibility, or *pro bono* service, has progressed in the legal profession, and why it is a vital element of professional responsibility. It will also examine examples of the exercise of social responsibility by lawyers, and review challenges and prospects for both private sector and corporate lawyers.

Current appraisals of the legal profession often express nostalgia for the 'Golden Age' of lawyering. Anthony Kronman, the former Dean of Yale Law School wrote an uplifting oft-quoted book praising the 'lawyer-statesman' of yesteryear, allegedly characterized by high standards of ethical propriety, public service and practical wisdom. In point of fact that vision of a Golden Age is only nostalgia for a myth that did not exist in reality, either in the United States or elsewhere.

---

* Jerome J. Shestack is a partner in Wolf Block Schorr & Solis-Cohen LLP, Philadelphia, PA and was President of The American Bar Association (1997–1998).
[1] F.R. Marks, K. Leswing, B.A. Fortinsky, *The Lawyer, The Public, and Professional Responsibility*, American Bar Foundation, p. 189 (1972).

Ramon Mullerat (ed.), Corporate Social Responsibility: The Corporate Governance of the 21st Century, 403–415.
© 2005 *International Bar Association. Printed in the Netherlands.*

403

Insofar as social responsibility is concerned by either the bar or business, the legal profession cannot boast of being initiator, pioneer, innovator, or even a firm supporter throughout most of the profession's history. This may be disconcerting to lawyers who like to think that they are the avant garde of society's progress. Regrettably, the legal profession is not entitled to make any such claim as to social responsibility.

Undoubtedly, the rose-colored view of the profession is rooted in the fact that there have always been admirable public figures who brought about social and economic progress, and who were lawyers. But for the most part, the achievements of these lawyers did not come because of their profession. Indeed, it could be waggishly said that their achievements came despite it. As to the legal profession as a whole, for most of its history, it has been parochial, insular and self-serving. And society recognized that condition and disapproved it, leading to the low esteem in which lawyers were held.

A.   HISTORICAL ANTECEDENTS

To understand the long time disconnect between lawyer and social responsibility, it is useful to delve a bit into the history of the profession. Santayana's well known aphorism is that those who forget the past are doomed to repeat it. Whether or not that aphorism has any validity, we would not want to repeat the past in this area. Remembering history is valuable beyond being an academic exercise, it presents us with insights into past error and suggests opportunities and measures for society to advance.

Historically, if we start with ancient Rome, there were, of course, lawyers who were highly regarded. But even then, lawyers as a class were looked upon unfavorably. Thus, young Pliny described the 'dodges' of a lawyer anxious to advertise himself and his practice. Quintilian's view of lawyers was that their pleadings were debased by villainous, colloquial barbarisms, and that lawyer oratory was one of the meanest of the mechanical arts. Seneca called lawyers a 'venal race'. Fronto wrote that their love of money is so great that their wives must be women of a very large appetite. Other Roman contemporary observers agreed.

Turning to England, the legal profession emerged by the end of the reign of Edward I in 1307. From its very beginning lawyers were targets of ridicule and satire. According to one popular 14th Century poem, pleaders will 'beguile you in your hand unless you beware' and 'speak for you a word or two and do you little good'. An attorney would 'get silver for naught' and 'no man should trust them so false are they in the bile'. As historian Barbara Tuchman succinctly stated, 'In the 14th Century doctors were admired, lawyers universally hated and mistrusted'.

The expanding use of lawyers with their low public esteem led to a series of regulations in England, restricting use of lawyers and even excluding them from appearing in some courts. This hostile, medieval attitude towards lawyers was justified on the ground that there were too many lawyers, and that their misconduct and poor training caused excessive and unmerited litigation. As Charles Dickens' novels well illustrate, such hostile attitudes continued in England in later years, even as the 20th Century began.

The English prejudice against lawyers found considerable strength in America's early history. Of course, many lawyers played a praiseworthy role in the American Revolution; indeed the majority of the signers of the American Declaration of Independence were lawyers. Still, in 1776, the very year that the Declaration was signed, Timothy Dwight, a prominent colonial educator, who later became President of Yale College, warned the commencement class of Yale to shun law as 'you would shun treason or infamy'.

The historian, Charles Warren, wrote that during the period after the American Revolutionary War the old dislike of lawyers flourished. As Warren put it, because of excessive litigation, the increase of suits and mortgage foreclosures, and the high fees and court costs, people attributed their evils to lawyers.[2] Many colonial legislatures adopted regulations restricting the practice of lawyers and limiting the amount of their fees.[3] Paradoxically, at the same time, lawyers enjoyed a high social status.

As the 19th Century unfolded, the hostility continued. The frontier lawyer in America was viewed with deep rooted unpopularity and considered a meddlesome fellow, the cause of all sorts of troubles, to be classed with land speculators, swindlers and other evil doers. Indeed, in America, the years between 1836 and 1870 were referred to by Roscoe Pound as the 'Era of Decadence' in the legal profession.[4] Those days are often referred to as 'golden' days; – tarnished brass would be a more relevant metal.

Although the elevated social status of lawyers continued and even improved by the beginning of the 20th Century, anti-lawyer attitudes remained imbedded in the social fabric. Perhaps representative of the prevailing attitude is the poem by Carl Sandburg asking, 'Why is there always a secret singing when a lawyer cashes in? Why does a hearse horse snicker hauling a lawyer away?'

Of course, there were always lawyers who recognized social responsibility. But most often, that consisted of giving charity to the poor. Charity was given as one might tithe, (if one believed in the biblical admonition), or because of a belief in helping the needy, or because philanthropy gave social status, or because it was a discreet form of advertising.

It was not until the late 19th Century that American legal organizations begin to recognize the need for meaningful public service by the profession which would contribute to the general welfare and in particular address the needs of the afflicted and less fortunate. In 1870, Samuel Tilden, at the first meeting of the New York City Bar, called upon the new organization to serve the common and public good. 'If the bar is to become merely a method of making money, making it in the most convenient way possible, but making it at all hazards, then the bar is degraded. If the bar is to be merely an institution that seeks to win causes and to win them by back door access to the judiciary, then it is not only degraded but it is corrupt'.[5]

---

2   See C. Warren, *A History of the American Bar* (1911).
3   For example, in 1786, in the town of Braintree, Massachusetts, close to Boston, the citizens voted as follows: 'We humbly request that there be such laws compiled as may crush lawyers, whose modern conduct appears to us to tend rather to the destruction than the preservation of the town'.
4   R. Pound, *The Lawyer From Antiquity to Modern Times* (1953).
5   G. Martin, *Causes and Conflicts: 'The Centennial History of the Association of The Bar of the City of New York, 1870–1971'* at 37–38 (1970).

But Tilden's call, although it stimulated the formation of some legal aid societies, was largely ignored. In 1888, Lord Bryce commented on the general decline of the American bar in the public influence. He attributed this decline mainly to the unwillingness or inability of the bar to deal with the political and social issues of the time.[6] Louis D. Brandeis, in 1905, eloquently deplored the bar's lack of concern with questions of public interest.[7] Others echoed the same lament.

Indeed, leading lawyers in the United States vigorously opposed and predicted dire consequences from such social reforms as women's suffrage, enactment of the homestead laws, liberal immigration, adoption of initiative and referendum, and creation of juvenile courts. The record was not better in other parts of the developed world.

To be sure, forward thinkers recognized the Bar's obligations to *pro bono* public service. In 1906, Roscoe Pound, addressing the causes of dissatisfaction with the legal profession, defined a professional lawyer as 'an expert in law pursuing a learned art in service to a client in the spirit of public service and engaging in these pursuits as part of a common calling to promote justice and public good'.[8]

Pound's definition met with some acclaim, but was hardly taken seriously. It is a fair recapitulation that throughout the 19th Century, and a large part of the 20th, most American lawyers showed little concern for the 'spirit of public service', did not welcome the large diverse citizenry that was transforming America,[9] and saw no need for the bar to provide legal services to the poor, the disabled and the disadvantaged. The American attitude was essentially reflected worldwide.

What happened to the profession? In short, the profession, in America in particular, and generally world-wide, became so obsessed with being a service profession to clients that it became a service profession and nothing else. Lawyers represented their clients well, but their concept of public service was to only represent their clients. In the adversary system, theoretically truth and justice emerge from the adversary system and so they reasoned that society was well enough served if lawyers represented their clients well.

But that attitude did little to enhance the reputation of the lawyer in the public eye. Professor Karl Llewelyn perceptively noted that the legal profession's lack of popular appeal resulted from the fact the lawyers specialize in human conflict. In litigation, losers felt that lawyers trampled them down and manipulated human rights. And even the winners often thought of law as a black art. Other professions were not subject to the same attack.

---

[6]   Lord Bryce, *The American Commonwealth*, at 306–307, 671–676 (1917).
[7]   L. Brandeis, Business – a Profession at 318, 321 (1944).
[8]   R. Pound, *The Lawyer from Antiquity to Modern Times* (1953).
[9]   In 1922, the President of the New York State Bar opposed admission of immigrants into the legal profession as a menace to the elite bar. In 1925, in Pennsylvania, a special Committee dealing with bar admission requirements stated: 'What concerns us ... is not keeping straight those who are already members of the bar, but keeping out of the profession those whom we do not want'. During the first half of the 20th Century, many US law schools and bar organizations (including the ABA) restricted admissions based on race, sex and ethnicity.

B.   A SEA CHANGE IN SOCIAL RESPONSIBILITY

However, far reaching changes were to come, particularly in the United States. These changes merit elaboration, since the United States example (with more lawyers than any other nation), influences the legal profession in other parts of the world. With the advent of Roosevelt's New Deal, thousands of young lawyers came to the government. They had a different attitude, an obligation to the spirit of public service and to the people at large. When these lawyers later went into the private sector, they helped raise the bar's sensitivity to public concerns.

Nonetheless, acceptance of the need for social responsibility and reform proceeded at a snail's pace. As late as the 1960s in the United States, except for issues affecting the bar directly, such as judicial independence – involvement in public interest issues was slight. Issues such as civil rights, human rights, discrimination against minorities, gender bias, lack of access to justice, neglect of the poor and disabled, went largely unaddressed by a generally apathetic bar. It is fair to say that such apathy towards social reform was universal in the profession.

A sea change began in the United States with the civil rights revolution of the early 1960s. When Martin Luther King began his peaceful civil rights revolution, few lawyers were involved. Civil rights protesters in the South were highly at risk, but Southern lawyers were unwilling to represent them and indeed, more than a few had contributed to the prevailing segregation laws.

In this charged atmosphere, on 21 June 1963, President John F. Kennedy convened an assembly of 244 lawyers, mostly leaders in the profession, to urge them to pay attention to the civil rights issues wracking the nation. Out of that meeting emerged the Lawyers' Committee for Civil Rights Under Law. For the first time, leaders of the profession, including some from the South, became involved in the civil rights movement. The American Bar Association began to endorse civil rights measures and to promote civil rights committees in bar associations, not just in the North, but throughout the nation. Many corporate executives joined in these efforts.

Another seminal development in America came with President Lyndon Johnson's War Against Poverty in 1965. Part of that war involved providing legal services to the poor. To the poor, the law was stacked against them, often leaving them alienated and hostile to our system of justice. We all know the consequences of deprivation of justice – disillusionment, despair, and potential violence.

Sargent Shriver, as head of the Office of Economic Opportunity, instituted a federally funded legal services program for the poor. It was a fragile enterprise, requiring a willing Congress and a supporting bar. Fortunately, a nationally funded program of Legal Services for the Poor, won the enthusiastic endorsement of the American Bar Association, as well as many state and local bar associations. The organized bar became the program's public advocate and promoted private lawyer involvement in *pro bono* service.

Still, even with these advances, in the United States – with the largest number of the world's lawyers – the involvement of the private bar in *pro bono* service was painfully slow. As late as 1970, less than a half dozen major law firms in the United States had established *pro bono* programs and there were none in major corporate legal departments.

In 1970, while Chair of the ABA Section of Individual Rights, I secured a grant from the Ford Foundation to fund a program to encourage law firms throughout the nation to engage in *pro bono* service. That program, then headed by Marna Tucker and Warren Christopher, (later US Secretary of State) was remarkably successful in energizing law firms to initiate *pro bono* activity.

Today, heavy involvement in *pro bono* service been institutionalized in many law firms, despite continued focus on billable hours.[10] Many firms have fulltime *pro bono* coordinators to manage the firm's projects in assisting the needy and contributing to the urban welfare.

A fair measure of credit for the increase in *pro bono* service goes to the organized bar. The organized bar was slow in endorsing *pro bono* activities, but ultimately guided by visionary leaders and propelled by the needs of the times during the mid 1970s and the 1980s,[11] the organized bar's endorsement of public interest activities steadily increased and mushroomed. Space does not allow details of that steady growth, but the coming of age of *pro bono* service is perhaps best seen in the fact that by the beginning of the 21st century, *pro bono* service was regarded as such a basic element of legal professionalism that it was incorporated in the ABA's Model Rules of Professional Responsibility. Thus, *pro bono* service in the United States was given a mandatory ethical dimension.

Pro bono service, while it may have had its initiation in the United States, is now a staple of lawyers in the private and corporate bar in a substantial number of nations, particularly Australia, Canada and the United Kingdom and many countries in the European Union. In a number of nations, *pro bono* organizations or groups have been formed to mobilize lawyers for *pro bono* service. For example, in the United Kingdom, Lord Goldsmith, Q.C., (now Attorney General of England), established the Bar Pro Bono Unit to call upon the services of barristers from England and Wales. The Law Society's Solicitor Pro Bono Group is another such organization, as are The Pro Bono Law Group in Ontario Canada, and the National Pro Bono Resource Centre of Australia. The number of such organizations continues to grow.

While *pro bono* services have primarily involved legal assistance to the needy, starting in the 1970s, the organized bar in the United States increasingly also became involved in other important social issues, such as gender and race diversity, reform of mental health, human rights, environmental protection and civil rights. This article will not review the contributions of the organized bar in furthering social responsibility among lawyers. Suffice it to say that the concern of the organized bar with such social justice issues has proved a significant stimulus for lawyers to become involved in such activities. The organized bar in the United States is now a significant voice in calls for social reform.

---

[10] For example, in my own firm, (Wolf Block Schorr & Solis-Cohen LLP), we expended nearly half a million dollars in time over several years in order to ultimately overturn a death penalty that had been unjustly imposed. Ken Frazier, General Counsel of Merck, worked for some nine years to overturn a death penalty. There are a substantial number of such cases.

[11] An example of an elegant call is US Supreme Court Justice Sandra Day O'Connor's statement: 'One distinguishing feature of any profession... is that membership entails an ethical obligation to temper one's selfish pursuit of economic success. Both the special privileges incident to membership in the profession and the advantages those privileges give in the necessary task of earning a living are means to a good that transcends the accumulation of wealth. That good is public service'. *Shapero v. Kentucky Bar Association* 86 US 488–489 (1986).

C.   THE CORPORATE BAR

Despite the increase of *pro bono* service by lawyers in private sector law firms, the immersion of corporate counsel in *pro bono* service, particularly that involving social reform, came slowly. Why it came so slowly can be attributed to a variety of factors, the primary one being the corporation's single-minded focus on profits. The corporate culture also was accustomed to a 9:00 a.m. to 5:00 p.m. workday culture, without the discretionary time available to private practitioners. Additionally, some of the key social issues needing reform were sometimes incompatible with the corporation's practices.

Gradually the reasons for *pro bono* services – by any lawyer, including corporate lawyers, – became increasingly clear and cogent and were persuasively advocated by idealistic bar leaders.[12] The basic reasons for promoting the public good can be succinctly summarized.

First, it is one's responsibility simply as a decent human being to help the afflicted or vulnerable members of society when it is in one's power to do so.

Second, lawyers increasingly recognized that achieving justice and access to justice is the central foundation of the legal profession and a bedrock principle of constitutional democracy. *Pro bono* service offers the opportunity to advance justice.

Third, lawyers are given privileges by society, and often a monopoly status. To give something back to society is only fair. The precept from the Gospel of Luke that those to whom much is given, much is expected, should indeed be gospel for the profession.

Fourth, the profession's desire to be highly regarded, (whether in a private or a corporate body) can hardly be achieved without contributing their special talents and skills to the public good.

And finally, any lawyer engaged in *pro bono* service surely knows the joy and sense of professional fulfillment it brings.

These professional reasons are compeling for the private lawyer. They have begun to be compelling for the corporate lawyer. Additionally, for the corporate bar, there are also a number of practical reasons for *pro bono* involvement.

One significant reason for a corporate law department to provide *pro bono* services to improve societal conditions is that providing such services is an important element in whether a company is perceived as a good corporate citizen. That perception bears on economic success. A Hill and Knowlton study in 2001 found that 79 percent of respondents considered 'good citizenship' factors in buying goods or services, and 71 percent considered that factor in buying a company's stock.

Of particular relevance to the corporate lawyer is the realization that it is not enough for a corporation to make charitable contributions through its

---

12   Lord McMillan, a Lord Advocate General in Scotland, in his 1934 address to Scottish law agents on law and history said: 'The difference between a trade and a profession is that the trader frankly carries on his business primarily for the sake of pecuniary profit while the members of a profession profess an art, their skill in which they no doubt place at the public service for remuneration, adequate or inadequate, but which is truly and end in itself. The professional man finds the highest rewards in a sense of his mastery of his subject and the absorbing interest of the pursuit of knowledge for its own sake and in a contribution which by reason of his attainments he can make to the proportion promotion of a general welfare. It is only by the liberality of our learning that we can hope to merit the place in public estimation which we claim and to render to the public the service which they are entitled to expect from us'. *Law and History,* Edison Books, October 1934, reproduced in *Law & Other Things,* p. 127 (1930).

Foundation or other company resources, or for a lawyer to contribute funds to a social cause. Today, what is expected by stockholders and stakeholders is a corporate social responsibility which includes volunteerism. Corporate lawyers, in particular, can engage in socially responsible *pro bono* work which demonstrates volunteerism.

Corporations have clearly benefited from successful volunteer involvement in *pro bono* work. A telling example is that of Sears Roebuck. In cities in which Sears partnered with a non-profit cancer group called The Gilda Club, Sears' annual sales increased by 56 percent as compared with 16 percent in cities where such a partnership did not exist.

Benjamin W. Heineman, Jr, Senior Vice President and General Counsel of General Electric Company put it succinctly. 'The potential rewards,' of *pro bono* service, he said, 'are enormous: helping the non-profit organizations that serve our communities; creating goodwill for our clients and our profession; and providing personal satisfaction and professional enrichment for the volunteer corporate lawyers'.

A second current reason for the corporation to engage in socially responsible *pro bono* programs stems from the recent scandals involving business leaders and also in-house general counsel. The scandals have caused a skeptical view of corporate conduct that corporations need to overcome. Social responsibility is something shareholders will increasingly demand and expect to get.

In short, *pro bono* volunteerism by a corporation's lawyers as part of a program of corporate social responsibility, strengthens a company's reputation for responsibility, wins consumer acceptance, boosts morale among the corporation's lawyers and other personnel, and takes into consideration the demands of shareholders.

To be sure, for the 21st Century corporate lawyer, the *pro bono* path is not always an easy one. Corporate lawyers often find it hard to find time for *pro bono* service. Lawyers get caught up in the ardor of practice. Pressure stalks the practitioner. Corporate cultures generally demand a full day at work. *Pro bono* service competes with the desire to have a life at home. But if a *pro bono* undertaking is made part of the in-house lawyer's roster of the tasks that need to be done, it can receive appropriate attention. What is required is an attitude that does not treat a *pro bono* assignment as an extra-curricular throwaway.

A recurring problem that faces a corporate law department is that principal areas of socially responsible *pro bono* service, such as legal services to the poor, the disabled, children, elderly, abused spouses, etc., generally involve areas of law outside the expertise of many of its lawyers. However, there are many areas in which corporate lawyers can provide *pro bono* service. For example, most corporate law departments have lawyers engaged in labor practice. Such lawyers, with little additional training, could handle asylum cases or immigration problems for the indigent. Business lawyers can help struggling minority businesses and impoverished civic enterprises in underdeveloped communities. Socially responsible corporate counsel can take the lead in drafting and monitoring codes of conduct in ethics, environment, labor and community relations.[13]

---

[13]   In law firms, too, *pro bono* service is chiefly done by litigators, with other lawyers claiming lack of litigation expertise as a reason for non-involvement. But as noted, this is a lame excuse. The areas open to non-litigation lawyers are vast and wanting.

D. EXAMPLES

Despite its slow start, current *pro bono* activity by corporate law departments, as well as by private sector lawyers, is now substantial. The Pro Bono Institute of Georgetown University Law Center and ACCA have identified a number of corporations as having the best practices in the *pro bono* field. Strikingly, in each case, it is the general counsel's leadership that has been the key factor.

One such corporation is Merck and Co. Inc. Kenneth C, Frazier, General Counsel of Merck, has provided what has come to be viewed as a preeminent model for corporate in-house *pro bono* work. The Merck Pro Bono Program has more than 50 attorneys who have covered matters involving bankruptcy, consumer credit, child custody, domestic violence hearings, and support of victims of the 9/11 disaster. Merck's Pro Bono Program has been extended to the international area in addition to the national one.

Another is Starbucks Coffee Company's Legal Department which the King County Bar Association of Washington selected as Pro Bono Firm of the Year for its work with the Housing Justice Project representing low-income tenants in eviction cases. Paula Boggs, the dynamic Vice President and General Counsel of Starbucks, said that her department has capitalized on the 'personal commitment of many of the lawyers and staff to *pro bono* and also to further the corporation's strong commitment to corporate social responsibilities'.

Abbott Laboratories V.P. and General Counsel, Jose de Lasa has made *pro bono* work a staple of his stellar career. His legal department encourages Abbott's attorneys to do *pro bono* work on company time and he does so himself. Most notable among Abbott's many project is its naturalization clinic which it partners with the Midwest Immigrant & Human Rights Center and with Baker & McKenzie, which provides training for Abbott's volunteers.

Pfizer, the world's largest pharmaceutical company, is relatively new to organized corporate *pro bono* activity. By now, under the leadership of its General Counsel, Jeffrey Kindler, Pfizer has assumed a leadership role with the establishment of a corporate *pro bono* coordinator. Pfizer has dozens of legal projects partnering with United Way of New York City.

Other notable programs are those of Aetna, Inc. (Louis Briskman, Senior Vice President and General Counsel), General Motors (Thomas A. Gottschalk, Executive Vice President and General Counsel), the Altria Group (including Kraft Foods, Inc. and Philip Morris USA) (Charles R. Wall, Senior Vice President and General Counsel) and the Australian-English corporation, BHP Billiton (John C. Fast, Chief General counsel). There are many other outstanding programs.[14]

Looking to other nations, one deterrent to *pro bono* service occurs where the government provides a rather comprehensive system of legal aid, particularly in the criminal field. That has led to the feeling of some lawyers there that the socially responsible field has been filled. But this is a narrow view of social responsibility. The need to improve the general welfare encompasses far more than legal services to the indigent.

---

[14] A striking example of a current focus on *pro bono* is the recent Harvard Law School 'Pro Bono Fair' for law firms to showcase their *pro bono* activities to recruit potential applicants.

While *pro bono* service has begun to have a significant role in legal practice in English-speaking and European nations, in the majority of other nations, *pro bono* service is negligible and only dimly on the horizon. The reasons for this are many: a bar that is not influential or economically comfortable, the absence of effective bar leaders or associations, a repressive government, the daunting scope of the social problems, and other deterrents. Unfortunately, that condition is not likely to significantly improve in the near future.

E.   HOW TO FURTHER *PRO BONO* SERVICE

True social responsibility must transcend promises. Often lawyers, as well as corporate executives, give lip service to the exercise of social responsibility but do little. If a corporate legal department or a law firm is seriously committed to *pro bono* activity by its organization, the following rather simple steps would evidence taking *pro bono* seriously:

1. Establish a *pro bono* culture in the organization. A *pro bono* committee or coordinator is beneficial, if feasible. In a corporation, the general counsel is best able to do this.
2. Assess the *pro bono* activity currently undertaken, the level of interest, the nature of the work the lawyers are equipped to handle, and its compatibility with the firm's or corporation's objectives. Generally, uncomplicated surveys provide that information.
3. Consult with bar associations and NGOs, both national and international, with programs in legal services, child advocacy, women's and minority rights, environmental protection, fair labor standards, etc., to ascertain areas in which a real contribution can be made.
4. For the corporate legal department, look for opportunities to partner with law firms in *pro bono* activities. Increasingly, such partnerships have been established for a whole variety of public interest projects.[15]
5. The *pro bono* activities must be visible within the firm or corporation and recognized as valuable at high levels.
6. Make clear that *pro bono* work in a law firm or corporate law department is not treated differently from regular office time assignments – both in theory and practice. Visible and cohesive management support is vital if lawyers are to take *pro bono* work seriously.
7. Insure full participation, including senior lawyers. Making financial contributions to legal services programs is commendable. But it is not a substitute for actual personal service at every level. Ethical obligations are not delegable.

---

[15] Some corporate counsel, before retaining the services of an outside law firm, now ask what that firm is doing in the *pro bono* area. Some have also begun asking what *pro bono* activity is undertaken by the very lawyers handling their matters. This is a salutary development; such inquiries will undoubtedly spur greater involvement by law firms in *pro bono* activities. While this is not 'partnering' as such, it demonstrates a professional solidarity towards the *pro bono* obligation. That solidarity is vital to the future of *pro bono* service.

F.   A PARTICULAR ROLE FOR THE CORPORATE LAWYER

There is a particular role in which the corporate lawyer can be effective in furthering the field of social responsibility . Corporate general counsel are often part of the executive team and have considerable influence in their corporations. They are no longer regarded as solely a staff function, but are now part of the *line?* leadership. Today, corporate general counsel and their departments often help formulate policy, draft codes of conduct, suggest areas of volunteerism, monitor practices, advise on social philanthropy and are otherwise consulted on issues of corporate responsibility. General counsel can lead their corporations in socially responsible directions by initiating reforms and guiding corporate executives in matters of CSR.

Many corporations have ethical codes of conduct that impact on areas of social responsibility. But as well put by Roderick A. Palmore, General Counsel of Sarah Lee Corporation, 'such a code must be more than a pious wish; it must be a reliability which everyone sees and which is seen to have universal application'.[16] The seriousness with which a code of conduct (e.g., labor, environment, etc.) is implemented may often depend on the vigilance of the corporation's general counsel.[17] As international corporate activities become more extended, more complex and more involved in the needs of the people in the countries in which the corporations operate, the role of lawyers is likely to increase. It is the corporate counsel who will often hold the position of guardian of the corporate conscience.

G.   INTERNAL RESPONSIBILITY

One final area that merits attention is the responsibility of the legal profession to improve its own conduct. While a full discussion of that subject is beyond the scope of this chapter, it cannot be wholly ignored. The area which seems most to need reform is ethics and, in particular, conflicts of interest and whistle blowing.

One would assume that ethics are the most developed portion of the lawyer's conduct. It is not. Indeed when the 20th Century began, there were no official ethical rules to speak of. When ethical codes were first drawn in the first half of the 20th Century, they remained largely discretionary. It is only within the past few decades that lawyers have begun to take ethics seriously and develop codes of ethical responsibility that are meaningful and obligatory. Review and revision of ethical codes is ongoing by numerous bar associations.

Particularly relevant to issues of social responsibility is the need to develop an ethic that relates to conflicts of interest. Put simply, conflicts of interest interfere with a lawyer's duty to be independent and erode the element of trust that is vital to the legal profession. There is little harmony in this area. In common law countries, conflicts of interest are, on the whole, waivable; in civil systems, generally not. Some jurisdictions allow 'Chinese Walls' to separate opposing lawyers, as if they were in separate venues, but there are serious questions whether that device provides a sufficient assurance of independence and confidentiality.

---

[16]   See e.g. The ABAs Ethics 2000 Commission, which revised the ABA Code of Professional Responsibilities.

[17]   The Metropolitan Corporate Counsel, May 2004, p. 55.

414 CSR – THE CORPORATE GOVERNANCE OF THE 21ST CENTURY

Conflict of interest is not only an issue of the profession's responsibility to its own standards of independence and trust, it also affects areas of social responsibility where the interests of the corporation may conflict with social programs to which the corporation has committed.

Is there a conflict of interest where a corporate company advertises in the United States about the harm of children smoking, but does not do so in other countries where smoking is universally encouraged? Is there a conflict where a company endorses fair labor standards, but then hires children for pitiful wages? Such questions are not easy to resolve.

Individual lawyers engaged in *pro bono* service often encounter the situation where the *pro bono* representation involves taking a position that may conflict with policies of corporate clients. Here waiver is a possibility, but not always. Even where there is a waiver, the *pro bono* lawyer risks the client's displeasure, if not an open objection.

The Council of the Bars and Law Societies of the European Union and the American Bar Association, among others, have been wresting with rules to cover the pitfalls of the conflict of interest issue, and I will not attempt to review them here,[18] but there is still little harmony on these issues.

Another high-profile ethical issue in the legal profession involves the clash between confidentiality and whistle-blowing.

Confidentiality, of course, is a bedrock principle of the legal profession. Here, too the concept of confidentiality in the common law system is not the same as in the civil law system. In the latter, professional confidentiality is generally an absolute ('erga omnes') with minimum exceptions. In the common law system, there has long been a series of exceptions to confidentiality to prevent the commission of some serious crimes.[19] Recently, the exceptions to confidentiality have been extended. The US Patriot Act imposes duties on professionals to identify, prevent and report money laundering. In Europe, an EEC Directive is similar.[20] In the UK, lawyers are obliged to report suspicions of laundering from drug trafficking and terrorism. In the United States, the recent Sarbanes-Oxley legislation imposes serious duties on the lawyer to 'whistle blow' on material violations of securities law, or breach of fiduciary duty, or similar violations by the corporation. In short, lawyers are increasingly required to be 'gatekeepers' with respect to corporate wrongdoing.[21] Many lawyers are concerned that gatekeeper duties diminish the traditional duties of confidentiality, but the trend favors these exceptions in the public interest.

H. CONCLUSION

The exercise of social responsibility by private sector lawyers, corporate lawyers and bar associations has grown considerably and will continue to grow.

[18] See R. Mullerat, *Lawyers' Conflicts of Interest.* (A proposal for the review of art. 3.2 of the CCBE Code of Conduct).

[19] See ABA Model Rules of Professional Conduct, Rule 1.6(b)(1).

[20] EEC Directive 41/308.

[21] For an excellent article on the ethical duties of lawyers in Corporate America, see Dick Thornburgh's (former Attorney General of the US) 'Empowering the "Good Guy"', *The Pennsylvania Lawyer* at 12 (July–August 2004).

Moreover, social responsibility has increasingly expanded from its dismal beginnings to reach broad areas of social reform and justice beyond legal aid to the needy. Still, for a large portion of the world's lawyers, social responsibility is not a critical element of their practice. Response to the 'higher calling of the law' is recognized as a professional obligation, but all too few are yet inclined to pursue it. Perhaps that will change as lawyers realize that their profession will never engender the respect from society that they would like until the lawyers are willing to exercise their talents on behalf of society.

Chapter 28

LAWYERS' RESPONSIBILITY FOR ADVISING ON CORPORATE SOCIAL RESPONSIBILITY

Jonathan Goldsmith

A. INTRODUCTION

1. Introduction to the CCBE

The Council of Bars and Law Societies of Europe (CCBE) was founded in 1960. It is the officially recognized representative organization for the legal profession in the European Union (EU) and the European Economic Area (EEA), and has observer members in a number of other European countries. Through its members bars, it represents over 700,000 European lawyers to the European institutions and internationally.

2. The European Position

European developments in the field of CSR began in 1995 when a group of EU companies and the President of the EU Commission launched a Manifesto, which was called 'the Manifesto of Enterprises against social exclusion'. This was followed by the creation of a European Business Network promoting a business-to-business dialogue and exchange of best practices on CSR-related issues. It was the European Lisbon Summit in March 2000, though, that put CSR at the top of the political agenda of the EU. For the first time, EU heads of state made a special appeal to companies' sense of responsibility to help in achieving the new EU strategic goal of becoming the most competitive and inclusive economy in the world by 2010.

The next step was the publication in July 2001 by the European Commission of a Green Paper on promoting a European framework for CSR. This covered a wide range of topics, including responsible actions during corporate restructuring,

Ramon Mullerat (ed.), Corporate Social Responsibility: The Corporate Governance of the 21st Century, 417–431.
© 2005 *International Bar Association. Printed in the Netherlands.*

promotion of 'work/life balance' and corporate codes of conduct and social rights. It was intended to function as a launch-pad for debate, encouraging companies to take the 'triple-bottom-line' approach, i.e. giving attention to social and environmental concerns in addition to economic goals. The Green Paper consisted of two sections: the *internal section* focusing on CSR practices involving employees relating to issues such as investing in human capital, health and safety, and managing change; and the *external section* focusing on CSR with a wider range of stakeholders, including local communities and international communities, business partners and human resources. The consultation process hoped to develop a new framework for the promotion of CSR based on European values.

Then, in July 2002, the European Commission published a new strategy to promote business contribution to sustainable development. This policy paper calls for a new social and environmental role for business, and sets up a 'European Multi-Stakeholder Forum' for all players, social partners, business networks, civil society, consumers and investors to exchange best practices, establish principles for codes of conduct, and seek consensus on objective evaluation methods and validation tools, such as 'social labels'.

The European Parliament has also been active in trying to bring about codes of conduct, and legislation to require companies publicly to report annually on their social and environmental performance, to make board members personally responsible for these practices, and to establish legal jurisdiction against European companies' abuses in developing countries.

3.   CCBEs Involvement

The CCBE came to the subject of corporate social responsibility in a curious way. It was aware of the activity of the European institutions in relation to the topic, as just described, and thought that it would be useful if its member bars became involved. It envisaged that bars might want to draw up guidelines to assist their bigger law firms that were operating overseas, for instance. The CCBE was very surprised when, after a call for experts, a number turned up to its office in Brussels – but with a very different view in mind. They came from Germany, Italy, France, Sweden and Denmark, but they did not want to talk about the activities of their bars. Rather, they preferred to talk about how lawyers can advise the boardrooms of companies about their CSR responsibilities. They were all involved in this area of work in their home countries, and felt that it was a neglected area. They wanted the CCBE to assist them to open it up to lawyers. Some had a human rights aim: they thought it would be good for the wider world if companies behaved better, and if lawyers assisted them to do so. Others wanted their brother and sister lawyers to become involved in an area of legal advice which was dominated by non-lawyers, seeing it as a way of adding a new topic to those which lawyers regularly cover.

As a result, the CCBE decided to issue guidelines specifically for lawyers, on how to advise companies of their CSR responsibilities. The CCBE deliberately wanted to avoid developing yet another code of conduct. It thought it was ill-equipped to do this in the first place, and in any case there are more than enough codes out there urging companies to behave in this way or that. Rather the

CCBE wanted to explain to European lawyers that there was an area of work which it was important for them to learn about. As a result, the CCBE guidelines are unique, in that they are addressed to lawyers and not to companies.

So, the CCBE established a Working Group to achieve the above aims. This Working-Group was comprised of Claes Cronstedt (Sweden), Claes Lundblad (Sweden), Yvon Martinet (France), Mauro Pizzigati (Italy), Birgit Spießhofer (Germany), Sune Skadegard Thorsen (Denmark), Marco Vianello (Italy) and Carita Wallgren (Finland).

The CCBE Working Group had its first meeting on 16 September 2002. The Working Group also agreed to make contact with the European Commission to establish what the Commission would be concentrating on in the future and to provide an input into the Commission's work. With these objectives in mind, the CCBE set about its work, and in particular began to draw up its guidelines.

B. CSR AND THE EXTERNAL LAWYER

To date, CSR has not generally been seen as an area for external lawyers, at any rate in Europe. One can see why in-house counsel might have been more involved in such work. But, when companies have looked for outside help with CSR, they have traditionally gone to management consultants, or consultants in fields such as environment or human resources. Yet much of the work is legally-based, and there are very good reasons why external lawyers should be involved. These are some of them:

(a) *Lawyers are in a privileged position in relation to the board of a company.* They have ready access to boards, and are trusted advisors to directors. This works both ways. It means that lawyers will be heard on the importance of CSR by companies who may not be yet engaged in the area, and it is also, therefore, easier for lawyers to market their own expertise in this field direct to the client.

(b) *Lawyers are expert drafters and advisers.* Those are among their chief skills, and they use them all day and every day. If one looks at the tasks in the short- and long-term outlined in the guidelines which follow, nearly all of them involve these skills. Who better to carry them out than a lawyer?

(c) *This is a growing area of work.* Globalization is expanding apace. One of the consequences of globalization is that the behaviour of companies, particularly large ones, and often when operating abroad, has come under the microscope. This examination of corporate behaviour has extended afterwards to smaller companies, and to those which are purely domestic in operation. It is obvious that CSR will grow in scope in the future.

(d) *The nature of the work is good.* It is not often that lawyers, and particularly commercial lawyers, can say only good things about the work that they do. But CSR seems to satisfy all criteria. Not only is it socially useful, it is in the best interests of clients. Not only is it interesting work, but it should be a remunerative expertise to develop.

C. THE CCBE GUIDELINES

1. Introduction

A good deal of the CCBE guidelines address themselves to explaining the importance of CSR, and its potential impact on clients. That is not surprising, given
that they are aimed at an audience unfamiliar with CSR. However, the core of
the guidelines is the advice to lawyers on how to approach their corporate clients
with counsel and tasks to assist them to be CSR-ready.

2. The Aim of the CCBE Guidelines

The guidelines explain two main issues

- why companies should be interested in CSR; and
- why lawyers should advise on CSR.

The guide also provides information on how to pursue this topic further and
explains the current CSR initiatives at a European and world-wide level.

The guidelines have been very well received.

What follows is a copy of the guidelines.

3. Understanding Corporate Social Responsibility

'Corporate social responsibility is now in every reasonable chief executives
agenda, not always at the top, but it is there'.[1]

When Warren Buffett took over the chairmanship of Salomon Brothers after
the bidding scandal on Wall Street in 1991, he told the assembled staff: '*Lose
money for the firm, I will be very understanding; lose a shred of reputation for the firm,
I will be ruthless*'.
   Buffett and other successful representatives of the business world instinctively
understand that values such as honesty, fairness and responsibility are necessary
to be able to run a successful business. Many fortunes have been made, and are
still being made, through unacceptable business methods. However, the development has been towards more transparency, more freedom, more democracy
and more laws. This makes it less attractive to conduct business that is contrary
to the values of society.
   Courts in a number of countries are using the standards of international
conventions on companies, although the vast majority of these standards are not
directly binding on companies. This is a trend that is spreading to other jurisdictions. Many companies are being subject to legal proceedings at home and
abroad – even though the alleged violations have been committed by its operations in other countries. Today, social responsibility is becoming a serious matter
for our corporate clients.

---

[1]   Steve Hilton and Giles Gibbons, *Good Business*, p. 55.

The US judiciary especially apply their legal regime in an extraterritorial way, and they judge the companies' conduct with regard to international law.

Shell, BP, Nike, GAP, Coca-Cola, JP Morgan Chase, Polo Ralph Lauren – the list could be made longer – have had their reputations severely damaged in recent times because they have acted contrary to current values.

In an opinion poll published in 2002, 25,000 individuals from 23 countries were asked about companies' roles in society. Eight out of ten employees in larger companies said that the more social responsibility the employer takes, the more motivated and loyal the employees become.

A majority of the questioned shareholders stated that they would consider selling their shares in a company that fails in respect of social responsibility, even if the earnings are good.[2]

4.   Current Developments

'Corporate Social Responsibility is something that companies operating internationally cannot ignore anymore'.[3]

More and more companies adopt and implement rules for social responsibility because they know only too well how the market really works today. It is a matter of risk management, of creating an effective organization and of creating a good market position.

A new legal landscape that extends liability for corporations concerned is emerging. Among other initiatives (see annex) we can see many obligations on companies, which have been imposed by national governments:

a.   Australia

In Australia the Corporate Code of Conduct Bill 2000 reflects the definite trend towards penalizing unacceptable and harmful behaviour that occurs overseas.[4] Australian companies with global operations and multinationals with Australian subsidiaries need to be aware that certain standards of conduct are increasingly expected of them in both the domestic and offshore operations. The Bill, although not yet enacted, sets codes of conduct that must be adhered to including environmental standards, health and safety standards, employment standards, human right standards, duty to observe tax laws, duty to observe consumer health and safety standards and consumer protection and trade practices standards. The Bill also provides for wide-ranging and onerous reporting obligations. This Bill is indicative of the trend and direction that CSR is taking.

Also in Australia, there are CSR reporting requirement currently in place for investments firms and listed companies.

---

[2]   See www.environicsinternational.com.
[3]   Doug Miller, CEO of Environment International, 'CSR is here to stay', *CSR Magazine*, October 2002.
[4]   See http://www.aph.gov.au/Senate.

b.   Denmark and the Netherlands

Denmark and the Netherlands have encouraged 'triple bottom line' reporting, whereby social and environmental information is disclosed alongside financial reports.

c.   France

In 2001, the French Parliament passed legislation requiring mandatory disclosure of social and environmental issues in companies' annual reports and accounts.[5] It requires all companies listed on the 'premier marché' (those with the largest capitalizations) to report against a template of social and environmental indicators, including those related to human resources, community issues and engagement, labour standards and key health, safety and environmental standards.[6]

d.   Germany

In Germany, CSR reporting requirements have been introduced and apply to companies involved with pension funds.

e.   United Kingdom

In 1999, the UK Parliament approved the Pensions Disclosure Regulation. The Regulation amended the 1995 Pensions Act, requiring all trustees of UK occupational pension funds to disclose 'the extent (if any), to which social, environmental or ethical considerations are taken into account in the selection, retention and realization of investments'.[7]

Furthermore, in 2002 a CSR Bill was introduced in the House of Commons as a private members' Bill. Although the Bill was not enacted, it gives a good indication of movement in the direction of CSR, and the Bill was proposed again in an amended version in June 2003 backed by numerous NGOs.[8]

The original Bill proposed to:

– Make social, financial and environmental reporting (the so-called 'triple bottom line') mandatory;
– Require companies to consider CSR on big projects;
– Place specific duties and liabilities on directors and companies, with respect to social, financial and environmental issues;
– Provide remedies and rights of redress for people negatively impacted by business activities;
– Establish a new regulatory body to oversee environmental and social standards.

---

5   See www.occes.asso.fr/fr/comm/nre.html.
6   Halina Ward, Legal issues in Corporate Citizenship, February 2003.
7   See http://www.legislation.hmso.gov.uk/si/si1999/19991849.htm.
8   See http://www.parliament.the-stationery-office.co.uk/pa/cm200102/cmbills/145/2002145.pdf.

f.   US Sarbanes-Oxley Act July 2002

On 30 July, 2002, the Sarbanes-Oxley Act of 2002 ('Sarbanes-Oxley Act') was enacted.[9] This imposed codes of conduct on companies in which they would be obliged to report on Corporate Social Responsibility requirements.

The final rules implementing Section 406 of the Sarbanes-Oxley Act require reporting issuers, including foreign private issuers, to disclose in their annual report whether they have adopted a written code of ethics that applies to the issuer's principal executive officer, principal financial officer, principal accounting officer or controller, or people performing similar functions.

The above-mentioned governmental developments are merely reflections of broader international and regional movements and various court decisions.

5.   Corporate Risks and Opportunities

'The 21st century company will be different. Many of the world's best-known companies are already redefining traditional perception of the will of the corporation. They are recognizing that every customer is part of the community, and that social responsibility is not an optional activity'.[10]

Companies that choose to ignore CSR may encounter many consequences. The risks can be summarized as follows:

- Increased civil and criminal litigation against companies and management;[11]
- Loss of top talents;
- Loss of investors;
- Increased cost of capital;
- Decline in stock value;
- Loss of customers and business partners;
- Loss of public contracts and public procurement procedures e.g. World Bank, European Union, European Bank for Reconstruction and Development;
- Loss of business partners;
- Exposure to naming and shaming campaigns and blacklisting campaigns;
- Loss of brand value.

On the other hand, there are many opportunities available to companies who choose to implement CSR strategies and incorporate CSR into company policies:

- Enhanced corporate image and added brand value;
- Attract and retain top talents;

---

[9]   Pub. L. 107-204, 116 Stat. 745 (2002).
[10]   Tony Blair, UK Prime Minister.
[11]   Business and Human Rights, A Progress Report, p.18, Office of the UN High Commissioner for Human Rights, January 2000.

- Enhancing job satisfaction, loyalty and identification;
- Access to quality business partners;
- Obtaining the status of a 'preferred partner';
- Customer satisfaction and loyalty;
- Improving risk management;
- Lower insurance fees;
- Favourable access to capital markets;
- Attracting Socially Responsible Investment (SRI), which is mushrooming;[12]
- Establishing a good footing with public authorities and the general public;
- Creating a basic reference point and language for partnerships;
- Public relations opportunities;
- Contribution to the development of stable global markets.

6. Why Lawyers Should Advise on Corporate Social Responsibility

'The main purpose of the board of directors is to seek to ensure the prosperity of the company by collectively directing the company's affairs, whilst meeting the appropriate expectations of its shareholders and relevant stakeholders'.[13]

Responsibility for advising on CSR issues has not always been seen as falling to the legal profession. The CCBE believes that this should change. Law is the codification of basic human values. The goal of CSR is to implement these values in corporations, thus CSR develops and functions in a legal framework. There is no other professional who both has such ready access to EU boardrooms, and enjoys legal privilege. As a result, advising on CSR issues should become an everyday matter for corporate lawyers.

Even voluntary approaches to CSR have a legal context. Laws on misrepresentation or false advertising frame voluntary company reporting, for example. And voluntary approaches such as company codes of conduct can shape the standards of care that are legally expected of businesses. In the workplace, agreements reached through collective bargaining between employers and trade unions can become legally binding through incorporation in employment contracts.[14]

CSR should be part of company policies and integrated into strategies and decision-making. In this regard, the lawyer has a number of boardroom responsibilities:

- The lawyer should make the company management aware that CSR is an issue, which they will have to deal with.
- As lawyers are specialist advisers to corporations this will reflect on their responsibilities when acting as member of, or secretary to, the Board of

---

[12] See for example survey by UK Social Investment Forum/Just Pensions that SRI investments in UK are up from £22.7bn in 1997 to £224.5BN in 2001.
[13] Institute of Directors, *Standards for the Board*, 1999.
[14] Halina Ward, Legal issues in Corporate Citizenship, February 2003.

Directors. CSR must be considered as an area where negligence may very well result in losses of a considerable size for the involved company. If the issues leading to the loss were treated during a board meeting, and the lawyer did not respond adequately, due to ignorance, this may very well lead to liability.

The lawyer also has a number of advising opportunities that might take place, as the case may be, together with other experts. These advising opportunities can be divided into long-term and short-term assignments.

For longer term assignments:[15]

- Analyze strengths, weaknesses, opportunities and threats (SWOT-analysis) of a given company in relation to CSR;
- Design CSR policies;
- Design a strategy for the company to address CSR adequately;
- Integrate CSR under existing risk management and compliance programmes;
- Design and implement concrete projects under CSR;
- Create CSR screening systems for investments;
- Develop a framework for supply chain management systems;
- Develop a framework for CSR as part of Quality Management;
- Implement in-house training on CSR;
- Integrate CSR into existing risks and quality management schemes and compliance programmes.

For short-term assignments:

- Consider the 'what, why and how' of a CSR approach – its challenges, dilemmas and opportunities;
- Undertake CSR assessments of affiliates, branches, investment opportunities, suppliers, licensees or other partners;
- Undertake CSR assessments as part of due diligence;
- Respond to media or NGO criticism;
- Provide assurance statements on CSR reporting in relation to scope, relevance and compliance with international standards;
- Undertake assessment of concrete CSR projects;
- Network with other companies and/or associations;
- Coordinate and supervise the CSR work of the company;
- Assess the legal implications of CSR reporting and advertising.

In *Kasky v. Nike*, Nike was sued under Californian State Law for false advertising. Kasky claimed that information on Nike's social performance was false and did not reflect the poor working conditions in its foreign factories. Nike defended itself based on the First amendment of the US Constitution on freedom of

---

[15] It is recommended that longer-term tasks be performed in co-operation with either in-house or external competencies in organization, management – including crisis management, communication, human resources, training etc. depending on the objectives of the client.

speech, but the Court ruled, in the first instance, against Nike to find that the company statements should be classified as 'commercial speech' (and not political). Thus Nike's statements would be subject to the stricter standard of truth required by advertising law. In June 2003 the US Supreme Court dismissed on technical grounds the action in which Nike was seeking to reaffirm the First Amendment right to free and open debate. Although the US Supreme Court issued no formal decision, a majority of the Court expressly rejected the central holding of the California Supreme Court that Nike's speech could be restricted as purely 'commercial'. The case now returns to the California courts, which will have the views of the US Supreme Court in deciding whether the case may proceed to trial.

This case illustrates that companies' statements can be challenged for misrepresentation, and further illustrates the need for a corporate lawyer to be involved in CSR.

7. CSR Standards

'A global human society based on poverty for many and prosperity for a few, characterized by islands of wealth, surrounded by a sea of poverty, is unsustainable'.[16]

Many companies have established codes of conduct and policies integrating CSR principles into their business practices. According to the OECD, in 2000 there were 296 different codes of conduct.[17] These codes reflect the growing pressure being placed on companies by NGOs, shareholders and socially responsible investment funds.

There are five basic types of codes:

* Company codes – e.g. Shell, Philips, Levi Strauss;
* Trade association codes – e.g. ICC, British Toy and Hobby Association, Bangladesh Garments Headquarters and Expatriates Association, Kenya Flower Council Code;
* Multi-stakeholder codes – e.g. AccountAbility 1000, good corporation.com, Project Sigma UK, Ethical Trading initiatives UK, Apparel Industry Partnership USA, Social Accountability 8000;
* Intergovernmental codes – e.g. the ILO Convention, OECD Guidelines on TNCs, EU Code of Conduct;
* World codes – e.g. ICFTU Code of Conduct Covering Labour Bodies, Principles in Global Corporate Responsibility, UN Norms of Responsibilities of Transnational Corporations and Other Business Enterprises with Regard to Human Rights.[18]

---

[16] President Thabo Mbeki of South Africa, *The New York Times*, 26 August 2002.
[17] OECD Codes of Conduct. An expanded review of their contents, working party of the committee 2000.
[18] Ralhp Jenkins, *Corporate Codes of Conduct: Self regulation in a global economy, business and society programme*, 2001 UN Research Institute in Social Development.

In general, codes of conduct should:

- Be applied at every level of the organization;
- Be based on the UN Norms of Responsibilities of Transnational Corporations and Other Business Enterprises with Regard to Human Rights;
- Be included in training for local management, workers and communities on implementation;
- Have emphasis on gradual improvements to standards, and to the code itself;
- Include ongoing verification, which should be developed and performed carefully following defined standards and rules;
- Enable benchmarking.

Based on these principles, each company should tailor its own code adapted to its specific environment and resources, to ensure acceptance and compliance with it. This code of conduct can take the form of a manual governing the day to day business of the company. It is the natural role of the lawyer to be involved in the drafting of such documents.

The first generation of codes were developed by individual companies. Starting with the 'credo' of Johnson & Johnson in the 1940s and Levi Strauss & Co., Starbucks Coffee Co., Shell and BP Amoco all following suit. The latter part of the 1990s displayed codes like SA8000 (the Council on Economic Priorities), the Fair Labour Association (US) and the Ethical Trading Initiative (UK), which were developed based on consensus from a range of stakeholders. Codes defined by single stakeholders including the Workers Rights Consortium and Clean Clothes Campaign also appeared, along with various trade or business associations like the Norwegian Confederation of Businesses' checklist for human rights practices, the Global Sullivan Principles and the Caux Principles for Business.

Finally, international organizations have begun to issue codes or standards to enhance corporate social responsibility. The OECD Guidelines for Multinational Enterprises (revised in 2000), the ILO 'Tripartite Declaration of Principles concerning Multinational Enterprises and Social Policy (1977) and the United Nations Global Compact are very important initiatives. The Global Compact officially co-operates with the multi-stakeholder Global Reporting Initiative (GRI). Notably, the UN have adopted guidelines in the form of Norms of Responsibilities of Transnational Corporations and Other Business Enterprises with Regard to Human Rights.

8. The Triple Bottom Line

Sustainable development for business is operationalized by the triple bottom line, popularly described by the three Ps; *People, Planet, Profit*. In short companies seek to find sustainable solutions for their relationship with the *economy* (including the economy of the community), with the *external environment* (including biodiversity and animal welfare), and with *human beings* (hereunder in the relationship with employees, suppliers, customers, local communities and other stakeholders).

The following boxes present indicative lists of areas under the triple bottom line reflecting present developments. The areas mentioned are not intended to be exhaustive, but merely to give a brief overview of current developments.

Social Responsibility (People)

- Labour rights: Slave, forced or compulsory labour; child labour; freedom of association/collective bargaining; non-discrimination/equal opportunities; rest, leisure and holidays; minimum wages; health and safety;
- Right to work: Protection against unjustified dismissals and technical/ vocational guidance and training;
- Right to life;
- Development rights: Right to education; to health; to adequate food and fair distribution of food; to clothing; to housing; to social security; to enjoy technological development;
- Right to hold opinions and freedom of expression, thought, conscience and religion;
- Right to a family life;
- Right to privacy, e.g. surveillance, personal information, drug testing;
- Minority rights to culture, religious practice and language and cultural rights (indigenous peoples);
- Right to peaceful assembly;
- Right to take part in political life;
- Informed consent to medical / biological trials;
- Moral and material interests form inventions.

Environmental Responsibility (Planet)

- UN Convention on Bio-Diversity: in-situ and ex-situ conservation, impact on diversity, use of genetic material, technology transfer;
- The Precautionary Principle (In doubt about negative environmental impact of a given action – abstain);
- Use and handling of GMOs (Genetically Modified Organisms);
- Air emissions and impact on global warming (greenhouse gases);
- Impact on the ozone layer (Montreal Protocol Annexes);
- Prohibition of use of certain materials and substances, hereunder safe handling/transport of dangerous substances;
- Distance to residential neighbourhoods for production sites;
- Soil, ground water and surface water contamination;
- Treatment and reduction of waste water;
- Water consumption and leakage;
- 'Eco-efficiency', consumption of raw materials, and consumption of energy;
- Export of waste and re-use of material;
- Subsidising of environmental projects (e.g. protection of the rainforest etc.);
- Animal welfare.

Economic Responsibility (Profit)

- Financial profit, economic growth and asset creation;
- Business ethics, corruption and bribery;
- Direct and indirect economic impact on communities through spending power (suppliers, consumers, investors, tax payments and investments), and geographic economic impact;
- Economic impact through business process: outsourcing, knowledge, innovation, social investments in employees and consumers;
- Monetary support for political parties, lobbying, and other 'political' activities;
- External economic impact from pollution, internalization of externalities, value of consuming products;
- Stock exchange behaviour, including insider trading;
- Economic regulation, tax incentives, redistribution;
- State contracts and state subsidies;
- Intellectual property rights, hereunder patents, pricing and the impact on economic and societal development potential;
- Anti-trust and competition, including market impact and 'alliances';
- Board and executive remuneration and role of accountants;
- Donations;
- Taxes, including 'transfer pricing'.

In practice it is not possible to describe each bottom line quite as simple as illustrated. Grey zones exist between the lines. For example, corruption and bribery will belong to the 'economic'-bottom line as having an immediate impact on the economy of the community, notwithstanding that the practice has human rights implications as well in the form of discrimination and non-equal access to law.[19] The 'environmental'-bottom line describes the impact on the external environment, notwithstanding that the environment has great impact on the right to health of people. Consequently, most reporting strives towards a holistic approach embracing all three bottom lines in one report.

---

[19] A few human rights are not of immediate concern for business and should remain the overriding obligation of the state structure. These rights are found in the International Covenant on Civil and Political Rights (ICCPR): Art 9–10: the rights to freedom and personal safety (arrest and detention), Art 11: prohibition against imprisonment for non-fulfillment of a contractual obligation, Art 12: the right to liberty of movement and freedom to choose residence, Art 13: the right to seek asylum, Art 14–15: the right to a fair trial and prohibition against retroactive punishment, Art 16: the right to recognition as a person before the law, Art 20: prohibition against inciting war and against hate speech, and Art 26: equality before the law. However, business should be conversant in relation to the rights as the State's performance in these areas may have an impact on business opportunities and certainly has an impact on the public's perception of the legitimacy of the company to conduct business in a certain territory. In a few incidences the company may even be directly involved when selling goods and providing services to the violating government or, with the pace of privatization, taking over the government function as such.

The figure below mentions some of the existing management tools in relation to the three bottom lines.

Economic responsibility	Environmental responsibility	Social responsibility
IAS (International Accounting Standards) ISO 9000 series	ISO 14000 series E-MAS Life Cycle Assessments Business in the Environment's Index	ISO 18000 SA 8000 AA 1000s ETI Base Code ILO standards Caux Principles Sigma Amnesty International Human Rights guidelines for Business

Global Reporting Initiative (for reporting)
Balanced Business Scorecard
Compliance Programmes
Dow Jones Sustainability Index
FTSE4good Index
EFQM Business Excellence model
PricewaterhouseCoopers Reputation Assurance framework
London Benchmarking Group
OECD Governance Principles

Finally, as a prerequisite, any company is expected to comply with international, regional, national and local laws and regulations *directly applicable* to the corporation.

Compliance to such regulation will in most societies fulfill several of the areas mentioned in the boxes above, but in many cases a company may not be able to prove CSR only by demonstrating legal compliance. Beyond this compliance, there is another area that we might describe as Corporate Social Opportunity, which is motivated by competitive advantages i.e. economic incentives.

9. Conclusion

'CSR may have entered our national vocabulary but it has not taken root in our consciousness'.[20]

CSR has increased in recent years as a result of the recognition of the essential contribution of business to social, environmental and Human Rights progress,

[20]   Ella Joseph, centre-left think-tank IPPR, *The Observer*, 2 February 2003.

and because of pressure from consumers, investors, employers, governments, NGOs and public opinion.

A growing number of businesses already have CSR as a priority in their agendas. It is the lawyers' role to assist their clients in positioning their business successfully in this new legal landscape.

D.   THE FUTURE

The CCBE sees CSR as forming an important part of its work.

The CCBE Working Group is currently working on an update to the guidelines. The CCBE recommends the guidelines to you, as a basis on which to promote the involvement of external lawyers in the field of CSR.

Chapter 29

CORPORATE SOCIAL RESPONSIBILITY IN LAWYERS' FIRMS*

Richard Taylor
Richard Brophy

A. INTRODUCTION

Whether a law practice is conducted by a sole practitioner or is a large multina-tional enterprise employing thousands of individuals, at the heart of its activities will be the provision of legal services by professionals whose licence to practise depends on compliance with certain minimum ethical standards. The hallmark of an independent legal profession is the observance of a code of conduct which has integrity as its basic principle. For example, the Solicitors' Practice Rules 1990 prohibit a solicitor from doing anything which compromises or impairs his independence or integrity or the good repute of the solicitor or the profession.

Ethical behaviour is thus not an optional extra for lawyers or law firms but a basic requirement. This obligation is a consequence of the special position that a lawyer holds in a free society. Lawyers, although most work fully independently from the state, are a part of the machinery of justice and in order to ensure that the justice system works well they must accept certain responsibilities which may at times limit their own freedom of action. This is recognized by the EC Recommendation on the Freedom of Exercise of the Profession of Lawyer[1] which, drawing on the CCBE Code of Conduct, states that '. . . a lawyer must

---

*   This section is based upon practice in the UK in general and London in particular. However, there is an even longer tradition of *pro bono* activities on the part of US law firms. For further information on *pro bono* activities in the US see the website of The Pro Bono Institute (http://www.probonist.org/).
[1]   Recommendation REC (2000) 21 of the Committee of Ministers to Member States on the Freedom of Exercise of the Profession of Lawyers, adopted on 25th October 2000.

Ramon Mullerat (ed.), Corporate Social Responsibility: The Corporate Governance of the 21st Century, 433–445.
© 2005 *International Bar Association. Printed in the Netherlands.*

service the interests of justice as well as those whose rights and liberties he is trusted to assess and defend and it is his duty not only to plead his client's cause but to be his adviser'.[2]

Notwithstanding that ethical obligations are rooted in lawyers' entitlement to practise, law firms have tended to avoid any public espousal of CSR or to use the term in relation to the conduct of their own practices.[3] This is not because law firms are too small to be able to introduce, organize and manage an explicit CSR policy. Indeed the largest law firms now have thousands of employees, a multiplicity of offices in different jurisdictions and a turnover greatly in excess of US$100 million. They are often larger enterprises than the clients that they serve. Neither is the reticence of law firms to publicize an explicit commitment to CSR a sign that firms fall behind enterprises in the commercial and industrial sectors in the degree of social responsibility that they demonstrate.[4]

The reason appears to be that law firms feel that they might be constrained with respect to the scope and ambit of their professional work if they were to take or be seen to take particular moral positions on practices or issues which might be the subject of proceedings involving their clients or, generally, to hold themselves out to the world as models of ethical behaviour. The degree of difficulty to which this gives raise differs according to the nature of the lawyer's practice. In criminal work it is often a professional obligation to represent a client irrespective of the nature of the offence which he or she is alleged to have committed and the lawyer's reputation is not sullied by involvement in the case.[5]

In the case of civil proceedings, or advice on civil law, the lawyer or law firm is not obliged to act for any particular client. However, given the fierce competition for work among business law firms a law firm which built up a reputation for not acting for particular types of proceedings or in relation to specific problems in a particular industry might regard itself as unnecessarily cutting off sources of potentially lucrative and entirely 'respectable' work. It is certainly possible to distinguish the question of legal liability from that of ethical responsibility and to maintain that there is nothing improper in using professional experience, skill and knowledge to give the clients the best possible legal position (e.g. asserting a prescription or limitation period as a defence to an otherwise meritorious claim) even where this might be judged as 'unfair' when viewed from a moral standpoint.

However, notwithstanding law firms' reluctance to vigorously wave the CSR banner, UK lawyers do in fact increasingly carry out a significant number of activities which can be regarded as falling under the overall CSR umbrella. According to a recent Law Society survey more than half of all solicitors have

---

2   This formulation addresses the possible conflict between a lawyer's duty to ensure justice and his duty to his clients. The duty to the client is reflected in the UK Law Society's Practice Rules 1990 by obligations to act in the best interests of the client, to avoid conflicts of interest and to keep client information confidential.

3   For a general survey of the interaction between CSR and lawyers see *Legal Issues in Corporate Citizenship* by Halina Ward, International Institute for Environment and Development, February 2003 – prepared for the Swedish Partnership for Global Responsibility.

4   A number of other professional service organisations – and particularly the international audit, management and IT based consultancies have put in place and published formal CSR policies.

5   This obligation is clearly necessary to ensure that all individuals prosecuted by the state have the opportunity to be defended.

undertaken *pro bono* work in the course of their careers. In addition some 1,400 barristers volunteer their services through the Bar Pro Bono Unit. There are a number of reasons for this but perhaps the most compelling is the competition between law firms to recruit the most able new talent for their practices.[6] Entrants to the legal profession have graduated recently from universities and colleges where issues of ethical behaviour on the part of governments and businesses are likely to have been extensively debated. There is a positive well of idealism in these young people which responds positively to the opportunity to play a constructive part in helping the less well off while training and working with a reputed provider of legal services.[7] Further, law firms benefit from the development of their people through involvement in *pro bono* activities where they receive valuable experience in handling clients earlier than they otherwise might. A further incentive for firms is the increasing trend of UK corporates to take account of involvement in *pro bono* programmes when selecting external counsel.

The remaining paragraphs of this section briefly describe some of the activities carried out by UK law firms some of which can be said to correspond to activities carried on by commercial enterprises under the CSR banner. They fall into four broad categories:

- Legal *pro bono* activities – where legal services are provided free of charge to needy individuals or organisations.
- Other *pro bono* activities – where volunteers from the firm assist deserving causes in other ways.
- Financial Support and Charitable Donations.
- Internal Policies with an ethical dimension – these include HR, risk management, environmental and governance policies applied within the firm itself.

B.   LEGAL *PRO BONO* ACTIVITIES

1.   Introduction

Most major London law firms support some form of legal *pro bono* activity.[8] Clearly, the size of the firm has an impact on how well it is able to manage and promote these activities, and whether or not it is able to dedicate partners and employ staff specifically to optimize and maximize its investment of professional time. The fact that not all law firms actively promote their legal *pro bono* activities on their websites or in other communication tools, should not necessarily be seen as an indication that they do not support or encourage this

---

[6]   The Solicitors Pro Bono Group is shortly to distribute to law school students in England and Wales a guide to law firm *pro bono* programmes.

[7]   The England and Wales Young Solicitors Group gives annual awards for outstanding *pro bono* activities.

[8]   One very large London headquartered international firm is offering the staff in its 24 offices an additional day's leave a year for voluntary work. It already undertakes more than £1 million of *pro bono* and community work.

activity, simply that they see no reason to promote it in anything other than an ad hoc way.

Historically, legal *pro bono* activities have originated spontaneously, with enthusiastic volunteers fitting community involvement into their fee earning activities.[9] It is only relatively recently – within the last five years or so – that UK law firms have begun to employ people specifically to encourage, support and manage this activity, and enhance the profile of corporate community involvement for the benefit of the firms' internal and external reputation.

The description which follows is not based on a scientific survey but is rather a snapshot of the range of work being completed on a regular basis at approximately 15 large to medium sized firms with headquarters in London.

Law firms' *pro bono* work tends to be carried out without any dedicated organizational structure being set up in the firm. One US headquartered firm has however established a number of specialist *pro bono* practice groups headed up by a partner and an associate to develop precedents and build specialized knowledge through training in specific areas.

Legal *pro bono* work largely falls within the following categories:

- Work with legal advice and representation agencies providing volunteers to attend evening or weekend advice sessions or 'clinics', to man legal advice telephone lines and low profile legal casework on behalf of litigants for whom publicly funded legal aid is not available.
- Either continuing or ad hoc advice to charities or community groups in a specific area of legal practice.
- High profile legal casework tackling alleged infringements of human rights or assisting in the commuting or annulling of death sentences.
- Work with young people providing general advice on rights and responsibilities.

In order to promote high standards on the part of lawyers' involved in *pro bono* work the Solicitors Pro Bono Group has drawn up a *pro bono* protocol which law firms and in-house legal teams engaged in such work are encouraged to sign. The protocol addresses matters such as staffing, file management, insurance and supervision.

2.   Legal Advice Agencies

Legal advice agencies take on a number of forms. There are well-established agencies like Law Centres or Citizens Advice Bureaux, which will often provide advice to individuals or groups based on an assessment of local need. The most common forms of advice include immigration, employment, housing, consumer, debt and small claims as well as advice and training to small businesses and community groups on governance issues and best practice.

---

[9]   There is of course no requirement for UK lawyers to be involved in *pro bono* activities, nor any professionally recommended target commitment. The US Model Code of Professional Responsibility by contrast has at its core an annual target of 50 hours of *pro bono* work for each lawyer.

City law firms contribute on a number of levels, the most common of which is providing volunteers to attend and advise clients as part of a LawWorks Clinic.[10]

The volunteers are typically trainee solicitors or young lawyers looking to develop skills in client interface and confidence. Training is provided in the areas of law likely to feature, and supervision is provided. In most cases, the volunteer will not meet the client more than once.

Since solicitors employed on a full time basis by law centres will be involved in representing clients at court, volunteers at evening sessions are less likely to be involved directly in this work. However, volunteers may be involved in court work through other agencies should a case be referred to court. Examples of these groups include the Royal Courts of Justice Advice Bureau and the Free Representation Unit, both of whom have long standing partnerships with a number of city law firms. Volunteer involvement includes preparing files of evidence on behalf of litigants and other paralegal support at tribunals ranging from the Court of Appeal to employment appeals and immigration appeals tribunals.

Volunteering opportunities are attractive to trainees because they are a basis for the acquisition of basic skills and confidence in dealing with clients, whilst also making a recognized contribution to the community. There is clearly also scope for acquiring specialist skills through advocacy experience gained through representing litigants appearing in court.

An interesting development in relation to training and development of staff, pursued by a few city law firms, is to have a closer relationship with the advice agency, under which trainees are actually seconded to it as part of their rotation within different practice areas of their firm.

3. Support to Charities and Community Groups

All of the large London law firms have relationships with charities, large and small, community groups, local government agencies and advisory panels, providing continuing or one-off pieces of advice on non-contentious issues. This might be in the form of generalist business advice or advice in specific areas of legal practice and, by definition, is likely to attract individuals with more experience for whom volunteering at a law centre or advice agency may not be regarded as sufficiently challenging.

A model for involvement of this kind consists of lawyers from a firm acting on behalf of charities in specific areas of legal practice in which their firm may specialize, or using their core skills as advocates to assist the charity's beneficiaries. An example might be a law firm specialising in healthcare issues manning telephone advice lines for a healthcare charity, or lawyers appearing at the behest of a charity for children with special educational needs at tribunals to secure the appropriate level of support from the local authority.

Another common approach involves working with the charity or community group in much the same way as the firm would work with a commercial client.

---

[10] LawWorks Clinics is a partnership initiative of the Solicitors Pro Bono Group – a registered charity that exists to encourage and support *pro bono* activity – and the Law Centres Federation – the umbrella group supporting the work of Law Centres around the UK.

Some typical examples might be an employment lawyer helping a charity to reflect specific areas of new legislation or best practice into their management of human resources; a property lawyer helping to negotiate leasing arrangements with a local authority on behalf of a community group or helping to establish the feasibility of expansion/refurbishment as part of an overall business plan; banking lawyers advising on the establishment of a co-operative bank or other local financial services; a corporate lawyer advising on specific areas of governance and drafting constitutional documents; or an intellectual property lawyer helping a social enterprise to protect its brand.

4.   International Human Rights Cases[11]

The most common feature of city law firms' work in the field of international human rights is their representation of clients on death row, typically in the United States and in Caribbean countries. This is the most obvious expression of the ethical strain that runs through the profession in its desire to address a possible injustice through the imposition of a mode of punishment which many find immoral and whose finality makes unimpeachable trial processes essential.

Firms will also act for those sentenced to life where the evidence is insufficient or there is a suggestion of injustice. In both areas, city lawyers acting on behalf of these individuals have had considerable success, either in having the convictions quashed or sentences severely reduced.

Often this work involves partnering a human rights charity like *Liberty* or *Amicus*, for example, where cases are screened against agreed principles (e.g. the EU Convention on Human Rights) before being referred to the law firm to manage the case.

C.   OTHER *PRO BONO* ACTIVITIES

Law firms are also involved in a very wide range of non-legal *pro bono* activities. Most of these are designed to help local communities and many focus on children, young adults and the homeless. Some examples of these activities are given in the following paragraphs.

1.   Primary School: Reading, Numbers and IT Partners

Volunteers typically meet with children from a local primary school once a week, and read with them for around half an hour. The firm will often provide transport, allowing volunteers to maximize the relatively short amount of time they have with the children. 'Reading Partners' as the scheme is known is a proven way of assisting those children who may just need some extra attention to fulfil their potential, or those children who are really struggling to make the grade.

---

[11]   For a review of the obligation of business lawyers to uphold human rights see Waljee, *New Academy Review* Spring 2003, Vol. 2 No. 1, p. 62.

Reported benefits to the children include increased motivation, a greater interest in reading and improvements in academic attainment, while the adult volunteers learn increased patience and the ability to motivate people, and improve their own communication skills and confidence.

Firms with well-developed reading partnerships have used this as a starting point to progress their relationship with the school and include support on the numeracy and IT sections of the curriculum.

2. Secondary School: Mentoring

Another very popular initiative on the part of law firm staff is mentoring teenagers, particularly those working towards their public examinations. Volunteers will be paired off, either one-to-one or in groups, with young people from a local secondary school. After initial ice-breaker sessions at the school, the pupils are asked to travel to the office of the mentor for meetings that take place after school hours and will normally be for around one hour. The mentees may not all want to be corporate lawyers at the end of the relationship, but they will learn something about what a law firm does, and there is clearly a benefit to be drawn from changing young peoples' view of business and the way it works.

3. Other Forms of Mentoring

Mentoring teenagers is unlikely to appeal to everybody, so firms have developed different models to appeal to a broader range of volunteers. For example, one law firm establishes relationships with ethnic minority undergraduates, offering expertize and guidance through their degree and into their early careers.

Activities likely to be more popular at the senior level in the firm include mentoring school head teachers – a recognition that the new generation of head teachers require business acumen, marketing, financial planning and people management skills, to run their schools effectively in the modern, more competitive market.

4. Board Membership

Sometimes the law firm will provide a trustee or director for the organization, so that an experienced lawyer sits on management committees of charities or community groups. The role is often concerned less with giving specific legal advice than with general support in matters of corporate governance. A charity that has a senior lawyer on its board, for example, is likely to be seen by stakeholders as a buoyant and professional organization able to function in a strategic way and plan objectively over long periods. There is a huge range of organizations being supported in this way. They include law centres and advice agencies, local community centres and youth clubs, primary care trusts, school governors, local government advisory groups, social enterprise initiatives and regeneration agencies.

D.   FINANCIAL SUPPORT AND DONATIONS

While *pro bono* work is the centrepiece of UK law firms involvement in CSR, direct financial support of worthy causes and charitable donations also play an important role. Fundraising initiatives permit the participation of all employees – not just fee earners with legal skills – and facilitate the support of a broader range of charities by including those which do not need *pro bono* legal expertise, but do need cash or other resources.

Many firms have formed their own charitable trust, a legal structure through which all fundraising is channelled. The trust often has a strategy to co-ordinate the raising of funds and their distribution, although it may also operate simply as a receptacle for ad hoc employee donations. Often the law firm matches the total amount of the donations so that the charity receives double the amounts collected.

Many fundraising initiatives which take place are linked to an activity – such as a sponsored walk or team event and donations in kind are also a popular means of charitable giving by law firms. Employees of one firm have donated computers to the United Nations for use in Sarajevo, as well as clothing for the accident and emergency department of the local hospital. Another firm has a program for the donation of computer equipment to community centres, while it also donates clothing, toys and furniture to Refuge, the charity for the homeless.

At the level of the individual employee, the practice of payroll giving is now widespread in law firms across the UK. The money is deducted from the employees' salary and there is a tax credit in the hands of the charity.

Large and small charities benefit from charitable giving by UK law firms, from local community centres and shelters, to large branded charities such as Tommy's, MacMillan's and Comic Relief. Some firms elect a 'charity of the year' and focus the majority of their efforts on a goal for that charity, while others support a wider range of charities through different initiatives.

E.   INTERNAL POLICIES AND GOVERNANCE

The preceding sections on *pro bono* activities have described essentially outward facing activities carried out by law firm staff and volunteers for the benefit of third parties. The sections which follow describe policies and practices forming part of a firms internal management procedures – for example those designed to positively improve the conditions of major stakeholders such as employees or to minimise the risk to the firm's reputation or other assets from non-compliance with statutory requirements (e.g. money laundering) or professional obligations (e.g. avoidance of conflicts of interest).

1.   Codes of Conduct

Many firms draw up codes of conduct with which their staff must comply. Typically these codes will require staff to behave ethically and report any instances of criminal, improper or unprofessional conduct or concealment which may come to their attention.

2. Health and Safety

Many UK law firms take active steps going beyond legal requirements to maximize employee health and safety. Firms are well aware of the risks to their employees of conditions such as repetitive strain injury or the debilitating symptoms of stress, and the expense that can result. Increasingly the office is being seen as a potentially dangerous environment.

In one large London firm, for example, all staff are trained in a broad spectrum of health and safety topics including fire safety, occupational health, accident reporting and stress management. New recruits are given a health and safety induction and managerial staff are given annual health and safety training. The emphasis is on educating the workforce to operate in a 'health-and-safety-conscious' manner, identifying the risks and either avoiding or dealing with them safely. A team of workstation assessors checks that all desks are at an appropriate height, chairs have appropriate support and that here are no other health and safety risks. Firms also typically ensure that a number of employees are trained in first aid.

3. Work/Life Balance

This is an area where law firms are paying increasing attention so as to be able to attract top graduates and prospective employees. The hard working ethos of the 80s and 90s has now been complemented by a greater emphasis on balancing efficient working practices with healthy living and fulfilling leisure time. There is clearly a realization that healthy workers are good workers. Many firms offer a full range of benefits and incentives to ensure that employees suffer less stress, eat more healthily, take regular exercise and as a result work more productively and have fewer absences through ill health. A small number of very large city firms have gyms on their premises which provide facilities for the staff at no cost. The majority of large London firms offer a gym subsidy so that employees wishing to take membership of a gym can do so at a significantly reduced price.

Nevertheless, for many lawyers their chosen career calls on them to make one major sacrifice – long hours. Every large law firm sets targets for their employees encouraging them to work a certain number of target hours sometimes as a condition of qualifying for an annual bonus. The number of hours set as a target varies from firm to firm, with 1,400 hours at the lower end of the spectrum and around 1,700 hours at the higher end. In practice, no matter what targets are set by the firm, a lawyer will be expected to work for as long as it takes to get the job done.

Some large firms are now beginning to accept that employees can deliver the same if not better results when they are able to structure their working life in a way that suits their personal life. For example lawyers can start their working day an hour later (or earlier) and finish an hour later (or earlier), or they could work from home for part of the week where this is a practical option given the demands of their clientele.

Some firms offer their staff access to confidential external counselling services and sources of information and advice on issues such as childcare, eldercare, debt, moving house, alcohol abuse, drugs and stress management.

4. Policies to Promote Equal Opportunities and Prevent Harassment or Bullying at Work

Many UK law firms draw up and publicise policies designed to ensure that no discrimination on the grounds of race, creed, colour, religion, sex, sexual orientation, age, national origin or disability is tolerated whether in the course of recruitment or career development. Typically, the policies will also emphasize that harassment, intimidation, victimization or bullying of any kind is unacceptable in the firm.

5. Employee Benefits

Law firms are constantly improving the conditions of their employees so as to preserve their position in a competitive market. Typical benefits in London are interest free loans for travel season tickets, medical and insurance benefits and enhanced holiday and maternity and paternity leave entitlements.

6. Compliance/Risk Management

Every business enterprise is subject to the risk of unforeseen events which can damage or even destroy it, and law firms are no exception to this. Events in recent years have shown that large professional organizations with worldwide practices and reputations can fail practically overnight if they appear to have been complicit in helping clients evade or infringe ethical standards, or have evaded or infringed such standards themselves. For law firms an effective risk management programme, as well as lowering the cost of professional indemnity insurance by making claims less likely, should reduce the chance of the firm's reputation becoming tarnished.

A law firm should apply to *pro bono* work the same risk management approach as it applies to its normal fee earning activities.

Three areas where risk management is particularly important are:

- Conflicts of interest
- Money laundering
- Engagement letters

a.   *Conflicts of Interest*[12]

The larger the firm the greater the possibility that lawyers within the firm may be working for clients with interests that may conflict. A law firm therefore needs to set up a procedure to minimize the risk of such a conflict arising, whether between the interests of two clients, or the interests of a client and a solicitor within the firm.[13]

---

[12]   The Law Society produced a consultation paper in December 2002 in relation to modifying these rules and these are expected to be introduced later in 2004 or in 2005.

[13]   Firms will typically prohibit their staff from investing in client companies or dealing in their shares.

In larger firms conflict committees are often created to resolve such situations, allowing an assessment to be made as to whether the firm can act for a new client where a conflict may potentially arise. Such committees can also draw up guidelines on the method of their assessment, thus minimizing the risk of decisions being made arbitrarily.

b. Money Laundering

The events of 11th September 2001 and the threat of international terrorism have intensified the international impetus for the effective tackling of money laundering and terrorist financing globally. UK law firms are required, by law, to have policies and procedures for identification, record keeping, reporting, training and awareness, and to designate an individual to receive reports of suspicions of money laundering activity.

As the legislation in this area is new and untested, and because of its implications for all law firms, fourteen firms in the City of London have worked together to develop an e-learning course to increase the awareness of their solicitors of their obligations under the legislation. This should be launched in the autumn of 2004.

c. Engagement Letters

It is sound professional practice to agree the terms of any instructions from a client in the form of an engagement or retainer letter. By outlining the scope of work that the lawyer has been instructed in and the basis of charging, such a letter reduces the risk of an argument that a solicitor has not acted according to a client's instructions and it also reduces the scope for disagreements on fees. Further, a retainer letter allows a law firm to incorporate a set of standard terms and conditions, much like any other business, thus creating uniformity in its client relationships.

7. Environmental Policies

Most London based firms, and a number elsewhere in the UK, have long since adopted environment friendly practices for recycling waste paper, which is a usual 'first step' towards a progressive environmental policy. In one London firm not only is all wastepaper recycled, but for each tonne recycled, a tree is planted. Other initiatives used throughout a number of London and regional firms include recycling light bulbs, batteries, glass and printer toner cartridges. One London based firm has replaced the use of plastic and wax coated cups with personal thermos cups and glasses for each employee, whilst another recycles the cups to make pens and rulers to be used in the firm. Some firms have now moved beyond the 'quick fix' initiatives of recycling their paper and other waste and have adopted an altogether broader approach to recycling and preserving the environment. One London based firm has advised and contributed to a scheme which reconditions old and used office equipment to be used in schools and hospitals in West Africa. Another 'recycled' their old computers to be used in legal aid centres in Bosnia, whilst others have done the same for the benefit of charities in the UK.

Many firms with environmental law departments make their expertise available on a *pro bono* basis. One London based firm supports the Environmental Law Foundation which is a non-profit company that represents community groups involved in environmental disputes. Other firms provide legal advice directly to environmental groups and charities on regulations, laws, enforcement actions and best practice for business so that these organizations can maximize their resources. The organisations involved range from Thames 21, an environmental group cleaning up the Thames River, to the Amazon Conservation Society.

8.   Governance and Reporting

Law firms are traditionally established as partnerships[14] with no obligation to publish their accounts or produce annual reports. Notwithstanding this their affairs are increasingly transparent in part as a result of the advent of a plethora of periodicals dedicated to publicising news about the activities of lawyers and law firms. A number of firms now produce the equivalent of a social report for the benefit of their staff and clientele providing information about their activities with a particular emphasis on their involvement in *pro bono* work and community orientated initiatives. Many also make this information available on their websites.

One of the 'themes' of Corporate Social Responsibility is the impact of corporate actions on an organization's structure including in particular its employees. Under current legislation employers in the UK are legally obliged to inform and/or consult with their employees only to a limited extent e.g. the provision of information and consultation requirements about health and safety, collective redundancies and transfers of business.[15] However, in order to promote the greater participation of its staff in its affairs and their commitment, some large firms have established a staff council to provide a forum for a joint review of a firm's strategy, its performance and employment policies by the management of the firm with its employee representatives. The employee representatives are usually elected from all sections of a firm's workforce, therefore not just representing the interests of the fee-earners. Establishing a 'brand image' is an important aspect for international firms and therefore including employee representatives from overseas offices helps to create a 'one firm' common strategy, engendering a sense that everyone is allowed input into that strategy.

---

[14]   A number of firms are now taking advantage of a recent change in professional rules which enables them to incorporate as limited liability partnerships but which, if they do so, will make them subject to statutory reporting requirements.

[15]   In the future, the EC Directive on Information and Consultation OJ L080, 23/3/2002 – 0034 will apply to firms with more than 50 employees. It establishes a general framework for informing and consulting employees in relation to an undertaking's economic situation, employment prospects, and decisions likely to lead to substantial changes in work organizations or contractual relations, including redundancies. The Directive will be applied in stages by reference to numbers of staff employed.

F.   CONCLUSION

The foregoing paragraphs illustrate the extent and variety of *pro bono* and other 'ethical' activities being carried out in one major European jurisdiction. The United States has led the way in this field but lawyers in other jurisdictions are making up the ground fast. The amount of *pro bono* work done by lawyers and law firms will certainly increase in the coming years as the profession responds to the growing interest and involvement in Corporate Social Responsibility on the part of society generally and also to the desire of those entering the profession to play their part and use their developing expertise and experience for the benefit of others.

Chapter 30

CORPORATE SOCIAL RESPONSIBILITY AND THE IN-HOUSE COUNSEL

Isaiah Odeleye*

A. INTRODUCTION

The concept or policy of Corporate Social Responsibility (CSR) gained prominence first in the US in the early 1950s from where it spread to other parts of
the world. This is not to say that social concerns are only a product of contemporary world or business entities. Evidence of support for social concerns and
conditions dating as far back as the 18th century, can be found in countries like
France, Britain, Germany, US etc. This was particularly reflected in the attitudes
and policies of the respective governments to education, transport, housing,
health and other welfare services. Today CSR is not only the concern of international organizations like the UN, OECD, EU, ILO; ECOWAS, business entities
and national governments, but has also received the attention of some religious
organizations like the Evangelical Lutheran Church in America. In addition,
many professional associations and NGOs have driven CRS issues to the front
burners of public opinion. For example the council of Bars and Law Societies of
the European Union (CCBE) is playing a vital role on CSR issues.

CSR today therefore is a global and multi dimensional issue. Many multinationals like Shell, Agip, Chevron-Texaco, Total, BP, ExxonMobil, Cadbury, etc.,
have CSR policies as do other MNCs like General Motors, Tesco, McDonald,
Kmart, Basf, Roche Volkswagen, Corvs, Matav, Acome.

While CSR is largely accepted as an integral part of business, there is, however,
still no single position on its scope and the extent to which it should change the
business landscape. Its scope, content application and implementation largely

*   Mr I. Odeleye is the Company Secretary of The Shell Petroleum Development Company of
     Nigeria Limited. The views and opinions expressed in this paper are his views and opinions and
     do not represent the views or opinions of The Shell Petroleum Development Company of
     Nigeria Limited.

*Ramon Mullerat (ed.), Corporate Social Responsibility: The Corporate Governance of
the 21st Century*, 447–469.
© 2005 *International Bar Association. Printed in the Netherlands.*

depend on the geographical location where a company is operating varying from country to country and from one corporate entity to another.

For companies operating in poor countries where, there is little or no respect for rule of law, serious corruption is the norm rather than exception, and security of life and property is a concern, the unemployment rate is in high double digits, ethnic strife is common, no freedom of speech and press and other infrastructural facilities are grossly inadequate or malfunctioning, the pressure on the few companies around to be involved in CSR is always extremely high if not out of proportion.

Government support for CSR in some of such countries is partly both as a result of concerns for the host communities and as a means of transferring some responsibilities of government to business entities. CSR should not be allowed to become an escape route for governments to abdicate their responsibilities at the door step of business entities.

Caught in the fire works of lack of funds to meet CSR and the consequences of neglecting CSR, the average company executive is often in a dilemma as to whether he should continue to operate in such business environments or make new investment decisions. In the meantime, companies in such environments may be faced with high litigation portfolio, adverse public opinions, sabotage, kidnapping, unofficial levies and demands and threat to license to operate and grow. With the realization that central economies cannot function efficiently, with more and more privatizations around the world, among other factors the chances are high that more pressure will come on business entities to discharge what they have accepted and or what the society has imposed on them as part of their CSR.

B.   WHAT IS CSR?

There is no consensus on the definition or the precise meaning of CSR. I make no attempt to define it here either, but I will describe it in line with my understanding of the concept in a general way. As I see, CSR is the policy through which a business entity seek to strike a balance under law and regulation in an atmosphere of fair competition between its economic objective of making profit and simultaneously paying due attention to the expectations of not just the shareholders but also of the stakeholders.

CSR is a way for a business entity to forge parity between the often competing and conflicting environmental, economic, human and societal imperatives. A typical CSR policy of a business entity therefore will address issues including sustainable development, HSE, personnel policy, community development, business principles, and ethics, diversity, contractors/suppliers relations, environmental protection, transparency, accountability etc. Today, it is no longer fashionable to regard CSR as corporate philanthropy or to equate corporate interest with just shareholders interest without considering the larger interest of the community of stakeholders. CSR therefore, includes the liberalization of corporate governance in such a way that it is answerable for the legitimate social concerns and interests of host communities in particular and the business environment as a whole.

Dr O. Igho Natufe realizing the difficulty in defining CSR, came to the conclusion, that, while there is no universally accepted definition of the concept, there is however a consensus that it implies a demonstration of certain responsible behavior on the part of governments and the business sector toward society and the environment.[1]

C.   WBCSD, OECD AND CSR

The World Business Council for Sustainable Development (WBCSD) is one of the foremost international organizations committed to the ideals of CSR. WBCSD is a coalition of several companies numbering about 170 multinational companies with commitment to SD and CSR through the tripod of economic growth, ecological balance and social progress. The mission of WBCSD is to provide business leadership as a catalyst for change toward SD and to promote the role of eco-efficiency, innovation and CSR.

WBCSD is of the view that, a coherent CSR strategy, based on sound ethics and core values, offers clear business benefits. The core values identified by WBCSD as integral to CSR include employee rights, supplier relations, shareholder rights, community development and environmental protection.

The organization for Economic cooperation and Development OECD is another international organization that is giving a lot of attention and focus to CSR and its associated issues. The OECD has produced the OECD Guidelines for Multinational Enterprises. The Guidelines is a set of voluntary principles and standards for responsible business conduct consistent with applicable laws. The purport of the Guidelines is to ensure that activities of MNE are in harmony with government policies and strengthens the basis of mutually beneficial confidence between enterprises and the societies or communities where they operate. In addition to the Guidelines for Multinational Enterprises, the OECD is equally involved in formulating other international policy frameworks, including the Convention on combating Bribery of Foreign public officials in International Business Transactions, the OECD principles of corporate Governance, the OECD Guidelines for Consumer Protection in Electronic Commerce etc. The General policies of OECD on CSR are that, Enterprises should take fully into account established policies in the countries in which they operate and therefore should:[2]

1. Contribute to Economic, social and environmental progress with a view to achieving sustainable development.
2. Respect the rights of those affected by their activities consistent with the host government's international obligations and commitments.
3. Encourage local capacity building through close co-operation with the local community, including business interests, as well as developing the

---

[1]   O. Igho Natufe, The problematic of sustainable Development and CSR. Policy Implications for the Niger Delta. Presented during the Urhobo Historical Society Annual Conference and General Meeting, 2–4 November 2001.
[2]   OECD Guidelines for Multinational Enterprises: General Policies.

enterprise's activities in domestic and foreign markets, consistent with the need for sound commercial practice.

4. Encourage human capital formation in particular by creating employment and facilitating training opportunities for employees.
5. Refrain from seeking or accepting exemptions not contemplated in the statutory framework related to environmental, health, safety, labour, taxation, financial incentives, or other issues.
6. Support and uphold good corporate governance principles and develop and apply good corporate governance practices.
7. Develop and apply effective self-regulatory practices and management systems that foster a relationship of confidence and mutual trust between enterprises and the societies in which they operate.
8. Promote employee awareness of, and compliance with, company policies through appropriate dissemination of these policies including through training programs.
9. Refrain from discriminatory or disciplinary action against employee who makes bonafide reports to management or, as appropriate, to the competent public authorities, on practices that contravene the law, the Guidelines, or the enterprise's policies.
10. Encourage, where practicable, business partners, including suppliers and sub-contractors, to apply principles of corporate conduct compatible with the Guidelines.
11. Abstain from any improper involvement in local political activities.

In addition, the OECD Guidelines prescribes the specific – responsibilities of enterprises on taxation, competition, science and technology, consumer interests, combating bribery, environment, employment and industrial relations and disclosure requirements.[3] Apart from OECD and WBCSD, other international organizations playing meaningful roles in CSR issues include, Amnesty International, the UN, ILO, EU and ISO and World Bank.

D.   THE BUSINESS CASE FOR CSR

Nowadays business enterprises are the singularly most important mode of harnessing and distributing economic resources. With the substantive collapse of communism coupled with the spate of privatization of state enterprises across the globe, the economic power of companies is far more important and stronger than before. It is opined that out of the 100 largest economies in the world today, 51 of them are corporate entities. Toyota corporation is bigger than Norway, while the resources of General Motors is more than that of Denmark.[4] In view of the economic and political powers of corporate entities today, it is unrealistic to regard corporate decision making power and influence as ordinary power of private individual.

---

[3]   Part III–X of the OECD Guidelines for Multinational Enterprises.
[4]   Sarah Anderson & John Cavanagh, '*The top 200 – The Rise of Global corporation Power*. www. ips-dc.org/reports/top 200 text.htm'.

Every opportunity must be accompanied by corresponding responsibility. It follows therefore that there are some social responsibilities associated with corporate power. Social responsibilities should involve corporate entities that is not free from criticisms up till date. Pope John Paul II once observed, 'when a firm makes a profit this means that productive factors have been properly employed and corresponding human needs have been duly satisfied'. In a spirited effort, Milton Friedman wrote inter alia that 'the social responsibility of business is to increase its profits subject to conforming to the basic rules of the society embodied in law and those embodied in ethical custom'.[5]

One problem with the view of Milton Friedman is that, it is shareholders focused in a world that is stakeholders focused. The kernel of stakeholder's theory in relation to CSR is that, business entities are communities of many constituencies or parts. Each constituency has a stake in the corporation and therefore should have a legitimate voice in its governance and destiny. The stakeholders who should have a say therefore includes shareholders, employees, host communities, investors, suppliers or contractors, partners, consumers, governments etc. A key argument against the stakeholder's theory is that, the shareholders must not be made to bear the cost of the decisions of the other stakeholders. Whatever may be the merits of the arguments against CSR, the point is that, CSR has come to stay as an integral part of business particularly the business of multinational corporations. Tony Blair, the UK Prime Minister once said, 'The 21st century company will be different. Many of the world's best-known companies are already redefining traditional perception of the will of the corporation. They are recognizing that every customer is part of the community and that social responsibility is not an optional activity'.[6]

E. ADVANTAGES OF IMPLEMENTING CSR TO BUSINESS

The advantages of having and implementing CSR in the interest of stakeholders by companies are many and by no means exhaustive. However, the list of the advantages compiled by CCBE is very comprehensive and I hereby adopt them. These are:

- Enhanced corporate image and added brand value
- Better ability to attract and retain talents
- Enhancement of job satisfaction and loyalty of employees
- Better access to quality business partners
- Obtaining the status of preferred partner/investor
- Customer loyalty and satisfaction
- Improvement on risk management
- Better access to capital and terms
- Good footing with public authorities, governments and the general public
- Enhancement of ability to make profits

---

[5]   Milton Friedman, *The Social Responsibility of Business is to Increase Profits*, The New York Times Magazine, 13 September 1970.

[6]   Council of the Bars and Law Societies of the European Union: CSR and the Role of the Legal Profession, September 2003.

452 CSR – THE CORPORATE GOVERNANCE OF THE 21ST CENTURY

- Better stock value
- Better asset preservation
- Less or nil disruption to operations
- Cost effective
- Reduction of Litigation.

F. POSSIBLE CONSEQUENCES OF NEGLECTING CSR AS A CORPORATE MANAGEMENT TOOL

- More litigation against the company and its key officers
- Loss of top talents
- Loss of credible investors
- Increased cost of capital
- Decline in stock value
- Loss of business partners and customers
- Loss of public contracts e.g. from international organization like World Bank, EU etc.
- Exposure to shaming/blacklisting campaigns
- Erosion of reputation and brand value
- Sabotage of facilities
- Kidnapping
- Risk of losing LTO/G
- Increased insurance premiums
- Staff strike – breach of contracts
- Risk of provoking more stringent regulations
- Courts may take failure to adopt CSR principles into consideration in deciding liability issues

G. THE ROLE OF IN-HOUSE COUNSEL

The in-house counsel in his capacity as either Legal Counsel or Company Secretary or otherwise, has a key role to play in CSR issues. But before then, it is necessary for the in-house counsel or Corporate Secretary to have first and foremost the right attitude toward CSR as an ingrained element of modern day business. With the proper or positive mind set on CSR as part of good business and wise management, the in-house counsel must be properly trained on CSR. Without a proper mind set and training of the in-house counsel on CSR issues, the in-house counsel will most likely perceive business as oil which cannot mix with anything but business. Such a lawyer will be consumed by the zeal of legalism and utilitarianism, which may be contrary at times to reality, and the business objectives of his client and employer – the company. It is therefore necessary for every in-house counsel to become an apostle of CSR as part of his or her responsibility to the company whether in the North or in the South. With the benefit of the advantages of implementing CSR policies and principles as part of good management, as well as the possible disadvantages of neglecting same, it is easier for us in a general sense to identify the role of in-house counsel in CSR issues. CSR is an instrument of positive change in business. It sets the social framework and defines the manner in which a well-run business should operate in order to meet the ethical, legal, commercial, and public expectations that a society has of any company. As recent as 2002 the European Commission made the following statement 'CSR can play an important role in advancing sustainable development. Many businesses have already recognized that CSR can be profitable and CSR schemes have mushroomed. .... CSR is no longer a job for marketing departments'.[7]

The key responsibilities of the in-house counsel in CSR may be summarized as follows:

1.   CSR Should be Part of In-house Counsel's Mandate

Traditionally some companies do not regard CSR as part of the mandate of the in-house counsel to the company. For the few that have accepted CSR as part of the sphere of influence of the in-house counsel; it is often as a result of bad experiences. A Company that neglects to drink out of the well of experience of others is most likely to die in the desert of ignorance. CSR is largely voluntary. But legal liabilities can arise even out of voluntary actions.

2.   Pre-emptive Measures in Memo and Articles

The in-house counsel especially for public quoted companies should ensure that when incorporating new investment vehicles, appropriate provisions are made under the Memorandum and Articles of the company to enable the company carry out its CSR obligations in order to prevent successful challenge of CSR activities by shareholders. This is particularly important in jurisdictions where the doctrine of ultra vires could be used to strike down CSR initiatives and programmes.

3.   Legal Audits

The in-house counsel could or should conduct periodic legal audits in the company. This should cover changes in law and procedure, changes or proposed changes in policies directly relevant to the business of the company. The audit should also cover present and potential key problems, and major misconducts. Directors, Company Secretary, and some Accountants should be involved. The audit should review all compliance including CSR compliance requirements, control procedures pending and potentially serious problems.

The aim of legal audit is to detect and prevent violations of laws and policies. Where a company can demonstrate that it conducts periodic legal audits

---

[7]   European Commission; Corporate Social Responsibility; New Commission Strategy to Promote Business Contribution to Sustainable Development, ip1021 985, 2 July 2002.

of itself, it is most likely that in the event that a breach occurs, authorities including the court may be willing to be less severe on their view of the breach. Other issues that a legal audit may look into include, codes of conduct, ethics, training sessions, disciplinary systems, mechanism to encourage employees to report violations without fear of retribution.[8] In order to curtail the ambit of this procedure, in Grahams V. Allis – Chalmers Manufacturing Co,[9] the Delaware Supreme Court in the US held that 'there is no duty on directors to install and operate a corporate system of episionage to ferret out wrongdoing which they have no reason to suspect exists.' It is therefore incumbent on the board of directors of each company to use sound business judgement in relation to the business of the company with a view to ensuring that, the company's systems and procedures are sufficiently robust to ensure the ability of the board to capture relevant information in a timely fashion as a matter of course.

4.   Compliance Monitoring

Law in a way is a set of values usually backed by sanctions. CSR issues to a large extent are ethical values. These values are not backed by legal sanctions as such but their neglect could subject a company to certain disabilities.

For example in the UK, all trustees of UK Pension Funds are required to disclose the extent to which social, environmental and ethical considerations are taken into account in the selection, retention and realization of investments. The effect of this legal provision is that, companies, that neglect CSR, may not receive access to capital from pension funds. This may increase the cost of capital for such companies.It should therefore be part of the duties of the in-house counsel to monitor CSR standards at local and international levels and advise the company on compliance.

Companies perceived as adopting international best corporate governance practices are more likely to attract international investors than those whose practices are perceived to be below international standards.[10] Currently, there are hundreds of CSR Standards, codes etc. Monitoring them is therefore a huge task, which the in-house counsel is best, equipped to carry out. It should be remembered that, international institutions like UN, OECD, ILO, ISO, etc. are behind a lot of CSR standards. These institutions are capable of persuading governments to adopt and enforce CSR standards or rules locally either through legislation or policies. For example in the Netherlands, companies seeking export credits and investment guarantees must state that they are aware of the OECD Guidelines and that they will endeavour to comply with the Guidelines to the best of their ability.[11]

---

[8]   *Kaplan, sentencing Guidelines: An Umprecedented Offer: from Governance 5 Ethikos* 12, 13 (No. 5, 1992).
[9]   188 A.2d 125, Del. 1963.
[10]   Atedo N.A. Peterside, OON at p. 2 of code of corporate Governance in Nigeria.
[11]   OECD Guidelines for Multinational Enterprises: 23–24 June 2003, Annual Meeting of the National Contact Points Report p. 7.

5. Formulation of CSR Policy

Currently CSR is largely a Northern policy. One of the reasons for this is that, a lot of business enterprises in the South or developing countries are small and still struggling to make profits. This should not be a valid reason for neglecting CSR. CSR should be a global policy for all businesses whether large, medium or small.

In jurisdictions where there is legal or contractual basis for companies to be involved in CSR, the in-house counsel should draw the attention of the Board of directors to it. Where there is no policy on CSR, the in-house counsel working in collaboration with other teams and officers in the company should stimulate and promote the formulation of policies on CSR issues. It is only then, that CSR and its benefits for the stakeholders will cease to be a fashion but a structured process capable of yielding the required dividends on long-term basis for the Company.

6. Legislative Proposal

As part of the mandate for CSR, the in-house counsel working in collaboration with his colleagues at professional or industry level can propose legislation that will give incentives to business entities in order to encourage them to be committed to CSR. Such legislation may also provide for certain reporting requirements by business organizations.

7. Review of Company Policies etc.

The policies of a company outlines its opinion and attitudes to the various issues addressed in the policies. The in-house counsel should review such policies from time to time with a view to ensuring that they are fair, just, current and acceptable under applicable CSR norms and policies. In particular, the in-house counsel should focus on: HSE policies of the company, personnel policy, diversity, security, collective bargaining, outsourcing policy in relation to HSE and fair wages in particular. This is also of importance to in-house counsel of privatized entities where there is need to ensure that relevant agreements take into consideration the welfare of staff.

8. Corporate Structure

The in-house counsel should take a hard look at the corporate structure of his or her organization especially during and after every reorganization with a view to ensuring that, the corporate structure does not constitute an impediment to compliance efforts and to dissemination of information on approaches to CSR and its implementation.

9. New Projects or Developments

In properly organized business entities, the in-house counsel has a key role to play with respect to major new projects. As an important member of the project team whether as a full or part time member, the in-house counsel should ensure CSR issues are taken into consideration in screening investment, legal due diligence, media and NGO relations, applicable CSR reporting requirements etc.

10.   Protection of Parent Companies

There is a growing culture of litigation against parent companies of multinational corporate entities. Such legal actions are substantially driven by CSR considerations by members of the public generally and special interest groups in particular. It is therefore necessary for in-house counsel who has a key role to play in the defence of such actions to be involved in the formulation and implementation of CSR policies of the organization. This will assist the company in preventing litigation against it, and where CSR policy formulation or implementation still results in litigation, the in-house counsel if involved in CSR issues of the company will be in a better position to formulate the defences of the company and manage such litigation.

11.   CSR Consequence Management

The implementation of any policy may be accompanied by certain consequences, CSR implementation inclusive. Again, the nature and scope of consequences resulting from CSR implementation will depend on number of factors including, level of poverty, education, culture, history, etc. of the business environment. In some developing countries the provision of amenities may lead to inter or intra ethic violence if there is a breach of custom or culture or where there is unresolved land dispute. The in-house counsel should realize that, culture which consists of norms, values, attitudes, role, expectations, taboos, symbols, heroes, beliefs, morals, customs, rituals etc. are very important. In some countries customs are customary laws. A violation of customary law with all good intentions may incur the wrath of the people including authorities. The in-house counsel should be familiar with the culture of the area where his or her company is operating and put this knowledge at the disposal of the business lines in the company. Where CSR implementation results in dispute, protest or violence, the starting point is for the in-house counsel assisted by relevant staff of the company to investigate whether there is a breach of any aspect of the culture of any or all of the parties involved.

Where there is, honest acknowledgement of the mistake and an apology may be all that is necessary to manage the situation successfully. A proper understanding of the culture of the people is very important for the resolution of CSR related disputes in the developing countries in particular.

12.   CSR and Settlement of Company Disputes

Every company should have a litigation policy. The litigation policy of a corporate entity should strike a good balance between the protection of its business interests, principles, ethics, values, and reputation on one hand and ensure that, stakeholders are not drawn into long and tedious legal battles just to establish an academic or valueless point on the other. Each time a company embark on litigation when it ought not to, and losses, the impact on reputation is negative. The in-house counsel should see his company as a settler and not a traveler in the business environment and ensure that, the litigation policy of the company and its implementation supports the other policies and objectives of the company taking into consideration in particular the reputation and long term business objectives of the company. There is time, to insist on legality or constitutionality and to be compassionate. Central to CSR is compromise and compassion, and to that, the in-house counsel should be central under law.

H. THE ROLE OF GOVERNMENT IN ENSURING THAT CSR WORKS

Without discouraging governments from enacting laws that could enforce CSR standards, codes, policies etc., it must be stated that, it is not likely that such laws will achieve maximum results if enacted. This is because, the best role of government in such issues is not to legislate but to encourage, counsel, facilitate and stimulate. The argument in support of this position is that, CSR is part of the production processes of any business entity. Only where necessary this should be left for private regulation with public intervention. Of course, it is in the best interest of corporations to take the lead in performing their own CSR.

If they do not, and stakeholders especially in the developing countries continue to mount serious pressure on government, government may be forced to make laws as enable would it to take part in business or introduce more control measures through laws. A reason government may advance in support of its action is the uncooperative attitude of the business community on CSR issues, and the fact that, if the built up pressure explodes it could worsen already bad public security concerns in the polity with grave political consequences. If government must inspire business entities to perform their social responsibilities, then, government should lead by good example. As a minimum, every government should:

- Ensure that social responsibility is not for corporations alone but for government, and its institutions and other organizations.
- Have appropriate welfare programmes particularly for the poor.
- Actively support and promote export of goods and services at its own expense.
- Ensure fair competition under competition law.
- Perform its contractual obligations to business entities.
- Ensure transparency and accountability in governance.
- Provide good and necessary infrastructures and ensure functionality of utilities.
- Ensure a conducive business environment under the rule of law.
- Generally ensure good governance.
- Reward moves to control irresponsible behaviour and promote calculated steps to ensure corporate culture of compliance, awareness of possibility of illegality, personal ethics of care, and culture of risk management.

- Use CSR to encourage and not to constrain improved business result and efficiency.
- Discourage law breaking by corporate entities.
- Make emergency Response Policy a must for companies.

I. EXAMPLES OF CSR ACTIVITIES FROM NIGERIA AND GHANA

When we talk about CSR in the developing countries, it is the same way of saying something about the role of business entities in alleviating poverty in the developing countries. If poverty must be alleviated and eradicated in the developing countries, there must be good governance, adherence to the rule of law, transparency and accountability in the public sector, good management of resources and eradication of corruption among others. For they are to be meaningful approach to CSR in the developing countries, there must be sustainable partnerships between the society or communities, the business entities and the government. One of the disincentives for many SMEs in the developing countries for not having aggressive approach to CSR is the fear of the possible end game of globalization. With globalization of trade, the size of many TNCs is increasing. At the same time, a lot of SME entities are loosing markets to TNCs in areas where they use to dominate. The effect of this on many small and medium enterprises is that, though they realize that there is a business case for investing in CSR, but, can investment in CSR retain them in business in the face of cheaper products due to globalization? In addition, being very responsible on CSR issues is not of high priority to most SMEs in the developing countries as it is not always considered as a must business development strategy.

Apart from companies in the mining industry in the developing countries, the level of public pressure in support of CSR is low. In the circumstance, a key factor driving CSR issues in the Northern countries is absent. The effect of this is that, many MNCs and local business entities are not alive to their social responsibilities as they ought to be.

There are various reasons for CSR in different parts of the world. As mentioned earlier, the main focus of CSR in the developing countries is poverty alleviation. This calls for a change in attitude, policy and legislation in order to create an enabling business environment for business entities in the developing countries in order that, they might have the focus of mind to approach CSR as a core business issue.

In this regard, my opinion is that, if CSR will become a policy of majority of the businesses operating in the developing countries and in particular the SMEs, factors that are currently hindering their ability to grow, expand, be competitive must be addressed.

Because the focus of CSR in the developing countries is to alleviate poverty and support the efforts of governments in the provision of infrastructure, I will discuss the New Partnership for Africa's Development (NEPAD) in relation to NEPAD's objective of alleviating poverty in the Region, the Niger Delta Development Commission as a good example of public and private sector partnership in CSR. Last, I will discuss the CSR activities of The Shell Petroleum

Development Company of Nigeria Limited in 2002, mention the recent Shell Ghana example in Social Responsibility as well as one or two entities in Nigeria. I should have discussed the CSR activities of more companies but for two key constraints. The first is space and the second is lack of documented facts on CSR activities of a lot of companies I contacted. It is however hoped that the examples discussed below will give a good indication of what CSR is about in the developing countries as well as its challenges.

J. THE NEW PARTNERSHIP FOR AFRICA's DEVELOPMENT

The reason that informed the formation of NEPAD is the need to address the challenges facing the African continent. These issues include escalating poverty, under development, and the continued marginalization of Africa. It is not surprising that the three prong primary objectives of NEPAD are poverty eradication, sustainable growth and development of African countries and the need to halt the marginalization process. One of the principles of NEPAD that is relevant for the topic under discussion is the realization of the fact that, good governance is a basic requirement for peace, security and sustainable political and socio-economic development.

If there is good governance in African countries, there will be peace, security, economic growth and development, more local and foreign investments, unemployment rate will fall drastically, there will be more revenues for the government, better infrastructure and improved ability of corporate entities to perform their CSR. However, in order that, NEPAD may be able to achieve its objectives NEPADs organs and leadership must be consistent in the pursuit of its set goals and objectives, and must make truth the foundation of its policies, practices and procedures. But without the support of the public, no policy can succeed. Most Africans have little or no knowledge of NEPAD and its objectives. It is difficult therefore to see how Africans can fully support an initiative they are neither aware of nor understand. This can still be corrected. Nevertheless NEPAD is an excellent initiative for the alleviation and eventual eradication of poverty in Africa.

K. THE NIGER DELTA DEVELOPMENT COMMISSION

The Niger Delta Development Commission (NDDC) was set up by an Act of the National Assembly in 2000. Before then, there was the Oil Mineral Producing Areas Development Commission. The main objective of NDDC and that of its predecessor is to serve as catalyst for the sustainable development of the Niger Delta Region of Nigeria on a non-exclusive basis. The mission of NDDC in relation to its duties is to facilitate the rapid development of the Niger Delta into a region that is economically prosperous, socially stable, ecologically regenerative and politically peaceful through a development plan for the Niger Delta and the implementation of development projects. One of the functions of

NDDC relevant for our present purpose is: 'Conceive, plan and implement, in accordance with set rules and regulations, projects and programmes for the sustainable development of the Niger Delta area in the field of transportation including roads, jetties and waterways, health, education, employment, industrialization, agriculture and fisheries, housing and urban development, water supply, electricity and telecommunications'.[12]

Section 14(2) of the Act provides for the sources of the fund of the commission. Under that section, the Federal Government contributes 15 per cent of the total monthly statutory allocations due to member states of the commission from the Federation Account, each company operating in the Niger Delta area including gas processing companies must contribute three per cent of the total annual budget, while every member state of the Commission must contribute 50 per cent of the total annual budget of monies due to the state from the Ecological Fund.

The above provision shows a good example of how government through policy or law in partnership with the private sector or a section of it could discharge CSRS to the communities where the companies are operating. In 2002, the SPDC JV in Nigeria contributed $14.4 million to the NDDC Fund. Other oil companies like Chevron, Exxon-Mobil, Agip, Total etc. also paid depending on budget level. With this money from oil companies and money from other sources available to NDDC, the NDDC was able to execute a lot of projects like roads, bridges, schools, water supply schemes, hospitals, market stalls, various training programmes etc. for the communities in the Niger Delta area of Nigeria. The Nigerian Bottling Company PLC, the producers of Coca Cola in Nigeria spent the sum of N5,751,575 on CSR in 2003.[13] In 1999, Nigerian Breweries PLC spent the sum of N5,865,000 on CSR'.[14]

L.   2002 CSR EFFORTS OF THE SHELL PETROLEUM DEVELOPMENT COMPANY OF NIGERIA LIMITED

CSR efforts of SPDC in Nigeria are almost as old as the company. CSR including SD and CD has become a business issue for the company over the years. It is not possible because of space and time to give a detailed account of SPDCs CSR efforts and achievement for year 2002 or the period before then. In the circumstance, I will only mention the key issues for 2002 in general terms. The facts mentioned in this part are as stated by SPDC in her 2002 'People and Environment Report' which is a public document. The Report is a succinct document on the CSR activities of the company for year 2002. It is published annually. Before publication, the facts were verified internally by officials of the company, stakeholders and a reputable firm of external auditors – KPMG.

---

[12]   Section 7(1)(a) of the NDDC Act 2000.
[13]   2003 Annual Report p. 8.
[14]   D. Oluwagbami, *Corporate Responsibilities to Shareholders and Society.* Inputs publishing Company Limited Lagos 2002, pp. 18–19.

1. Stakeholders Engagement and Workshop

SPDC is committed to working with all Stakeholders especially stakeholders in the Niger Delta in order to share information of mutual interest between the Company and the stakeholders with a view to promoting Sustainable Development (SD) and good relationship between the Company and the stakeholders. For this purpose SPDC has a lot of engagement activities with the stakeholders from time to time. These include community open fora, people's parliaments, Environmental, Social and Health Impact Assessment reviews, oil seminars, NGO and CBO engagements and regular meetings with relevant institutions including governments. Participants at the engagement activities include, community leaders, women, youth organizations, CBOs and government agencies.

Every year since 1997, SPDC conducts an annual stakeholders workshop. The theme for the 2002 stakeholders Workshop was 'Building Partnerships for Sustainable Development' There were more than 700 participants at the Workshop from Communities, local, state, and Federal authorities including parliamentarians, CBOs, local and international NGOs, development agencies, regulatory authorities, industry specialists, unions, staff, academics, news media. The workshop focused on ways to continue fostering partnerships with stakeholders for sustainable growth and development in the Niger Delta. The Workshop also served the dual purpose of providing comments and feedbacks on SPDC's activities, plans, programmes and performance.

2. Community Development Programme

SPDC's Community Development Programme is based on the need to reduce poverty in the Niger Delta, promote economic empowerment, improve quality of life, stimulate employment for youths and women and supplement government's efforts in the provision of key infrastructure and facilities like water, roads, hospitals, schools, electricity, and market stalls. In doing this, it is expected that SPDC will earn the support of the communities for a peaceful and stable business environment.

3. Safeguarding People

Occupational Health: As a matter of Policy, SPDC plans and executes its activities in a manner that protects employees, contractors and the public at large against possible hazards that might arise from its operations. In 2002, SPDC started implementing the Royal Dutch/Shell Group's new Minimum Health Management Standards which comprise: Health Risk Assessment, Monitoring of Health Performance and Incident Reporting and Investigation, Health impact Assessment, Human Factors Engineering in New Projects, Fitness to Work and Local Health Facilities and Medical Emergency Response.

In 2002, many SPDC and contractors staff attended some 240 lectures on topics such as malaria, stress, chemical exposure, health, life style and general medical topics. Awareness sessions for staff and contractors on the prevention of HIV/AIDs and care were held. SPDC contributed to Warri Youth Health Forum 2002 on HIV/AIDs.

4. Safety

There were more fatalities associated with the operations of the Company in 2002 than 2001. The company has since renewed her aggressive policy of reducing fatalities to zero. However, lost time injury frequency (LTIF) which measures the number of injuries per million man-hours worked by staff and contractors dropped further from the 2001 level. Some of the initiatives that led to this improved performance include: The development of a structured corporate HSE plan and the enforcement of the ownership culture and delivery policy by the various business units in the company, and the verification of reported performance from the business units, the development, roll out and implementation of a Contract Management Guide with mandatory training, testing and certification of all staff who are contract holders or company site representatives and a sustained campaign on transport safety with seminars, training for drivers, good journey management including audits and compliance reviews.

5. Security

SPDC has a Security Policy, which took into consideration Nigerian laws, international, and Group Guidelines and Standards. Consequently, SPDC has adopted the joint US/UK Voluntary Principles on Security and Human Rights in the Extractive Sectors. Staff security while at work in particular is a shared responsibility of the company. In 2002, SPDC conducted more security awareness seminars for staff. In addition, the company took steps that improved access to buildings, sites, premises and facilities. A number of early warning and preventive measures were introduced.

6. Women Empowerment

Because of the importance of women as a group within communities and their role and influence in peace building and conflict resolution, SPDC has a Women Empowerment programme as a way of shielding them from the effects of underdevelopment. Between 1999 and 2001, 7,000 women were trained in various capacity building schemes. In 2002, about 1,000 women were trained in participatory project planning, project and enterprise management, personnel recruitment, safety and basic first aid. SPDC facilitated access to credit for women groups to start or expand existing business. SPDC supported the building of more development centres for the purpose of training women in skills such as bakery, sewing, hairdressing, and soap making. The company also supported income generation and micro-credit projects including food processing and preservation schemes, cargo transportation and retail trading.

7. Youth Empowerment and Skills Development

SPDC's Youth Empowerment Programme is designed to reduce youth unemployment in the host communities through employment opportunities, skills training, business support and access to credit. In 2002, under the SPDC Youth Training Scheme, 850 Youths were trained at five Centres for skills acquisition in welding, sewing, auto mechanics, computer, hair dressing, building, bakery, soap making, plumbing and fitting. The training schemes were managed in partnerships with local NGOs. In addition, SPDC supported the training of 200 youths under the Youth Oil and Gas Training Scheme with two government craft centres in Rivers and Bayelsa States.

8. Agriculture and Youth Empowerment

Agriculture is the mainstay of the non-oil sector of the Nigerian and the Niger Delta economy, and has been a longstanding area of support by SPDC. In 2002, SPDC provided support to farmers through agricultural extension advisers. Farmers in the Niger Delta received advice on improved planting technicians, livestock husbandry, post harvest loss reduction, organic agriculture practice, seed multiplication and snail husbandry.

Over 5,000 farm families benefited directly from the services provided. SPDC in collaboration with research institutes distributed high yielding disease resistant crop varieties. In 2002, SPDC helped to establish 28 agribusiness enterprises, creating direct and indirect job opportunities for over 800 people. The enterprises established included community poultry projects, creek fishing, community model farms schemes, offshore fishing, integrated fish hatchery, oil palm nursery out-growers scheme, oil palm mill and fish ponds.

As a way of supporting continuous improvement in agricultural production in Niger Delta, SPDC adopted new initiatives. These include mushroom production in partnership with Helta International Company, a new approach for community agriculture development intervention was designed in collaboration with Royal Institute of Tropical Agriculture (KIT) Amsterdam, a unique collaboration with Citizens International and the International Institute of Tropical Agriculture helped to encourage farmers to earn additional income by mass producing improved cassava strain for export, a tractor hiring business was started by a Shell farmers' Union with a tractor and accessories donated by SPDC, a pilot fresh water shrimp culture project was opened in collaboration with Kentucky University USA and Multilynx Enterprises Nigeria who are providing technical support.

9. Micro-Credit and Business Development Programme

In the developing countries in particular, medium and small-sized enterprises play important roles in economic development. Apart from their income generation abilities, they are vital agents of employment generation in the process of producing goods and services for the market. In order to further bring the advantages of small and medium sized enterprises to Niger Delta Stakeholders in the operations of SPDC, SPDC in 1998 started its micro-credit and business development programme as a way of empowering communities economically.

This scheme or goal is being pursued through three broad categories of service which are: community based enterprises, micro-credit schemes and youth business development programmes. A total of 146 community-based enterprises (26 in 2002) have been established in 115 host communities and 513 micro-entrepreneur groups from 50 host communities (153 groups in 2002) have benefited from loans through the revolving loans schemes. Another 29 agricultural cooperatives have accessed loans under the micro-credit scheme which is a partnership between SPDC the Central Bank of Nigeria, First Bank of Nigeria PLC and Cooperative Development Bank.

10. Education

During the 2001/2002 academic year, SPDC awarded 2,600 Secondary and 863 University scholarships. A total of 13,000 secondary school students and 2,500 University students are supported by SPDC through SPDC scholarships at any one time. SPDC donated over 120,000 text books on various subjects to 70 secondary schools in the Niger Delta region. A total of 374 professional science teachers were deployed by SPDC to teach science subjects at 42 schools in Niger Delta. In addition, 213 National Youth Service Corps graduates were deployed to 37 schools to boost English and Science education in host communities' schools. SPDC's adult literacy programme was expanded in 2002 with the establishment of four additional centres which brought the number of centers in operation to 14. About 1,400 participants benefited from this programme in 2002. SPDC completed and donated science laboratories to three community schools. Sixteen classroom blocks were constructed while six others were renovated across host communities. To encourage the rural areas, SPDC began the construction of teachers, quarters in four towns serving 20 host communities. In addition SPDC, supported five professional chairs in geology, geophysics, mechanical engineering and petroleum engineering in five Nigerian Universities.

11. Sports and Competition

The Annual Shell Cup football competition for secondary schools in Nigeria took place in 2002. Over 3,000 secondary schools took part in the 2002 competition. It is gratifying to note that, Femi Opabunmi a member of the Nigerian National team (the Super Eagles) who took part in the 2002 Korea/Japan World Cup was discovered during the year 2000 Shell Cup football competition. Annually SPDC organizes choral and science quiz competitions for secondary schools in three locations in Nigeria.

12. Health

SPDC has a community health services policy which conforms to the National Health Care Policy and international development practice. In 2002, SPDC maintained support for five general hospitals, 15 cottage hospitals and 12 health centers in the host communities. A total of 265,000 patients were treated in these hospitals. In 2002, SPDC supported the National Immunization day as in the past with $172,000 which helped to immunize about 1.8 million children against poliomyelitis. In the same year, SPDC commenced a pilot behavioural change project for University students as part of the World Summit on Sustainable Development (WSSD) and Heritage Project on HIV/AIDs. SPDC is of the view that, the provision of adequate potable water and good sanitation practices will reduce the relatively high incidence of infant mortality and morbidity attributable to water borne and human waste related diseases. In 2002 therefore, SPDC rehabilitated 32 water schemes and hand pumps in 20 communities with over 40,000 people.

13.   Social and Economic Infrastructure

The policy of SPDC with respect to the delivery of social and economic infrastructure is engagement, participation and partnership. In 2002 some 116 Km of community roads were constructed. In the same year 21 rural electrification projects were completed.

SPDC also assisted four host communities located in low-lying terrains and therefore subject to seasonal flooding to sand fill their areas in order to prevent erosion and provide better land for future growth and development. On the whole in 2002, SPDC spent 66.9 million USD on community development.

14.   Protecting the Environment

In 2002, SPDC continued monitoring the regulatory compliance of its operations using a transparent reporting format.

The HSE data of the company was audited in 2002. The result of the audit confirmed that some parameters of the data quality improved when compared with 2001 though some areas need to be improved upon. During 2002 SPDC achieved 19 new ISO certificates in respect of some facilities and eight Operations/Services certified to ISO 14001 standard by the end of 2002.

In collaboration with Work Bank's Business Partners for Development, SPDC continued its EIA improvement project. During the year, the company concluded the capacity building aspects of the programme. Through a competent third party, SPDC commenced training of its staff, regulatory staff and chief executives of EIA consulting companies on environmental, social and health impact assessment. A total of 300 persons were trained.

15.   Health, Safety and Environmental Awareness Training (HSEAT)

Over the years, the scope of environmental awareness training in SPDC expanded to include training for external stakeholders including communities, school environmental conservation clubs and contractors. Over 1,000 training sessions were conducted for 17,500 participants. In 2002, 55 additional Environmental Conservation Clubs (ECC) were inaugurated. Six ECC members participated in the National High Schools Model United Nations Conference held in New York.

16.   Flares – Down Programme

SPDC in 2002 intensified its efforts to end all routine gas flaring by 2008. SPDC further intensified its efforts to put into economic use the gas otherwise flared from its facilities. Hence the volume of gas flared in 2002 was less than the volume flared in 2001 by 33 per cent due mainly to the effect of the Associated Gas Gathering projects of the company.

17.   Oil Spills

Compared with 2001 data, in 2002 there was a 13 per cent and 74 per cent reduction in the number of oil spill incidents and volume spilled, respectively. There was also a significant reduction in the volume of oil spill incidents caused by corrosion. Sabotage accounted for 61 per cent, of total oil spill incidents in 2002. The overall improvement in the company's record in 2002 was due to the progress made by SPDC in her asset integrity programme. This includes pipeline and flowline replacement, flowstation upgrade, improved wellhead control system and better proactive inspections. In 2002 about 400 people majority of who are field based staff of the company were trained in oil spill response capabilities and preparedness. To improve the spill response time, the company established six additional field logistics bases in 2002. Total carbon dioxide emissions associated with oil and gas production by SPDC fell by 45 per cent in 2002. One of the reasons responsible for this is the increase in the utilization of more associated gas from the operations of the company. With respect to produced water, the concentration of oil in water in the produced water discharged by SPDC into the environment was lower than the regulatory limits in 2002.

M.   AN EXAMPLE FROM GHANA

One of the recent examples of Shell Ghana Limited efforts in CSR is the provision of two 20 ft long cold storage facilities for the immediate host community of the company in Accra Ghana. The project became a reality as a result of tripartite co-operation between the Ashieolu-keteke sub-metro communities. MURAG (an NGO) and Shell Ghana Limited.

The purpose of providing the cold room was to enable members of the host community improves their fish storage and preservation capability, generate more income and thus reduce poverty. In addition to the two, each 20 ft long cold storage facilities, Shell Ghana also provided a suitable generator, and office facility, all securely fenced. Shell Ghana also provided start up funds and technical support for the operation of the facilities and it was the duty of the community to operate the facility efficiently. Speaking at the commissioning ceremony, Dr Roy Kretzen the Managing Director of Shell Ghana said 'This just demonstrated yet again that carefully identified catalysts rather than handouts, are required to assist communities to look after their own needs with pride, dignity and sustainability.... The facility is merely a Pilot project that can be duplicated and replicated fairly quickly and this is what makes it very exciting. ... It is in this regard that I want to appeal to the private sector to join hands based on the outcome of this project as no single organization can do it alone'.

N. CONCLUSION

'A global human society based on poverty for many and prosperity for a few characterized by islands of wealth, surrounded by a sea of poverty is unsustainable'.[15] The issue today therefore is not whether CSR is necessary or not as the majority of the stakeholders especially, shareholders, corporate entities, consumers, governments, and other stakeholders have come to a realization that, CSR is vital for business success and good business relations. CSR as one of the key roles of a Board of Directors of a corporate entity is part of the managerial responsibilities to meet society's demand for accountability and to reduce corporate risks. There are three main dimensions to this: the first is legal responsibility, which consists of obeying the law and complying with mandatory codes of conduct. The second is discretionary and it consists of building goodwill with stakeholders by being a good corporate citizen. The third dimension to CSR is strategic.

This is about corporate value building with a view to ensuring long term sustainability of a company by increasing or improving its economic and ecological efficiency.[16]

CSR is good business. A real challenge on CSR for corporate entities and lawyers is how to create synergy between the imperatives of legal risks management and reputation risks management. That synergy is necessary in order to ensure that, legal risks management which does not impair reputation risks management which does not lead to additional litigation for the company. As lawyers we should embrace the fact that, we can learn a lot from experts on external relations on reputation issues and management. The primary responsibility for CSR in a corporate entity lies with the board of directors of the company. However, lawyers have a key role to play if the milk of human kindness of the company in formulating and implementing its CSR policies will not turn into a sour taste.

Apart from the lawyers, human resources, commercial and external relations professionals and external advisers have an important role to play in CSR issues. There is a good debate now on whether or not government should compel corporate entities to comply with CSR imperatives. There are good arguments for and against this issue. But I will urge that we err on the side of caution on this matter because force may conquer, but its victories are often short-lived.

A good number of corporate organizations are showing more than expected and beyond the law commitments to CSR already. It is therefore necessary that the direction of policy formulation on CSR should aim at striking a balance between the sometimes conflicting interests of some stakeholders who believe in making a living by what they get and the investors or shareholders who want to give what they can share in order to make a life for the corporate entity by what they give.

It is for this reason that I fully agree with the observation of Grabosky when he asked the question: what is the role of government in an era of less regulation in relation to the use of incentives as regulatory instruments? and answered as follows:

'A regulatory system in which they themselves play a less dominant role, facilitating the constructive regulatory participation of private interests – monitoring the overall regulatory system, broadly defined, and one of fine tuning – manipulating incentives in order to facilitate the constructive contributions of non-government interests'.[17]

Government regulatory agencies will no longer occupy center stage, but rather will be unobtrusively influential from a position offstage – Governments can vary their degree of investment, both symbolic and material in forums for consultation and decision, and in the interests of intermediaries themselves.

As such they can give a new voice to the previously disenfranchised, and can tone down those interests which would unreasonably dominate'.[18]

I am of the opinion that business entities will continue to face more challenges and pressure from the stakeholders on CSR. Currently, new forms of sanctions against corporate misconducts are being devised and implemented. The trend now is not just to fine a corporate entity or imprison key corporate officers in cases of serious corporate misconducts but also to impose sanctions of stigma such as adverse publicity. The threat of adverse publicity for example forced Black and Decker to settle a lawsuit filed against it by US Consumer Safety Commission in respect of defective toasters. Another form of sanction emerging now is the sanction of community service against companies by law courts. In *United States v. Dan low Pastry Co.*,[19] six bakeries pleaded *novo contendere* to a charge that they violated the Sherman Act. The court ordered them to provide community services by donating baked products to the needy.

As in-house counsel or external counsel, if our employer or client should be subjected to such sanctions by the court, that will have a rob on effect on our professional effectiveness and efficiency. Such a counsel may also suffer personal abasement. As in house counsel and lawyers anywhere, we have a duty at all

---

[17]   P. Grabosky, *Regulation by Reward: On The Use of Incentives as Regulatory Instruments,* Law and Policy, Vol. 17, No. 3, 1995, pp. 543–544.

[18]   P. Grabosky Regulation by reward. *Law policy,* Vol. 17, No. 3, 1995, p. 273.

[19]   563 F. Supp 1159 (1983).

times to support the cause of justice and fair play and to remember at the same time that, our clients are entitled to the best of our professional knowledge, skill and judgement which must be thorough and fit for good purpose at all times. We have a duty within the scope of our professional duties, ethics and law to ensure that, the reputation of our employer or client is deservedly kept spotless. One way of doing this is by playing active roles in CSR issues of our employers or clients.

PART VIII

CRITICISM OF THE CORPORATE SOCIAL RESPONSIBILITY MOVEMENT

Chapter 31

CRITICISM OF THE CORPORATE SOCIAL RESPONSIBILITY MOVEMENT

Michael Hopkins

A. INTRODUCTION

To end this book, it is appropriate to review some of the key criticisms with the concept and application of corporate social responsibility (CSR). However, to preface my remarks, it is always easy to criticize concepts especially those that rise to rapid prominence.

The attraction of CSR, as defined in this chapter, is that it is a systems approach[1] to the issue of business in society. Many of the criticisms, as will be seen, stem from problems with concepts and definitions. Now business, in general, is more concerned to stay in business and be profitable than to be concerned with such seemingly academic discussions. This is unusual, since business is usually a stickler for detail – a company can hardly prepare accounts, sell pharmaceuticals, computer software, copper tubing or whatever without knowing exactly the definition of the product they are selling.

Yet, somehow, management concepts are manipulated at ease to fit in with some pre-conceived notion or other that will please the chairman or some shareholders. This translates into a confusing set of definitions for the same concept. For instance some define CSR as a systems approach taking into account both internal and external stakeholders, while others define it as purely voluntary. This confusion leads to a proliferation of concepts in the business in society area – corporate sustainability, corporate citizenship, corporate responsibility, business responsibility, business social responsibility, business reputation, the ethical corporation etc.

---

[1]   In the systems approach the problem is defined and the systems boundary delineated so that all important influences on resolving the problem are taken into consideration – see, for instance the systems approach defined in: *Global Simulation Models* (John Wiley, New York, 1975), J. Clark, S. Cole, R. Curnow and M. Hopkins.

Ramon Mullerat (ed.), Corporate Social Responsibility: The Corporate Governance of the 21st Century, 473–482.
© 2005 *International Bar Association. Printed in the Netherlands.*

In this chapter some of the criticisms of CSR are channelled, into seven essentially different statements. In brief they are:

1. Lack of definition, everyone seems to have their own concept or definition.
2. CSR is just part of public relations to bamboozle an increasingly sceptical public.
3. CSR is just another word for corporate philanthropy and that the contribution that a business directly makes to the welfare of society (or 'the planet') is to be viewed as largely independent of its profitability.
4. CSR is misleading as it diverts attention from key issues, it is a curse rather than a cure.
5. CSR ignores development economics and its concerns with capitalism, neo-liberalism and, anyway, is just a proxy to introduce socialism through the backdoor.
6. The social responsibility of business begins and ends with increasing profits. CSR is an unnecessary distraction.
7. CSR is sham because companies cannot be left to self-regulate.

Next, I look at each of these concerns in more detail.

1. Lack of definition, everyone seems to have their own concept or definition.
As already noted, there are a wide variety of concepts and definitions associated with the term *corporate social responsibility*. However, there is no general agreement of terms and one well-known CSR manager told this author that it was all a question of 'semantics' and therefore definitions were not important.

But, without a common language we don't really know that our dialogue with companies is being heard and interpreted in a consistent way. These flaws lead some companies to consider CSR as purely corporate philanthropy while others dismiss the notion entirely. But there are some, such as Shell, BP-Amoco, Co-operative Bank etc. that see CSR as a new corporate strategic framework.

In this context, a lively debate has led some authors, mainly US based academics, to prefer to use the concept of 'corporate social responsiveness', rather than corporate social responsibility *per se*. Ackerman and Bauer,[2] for instance, note that the notion of 'responsibility' is that of a process that merely assumes an obligation. It places an emphasis on motivation rather than performance and, they believe, this motivation is not enough, because responding to social demands is much *more* than deciding what to do. There remains the management task of *doing* what one has decided to do: *this* is social responsiveness. However, the view here is that managers need to accept the notion of social responsibility *before* they work out what to do. There is no argument about the fact that once this has been accepted, *then* the next step is the response, in other words that acceptance of the motivation to be socially responsible *immediately leads* the manager into what should be done next, i.e. into social responsiveness. Acceptance, of course, does not come easily, and the point of this booklet is to show that CSR makes sound economic as well as social, ethical, political and philosophical sense.

---

[2]   Robert Ackerman and Raymond Bauer (1976): *Corporate Social Responsiveness*, Reston Publishing, Prentice-Hall, Reston, Virginia.

The definition that this author finds most appealing[3] is the stakeholder definition:

'CSR is concerned with treating the stakeholders of the firm ethically or in a socially responsible manner. Stakeholders exist both within a firm and outside. The aim of social responsibility is to create higher and higher standards of living, while preserving the profitability of the corporation, for its stakeholders both within and outside the corporation'.

This definition, of course, begs the question what is meant by 'ethical' and what is meant by 'stakeholder'. Without going into a long discourse on ethics, ethical behaviour is clearly in the eye of the beholder and, like beauty, we know it when we see it but find it difficult to define. Who are the stakeholders of a company has also sparked intense debate but, at minimum they include those *within* the company: the board of directors, shareholders, investors, managers and employees; and *outside* the company: suppliers, customers, the natural environment, Government, and local community.

2. CSR is just part of public relations to bamboozle an increasingly sceptical public.
Is CSR just fodder for a company's PR department? Tim Wright thinks so. In his prize winning essay[4] he states: 'The number of public relations companies adding CSR practices or strengthening existing offerings endorses the assertion that corporations desire to seize and dictate the agenda through savvy media management. For example Edelman Public Relations, which has hired non-profit veteran Steven Voien to launch First and 42nd, its first national CSR practice and management consultancy. Similarly WPP Group's BursonMarsteller brought Bennett Freeman aboard as managing director for corporate responsibility, based in Washington, D.C., and Hill and Knowlton Canada created a global CSR practice'.

These concerns were also voiced in a recent World Bank sponsored internet conference on CSR and the media. Rachel Olivier, a journalist from Hong Kong who jointly moderated the conference with the current author remarked about CSR information from companies in Asia:

'It is all very well to promote easy access to sources of information, but the public relations industry would have you believe that is what they already do. And their very existence more often than not hampers the development of a story instead of encouraging it. One of the key problems I have faced (as have many, many others) is the institutionalisation of spin which gives the appearance of increased access to information through heavily staffed internal and external PR offices, but the reality often means these individuals serve more to control the flow of their own messages as opposed to facilitating deeper relationships between the media and those in the know. That then puts them in the position of gatekeeper. ... Unfortunately, for non-listed companies, there is little incentive for the dissemination of information to the public – why would they do something they are not legally required to do?'

---

[3]   From Michael Hopkins, *The Planetary Bargain: CSR Matters* (Earthscan, London, 2003).

[4]   Tim Wright, *Plus ça change, plus c'est la meme chose: The grand illusion of corporate social responsibility*, Leicester University Management Centre, Winner, Guardian/Ashridge MBA Essay Competition, 2003.

So, no doubt that companies use CSR in their PR to promote their reputation. Yet, is there no more to CSR than just that? Evidence I have produced elsewhere using sources such as the Dow Jones Sustainability indices[5] led me to conclude that the top companies are becoming more socially responsible over time. This does not mean that all is well with the corporate world but might just suggest that all the actions, protests, analysis etc. ... of disparate groups all over the world might just be having a positive effect. In fact, my article showed that, on balance, companies are becoming more and more responsible on *average* In fact the word *average* is the key to unlock what is going on. Now, it is always easy to start to get better CSR rankings in the beginning than as time goes on. For instance, cleaning up a leaking pipeline, producing a code of ethics that nobody reads, producing a glossy CSR report, making extra sure that your product doesnot kill your customers, closing down that supplier in Bangladesh that uses child labour etc. So, on *average* it is relatively easy to make progress on CSR. But how to embed the ideas throughout the organization? That is the problem and that is why scandals will erupt in supposedly 'clean' organizations such as Shell, Enron or World Com.

3. CSR is just another word for corporate philanthropy – the contribution that a business directly makes to the welfare of society (or 'the planet') is to be viewed as largely independent of its profitability.

This is a popular view also recently pronounced by *The Economist* in an article entitled *Two faced capitalism*. They stated: 'CSR is philanthropy with a few bits added on.[6] CEOs should ignore this and go back to doing their jobs'.

Thus, *The Economist* seems to imply that a company that pays starvation wages, pollutes, treats employees as slaves, ignores customer complaints, bribes Governments, leaves human rights issues to Bush etc. and makes glorious profits is fine. Anyone who opposes that model is anti-capitalist.

That CSR is purely voluntary is also the view of Michael Porter. He states that *Corporate philanthropy – or CSR – is becoming an ever more important field for business. Today's companies ought to invest in CSR as part of their business strategy to become more competitive.*[7] But I believe he has got this wrong.[8] However, when even an internationally respected management guru mentions philanthropy and CSR as being the same, it is hardly surprising that business leaders, academics and politicians confuse them. Nevertheless, CSR is *not* the same as corporate philanthropy.

CSR, as noted above, is a system-wide concept that touches all the stakeholders of a corporation. CSR does not concentrate on only one stakeholder whereas philanthropy, 'the practice of performing charitable or benevolent actions' according to the Oxford English Dictionary, does. Most, if not all, philanthropy is devoted to items that governments should be doing (health grants to developing countries, help to the handicapped, drugs for HIV/AIDS for example). The

5   Michael Hopkins: *Measurement and Progress of Corporate Social Responsibility*, March 2004, www.mhcinternational.com.
6   *The Economist*, 24th January 2004.
7   See Michael Porter, http://www.ebfonline.com/debate/debate.asp.
8   Michael Hopkins: *Corporations Should Abandon Philanthropy and Concentrate on CSR*, Monthly Feature, April 2004, www.mhcinternational.com.

failure of governments should not be the preserve of corporations. Moreover, since government is one of the stakeholders of a corporation there is nothing to stop corporations offering their management and technical skills to government to improve or introduce programmes to help vulnerable groups. Corporations exist to make profits. There is nothing wrong with that, only the *way* profits are made is the concern of CSR practitioners. Philanthropy does little or nothing to help companies make profits, while *all* CSR activities are linked to improving a company's bottom line.

Consequently, an alternative view to that of *The Economist* is that CSR is not anti-capitalist since it questions not profit-making in itself but how profits are made. Long staying companies have focussed on values as well as their social responsibilities – work at Boston and Yale Universities based upon the book *Built to Last* found that visionary companies achieved their extraordinary performance by working productively and positively with other primary stakeholders such as customers, employees, communities and the environment. Identifying key stakeholders, evaluating what works better while keeping an eye on costs is what CSR is all about.

4. CSR is misleading since it diverts attention from key issues, it is a curse rather than a cure.

The curse, as elaborated in an article by Geoffrey Chandler,[9] is that with 'the absence of a clear definition... CSR is likely to delay the introduction of a regulatory framework...the shirt of Nessus poisoned those who wore it'. He continues: '...the prevalent interpretation is that 'CSR' is simply a voluntary add-on'. This is not the total concept of corporate responsibility which he believes, as I do, to be the necessary basis for corporate success and survival in the 21st century. The curse, he says,[10] has yet to run itself out: the misinterpretation of 'CSR' is a continuing diversion for companies from the reality that regulation has throughout corporate history been necessary to get the corporate world to fulfill its non-monetary responsibilities. 'CSR' is giving employment to many and has raised the profile of debate. Its impact in practice has been to divert attention from what is fundamentally required.

Unfortunately, Chandler's flowing words are likely to harm his vision of CSR as a total concept. Using strong words such as 'curse' misleads companies and provides them with ammunition to avoid CSR – not something that either of us want.

5. CSR ignores what has gone on before, in particular, development economics.

Bryane Michael writes[11] that within the literature focussing on CSR's role in development, 'three 'schools of practice' appear to be emerging: the neo-liberal school (focussed on self-regulation by industry according to the risks and rewards of CSR activity), the state-led school (focussed on national and international regulation and co-operation), and the 'third way' school (focussed on the

---

[9] Geoffrey Chandler: 'The curse of CSR', *New Academy Review*, Vol. 2, No. 1, Spring 2003.
[10] Personal communication, Spring, 2004.
[11] Bryane Michael, *Corporate Social Responsibility in International Development: An Overview and Critique*, Linacre College, Oxford, see http://users.ox.ac.uk/~scat1663/.

role of for profit and not-for-profit organizations). Yet, each of these schools of practice may be critiqued using theories applicable to the broader field of development. Namely, the neo-liberal school fails to address the resource misallocations caused by CSR. The state-led school fails to address the underlying politics behind government encouraged CSR. The 'third way' school fails to address the self-interest involved in CSR'. Michael continues that 'the CSR discourse appears to signal a new form of co-operation between government, business, and civil society in the promotion of social objectives. Yet, left out of the discourse are all the difficulties and complexities which development theory has been debating for a century. The neo-liberal school stresses the adequacy of the incentives versus insurance model – yet fails to address important resource misallocations. The state-led school emphasises the balance between co-operation versus control exercised by the state – yet ignores important contestation of political power by international organizations, national governments, and business interests. The 'third sector' school notes the new potential for public engagement in policymaking, but ignores the highly politicized and conflictual nature of that engagement. CSR is part of a larger transformation in the relations between government, business and civil society'.

Michael points are interesting and he is correct to note that there is a tendency for CSR practitioners to ignore history as well as theory. But Michael's three models are not necessarily discrete. Academics often use stylized facts to conceptualize difficult issues. CSR is no exception to this trend. Moreover, transposing into the current CSR debate as: (1) legislate for CSR (state school), (2) no legislation (voluntary or self-regulation school) and (3) some legislation to ensure a level playing field (third way) actually captures the debate on legislate or not, quite well.[12]

6. The social responsibility of business begins and ends with increasing profits. CSR is an unnecessary distraction.
Milton Friedman's oft-cited pronouncement that the 'social responsibility of business begins and ends with increasing profits' implies that social issues are best left for anyone but business. But, as the pressure increases on governments to spend less and less to rectify social problems these problems refuse to go away – third world underdevelopment and unemployment refuse to go away, HIV/AIDS has defeated many governments especially in Africa etc. It is logical, therefore, in the absence of public funds, or even in partnership with existing institutions,[13] that business must play a larger part in human development issues than ever before. In the longer term richer consumers and an improved world wide income distribution is obviously good for business. But should business be directly involved in these issues or simply pay their taxes and rely upon governments and public organizations to use these taxes wisely? i.e. is it simply enough for business to maximize profits in the anticipation that this is in the best interest of human development?

---

[12]   See my evolving views on this debate in Michael Hopkins: *CSR and Legislation*, Monthly Feature, www.mhcinternational.com, July 2002.
[13]   It is noteworthy that the World Bank has an evolving programme on partnership with the private sector and corporate social responsibility called 'Business Partners for Development', and the UN has embarked on a Global Partnership that requires business partners to sign up for good practice in labour, human rights and the environment.

On 16th, May 2001, Martin Wolf of the Financial Times wrote a provocative article criticizing CSR since he argued, based on a pamphlet by David Henderson former Chief Economist of the OECD, that social responsibility distorts the market by deflecting business from its primary role of profit generation.[14]

Wolf's main concern was that CSR is conducted by activist groups, who are 'with few exceptions...hostile to, or highly critical of, multinational enterprises, capitalism, freedom of cross-border trade and capital flows and the idea of a market economy. One might expect, and indeed hope, that the business community would effectively contest such anti-business views. But...the emphasis is on concessions and accommodation'.

Henderson, unlike, Wolf, realized that CSR was not confined to so-called 'anti-capitalists' and set up a number of more reasonable assertions. Henderson's view[15] is that businesses should 'act responsibly, and should be seen to do so' but not that 'responsible behaviour today need mean endorsing the current doctrine of CSR'. Henderson did not define what he meant by 'responsible behaviour' although he listed eleven points that he thought were unwise for corporations to accept. His main points are listed next together with my response:

i. That the objective of 'sustainable development', and the means to achieving it, are well defined and generally agreed.

Response: The term sustainable development originally emanated from the environment movement. Even through the term 'sustainable' had been criticized as ambiguous and open to a wide range of interpretations many of which were contradictory.[16] Confusion was because 'sustainable development', 'sustainable growth' and 'sustainable use' were used interchangeably as if their meanings were the same. The International Union for the Conservation of Nature (IUCN) rejected this and argued that 'sustainable growth' is a contradiction in terms since nothing can grow indefinitely. While 'sustainable use' was applicable only to natural resources so that they may be used at rates within their capacity for renewal. Sustainable development means improving the quality of human life while living within the carrying capacity of supporting ecosystems. More and more we hear of the term corporate sustainability and no-one is against their own corporation being sustainable i.e. continuing for ever. Hence Henderson's gripe is well-founded in this case.

ii. That the contribution that a business directly makes to the welfare of society (or 'the planet') is to be viewed as largely independent of its profitability.

Response: The implication is that so-called 'activists' require corporations to be philanthropic even when they are unprofitable. Few are as silly as this.

iii. That 'corporate citizenship', which is now to be endorsed, carries with it an obligation to redefine the goals of businesses, in terms of 'meeting the triple bottom line' and pursuing 'social justice'.

Response: There is a worrying unconcern with definitions and concepts – when challenged on this one CSR manager stated that her 'corporation was more

---

14   See Martin Wolf (2001), *Sleeping with the Enemy* in www.ft.com.
15   David Henderson (2001): *False Notions of Corporate Social Responsibility*, Institute of Economic Affairs (IEA), London, UK.
16   IUCN (1991), *Caring for the Earth*, Gland, Switzerland.

interested in the issues than worrying about semantics'. But the definition cited above that 'corporate citizenship implies a strategy that moves from a focus on short-term transaction to longer-term, values-based relationships with these stakeholders and that loyalty will be based on a company's ability to build a sense of shared values and mission with key stakeholders' is sensible and hardly requires corporations to meet 'triple bottom line (TBL)' considerations. It is true that TBL has become prominent and stems from John Elkington's book *Cannibals with Forks* which itself arose from the NGO environmental movement. CSR itself, as defined above, carries no such obligation.

iv. That new planning, monitoring and review systems should be introduced into businesses to ensure that they meet a range of often questionable environmental and 'social' targets.

Response: This point is similar to the previous point and it is true that environmentalists wish to reduce polluting emissions and so on, but there is widespread agreement on the need to do this. To date CSR implies treating stakeholders in an ethical manner, but no 'social targets' have been set except for the need to open this dialogue.

v. That an array of 'stakeholders' should now be closely and formally involved in the conduct and oversight of businesses.

Response: Stakeholders include internal ones such as owners, shareholders, management including the board of directors and also external stakeholders such as government, local communities and consumers. Clearly, internal stakeholders need to be 'closely and formally involved in the conduct and oversight' of their own business. External stakeholders will have different perceptions but, in each case, legislation does have a role to play in how business is conducted so as to protect the externals – consumer safety, ethically produced products and so on.

vi. That society has conferred on businesses special privileges and benefits, in return for which each of them must obtain from it an informal 'licence to operate', by engaging in good works that are not directly related to profitability.

Response: Much has been written about the phrase 'licence to operate' but, in fact, no business actually requires a licence to operate in the sense of a driving or pilot's licence. Therefore to link a 'licence' to operate with a 'must' obligation for good works does not characterize the main players. There continues to be much discussion on what aspects of CSR should lead to regulation and what voluntary to ensure a 'level playing field' for companies to operate in.

vii. That 'society's expectations', which are not to be questioned and which have to be met if businesses are to earn and keep their 'licence to operate', can be largely identified with the current demands made by NGOs, 'ethical' investment funds, and other radical critics of the market economy.

Response: Ethical (and social) investment funds are rapidly gaining ground (see below) but work within the market economy so can hardly be associated with 'radical critics of the market economy'.

viii. That grave environmental damage has been done, and is being done, as a result of economic activity in general and the profit-directed operations of companies in particular.

Response: The concern for these issues stands by itself and is not easy to dismiss. Clearly, Henderson falls into the radical camp of free marketers so characterized by the Bush administration's rejection of international treaties on the environment such as Kyoto.

ix. That recent globalization has brought with it (1) disproportionate gains to multinational enterprises, (2) 'social exclusion' everywhere, (3) 'marginalization' of poor countries, and (4) a transfer of the power to act and decide from governments to multinational enterprises, so that the role and responsibilities of these latter now have to be conceived in more ambitious terms.

Response: There is truth to each of these concerns stemming from the so-called anti-globalization lobby. However, not everyone who is in support of CSR is necessarily against globalization.

x. That progress within national economies, and in the world as a whole, is to be largely identified with the adoption and enforcement of ever more stringent and more uniform norms and standards, environmental and social, both within and across national frontiers.

Response: The discussion on norms and standards has been a regular feature of international organizations such as the ILO, OECD (where Henderson used to work) and EU. Some proponents of CSR are very hesitant to suggest ever more stringent standards and are aware that business should not be enveloped in a fog of new rules and regulations.

xi. That it has become the duty of businesses to work with governments, moderate NGOs and international agencies, in the name of improved 'global governance' and 'global corporate citizenship', to realize such standards internationally.

Response: There is increasing agreement that improved corporate governance is necessary to prevent abuse not only by the rich and powerful but also by large corporations in countries in the Third World which, hitherto, have been powers in themselves – the OECD corporate governance principles are contemporary examples of this process.

In summary, Henderson's views can be easily situated within the school of radical market capitalism where any hint of regulation is seen as an attack on the market economy. Consequently, CSR cannot be considered completely in isolation from the business case. It is, therefore, more appropriate to revise Friedman's aphorism from one of social responsibility *or* profits to one of social responsibility *and* profits!

7. CSR is a sham because companies cannot be left to self-regulate.
So Oxfam argues in their report *Behind the mask: the Real Face of CSR*.[17] Citing among the other case of Shell, Oxfam argues that Shell's recent fall from grace

---

17   *Behind the mask: the Real Face of CSR*, Oxfam, Oxford, UK, 2004 and argued by Andrew Pendleton, the author of the report, and David Vidal of the Conference Board in New York in 'Beyond the bottom line' *The Guardian*, London, UK, p.18, 12 June 2004.

over the misreporting of its oil reserves showed that its CSR policy was not work-ing. If CSR was going to have any teeth then there must be legislation that forces companies to adhere to its precepts. In response, David Vidal argued (see previ-ous footnote) that it is dangerous to make the 'perfect the enemy of the good. Holding companies to a standard of perfection in CSR performance is a false promise'. As argued above, I make the case that CSR still has a long way to go from a few statements at the top of the company and from a few in-house activists to being embedded in a company's ethos. On average a company may seem to be following CSR policies but the average, as we know from statistics, covers a variety of sins. Further, no-one is particularly against legislation that moves toward a level playing field for all companies. Indeed, some corporate leaders of the CSR movement welcome legislation that would bring their competitors in line with their own best practice. But the story on legislation is not one of voluntary vs legislate. There is a continuum between purely voluntary and total legislation. The current pointer is probably nearer the former than the latter and will, over time, gradually move toward the latter.

B.   CONCLUDING REMARKS

CSR is not a new concept, but has rapidly come to prominence in the past few years with hardly a day going past without a new report on CSR by a leading company, international organization, NGO or journalist. But, given the above criticisms, is CSR here to stay or will it disappear into the mists of time as just another fad. More likely than the latter view is that CSR will transform into different concepts but not disappear entirely. Since the realm of business in society is so crucial, CSR and its entrails will eventually become embedded in all organisations rather like the concern with the environment is right now. Consequently, in the future there will be less talk about CSR simply because it will become just part of routine daily operations.

PART IX
CONCLUSIONS

Chapter 32

A FEW CONCLUDING REMARKS

Ramon Mullerat

When asked about the definition of a 'deacon', Jonathan Swift answered that 'a deacon is one who carries out diaconal functions'. I hope that after reading this book, the reader will be able to be less cryptic when defining CSR.

After reading the interesting essays compiled in this book, I have reached some personal inferences, and I would like to share at least a few of them with the reader. It is clear that business enterprises have conquered, in the world of the 21st century, a prominent position among other human activities and that the power and influence exerted by business corporations, in the developing and in the developed world, is paramount. As John McDermott put it already in 1991, 'the modern corporation is the central institution of contemporary society'.

Today there is a very extended conviction in the world society that business corporations, in addition to strictly fulfilling the economic objectives of their by-laws, unquestionably have broader duties and responsibilities, internally and towards the local community and the global community at large, be it in their social facet, environmental facet or human rights facet – the CSR's triple bottom line. No board of directors, no business manager today can any longer restrict themselves to just looking at the company's production line and sales report and the reality is that their obligation has clearly expanded to form a much broader and more complex circle including contributing actively and directly to the public good. If these duties mainly fall with a particular weight on the board of directors, CEOs and managers – as epicentre of the corporation's decisions – the conviction is also permeating the minds of the employees, suppliers, customers and other stakeholders more and more, who, at the same time, are both beneficiaries and instigators of CSR. It is not a heresy to affirm that this 21st century world will be as bad or as good as the business community – the boards, the stockholders and the stakeholders – will decide to make it.

That is the idea that underpins the title of this book, 'CSR: the Corporate Governance of the 21st century'. That does not mean that these prominent roles and duties that business enterprises have assumed today should replace the

Ramon Mullerat (ed.), Corporate Social Responsibility: The Corporate Governance of the 21st Century, 485–486.
© 2005 *International Bar Association. Printed in the Netherlands.*

states' archetypal obligations but, by the same token that governments cannot off-load their traditional responsibilities on to companies, companies cannot exempt themselves from these new duties and hide behind the governments' responsibilities.

As I said in the introduction, I believe that the approach to CSR is not and should not be a dichotomised ethics or legal rules position, but is and should be an interweaving and interchanging of ethics and law and that governments and business corporations should honestly and decidedly hand in hand face the enormous and unacceptable inequalities and injustices that characterize the Earth within local communities, within states and throughout the whole of the 6 billion human beings that make up our human race that underlie so many world evils. I believe that CSR even goes beyond legal and ethical rules. It is more of an intimate conviction and an attitude towards our neighbours, mankind and towards human existence itself and an indisputable tool to improve the present deplorable situation of the world.

Finally, let me highlight the exceptional vocation of lawyers in this crusade, which has been so clearly illustrated by many of the contributors. Lawyers perform an excellent altruistic mission in society: to defend the rights and liberties of the citizens through the development of the vital function to give advice and impart their expertise to their clients. Their mediating task between clients, courts and governments is crucial for the new world order.

I hope that both the cultivators of both business and law will be more and more enticed by the CSR doctrine and will be decisive in taking the step that will lead to the world becoming a better place.

PART X

ANNEXES

We have decided to annex some of the key sets of principles/guidelines/norms that have been referred to by the authors of this book. This is a mere selection that the editor feels may be of interest to the readers, and he by no means intends it to be a comprehensive set of guidelines, there simply being too great a number to include in one book.

Due to practical reasons of lack of space, we have extracted what we feel to be the essence of what these international organizations propose on CSR and what we feel to be most relevant in respect of the contents of this book. However, given that the readers may well want a more comprehensive insight into these principles, we have provided a link to the web page of the organization at the end of every annex.

CONTENTS

Annex	Name of Organization/Principles	Year	Page
1	The ILO Tripartite Declaration of Principles Concerning Multinational Enterprises and Social Policy	1977	489
2	The Global Sullivan Principles	1977	497
3	The Caux Round Table Principles for Business	1994	499
4	Amnesty International Guidelines for Companies	1997	505
5	Social Accountability 8000	1998	511
6	OECD Guidelines for Multinational Enterprises	2000	517
7	The Global Compact Launched by the United Nations	2000	527
8	The ICC's Nine Steps to Responsible Business Conduct	2002	529
9	Global Reporting Initiative Guidelines	2002	533
10	CCBE Guide for European Lawyers advising on Corporate Social Responsibility Issues	2003	541
11	UN Norms on Responsibilities of Transnational Corporations and other Business Enterprises with regard to Human Rights	2003	549

Annex 1

THE ILO TRIPARTITE DECLARATION OF PRINCIPLES CONCERNING MULTINATIONAL ENTERPRISES AND SOCIAL POLICY*,†

1. Multinational enterprises play an important part in the economies of most countries and in international economic relations. This is of increasing interest to governments as well as to employers and workers and their respective organizations. Through international direct investment and other means such enterprises can bring substantial benefits to home and host countries by contributing to the more efficient utilization of capital, technology and labour. Within the framework of development policies established by governments, they can also make an important contribution to the promotion of economic and social welfare; to the improvement of living standards and the satisfaction of basic needs; to the creation of employment opportunities, both directly and indirectly; and to the enjoyment of basic human rights, including freedom of association, throughout the world. On the other hand, the advances made by multinational enterprises in organizing their operations beyond the national framework may lead to abuse of concentrations of economic power and to conflicts with national policy objectives and with the interest of the workers. In addition, the complexity of multinational enterprises and the difficulty of clearly perceiving their diverse structures, operations and policies sometimes give rise to concern either in the home or in the host countries, or in both.
2. The aim of this Tripartite Declaration of Principles is to encourage the positive contribution which multinational enterprises can make to economic and social progress and to minimize and resolve the difficulties to which their various operations may give rise, taking into account the United Nations resolutions advocating the Establishment of a New International Economic Order.
3. This aim will be furthered by appropriate laws and policies, measures and actions adopted by the governments and by cooperation among the governments and the employers' and workers' organizations of all countries.
4. The principles set out in this Declaration are commended to the governments, the employers' and workers' organizations of home and host countries and to the multinational enterprises themselves.
5. These principles are intended to guide the governments, the employers' and workers' organizations and the multinational enterprises in taking such measures and actions

---

* Copyright International Labour Organization.
† The Tripartite Declaration became adopted in 1997 by the governing body of the ILO.

and adopting such social policies, including those based on the principles laid down in the Constitution and the relevant Conventions and Recommendations of the ILO, as would further social progress.

6. To serve its purpose this Declaration does not require a precise legal definition of multinational enterprises; this paragraph is designed to facilitate the understanding of the Declaration and not to provide such a definition. Multinational enterprises include enterprises, whether they are of public, mixed or private ownership, which own or control production, distribution, services or other facilities outside the country in which they are based. The degree of autonomy of entities within multi-national enterprises in relation to each other varies widely from one such enterprise to another, depending on the nature of the links between such entities and their fields of activity and having regard to the great diversity in the form of ownership, in the size, in the nature and location of the operations of the enterprises concerned. Unless otherwise specified, the term 'multinational enterprise' isused in this Declaration to designate the various entities (parent companies or local entities or both or the organization as a whole) according to the distribution of responsibilites among them, in the expectation that they will cooperate and provide assistance to one another as necessary to facilitate observance of the principles laid down in the Declaration.

7. This Declaration sets out principles in the fields of employment, training, conditions of work and life and industrial relations which governments, employers' and workers' organizations and multinational enterprises are recommended to observe on a voluntary basis; its provisions shall not limit or otherwise affect obligations arising out of ratification of any ILO Convention.

GENERAL POLICIES

8. All the parties concerned by this Declaration should respect the sovereign rights of States, obey the national laws and regulations, give due consideration to local prac-tices and respect relevant international standards. They should respect the Universal Declaration of Human Rights and the corresponding International Covenants adopted by the General Assembly of the United Nations as well as the Constitution of the International Labour Organization and its principles according to which freedom of expression and association are essential to sustained progress. They should also honour commitments which they have freely entered into, in conformity with the national law and accepted international obligations.

9. Governments which have not yet ratified Conventions Nos. 87, 98, 111 and 122 are urged to do so and in any event to apply, to the greatest extent possible, through their national policies, the principles embodied therein and in Recommendations Nos. 111, 119 and 122. Without prejudice to the obligation of governments to ensure compliance with Conventions they have ratified, in countries in which the Conventions and Recommendations cited in this paragraph are not complied with, all parties should refer to them for guidance in their social policy.

10. Multinational enterprises should take fully into account established general policy objectives of the countries in which they operate. Their activities should be in harmony with the development priorities and social aims and structure of the country in which they operate. To this effect, consultations should be held between multinational enterprises, the government and, wherever appropriate, the national employers' and workers' organizations concerned.

11. The principles laid down in this Declaration do not aim at introducing or main-taining inequalities of treatment between multinational and national enterprises. They reflect good practice for all. Multinational and national enterprises, wherever

the principles of this Declaration are relevant to both, should be subject to the same expectations in respect of their conduct in general and their social practices in particular.

12. Governments of home countries should promote good social practice in accordance with this Declaration of Principles, having regard to the social and labour law, regulations and practices in host countries as well as to relevant international standards. Both host and home country governments should be prepared to have consultations with each other, whenever the need arises, on the initiative of either.

EMPLOYMENT PROMOTION

13. With a view to stimulating economic growth and development, raising living standards, meeting manpower requirements and overcoming unemployment and underemployment, governments should declare and pursue, as a major goal, an active policy designed to promote full, productive and freely chosen employment.

14. This is particularly important in the case of host country governments in developing areas of the world where the problems of unemployment and underemployment are at their most serious. In this connection, the general conclusions adopted by the Tripartite World Conference on Employment, Income Distribution and Social Progress and the International Division of Labour (Geneva, June 1976) should be kept in mind.

15. Paragraphs 13 and 14 above establish the framework within which due attention should be paid, in both home and host countries, to the employment impact of multinational enterprises.

16. Multinational enterprises, particularly when operating in developing countries, should endeavour to increase employment opportunities and standards, taking into account the employment policies and objectives of the governments, as well as security of employment and the long-term development of the enterprise.

17. Before starting operations, multinational enterprises should, wherever appropriate, consult the competent authorities and the national employers' and workers' organizations in order to keep their manpower plans, as far as practicable, in harmony with national social development policies. Such consultation, as in the case of national enterprises, should continue between the multinational enterprises and all parties concerned, including the workers' organizations.

18. Multinational enterprises should give priority to the employment, occupational development, promotion and advancement of nationals of the host country at all levels in cooperation, as appropriate, with representatives of the workers employed by them or of the organizations of these workers and governmental authorities.

19. Multinational enterprises, when investing in developing countries, should have regard to the importance of using technologies which generate employment, both directly and indirectly. To the extent permitted by the nature of the process and the conditions prevailing in the economic sector concerned, they should adapt technologies to the needs and characteristics of the host countries. They should also, where possible, take part in the development of appropriate technology in host countries.

20. To promote employment in developing countries, in the context of an expanding world economy, multinational enterprises, wherever practicable, should give consideration to the conclusion of contracts with national enterprises for the manufacture of parts and equipment, to the use of local raw materials and to the progressive promotion of the local processing of raw materials. Such arrangements should not be used by multinational enterprises to avoid the responsibilities embodied in the principles of this Declaration.

EQUALITY OF OPPORTUNITY AND TREATMENT

21. All governments should pursue policies designed to promote equality of opportunity and treatment in employment, with a view to eliminating any discrimination based on race, colour, sex, religion, political opinion, national extraction or social origin.
22. Multinational enterprises should be guided by this general principle throughout their operations without prejudice to the measures envisaged in paragraph 18 or to government policies designed to correct historical patterns of discrimination and thereby to extend equality of opportunity and treatment in employment. Multinational enterprises should accordingly make qualifications, skill and experience the basis for the recruitment, placement, training and advancement of their staff at all levels.
23. Governments should never require or encourage multinational enterprises to discriminate on any of the grounds mentioned in paragraph 21, and continuing guidance from governments, where appropriate, on the avoidance of such discrimination in employment is encouraged.

SECURITY OF EMPLOYMENT

24. Governments should carefully study the impact of multinational enterprises on employment in different industrial sectors. Governments, as well as multinational enterprises themselves, in all countries should take suitable measures to deal with the employment and labour market impacts of the operations of multinational enterprises.
25. Multinational enterprises equally with national enterprises, through active manpower planning, should endeavour to provide stable employment for their employees and should observe freely negotiated obligations concerning employment stability and social security. In view of the flexibility which multinational enterprises may have, they should strive to assume a leading role in promoting security of employment, particularly in countries where the discontinuation of operations is likely to accentuate long-term unemployment.
26. In considering changes in operations (including those resulting from mergers, takeovers or transfers of production) which would have major employment effects, multinational enterprises should provide reasonable notice of such changes to the appropriate government authorities and representatives of the workers in their employment and their organizations so that the implications may be examined jointly in order to mitigate adverse effects to the greatest possible extent. This is particularly important in the case of the closure of an entity involving collective layoffs or dismissals.
27. Arbitrary dismissal procedures should be avoided.
28. Governments, in cooperation with multinational as well as national enterprises, should provide some form of income protection for workers whose employment has been terminated.

TRAINING

29. Governments, in cooperation with all the parties concerned, should develop national policies for vocational training and guidance, closely linked with employment.) This is the framework within which multinational enterprises should pursue their training policies.
30. In their operations, multinational enterprises should ensure that relevant training is provided for all levels of their employees in the host country, as appropriate, to

meet the needs of the enterprise as well as the development policies of the country. Such training should, to the extent possible, develop generally useful skills and promote career opportunities. This responsibility should be carried out, where appropriate, in cooperation with the authorities of the country, employers' and workers' organizations and the competent local, national or international institutions.

31. Multinational enterprises operating in developing countries should participate, along with national enterprises, in programmes, including special funds, encouraged by host governments and supported by employers' and workers' organizations. These programmes should have the aim of encouraging skill formation and development as well as providing vocational guidance, and should be jointly administered by the parties which support them. Wherever practicable, multinational enterprises should make the services of skilled resource personnel available to help in training programmes organized by governments as part of a contribution to national development.

32. Multinational enterprises, with the cooperation of governments and to the extent consistent with the efficient operation of the enterprise, should afford opportunities within the enterprise as a whole to broaden the experience of local management in suitable fields such as industrial relations.

CONDITIONS OF WORK AND LIFE

Wages, Benefits and Conditions of Work

33. Wages, benefits and conditions of work offered by multinational enterprises should be not less favourable to the workers than those offered by comparable employers in the country concerned.

34. When multinational enterprises operate in developing countries, where comparable employers may not exist, they should provide the best possible wages, benefits and conditions of work, within the framework of government policies. These should be related to the economic position of the enterprise, but should be at least adequate to satisfy basic needs of the workers and their families. Where they provide workers with basic amenities such as housing, medical care or food, these amenities should be of a good standard.

35. Governments, especially in developing countries, should endeavour to adopt suitable measures to ensure that lower income groups and less developed areas benefit as much as possible from the activities of multinational enterprises.

Safety and Health

36. Governments should ensure that both multinational and national enterprises provide adequate safety and health standards for their employees. Those governments which have not yet ratified the ILO Conventions on Guarding of Machinery (No. 119), Ionizing Radiation (No. 115), Benzene (No. 136) and Occupational Cancer (No. 139) are urged nevertheless to apply to the greatest extent possible the principles embodied in these Conventions and in their related Recommendations (Nos. 118, 114, 144 and 147). The Codes of Practice and Guides in the current list of ILO publications on Occupational Safety and Health should also be taken into account.

37. Multinational enterprises should maintain the highest standards of safety and health, in conformity with national requirements, bearing in mind their relevant experience within the enterprise as a whole, including any knowledge of special hazards. They should also make available to the representatives of the workers in the enterprise, and upon request, to the competent authorities and the workers' and

employers' organizations in all countries in which they operate, information on the safety and health standards relevant to their local operations, which they observe in other countries. In particular, they should make known to those concerned any special hazards and related protective measures associated with new products and processes. They, like comparable domestic enterprises, should be expected to play a leading role in the examination of causes of industrial safety and health hazards and in the application of resulting improvements within the enterprise as a whole.

38. Multinational enterprises should cooperate in the work of international organizations concerned with the preparation and adoption of international safety and health standards.

39. In accordance with national practice, multinational enterprises should cooperate fully with the competent safety and health authorities, the representatives of the workers and their organizations, and established safety and health organizations. Where appropriate, matters relating to safety and health should be incorporated in agreements with the representatives of the workers and their organizations.

INDUSTRIAL RELATIONS

40. Multinational enterprises should observe standards of industrial relations not less favourable than those observed by comparable employers in the country concerned.

Freedom of Association and The Right To Organize

41. Workers employed by multinational enterprises as well as those employed by national enterprises should, without distinction whatsoever, have the right to establish and, subject only to the rules of the organization concerned, to join organizations of their own choosing without previous authorisation. They should also enjoy adequate protection against acts of anti-union discrimination in respect of their employment.

42. Organizations representing multinational enterprises or the workers in their employment should enjoy adequate protection against any acts of interference by each other or each other's agents or members in their establishment, functioning or administration.

43. Where appropriate, in the local circumstances, multinational enterprises should support representative employers' organizations.

44. Governments, where they do not already do so, are urged to apply the principles of Convention No. 87, Article 5, in view of the importance, in relation to multinational enterprises, of permitting organizations representing such enterprises or the workers in their employment to affiliate with international organizations of employers and workers of their own choosing.

45. Where governments of host countries offer special incentives to attract foreign investment, these incentives should not include any limitation of the workers' freedom of association or the right to organize and bargain collectively.

46. Representatives of the workers in multinational enterprises should not be hindered from meeting for consultation and exchange of views among themselves, provided that the functioning of the operations of the enterprise and the normal procedures which govern relationships with representatives of the workers and their organizations are not thereby prejudiced.

47. Governments should not restrict the entry of representatives of employers' and workers' organizations who come from other countries at the invitation of the local or national organizations concerned for the purpose of consultation on matters of mutual concern, solely on the grounds that they seek entry in that capacity.

Collective Bargaining

48. Workers employed by multinational enterprises should have the right, in accordance with national law and practice, to have representative organizations of their own choosing recognized for the purpose of collective bargaining.

49. Measures appropriate to national conditions should be taken, where necessary, to encourage and promote the full development and utilization of machinery for voluntary negotiation between employers or employers' organizations and workers' organizations, with a view to the regulation of terms and conditions of employment by means of collective agreements.

50. Multinational enterprises, as well as national enterprises, should provide workers' representatives with such facilities as may be necessary to assist in the development of effective collective agreements.

51. Multinational enterprises should enable duly authorized representatives of the workers in their employment in each of the countries in which they operate to conduct negotiations with representatives of management who are authorized to take decisions on the matters under negotiation.

52. Multinational enterprises, in the context of bona fide negotiations with the workers' representatives on conditions of employment, or while workers are exercising the right to organize, should not threaten to utilize a capacity to transfer the whole or part of an operating unit from the country concerned in order to influence unfairly those negotiations or to hinder the exercise of the right to organize; nor should they transfer workers from affiliates in foreign countries with a view to undermining bona fide negotiations with the workers' representatives or the workers' exercise of their right to organize.

53. Collective agreements should include provisions for the settlement of disputes arising over their interpretation and application and for ensuring mutually respected rights and responsibilities.

54. Multinational enterprises should provide workers' representatives with information required for meaningful negotiations with the entity involved and, where this accords with local law and practices, should also provide information to enable them to obtain a true and fair view of the performance of the entity or, where appropriate, of the enterprise as a whole.

55. Governments should supply to the representatives of workers' organizations on request, where law and practice so permit, information on the industries in which the enterprise operates, which would help in laying down objective criteria in the collective bargaining process. In this context, multinational as well as national enterprises should respond constructively to requests by governments for relevant information on their operations.

Consultation

56. In multinational as well as in national entrprises, systems devised by mutual agreement between employers and workers and their representatives should provide, in accordance with national law and practice, for regular consultation on matters of mutual concern. Such consultation should not be a substitute for collective bargaining.

Examination of Grievances

57. Multinational as well as national enterprises should respect the right of the workers whom they employ to have all their grievances processed in a manner consistent with the following provision: any worker who, acting individually or jointly

with other workers, considers that he has grounds for a grievance should have the right to submit such grievance. without suffering any prejudice whatsoever as a result, and to have such grievance examined pursuant to an appropriate procedure. This is particularly important whenever the multinational enterprises operate in countries which do not abide by the principles of ILO Conventions pertaining to freedom of association, to the right to organize and bargain collectively and to forced labour.

Settlement of Industrial Disputes

58. Multinational as well as national enterprises jointly with the representatives and organizations of the workers whom they employ should seek to establish voluntary conciliation machinery, appropriate to national conditions, which may include provisions for voluntary arbitration, to assist in the prevention and settlement of industrial disputes between employers and workers. The voluntary conciliation machinery should include equal representation of employers and workers.

The full text of this document including the addendum and additional footnote references can be found online at: http://www.ilo.org/public/english/standards/norm/sources/ mne.htm

For further information please visit the ILO website: www.ilo.org

THE GLOBAL SULLIVAN PRINCIPLES*

As a company which endorses the Global Sullivan Principles we will respect the law, and as a responsible member of society we will apply these Principles with integrity consistent with the legitimate role of business. We will develop and implement company policies, procedures, training and internal reporting structures to ensure commitment to these Principles throughout our organization. We believe the application of these Principles will achieve greater tolerance and better understanding among peoples, and advance the culture of peace.

Accordingly, we will:

- Express our support for universal human rights and, particularly, those of our employees, the communities within which we operate, and parties with whom we do business.
- Promote equal opportunity for our employees at all levels of the company with respect to issues such as color, race, gender, age, ethnicity or religious beliefs, and operate without unacceptable worker treatment such as the exploitation of children, physical punishment, female abuse, involuntary servitude, or other forms of abuse.
- Respect our employees' voluntary freedom of association.
- Compensate our employees to enable them to meet at least their basic needs and provide the opportunity to improve their skill and capability in order to raise their social and economic opportunities.
- Provide a safe and healthy workplace; protect human health and the environment; and promote sustainable development.
- Promote fair competition including respect for intellectual and other property rights, and not offer, pay or accept bribes.
- Work with governments and communities in which we do business to improve the quality of life in those communities – their educational, cultural, economic and social well being – and seek to provide training and opportunities for workers from disadvantaged backgrounds.
- Promote the application of these Principles by those with whom we do business.

We will be transparent in our implementation of these Principles and provide information which demonstrates publicly our commitment to them.

This document can be found online at:
http://globalsullivanprinciples.org/principles.htm

For further information please visit the website:
www.glogalsullivanprinciples.org

---

* The Global Sullivan Principles were originally drafted and submitted in 1997, being re-launched by Reverend Lean Sullivan in 1999.

Annex 3

THE CAUX ROUND TABLE PRINCIPLES FOR BUSINESS*

INTRODUCTION

The Caux Round Table believes that the world business community should play an important role in improving economic and social conditions. As a statement of aspirations, this document aims to express a world standard against which business behavior can be measured. We seek to begin a process that identifies shared values, reconciles differing values, and thereby develops a shared perspective on business behavior acceptable to and honored by all.

These principles are rooted in two basic ethical ideals: kyosei and human dignity. The Japanese concept of kyosei means living and working together for the common good enabling cooperation and mutual prosperity to coexist with healthy and fair competition. 'Human dignity' refers to the sacredness or value of each person as an end, not simply as a mean to the fulfillment of others' purposes or even majority prescription.

The General Principles in Section 2 seek to clarify the spirit of kyosei and 'human dignity', while the specific Stakeholder Principles in Section 3 are concerned with their practical application.

In its language and form, the document owes a substantial debt to The Minnesota Principles, a statement of business behavior developed by the Minnesota Center for Corporate Responsibility. The Center hosted and chaired the drafting committee, which included Japanese, European, and United States representatives.

Business behavior can affect relationships among nations and the prosperity and well-being of us all. Business is often the first contact between nations and, by the way in which it causes social and economic changes, has a significant impact on the level of fear or confidence felt by people worldwide. Members of the Caux Round Table place their first emphasis on putting one's own house in order, and on seeking to establish what is right rather than who is right.

Section 1. Preamble

The mobility of employment, capital, products and technology is making business increasingly global in its transactions and its effects.

Law and market forces are necessary but insufficient guides for conduct.

Responsibility for the policies and actions of business and respect for the dignity and interests of its stakeholders are fundamental.

Shared values, including a commitment to shared prosperity, are as important for a global community as for communities of smaller scale.

---

* The CRT Principles for business were published in 1994.

For these reasons, and because business can be a powerful agent of positive social change, we offer the following principles as a foundation for dialogue and action by business leaders in search of business responsibility. In so doing, we affirm the necessity for moral values in business decision making. Without them, stable business relationships and a sustainable world community are impossible.

Section 2. General Principles

Principle 1. The Responsibilities of Businesses: Beyond Shareholders toward Stakeholders

The value of a business to society is the wealth and employment it creates and the marketable products and services it provides to consumers at a reasonable price commensurate with quality. To create such value, a business must maintain its own economic health and viability, but survival is not a sufficient goal.

Businesses have a role to play in improving the lives of all their customers, employees, and shareholders by sharing with them the wealth they have created. Suppliers and competitors as well should expect businesses to honor their obligations in a spirit of honesty and fairness. As responsible citizens of the local, national, regional and global communities in which they operate, businesses share a part in shaping the future of those communities.

Principle 2. The Economic and Social Impact of Business: Toward Innovation, Justice and World Community

Businesses established in foreign countries to develop, produce or sell should also contribute to the social advancement of those countries by creating productive employment and helping to raise the purchasing power of their citizens. Businesses also should contribute to human rights, education, welfare, and vitalization of the countries in which they operate.

Businesses should contribute to economic and social development not only in the countries in which they operate, but also in the world community at large, through effective and prudent use of resources, free and fair competition, and emphasis upon innovation in technology, production methods, marketing and communications.

Principle 3. Business Behavior: Beyond the Letter of Law Toward a Spirit of Trust

While accepting the legitimacy of trade secrets, businesses should recognize that sincerity, candor, truthfulness, the keeping of promises, and transparency contribute not only to their own credibility and stability but also to the smoothness and efficiency of business transactions, particularly on the international level.

Principle 4. Respect for Rules

To avoid trade frictions and to promote freer trade, equal conditions for competition, and fair and equitable treatment for all participants, businesses should respect international and domestic rules. In addition, they should recognize that some behavior, although legal, may still have adverse consequences.

Principle 5. Support for Multilateral Trade

Businesses should support the multilateral trade systems of the GATT/World Trade Organization and similar international agreements. They should cooperate in efforts to promote the progressive and judicious liberalization of trade and to relax those domestic measures that unreasonably hinder global commerce, while giving due respect to national policy objectives.

Principle 6.   *Respect for the Environment*

A business should protect and, where possible, improve the environment, promote sustainable development, and prevent the wasteful use of natural resources.

Principle 7.   *Avoidance of Illicit Operations*

A business should not participate in or condone bribery, money laundering, or other corrupt practices: indeed, it should seek cooperation with others to eliminate them. It should not trade in arms or other materials used for terrorist activities, drug traffic or other organized crime.

Section 3.   Stakeholder Principles

Customers

We believe in treating all customers with dignity, irrespective of whether they purchase our products and services directly from us or otherwise acquire them in the market. We therefore have a responsibility to:

- provide our customers with the highest quality products and services consistent with their requirements;
- treat our customers fairly in all aspects of our business transactions, including a high level of service and remedies for their dissatisfaction;
- make every effort to ensure that the health and safety of our customers, as well as the quality of their environment, will be sustained or enhanced by our products and services;
- assure respect for human dignity in products offered, marketing, and advertising; and respect the integrity of the culture of our customers.

Employees

We believe in the dignity of every employee and in taking employee interests seriously. We therefore have a responsibility to:

- provide jobs and compensation that improve workers' living conditions;
- provide working conditions that respect each employee's health and dignity;
- be honest in communications with employees and open in sharing information, limited only by legal and competitive constraints;
- listen to and, where possible, act on employee suggestions, ideas, requests and complaints;
- engage in good faith negotiations when conflict arises;
- avoid discriminatory practices and guarantee equal treatment and opportunity in areas such as gender, age, race, and religion;
- promote in the business itself the employment of differently abled people in places of work where they can be genuinely useful;
- protect employees from avoidable injury and illness in the workplace;
- encourage and assist employees in developing relevant and transferable skills and knowledge; and
- be sensitive to the serious unemployment problems frequently associated with business decisions, and work with governments, employee groups, other agencies and each other in addressing these dislocations.

Owners/Investors

We believe in honoring the trust our investors place in us. We therefore have a responsibility to:

* apply professional and diligent management in order to secure a fair and competitive return on our owners' investment;
* disclose relevant information to owners/investors subject to legal requirements and competitive constraints;
* conserve, protect, and increase the owners/investors' assets; and
* respect owners/investors' requests, suggestions, complaints, and formal resolutions.

Suppliers

Our relationship with suppliers and subcontractors must be based on mutual respect. We therefore have a responsibility to :

* seek fairness and truthfulness in all our activities, including pricing, licensing, and rights to sell;
* ensure that our business activities are free from coercion and unnecessary litigation;
* foster long-term stability in the supplier relationship in return for value, quality, competitiveness and reliability;
* share information with suppliers and integrate them into our planning processes;
* pay suppliers on time and in accordance with agreed terms of trade; and
* seek, encourage and prefer suppliers and subcontractors whose employment practices respect human dignity.

Competitors

We believe that fair economic competition is one of the basic requirements for increasing the wealth of nations and ultimately for making possible the just distribution of goods and services. We therefore have a responsibility to:

* foster open markets for trade and investment;
* promote competitive behavior that is socially and environmentally beneficial and demonstrates mutual respect among competitors;
* refrain from either seeking or participating in questionable payments or favors to secure competitive advantages;
* respect both tangible and intellectual property rights; and
* refuse to acquire commercial information by dishonest or unethical means, such as industrial espionage.

Communities

We believe that as global corporate citizens we can contribute to such forces of reform and human rights as are at work in the communities in which we operate. We therefore have a responsibility in those communities to:

* respect human rights and democratic institutions, and promote them wherever practicable;
* recognize government's legitimate obligation to the society at large and support public policies and practices that promote human development through harmonious relations between business and other segments of society;
* collaborate with those forces in the community dedicated to raising standards of health, education, workplace safety and economic well-being;

- promote and stimulate sustainable development and play a leading role in preserving and enhancing the physical environment and conserving the earth's resources;
- support peace, security, diversity and social integration; and
- respect the integrity of local cultures.
- be a good corporate citizen through charitable donations, educational and cultural contributions, and employee participation in community and civic affairs.

Please find further information relating to these principles at:
http://www.cauxroundtable.org/

This document also appears at:
http://www.cauxroundtable.org/documents/PrinciplesforBusiness.doc

AMNESTY INTERNATIONAL GUIDELINES FOR COMPANIES[*]

INTRODUCTION

The protection of human rights is the responsibility of all sectors of society. The *Universal Declaration of Human Rights*, adopted by the United Nations (UN) General Assembly in 1948, calls on '*every individual and every organ of society*' to play their part in securing the observance of these rights.

Companies have a direct responsibility for the impact of their activities on their employees, on consumers of their products and on the communities within which they operate. This means ensuring the protection of human rights in their own operations. They also have a broad responsibility, embodied in the expectations of civilized society and in international protocols, to use their influence to mitigate the violation of human rights. This applies whether these violations are committed by governments, by the forces of law and order, or by opposition groups in the countries where companies have a presence.

International companies are likely to operate in countries where there are serious and frequent human rights violations. Such violations inevitably contribute to civil instability and to uncertainty in the investment climate. Companies therefore have a direct self-interest in using their influence to promote respect for human rights. Moreover, the world is increasingly critical of corporate silence and inaction in these matters. The presence of companies can be interpreted as providing essential support to oppressive regimes and being aligned with those regimes and their standards. A company's reputation will be increasingly affected by its response – in word and deed – to the violation of human rights and the defence of such rights. Companies may also be at risk of inadvertently contributing to the violation of human rights through their security arrangements if these are not carefully safeguarded. The publicising of such incidents can be hugely damaging to reputation.

Companies may argue that they should not take action in these areas because to do so would be to interfere in domestic politics or to offend the values of other cultures. However, the international community has decided, through a variety of covenants and agreements, that certain fundamental rights transcend national and cultural boundaries. The *Universal Declaration of Human Rights* has pronounced a number of fundamental rights which must be respected in all circumstances including:

- the right to life
- the right to legal recognition as a person
- freedom of thought, conscience and religion
- freedom of opinion and expression

[*] The Amnesty International Guidelines for companies were originally published in 1997 and reprinted in September 1998.

- freedom from torture
- freedom from cruel, inhumane or degrading treatment
- freedom from slavery and servitude
- freedom from retroactive penal legislation

The following are intended as guidelines, excerpted from international protocols, to assist companies in confronting situations of human rights violations or the potential for such violations.

Checklist of Human Rights Principles

Background information on the international human rights standards on which this checklist is based is included in the section entitled '*Sources of International Human Rights Standards*'.

1. **Company policy on human rights**
    All companies should adopt an explicit company policy on human rights which includes public support for the *Universal Declaration of Human Rights*. Companies should establish procedures to ensure that all operations are examined for their potential impact on human rights, and establish safeguards to ensure that company staff are never complicit in human rights abuses. The company policy should enable discussion with the appropriate authorities at local, regional and national levels of specific cases of human rights violations and of the need for safeguards to protect human rights. It should enable the establishment of programmes for the effective human rights education and training of all employees.

2. **Security**
    All companies should ensure that any security arrangements protect human rights and are consistent with international standards for law enforcement. Any security personnel employed or contracted should be adequately trained. Procedures should be consistent with *UN Basic Principles on the Use of Firearms by Law Enforcement Officials* and the *UN Code of Conduct for Law Enforcement Officials*. They should include measures to prevent excessive force, as well as torture and cruel, inhuman or degrading treatment. Companies should develop clear rules for calling in or contracting with state security forces and for not hiring security personnel who have been responsible for serious human rights violations. Any complaint about security procedures or personnel should be promptly and independently investigated. Companies which supply military, security or police products or services should take stringent steps to prevent those products and services from being misused to commit human rights violations.

3. **Community engagement**
    All companies should take reasonable steps to ensure that their operations do not have a negative impact on the enjoyment of human rights by the communities in which they operate. This should include a willingness to meet with community leaders and voluntary organizations to discuss the impact of the company's activities on the broader community. Companies should seek to support initiatives which promote or defend human rights, for example by sponsoring education, training or citizenship programmes which incorporate human rights issues.

4. **Freedom from discrimination**
    All companies should ensure that their policies and practices prevent discrimination based on ethnic origin, gender, sexuality, colour, language, national or social origin, economic status, religion, political or other conscientiously held beliefs. These policies should be applied within the spheres of recruitment, marketing, remuneration, working conditions, customer relations and also to the practices of contractors,

suppliers and partners. They should include measures to deal with sexual or racial harassment and to prohibit the propagation of national, racial or religious hatred.

5. **Freedom from slavery**

   All companies should ensure that their policies and practices prohibit the use of chattel slaves, forced labour, bonded child labourers or coerced prison labour. This should include the imposition of conditions on suppliers, partners and sub-contractors that they do not use such labour.

6. **Health and safety**

   All companies should ensure that their policies and practices provide for safe and healthy working conditions and products. The company should not engage in or support the use of corporal punishment, mental or physical coercion, or verbal abuse.

Strategic Planning and Policy Framework

Companies may operate under circumstances where they find themselves in a situation of conflict, or where legislation, governmental practice or other constraints make it difficult to ensure the protection of human rights. Companies therefore need to plan carefully how they will respond to such conflicts which may also affect their own employees. Frameworks to integrate social concerns into their project planning and implementation strategies are currently being developed by a number of forward-looking companies and by the World Bank.

The integration of human rights considerations into the fabric of a company's operations requires the same kind of tools and methodologies as for any other area of policy. The key indicators of the extent to which human rights policies are embedded in corporate structures and strategies will be found in the attitude of the company's leadership, in its core business principles, in internal communication, in training programmes, in management information systems and in the internal audit function.

An explicit policy on human rights should:

- include public support for the *UN Universal Declaration of Human Rights* (1948);
- address how human rights issues and safeguards will be raised with the authorities;
- communicate internationally accepted human rights standards internally;
- assess the human rights implications of the company's activities;
- identify stakeholders whose rights may be affected by the company's operations;
- develop mechanisms for consultation and for resolution of conflict;
- determine clear delineations of responsibility for dealing with human rights matters;
- ensure that managers receive adequate training to implement company policy;
- introduce a system for monitoring and reviewing the policy.

It is in a company's interest to assist in resolving tensions arising from its presence and from the nature of its activities in a particular country/region.[1] Approaches are likely to be different in different situations, but willingness to initiate discussions is essential. The costs of not doing so are likely to be reflected in:

- high security costs to protect staff and property;
- high insurance premiums and risk to investments;
- disruption of labour markets and productivity;
- the weakening of local markets;
- damage to local infrastructure;
- the potential for damage to reputation in other markets.

---

[1]   *It is important to note that Amnesty International does not support or oppose calls for economic sanctions, disinvestment or trade embargoes.*

Personnel Policies and Practices

Standards relating to these issues have been establizhed by a variety of international organizations. In general, the following rights need to be respected as part of corporate personnel policies and practices:

* health and safety;
* freedom of association and right to collective bargaining;
* non-discrimination;
* disciplinary practices;
* avoidance of child labour;
* avoidance of prison labour and products;
* avoidance of forced labour.

Most of these rights are covered in the *Introductory Checklist*. On complex and sensitive issues, such as child labour, companies would find it useful to consult relevant non-governmental organizations. The scope and extent of personnel policy is a particularly complex area in view of a number of recent high profile cases where companies have been held responsible for the treatment of individuals who are not employees but who nevertheless contribute to the production process.

The performance of a company's contractors, suppliers and partners (whether these are governments, governmental agencies or businesses) is perceived to reflect the performance of the company. The general public does not draw a distinction between them and the transnational corporations to whom they are contracted. Companies should therefore promote similar standards through all third parties who act with them or on their behalf.

Companies should also be prepared to act for their own staff, and for joint venture staff, in cases of arrest and detention without due procedure, or in the case of unexplained disappearance.

Security Arrangements in General

Violence and instability in a number of countries today make it necessary for many companies to defend their personnel and property by armed guards and/or by arrangements with state security forces. These arrangements can be among the most dangerous in terms of human rights violations and harm to the company, its employees and its reputation.

A company should therefore ensure that its own personnel and any security forces engaged by them should be familiar with and committed to international guidelines and standards for the use of force in policing, in particular the *UN Basic Principles on the use of Force and Firearms* and the *UN Code of Conduct for Law Enforcement Officials*, which:

* set strict limitations on when force and firearms can be used;
* require a reporting/review process when they are used;
* require that abusive or unlawful use is punishable.

Companies should develop their own rules of engagement for calling in or contracting with state security forces and for the company's own security forces, should make public the terms of any such contracts, and take positive steps to ensure that any training or equipment provided by them to public or private security forces is not used to violate human rights. These would include rules on who carries arms, what the company supplies in kind to security forces, and the amount and nature of the control and influence exerted by the company over the security forces.

Companies should also, when recruiting staff, screen backgrounds for any previous violations of human rights.

In addition to the above areas, for many of which agreed international standards now exist, companies can improve their ability to promote human rights by:

a) including security arrangements in their strategic planning and policy-making processes;
b) consulting international and local NGOs on country-specific factors relating to the human rights climate that may influence or that may be affected by business decisions;
c) providing training for their managers and their staff in these matters, preferably with input and assistance from appropriate NGOs.

Security Arrangements – Specific Recommendations

There will be significant variations from country to country in the type of security arrangements that are most appropriate, but the following recommendations are likely to be widely applicable in areas of conflict:

a) companies should insert appropriate clauses into any security agreement signed with a government or any state entity. These should require, as a condition of contract, that state security forces operating in the area of company installations conform to the human rights obligations the government has assumed under the *International Covenant on Civil and Political Rights,* as well as other international human rights and humanitarian norms. These security agreements should be made public to allow for external monitoring, apart from operational details that could jeopardize lives.
b) companies should insist on screening the military, police and security officials who are assigned for their protection, whether they are part of the state security apparatus, company staff or private contractors. Careful background checks should be undertaken to ensure that no soldier, police agent or security official who has been credibly implicated in human rights abuses, or involved in para-military squads with a history of violations, should be engaged in their protection;
c) companies must make absolutely clear to the police and military defending them – as well as to company staff and sub-contracted personnel – that human rights violations will not be tolerated, and that companies will be the first to press for investigation and prosecution if any abuses occur;
d) whenever credible allegations of human rights abuses surface, companies should insist that the security force members implicated be immediately suspended and that appropriate internal and criminal investigations be launched;
e) companies should actively monitor the status of the investigations and press for resolution of the cases. If the investigations or prosecutions are stalled, the companies should publicly condemn the failure to conduct or complete the investigations;
f) any material assistance by companies to the security forces should be the subject of external auditing on a regular basis.

Implementation and Monitoring

The primary responsibility for monitoring company policy and practice lies with the company itself. However, Amnesty International recommends that there be in place credible systems for monitoring compliance with corporate codes of behaviour and that their reports be independently verifiable. There is an analogy between financial audits and social audits. Companies maintain their own internal accounting controls which are periodically verified by outside independent auditors in order to ensure their integrity. Similarly, while companies should have internal social auditing procedures by which they can determine the degree of compliance with the organization's code of conduct, there should also be periodic independent verification of these procedures and the reports they generate. In this there is also a role for other stakeholders, such as NGOs or members of the local community in which the company operates, in order to give greater transparency and credibility to the operation.

In those few countries where independent human rights or humanitarian groups are refused entry and there is therefore no possibility of any legitimate external monitoring, public opinion may well suspect abusive practices. It is therefore in the interest of companies to encourage such governments to allow access to organizations such as Amnesty International or the Red Cross.

Sources of International Human Rights Standards

The principles contained in this document are based on international human rights standards which are embodied in the following protocols:

* the *UN Universal Declaration of Human Rights*;
* conventions of the International Labour Organization (ILO);
* the *UN Basic Principles on the Use of Force and Firearms*;
* the *UN Code of Conduct for Law Enforcement Officials*;
* the *ILO Tripartite Declaration of Principles Concerning Multinational Enterprises and Social Policy*.

There are other human rights standards contained in international treaties which might also provide relevant terms of reference for companies wishing to develop human rights policies. These treaties are:

* the *International Covenant on Civil and Political Rights*;
* the *International Covenant on Economic, Cultural and Social Rights*;
* the *Convention Against Torture and Other Cruel, Inhuman or Degrading Treatment or Punishment*;
* the *Convention on the Elimination of all Forms of Discrimination Against Women*;
* the *Convention on the Rights of the Child*;
* the *International Convention on the Elimination of All Forms of Racial Discrimination*;
* the *International Convention on the Rights of all Migrant Workers and Members of their families*.

There are further relevant international standards which are not enshrined in international law, such as the *O.E.C.D. Guidelines for Multinational Enterprises*, and the *Principles Governing Conventional Arms Transfers* of the Organization for Security Cooperation in Europe.

For further information please visit the Amnesty International website: www.amnesty.org

Annex 5

SOCIAL ACCOUNTABILITY 8000*

1. CHILD LABOUR

Criteria:

1.1 The company shall not engage in or support the use of child labour as defined above.

1.2 The company shall establish, document, maintain, and effectively communicate to personnel and other interested parties policies and procedures for remediation of children found to be working in situations which fit the definition of child labour above, and shall provide adequate support to enable such children to attend and remain in school until no longer a child as defined above.

1.3 The company shall establish, document, maintain, and effectively communicate to personnel and other interested parties policies and procedures for promotion of education for children covered under ILO Recommendation 146 and young workers who are subject to local compulsory education laws or are attending school, including means to ensure that no such child or young worker is employed during school hours and that combined hours of daily transportation (to and from work and school), school, and work time does not exceed 10 hours a day.

1.4 The company shall not expose children or young workers to situations in or outside of the workplace that are hazardous, unsafe, or unhealthy.

2. FORCED LABOUR

Criterion:

2.1 The company shall not engage in or support the use of forced labour, nor shall personnel be required to lodge 'deposits' or identity papers upon commencing employment with the company.

3. HEALTH AND SAFETY

Criteria:

3.1 The company, bearing in mind the prevailing knowledge of the industry and of any specific hazards, shall provide a safe and healthy working environment and shall take adequate steps to prevent accidents and injury to health arising out of, associated with or occurring in the course of work, by minimizing, so far as is reasonably practicable, the causes of hazards inherent in the working environment.

3.2 The company shall appoint a senior management representative responsible for the health and safety of all personnel, and accountable for the implementation of the Health and Safety elements of this standard.

*   The SA 8000 became fully operational in 1998 and the principles were published in 2002.

3.3 The company shall ensure that all personnel receive regular and recorded health and safety training, and that such training is repeated for new and reassigned personnel.

3.4 The company shall establish systems to detect, avoid or respond to potential threats to the health and safety of all personnel.

3.5 The company shall provide, for use by all personnel, clean bathrooms, access to potable water, and, if appropriate, sanitary facilities for food storage.

3.6 The company shall ensure that, if provided for personnel, dormitory facilities are clean, safe, and meet the basic needs of the personnel.

4. FREEDOM OF ASSOCIATION AND RIGHT TO COLLECTIVE BARGAINING

Criteria:

4.1 The company shall respect the right of all personnel to form and join trade unions of their choice and to bargain collectively.

4.2 The company shall, in those situations in which the right to freedom of association and collective bargaining are restricted under law, facilitate parallel means of independent and free association and bargaining for all such personnel.

4.3 The company shall ensure that representatives of such personnel are not the subject of discrimination and that such representatives have access to their members in the workplace.

5. DISCRIMINATION

Criteria:

5.1 The company shall not engage in or support discrimination in hiring, remuneration, access to training, promotion, termination or retirement based on race, caste, national origin, religion, disability, gender, sexual orientation, union membership, political affiliation, or age.

5.2 The company shall not interfere with the exercise of the rights of personnel to observe tenets or practices, or to meet needs relating to race, caste, national origin, religion, disability, gender, sexual orientation, union membership, or political affiliation.

5.3 The company shall not allow behaviour, including gestures, language and physical contact, that is sexually coercive, threatening, abusive or exploitative.

6. DISCIPLINARY PRACTICES

Criterion:

6.1 The company shall not engage in or support the use of corporal punishment, mental or physical coercion, and verbal abuse.

7. WORKING HOURS

Criteria:

7.1 The company shall comply with applicable laws and industry standards on working hours. The normal workweek shall be as defined by law but shall not on a regular basis exceed 48 hours. Personnel shall be provided with at least one day off in every seven-day period. All overtime work shall be reimbursed at a premium rate and under no circumstances shall exceed 12 hours per employee per week.

7.2 Other than as permitted in Section 7.3 (below), overtime work shall be voluntary.

7.3 Where the company is party to a collective bargaining agreement freely negotiated with worker organizations (as defined by the ILO) representing a significant portion of its workforce, it may require overtime work in accordance with such agreement to meet short-term business demand. Any such agreement must comply with the requirements of Section 7.1 (above).

8. REMUNERATION

Criteria:

8.1 The company shall ensure that wages paid for a standard working week shall always meet at least legal or industry minimum standards and shall be sufficient to meet basic needs of personnel and to provide some discretionary income.

8.2 The company shall ensure that deductions from wages are not made for disciplinary purposes, and shall ensure that wage and benefits composition are detailed clearly and regularly for workers; the company shall also ensure that wages and benefits are rendered in full compliance with all applicable laws and that remuneration is rendered either in cash or check form, in a manner convenient to workers.

8.3 The company shall ensure that labour-only contracting arrangements and false apprenticeship schemes are not undertaken in an effort to avoid fulfilling its obligations to personnel under applicable laws pertaining to labour and social security legislation and regulations.

9. MANAGEMENT SYSTEMS

Criteria:

Policy

9.1 Top management shall define the company's policy for social accountability and labour conditions to ensure that it:
a) includes a commitment to conform to all requirements of this standard;
b) includes a commitment to comply with national and other applicable law, other requirements to which the company subscribes and to respect the international instruments and their interpretation (as listed in Section II);
c) includes a commitment to continual improvement;
d) is effectively documented, implemented, maintained, communicated and is accessible in a comprehensible form to all personnel, including, directors, executives, management, supervisors, and staff, whether directly employed, contracted or otherwise representing the company;
e) is publicly available.

Management Review

9.2 Top management shall periodically review the adequacy, suitability, and continuing effectiveness of the company's policy, procedures and performance results vis-à-vis the requirements of this standard and other requirements to which the company subscribes. System amendments and improvements shall be implemented where appropriate.

Company Representatives

9.3 The company shall appoint a senior management representative who, irrespective of other responsibilities, shall ensure that the requirements of this standard are met.

9.4 The company shall provide for non-management personnel to choose a representative from their own group to facilitate communication with senior management on matters related to this standard.

Planning and Implementation

9.5 The company shall ensure that the requirements of this standard are understood and implemented at all levels of the organization; methods shall include, but are not limited to:
a) clear definition of roles, responsibilities, and authority;
b) training of new and/or temporary employees upon hiring;
c) periodic training and awareness programs for existing employees;
d) continuous monitoring of activities and results to demonstrate the effectiveness of systems implemented to meet the company's policy and the requirements of this standard.

Control of Suppliers/Subcontractors and Sub-Suppliers

9.6 The company shall establish and maintain appropriate procedures to evaluate and select suppliers/subcontractors (and, where appropriate, sub-suppliers) based on their ability to meet the requirements of this standard.

9.7 The company shall maintain appropriate records of suppliers/subcontractors (and, where appropriate, sub-suppliers') commitments to social accountability, including, but not limited to, the written commitment of those organizations to:
a) conform to all requirements of this standard (including this clause);
b) participate in the company's monitoring activities as requested;
c) promptly implement remedial and corrective action to address any nonconformance identified against the requirements of this standard;
d) promptly and completely inform the company of any and all relevant business relationship(s) with other suppliers/subcontractors and sub-suppliers.

9.8 The company shall maintain reasonable evidence that the requirements of this standard are being met by suppliers and subcontractors.

9.9 In addition to the requirements of Sections 9.6 and 9.7 above, where the company receives, handles or promotes goods and/or services from suppliers/subcontractors or sub-suppliers who are classified as homeworkers, the company shall take special steps to ensure that such homeworkers are afforded a similar level of protection as would be afforded to directly employed personnel under the requirements of this standard. Such special steps shall include but not be limited to:
(a) establishing legally binding, written purchasing contracts requiring conformance to minimum criteria (in accordance with the requirements of this standard);
(b) ensuring that the requirements of the written purchasing contract are understood and implemented by homeworkers and all other parties involved in the purchasing contract;
(c) maintaining, on the company premises, comprehensive records detailing the identities of homeworkers; the quantities of goods produced/services provided and/or hours worked by each homeworker;
(d) frequent announced and unannounced monitoring activities to verify compliance with the terms of the written purchasing contract.

Addressing Concerns and Taking Corrective Action

9.10 The company shall investigate, address, and respond to the concerns of employees and other interested parties with regard to conformance/nonconformance with the company's policy and/or the requirements of this standard; the company shall refrain from disciplining, dismissing or otherwise discriminating against any employee for providing information concerning observance of the standard.

9.11 The company shall implement remedial and corrective action and allocate adequate resources appropriate to the nature and severity of any nonconformance identified against the company's policy and/or the requirements of the standard.

Outside Communication

9.12 The company shall establish and maintain procedures to communicate regularly to all interested parties data and other information regarding performance against the requirements of this document, including, but not limited to, the results of management reviews and monitoring activities.

Access for Verification

9.13 Where required by contract, the company shall provide reasonable information and access to interested parties seeking to verify conformance to the requirements of this standard; where further required by contract, similar information and access shall also be afforded by the company's suppliers and subcontractors through the incorporation of such a requirement in the company's purchasing contracts.

Records

9.14 The company shall maintain appropriate records to demonstrate conformance to the requirements of this standard.

This page can be found at: http://www.sa-intl.org/DocumentPercent20Center/2001StdEnglishFinal.doc

For further information please go to: www.sa-intl.org

Annex 6

OECD GUIDELINES FOR MULTINATIONAL ENTERPRISES*

PREFACE

1. The *OECD Guidelines for Multinational Enterprises* (the *Guidelines*) are recommendations addressed by governments to multinational enterprises. They provide voluntary principles and standards for responsible business conduct consistent with applicable laws. The *Guidelines* aim to ensure that the operations of these enterprises are in harmony with government policies, to strengthen the basis of mutual confidence between enterprises and the societies in which they operate, to help improve the foreign investment climate and to enhance the contribution to sustainable development made by multinational enterprises. The *Guidelines* are part of the *OECD Declaration on International Investment and Multinational Enterprises* the other elements of which relate to national treatment, conflicting requirements on enterprises, and international investment incentives and disincentives.

2. International business has experienced far-reaching structural change and the *Guidelines* themselves have evolved to reflect these changes. With the rise of service and knowledge-intensive industries, service and technology enterprises have entered the international marketplace. Large enterprises still account for a major share of international investment, and there is a trend toward large-scale international mergers. At the same time, foreign investment by small- and medium-sized enterprises has also increased and these enterprises now play a significant role on the international scene. Multinational enterprises, like their domestic counterparts, have evolved to encompass a broader range of business arrangements and organizational forms. Strategic alliances and closer relations with suppliers and contractors tend to blur the boundaries of the enterprise.

3. The rapid evolution in the structure of multinational enterprises is also reflected in their operations in the developing world, where foreign direct investment has grown rapidly. In developing countries, multinational enterprises have diversified beyond primary production and extractive industries into manufacturing, assembly, domestic market development and services.

4. The activities of multinational enterprises, through international trade and investment, have strengthened and deepened the ties that join OECD economies to each other and to the rest of the world. These activities bring substantial benefits to home and host countries. These benefits accrue when multinational enter-prises supply the products and services that consumers want to buy at competitive prices and when they provide fair returns to suppliers of capital.

---

*   The latest version of the Guidelines was printed in 2000, and varies substantially from the 1976 adoption.

517

Their trade and investment activities contribute to the efficient use of capital, technology and human and natural resources. They facilitate the transfer of technology among the regions of the world and the development of technologies that reflect local conditions. Through both formal training and on-the-job learning enterprises also promote the development of human capital in host countries.

5. The nature, scope and speed of economic changes have presented new strategic challenges for enterprises and their stakeholders. Multinational enterprises have the opportunity to implement best practice policies for sustainable development that seek to ensure coherence between social, economic and environmental objectives. The ability of multinational enterprises to promote sustainable development is greatly enhanced when trade and investment are conducted in a context of open, competitive and appropriately regulated markets.

6. Many multinational enterprises have demonstrated that respect for high standards of business conduct can enhance growth. Today's competitive forces are intense and multinational enterprises face a variety of legal, social and regulatory settings. In this context, some enterprises may be tempted to neglect appropriate standards and principles of conduct in an attempt to gain undue competitive advantage. Such practices by the few may call into question the reputation of the many and may give rise to public concerns.

7. Many enterprises have responded to these public concerns by developing internal programmes, guidance and management systems that underpin their commitment to good corporate citizenship, good practices and good business and employee conduct. Some of them have called upon consulting, auditing and certification services, contributing to the accumulation of expertise in these areas. These efforts have also promoted social dialogue on what constitutes good business conduct. The *Guidelines* clarify the shared expectations for business conduct of the governments adhering to them and provide a point of reference for enterprises. Thus, the *Guidelines* both complement and reinforce private efforts to define and implement responsible business conduct.

8. Governments are co-operating with each other and with other actors to strengthen the international legal and policy framework in which business is conducted. The post-war period has seen the development of this framework, starting with the adoption in 1948 of the Universal Declaration of Human Rights. Recent instruments include the ILO Declaration on Fundamental Principles and Rights at Work, the Rio Declaration on Environment and Development and Agenda 21 and the Copenhagen Declaration for Social Development.

9. The OECD has also been contributing to the international policy framework. Recent developments include the adoption of the Convention on Combating Bribery of Foreign Public Officials in International Business Transactions and of the OECD Principles of Corporate Governance, the OECD Guidelines for Consumer Protection in the Context of Electronic Commerce, and ongoing work on the OECD Guidelines on Transfer Pricing for Multinational Enterprises and Tax Administrations.

10. The common aim of the governments adhering to the *Guidelines* is to encourage the positive contributions that multinational enterprises can make to economic, environmental and social progress and to minimise the difficulties to which their various operations may give rise. In working towards this goal, governments find themselves in partnership with the many businesses, trade unions and other non-governmental organizations that are working in their own ways toward the same end. Governments can help by providing effective domestic policy frameworks that include stable macroeconomic policy, non-discriminatory treatment of firms, appropriate regulation and prudential supervision, an impartial system of courts

and law enforcement and efficient and honest public administration. Governments can also help by maintaining and promoting appropriate standards and policies in support of sustainable development and by engaging in ongoing reforms to ensure that public sector activity is efficient and effective.

Governments adhering to the *Guidelines* are committed to continual improvement of both domestic and international policies with a view to improving the welfare and living standards of all people.

I. Concepts and Principles

1. The *Guidelines* are recommendations jointly addressed by governments to multinational enterprises. They provide principles and standards of good practice consistent with applicable laws. Observance of the *Guidelines* by enterprises is voluntary and not legally enforceable.

2. Since the operations of multinational enterprises extend throughout the world, international co-operation in this field should extend to all countries. Governments adhering to the *Guidelines* encourage the enterprises operating on their territories to observe the *Guidelines* wherever they operate, while taking into account the particular circumstances of each host country.

3. A precise definition of multinational enterprises is not required for the purposes of the *Guidelines*. These usually comprise companies or other entities established in more than one country and so linked that they may co-ordinate their operations in various ways. While one or more of these entities may be able to exercise a significant influence over the activities of others, their degree of autonomy within the enterprise may vary widely from one multinational enterprise to another. Ownership may be private, state or mixed. The *Guidelines* are addressed to all the entities within the multinational enterprise (parent companies and/or local entities). According to the actual distribution of responsibilities among them, the different entities are expected to co-operate and to assist one another to facilitate observance of the *Guidelines*.

4. The *Guidelines* are not aimed at introducing differences of treatment between multinational and domestic enterprises; they reflect good practice for all. Accordingly, multinational and domestic enterprises are subject to the same expectations in respect of their conduct wherever the *Guidelines* are relevant to both.

5. Governments wish to encourage the widest possible observance of the *Guidelines*. While it is acknowledged that small- and medium-sized enterprises may not have the same capacities as larger enterprises, governments adhering to the *Guidelines* nevertheless encourage them to observe the *Guidelines* recommendations to the fullest extent possible.

6. Governments adhering to the *Guidelines* should not use them for protectionist purposes nor use them in a way that calls into question the comparative advantage of any country where multinational enterprises invest.

7. Governments have the right to prescribe the conditions under which multinational enterprises operate within their jurisdictions, subject to international law. The entities of a multinational enterprise located in various countries are subject to the laws applicable in these countries. When multinational enterprises are subject to conflicting requirements by adhering countries, the governments concerned will co-operate in good faith with a view to resolving problems that may arise.

8. Governments adhering to the *Guidelines* set them forth with the understanding that they will fulfil their responsibilities to treat enterprises equitably and in accordance with international law and with their contractual obligations.

9. The use of appropriate international dispute settlement mechanisms, including arbitration, is encouraged as a means of facilitating the resolution of legal problems arising between enterprises and host country governments.
10. Governments adhering to the *Guidelines* will promote them and encourage their use. They will establish National Contact Points that promote the *Guidelines* and act as a forum for discussion of all matters relating to the *Guidelines*. The adhering Governments will also participate in appropriate review and consultation procedures to address issues concerning interpretation of the *Guidelines* in a changing world.

II. General Policies

Enterprises should take fully into account established policies in the countries in which they operate, and consider the views of other stakeholders. In this regard, enterprises should:

1. Contribute to economic, social and environmental progress with a view to achieving sustainable development.
2. Respect the human rights of those affected by their activities consistent with the host government's international obligations and commitments.
3. Encourage local capacity building through close co-operation with the local community, including business interests, as well as developing the enterprise's activities in domestic and foreign markets, consistent with the need for sound commercial practice.
4. Encourage human capital formation, in particular by creating employment opportunities and facilitating training opportunities for employees.
5. Refrain from seeking or accepting exemptions not contemplated in the statutory or regulatory framework related to environmental, health, safety, labour, taxation, financial incentives, or other issues.
6. Support and uphold good corporate governance principles and develop and apply good corporate governance practices.
7. Develop and apply effective self-regulatory practices and management systems that foster a relationship of confidence and mutual trust between enterprises and the societies in which they operate.
8. Promote employee awareness of, and compliance with, company policies through appropriate dissemination of these policies, including through training programmes.
9. Refrain from discriminatory or disciplinary action against employees who make *bona fide* reports to management or, as appropriate, to the competent public authorities, on practices that contravene the law, the *Guidelines* or the enterprise's policies.
10. Encourage, where practicable, business partners, including suppliers and subcontractors, to apply principles of corporate conduct compatible with the *Guidelines*.
11. Abstain from any improper involvement in local political activities.

III. Disclosure

1. Enterprises should ensure that timely, regular, reliable and relevant information is disclosed regarding their activities, structure, financial situation and performance. This information should be disclosed for the enterprise as a whole and, where appropriate, along business lines or geographic areas. Disclosure policies of enterprises should be tailored to the nature, size and location of the enterprise, with due regard taken of costs, business confidentiality and other competitive concerns.

2. Enterprises should apply high quality standards for disclosure, accounting, and audit. Enterprises are also encouraged to apply high quality standards for non-financial information including environmental and social reporting where they exist. The standards or policies under which both financial and non-financial information are compiled and published should be reported.

3. Enterprises should disclose basic information showing their name, location, and structure, the name, address and telephone number of the parent enterprise and its main affiliates, its percentage ownership, direct and indirect in these affiliates, including shareholdings between them.

4. Enterprises should also disclose material information on:
   a) The financial and operating results of the company.
   b) Company objectives.
   c) Major share ownership and voting right.
   d) Members of the board and key executives, and their remuneration.
   e) Material foreseeable risk factors.
   f) Material issues regarding employees and other stakeholders.
   g) Governance structures and policies.

5. Enterprises are encouraged to communicate additional information that could include:
   a) Value statements or statements of business conduct intended for public disclosure including information on the social, ethical and environmental policies of the enterprise and other codes of conduct to which the company subscribes. In addition, the date of adoption, the countries and entities to which such statements apply and its performance in relation to these statements may be communicated.
   b) Information on systems for managing risks and complying with laws, and on statements or codes of business conduct.
   c) Information on relationships with employees and other stakeholders.

IV. Employment and Industrial Relations

Enterprises should, within the framework of applicable law, regulations and prevailing labour relations and employment practices:

1. a) Respect the right of their employees to be represented by trade unions and other bona fide representatives of employees, and engage in constructive negotiations, either individually or through employers' associations, with such representatives with a view to reaching agreements on employment conditions;
   b) Contribute to the effective abolition of child labour.
   c) Contribute to the elimination of all forms of forced or compulsory labour.
   d) Not discriminate against their employees with respect to employment or occupation on such grounds as race, colour, sex, religion, political opinion, national extraction or social origin, unless selectivity concerning employee characteristics furthers established governmental policies which specifically promote greater equality of employment opportunity or relates to the inherent requirements of a job.

2. a) Provide facilities to employee representatives as may be necessary to assist in the development of effective collective agreements.
   b) Provide information to employee representatives which is needed for meaningful negotiations on conditions of employment.
   c) Promote consultation and co-operation between employers and employees and their representatives on matters of mutual concern.

3. Provide information to employees and their representatives which enables them to obtain a true and fair view of the performance of the entity or, where appropriate, the enterprise as a whole.

4. a) Observe standards of employment and industrial relations not less favourable than those observed by comparable employers in the host country.
   b) Take adequate steps to ensure occupational health and safety in their operations.
5. In their operations, to the greatest extent practicable, employ local personnel and provide training with a view to improving skill levels, in co-operation with employee representatives and, where appropriate, relevant governmental authorities.
6. In considering changes in their operations which would have major effects upon the livelihood of their employees, in particular in the case of the closure of an entity involving collective lay-offs or dismissals, provide reasonable notice of such changes to representatives of their employees, and, where appropriate, to the relevant governmental authorities, and co-operate with the employee representatives and appropriate governmental authorities so as to mitigate to the maximum extent practicable adverse effects. In light of the specific circumstances of each case, it would be appropriate if management were able to give such notice prior to the final decision being taken. Other means may also be employed to provide meaningful co-operation to mitigate the effects of such decisions.
7. In the context of bona fide negotiations with representatives of employees on conditions of employment, or while employees are exercising a right to organise, not threaten to transfer the whole or part of an operating unit from the country concerned nor transfer employees from the enterprises' component entities in other countries in order to influence unfairly those negotiations or to hinder the exercise of a right to organise.
8. Enable authorised representatives of their employees to negotiate on collective bargaining or labour-management relations issues and allow the parties to consult on matters of mutual concern with representatives of management who are authorised to take decisions on these matters.

V. Environment

Enterprises should, within the framework of laws, regulations and administrative practices in the countries in which they operate, and in consideration of relevant international agreements, principles, objectives, and standards, take due account of the need to protect the environment, public health and safety, and generally to conduct their activities in a manner contributing to the wider goal of sustainable development. In particular, enterprises should:

1. Establish and maintain a system of environmental management appropriate to the enterprise, including:
   a) Collection and evaluation of adequate and timely information regarding the environmental, health, and safety impacts of their activities;
   b) Establishment of measurable objectives and, where appropriate, targets for improved environmental performance, including periodically reviewing the continuing relevance of these objectives; and
   c) Regular monitoring and verification of progress toward environmental, health, and safety objectives or targets.
2. Taking into account concerns about cost, business confidentiality, and the protection of intellectual property rights:
   a) Provide the public and employees with adequate and timely information on the potential environment, health and safety impacts of the activities of the enterprise, which could include reporting on progress in improving environmental performance; and
   b) Engage in adequate and timely communication and consultation with the communities directly affected by the environmental, health and safety policies of the enterprise and by their implementation.

3. Assess, and address in decision-making, the foreseeable environmental, health, and safety-related impacts associated with the processes, goods and services of the enterprise over their full life cycle. Where these proposed activities may have significant environmental, health, or safety impacts, and where they are subject to a decision of a competent authority, prepare an appropriate environmental impact assessment.

4. Consistent with the scientific and technical understanding of the risks, where there are threats of serious damage to the environment, taking also into account human health and safety, not use the lack of full scientific certainty as a reason for postponing cost-effective measures to prevent or minimise such damage.

5. Maintain contingency plans for preventing, mitigating, and controlling serious environmental and health damage from their operations, including accidents and emergencies; and mechanisms for immediate reporting to the competent authorities.

6. Continually seek to improve corporate environmental performance, by encouraging, where appropriate, such activities as:

   a) Adoption of technologies and operating procedures in all parts of the enterprise that reflect standards concerning environmental performance in the best performing part of the enterprise;

   b) Development and provision of products or services that have no undue environmental impacts; are safe in their intended use; are efficient in their consumption of energy and natural resources; can be reused, recycled, or disposed of safely;

   c) Promoting higher levels of awareness among customers of the environmental implications of using the products and services of the enterprise; and

   d) Research on ways of improving the environmental performance of the enterprise over the longer term.

7. Provide adequate education and training to employees in environmental health and safety matters, including the handling of hazardous materials and the prevention of environmental accidents, as well as more general environmental management areas, such as environmental impact assessment procedures, public relations, and environmental technologies.

8. Contribute to the development of environmentally meaningful and economically efficient public policy, for example, by means of partnerships or initiatives that will enhance environmental awareness and protection.

VI. Combating Bribery

Enterprises should not, directly or indirectly, offer, promise, give, or demand a bribe or other undue advantage to obtain or retain business or other improper advantage. Nor should enterprises be solicited or expected to render a bribe or other undue advantage. In particular, enterprises should:

1. Not offer, nor give in to demands, to pay public officials or the employees of business partners any portion of a contract payment. They should not use subcontracts, purchase orders or consulting agreements as means of channelling payments to public officials, to employees of business partners or to their relatives or business associates.

2. Ensure that remuneration of agents is appropriate and for legitimate services only. Where relevant, a list of agents employed in connection with transactions with public bodies and state-owned enterprises should be kept and made available to competent authorities.

3. Enhance the transparency of their activities in the fight against bribery and extortion. Measures could include making public commitments against bribery and extortion and disclosing the management systems the company has adopted in order

to honour these commitments. The enterprise should also foster openness and dialogue with the public so as to promote its awareness of and co-operation with the fight against bribery and extortion.

4. Promote employee awareness of and compliance with company policies against bribery and extortion through appropriate dissemination of these policies and through training programmes and disciplinary procedures.
5. Adopt management control systems that discourage bribery and corrupt practices, and adopt financial and tax accounting and auditing practices that prevent the establishment of 'off the books' or secret accounts or the creation of documents which do not properly and fairly record the transactions to which they relate.
6. Not make illegal contributions to candidates for public office or to political parties or to other political organizations. Contributions should fully comply with public disclosure requirements and should be reported to senior management.

VII.   Consumer Interests

When dealing with consumers, enterprises should act in accordance with fair business, marketing and advertising practices and should take all reasonable steps to ensure the safety and quality of the goods or services they provide. In particular, they should:

1. Ensure that the goods or services they provide meet all agreed or legally required standards for consumer health and safety, including health warnings and product safety and information labels.
2. As appropriate to the goods or services, provide accurate and clear information regarding their content, safe use, maintenance, storage, and disposal sufficient to enable consumers to make informed decisions.
3. Provide transparent and effective procedures that address consumer complaints and contribute to fair and timely resolution of consumer disputes without undue cost or burden.
4. Not make representations or omissions, nor engage in any other practices, that are deceptive, misleading, fraudulent, or unfair.
5. Respect consumer privacy and provide protection for personal data.
6. Co-operate fully and in a transparent manner with public authorities in the prevention or removal of serious threats to public health and safety deriving from the consumption or use of their products.

VIII.   Science and Technology

Enterprises should:

1. Endeavour to ensure that their activities are compatible with the science and technology (S&T) policies and plans of the countries in which they operate and as appropriate contribute to the development of local and national innovative capacity.
2. Adopt, where practicable in the course of their business activities, practices that permit the transfer and rapid diffusion of technologies and know-how, with due regard to the protection of intellectual property rights.
3. When appropriate, perform science and technology development work in host countries to address local market needs, as well as employ host country personnel in an S&T capacity and encourage their training, taking into account commercial needs.
4. When granting licenses for the use of intellectual property rights or when otherwise transferring technology, do so on reasonable terms and conditions and in a manner that contributes to the long term development prospects of the host country.

5. Where relevant to commercial objectives, develop ties with local universities, public research institutions, and participate in co-operative research projects with local industry or industry associations.

IX. Competition

Enterprises should, within the framework of applicable laws and regulations, conduct their activities in a competitive manner. In particular, enterprises should:

1. Refrain from entering into or carrying out anti-competitive agreements among competitors:
   a) To fix prices.
   b) To make rigged bids (collusive tenders).
   c) To establish output restrictions or quotas; or
   d) To share or divide markets by allocating customers, suppliers, territories or lines of commerce.
2. Conduct all of their activities in a manner consistent with all applicable competition laws, taking into account the applicability of the competition laws of jurisdictions whose economies would be likely to be harmed by anti-competitive activity on their part.
3. Co-operate with the competition authorities of such jurisdictions by, among other things and subject to applicable law and appropriate safeguards, providing as prompt and complete responses as practicable to requests for information.
4. Promote employee awareness of the importance of compliance with all applicable competition laws and policies.

X. Taxation

It is important that enterprises contribute to the public finances of host countries by making timely payment of their tax liabilities. In particular, enterprises should comply with the tax laws and regulations in all countries in which they operate and should exert every effort to act in accordance with both the letter and spirit of those laws and regulations. This would include such measures as providing to the relevant authorities the information necessary for the correct determination of taxes to be assessed in connection with their operations and conforming transfer pricing practices to the arm's length principle.

The full text of the principles can be found online at: http://www.oecd.org/dataoecd/56/36/1922428.pdf

For more information please visit the OECD website: http://www.oecd.org/

Annex 7

THE GLOBAL COMPACT LAUNCHED BY THE UNITED NATIONS*

The Global Compact's ten principles in the areas of human rights, labour, the environment and anti-corruption enjoy universal consensus and are derived from:

* *The Universal Declaration of Human Rights*
* *The International Labour Organization's Declaration on Fundamental Principles and Rights at Work*
* *The Rio Declaration on Environment and Development*
* *The United Nations Convention Against Corruption*

The Global Compact asks companies to embrace, support and enact, within their sphere of influence, a set of core values in the areas of human rights, labour standards, the environment, and anti-corruption:

Human Rights
* *Principle 1*: Businesses should support and respect the protection of internationally proclaimed human rights; and
* *Principle 2*: make sure that they are not complicit in human rights abuses.

Labour Standards
* *Principle 3*: Businesses should uphold the freedom of association and the effective recognition of the right to collective bargaining;
* *Principle 4*: the elimination of all forms of forced and compulsory labour;
* *Principle 5*: the effective abolition of child labour; and
* *Principle 6*: the elimination of discrimination in respect of employment and occupation.

Environment
* *Principle 7*: Businesses should support a precautionary approach to environmental challenges;
* *Principle 8*: undertake initiatives to promote greater environmental responsibility; and
* *Principle 9*: encourage the development and diffusion of environmentally friendly technologies.

---

*   Launched in 2000 at the initiative of UN General Secretary, Kofi Annan.

Anti-Corruption
- *Principle 10*: Businesses should work against all forms of corruption, including extortion and bribery.

The full text of the Principles and further information can be obtained from the GRI website: www.unglobalcompact.org

Annex 8

THE ICC'S NINE STEPS TO RESPONSIBLE BUSINESS CONDUCT*

NINE PRACTICAL STEPS TO RESPONSIBLE BUSINESS CONDUCT

If a company is considering whether to develop its own business principles or to support external codes of conduct, the following steps are suggested.

1. *Confirm CEO/board commitment to give priority to responsible business conduct*
A basic requirement is the commitment of senior management to treat responsible business conduct as a corporate priority. Rather than reacting to outside pressures, a company's voluntary adoption of its own business principles should be motivated by the desire to express the values that guide its approach to doing business.

2. *State company purpose and agree on company values*
Responsible business conduct is built upon the values and goals of the company itself, as well as on legal requirements and stakeholder expectations. Business principles commonly include a statement of mission, values and operating principles. All companies should consider articulating their core values as an underpinning for their own principles.

3. *Identify key stakeholders*
Business principles set out what companies see as their responsibilities to employees, shareholders, customers, business partners and other groups in society. Finding out from stakeholders what issues are important to them is therefore essential. Stakeholders – defined as those constituencies that have a direct stake in a company – typically can include shareholders and investors, company employees, trade unions, client companies and consumers, and local communities directly affected by a company's operations. A company may also wish to broaden its consultations to include other participants in the production chain, as well as government authorities, the media and non-governmental organizations. Companies should be mindful of the differences that may exist within stakeholder groups such as local communities who are becoming increasingly emphatic about their concerns and with whom it may be useful to establish a dialogue.

4. *Define business principles and policies*
Each company needs to think through its principles for itself (rather than just take an existing code 'off the shelf'). Some companies choose to do this through open dialogue and collaboration with selected stakeholders. Some companies' business principles are just high-level statements of principle. Others contain more detailed statements of policy,

---

*   Published in 2002.

while some prepare separate materials on policies, management systems, implementation and monitoring procedures. The underlying reasons why business principles make good economic sense should be borne in mind in defining the principles. Companies should consider legislation, social expectations, reputation indicators, risk management, bottom-line benefits, corporate and product image and strategic advantage.

5.   *Establish implementation procedures and management systems*
Companies must raise awareness among their own personnel and other stakeholders if business principles are to be effective and command wide support. Processes or formal management systems for developing, adopting and implementing individual principles should therefore include internal consultation and communication. Companies offer many examples of management systems covering areas ranging from health, safety and the environment to business integrity, human resources and sustainable development. There are also international standards for these systems, such as those of the International Organization for Standardization (ISO). In some sectors, management processes and guidelines also apply both to joint ventures and to contractors and suppliers. The range of issues covered varies between sectors but continues to develop to include, for example, diversity of the work force, climate change, biodiversity, waste management and recycling. In order to implement effectively its business principles a company should define objectives and targets and a structured programme to achieve them.

6.   *Benchmark against selected external codes and standards*
Government-mandated or other external codes are unlikely to be a viable alternative to voluntary business principles developed by the company itself, although these may have significant value as external benchmarks. Some companies choose to express public support for one or more of these external codes. It is for an individual company or industry sector to decide what the most useful benchmark codes are and to develop their own understanding of how business principles relate to external codes and guidelines, and to societal expectations. Support for external codes can be time-consuming since they may imply additional commitments. Companies should be selective, bearing in mind their own needs. ICC can provide guidance on the implications of supporting some of the existing international code offerings.

7.   *Set up internal monitoring*
Corporate policies and their implementation need to be kept under constant review to keep abreast of developments in technology and scientific understanding, customer needs and wider societal expectations. It is for the company to assess its social performance through internal consultation and periodic review by management. Equally, it is the company's responsibility to check that its business principles are being acted upon. The extent and manner of external reporting of performance is, of course, for the company to decide. Given the wide differences between industries and individual companies, the contents of such reports are bound to vary. Various international initiatives are being undertaken to develop a common yardstick for voluntary reporting of the economic, environmental and social impact of company activity. An example is the work being done by the Global Reporting Initiative, which is supported by the UN and other international organizations, to agree on a set of common core indicators. They would enable investors and other stakeholders to make global comparisons. Companies should retain the flexibility to adapt such voluntary indicators to their particular circumstances. A key way for companies to create confidence and trust in their commitment to responsible business conduct is to provide timely and reliable information on their financial, environmental and social performance and to communicate this to their stakeholders. Markets all over the world provide examples of companies who enjoy sustained public goodwill and respect by doing this successfully.

8. *Use language that everyone can understand*
Principles, policies and guidelines must be clearly expressed, particularly if the material is to be translated. The same is true of any external reports.

9. *Set pragmatic and realistic objectives*
These recommendations require the commitment of executives running the business and the development of expertise and internal processes. Above all, responsible business conduct requires a sustained effort by everybody in the company. A key element of a company's organizational development is promoting the importance of responsible business conduct and ensuring that new managers are well versed in this area.

This document can be found at: http://www.iccwbo.org/home/news_archives/2002/businsocdoc.asp

For the full text of the 9 steps please go to: http://www.iccwbo.org/corporate-responsibilityguide/

Annex 9

GLOBAL REPORTING INITIATIVE GUIDELINES*

TRANSPARENCY:

Full disclosure of the processes, procedures, and assumptions in report preparation are essential to its credibility.

Transparency is an overarching principle and is the centrepiece of accountability. It requires that, regardless of the format and content of reports, users are fully informed of the processes, procedures, and assumptions embodied in the reported information. For example, a report must include information on the stakeholder engagement processes used in its preparation, data collection methods and related internal auditing, and scientific assumptions underlying the presentation of information. This transparency in reporting is an exercise in accountability — the clear and open explanation of one's actions to those who have a right or reason to inquire.

Transparency is central to any type of reporting or disclosure. In the case of financial reporting, over many decades governments and other organizations have created, and continue to enhance, disclosure rules affecting financial reports to increase the transparency of the reporting process. These generally accepted accounting principles and evolving international accounting standards seek to ensure that investors are given a clear picture of the organization's financial condition, one that includes all material information and the basis upon which this depiction is developed.

GRI seeks to move reporting on economic, environmental, and social performance in a similar direction by creating a generally accepted framework for economic, environmental, and social performance disclosure. As this framework continues to evolve rapidly, general practices will evolve in parallel, based on best practice, best science, and best appraisal of user needs. In this dynamic environment, it is essential that reporting organizations are transparent regarding the processes, procedures, and assumptions that underlie their reports so that users may both believe and interpret reported information. In this sense, transparency transcends any one principle, but affects all.

INCLUSIVENESS

The reporting organization should systematically engage its stakeholders to help focus and continually enhance the quality of its reports.

The inclusiveness principle is rooted in the premise that stakeholder views are integral to meaningful reporting and must be incorporated during the process of designing a report. Reporting organizations should seek to engage stakeholders who are both directly and indirectly affected. Aspects of reporting enriched by stakeholder consultation include

---

*   Published in 2002. The next version of the Guidelines will come into print in 2006.

533

(but are not limited to) the choice of indicators, the definition of the organization's reporting boundaries, the format of the report, and the approaches taken to reinforce the credibility of the reported information. Characteristics relevant to designing stakeholder consultation processes include the nature and diversity of products and services, the nature of the reporting organization's operations and activities, and the geographic range of operations. Stakeholder engagement, like reporting itself, is a dynamic process. Executed properly, it is likely to result in continual learning within and outside the organization, and to strengthen trust between the reporting organization and report users. Trust, in turn, fortifies report credibility, itself a key goal of GRI's reporting framework.

The principle of inclusiveness also addresses the diverse needs of stakeholders who use sustainability reports. The range of users of a sustainability report is broader than that of financial reports. Inclusiveness is essential to ensuring that the reporting process and content reflect the needs of these diverse users. Each user group has specific information expectations – at times overlapping with those of other groups, at times distinct.

Failure to identify and consult with stakeholders is likely to result in reports that are less relevant to users' needs and thereby less credible to external parties. In contrast, systematic stakeholder engagement enhances receptivity and usefulness across user groups. This engagement may also include soliciting views regarding the utility and credibility of sustainability reports issued by the reporting organization. GRI recognises that many reporting organizations have a wide range of potential stakeholders.

Any systematic approach to inclusiveness will require an organization to define an approach for grouping and prioritising stakeholders for purposes of engagement. In the spirit of the inclusiveness and transparency principles, it is important for reporting organizations to clearly and openly explain their approach to defining whom to engage with and how best to engage.

AUDITABILITY

Reported data and information should be recorded, compiled, analysed, and disclosed in a way that would enable internal auditors or external assurance providers to attest to its reliability.
The auditability principle refers to the extent to which information management systems and communication practices lend themselves to being examined for accuracy by both internal and external parties. Reports using the Guidelines contain data that is both qualitative and quantitative in nature. In designing data collection and information systems, reporting organizations therefore should anticipate that internal auditing and external assurance processes may be used in the future.

In preparing reports, organizations should continually ask the question: Is the response to an information query presented in such a way that an internal or external party in the future could examine its accuracy, completeness, consistency, and reliability? Unverifiable statements or data that affect the broad messages contained in a report using the Guidelines may compromise its credibility. In addition to accuracy and reliability, the completeness of information may also affect the ability of an auditor to render an assessment.

The Verification Working Group

In response to user requests, GRI formed a working group in 1999 to explore issues and options for strengthening the credibility of sustainability reports through various assurance mechanisms. The results of these consultations are reflected in the statements in Part A (Credibility of Reports) and in Annex 4 on assurance processes. The working group also has prepared an advisory assurance strategy paper (available on www.globalreporting.org) for consideration by the GRI Board of Directors. Beginning in

September 2002, the Board will consider options for how GRI might continue to play a constructive role in advancing the assurance of sustainability reports.

COMPLETENESS

All information that is material to users for assessing the reporting organization's economic, environmental, and social performance should appear in the report in a manner consistent with the declared boundaries, scope, and time period.

This principle refers to accounting for and disclosing, in sufficient detail, all information of significant concern to stakeholders within the declared boundaries (i.e., operational, scope, and temporal) of the report. Defining whether such information meets the test of significance to stakeholders should be based on both stakeholder consultation as well as broad-based societal concerns that may not have surfaced through the stakeholder consultation process. Such broad-based concerns may derive, for example, from national policy and international conventions.

The completeness principle is three-dimensional:

Operational boundary dimension: Reported information should be complete in relation to the operational boundaries of the reporting organization, in other words, the range of entities for which the reporting organization gathers data. These boundaries should be selected with consideration of the economic, environmental, and social impacts of the organization. Such boundaries may be defined based on financial control, legal ownership, business relationships, and other considerations. The boundaries may vary according to the nature of the reported information. In some cases, the most appropriate boundaries for meeting the expectations outlined by other reporting principles may extend beyond traditional financial reporting boundaries.

Scope dimension: Scope is distinct from boundaries in that an organization could choose extended reporting boundaries (e.g., report data on all the organizations that form the supply chain), but only include a very narrow scope (e.g., only report on human rights performance). In the context of GRI, 'scope' refers to aspects such as energy use, health and safety, and other areas for which the Guidelines include indicators and queries. Despite the fact that the reporting boundary may be complete, the scope (e.g., human rights aspects only) may not be complete. The process for determining a complete scope may include, for example, the results of lifecycle analysis of products or services and assessment of the full range of direct and indirect social or ecological impacts of the reporting organization. Some of these same tools may also influence decisions about the other dimensions of completeness discussed here. The report should disclose all relevant information within the context of the scope (i.e., aspects) covered.

Temporal dimension: Reported information should be complete with reference to the time period declared by the reporting organization. As far as possible, reportable activities, events, and impacts should be presented for the reporting period in which they occur. This may involve reporting on activities that produce minimal short-term impact, but will have a cumulative effect that may become material, unavoidable, or irreversible in the longer term. Such activities might include, for example, the release of certain bioaccumulative or persistent pollutants. Disclosure of the nature and likelihood of such impacts, even if they may only materialize in the future, comports with the goal of providing a balanced and reasonable representation of the organization's current economic, environmental, and social performance. In making estimates of future impacts (both positive and negative), the reporting organization should be careful to make well-reasoned estimates that reflect the best understanding of the likely size, nature, and scope of impacts. Although speculative in nature, such estimates can provide useful and relevant information for decision-making as long as the limitations of the estimates are clearly acknowledged.

Information within the organization often flows from management systems that operate on a regular, short-term cycle, typically one year. However, a single reporting cycle often is too brief to capture many important economic, environmental, and social impacts. This type of performance, by nature, focuses on the long-term, with forward-looking trends at least as important as lagging, or historical, ones. Thus, reporting organizations should strive to gradually align information systems to account for these forward-looking trends in addition to historical trends.

Defining Boundaries

Defining boundary conditions for reporting on economic, environmental, and social performance is a complex challenge. Complicating factors include the diverse nature of the information and the intimate relationship between the organization and the larger economic, environmental, and social systems within which it operates. Boundary research is a high priority in GRIs work programme. Discussion papers, exposure drafts and testable protocols will appear during 2002–2003, leading to more systematic and precise treatment of this critical reporting issue.

RELEVANCE

Relevance is the degree of importance assigned to a particular aspect, indicator, or piece of information, and represents the threshold at which information becomes significant enough to be reported.

Relevance in sustainability reporting is driven by the significance attached to a piece of information to inform the user's decision-making processes. Stakeholders use information on economic, environmental, and social performance in a variety of ways, some of which may differ substantially from that of the reporting organization. The significance of information can be judged from a number of perspectives; however, in any reporting system, the key perspective is that of the information user. The primary purpose of reporting (as opposed to other types of outreach and communication) is to respond to user information needs in a neutral and balanced manner. Reporting must therefore place a strong emphasis on serving users' specific needs.

In considering relevance, it is important to remain sensitive to differences in how users and reporting organizations apply information. Through stakeholder consultation, a reporting organization can better understand stakeholders' information needs and how best to respond to them. Ideally, reports should contain information that is useful and relevant to both the reporting organization and the report users. However, in some cases, information may be relevant to the report user, but may not be of the same value to the reporting organization. It is important to differentiate between situations where reporting expectations differ and those where information is irrelevant.

SUSTAINABILITY CONTEXT

The reporting organization should seek to place its performance in the larger context of ecological, social, or other limits or constraints, where such context adds significant meaning to the reported information.

Many aspects of sustainability reporting draw significant meaning from the larger context of how performance at the organizational level affects economic, environmental, and social capital formation and depletion at a local, regional, or global level. In such cases, simply reporting on the trend in individual performance (or the efficiency of the organization) leaves open the question of an organization's contribution to the total amount of these different types of capital. For some users, placing performance information in the broader biophysical, social, and economic context lies at the heart of sustainability reporting and is one of the key differentiators between this type of reporting and financial reporting. Moreover, while the ability of an organization to 'sustain' itself is obviously important to a range of stakeholders, it is unlikely that any individual organization will remain in existence indefinitely. This principle emphasises the sustainability of the broader natural and human environment within which organizations operate. Where relevant and useful, reporting organizations should consider their individual performance in the contexts of economic, environmental, and social sustainability. This will involve discussing the performance of the organization in the context of the limits and demands placed on economic, environmental, or social resources at a macro-level. This concept is most clearly articulated in the environmental area in terms of global limits on resource use and pollution levels, but also may be relevant to social and economic issues.

The understanding of how best to link organizational performance with macro-level concerns will continue to evolve. GRI recommends that individual reporting organizations explore ways to incorporate these issues directly into their sustainability reports in order to advance both reporting organizations' and users' understanding of these linkages.

ACCURACY

The accuracy principle refers to achieving the degree of exactness and low margin of error in reported information necessary for users to make decisions with a high degree of confidence.
Economic, environmental, and social indicators can be expressed in many different ways, ranging from qualitative responses to detailed quantitative measurements. The characteristics that determine accuracy vary according to the nature of the information. For example, the accuracy of qualitative information is largely determined by the degree of clarity, detail, and balance in presentation. The accuracy of quantitative information, on the other hand, may depend on the specific sampling methods used to gather hundreds of data points from multiple operating units. The specific threshold of accuracy that is necessary will depend in part on the intended use of the information. Certain decisions will require higher levels of accuracy in reported information than others.

Application of the accuracy principle requires an appreciation of:

- the intentions and decision-making needs of the users; and
- the different conditions under which information is gathered.

As with other principles, it is important to be transparent in how this principle is applied.

Explaining the approaches, methods, and techniques that the reporting organization uses to achieve satisfactory levels of accuracy will help improve the credibility of the report and the acceptance of the reported information.

NEUTRALITY

Reports should avoid bias in selection and presentation of information and should strive to provide a balanced account of the reporting organization's performance.
The neutrality principle refers to the fair and factual presentation of the organization's economic, environmental, and social performance. Embodied in the principle of neutrality is the notion that the core objective behind a reporting organization's selection and communication of information is to produce an unbiased depiction of its performance.

This means presenting an account that includes both favourable and unfavourable results, free from intentional tilt or under- or overstatement of the organization's performance. The report should focus on neutral sharing of the facts for the users to interpret.

Environmental reporting, the precursor to sustainability reporting, has demonstrated this type of gradual evolution from anecdotal and selective disclosure toward a more neutral, factual presentation of data. While reporting practices still vary significantly among reporting organizations, many have recognized that achieving and maintaining credibility among users hinges on the commitment of the reporting organization to a neutral and fair depiction. Under the neutrality principle, the overall report content must present an unbiased picture of the reporting organization's performance, avoiding selections, omissions, or presentation formats that are intended to influence a decision or judgement by the user.

Where the reporting organization wishes to present its perspective on an aspect of performance, it should be clear to the reader that such information is separate and distinct from GRIs reporting elements. In the same way that annual financial reports typically contain interpretive material in the front end and financial statements in the back, so too should GRI-based reports strive for a clear distinction between the reporting organization's interpretation of information and factual presentation.

COMPARABILITY

The reporting organization should maintain consistency in the boundary and scope of its reports, disclose any changes, and re-state previously reported information.

This principle refers to ensuring that reports on economic, environmental, and social performance support comparison against the organization's earlier performance as well as against the performance of other organizations. This allows internal and external parties to benchmark performance and assess progress as part of supporting rating activities, investment decisions, advocacy programmes and other activities. Comparability and associated demands for consistency are a pre-requisite to informed decision making by users.

When changes in boundary, scope, and content of reporting occur (including in the design and use of indicators), reporting organizations should, to the maximum extent practicable, re-state current accounts to ensure that time series information and cross-organizational comparisons are both reliable and meaningful. Where such re-statements are not provided, the reporting organization should disclose such circumstances, explain the reasons, and discuss implications for interpreting current accounts.

CLARITY

The reporting organization should remain cognizant of the diverse needs and backgrounds of its stakeholder groups and should make information available in a manner that is responsive to the maximum number of users while still maintaining a suitable level of detail.

The clarity principle considers the extent to which information is understandable and usable by diverse user groups. In financial reporting, there is an unspoken assumption concerning the general level of background knowledge and experience of the assumed 'primary' user group, namely, investors. No such 'primary' user group exists for GRI at this juncture. In fact, it may never exist owing to the diversity of user groups that are consumers of economic, environmental, and social performance information. In using the GRI Guidelines, it is reasonable to assume that all users have a working knowledge of at least a portion of the economic, environmental, and social issues faced by the reporting organization. However, not all user groups will bring the same level of experience or even the same language to the reading of the report. Thus, reporting organizations, through assessing stakeholder capabilities, should design reports that respond to the maximum number of users without sacrificing important details of interest to a subset of user groups. Technical and scientific terms should be explained within the report, and clear, suitable graphics should be used where appropriate. Providing information that is not understandable to stakeholders does not contribute to successful engagement.

Clarity is therefore an essential characteristic of any reporting effort.

TIMELINESS

Reports should provide information on a regular schedule that meets user needs and comports with the nature of the information itself.
The usefulness of information on economic, environmental, and social performance is closely tied to its timely availability to user groups. Timeliness ensures maximum uptake and utility of the information, enabling users to effectively integrate it into their decision-making. As with financial disclosures, reporting on economic, environmental, and social performance is most valuable when users can expect a predictable schedule of disclosures. Special updates can be issued if and when unexpected developments of material interest to users occur.

Reporting organizations should structure disclosures to accord with the nature of the information. Certain environmental information, for example, may be most useful on a quarterly, monthly or continuous ('real time') basis, while other environmental information is most suitable for an annual report. Similarly, reporting on economic performance may parallel financial reporting: annual disclosures can summarise economic performance during the prior 12 months, while quarterly updates can be issued in parallel with quarterly earnings reports to investors. With the menu of new communications technologies available to reporting organizations, adjusting the timing of disclosures to reflect the varying nature of an organization's impacts is now more feasible than ever before. However, the degree to which any technology approach can be applied depends on stakeholders having access to the necessary technology.

This document can be viewed in its entirety at: http://www.globalreporting.org/guidelines/2002/gri_2002_guidelines.pdf

For further information please go to the GRI website: www.globalreporting.org

Annex 10

CCBE GUIDE FOR EUROPEAN LAWYERS ADVISING ON CORPORATE SOCIAL RESPONSIBILITY ISSUES*

PREFACE

The Council of Bars and Law Societies of the European Union (CCBE) has issued this guidance to European lawyers advising corporations on Corporate Social Responsibility (CSR).

CSR is an instrument of positive change inside businesses. It sets the framework and defines the manner in which a business must operate to be able to meet the ethical, legal, commercial and public expectations that a society has of any company. These guidelines serve as a starting point for the corporate lawyer in creating new legal solutions for his client.

This guide explains:

- why companies should be interested in CSR; and
- why lawyers should advise on CSR.

The guide also provides information on how to pursue this topic further and explains the current CSR initiatives at a European and world-wide level.

The CCBE recently established a CSR discussion group for drafting this guide. The CCBE would like to thank Claes Cronstedt, Claes Lundblad, Yvon Martinet, Mauro Pizzigati, Birgit Spießhofer, Sune Skadegard Thorsen, Marco Vianello and Carita Wallgren for their participation in this discussion group.

The CCBE would appreciate any comments on the guide, and your feedback on this initiative.

For your comments or further information, please contact the CCBE at ccbe@ccbe.org

I: UNDERSTANDING CORPORATE SOCIAL RESPONSIBILITY

'Corporate social responsibility is now in every reasonable chief executives agenda, not always at the top, but it's there'.[1]

When Warren Buffett took over the chairmanship of Salomon Brothers after the bidding scandal on Wall Street in 1991, he told the assembled staff: *'Lose money for the firm, I will be very understanding; lose a shred of reputation for the firm, I will be ruthless'*. Buffett and other successful representatives of the business world instinctively understand that values such as honesty, fairness and responsibility are necessary to be able to run a successful business. Many fortunes have been made, and are still being made, through unacceptable business

---

*   Published in 2002.
[1]   Steve Hilton and Giles Gibbons, Good Business, p. 55.

541

methods. However, the development has been towards more transparency, more freedom, more democracy and more laws. This makes it less attractive to conduct business that is contrary to the values of society. Courts in a number of countries are using the standards of international conventions on companies, although the vast majority of these standards are not directly binding on companies. This is a trend that is spreading to other jurisdictions. Many companies are being subject to legal proceedings at home and abroad – even though the alleged violations have been committed by its operations in other countries. Today, social responsibility is becoming a serious matter for our corporate clients.

The US judiciary especially apply their legal regime in an extraterritorial way, and they judge the companies' conduct with regard to international law.

Shell, BP, Nike, GAP, Coca-Cola, JP Morgan Chase, Polo Ralph Lauren – the list could be made longer – have had their reputations severely damaged in recent times because they have acted contrary to current values.

In an opinion poll published in 2002, 25,000 individuals from 23 countries were asked about companies' roles in society. Eight out of ten employees in larger companies said that the more social responsibility the employer takes, the more motivated and loyal the employees become. A majority of the questioned shareholders stated that they would consider selling their shares in a company that fails in respect of social responsibility, even if the earnings are good.

II: CURRENT DEVELOPMENTS

'Corporate Social Responsibility is something that companies operating internationally cannot ignore anymore'.[2]

More and more companies adopt and implement rules for social responsibility because they know only too well how the market really works today. It is a matter of risk management, of creating an effective organisation and of creating a good market position. A new legal landscape that extends liability for corporations concerned is emerging. Among other initiatives we can see many obligations on companies, which have been imposed by national governments:

1.   Australia

In Australia the Corporate Code of Conduct Bill 2000 reflects the definite trend towards penalising unacceptable and harmful behaviour that occurs overseas. Australian companies with global operations and multinationals with Australian subsidiaries need to be aware that certain standards of conduct are increasingly expected of them in both the domestic and offshore operations. The Bill, although not yet enacted, sets codes of conduct that must be adhered to including environmental standards, health and safety standards, employment standards, human right standards, duty to observe tax laws, duty to observe consumer health and safety standards and consumer protection and trade practices standards. The Bill also provides for wide-ranging and onerous reporting obligations. This Bill is indicative of the trend and direction that CSR is taking. Also in Australia, there are CSR reporting requirement currently in place for investments firms and listed companies.

2.   Denmark And The Netherlands

Denmark and the Netherlands have encouraged 'triple bottom line' reporting, whereby social and environmental information is disclosed alongside financial reports.

---

[2]   Doug Miller, CEO of Environment International, 'CSR is here to stay', CSR Magazine, October 2002.

3.   France

In 2001, the French Parliament passed legislation requiring mandatory disclosure of social and environmental issues in companies' annual reports and accounts. It requires all companies listed on the 'premier marché' (those with the largest capitalisations) to report against a template of social and environmental indicators, including those related to human resources, community issues and engagement, labour standards and key health, safety and environmental standards.

4.   Germany

In Germany, CSR reporting requirements have been introduced and apply to companies involved with pension funds.

5.   United Kingdom

In 1999, the UK Parliament approved the Pensions Disclosure Regulation. The Regulation amended the 1995 Pensions Act, requiring all trustees of UK occupational pension funds to disclose 'the extent (if any), to which social, environmental or ethical considerations are taken into account in the selection, retention and realisation of investments'.

Furthermore, in 2002 a CSR Bill was introduced in the House of Commons as a private members' Bill. Although the Bill was not enacted, it gives a good indication of movement in the direction of CSR, and the Bill was proposed again in an amended version in June 2003 backed by numerous NGOs. The original Bill proposed to:

- Make social, financial and environmental reporting (the so-called 'triple bottom line') mandatory;
- Require companies to consider CSR on big projects;
- Place specific duties and liabilities on directors and companies, with respect to social, financial and environmental issues;
- Provide remedies and rights of redress for people negatively impacted by business activities;
- Establish a new regulatory body to oversee environmental and social standards. 6. US Sarbanes-Oxley Act July 2002 On July 30, 2002, the Sarbanes-Oxley Act of 2002 ('Sarbanes-Oxley Act') was enacted. 10. This imposed codes of conduct on companies in which they would be obliged to report on Corporate Social Responsibility requirements. The final rules implementing Section 406 of the Sarbanes-Oxley Act require reporting issuers, including foreign private issuers, to disclose in their annual report whether they have adopted a written code of ethics that applies to the issuer's principal executive officer, principal financial officer, principal accounting officer or controller, or people performing similar functions. The above-mentioned governmental developments are merely reflections of broader international and regional movements and various court decisions.

III: CORPORATE RISKS AND OPPORTUNITIES

'The 21st century company will be different. Many of the world's best-known companies are already redefining traditional perception of the will of the corporation. They are recognising that every customer is part of the community, and that social responsibility is not an optional activity'.[3]

---

[3]   Tony Blair, UK Prime Minister.

Companies that choose to ignore CSR may encounter many consequences. The risks can be summarised as follows:

- Increased civil and criminal litigation against companies and management;
- Loss of top talents;
- Loss of investors;
- Increased cost of capital;
- Decline in stock value;
- Loss of customers and business partners;
- Loss of public contracts and public procurement procedures e.g. Word Bank, European Union, European Bank for Reconstruction and Development;
- Loss of business partners;
- Exposure to naming and shaming campaigns and blacklisting campaigns;
- Loss of brand value. On the other hand, there are many opportunities available to companies who choose to implement CSR strategies and incorporate CSR into company policies;
- Enhanced corporate image and added brand value;
- Attract and retain top talents;
- Enhancing job satisfaction, loyalty and identification;
- Access to quality business partners;
- Obtaining the status of a 'preferred partner';
- Customer satisfaction and loyalty;
- Improving risk management;
- Lower insurance fees;
- Favourable access to capital markets;
- Attracting Socially Responsible Investment (SRI), which is mushrooming;
- Establishing a good footing with public authorities and the general public;
- Creating a basic reference point and language for partnerships;
- Public relations opportunities;
- Contribution to the development of stable global markets.

IV: WHY LAWYERS SHOULD ADVISE ON CORPORATE SOCIAL RESPONSIBILITY

'The main purpose of the board of directors is to seek to ensure the prosperity of the company by collectively directing the company's affairs, whilst meeting the appropriate expectations of its shareholders and relevant stakeholders'.[4]

Responsibility for advising on CSR issues has not always been seen as falling to the legal profession. The CCBE believes that this should change. Law is the codification of basic human values. The goal of CSR is to implement these values in corporations, thus CSR develops and functions in a legal framework. There is no other professional who both has such ready access to EU boardrooms, and enjoys legal privilege. As a result, advising on CSR issues should become an everyday matter for corporate lawyers.

Even voluntary approaches to CSR have a legal context. Laws on misrepresentation or false advertising frame voluntary company reporting, for example. And voluntary approaches such as company codes of conduct can shape the standards of care that are legally expected of businesses. In the workplace, agreements reached through collective bargaining between employers and trade unions can become legally binding through incorporation in employment contracts.

---

[4]   Institute of Directors, Standards for the Board, 1999.

CSR should be part of company policies and integrated into strategies and decision-making. In this regard, the lawyer has a number of boardroom responsibilities: The lawyer should make the company management aware that CSR is an issue, which they will have to deal with. As lawyers are specialist advisers to corporations this will reflect on their responsibilities when acting as member of, or secretary to, the Board of Directors. CSR must be considered as an area where negligence may very well result in losses of a considerable size for the involved company. If the issues leading to the loss were treated during a board meeting, and the lawyer did not respond adequately, due to ignorance, this may very well lead to liability.

The lawyer also has a number of advising opportunities that might take place, as the case may be, together with other experts. These advising opportunities can be divided into long-term and short-term assignments. For longer term assignments:

- Analyse strengths, weaknesses, opportunities and threats (SWOT-analysis) of a given company in relation to CSR;
- Design CSR policies;
- Design a strategy for the company to address CSR adequately; Integrate CSR under existing risk management and compliance programmes;
- Design and implement concrete projects under CSR;
- Create CSR screening systems for investments;
- Develop a framework for supply chain management systems;
- Develop a framework for CSR as part of Quality Management;
- Implement in-house training on CSR;
- Integrate CSR into existing risks and quality management schemes and compliance programmes. For short-term assignments;
- Consider the 'what, why and how' of a CSR approach – its challenges, dilemmas and opportunities;
- Undertake CSR assessments of affiliates, branches, investment opportunities, suppliers, licensees or other partners;
- Undertake CSR assessments as part of due diligence;
- Respond to media or NGO criticism;
- Provide assurance statements on CSR reporting in relation to scope, relevance and compliance with international standards;
- Undertake assessment of concrete CSR projects;
- Network with other companies and/or associations;
- Coordinate and supervise the CSR work of the company;
- Assess the legal implications of CSR reporting and advertising.

In *Kasky v. Nike*, Nike was sued under Californian State Law for false advertising. Kasky claimed that information on Nike's social performance was false and did not reflect the poor working conditions in its foreign factories. Nike defended itself based on the First amendment of the US Constitution on freedom of speech, but the Court ruled, in the first instance, against Nike to find that the company statements should be classified as 'commercial speech' (and not political). Thus Nike's statements would be subject to the stricter standard of truth required by advertising law. In June 2003 the US Supreme Court dismissed on technical grounds the action in which Nike was seeking to reaffirm the First Amendment right to free and open debate. Although the US Supreme Court issued no formal decision, a majority of the Court expressly rejected the central holding of the California Supreme Court that Nike's speech could be restricted as purely 'commercial'. The case now returns to the California courts, which will have the views of the US Supreme Court in deciding whether the case may proceed to trial.

This case illustrates that companies' statements can be challenged for misrepresentation, and further illustrates the need for a corporate lawyer to be involved in CSR.

V: CSR STANDARDS

'A global human society based on poverty for many and prosperity for a few, characterised by islands of wealth, surrounded by a sea of poverty, is unsustainable'.[5]

Many companies have established codes of conduct and policies integrating CSR principles into their business practices. According to the OECD, in 2000 there were 296 different codes of conduct. These codes reflect the growing pressure being placed on companies by NGOs, shareholders and socially responsible investment funds.

There are five basic types of codes:

* Company codes – e.g. Shell, Philips, Levi Strauss;
* Trade association codes – e.g. ICC, British Toy and Hobby Association, Bangladesh Garments Headquarters and Expatriates Association, Kenya Flower Council Code;
* Multi-stakeholder codes – e.g. Accountability 1000, good corporation.com, Project Sigma UK, Ethical Trading initiatives UK, Apparel Industry Partnership USA, Social Accountability 8000;
* Intergovernmental codes – e.g. the ILO Convention, OECD Guidelines on TNCs, EU Code of Conduct;
* World codes – e.g. ICFTU Code of Conduct Covering Labour Bodies, Principles in Global Corporate Responsibility, UN Norms of Responsibilities of Transnational Corporations and Other Business Enterprises with Regard to Human Rights.

VI: THE TRIPLE BOTTOM LINE

Sustainable development for business is operationalised by the triple bottom line, popularly described by the three Ps; *People, Planet, Profit*. In short companies seek to find sustainable solutions for their relationship with the *economy* (including the economy of the community), with the *external environment* (including biodiversity and animal welfare), and with *human beings* (hereunder in the relationship with employees, suppliers, customers, local communities and other stakeholders). The following boxes present indicative lists of areas under the triple bottom line reflecting present developments. The areas mentioned are not intended to be exhaustive, but merely to give a brief overview of current developments.

Social Responsibility (People)

* Labour rights: Slave, forced or compulsory labour; child labour; freedom of association/collective bargaining; non-discrimination/equal opportunities; rest, leisure and holidays; minimum wages; health and safety;
* Right to work: Protection against unjustified dismissals and technical/vocational guidance and training;
* Right to life;
* Development rights: Right to education; to health; to adequate food and fair distribution of food; to clothing; to housing; to social security; to enjoy technological development;
* Right to hold opinions & freedom of expression, thought, conscience and religion;
* Right to a family life;

---

5   President Thabo Mbeki of South Africa, The New York Times, 26 August 2002.

- Right to privacy, e.g. surveillance, personal information, drug testing;
- Minority rights to culture, religious practise & language and cultural rights (indigenous peoples);
- Right to peaceful assembly;
- Right to take part in political life;
- Informed consent to medical / biological trials;
- Moral and material interests form inventions.

Environmental Responsibility (Planet)

- UN Convention on Bio-Diversity: in-situ and ex-situ conservation, impact on diversity, use of genetic material, technology transfer;
- The Precautionary Principle (In doubt about negative environmental impact of a given action – abstain);
- Use and handling of GMOs (Genetically Modified Organisms);
- Air emissions and impact on global warming (greenhouse gases);
- Impact on the ozone layer (Montreal Protocol Annexes);
- Prohibition of use of certain materials and substances, hereunder safe handling/transport of dangerous substances;
- Distance to residential neighbourhoods for production sites;
- Soil, ground water and surface water contamination;
- Treatment and reduction of waste water;
- Water consumption and leakage;
- 'Eco-efficiency', consumption of raw materials, and consumption of energy;
- Export of waste and re-use of material;
- Subsidising of environmental projects (e. g. protection of the rainforest etc.);
- Animal welfare.

Economic Responsibility (Profit)

- Financial profit, economic growth and asset creation;
- Business ethics, corruption and bribery;
- Direct and indirect economic impact on communities through spending power (suppliers, consumers, investors, tax payments and investments), and geographic economic impact;
- Economic impact through business process: outsourcing, knowledge, innovation, social investments in employees and consumers;
- Monetary support for political parties, lobbying, and other 'political' activities;
- External economic impact from pollution, internalisation of externalities, value of consuming products;
- Stock exchange behaviour, including insider trading;
- Economic regulation, tax incentives, redistribution;
- State contracts and state subsidies;
- Intellectual property rights, hereunder patents, pricing and the impact on economic and societal development potential;
- Anti-trust & competition, including market impact and 'alliances';
- Board and executive remuneration and role of accountants;
- Donations;
- Taxes, including 'transfer pricing'.

In practice it is not possible to describe each bottom line quite as simple as illustrated. Grey zones exist between the lines. For example, corruption and bribery will belong to the 'economic'-bottom line as having an immediate impact on the economy of the community, notwithstanding that the practice has human rights implications as well in the form of discrimination and non-equal access to law 20. The 'environmental'-bottom line describes the impact on the external environment, notwithstanding that the environment has great impact on the right to health of people. Consequently, most reporting strives towards a holistic approach embracing all three bottom lines in one report.

Finally, as a prerequisite, any company is expected to comply with international, regional, national and local laws and regulations *directly applicable* to the corporation. Compliance to such regulation will in most societies fulfil several of the areas mentioned in the boxes above, but in many cases a company may not be able to prove CSR only by demonstrating legal compliance. Beyond this compliance, there is another area that we might describe as Corporate Social Opportunity, which is motivated by competitive advantages i.e. economic incentives.

VII: CONCLUSION

'CSR may have entered our national vocabulary but it has not taken root in our consciousness'.[6]

CSR has increased in recent years as a result of the recognition of the essential contribution of business to social, environmental and Human Rights progress, and because of pressure from consumers, investors, employers, governments, NGOs and public opinion. A growing number of businesses already have CSR as a priority in their agendas. It is the lawyers' role to assist their clients in positioning their business successfully in this new legal landscap

Please find the complete and unabridged version of this document at: http://www.ccbe. org/doc/En/guidelines_csr_en.pdf

For further information please consult the CCBE website: http://www.ccbe.org

---

[6]   Ella Joseph, centre-left think-tank IPPR, The Observer, 2 February 2003.

UN NORMS ON RESPONSIBILITIES OF TRANSNATIONAL CORPORATIONS AND OTHER BUSINESS ENTERPRISES WITH REGARD TO HUMAN RIGHTS*, †

ECONOMIC, SOCIAL AND CULTURAL RIGHTS

Preamble

Bearing in mind the principles and obligations under the Charter of the United Nations, in particular the preamble and Articles 1, 2, 55 and 56, inter alia to promote universal respect for, and observance of, human rights and fundamental freedoms.

Recalling that the Universal Declaration of Human Rights proclaims a common standard of achievement for all peoples and all nations, to the end that Governments, other organs of society and individuals shall strive, by teaching and education to promote respect for human rights and freedoms, and, by progressive measures, to secure universal and effective recognition and observance, including of equal rights of women and men and the promotion of social progress and better standards of life in larger freedom.

Recognizing that even though States have the primary responsibility to promote, secure the fulfilment of, respect, ensure respect of and protect human rights, transnational corporations and other business enterprises, as organs of society, are also responsible for promoting and securing the human rights set forth in the Universal Declaration of Human Rights.

Realizing that transnational corporations and other business enterprises, their officers and persons working for them are also obligated to respect generally recognized responsibilities and norms contained in United Nations treaties and other international instruments such as the Convention on the Prevention and Punishment of the Crime of Genocide; the Convention against Torture and Other Cruel, Inhuman or Degrading Treatment or Punishment; the Slavery Convention and the Supplementary Convention on the Abolition of Slavery, the Slave Trade, and Institutions and Practices Similar to Slavery; the International Convention on the Elimination of All Forms of Racial Discrimination; the Convention on the Elimination of All Forms of Discrimination against Women; the International Covenant on Economic, Social and Cultural Rights; the International Covenant on Civil and Political Rights; the Convention on the Rights of the Child; the International Convention on the Protection of the Rights of All Migrant Workers and Members of Their Families; the four Geneva Conventions of 12 August

---

1949 and two Additional Protocols thereto for the protection of victims of war; the Declaration on the Right and Responsibility of Individuals, Groups and Organs of Society to Promote and Protect Universally Recognized Human Rights and Fundamental Freedoms; the Rome Statute of the International Criminal Court; the United Nations Convention against Transnational Organized Crime; the Convention on Biological Diversity; the International Convention on Civil Liability for Oil Pollution Damage; the Convention on Civil Liability for Damage Resulting from Activities Dangerous to the Environment; the Declaration on the Right to Development; the Rio Declaration on the Environment and Development; the Plan of Implementation of the World Summit on Sustainable Development; the United Nations Millennium Declaration; the Universal Declaration on the Human Genome and Human Rights; the International Code of Marketing of Breast-milk Substitutes adopted by the World Health Assembly; the Ethical Criteria for Medical Drug Promotion and the 'Health for All in the Twenty-First Century' policy of the World Health Organization; the Convention against Discrimination in Education of the United Nations Educational, Scientific, and Cultural Organization; conventions and recommendations of the International Labour Organization; the Convention and Protocol relating to the Status of Refugees; the African Charter on Human and Peoples' Rights; the American Convention on Human Rights; the European Convention for the Protection of Human Rights and Fundamental Freedoms; the Charter of Fundamental Rights of the European Union; the Convention on Combating Bribery of Foreign Public Officials in International Business Transactions of the Organization for Economic Cooperation and Development; and other instruments.

Taking into account the standards set forth in the Tripartite Declaration of Principles Concerning Multinational Enterprises and Social Policy and the Declaration on Fundamental Principles and Rights at Work of the International Labour Organization.

Aware of the Guidelines for Multinational Enterprises and the Committee on International Investment and Multinational Enterprises of the Organization for Economic Cooperation and Development.

Aware also of the United Nations Global Compact initiative which challenges business leaders to 'embrace and enact' nine basic principles with respect to human rights, including labour rights and the environment.

Conscious of the fact that the Governing Body Subcommittee on Multinational Enterprises and Social Policy, the Governing Body, the Committee of Experts on the Application of Standards, as well as the Committee on Freedom of Association of the International Labour Organization have named business enterprises implicated in States' failure to comply with Conventions No. 87 concerning the Freedom of Association and Protection of the Right to Organize and No. 98 concerning the Application of the Principles of the Right to Organize and Bargain Collectively, and seeking to supplement and assist their efforts to encourage transnational corporations and other business enterprises to protect human rights.

Conscious also of the Commentary on the Norms on the responsibilities of transnational corporations and other business enterprises with regard to human rights, and finding it a useful interpretation and elaboration of the standards contained in the Norms.

Taking note of global trends which have increased the influence of transnational corporations and other business enterprises on the economies of most countries and in international economic relations, and of the growing number of other business enterprises which operate across national boundaries in a variety of arrangements resulting in economic activities beyond the actual capacities of any one national system.

Noting that transnational corporations and other business enterprises have the capacity to foster economic well-being, development, technological improvement and wealth as well as the capacity to cause harmful impacts on the human rights and lives of individuals through their core business practices and operations, including employment practices, environmental policies, relationships with suppliers and consumers, interactions with Governments and other activities.

Noting also that new international human rights issues and concerns are continually emerging and that transnational corporations and other business enterprises often are involved in these issues and concerns, such that further standard-setting and implementation are required at this time and in the future.

Acknowledging the universality, indivisibility, interdependence and interrelatedness of human rights, including the right to development, which entitles every human person and all peoples to participate in, contribute to and enjoy economic, social, cultural and political development in which all human rights and fundamental freedoms can be fully realized.

Reaffirming that transnational corporations and other business enterprises, their officers – including managers, members of corporate boards or directors and other executives – and persons working for them have, inter alia, human rights obligations and responsibilities and that these human rights norms will contribute to the making and development of international law as to those responsibilities and obligations.

Solemnly proclaims these Norms on the Responsibilities of Transnational Corporations and Other Business Enterprises with Regard to Human Rights and urges that every effort be made so that they become generally known and respected.

A. General Obligations

1. States have the primary responsibility to promote, secure the fulfilment of, respect, ensure respect of and protect human rights recognized in international as well as national law, including ensuring that transnational corporations and other business enterprises respect human rights. Within their respective spheres of activity and influence, transnational corporations and other business enterprises have the obligation to promote, secure the fulfilment of, respect, ensure respect of and protect human rights recognized in international as well as national law, including the rights and interests of indigenous peoples and other vulnerable groups.

B. Right to Equal Opportunity And Non-Discriminatory Treatment

2. Transnational corporations and other business enterprises shall ensure equality of opportunity and treatment, as provided in the relevant international instruments and national legislation as well as international human rights law, for the purpose of eliminating discrimination based on race, colour, sex, language, religion, political opinion, national or social origin, social status, indigenous status, disability, age – except for children, who may be given greater protection – or other status of the individual unrelated to the inherent requirements to perform the job, or of complying with special measures designed to overcome past discrimination against certain groups.

C. Right To Security of Persons

3. Transnational corporations and other business enterprises shall not engage in nor benefit from war crimes, crimes against humanity, genocide, torture, forced disappearance, forced or compulsory labour, hostage-taking, extrajudicial, summary or arbitrary executions, other violations of humanitarian law and other international crimes against the human person as defined by international law, in particular human rights and humanitarian law.

4. Security arrangements for transnational corporations and other business enterprises shall observe international human rights norms as well as the laws and professional standards of the country or countries in which they operate.

D.   Rights of Workers

5. Transnational corporations and other business enterprises shall not use forced or compulsory labour as forbidden by the relevant international instruments and national legislation as well as international human rights and humanitarian law.

6. Transnational corporations and other business enterprises shall respect the rights of children to be protected from economic exploitation as forbidden by the relevant international instruments and national legislation as well as international human rights and humanitarian law.

7. Transnational corporations and other business enterprises shall provide a safe and healthy working environment as set forth in relevant international instruments and national legislation as well as international human rights and humanitarian law.

8. Transnational corporations and other business enterprises shall provide workers with remuneration that ensures an adequate standard of living for them and their families. Such remuneration shall take due account of their needs for adequate living conditions with a view towards progressive improvement.

9. Transnational corporations and other business enterprises shall ensure freedom of association and effective recognition of the right to collective bargaining by protecting the right to establish and, subject only to the rules of the organization concerned, to join organizations of their own choosing without distinction, previous authorization, or interference, for the protection of their employment interests and for other collective bargaining purposes as provided in national legislation and the relevant conventions of the International Labour Organization.

E.   Respect For National Sovereignty And Human Rights

10. Transnational corporations and other business enterprises shall recognize and respect applicable norms of international law, national laws and regulations, as well as administrative practices, the rule of law, the public interest, development objectives, social, economic and cultural policies including transparency, accountability and prohibition of corruption, and authority of the countries in which the enterprises operate.

11. Transnational corporations and other business enterprises shall not offer, promise, give, accept, condone, knowingly benefit from, or demand a bribe or other improper advantage, nor shall they be solicited or expected to give a bribe or other improper advantage to any Government, public official, candidate for elective post, any member of the armed forces or security forces, or any other individual or organization. Transnational corporations and other business enterprises shall refrain from any activity which supports, solicits, or encourages States or any other entities to abuse human rights. They shall further seek to ensure that the goods and services they provide will not be used to abuse human rights.

12. Transnational corporations and other business enterprises shall respect economic, social and cultural rights as well as civil and political rights and contribute to their realization, in particular the rights to development, adequate food and drinking water, the highest attainable standard of physical and mental health, adequate housing, privacy, education, freedom of thought, conscience, and religion and freedom of opinion and expression, and shall refrain from actions which obstruct or impede the realization of those rights.

F.   Obligations With Regard To Consumer Protection

13. Transnational corporations and other business enterprises shall act in accordance with fair business, marketing and advertising practices and shall take all necessary steps to ensure the safety and quality of the goods and services they provide, including observance of the precautionary principle. Nor shall they produce, distribute, market, or advertise harmful or potentially harmful products for use by consumers.

G.   Obligations With Regard To Environmental Protection

14. Transnational corporations and other business enterprises shall carry out their activities in accordance with national laws, regulations, administrative practices and policies relating to the preservation of the environment of the countries in which they operate, as well as in accordance with relevant international agreements, principles, objectives, responsibilities and standards with regard to the environment as well as human rights, public health and safety, bioethics and the precautionary principle, and shall generally conduct their activities in a manner contributing to the wider goal of sustainable development.

H.   General Provisions of Implementation

15. As an initial step towards implementing these Norms, each transnational corporation or other business enterprise shall adopt, disseminate and implement internal rules of operation in compliance with the Norms. Further, they shall periodically report on and take other measures fully to implement the Norms and to provide at least for the prompt implementation of the protections set forth in the Norms. Each transnational corporation or other business enterprise shall apply and incorporate these Norms in their contracts or other arrangements and dealings with contractors, subcontractors, suppliers, licensees, distributors, or natural or other legal persons that enter into any agreement with the transnational corporation or business enterprise in order to ensure respect for and implementation of the Norms.

16. Transnational corporations and other business enterprises shall be subject to periodic monitoring and verification by United Nations, other international and national mechanisms already in existence or yet to be created, regarding application of the Norms. This monitoring shall be transparent and independent and take into account input from stakeholders (including non-governmental organizations) and as a result of complaints of violations of these Norms. Further, transnational corporations and other business enterprises shall conduct periodic evaluations concerning the impact of their own activities on human rights under these Norms.

17. States should establish and reinforce the necessary legal and administrative framework for ensuring that the Norms and other relevant national and international laws are implemented by transnational corporations and other business enterprises.

18. Transnational corporations and other business enterprises shall provide prompt, effective and adequate reparation to those persons, entities and communities that have been adversely affected by failures to comply with these Norms through, inter alia, reparations, restitution, compensation and rehabilitation for any damage done or property taken. In connection with determining damages, in regard to criminal sanctions, and in all other respects, these Norms shall be applied by national courts and/or international tribunals, pursuant to national and international law.

19. Nothing in these Norms shall be construed as diminishing, restricting, or adversely affecting the human rights obligations of States under national and international law, nor shall they be construed as diminishing, restricting, or adversely affecting more protective human rights norms, nor shall they be construed as diminishing, restricting, or adversely affecting other obligations or responsibilities of transnational corporations and other business enterprises in fields other than human rights.

I.   Definitions

20. The term 'transnational corporation' refers to an economic entity operating in more than one country or a cluster of economic entities operating in two or more countries – whatever their legal form, whether in their home country or country of activity, and whether taken individually or collectively.

21. The phrase 'other business enterprise' includes any business entity, regardless of the international or domestic nature of its activities, including a transnational corporation, contractor, subcontractor, supplier, licensee or distributor; the corporate, partnership, or other legal form used to establish the business entity; and the nature of the ownership of the entity. These Norms shall be presumed to apply, as a matter of practice, if the business enterprise has any relation with a transnational corporation, the impact of its activities is not entirely local, or the activities involve violations of the right to security as indicated in paragraphs 3 and 4.

22. The term 'stakeholder' includes stockholders, other owners, workers and their representatives, as well as any other individual or group that is affected by the activities of transnational corporations or other business enterprises. The term 'stakeholder' shall be interpreted functionally in the light of the objectives of these Norms and include indirect stakeholders when their interests are or will be substantially affected by the activities of the transnational corporation or business enterprise. In addition to parties directly affected by the activities of business enterprises, stakeholders can include parties which are indirectly affected by the activities of transnational corporations or other business enterprises such as consumer groups, customers, Governments, neighbouring communities, indigenous peoples and communities, non-governmental organizations, public and private lending institutions, suppliers, trade associations, and others.

23. The phrases 'human rights' and 'international human rights' include civil, cultural, economic, political and social rights, as set forth in the International Bill of Human Rights and other human rights treaties, as well as the right to development and rights recognized by international humanitarian law, international refugee law, international labour law, and other relevant instruments adopted within the United Nations system.

This document can also be accessed through online resources and was derived from: http://www.unhchr.ch/Huridocda/Huridoca.nsf/TestFrame/64155e7e8141b38cc1256d63 002c55e8?Opendocument

Please see the UN website for further information: www.un.org

Index

Access to health 307–308
Africa 323–337
  autocratic governments, and 323
  broad focus of CSR 325–326
    domestic laws, and 326
    meaning 325
  colonialism, and 323
  CSC, concept of 336
  CSR failures in energy 324
    collapse of companies, and 324
  economic regulation 326
    competition, and 326
    inefficiency, and 326
  Ghana, *see* Ghana
  implementation of CSR,
    challenge 335
  initiatives to support transparency and
    development 334–335
    EITI 334
    Nigeria's transparency commitments
      334–335
    promoting transparency in African Oil
      sector 335
  'magic bullet' solution, lack of 336
  mining, and 329–331
    destructive nature of 331
    economic common sense, and 331
    governance 330
    importance of CSR in 330
    multinational initiatives 330
  new emphasis on CSR 329
  new political arena 331–332
    NEPAD process, and 331
    sustainable development, and 331
  repairing corporate accountability 325
  specific NEPAD initiatives 332–334
    African Peer Review Mechanism (APRM)
      332–333
    Infrastructure Initiative 333
    PPP Initiative 334
  state-owned monopolies 327–329
    'bright lines' 328
    focus in infrastructure areas 328
    improving economic efficiency 329
    inefficiency and corruption in 327
    management of 327
    'natural monopoly' 328
    'sector reform' initiatives 327
    US electricity sector, and 329

Amnesty International Guidelines for
  Companies
  text 507–512
Audit committees 58
Auditors
  corporate governance, and 57–58
Australia
  CCBE Guidelines, and 423

Belgium
  pension fund disclosure 291–292
  social label law 291–292
Biodiversity
  CSR and the environment, and 181
Black economic empowerment
  corporate assistance for 137–139
Board membership
  pro bono work, and 441
Brand equity
  managing 122–123
Brennan, Daniel, QC
  business in the community, on 16–17
Brophy, Richard
  lawyers' forms, on 25
Brumm, James E.
  Japanese perspective, on 20
Business ethics 31–36
  Code of Ethics 31, 34–35
    OECD Guidelines 35
    strengths 34
    weaknesses 34–35
  corporate governance 32, 35
  CSR, and 32–33
  integrity 33–34
  matters comprising 31–32
  meaning 31
  measurable indicators 36
  moral values 33–34
  morality, and 36
  motivation 35–36
  post-Watergate 32
  trust 33
    reciprocity 33
  understanding, and 35–36
  values 31

Caux Round Table Principles 225–234, 372
  assessing CSR standards, and 265–269
    general principles 266–267

preamble   266
stakeholder principles   267–269
assessment framework-criteria matrix   233
avoidance of illicit operations   230–231
business behaviour: beyond the letter of the
    law toward a spirit of trust   229
economic and social impact of business:
    toward innovation, justice and world
    community   228–229
from aspirations to action   231–232
general principles   226–234
improvement process   232–234
moral capitalism   232
origins   225
preamble   226
respect for the environment   230
respect for rules   229–230
responsibilities of business: beyond
    share-holders toward stakeholders   228
self-assessment process   232–234
stakeholder ethic   227
support for multilateral trade   230
text   501–505
CCBE Guide for European Lawyers Advising
    on CSR Issues
text   543–550
CCBE Guidelines   422–433
aim   422
corporate risks and opportunities   425–426
CSR standards   428–429
current developments   423–425
    Australia   423
    Denmark and the Netherlands   424
    France   424
    Germany   424
    United Kingdom   424
    US Sarbanes-Oxley Act   425
lawyers obligation to advise on CSR   426–428
meaning   422
triple bottom line   429–432
    economic responsibility   431
    environmental responsibility   430
    social responsibility   430
understanding CSR   422–423
Charities
    pro bono work, and   439–440
China
    influence over Japan   339
Codes of conduct
    addressees   390–391
    advantages of   378–381
        behaving consistently with company's
            principles and ethics   380
        maintaining relationships with partners
            378
        managing relations with NGOs   379
        minimizing friction with shareholders
            379–380

production efficiency   379
reducing legal risk   380–381
reputation   378
risk management   379
safeguarding brand equity   378
supply chain management   378
contents   390–391
definition   389–390
differences from legal rules   388–389
future of   385–386
history   368–371
    beginning of   368
    corporate scandals   370
    cross-border economic enterprises   369
    economic disparities between developed
        and developing countries   370
    Johnson and Johnson Credo   368
    post-World War Two   369
    Universal Declaration of Human Rights,
        and   368–369
intergovernmental organizations, originating
    from   399–401
    legal sanctions, and   400
    National Contact Point (NCP)   400
    OECD Guidelines, and   399–401
issued by companies   392–399
    complement to law, as   392–393
    contracts with business partners in supply
        chain, and   396–397
    contracts with investors and financial
        markets, and   397–398
    contractual commitment required by
        regulators   394
    contractual relevance   395–398
    employees' duty to follow law   393
    encouraged by law   394
    external contracts   396–398
    instructions to corporate organs   399
    labour contracts   395–396
    legal systems, and   392–393
    marketing   398
    reduction of legal risk   393
    standards of care   398–399
lawyers' firms, for   442
legal dimensions of   387–401
    driving factors behind development of
        387–388
legal dimensions, whether   391–392
meaning   389–391
objectives   388
originators   390
self regulation, and   367
stakeholder challenges   381–384
    companies   383–384
    factory management and owners   382
    NGOs   383
    SRIs   383
    vendor employees   381–382

standardization and harmonization
    384–385
types of 371–377
    Caux Round Table Principles 372
    company codes 377
    Ethical Trading Initiative Base Code 375
    European Commission, and 374
    Global Sullivan Principles 371–372
    intergovernmental codes 373–375
    model codes 371–373
    multi-stakeholder codes 375–376
    NGOs, and 372
    OECD Guidelines 373–374
    Social Accountability 8000 (SA8000) 373
    trade association codes 376
    UK Banana Industry Code of Best
        Practice 376
    UN Global Compact 371
    United Nations, and 374–375
    voluntary commitments, as 391
Command and control
    environmental protection through 160–163
Community groups
    pro bono work, and 439–440
Compensation
    social responsibility, and 130–131
Contracts
    codes of conduct, and 395–397
Corell, Hans
    Global Compact, on 14
Corporate citizenship, *see* Shareholder value
Corporate governance 37–60
    assessing CSR standards 263–271
        business in the community 263–264
        Caux Round Table 265–269, *see also*
            Caux Round Table Principles
        CRI, working of 264–265
        improvement process 269–271
        self-assessment process 269–271
    auditors, and 57–58
    directors, and 46–50
        additional requirements 50
        audit committees 48
        board committees 49
        chairman, role of 49–50
        corporate governance committees 48–49
        duties 46–48
    European Union 45–46
    external lawyers, and 59
    initiatives 274–275
    international initiatives 271–274
    investment professionals, and 58
    management, and 50–53
        certification of financial statements 51
        certification of reports 51
        codes of ethics 52–53
        disclosure committees 51
        duty on lawyers to report violations 53

forfeiture of bonuses 51–52
forfeiture of profits 51–52
improper influence on conduct of audits
    53
pension fund blackout restrictions 52
prohibition against personal loans 52
new ideas 263–276
practical applications 263–276
precondition to social responsibility, as
    117–120
    Board of Directors oversight 118–119
    management committee to Corporate
        Purpose and Core Values 117–118
    policies 119–120
    procedures 119–120
rating agencies, and 58–59
rating systems 59
shareholders 53–57
    disclosure controls 56
    enhanced shareholder activism 57
    improved disclosure 55–56
    internal controls 56
    right of access to information 54–55
third parties, and 57–59
UK, in 42–45
    Combined Code 43
    company law 42–43
    financial services law enforcement 44–45
    Higgs Review 44
    Listing Rules 43
    recent reforms 44
    Reports of 1990s 43–44
    Smith Review 44
US, in 39–42
    federal laws 40
    recent developments 41–42
    securities law enforcement 40–41
    state corporate and securities laws 39
    Stock Exchange listing requirements 41
Corporate governance committees 48–49
Corporate philanthropy
    CSR, and 103
CSR
    corporate governance distinguished 4
    criticisms of 99–100
    history 98–100
    legislation, and 4
    marketing, and 5
    meaning 97, 3–4
    public relations smokescreen, as 131–132
CSR and corporate governance 37–60
    relationship between 38–39
CSR and public policy 77–95
    aligning CSR with public policy
        objectives 88
    championing best practice 82–83
    co-ordinating CSR practice 85–86
    company accounts, disclosures in 92

enabling smaller companies 84
engaging champions 81–84
engaging the financial community 83–84
ensuring transparency in CSR practice
    84–85
foreign direct liability 93–94
fostering integrity 84–87
government action
    summary 89–90
international agencies, role of 88–89
leading by example 86–87
legislation v trade 77–78
legislative approach 90–94
NGOs, facilitating relationships with 87–88
role of public policy in promotion of
    CSR 80
selling the message 81–82
shareholder value 78–80
stakeholders, facilitating relationships with
    87–88
sustainability 77–78
transforming business culture 77–80
transforming society 94–95
voluntary approach 80–90
working together 87–90
CSR and the environment 159–182
characteristics of responsible environmental
        performance 168–181
    accountability 168–171
    assessing, managing and disclosing risk of
        environmental issues to business
        175–176
    assessing and managing risk to
        environment 174–175
    biodiversity 181
    eco-efficiency 178–179
    engaging stakeholders 168–171, 171–172
    extended producer responsibility (EPR)
        180
    life cycle assessments 179
    management systems 173–174
    measuring performance 171
    opportunity identification 174–176
    product stewardship 178–180
    providing for continuous improvement
        171
    reporting performance 168–171
    risk management 174–176
    setting objectives and targets 171
    supply chains 180–181
    technology 176–178
    transparency 168–171
environmental performance 163–181
    business case for environmental
        responsibility 163–166
    characteristics of responsible
        environmental performance 168–181
    codes 166–168

commitments 166–168
principles 166–168
voluntary compacts 166–168
environmental protection 160–163
    command and control 160–161
    international co-operative efforts
        161–163
CSR in a changing corporate world 97–109
achievements of globalization 107–109
advantages of CSR 108
Berle, Adolf A. on 98
business incentives 104
Canon 105
corporate climate, and 104
corporate philanthropy, and 103
criticisms of CSR 99–100
cynicism in relation to 108
Dodd, E. Mernick on 98
Drucker, Peter on 98–99
gap between rich and poor, and 108–109
Gilda Club, and 104
globalization 102–103
globalized climate, and 106–107
'good citizenship', and 106
history of CSR 98–100
human rights, 100–102, *see also* Human
    Rights
hypocrisy, and 108
Kyosei 105
meaning of CSR 97
NGOs, and 104
pro bono programs 106
reasons for pursuit of CSR 103–106
reputation, and 105
stakeholders, and 100
voluntary codes 107
CSR movement
criticism of 475–484
    corporate citizenship, and 481–482
    diverting attention from key issues 479
    economic progress, and 483
    environmental damage, and 483
    'global governance', and 483
    globalization, and 483
    ignorance of development economics
        479–480
    lack of definition 476–477
    licence to operate, and 482
    management concepts 475
    new systems to monitor 'social'
        targets 482
    philanthropy, CSR as 478–479
    public relations exercise, CSR as
        477–478
    self-regulation, and 483–484
    'society's expectations', and 482
    stakeholders, and 482
    sustainable development, and 481

unnecessary distraction, CSR as 480–481
  welfare of society, and 481
CSR standards 428–429
  assessing 263–271, *see also* Corporate
    governance

Denmark
  Business and Human Rights Project 293
  CCBE Guidelines, and 424
  Copenhagen Centre 292
  Our Common Concern Campaign 292
Directors
  corporate governance, and, *see* Corporate
    governance
Donations
  lawyers firms, and 442

Eco-efficiency 178–179
Economic development
  triple bottom line, and 132–133
Employees
  attracting, motivating and retaining
    social responsibility, and 123–124
Environment
  CSR, and, *see* CSR and the environment
Environmental commitments
  triple bottom line, and 135–137
Equal opportunities 308
Ethical Trading Initiative Base Code 375
European Initiatives 279–299
  BLIHR 289–290
  Communications of EU Commission
    concerning CSR July 2002, 286–287
  Council Resolution December
    2001, 284
  Council Resolution February 2003, 287
  CSR, and 279
  discussion on legislation measures to
    promote CSR 298–299
  EU Charter of Fundamental Rights
    290–291
  EU Commission's Green Paper on
    Promoting European Framework for
    CSR, 2001, 281–284
  European Academy of Business in
    Society 288
  European Business Campaign on
    CSR 287–288
  European Parliament's Code of Conduct
    December 1998 and June 2002, 285
  Lisbon summit March 2000, 281
  manifesto of enterprises against social
    exclusion 280
European perspectives 299–310
  compliance vs opportunity (CSO) 305–310
    access to health 307–308
    equal opportunities 308
    external funding 306

freedom of information 309
freedom of speech 309
Novo Nordisk 307–308
proactive approach 305–306
relevance of values to specific sector 306
right to health 307–308
right to privacy 309
right to take part in technological
  development 310
Sonofon 308–310
discourse on CSR 299
establishing responsibilities 299
'human rights'-based approach 300–304
  company liability 303
  engagement in developing world 302–303
  EU constitutional process 302
  FTSE4good index 302
  implementation of core values 301
  international agreements 303–304
  international instruments 301
  international regulation on companies 303
  negative obligations 302
  recent initiatives 302
  recognition of human rights 301
  rising social gaps 303
  sustainable development 300
  triple bottom line 300–302
  'us and them' approach 302–303
  voluntary codes of conduct 304
lawyer, responsibilities 304–305
  awareness of cases 305
  challenges on human rights agenda 305
  reasons for 304
lawyers' involvement in 299
European Union
  corporate governance 45–46
Extended producer responsibility (EPR) 180

Financial sector initiatives
  triple bottom line, and 135–137
France
  CCBE Guidelines, and 424
  mandatory sustainability reporting 293–294
  study centre for CSR 294
Freedom of information 309
Freedom of speech 309
FTSE4good index 302

Germany
  CCBE Guidelines, and 424
  pension fund disclosure 295
  round table on code of conduct 294
  Rugmark 294
Ghana, CSR and human rights in 349–364,
  460–461, 468–469
  constitution 351–355
    acquiring mineral right 354
    article 18 351

Labour standards and CSR 141–158
  meaning 141
Lawyers
  appraisals of legal profession 405–406
  corporate bar 411–412
    corporate scandals, and 412
    pro bono service, and 411
    responsibilities, and 411
    Sears Roebuck, and 412
  corporate governance, and 59
  CSR in lawyers' firms, *see* Lawyers' firms
  furthering *pro bono* service 414
  historical antecedents 406–408
    ancient Rome 406
    England 1307, in 406
    expanding use 406
    formation of legal aid societies 408
    hostility to lawyers 406–407
    lawyers' role in American Revolution 407
  in-house counsel, *see* In-house counsel
  internal responsibility 415–416
    confidentiality and whistle-blowing, clash
      between 416
    conflicts of interest 415–416
    ethics, and 415
  particular role for corporate lawyers 415
  pro bono examples 413–414
    Abott Laboratories V.P. 413
    international 414
    Merck and Co. Inc 413
    Pfizer 413
    Starbucks 413
  responsibility for advising on CSR 419–433
    CCBE Guidelines, *see* CCBE Guidelines
    CCBE, introduction to 419
    CCBEs involvement 420–421
    European position 419–420
    external lawyers, and 421
  role of
    US perspective, *see* US perspective
  sea change in social responsibility 409–410
    organized bar, role in 410
    pro bono service, and 409
    slow pace of reform 409
  social responsibility, and 405
Lawyers' firms
  bullying at work, prevention of 444
  charities and community groups, support
    to 439–440
    model for 439
  civil proceedings, and 436
  codes of conduct 442
  compliance with ethical standards, and 435
  compliance/ risk management 444–445
    conflicts of interest 444–445
    engagement letters 445
    money laundering 445
  employee benefits 444

  environmental policies 445–446
  equal opportunities 444
  ethical behaviour, obligation 435–436
  financial support and donations 442
  governance and reporting 446
  harassment, prevention of 444
  health and safety 443
  internal policies and governance 442–446
  international human rights cases 440
  legal advice agencies 438–439
    forms of 438
    volunteers, and 439
  legal *pro bono* activities 437–440
    categories of 438
    size of firm, and 437–438
  pro bono activities, other 440–441
    board membership 441
    mentoring 441
    primary school 440–441
    secondary schools 441
  pro bono work, undertaking 437
  use of term CSR by 436
  work/ life balance 443
Legal advice agencies, *see* Lawyers firms
License to operate
  protecting
    social responsibility, and 124–126
Life cycle assessments 179
Lock, Reinier
  African perspective, on 19
Lowry, John
  corporate governance, on 6
Lozano, Josep
  human rights, on 10–11
Lundblad, Claes
  codes of conduct, on 22–23
Lux, Johnathan
  European initiatives, on 17–18

Management
  corporate governance, and, *see* Corporate
    governance
Management systems
  CSR and the environment, and 173–174
Marketing
  codes of conduct, and 398
Martin, Felix
  CSR and public policy, and 7
Milward-Oliver, Gerald, 75
  soul of the corporation, on 6–7

NEPAD process, 331, *see also* Africa
Netherlands
  CCBE Guidelines, and 424
New Partnership for Africa's Development,
    461, *see also* NEPAD process; Africa
Niger Delta Development Commission
    461–462

Nigeria
  CSR activities in   460–461
  CSR efforts of Shell Petroleum Development
      Company of Nigeria Ltd   462–468
    agriculture and youth empowerment   465
    community development programme   463
    education   466
    flares–down programme   468
    health   466–467
    Health, Safety and Environmental
        Awareness Training (HSEAT)
        467–468
    micro-credit and business development
        programme   465–466
    oil spills   468
    protecting the environment   467
    safeguarding people   463–464
    safety   464
    security   464
    social and economic infrastructure   467
    sports and competition   466
    stakeholders engagement and
        workshop   463
    women empowerment   464
    youth empowerment and skills
        development   465
  transparency commitments, 334–335, see also
      Africa
Norway
  Kompakt   295
Ntrakwah, Felix
  Ghana, on   20–21

Odeleye, Isaiah
  in-house counsel, on   25–26
OECD Guidelines for Multinational
    Enterprises   243–250
  adherents   243
  anti-consumption statements by sector of
      activity   245
  binding regulation, and   246
  corporate responsibility and the international
      economy   243–247
  effectiveness   244
  effectiveness of NCPs   250
  enhancing contributions of business in weak
      governance zones   250
  formal deterrence, and   246
  implementation   249
  key features   247–248
  Kortan suppliers in Guatemalan export
      processing zone   248
  legal aspects of,   399–401, see also Codes of
      conduct
  ongoing challenges   249–250
  parallel legal procedures   250
  partnership with other international
      organizations   250
  policy statements by issue area   245
  positive developments   249
  results   248
  Swedish business service provisions in
      Ghana's gold sector   248
  text   519–527
  transparency of NCPs   250
  Zambian copper mining   248
Offshoring issue   135
Opportunity identification

Performance plans
  social responsibility, and   130–131
Prandi, Maria
  human rights, on   10–11
Pro bono
  lawyers and CSR, and, see Lawyers; Lawyers
      firms
Product stewardship
  CSR and the environment, and
      178–180
Profit motive
  linking social responsibility to   127
Public policy, see CSR and public policy

Ragnwaldh, Jacob
  UN Norms, on   15–16
Rating agencies
  corporate governance, and   58–59
Reputation
  managing   122–123
Right to health   307–308
Right to privacy   309
Right to take part in technological development
    310
Risk management
  CSR and the environment, and   174
Roselle, James E.
  shareholder value, on   8
Rudolph, Phillip H.
  codes of conduct, on   21–22
  global Sullivan principles, on   13
  role of lawyers, on   18–19
  Tripartite Declaration, on   12–13

Schools
  pro bono work, and   441
Self-regulation, see Codes of conduct
Shareholder value   113–139
  corporate citizenship   113–120
    business judgment   115–117
    corporate governance as precondition to
        social responsibility, 117–120, see also
        Corporate governance
    paradigm shift   113–114
    recent guidelines   116
    social responsibility, and   114–115
  CSR, and   78–80

social responsibility
    business case for, *see* Social responsibility
Shareholders
    corporate governance, and, *see* Corporate
        governance
Shell Petroleum Development Company of
    Nigeria Ltd
    CSR efforts of, *see* Nigeria
Shestack, Jerome J
    CSR in a changing corporate world, on   7–8
    role of lawyer, on   23–24
Shoop, Marcelle
    environment, on   9–10
Social Accountability   8000
    text   513–517
Social responsibility
    business case for   120–127
        effect of Socially Responsible Investing
            (SRI) 120–121
        employees, and   123–124
        enhancing competitiveness   126–127
        key business factors   121–127
        license to operate, protecting   124–126
    corporate citizenship, and   114–115
    linking to profit motive   127
    obligation   134
    tracking progress   127–131
        compensation   130–131
        performance plans   130–131
        public disclosure   128–129
        social responsibility reporting   129–130
    triple bottom line, *see* Triple bottom line
Socially Responsible Investing (SRI)   120–121
Soul of the corporation   61–75
    Bernays, Edward on   64
    business education, and   72–73
    Confederation of British Industry   69
    consumers, and   71–72
    Corporate Reputation Watch   65
    corporate social responsibility, and   61–65
    Environmental Children's Organization   74
    Fetzer Vineyards   69
    Generation Y   72
    Google   73
    Hewlett Packard   68–69
    interests of shareholders, and   67–68
    legal issues   68
    meaning   67
    mission statements   66–67
    Orange   69
    PR publicity material, and   64–65
    Recording Industry of America   62–63
    Selden Patent   63
    Size of Earth, and   74
    'spiritual values-based model'   70–71
    Taylor Woodrow   65–66
    technological change, and   71–72
    Time Warner   62

    UK Green Alliance, and   63–64
    value of ethical business   71
    values, integration of   70
South Africa
    corporate assistance for black economic
        empowerment   137–139
Standards of care
    codes of conduct, and   398–399
State-owned monopolies
    Africa, and   327–329
Supply chains
    CSR and the environment, and   180–181
Sweden
    Swedish partnership for global responsibility
        295–296

Taylor, Richard
    lawyers firms, on   25
Technology
    CSR and the environment, and   176–178
Thomas, Rosamund
    business ethics, on   5–6
Thorsen, Sune Skadegard
    European perspectives, on   18
Tripartite Declaration of Principles concerning
    Multinational Enterprises   217–219
Triple bottom line
    CCBE Guidelines, and, *see* CCBE
        Guidelines
    corporate assistance for black economic
        empowerment   137–139
    corporate social responsibility, obligation
        134
    economic development   132–133
    environmental commitments   135–137
    European perspectives, and   299
    financial sector initiatives   135–137
    'offshoring' issue   135
    social responsibility   132–133

UK Banana Industry Code of Best
    Practice   376
UN Global Compact   371, *see also* Human
    rights
UN Norms   251–262
    adoption   252
    businesses covered by   253
    consumer protection   256–257
    criticism of   252
    environmental protection   257
    equal opportunities   255
    helpful tool, whether   259–260
    implementation   258–259
    increasing corporate accountability, and
        260–261
    monitoring   258–259
    non-discrimination   255
    obligations of companies   255–257

origins 251–252
reparation 257
reporting 258–259
scope 253–254
security of persons 255–256
workers' rights 256
UN Norms on Responsibilities of Transnational
    Corporations and Other Business
    Enterprises with regard to Human Rights
text 551–556
United Kingdom
    CCBE Guidelines, and 424
    corporate responsibility bill 297
    financial reviews 298
    Minister for corporate social responsibilities
        296–297
    pension fund disclosant 296
United States
    electricity sector
        CSR in Africa, and 329
    occupation of Japan 339–340
    perspective, *see* US perspective
    Sarbanes-Oxley Act 425
US perspective 313–321
    business issues 319–320
        development of documents 320
        opportunities for lawyers, and 319–320
    lawyers, role of 313–321
        characteristics of US justice system,
            and 313

interaction with other companies,
    and 314
litigation, use of 314
regulatory schemes, and 314
litigation issues 314–318
    Alien Tort Claims Act (1789),
        use of 317
    class action lawsuit, and 316
    contingency fees, and 315
    costs, and 316
    Earthrights International 'how-to' manual
        318
    exemplary damages, and 315
    Federal RICO statute, claims brought
        under 317
    freedom of speech, and 317–318
    juries, and 315–316
    television, and 314–315
regulatory issues 318–319
    implementation of recent regulations
        318–319
    organizations driven by values, not rules
        319

Walsh, Mark
    corporate governance, on 6

Young, Stephen
    Caux Round Table Principles, on 13–14

THE INTERNATIONAL BAR ASSOCIATION SERIES

Other titles in this series:

Acquisitions of Shares in a Foreign Country (Editors, M. Gruson, S. Hutter), March 1993
ISBN 1 85333 755 2

Agency and Distribution Agreements – An International Survey (Editor, A. Jausàs), October 1994
ISBN 1 85966 100 9

The Alleged Transnational Criminal (Editor, R.D. Atkins), August 1995
ISBN 0 7923 3409 4

Anti-Dumping under the WTO: A Comparative Review (Editor, K. Steele), July 1996
ISBN 90 411 0915 3

Arab Comparative and Commercial Law – The International Approach, September 1987
Volumes 1 and 2
Volume 1 ISBN 0 86010 977 1
Volume 2 ISBN 0 86010 987 X

Art Loans (N. Palmer), July 1997
ISBN 90 411 0667 7

Capital Markets Forum Yearbook vol 1/1993 (Editor, S.M. Revell), September 1994
ISBN 1 85966 066 5

Capital Markets Forum Yearbook vol 2/1994, 1995, 1996 (Editor, S.M. Revell), February 1997
ISBN 90 411 06596

Civil Appeal Procedures Worldwide (Editor, C. Platto), October 1992
ISBN 1 85333 958 X

Current Issues in Cross-Border Insolvency and Reorganisations (Editors, F.B. Leonard, C.W. Besant), July 1994
ISBN 1 85333 958 X

The Developing Global Securities Market (Editor, F.W. Neate), September 1987
ISBN 0 86010 979 8

Due Diligence, Disclosures and Warranties in the Corporate Acquisitions Practice (2nd ed.) (Editors, D. Baker, R. Jillson), June 1992
ISBN 1 85333 633 5

Economic Consequences of Litigation Worldwide (Editor, C. Platto), July 1999
ISBN 90 411 1095 X

Economic Development, Foreign Investment and the Law (Editor, Robert Pritchard), March 1996
ISBN 90 411 0891 2

E-Health and the Law (Editor, Stefaan Callens), August 2003
ISBN 90 411 9927 6

Energy Law '88 (Section on Energy & Natural Resources Law), September 1988
ISBN 1 85333 097 3

Energy Law '90 (Section on Energy & Natural Resources Law), November 1990
ISBN 1 85333 477 4

Energy Law '92 (Section on Energy & Natural Resources Law), October 1992
ISBN 1 85333 759 5

Enforcement of Foreign Judgments Worldwide (2nd ed.) (Editors, C. Platto, W.G. Horton), October 1993
ISBN 1 85333 757 9

Environmental Issues in Insolvency Proceedings (Editor, J. Barrett), December 1997
ISBN 90 411 0722 3

Environmental Liability (Editor, P. Thomas), June 1991
ISBN 1 85333 561 4

Exploiting Images and Image Collections in the New Media: Gold Mine or Legal Minefield? (Editor, B. Hoffman), June 1999
ISBN 90 411 9721 4

FIDIC: An Analysis of International Construction Contracts (Editor, Robert Knutson), December 2004
ISBN 90 411 2323 7

Global Offerings of Securities: Access to World Equity Capital Markets (Editors, M. Brown, A. Paley), August 1994
ISBN 1 85966 045 2

The Impact of the Freeze of Kuwaiti and Iraqi Assets (Editors, B. Campbell, D. Newcomb), November 1990
ISBN 1 85333 558 4

Industrial Design Rights: An International Perspective (Editors, B.W. Gray, E. Bouzalas), May 2001
ISBN 90 411 9684 6

Insider Trading in Western Europe (Editors, G. Wegen, H-D Assmann), August 1994
ISBN 1 85966 079 7

Joint Ventures in East Asia (Editor, J. Buhart), June 1992
ISBN 1 85333 739 0

Kyoto: From Principles to Practice (Editors, P. D. Cameron, D. Zillman), December 2001
ISBN 90 411 1689 3

Law Without Frontiers (Editor, E. Godfrey), April 1995
ISBN 90 411 0851 3

Legal Opinions in International Transactions (3rd ed.) (Editors, M. Gruson, S. Hutter, M. Kutschera), November 1997
ISBN 90 411 0944 7

Legal Opinions in International Transactions (4th ed.) (Editors, Michael Gruson, Stephan Hutter, Michael Kutschera), November 2003
ISBN 90-411-9902-0

Liability of Lawyers and Indemnity Insurance (Editors, A. Rogers, J. Trotter, W.G. van Hassel, J.R. Walsh, R.P. Kröner; Co-edited by K.C.J. Frikkee), November 1995
ISBN 90-411-0876-9

Life After Big Bang (Editor, S. MacLachlan), January 1988
ISBN 0 86010 982 8

Litigation and Arbitration in Central and Eastern Europe (Editors, D.W. Rivkin, C. Platto), September 1998
ISBN 90 411 0583 2

Litigation Issues in the Distribution of Securities: An International Perspective (Editors, W.G. Horton, G. Wegen), April 1997
ISBN 90 411 0950 1

Managing and Disclosing Risks of Investing in Derivatives (Editor, M. Brown), August 1996
ISBN 90 411 0930 7

Mechanics of Global Equity Offerings (Editor, M. Brown), August 1995
ISBN 90 411 0855 6

Nuclear Energy Law After Chernobyl (Editors, P. Cameron, L. Hancher, W. Kühn),
    September 1988
    ISBN 1 85333 110 4

Obtaining Evidence in Another Jurisdiction in Business Disputes (2nd ed.) (Editors,
    C. Platto, M. Lee), October 1993
    ISBN 1 85333 082 5

Pre-Trial and Pre-Hearing Procedures Worldwide (Editor, C. Platto), July 1990
    ISBN 1 85333 758 7

Privatisation – Current Issues (Editors, M. M. Brown, G. Ridley), January 1994
    ISBN 1 85966 049 5

Remedies under Security Interests (Editors, I. Fletcher, O. Swarting), October 2002
    ISBN 90 411 9877 6

Research and Invention in Outer Space – Liability and Intellectual Property Rights
    (Editor, Sai'd Mosteshar), March 1995
    ISBN 0 7923 2982 1

Transnational Environmental Liability and Insurance (Editor, R.P. Kröner),
    February 1993
    ISBN 1 85333 778 1

Trial and Court Procedures Worldwide (Editor, C. Platto), September 1991
    ISBN 1 85333 608 4

Using Set-Off as Security – A Comparative Survey for Practitioners (Editor,
    F.W. Neate), June 1990
    ISBN 1 85333 363 8

Warranties in Cross-Border Acquisitions (Editor, M. Rubino-Sammartano),
    November 1993
    ISBN 1 85333 946 6

Warranties and Disclaimers: Limitations of Liability in Consumer-Related Transactions
    (Editors, M. Kurer, S. Codoni, K. Günther, J. Santiago Neves, L. Teh), June
    2002
    ISBN 90 411 9856 3

Water Pollution – Law and Liability (Editor, P. Thomas), February 1993
    ISBN 1 85333 874 5